P9-CCL-638

10332/3/3 85

Novels
for Students

for Novels *Students*

**Presenting Analysis, Context and Criticism on
Commonly Studied Novels**

Volume 4

Marie Rose Napierkowski Editor

Foreword by Anne Devereaux Jordan, Teaching and Learning Literature

GALE

DETROIT · LONDON

GLEN BURNIE H.S. MEDIA CENTER

Novels for Students

Staff

Series Editor: Marie Rose Napierkowski.

Contributing Editors: Sheryl Ciccarelli, Sara L. Constantakis, Catherine L. Goldstein, Margaret Haerens, Motoko Fujishiro Huthwaite, Arlene M. Johnson, Paul Loeber, Diane Telgen, and Stephen Thor Tschirhart.

Editorial Technical Specialist: Karen Uchic

Managing Editor: Joyce Nakamura.

Research: Victoria B. Cariappa, *Research Team Manager*. Andy Malonis, *Research Specialist*. Julia C. Daniel, Tamara C. Nott, Tracie A. Richardson, and Cheryl L. Warnock, *Research Associates*. Jeffrey Daniels, *Research Assistant*.

Permissions: Susan M. Trosky, *Permissions Manager*. Maria L. Franklin, *Permissions Specialist*. Sarah Chesney, *Permissions Associate*.

Production: Mary Beth Trimper, *Production Director*. Evi Seoud, *Assistant Production Manager*. Shanna Heilveil, *Production Assistant*.

Graphic Services: Randy Bassett, *Image Database Supervisor*. Robert Duncan and Michael Logusz, *Imaging Specialists*. Pamela A. Reed, *Photography Coordinator*. Gary Leach, *Macintosh Artist*.

Product Design: Cynthia Baldwin, *Product Design Manager*. Cover Design: Michelle DiMercurio, *Art Director*. Page Design: Pamela A. E. Galbreath, *Senior Art Director*.

Copyright Notice

Since this page cannot legibly accommodate all copyright notices, the acknowledgments constitute an extension of the copyright notice.

While every effort has been made to secure permission to reprint material and to ensure the reliability of the information presented in this publication, Gale Research neither guarantees the accuracy of the data contained herein nor assumes any responsibility for errors, omissions, or discrepancies. Gale accepts no payment for listing; and inclusion in the publication of any organization, agency, institution, publication, service, or individual does not imply endorsement of the editors or publisher. Errors brought to the attention of the publisher and verified to the satisfaction of the publisher will be corrected in future editions.

This publication is a creative work fully protected by all applicable copyright laws, as well as by misappropriation, trade secret, unfair competition, and other applicable laws. The authors and editors of this work have added value to the underlying factual material herein through one or more of the following: unique and original selection, coordination, expression, arrangement, and classification of the information. All rights to this publication will be vigorously defended.

Copyright © 1998
Gale Research
27500 Drake Rd.
Farmington Hills, MI 48331-3535

All rights reserved including the right of reproduction in whole or in part in any form.

ISBN 0-7876-2114-5
ISSN 1094-3552
Printed in the United States of America.

10 9 8 7 6 5 4 3 2 1

National Advisory Board

Dale Allender: Teacher, West High School, Iowa City, Iowa.

Dana Gioia: Poet and critic. His books include *The Gods of Winter* and *Can Poetry Matter?* He currently resides in Santa Rosa, CA.

Carol Jago: Teacher, Santa Monica High School, Santa Monica, CA. Member of the California Reading and Literature Project at University of California, Los Angeles.

Bonnie J. Newcomer: English teacher, Beloit Junior-Senior High School, Beloit, Kansas. Editor of KATE UpDate, for the Kansas Association of Teachers of English. Ph.D. candidate in information science, Emporia State University, Kansas.

Katherine Nyberg: English teacher. Coordinator of the language arts department of Farmington Public Schools, Farmington, Michigan.

Nancy Rosenberger: Former English teacher and chair of English department at Conestoga High School, Berwyn, Pennsylvania.

Dorothea M. Susag: English teacher, Simms High School, Simms, Montana. Former president of the Montana Association of Teachers of English Language Arts. Member of the National Council of Teachers of English.

Table of Contents

Guest Foreword
"The Informed Dialogue: Interacting with
Literature" by Anne Devereaux Jordan x

Introduction xii

Literary Chronology xv

Acknowledgments xvii

Contributors xx

All Quiet on the Western Front (by
Erich Maria Remarque) 1
    Author Biography 2
    Plot Summary 3
    Characters 4
    Themes 6
    Style 8
    Historical Context 8
    Critical Overview 11
    Criticism 12

Ceremony (by Leslie Marmon Silko) 19
    Author Biography 20
    Plot Summary .20
    Characters 22
    Themes 25
    Style 28
    Historical Context 29
    Critical Overview 31
    Criticism 32

The Chosen (by Chaim Potok) 42
  Author Biography 43
  Plot Summary 44
  Characters .45
  Themes 48
  Style 50
  Historical Context 51
  Critical Overview 53
  Criticism 54

Go Tell It on the Mountain (by James
Baldwin) 65
  Author Biography 66
  Plot Summary 66
  Characters .68
  Themes 72
  Style 74
  Historical Context 74
  Critical Overview 77
  Criticism 78

Great Expectations (by Charles Dickens) 88
  Author Biography 89
  Plot Summary 90
  Characters .92
  Themes 97
  Style 100
  Historical Context 102
  Critical Overview 103
  Criticism 104

The Handmaid's Tale (by Margaret
Atwood) 114
  Author Biography 115
  Plot Summary 115
  Characters 117
  Themes 121
  Style 123
  Historical Context 124
  Critical Overview 126
  Criticism 127

In Country (by Bobbie Ann Mason) 137
  Author Biography 138
  Plot Summary 138
  Characters 140
  Themes 143
  Style 144
  Historical Context 145
  Critical Overview 148
  Criticism 149

Jane Eyre (by Charlotte Brontë) 159
  Author Biography 160

  Plot Summary 161
  Characters 163
  Themes 168
  Style 171
  Historical Context 174
  Critical Overview 176
  Criticism 177

July's People (by Nadine Gordimer) 188
  Author Biography 189
  Plot Summary 189
  Characters 191
  Themes 193
  Style 195
  Historical Context 196
  Critical Overview 198
  Criticism 199

The Natural (by Bernard Malamud) 211
  Author Biography 211
  Plot Summary 212
  Characters 213
  Themes 216
  Style 217
  Historical Context 217
  Critical Overview 218
  Criticism 219

Night (by Eliezer Wiesel) 229
  Author Biography 230
  Plot Summary 230
  Characters 232
  Themes 235
  Style 237
  Historical Context 238
  Critical Overview 240
  Criticism 241

The Red Badge of Courage (by Stephen
Crane) 253
  Author Biography 254
  Plot Summary 255
  Characters 256
  Themes 259
  Style 260
  Historical Context 261
  Critical Overview 263
  Criticism 264

Seize the Day (by Saul Bellow) 276
  Author Biography 277
  Plot Summary 277
  Characters 279
  Themes 281

Style 283
Historical Context 284
Critical Overview 286
Criticism 287

The Sound and the Fury (by William
Faulkner) 297
Author Biography 298
Plot Summary .298
Characters 300
Themes 305
Style 306
Historical Context 307
Critical Overview 310
Criticism 310

Winesburg, Ohio (by Sherwood
Anderson) 322
Author Biography 323
Plot Summary .323
Characters 325
Themes 329
Style 330

Historical Context 331
Critical Overview 334
Criticism 335

The Women of Brewster Place (by
Gloria Naylor) .348
Author Biography 349
Plot Summary .349
Characters 351
Themes 354
Style 356
Historical Context 357
Critical Overview 358
Criticism 359

Glossary of Literary Terms 371

Cumulative Author/Title Index 383

**Cumulative Nationality/
Ethnicity Index** 385

Subject/Theme Index 387

The Informed Dialogue: Interacting with Literature

When we pick up a book, we usually do so with the anticipation of pleasure. We hope that by entering the time and place of the novel and sharing the thoughts and actions of the characters, we will find enjoyment. Unfortunately, this is often not the case; we are disappointed. But we should ask, has the author failed us, or have we failed the author?

We establish a dialogue with the author, the book, and with ourselves when we read. Consciously and unconsciously, we ask questions: "Why did the author write this book?" "Why did the author choose that time, place, or character?" "How did the author achieve that effect?" "Why did the character act that way?" "Would I act in the same way?" The answers we receive depend upon how much information about literature in general and about that book specifically we ourselves bring to our reading.

Young children have limited life and literary experiences. Being young, children frequently do not know how to go about exploring a book, nor sometimes, even know the questions to ask of a book. The books they read help them answer questions, the author often coming right out and *telling* young readers the things they are learning or are expected to learn. The perennial classic, *The Little Engine That Could, tells* its readers that, among other things, it is good to help others and bring happiness:

"Hurray, hurray," cried the funny little clown and all the dolls and toys. "The good little boys and girls in the city will be happy because you helped us, kind, Little Blue Engine."

In picture books, messages are often blatant and simple, the dialogue between the author and reader one-sided. Young children are concerned with the end result of a book—the enjoyment gained, the lesson learned—rather than with how that result was obtained. As we grow older and read further, however, we question more. We come to expect that the world within the book will closely mirror the concerns of our world, and that the author will *show* these through the events, descriptions, and conversations within the story, rather than *telling* of them. We are now expected to do the interpreting, carry on our share of the dialogue with the book and author, and glean not only the author's message, but comprehend how that message and the overall affect of the book were achieved. Sometimes, however, we need help to do these things. *Novels for Students* provides that help.

A novel is made up of many parts interacting to create a coherent whole. In reading a novel, the more obvious features can be easily spotted—theme, characters, plot—but we may overlook the more subtle elements that greatly influence how the novel is perceived by the reader: viewpoint, mood and tone, symbolism, or the use of humor. By focusing on both the obvious and more subtle literary elements within a novel, *Novels for Students* aids readers in both analyzing for message and in determining how and why that message is communicated. In the discussion on Harper Lee's *To*

Kill a Mockingbird (Vol. 2), for example, the mockingbird as a symbol of innocence is dealt with, among other things, as is the importance of Lee's use of humor which "enlivens a serious plot, adds depth to the characterization, and creates a sense of familiarity and universality." The reader comes to understand the internal elements of each novel discussed—as well as the external influences that help shape it.

"The desire to write greatly," Harold Bloom of Yale University says, "is the desire to be elsewhere, in a time and place of one's own, in an originality that must compound with inheritance, with an anxiety of influence." A writer seeks to create a unique world within a story, but although it is unique, it is not disconnected from our own world. It speaks to us *because* of what the writer brings to the writing from our world: how he or she was raised and educated; his or her likes and dislikes; the events occurring in the real world at the time of the writing, and while the author was growing up. When we know what an author has brought to his or her work, we gain a greater insight into both the "originality" (the world of the book), and the things that "compound" it. This insight enables us to question that created world and find answers more readily. By informing ourselves, we are able to establish a more effective dialogue with both book and author.

Novels for Students, in addition to providing a plot summary and descriptive list of characters—to remind readers of what they have read—also explores the external influences that shaped each book. Each entry includes a discussion of the author's background, and the historical context in which the novel was written. It is vital to know, for instance, that when Ray Bradbury was writing *Fahrenheit 451* (Vol. 1), the threat of Nazi domination had recently ended in Europe, and the McCarthy hearings were taking place in Washington, D.C. This information goes far in answering the question, "Why did he write a story of oppressive government control and book burning?" Similarly, it is important to know that Harper Lee, author of *To Kill a Mockingbird,* was born and raised in Mon-

roeville, Alabama, and that her father was a lawyer. Readers can now see why she chose the south as a setting for her novel—it is the place with which she was most familiar—and start to comprehend her characters and their actions.

Novels for Students helps readers find the answers they seek when they establish a dialogue with a particular novel. It also aids in the posing of questions by providing the opinions and interpretations of various critics and reviewers, broadening that dialogue. Some reviewers of *To Kill A Mockingbird,* for example, "faulted the novel's climax as melodramatic." This statement leads readers to ask, "Is it, indeed, melodramatic?" "If not, why did some reviewers see it as such?" "If it is, why did Lee choose to make it melodramatic?" "Is melodrama ever justified?" By being spurred to ask these questions, readers not only learn more about the book and its writer, but about the nature of writing itself.

The literature included for discussion in the *Novels for Students* series has been chosen because it has something vital to say to us. *Of Mice and Men, Catch-22, The Joy Luck Club, My Antonia, A Separate Peace* and the other novels here speak of life and modern sensibility. In addition to their individual, specific messages of prejudice, power, love or hate, living and dying, however, they and all great literature also share a common intent. They force us to *think*—about life, literature, and about others, not just about ourselves. They pry us from the narrow confines of our minds and thrust us outward to confront the world of books and the larger, real world we all share. *Novels for Students* helps us in this confrontation by providing the means of enriching our conversation with literature and the world, by creating an *informed* dialogue, one that brings true pleasure to the personal act of reading.

Sources

Harold Bloom, *The Western Canon, The Books and School of the Ages,* Riverhead Books, 1994.

Watty Piper, *The Little Engine That Could,* Platt & Munk, 1930.

Anne Devereaux Jordan
Senior Editor, *TALL*
(*Teaching and Learning Literature*)

Introduction

Purpose of the Book

The purpose of *Novels for Students* (*NfS*) is to provide readers with a guide to understanding, enjoying, and studying novels by giving them easy access to information about the work. Part of Gale's "For Students" Literature line, *NfS* is specifically designed to meet the curricular needs of high school and undergraduate college students and their teachers, as well as the interests of general readers and researchers considering specific novels. While each volume contains entries on "classic" novels frequently studied in classrooms, there are also entries containing hard-to-find information on contemporary novels, including works by multicultural, international, and women novelists.

The information covered in each entry includes: an introduction to the novel and the novel's author; a plot summary, to help readers unravel and understand the events in a novel; descriptions of important characters, including explanation of a given character's role in the novel as well as discussion about that character's relationship to other characters in the novel; analysis of important themes in the novel; and an explanation of important literary techniques and movements as they are demonstrated in the novel.

In addition to this material, which helps the readers analyze the novel itself, students are also provided with important information on the literary and historical background informing each work. This includes a historical context essay, a box comparing the time or place the novel was written to modern Western culture, a critical overview essay, and excerpts from critical essays on the novel. A unique feature of *NfS* is a specially commissioned overview essay on each novel by an academic expert, targeted toward the student reader.

To further aid the student in studying and enjoying each novel, information on media adaptations is provided, as well as reading suggestions for works of fiction and nonfiction on similar themes and topics. Classroom aids include ideas for research papers and lists of critical sources that provide additional material on the novel.

Selection Criteria

The titles for each volume of *NfS* were selected by surveying numerous sources on teaching literature and analyzing course curricula for various school districts. Some of the sources surveyed included: literature anthologies; *Reading Lists for College-Bound Students: The Books Most Recommended by America's Top Colleges;* textbooks on teaching the novel; a College Board survey of novels commonly studied in high schools; a National Council of Teachers of English (NCTE) survey of novels commonly studied in high schools; the NCTE's *Teaching Literature in High School: The Novel;* and the Young Adult Library Services Association (YALSA) list of best books for young adults of the past twenty-five years.

Input was also solicited from our expert national advisory board, as well as educators from various areas. From these discussions, it was determined that each volume should have a mix of "classic" novels (those works commonly taught in literature classes) and contemporary novels for which information is often hard to find. Because of the interest in expanding the canon of literature, an emphasis was also placed on including works by international, multicultural, and women authors. Our advisory board members helped pare down the list for each volume. If a work was not selected for the present volume, it was often noted as a possibility for a future volume. As always, the editor welcomes suggestions for titles to be included in future volumes.

How Each Entry Is Organized

Each entry, or chapter, in *NfS* focuses on one novel. Each entry heading lists the full name of the novel, the author's name, and the date of the novel's publication. The following elements are contained in each entry:

• Introduction: a brief overview of the novel which provides information about its first appearance, its literary standing, any controversies surrounding the work, and major conflicts or themes within the work.

• Author Biography: this section includes basic facts about the author's life, and focuses on events and times in the author's life that inspired the novel in question.

• Plot Summary: a description of the major events in the novel, with interpretation of how these events help articulate the novel's themes. Lengthy summaries are broken down with subheads.

• Characters: an alphabetical listing of major characters in the novel. Each character name is followed by a brief to an extensive description of the character's role in the novel, as well as discussion of the character's actions, relationships, and possible motivation.

Characters are listed alphabetically by last name. If a character is unnamed—for instance, the narrator in *Invisible Man*—the character is listed as "The Narrator" and alphabetized as "Narrator." If a character's first name is the only one given, the name will appear alphabetically by the name.

Variant names are also included for each character. Thus, the full name "Jean Louise Finch" would head the listing for the narrator of *To Kill a Mockingbird,* but listed in a separate cross-reference would be the nickname "Scout Finch."

• Themes: a thorough overview of how the major topics, themes, and issues are addressed within the novel. Each theme discussed appears in a separate

subhead, and is easily accessed through the boldface entries in the Subject/Theme Index.

• Style: this section addresses important style elements of the novel, such as setting, point of view, and narration; important literary devices used, such as imagery, foreshadowing, symbolism; and, if applicable, genres to which the work might have belonged, such as Gothicism or Romanticism. Literary terms are explained within the entry, but can also be found in the Glossary.

• Historical and Cultural Context: This section outlines the social, political, and cultural climate *in which the author lived and the novel was created.* This section may include descriptions of related historical events, pertinent aspects of daily life in the culture, and the artistic and literary sensibilities of the time in which the work was written. If the novel is a historical work, information regarding the time in which the novel is set is also included. Each section is broken down with helpful subheads.

• Critical Overview: this section provides background on the critical reputation of the novel, including bannings or any other public controversies surrounding the work. For older works, this section includes a history of how novel was first received and how perceptions of it may have changed over the years; for more recent novels, direct quotes from early reviews may also be included.

• Sources: an alphabetical list of critical material quoted in the entry, with full bibliographical information.

• For Further Study: an alphabetical list of other critical sources which may prove useful for the student. Includes full bibliographical information and a brief annotation.

• Criticism: an essay commissioned by *NfS* which specifically deals with the novel and is written specifically for the student audience, as well as excerpts from previously published criticism on the work.

In addition, each entry contains the following highlighted sections, set apart from the main text as sidebars:

• Media Adaptations: a list of important film and television adaptations of the novel, including source information. The list also includes stage adaptations, audio recordings, musical adaptations, etc.

• Compare and Contrast Box: an "at-a-glance" comparison of the cultural and historical differences between the author's time and culture and late twentieth-century Western culture. This box includes pertinent parallels between the major scientific, political, and cultural movements of the time or place the novel was written, the time or place the novel was set (if a historical work), and modern Western culture. Works written after the mid-1970s may not have this box.

• What Do I Read Next?: a list of works that might complement the featured novel or serve as a contrast to it. This includes works by the same author and others, works of fiction and nonfiction, and works from various genres, cultures, and eras.

• Study Questions: a list of potential study questions or research topics dealing with the novel. This section includes questions related to other disciplines the student may be studying, such as American history, world history, science, math, government, business, geography, economics, psychology, etc.

Other Features

NfS includes "The Informed Dialogue: Interacting with Literature," a foreword by Anne Devereaux Jordan, Senior Editor for *Teaching and Learning Literature (TALL)*, and a founder of the Children's Literature Association. This essay provides an enlightening look at how readers interact with literature and how *Novels for Students* can help teachers show students how to enrich their own reading experiences.

A Cumulative Author/Title Index lists the authors and titles covered in each volume of the *NfS* series.

A Cumulative Nationality/Ethnicity Index breaks down the authors and titles covered in each volume of the *NfS* series by nationality and ethnicity.

A Subject/Theme Index, specific to each volume, provides easy reference for users who may be studying a particular subject or theme rather than a single work. Significant subjects from events to broad themes are included, and the entries pointing to the specific theme discussions in each entry are indicated in **boldface.**

Each entry has several illustrations, including photos of the author, stills from film adaptations (when available), maps, and/or photos of key historical events.

Citing Novels for Students

When writing papers, students who quote directly from any volume of *Novels for Students* may use the following general forms. These examples are based on MLA style; teachers may request that students adhere to a different style, so the following examples may be adapted as needed.

When citing text from *NfS* that is not attributed to a particular author (i.e., the Themes, Style, Historical Context sections, etc.), the following format should be used in the bibliography section:

"Night." *Novels for Students.* Ed. Marie Rose Napierkowski. Vol. 4. Detroit: Gale, 1998. 34–5.

When quoting the specially commissioned essay from *NfS* (usually the first piece under the "Criticism" subhead), the following format should be used:

Miller, Tyrus. Essay on "Winesburg, Ohio." *Novels for Students.* Ed. Marie Rose Napierkowski. Vol. 4. Detroit: Gale, 1997. 218–9.

When quoting a journal or newspaper essay that is reprinted in a volume of *NfS,* the following form may be used:

Malak, Amin. "Margaret Atwood's 'The Handmaid's Tale' and the Dystopian Tradition," in *Canadian Literature,* No. 112, Spring, 1987, 9–16; excerpted and reprinted in *Novels for Students,* Vol. 4, ed. Marie Rose Napierkowski (Detroit: Gale, 1998), pp. 61–64.

When quoting material reprinted from a book that appears in a volume of *NfS,* the following form may be used:

Adams, Timothy Dow. "Richard Wright: 'Wearing the Mask," in *Telling Lies in Modern American Autobiography* (University of North Carolina Press, 1990), 69–83; excerpted and reprinted in *Novels for Students,* Vol. 4, ed. Marie Rose Napierkowski (Detroit: Gale, 1998), pp. 59–61.

We Welcome Your Suggestions

The editor of *Novels for Students* welcomes your comments and ideas. Readers who wish to suggest novels to appear in future volumes, or who have other suggestions, are cordially invited to contact the editor. You may contact the editor via e-mail at: **CYA@gale.com.** Or write to the editor at:

Editor, *Novels for Students*
Gale Research
27500 Drake Rd.
Farmington Hills, MI 48331-3535

Literary Chronology

1812: Charles Dickens is born February 7, 1812, at Portsea near Rochester, England.

1816: Charlotte Brontë is born on April 21, 1816, to the Reverend Patrick and Maria Branwell Brontë.

1847: Charlotte Brontë's *Jane Eyre: An Autobiography* is immediately accepted for publication by Smith, Elder & Co. upon its completion in August, 1847.

1855: Charlotte Brontë dies of toxemia of pregnancy on March 31, 1855.

1860: Charles Dickens's *Great Expectations* is published in the weekly series *All the Year Round.*

1861: Charles Dickens's *Great Expectations* is published in book form.

1863: On April 30, 1863, the Battle of Chancellorsville begins, a Civil War event which will inspire Stephen Crane's novel *The Red Badge of Courage* thirty-two years later.

1870: Charles Dickens dies of a stroke on June 9, 1870. He is buried in Westminster Abbey on June 14, 1870. *The Mystery of Edwin Drood* is left unfinished.

1871: Stephen Crane is born on November 1, 1871, in Newark, New Jersey, the fourteenth child of Pastor Jonathan Townley and Mary Helen (Peck) Crane.

1876: Sherwood Anderson is born in Camden, Ohio in 1876.

1895: A truncated version of Stephen Crane's *The Red Badge of Courage: An Episode of the American Civil War* appeared in the Philadelphia *Press* and the New York *Press,* among others in December 1894, before it is published fully in 1895.

1897: William Faulkner is born September 25, 1897 to Murray C. and Maud Butler Falkner in New Albany, Mississippi. He changed the spelling of his surname.

1898: Born Erich Paul Remark on June 22, 1898, to Peter Franz and Anna Maria Remark, in Osnabrück. Remarque later took his mother's middle name for his own and changed the spelling of Remark to the French version.

1900: Stephen Crane dies of tuberculosis on June 5, 1900, in a sanatorium at Badenweiler, Germany.

1914: Bernard Malamud is born in New York City in 1914.

1914: Austrian archduke Francis Ferdinand and his wife Sophie are assassinated on June 28, 1914, triggering the First World War. Over 10,000,000 soldiers lost their lives, many of them by fighting in the trench warfare depicted in Erich Maria Remarque's 1928 book, *All Quiet on the Western Front.*

1915: Saul Bellow is born in Lachine, Quebec, Canada in 1915.

1919: Sherwood Anderson's novel, *Winesburg, Ohio* is published in 1919.

1923: Nadine Gordimer is born in Springs, South Africa in 1923.

1924: James Baldwin is born in 1924 in Harlem, New York.

1928: Elie Wiesel is born in Sighet, Romania in 1928.

1928: Erich Maria Remarque's *Im Westen nichts Neues* (*All Quiet on the Western Front*) is serialized in *Die Vossische Zeitung* from November 10 through December 9, 1928. It appeared in book form on January 31, 1929.

1929: Born Herman Harold Potok on February 17, 1929, in New York City, to Benjamin Max and Mollie Friedman Potok. He later changed his first name to the Hebrew Chaim.

1929: William Faulkner's *The Sound and the Fury* is published. It is one of the first novels set in his fictional Yoknapatawpha County.

1939: Margaret Atwood is born in Ottawa, Canada in 1939.

1940: Bobbie Ann Mason is born in Mayfield, Kentucky in 1940.

1941: Sherwood Anderson dies in 1941.

1941: After the December 7, 1941 bombing of Pearl Harbor, President Franklin Delano Roosevelt announces that the United States will enter World War II on the side of the Allied Powers.

1945: On April 11, 1945, Allied forces liberate Buchenwald, a concentration camp where thousands of Jews, homosexuals, Roma (Gypsies), and other enemies of the Nazis were put to death. The events in Elie Wiesel's *Night* are based on his experiences in the German concentration camps, including Buchenwald.

1948: Leslie Marmon Silko is born in March, 1948 in Albuquerque, New Mexico.

1949: William Faulkner wins the Nobel Prize for Literature, which recognizes an author whose complete work is of the most distinguished idealistic nature in the field of literature.

1950: Gloria Naylor is born on January 25, 1950, in New York City.

1952: Bernard Malamud's novel, *The Natural,* is published in 1952.

1953: James Baldwin's first novel, *Go Tell It on the Mountain,* is published to critical acclaim.

1956: Saul Bellow's novel, *Seize the Day* is published in 1956.

1960: First published in Yiddish in 1956, Elie Wiesel's memoir, *Night* is published in English.

1962: William Faulkner dies of a heart attack in Byhalia, Mississippi on July 6, 1962.

1965: The United States military sends the first combat troops to Vietnam in 1965. Over fifty-eight thousand American troops were killed before a cease fire was reached with North Vietnam in January of 1975. Bobbie Ann Mason's first novel, *In Country,* deals with the difficult transition many Vietnam Veterans faced when returning to civilian life.

1967: *The Chosen,* published in 1967, is Chaim Potok's first novel.

1967: Chaim Potok's *The Chosen* wins the Edward Lewis Wallant Award, which recognizes an American author for a work of creative fiction similar to Wallant's writing. The annual winner receives $250 and a framed scroll.

1969: *The Promise,* Potok's sequel to The Chosen, is published.

1970: Erich Maria Remarque dies on September 25, 1970, in Saint Agnese Hospital in Locarno, Switzerland.

1976: In 1976, Saul Bellow wins the Nobel Prize for Literature.

1977: Leslie Marmon Silko's novel, *Ceremony* is published in 1977.

1981: Nadine Gordimer's novel *July's People* is published in 1981.

1982: Gloria Naylor's first novel, *The Women of Brewster Place,* is published in 1982.

1983: Gloria Naylor's first novel, *The Women of Brewster Place,* wins the American Book Award for Best First Novel in 1983.

1985: Margaret Atwood's novel, *The Handmaid's Tale* is published in 1985.

1985: Bobbie Ann Mason's first novel, *In Country,* is published in 1985.

1986: Bernard Malamud dies in 1986.

1986: Elie Wiesel wins the Nobel Peace Prize in 1986.

1987: James Baldwin dies of cancer at his house in southern France in 1987.

1990: Saul Bellow wins the National Book Foundation Medal for distinguished contribution to American letters in 1990.

Acknowledgments

The editors wish to thank the copyright holders of the excerpted criticism included in this volume and the permissions managers of many book and magazine publishing companies for assisting us in securing reproduction rights. We are also grateful to the staffs of the Detroit Public Library, the Library of Congress, the University of Detroit Mercy Library, Wayne State University Purdy/Kresge Library Complex, and the University of Michigan Libraries for making their resources available to us. Following is a list of the copyright holders who have granted us permission to reproduce material in this volume of NFS. Every effort has been made to trace copyright, but if omissions have been made, please let us know.

COPYRIGHTED EXCERPTS IN *NFS*, VOLUME 4, WERE REPRODUCED FROM THE FOLLOWING PERIODICALS:

American Literature, v. 62, December, 1990. Copyright 1990, Duke University Press. Reprinted with permission.—*Black American Literature Forum,* v. 24, Spring, 1990 for "Dream, Deferral, and Closure in 'The Women of Brewster Place'" by Jill M. Matus. Reproduced by permission.— *Canadian Literature,* Spring, 1987, for Margaret Atwood's 'The Handmaid's Tale' and the Dystopian Tradition" by Amin Malak. Reproduced by permission of the author.—*The Christian Century,* v. 104, November 4, 1987. Reproduced by permission.—*CLA Journal,* v. XIV, June, 1971. Copyright, 1971 by The College Language Association. Used by permission of The College Language Association.— *Dickens Studies Annual,* v. I, 1970. Copyright (c) 1970 by Southern Illinois University Press. All rights reserved. Reproduced by permission of AMS Press, Inc.—*English Studies,* v. 57, June, 1976. (c) 1976 by Swets & Zeitlinger B. V. Reproduced by permission.—*The Explicator,* v. 43, Winter, 1985. Copyright (c) 1985 Helen Dwight Reid Educational Foundation. Reproduced with permission of the Helen Dwight Reid Educational Foundation, published by Heldref Publications, 1319 18th Street, NW, Washington, DC 20036-1802.—*Massachusetts Studies in English,* v. III, Fall, 1972 for "The Character of Estella in 'Great Expectations'" by Lucille P. Shores. Copyright (c) 1972 by Lucille P. Shores. Reproduced by permission of the author.—*Melus,* v. 12, Spring, 1985; v. 15, Spring, 1988. Copyright, MELUS, The Society for the Study of Multi-Ethnic Literature of the United States, 1985, 1988. Both reproduced by permission.—*Modern Fiction Studies,* v. XIII, Summer, 1967. (c) 1967. Reproduced by permission of The Johns Hopkins University Press.—*MOSAIC: A Journal for the Comparative Study of Literature and Ideas,* v. VII, Fall, 1973. (c) MOSAIC, 1973. Acknowledgment of previous publication is herewith made.—*The Nation,* New York, v. 262, February 26, 1996. (c) 1996 The Nation magazine/ The Nation Company, Inc. Reproduced by permission.—*South Atlantic Review,* v. 56, May, 1991. Copyright (c) 1991 by the South Atlantic Modern Language Association. Reproduced by permission.—*The Southern Literary Journal,* v. XXII, Spring, 1990. Copyright 1990 by the Department of English, University of North Carolina at Chapel Hill. Reproduced by permission. World Literature Written in English, v. 24, Autumn, 1984. Reproduced by permission.—*Studies in American Fiction,* v. 9, Autumn, 1981. Copyright (c) 1981 Northeastern University. Reproduced by permission.—*Studies in the Novel,* v. XX, Summer, 1988; v. XXIV, Winter, 1992. Copyright 1988, 1992 by North Texas State University. Both reproduced by permission.—*The Yale Review,* v. LXVI, December, 1976 for "Courage and Convention: The Red Badge of Courage" by Paul Breslin. Copyright 1975, by Yale University. Reproduced by permission of the author.

COPYRIGHTED EXCERPTS IN *NFS,* VOLUME 4, WERE REPRODUCED FROM THE FOLLOWING BOOKS:

Allen, Shirley S. From *James Baldwin: A Critical Evaluation.* Edited by Therman B. O'-Daniel. Howard University Press, 1977. Copyright (c) 1977 by the College Language Association. Reproduced by permission of the publisher.—Bawer, Bruce. From *Diminishing Fictions: Essays on the Modern American Novel and Its Critics.* Graywolf Press, 1988. Reproduced by permission of the author.—Bawer, Bruce. From *The Aspect of Eternity: Essays by Bruce Bawer.* Graywolf Press, 1993. Reproduced by permission of the author.—Hamaoui, Lea. From *Elie Wiesel: Between Memory and Hope.* Edited by Carol Rittner. New York University Press, 1990. Copyright (c) 1990 by New York University. Reproduced by permission.—Ozick, Cynthia. From "Saul Bellows's 'Broadway'," in *Fame & Folly.* Knopf, 1996. Copyright (c) 1996 by Cynthia Ozick. Reproduced by permission of Alfred A. Knopf Inc and Raines & Raines, on behalf of the author.—Turner, III, Frederick W. From *Bernard Malamud and the Critics.* Edited with an introduction by Leslie A. Field and Joyce W. Field. New York University Press, 1970. Copyright (c), 1970 by New York University. Reproduced by permission.—Visser, Nicholas. From *Rendering Things Visible: Essays on South African Literary Culture.* Edited by Martin Trump. Ohio University Press, 1990. (c) Martin Trump, 1990. All rights reserved. Reproduced by permission.—Wasserman, Earl R. From *Bernard Malamud and the Critics.* Edited with an introduction by Leslie A. Field and Joyce W. Field. New York University Press, 1970. Copyright (c), 1970 by New York University. Reproduced by permission.—Wood, Diane S. From "Bradbury and Atwood: Exile as Rational Decision," in *The Literature of Emigration and Exile.* Edited by James Whitlark and Wendall Aycock. Texas Tech University Press, 1992. Copyright 1992 Texas Tech University Press. All rights reserved. Reproduced by permission of the publisher.

PHOTOGRAPHS AND ILLUSTRATIONS APPEARING IN *NFS,* VOLUME 4, WERE RECEIVED FROM THE FOLLOWING SOURCES:

Haworth Village, home of the Bronte family, 19th century, engraving.—Man standing with top hat in hand, and an elderly woman, seated, illustration by Frederic W. Pailthorpe. From Great Expectations, by Charles Dickens. Dodd, Mead & Company, 1942.—Child refugees fleeing a torched camp, 1991, South Africa, photograph. AP/Wide World Photos. Reproduced by permission.—Crowds outside Abysinnian Baptist Church, photograph. AP/Wide World Photos. Reproduced by permission.—"March for Life" Demonstration, photgraph. AP/Wide World Photos. Reproduced by permission.—Navajo medicine man at dedication ceremony, photograph. AP/Wide World Photos. Reproduced by permission.—Naylor, Gloria, photograph. AP/Wide World Photos. Reproduced by permission.—Remarque, Erich Maria (with dog), photograph. AP/Wide World Photos. Reproduced by permission.—Vietnam Veterans Memorial, photograph. AP/Wide World Photos. Reproduced by permission.—Anderson, Sherwood, photograph. Archive Photos, Inc. Reproduced by permission.—Baldwin, James, photograph. Archive Photos, Inc. Reproduced by permission.—Benson, Robby and Barry Miller, in the film "The Chosen", photograph. Archive Photos, Inc. Reproduced by permission.—Bronte, Charlotte (engraved according to an act of Congress), 1873, engraving. Archive Photos/Kean. Reproduced by permission.—Busy New York City street scene, photograph. Archive Photos, Inc. Reproduced by permission.— Fontaine, Joan and Orson Welles in the film "Jane Eyre,", 1944, photograph. Archive Photos, Inc. Reproduced by permission.—Jewish women and children, en route to Auschwitz, photograph. (c) Archive Photos, Inc. Reproduced by permission.—Oliver E. Almis's Dairy Farm in Power, North Dakota, photograph. From the Potter Collection/Archive Photos, Inc. Reproduced by permission.—South African policeman, (wielding a whip), photograph. (c) Archive Photos, Inc. Reproduced by permission.—Street scene of 5th Avenue in Clinton, Ohio in 1936, photograph. Archive Photos, Inc. Reproduced by permission.—Wiesel, Elie, photograph by Nancy Rica Schiff. Archive

Photos, Inc. Reproduced by permission.—Gordimer, Nadine (in corduroy shirt), photograph by Jerry Bauer. (c) Jerry Bauer. Reproduced by permission.—Mason, Bobbie Anne, photograph by Jerry Bauer. (c) Jerry Bauer. Reproduced by permission.—Potok, Chaim, photograph by Jerry Bauer. (c) Jerry Bauer. Reproduced by permission.—American troops during World War I gas attack, 1918, France, photograph. Corbis-Bettmann. Reproduced by permission.—Battle of Chancellorsville, May 3, 1863, lithograph by Currier and Ives. Corbis-Bettman. Reproduced by permission.—Brynner, Yul and Joanne Woodward, in the film "The Sound and the Fury", 1959, photograph. Springer/Corbis-Bettmann. Reproduced by permission.—Faulkner, William (with Eddie Arcaro at Kentucky Derby), 1955, photograph. UPI/Corbis-Bettmann. Reproduced by permission.—Harlem, New York, photograph. UPI/Corbis-Bettmann. Reproduced by permission.—Hassidim dancing at the Western Wall, 1973, Jerusalem, photograph. UPI/Corbis-Bettmann. Reproduced by permission.—Scene from film "Red Badge of Courage" (older soldier marching with younger), photograph. Springer/Corbis-Bettmann. Reproduced by permission.—Wager, Anthony, as Magwich, grabbing Pip, in the film "Great Expectations," 1946, photograph. Springer/Corbis-Bettmann. Reproduced by permission.—Redford, Robert, in the film "The Natural," 1984, photograph. The Kobal Collection. Reproduced by permission.—Thomas, Richard (in the trenches) in the television movie "All Quiet on the Western Front", 1979, photograph. The Kobal Collection. Reproduced by permission.—Willis, Bruce and Emily Lloyd in the film "In Country,", 1989, photograph. The Kobal Collection. Reproduced by permission.—Winfrey, Oprah, starring in film "The Women of Brewster Place", photograph. The Kobal Collection. Reproduced by permission.—Atwood, Margaret, photograph. The Library of Congress.—Bellow, Saul (seated on chair arm), photograph. The Library of Congress.—Crane, Stephen (weariung dark suit, hair parted down center), photograph. The Library of Congress.—Dickens, Charles, photograph. The Library of Congress.—Faulkner, William, photograph by Carl Van Vechten. The Library of Congress.—Malamud, Bernard, photograph. The Library of Congress.—Ruth, Babe (in uniform), photograph. The Library of Congress.—Urban decay, broken windows, street corner ("Mike's Cut-Rate"), photograph. The Library of Congress.—Prisoners of war on the Bataan Death March, 1942, photograph. National Archives and Records Administration.—Wiesel, Elie (with fellow inmates, Buchenwald, Germany), photograph. National Archives and Records Administration.—Woman of the Laguna Pueblo (holding jar), photograph. National Archives and Records Administration.—Silko, Leslie Marmon (looking right, in black shirt), photograph by Robyn McDaniels. (c) Robyn McDaniels.

Contributors

Anne Hiebert Alton: Instructor, Central Michigan University; Ph.D. from University of Toronto. Original essay on *The Chosen*.

Betsy Currier Beacom: Freelance writer, North Haven, CT. Entry on *Seize the Day*.

Robert Bennett: Doctoral candidate in English Literature, University of California at Santa Barbara. Original essay on *Ceremony*.

Sharon Cumberland: Assistant professor of English, Seattle University. Original essay on *The Red Badge of Courage*.

Jane Dougherty: Freelance writer, Medford, MA. Original essay on *Night*.

John Drexel: Freelance writer and editor, Glen Ridge, NJ. Entry on *Jane Eyre*.

Darren Felty: Visiting instructor, College of Charleston (SC); Ph.D. in Literature, University of Georgia. Original essay on *July's People*.

Diane Andrews Henningfeld: Professor of English, Adrian College (MI). Original essays on *In Country, The Natural,* and *All Quiet on the Western Front*.

Jeremy W. Hubbell: Freelance writer, Minneapolis, MN. Entries on *Ceremony, Night,* and *July's People*.

David J. Kelly: Professor of English, College of Lake County (IL). Entries on *Go Tell It on the Mountain, In Country, The Handmaid's Tale,* and *Winesburg, Ohio*.

Jeffrey M. Lilburn: Writer and translator specializing in twentieth-century American and Canadian literature; M.A., University of Western Ontario. Original essay on *The Sound and the Fury*.

Arnold A. Markley: Assistant Professor of English, Pennsylvania State, Delaware County. Original essays on *Great Expectations* and *Jane Eyre*.

Nancy C. McClure: Educational consultant and freelance writer, Clarksburg, WV; Ed.D, West Virginia University. Entry on *The Women of Brewster Place*.

Tyrus Miller: Assistant Professor of Literature, English, and Film Studies, Yale University; Ph.D. in English, Stanford University. Original essay on *Winesburg, Ohio*.

Marilyn Nowak: Freelance writer, Branchport, NY. Entry on *Great Expectations*.

Wendy Perkins: Assistant Professor of English, Prince George's Community College, MD; Ph.D. in English, University of Delaware. Original essays on *The Handmaid's Tale* and *Go Tell It on the Mountain;* entry on *The Natural*.

Jordan Richman: Freelance editor and writer; Ph.D. in English and Philosophy, University of New Mexico. Entry on *The Sound and the Fury*.

Vita Richman: Freelance editor and writer, Phoenix, AZ. Entry on *The Chosen*.

Elizabeth Anne Weston: Freelance writer, New York, NY; Ph.D. in English, New York University. Entries on *All Quiet on the Western Front* and *The Red Badge of Courage*.

Donna Woodford: Doctoral candidate, Washington University, St. Louis, MO. Original essays on *Seize the Day* and *The Women of Brewster Place*.

All Quiet on the Western Front

Erich Maria Remarque
1929

Published in 1929, *All Quiet on the Western Front* masterfully depicts the horror of war. Erich Maria Remarque based the book on his own experience as a young infantryman in the German army during World War I, and was partially influenced by Henri Barbusse's "Le Feu Journal d'une Escouade," (1916) a war novel published while the war was still being fought. His avowed purpose in writing the novel was "to report on a generation that was destroyed by the war—even when it escaped the shells." More than a million copies of the book were sold in Germany the first year it appeared, followed by millions more when translated and distributed in the other nations. However, Nazi Germany took away Remarque's citizenship in 1938. Later on, he became a citizen of Switzerland and the United States. Though Remarque published ten novels and various screenplays, he was known primarily as the author of this novel.

The story is about a lost generation, as seen through the eyes of Paul Bäumer, a nineteen-year-old German volunteer, during the last two years of World War I. The book alternates between periods at the Western front and peaceful interludes, horrifying battles and scenes of young comrades passing time together, episodes in the field hospital and at home on furlough. Fresh out of high school, Paul and his classmates idealistically enter military service, but the realities of war soon transform Paul and his comrades into "old folk" and "wild beasts." War destroys these men: their hope in a seemingly

hopeless situation attests to the endurance of the human spirit.

In his vivid chronicling of the infantryman's view of the German experience in this century, the book found a major audience in non-German readers; Remarque's episodic style and use of both the first person and present tense endowed the novel, published in German as *Im Westen nichts Neues,* with an eyewitness authenticity and added to its enduring appeal.

Erich Maria Remarque with dog

Author Biography

Erich Maria Remarque is considered one of the most significant war novelists in contemporary literature. In his works, he displayed his concern for the physical and spiritual effects of the First World War on a generation in Germany. Born in Osnabruck, Germany on June 22, 1908, Remarque came from a poor family; his father, Peter Franz Remark, was a bookbinder who supported Erich, his mother Anna Maria, and two sisters. The writer took the name of his mother and the spelling of his family name, Remarque, from his French ancestors. At school, he clashed with authorities (whom he later criticized in his character Kantorek). Remarque began writing at sixteen years of age and published his essays, poems, and an early novel later in *Die Traumbude* or "The Dream Room." (1920) Though he began training as an elementary school teacher at the University of Munster, he was unable to finish, since he was drafted at the age of nineteen into the German army to serve on the Western front. Wounded five times, Remarque, like his protagonist, Paul Bäumer, swallowed poison gas and sustained injury to his lungs. Both visited their mother, to whom they were close, during leave. The similarity ends there, of course, since Baumer makes the ultimate sacrifice. However, shortly after Remarque returned home from duty, his mother passed away in September, 1917.

Only months earlier, Remarque participated in the Battle of Flanders against the British. While carrying a wounded comrade back from the attack, he suffered shrapnel wounds that sent him to a hospital in Germany. He spent most of the war recuperating, writing music, and working on *Die Traumbude.* After his discharge in 1918, he suffered postwar trauma and disillusionment, complicated by regret that his wounds ended his hopes for a career as a concert pianist as well as by grief over his mother's death. He worked in a variety of positions ranging from an itinerant peddler and organist in an insane asylum to an advertising copywriter. He then moved to Berlin in 1925, where he wrote about car races in and edited the magazine *Sport im Bild* while continuing to write fiction. Remarque married a dancer, Jutta Zambona. Drawn to local social events, he developed a reputation for high living.

Im Westen nichts Neues (literally "In the West, nothing new"), his first and most famous work of fiction, was written in five weeks in 1927. Following serial publication in a magazine, the book was published in January 1929. The publishers were initially skeptical of the postwar reaction to the book, wondering if readers were still interested in World War I. However, a half million copies were sold in Germany within three months. After eighteen months, the worldwide sales totalled three-and-a-half million copies.

With achieving fame and fortune, Remarque began to live an upscale lifestyle. He bought a Lancia convertible and moved to Casa Remarque in Porto Ronco, on Switzerland's Lake Maggiore. He ended his marriage but still lived with his wife. Though he lived among priceless paintings and antique Egyptian artifacts, Remarque was unable to avoid the hatred against him by a new force in his native country. In 1933, the National Socialist Party came to power in Germany. Hitler's propagandist, Josef Goebbels, plotted to punish the writer for his anti-war sentiments. In the Obernplatz, facing Berlin's opera house, Goebbels burned Remarque's book and the film that was based on it along with books by Thomas Mann, Ernest Hemingway, James Joyce, Maxim Gorki, Bertolt Brecht, and Albert Einstein. Shortly before Hitler invaded Poland, Remarque fled the Gestapo by escaping through France and sailing to America on the Queen Mary. Unfortunately, his sister was murdered by the Nazis, for which he felt personally guilty for the rest of his life.

When Remarque arrived in New York, he was a literary star. Along with other writers in self-imposed exile, he continued to write about the war, worked for various movie studios, and settled in a colony of German expatriates in west Los Angeles until 1942. Remarque became a U.S. citizen in 1947 and married actress Paulette Goddard in 1958. After 1960, he spent more and more time in Italy and returned less often to the U.S. He was awarded the Great Order of Merit of Germany. He wrote ten books after his best seller, but none of them received the acclaim of *All Quiet*. A sequel, *The Road Back,* recounts the collapse of the German army and the efforts of returning soldiers to adjust to civilian life.

Remarque died of a heart attack on Sept. 24, 1970 in Locarno, Switzerland. In Germany, he was described as a successful writer of pulp love stories and popular thrillers but was recognized abroad as the chronicler of German destiny from 1914 through 1945. Above all, he was lauded as the writer of *All Quiet on the Western Front.*

Plot Summary

Part I—Behind the Lines

All Quiet on the Western Front is the story of a young German foot soldier, Paul Bäumer, during the waning days of the First World War. Since Paul narrates his story—which consists of a series of short episodes—in the first person and in present tense, the novel has the feel of a diary, with entries on everyday life interspersed with horrifying battle episodes.

We find that Paul joined the army with his classmates Müller, Kropp, and Leer at the urging of their schoolmaster. In the first section, Paul also introduces his friends Tjaden, Westhus, and Katczinski, called Kat. At forty, Kat is the oldest of the soldiers and is skilled in the practicalities of life. As the book opens, the solders concern themselves with food, cigarettes and thoughts of home.

While resting, Bäumer and his friends decide to visit Kemmerich, a wounded comrade, at the field hospital. They discover that he has had his leg amputated and that he is dying. Although they are concerned with Kemmerich's pain, they are more concerned with what will become of his boots. Müller, in particular, covets the soft leather. Paul explains to the reader that Müller would go to any lengths to save a comrade's life; but it is clear that Kemmerich will die and "good boots are scarce."

Frequently during the rest period, Paul's thoughts turn back to his days at school and to the lofty, philosophical ideals he and his classmates learned. However, nothing that he learned in school or in basic training have prepared him for life at the front. He attributes his survival not to his education, but to pure animal instinct. Paul contrasts his former life to the harsh, emotion-numbing conditions he now endures.

When the soldiers' rest comes to an end, they are sent to the front on wiring detail. Their job is to string barbed wire along the German lines. Paul and Kat are caught in a large battle. In graphic detail, Paul describes the trenches, the shelling, the screams of wounded horses and men, the poison gas attack, and the rain that drenches everything.

After a brief respite behind the lines during which the soldiers eat roast goose, smoke cigars, and talk of what they will do after the war, the men return to the front. This time they are sent up two days earlier than usual due to the rumor of a large offensive. In the trenches, morale is low and becomes lower as German shells fall on their own lines. Paul describes the tension and the horror of a major battle, with the confusion, the noise, and death turning the soldiers into numbed, unthinking machines.

Part II—On Leave

After the battle, Paul receives leave to visit home. His friends Kropp and Kat see him off, and Paul starts his journey. As he travels by train, he looks at the landscape, at once so normal and, at the same time, so changed.

At home, he finds his sister cooking and his mother ill with cancer. For the first time, Paul dissolves into tears as his emotions overwhelm him. Even when he recovers and is able to speak, he finds that he is unable to answer his family's questions about his experiences at the front.

Throughout his leave, Paul finds himself unable to get along with his family and friends. His father takes him to a pub and urges Paul to share detailed descriptions of the fighting with the older men there. Paul cannot do this. In addition, the noises of everyday life startle and frighten him. When he visits his old room at home, he feels a gulf open between himself and the person he was before the leave.

In the final scene of his leave, Paul bids farewell to his mother. Both know they will never see each other again. Later the same night, as Paul lies in his bed, he knows he should never have come home. "Out there I was indifferent and often hopeless," he thinks, knowing he will never be so again. "I was a soldier, and now I am nothing but an agony for myself, for my mother, for everything that is comfortless and without an end."

Part III—The Return to the Front

After Paul's return to the front, he feels himself more strongly attached to his friends than ever. They alone can understand what he has endured. Consequently, he volunteers to go on a patrol with them. Separated from the others in the dark, Paul finds himself suddenly paralyzed with fear as another battle begins. He throws himself into a shell crater for protection. Almost immediately, a French soldier jumps in on top of him. Paul stabs the Frenchman and then spends the rest of the night and the whole next day watching him die slowly and in great pain. It is the first time Paul has killed with his hands, and the man's dying is excruciating for Paul to witness. He tries to help his victim, but to no avail. Remorse fills Paul and he thinks of the man's wife and life at home. Eventually, Kropp and Kat find Paul and rescue him.

The men are next assigned to guard a deserted town where they loot houses and have a grand feast. However, as they leave the village, both Kropp and Paul are wounded.

In the subsequent weeks in the hospital, Kropp's leg is amputated and Paul's wounds heal. Eventually, Kropp is sent home, and Paul returns to the front. It is now 1918, and the days blend together in bombardment, death, and defeat. The German troops, tired and hungry, lose ground daily to the fresh American troops. Paul and Kat are the last two alive of the original group; and then the day comes when Kat is wounded. As Paul carries Kat to look for medical help, a shell fragment hits the older man in the skull, instantly killing him. Paul is alone.

Part IV—Conclusion

It is now the autumn of 1918. The war is winding down and Paul, recovering from a gas attack, knows that the armistice will come soon and that he will go home. He reflects on what it means to go home, not only for himself, but for all of those of his generation:

> Had we returned home in 1916, out of the suffering and the strength of our experience we might have unleashed a storm. Now if we go back we will be weary, broken, burnt out, rootless, and without hope. We will not be able to find our way any more.

> And men will not understand us—for the generation that grew up before us, though it has passed these years with us already had a home and a calling; now it will return to its old occupations, and the war will be forgotten—and the generation that has grown up after us will be strange to us and push us aside. We will be superfluous even to ourselves, we will grow older, a few will adapt themselves, some others will merely submit, and most will be bewildered;—the years will pass by and in the end we shall fall into ruin....

> I am very quiet. Let the months and years come, they can take nothing from me, they can take nothing more. I am so alone, and so without hope that I can confront them without fear.

These are Paul's last thoughts. The book shifts abruptly and the next page opens with a new narrator who takes over the story for the final two paragraphs. It is this voice that tells us of Paul Bäumer's death in October of 1918, on a "day that was so quiet and still on the whole front that the army report confined itself to the single sentence: All quiet on the Western Front."

Characters

Paul Bäumer

The sensitive twenty-year-old narrator (he has written poems and a play called "Saul") reaches manhood through three years of service as a soldier in the second company of the German army during World War I. His loss of innocence during the cataclysm is the focus of the author's anti-war sentiment. If one views this book as a *roman a clef* (a thinly veiled autobiographical novel), he is telling the basic story of Erich Maria Remarque. Although he feels cut off and alienated from past values two years after the war begins, Paul is compassionate to his dying friends. In camaraderie, the author suggests, is salvation. One by one, Paul sees his comrades die; he also stabs a French soldier, a death that torments him profoundly. He is killed by a stray bullet just before the declaration of the armistice. Critics differ on the degree to which Bäumer is Remarque, but the general consensus is that Paul Bäumer is foremost a fictional creation who recounts a story that evokes the absurdity of war.

Lt. Bertinck

He is the company commander and is regarded as a magnificent front-line officer. His heroism is shown through his knocking out an advancing flame thrower.

Detering

He is a peasant from Oldenburg, who worries about his wife alone in their farm. He grows particularly nostalgic when the cherry blossoms are in bloom, and he hates to hear the horses bellowing in agony. After he deserts, he is captured and never heard from again. As in the case of most of the characters in the novel, he is another example of someone without a future who simply exists in a meaningless world.

Gérard Duval

Lying in a shell hole during a bombardment, Paul suddenly finds the French soldier Gérard Duval on top of him. Instinctively Paul kills Duval, a typesetter in civilian life, by knifing him to death. The soldier's demise is slow and painful, and, overcome by guilt, Paul tries to ease his suffering. After the Frenchman dies, he searches his wallet for an address and finds letters and pictures of his wife and child.

Kantorek

The patriotic schoolteacher, who instructs Paul and his twenty classmates to sign up for military duty, typifies the many such teachers in Germany during World War I. While their idealism was sincere, it was also misguided. Paul expresses his rage at Kantorek's unrealistic view of war that proved dangerous and fatal to most of his class, the "Iron Youth," as Kantorek calls them. Instead, Paul wishes that Kantorek had guided them to a life of maturity and constructive actions. As a member of the local reserves, he is a poor soldier.

Kat

See Stanislaus Katczinsky.

Media Adaptations

- *All Quiet on the Western Front* was adapted as a film in 1930 by Lewis Milestone, who won an Academy Award for his direction. The movie, which won the Academy Award for Best Picture of the year despite controversy in both the United States and Germany, starred Lew Ayres, John Wray, and Louis Wolheim and is available from MCA/Universal Home Video.

- The film was remade into a television movie in 1979. Directed by Delbert Mann and produced by Norman Rosemont, it starred Richard Thomas, Donald Pleasence, Ernest Borgnine, and Patricia Neal and is available from CBS/Fox Video.

- A recording was produced by Prince Frederick, with Frank Muller narrating, 1994, five cassettes.

Stanislaus Katczinsky

Nicknamed "Kat," Katczinsky is one of the main characters of the novel. A forty-year-old reservist, he is an experienced man who is unselfish to his fellow soldiers and also seems to have a sixth sense for food, danger, and soft jobs. Kat serves as a tutor and father figure to Paul and the others, who depend on him for humor. He eases their minds during the bombardment.

Franz Kemmerich

A childhood friend of Paul Bäumer, Kemmerich longs to be a forester. Unfortunately, his dreams are dashed by the war, where he undergoes a leg amputation and then dies. He is Paul's first eyewitness experience with personal loss.

Albert Kropp

Kropp is the best student in Paul's class and joins him in rebelling against Himmelstoss. When he has to have part of his leg amputated, he threatens to kill himself. Eventually, with the help of his comrades, he resigns himself to his new condition and accepts an artificial limb.

Still from the 1979 movie All Quiet on the Western Front, *starring Richard Thomas.*

Müller

Müller is a young soldier who continues to study physics and think of exams during the war. He inherits Kemmerich's soft airman's boots; as he lies dying with an agonizing stomach wound, he wills the boots to Paul.

Paul's mother

She is a self-sacrificing and long-suffering woman who tries to give Paul what he needs, including potato cakes, whortleberry jam, and warm woolen underpants. His last night at home on leave, she sits by his bedside to express her concerns for his welfare. She later receives treatment for cancer at a charity ward in Luisa Hospital.

Tiedjen

Tiedjen is a soldier with whom Paul serves. When he is hit, he cries out for his mother and holds off a doctor with a dagger before collapsing. Paul describes this experience as his "most disturbing and hardest parting" until the one he experiences with Franz Kemmerich.

Tjaden

He is a thin, nineteen-year-old soldier with an immense appetite. A former locksmith, he is un-able to prevent himself from bed-wetting and is criticized by Himmelstoss. When Himmelstoss is ambushed by some of the soldiers and given a whipping as a comeuppance, Tjaden is the first to whip him.

Haie Westhus

Haie prefers military service to his civilian job as a peat digger. Hoping to become a village policeman, he dies at nineteen from a back wound.

Themes

Individual vs. Machine

The patriotism of war is a thing of the past, Remarque suggests, as the young recruits quickly learn about the reality of trench warfare. Paul Bäumer, fresh from Bäumerchool at the beginning of the novel, is sent after skimpy but brutal basic training to the trenches in France. He quickly learns that living or dying has little to do with one's prowess as a soldier but more as a conditioned reflex. Since the Allies outgunned the Axis in artillery and machinery, the German youth took refuge in trenches that were no match for the kind of warfare waged. As more and more of his comrades are killed, Bäumer sees that death comes from afar in the artillery shells and the bombs, and as the trenches offer less and less refuge from the other side's new tanks and airplanes and its better guns, survival becomes little more than a chance.

Thus, the theme of *All Quiet on the Western Front* is the individual's struggle against forces beyond his control: technology, institutions, politics, social conventions, disease, and death. The soldiers become automata, trying to avoid death more than actually fighting. Rapid changes of scene take the reader to the front—sheltering from shell-fire in a cemetery, under gas attack, behind the lines—on leave to a Germany that cannot conceive of life at the front, into contact with Russian POWs, and to the hospital, where the consequences of war are among the severest and clearest. The increasingly condensed final chapters show the young German troops defeated in the field, clearly unable to win in the face of livelier and better fed Allied troops, and Bäumer dies before the actual armistice. His death in the end, the author seems to say, is not even worth reporting.

The atmosphere of death, the callousness of Müller's request for Kenneth's boots, the theft of his watch, and the eagerness of a soldier to exchange cigarettes for morphine to aid a dying soldier add to the theme of the absurdity of modern existence, where man is forced to combat impersonal mechanistic forces.

Friendship

The one element that retains its positive value in the novel is friendship between the comrades. A difference in generation developed, and ties between the young soldiers solidified. Carl Zuckmayer, a playwright and friend of Remarque, writes in *A Part of Myself,* "The heroic gestures of the volunteers was barred to Erich Maria Remarque and his age group; they had to sweat out their normal time in school and then be unwillingly drafted, drilled, and harassed, and they went into the field without illusions, for they had some inkling of the horrors that awaited them there. For us the brief training period was a strenuous but also an amusing transition, a great joke, much as if we were playing parts in a highly realistic military comedy."

Topics for Further Study

- Compare the soldier's viewpoint in *The Red Badge of Courage* with *All Quiet on the Western Front.* Examine the similarities and differences of battle in the Civil War and World War I. Compare as well the quality of camaraderie, as presented by Stephen Crane and Erich Maria Remarque.

- Analyze the historical events of World War I in relation to Paul Baümer's personal history, and how his life reflects the changes taking place around him: the military force of Germany, its bravado and destruction, the tyranny of schoolteachers and other influential adults, and the insanity of modern warfare.

- Explain why Remarque expressed pity for the post-World War I "lost generation."

Alienation and Loneliness

Paul retreats from civilian life into the isolated world of the soldier. Following his leave, he grieves over his second departure to the front, which separates him from his mother. He is sad to lose his friends. In the same vein, the wistful, elegiac mood persists in the novel in the allusions to the lost generation. Paul accepts the fact that his generation is burned out and emotionally stifled. During his guard duty, he sees men scurry in terror in a rat-infested trench as they hide next to cadavers of their comrades. Chapter 12, the last, is a compelling existential cry of abandonment. Paul perceives his generation as "weary, broken, burnt out, rootless, and without hope." Against a red rowan tree, he sees nature through new, objective eyes. "I am so alone," he concludes, lacking a will to live.

When Bäumer returns home on leave, he is unable to identify with memories of his youth nor understand the patriotic enthusiasm of the older generation. The lost generation essentially includes the students whose youth is cut short and ruined by war.

Style

Point of View

Remarque has been praised for the simple, direct language of his war novels in contrast to their often violent subject matter; he is also acknowledged for his ability to create moving, realistic characters and situations. His prose style is punctuated with fragmented narrative passages that mirror Paul's often disoriented state of mind. The plot moves in a "bildungsroman" format, demonstrating a young man's personal development. There are impressionist details that move in tableau fashion. Remarque's choice of a first-person narrator does, however, create one possible problem: the two concluding paragraphs have to stem from a new, apparently omniscient third-person narrator whose intervention is needed after the death of the first-person narrator. The story does not suffer from this change of viewpoint or from the absence of any explanation of the mechanics by which it came to be set down.

The narrative stance provides Remarque with a realistic context for a naive and simple style, which is part of the novel's popular appeal, as well as a fragmented, uncoordinated syntax and use of the present tense, a form that reflects immediacy; these features thus became part of the famous 'frog's eye view' of the war. He is able to comment on events through Paul Bäumer himself—and through him of the other characters—without the need to provide an omniscient narrative perspective: indeed with a requirement not to do so. Style and point of view are matched, and both reflect the incomprehensibility of war.

Structure

Narrative viewpoint and the focus on the central character are also closely linked with structure. The work is divided into small sections, separated by asterisks. This feature makes it easier to read but it also makes for a realistic effect—that of a journal entry or a brief conversation. The novel operates structurally, in fact, on an alternation between the cruelty and despair of the battle scenes, and a gradual return to life during periods in reserve. The book is divided into short episodes and has a heavy reliance on conversation, characteristic of Remarque's style in general.

Description alternates with speculative passages by Bäumer, and there are inconclusive discussions on the futility of the whole war. There are no historical details, certainly no heroics, and not even a real enemy except death, although Bäumer is forced to kill an equally terrified Frenchman.

Setting

Though the novel is set during World War I, in the northern Belgian border between Langemark and Bixschoote, Flanders, Remarque does not really present the conflict of a war between the Germans and Allied forces. The battles are almost never identified and dates are rarely given; he writes of "the troops over there" more often than he does of specific nationalities, for they are not the real enemy. Speaking in a foxhole in no-man's land to the Frenchman he has killed, Paul blames the carnage on the desire for profit and on "national interest" as defined by authorities and institutions on both sides.

Imagery

The symbols in the novel are mundane yet striking: for example, the soldiers' boots, which pass from one man to the next as each man dies violently; and potato cakes, which represent home and comfort to Paul. Indeed, the boots pass from Kemmerich to Müller to Tjaden to Paul (and thus foreshadow his death). For Bäumer, the trenches represent the antithesis of the fragile, gentle, and ever-present beauty of nature, the "lost world of beauty." On the other hand, nature, in the form of butterflies and poplar trees, provides Paul with a reminder of innocence and peace.

Remarque also employs personification—endowing inanimate objects with human qualities—to describe the wind (playing with the soldiers' hair), and the darkness that blackens the night with giant strides. An example of his use of simile is his description of a man collapsing like a rotten tree. Apostrophes like "Ah, mother, mother! You still think I am a child—why can I not put my head in your lap and weep?" evoke the epic tragedies of ancient Greece.

Historical Context

World War I

Named for its complex involvement of countries from Northern Europe to Africa, western Asia, and the U.S., World War I, called the Great War, was ignited by a single episode. On June 28, 1914, Archduke Franz Ferdinand of Austria-Hungary was assassinated by a Serbian nationalist in Sarajevo, Bosnia. As the Austrian government plotted a suit-

American troops fighting in France during World War I, the war at the center of Erich Maria Remarque's book All Quiet on the Western Front.

able retribution against the Serbs, the effect on Russia was taken into consideration. Because Russia was closely allied with Serbia, Austrian officials worried that the slightest aggression against the Serbs would result in Russian involvement. As a precaution, Austria sought support from Germany, its most powerful ally. Kaiser Wilhelm II immediately vouched for Germany's assistance, telling the Austrian powers that his nation would support whatever action the Austrian government might take.

On July 23, 1914, the Austrian empire presented an ultimatum to the Serbs, demanding that they suppress Serbian nationalist activity by punishing activists, prosecuting terrorists, squashing anti-Austrian propaganda, and even allowing Austrian officials to intrude into Serbian military affairs. Two hours before the expiration of the forty-eight hour deadline on the ultimatum, Serbia responded. However, its response fell short of complete acceptance of the terms and so was rejected by the Austrian authorities. As war between Austria and Serbia loomed on the horizon, both sides experienced a massive groundswell of optimism and patriotism regarding the impending conflict.

The Austrians declared war on Serbia and began shelling Serbian defenses. As these aggressions began, the Russian army started mobilizing to aid the Serbs, and it was soon clear that Russia was going to become involved in the war. Two days later, the German army began to mobilize and entered the war to support Austria. Germany was jubilant about the prospect of war and believed that its entrance into the conflict was perfectly justified. Kaiser Wilhelm II stated: "A fateful hour has fallen upon Germany. Envious people on all sides are compelling us to resort to a just defense ... war will demand enormous sacrifices in blood and treasure but we shall show our foes what it means to provoke Germany."

Germany began a heavy assault on France, an ally of the Russians. To facilitate this assault, the German troops marched through Belgium. Great Britain, Belgium's ally, sent an ultimatum to the German army to withdraw from Belgian soil. When the ultimatum went unanswered, Britain entered the war, which had already included Czechs, Poles, Rumanians, Russians, Bulgarians, Greeks, Arabs, and eventually the Italians and Turks. Germany faced Russian, French, and British enemies, who outnumbered their army 10 million to 6 million.

War in the Trenches

As Germany engaged the French and British armies in the West, it became clear that a decisive

Compare & Contrast

- **1920s:** In the world of finance, the Dow Jones Industrial Average hits 381. A period of general prosperity for the country (except for the farmer), the government adopts a "laissez-faire" attitude towards big business. This policy ends with the collapse of the economy following October 29, 1929, the stock market crash, when $30 billion disappears, a sum equal to what the war cost America.

  Today: The Dow Jones Industrial Average reaches 7,000, as Federal Reserve Chairman Alan Greenspan keeps a steady watch on the burgeoning economy and cautions investors of the ever-present possibility of high inflation and interest rates that could adversely affect the market. The Securities and Exchange Commission and Banking Acts established by Franklin Delano Roosevelt's Administration set the precedent for improved vigilance in the stock market.

- **1920s:** The German dirigible, Graf Zeppelin, arrives October 15, 1992 after covering 1630 miles in 121 hours on its first commercial flight. The voyage from Friedrickshafen inaugurates transatlantic service by aircraft. The balloon-like airship, the zeppelin, is used in World War I to move silently over enemy territory and drop bombs.

  Today: The Concorde enables passengers to fly twice the speed of sound between Paris and New York in three and a half hours. Developed by Col. John Boyd, a legendary U.S. Air Force fighter pilot, the F16, used in the Persian Gulf War, has the capability to change course more quickly and climb faster than any war plane before, thus revolutionizing military strategy.

- **1920s:** *The Three Penny Opera* opens at Berlin's Theatre. Starring Lotte Lenya as Jenny, the show includes music by Lenya's husband Kurt Weill. The libretto is by Bertolt Brecht, who transposed the "Beggar's Opera" of 1728 into the idiomof Germany's Weimar Republic.

  Today: *Cabaret,* the hit musical starring Liza Minnelli and Joel Grey, based on Christopher Isherwood's "I am a Camera," records the story of an Englishman's initiation into the decadent, club scene of 1920s Berlin. The musical, which opened at the Broadhurst Theatre in New York City on Nov. 20, 1966, ran for 1,165 performances, and inspired an award-winning Hollywood film.

- **1920s:** The Leica introduced by E. Leitz G. m.b.H. of Wetzlar, Germany, is a revolutionary miniature 35 millimeter camera invented by Oskar Bernack. It takes a thirty-six-frame film roll and has a lens that can be closed down to take pictures with great depth of field or opened for dim lighting conditions, fast and slow shutter speeds, and interchangeable lenses that permit close-ups and telephotography.

  Today: Ken Perlin, a New York University professor, discovers a technique in computer science that makes computer-generated images look natural, as, for example, the roughing up of dinosaurs' skin in the film "Jurassic Park."

---

victory was not an immediate possibility. Both sides in the conflict settled themselves into trenches and dugouts in preparation for a war of attrition. New weapons such as the machine gun and more efficient artillery made the trenches a necessity. Soldiers on open ground would be decimated by the newfangled instruments of death. Opposing trenches were typically several hundred yards apart. The middle ground, which was laced with barbed wire, soon became known as "no-man's land." Constant firefights and artillery barrages removed all foliage from this area and made it nearly impossible to cross. Daring raids across this deadly no-man's land became one of the chief pursuits of infantrymen in the trenches. During these raids, soldiers would cross the treacherous ground, penetrating enemy barbed wire either with well-placed artillery attacks or with special rifle attachments that gathered several strands of wire together and the fired a bullet, severing them. Upon reaching the enemy lines, soldiers would first throw a volley of hand grenades into the trenches and then attack the surprised defenders with bayonets. While these raids did not typically result in major casualties to defenders, they devastated enemy morale and bolstered the confidence of the attackers. In *All Quiet on the Western Front,* Paul Bäumer participates in such a raid. Caught in a no-man's land by shellfire, Bäumer takes shelter in a shallow hole. When a French soldier also seeks shelter there, Bäumer stabs him and feels tormented by guilt as he watches the young man die. This scene especially illustrates the traumatic nature of the raids.

The Western Front

The Western front was a 475-mile-long battle line between the Germans and the Allied forces. Along this line of fighting were 900,000 German troops and 1.2 million Allied soldiers, or roughly 1,900 and 2,500 men per mile of front. Overall, the western front was not a continuous trench, but rather a string of unconnected trenches and fortifications.

The round of duty along the Western front differed little for soldier on either side of the conflict. Most of the night would be spent at hard labor, repairing the trench wall, laying barbed wire, and packing sandbags. After the dawn stand-to, when every man would line up on the firing step against the possibility of a morning attack, the rest of the day would generally be spent in sleep or idleness, occasionally interrupted by sentry duty or another stand-to when enemy activity was suspected. Despite the sometimes lengthy periods of calm along the front, life in the trenches was filled with constant dangers. In addition to artillery attacks and surprise raids, soldiers suffered afflictions brought on by a daily existence in wet and unsanitary conditions. The lack of fresh foods and soggy environment in the trenches resulted in "trench foot," an affliction that turned the feet green, swollen, and painful. Another ailment suffered by soldiers in the trenches was the debilitating, though not fatal, trench fever, transmitted by the lice that infested everyone after a day or two in the line. Bäumer and his comrades in the novel take several trips to the delousing stations during their service on the front.

The Human Cost of the War

On the Allies side, the total casualties suffered were as follows: Russia, 9,150,000; England, 3,190,235; France, 6,160,000; Italy, 2,197,000; the U.S., 323,018, and Serbia, 331,106. On the Axis side, Germany lost 7,142,558; and Austria-Hungary, 7,020,000.

The Influence of the Older Generation

Central to Remarque's novel is the attack on members of Germany's older generation for imposing their false ideals of war on their children. The older generation's notions of a patriotism and their assumptions that war was indeed a valorous pursuit played a crucial role in the conflict. The chief sources of this pro-war ideology were the older men of the nation: professor, publicists, politicians, and even pastors. As the war began, these figures intensified the rhetoric, providing all the right reasons why killing the young men of France and Britain was a worthy endeavor. One Protestant clergyman spoke of the war as "the magnificent preserver and rejuvenator." Government authorities in Germany did everything in their power to try and get the young men to enlist, even granting students special dispensation to complete final exams early so as to be able to join up sooner. As the war broke out, more than a million young men volunteered for service.

In his book, Remarque uses the character of the schoolteacher Kantorek to develop the novel's attack against the older generation. Kantorek's persistent encouragement of the young men to enlist prompted Bäumer's entire class to volunteer for service. With each successive death of Bäumer's classmates, the novel further condemns the attitudes and influences of the older generation. Bäumer himself denounces the pressure they exerted. "For us lads of eighteen," he observes, "they ought to have been mediators and guides to the world of maturity, the world of work, of duty, of culture, of progress—to the future."

Critical Overview

When Erich Maria Remarque published his first novel serially in Berlin's magazine *Vossische Zeitung* (November 10 to December 9, 1928), he immediately aroused interest. Politically, he was considered a rather courageous new writer who dared to question the mechanical militaristic tendencies of the German state, and, artistically, he possessed a facility in written expression that used various rhetorical devices in an impressionistic mode. In short, he could not be perceived by his reading public as a run-of-the-mill war novel romantic. The work appeared the next year in English and sold a million and a half copies that same year and in time was translated into twenty-nine languages.

Initially, the book was enthusiastically received by critics for its realistic presentation of the war and what it meant to the average soldier. Joseph Wood Krutch of *Nation* centered his commentary on Remarque, noting that the author spoke from experience and that he avoided rhetoric (artificial eloquence in speech or writing) and analysis in favor of a simplicity so devastating "as to make the unspeakable commonplace." Favorable reviews also came from such luminaries as William Faulkner, Maxwell Geismar, and Bernard DeVoto. Louis Kronenberger, commenting in the *New York Times Book Review,* called the soldier's experience a kind of "Everyman's pilgrimage," a compressed and intensive coming-of-age story.

Clearly, Remarque's journalistic training contributed to the popular appeal of *All Quiet on the Western Front.* According to Brian A. Rowley, the book's "particular blend of suffering, sensuality and sentiment suggests that Remarque had gauged public taste. The horror and degradation of war is represented, but it is shown with irony, wit, and even humor." Remarque's command of "a clear but lively, indeed pungent, style," says the critic, "owe something to journalism."

On the other hand, contemporary critics of Remarque faulted his work for its first-person narrative style, sensationalism, and distortion. His work was also parodied. Yet the historical nature of this criticism reflects the fact that the work is not a piece of historical documentation from 1917, but a novel written in 1928. Remarque's preface is telling in this case. While it declares the novel to be a report on the generation destroyed by the war (whether or not they survived physically), the bulk of the preface portrays the war through the eyes of a sensitive and literary young man.

Eventually, *All Quiet on the Western Front* was attacked by certain factions in Europe, censored by the Nazis, and publicly burned by their regime in 1933 for its pacifist denunciation of the war. Remarque was accused of being a Marxist sympathizer, who besmirched the memory of heroes killed on the World War I battlefields. In 1938, Nazi Germany deprived Remarque of German citizenship. While he received hefty royalties, he received few honors, since a percentage of the German population continued to perceive his novel as denigrating German militarism.

Later twentieth-century criticism carries with it the perspective of greater cataclysms—World War II, the Korean War, Vietnam, the Persian Gulf War—and the advent of more horrific and powerful weapons, including the atom bomb, biological warfare, and computerized missiles. Rowley views Remarque's novel as a gradual "alienation from any world but that of war … the sterility of [Bäumer's] leave." Biographers Christine R. Barker and R.W. Last note that "Remarque succeeded in transcending his own personal situation; he touched on a nerve of his time, reflecting the experiences of a whole generation of young men on whom the war had left an indelible mark." Modris Eksteins observes that the book merged with the *Zeitgeist* (spirit of the time) of 1929, when "war survivors searched for answers to their inmost disquietude." From a structural point of view, critics classify the book as a *roman a clef* (a thinly veiled autobiographical story), a *stationroman* (a book that centers on themes, without a plot), and a *bildungsroman* (the personal growth of the main character). German critic Hans Wagener finds that any reading of the novel requires an understanding of the time in which it was written and when it took place, and, as most critics concur, consider the book to be simply one of the best, if not the best, antiwar, pacifist novels ever written.

Criticism

Diane Henningfeld

In the following essay, Henningfeld, an assistant professor of English at Adrian College, points out that Remarque's book, based on the novelist's own war experiences, was the first of its kind, and she notes that Remarque's main concern was for the way war irreparably damaged the lives of the survivors.

Erich Maria Remarque's *All Quiet on the Western Front* offers readers a fictional yet accurate account of the life of a common soldier in the trenches during final two years of the First World War. Like the book's narrator, Paul Bäumer, Remarque was a German soldier himself. During the decade following the German defeat, he suffered from depression and a sense of loss. Finally, in 1928, he wrote *Im Westen nichts Neues*, translated into English in 1929 as *All Quiet on the Western Front.* It quickly became an international best-seller. Soon after the publication of the book, the American-made film of *All Quiet on the Western Front* was released to international acclaim.

Response to Remarque's work was not all positive, however. In Germany, older people detested the negative portrait of the war and of their generation. In 1933, the German Nazi regime banned and burned the book, as Hans Wagener notes in his *Understanding Erich Maria Remarque.* Even the showing of the film met with controversy in Berlin; subsequently, the film was banned in Germany.

Paul Fussell notes that the 1928 publication of Remarque's work coincided with the first memoirs of the war written by veterans who wanted the civilian population to know "the truth." Likewise, Brian Rowley partially attributes the success of *All Quiet on the Western Front* to its timing: "The interval of ten years since the war was short enough for the memoires of participants not to have faded, but long enough for the ex-servicemen to have recovered from their immediate post-war desire to forget."

Remarque's book drew on his first-hand knowledge of the war. He saw in others of his own generation the same hopelessness and lack of roots that he himself felt. Writing the book was his way of speaking for this generation. In a brief preface to *All Quiet on the Western Front* he writes, "This book is to be neither an accusation nor a confession, and least of all an adventure for death is not an adventure to those who stand face to face with it. It will try simply to tell of a generation of men who, even though they may have escaped shells, were destroyed by the war."

Although Remarque's book is filled with death, it is not intended as a memorial to the eight million who died. Rather, for Remarque, the real tragedy of the war was in the destruction of the survivors, men who returned home from the war utterly changed and unable to resume their roles in society. As Christine R. Barker and R. W. Last write, "What Remarque is asserting in his novel is that, so extreme were the experiences of Bäumer and his comrades that they were utterly devasted by their recognition of the discontinuity of life and the absence of any ultimate meaning in the universe." Through the setting, the structure, the tone of narration and dialogue, the descriptions of modern warfare, and the use of irony, Remarque demonstrates the ways in which the First World War profoundly changed the lives of a whole generation.

Remarque sets *All Quiet on the Western Front* during the last two years of the war. Germany's strength wanes while that of the Allieds grows from

What Do I Read Next?

- *The Road Back* is Remarque's sequel to his most famous novel. Published in 1931, the story describes the reactions and adjustments of Ernst, another sensitive young soldier, and his comrades as they return to a postwar world.

- *A Farewell to Arms* is Ernest Hemingway's novel about a young American lieutenant in World War I, his experience at the Italian front, and his sad but beautiful love affair with a British nurse.

- *The Captain of Kopenick,* by playwright Carl Zuckmayer, a close friend of Remarque and also a soldier in the same war, is a true story of an ex-convict who donned the uniform of an army captain and held the mayor of Kopenick to ransom. It is also a satire of the German people's willingness to take orders from anyone in military uniform.

- *Catch 22* by Joseph Heller is about the initiation of Captain John Yossarian, U.S. Air Force officer, into the grim realities of war and describes, in hilarious prose, the mechanical society in which we live today.

the American entry into the war in 1917. The location Remarque gives his story is the Western Front, along the German lines in France. However, although Remarque's story is that of a German soldier, his descriptions of the trenches and of the battles cross national boundaries. The tense, claustrophobic hours in the trenches waiting for the battle to begin; the huge rats stealing food from the soldiers; the corpses lying mutilated on the battlefield; the daily horrors of war taking on an air of normalcy: these are the experiences of all soldiers of the First World War.

As noted above, the first person narrator of the story is Paul Bäumer, a young German foot soldier. Paul tells his story in plain language, short sentences, and in the present tense. Remarque structures the book in short episodes, with periods of intense, horrific battles alternating with episodes of life at the rear in recovery. The overall effect of this contrast is to make the stark details of life at the front even more disturbing than they would be otherwise. Further, the fragmentary structure mirrors the soldiers' experiences as they shuttle between the relative peace and safety of the rear and the horror of the front. Just as Paul experiences the war in fragments, the reader comes to an understanding of the war through the slow accumulation of the fragmented episodes. In many ways, the structure of the book resembles a collage, a work of art created by pasting together small, finely detailed vignettes to create a whole picture of the war.

The narrator's voice is a recorder's voice, the voice of someone trying to convey the truth without embellishment. As the troops move up to the front, for example, Paul tells us, "On the way we pass a shelled out school-house. Stacked up against its longer side is a high double wall of unpolished, brand-new coffins. They still smell of resin, and pine, and the forest. There are at least a hundred." He does not dwell on the implications of the coffins; he merely reports their presence. Paul's voice is emotionally flat. Even when his close friend Müller dies, he does not reveal his inner feelings: "Müller is dead. Someone shot him point-blank in the stomach with a Verey light. He lived for half an hour, quite conscious, and in terrible pain."

Likewise, the dialogue between the men never becomes maudlin or sentimental. The men keep their fears and deep thoughts to themselves. In one instance, Paul must spend the night in a shell crater with a Frenchman he has killed with his bare hands. The man's painful death affects him greatly. Shortly after Kat and Albert find him, Paul tries to explain to them how he felt. They stop him from speaking:

"'You don't need to lose any sleep over your affair,' nods Albert.

And now I hardly understand it myself anymore.

"'It was only because I had to lie there with him so long,' I say. 'After all, war is war.'"

One notable exception to the generally emotionless narration is during Paul's last night at home during his leave. Paul shares with the reader not only the controlled, outward responses he gives to his mother but also his internal suffering at the parting. Yet neither he nor his mother will put into words the agony each feels. "Here I sit," Paul thinks, "and there you are lying; we have so much to say, and we shall never say it."

Remarque also includes descriptions of the new warfare to which the soldiers of the First World War were exposed. This warfare included the first use of machine guns, tanks, sophisticated explosives, airplanes, and poison gas. Technology outstripped tactics, causing battle losses on a greater scale than Europeans had ever seen. *All Quiet on the Western Front* moves the impersonal technology of war to a personal level. Through Paul's eyes, the reader is able to witness the technology on a small scale, through one man's experience. For example, when the French launch gas canisters into the German trenches, there is a scramble to put on the gas masks. Then the wait: "These first minutes with the mask decide between life and death: is it air-tight? I remember the awful sights in the hospital: the gas patients who in day-long suffocation cough up their burnt lungs in clots."

Although the book accurately portrays the experiences of soldiers under extreme pressure, *All Quiet on the Western Front* is not a history or a memoir of the events of the war, as Modris Eksteins points out. Rather, the events Paul relates serve to underscore the broader theme: the senselessness of all wars. Remarque effectively uses irony as a means of driving home this point. The irony is often bitter. For example, when a wounded messenger dog lies a hundred yards from the trenches, Berger decides to go and either "to fetch the beast in or to shoot it." In the attempt, he is killed with a wound to the pelvis, and the man who is sent to fetch Berger is also shot. In another instance, early in the book, Paul and Müller go to visit their friend Kemmerich, who has had a leg amputated. His most valuable possession is his pair of fine leather boots, boots that are useless now because " … even if he should get better, he would be able to use only one—they are no use to him." Müller inherits the boots; when he is killed, he bequeaths the boots to Paul. "I wear them, for they fit me quite well," Paul writes. As readers, we know the irony of this inheritance, something that Paul does not know himself: the acquisition of the boots is a clear signal that he is the next to die. Finally, Paul's death itself is bitterly ironic. He falls in the autumn of 1918, just weeks before the Armistice. Paul dies not in a big battle, but rather "on a day that was so quiet and still on the whole front, that the army report confined itself to the single sentence: "All quiet on the Western Front."

The closing lines of the novel are doubly ironic, however. We recall that Remarque opens his book with a promise to tell the story of those who have survived the war and have been destroyed by it. Because he dies, Paul is obviously not one of the survivors whose story Remarque promises to tell. Rather, Remarque grants Paul death, but not the horrid, slow death of the French printer, or of the young recruits splattered against the trenches. "Turning him over," the nameless narrator reports, "one saw that he could not have suffered long; his face had an expression of calm, as though almost glad the end had come." For Remarque, this seems to be the ultimate irony: that in the senselessness and brutality of war, there is something much worse than death, and that is survival.

Source: Diane Henningfeld in an essay for *Novels for Students,* Gale, 1998.

Diane Henningfeld

In the following essay, Henningfeld, an assistant professor of English at Adrian College, evaluates the roles of the secondary characters in Remarque's novel.

Erich Maria Remarque's *All Quiet on the Western Front* has as its narrator the young German foot soldier, Paul Bäumer. However, in addition to Paul, there are a number of other important characters who function in a variety of ways throughout the book. These secondary characters tend toward stereotypical representations of particular types Remarque wanted present in his account of life at the front.

The secondary characters can be grouped in several distinct categories. First, there are the young soldiers who were friends with Paul in school and decided to enlist at the same time. These include Muller, Albert Kropp, and Leer. The second group includes the friends of the school mates: Tjaden, Haie Westhus, and Stanislaus Katczinsky, called Kat. The third group of secondary characters are what could be termed "outsiders" by virtue of age and their relationships to the soldiers. This group includes Kantorek, the boys' former schoolteacher; Himmelstoss, the sadistic drill instructor; and Paul's family at home.

Remarque reserves some of his most biting commentary for the members of the last group. Kantorek, with his "face like a shrew mouse," is a small, bossy man who convinces his class that they should join the army for the glory of their country. A member of the older generation, he stands for all those men who urge younger men to give up everything in defense of their countries. As Paul reflects, "There were thousands of Kantoreks, all of whom were convinced that they were acting for the best—

in a way that cost them nothing." When Kantorek ends up in the army himself, he is totally unsuited for the life. One of his former students is given charge of training him and, in a reversal of roles, Kantorek becomes the powerless student.

Likewise, the training instructor Himmelstoss is a member of the older generation who attempts to teach the young men what he thinks they ought to know. However, it quickly becomes clear during their time at the front that Himmelstoss has taught them nothing worthwhile. When Himmelstoss himself is sent to the front, the men he previously mistreated ambush and beat him severely. Eventually, Himmelstoss distinguishes himself under fire by saving Westhus. With this character, Remarque demonstrates how only experience under fire can properly train a man for the brutality of war.

Paul's father is another of the older generation who seems to have no idea what his son must endure. When Paul comes home for leave, he realizes that a gulf has widened between them. His father wants him to share the details of life in battle with his friends, men of his own generation who stay at home. Paul's father symbolizes the whole generation of men who are willing to send their sons off to war but who, nonetheless, want to control the narration of their sons's experiences. Like Paul's father, older Germans did not want to read Remarque's book because of its brutality and lack of glory. They preferred to believe in what the poet Wilfred Owen called "the old lie": it is sweet and fitting to die for one's country.

Of those at home, Paul's mother is the only one who does not press him for details of the front. Hers is the traditional plight of women who are expected to sacrifice their sons in the name of patriotic duty. The hardships of the war have made it impossible for her even to feed her family adequately. Thus, her traditional role of family nurturer has been taken from her. Further, in giving her son to the state, she erases her role as mother. Her cancer, then, can be read symbolically: it eats her from within, just as pain, grief, and guilt eat at women from all nations engaged in war.

At the front, the men grow in comradeship. Because they believe that only men who have experienced what they have experienced can understand each other, they find themselves increasingly cut off from their previous lives. While Müller, for example, cannot look back, he does look forward. Paul describes him as a man of "foresight." This foresight at times makes him appear cold and tactless. When he and Paul visit their dying comrade Kemmerich, Müller notices immediately that Kemmerich will no longer need his soft leather boots and so he asks for them. In addition, during a period of rest, Müller pushes each man in the group to describe what he will do in the future, when the war is over. He insists that each man will need a job in the future that he imagines. Ironically, he dies with his new boots, demonstrating how even those with foresight may not survive the war.

The men that the school chums befriend at the front are an assorted lot. Detering, for example, is a peasant farmer. His concerns are in marked contrast to those of Paul and his school friends. As a farmer, Detering's life revolves around sowing, reaping, and harvesting. Farmers are concerned with fertility and growth, not the sterility of war. At one point, Detering becomes enraged when horses are wounded in a battle: "His voice is agitated, it sounds almost dignified as he says, 'I tell you it is the vilest baseness to use horses in the war.'" When asked what he would do if peace were declared he responds, " 'I would go straight on with harvesting.'" The tension between Detering the farmer who brings forth life through his husbandry of the earth's resources and Detering the soldier forced to witness the death of creatures of the earth finally becomes too great. He goes mad and deserts the troop after seeing a cherry tree in blossom. The men believe that he is dead.

Perhaps the most important character at the front is Katczinsky, known as Kat. He is a forty–year–old, shrewd, cunning, hardbitten soldier. Under his tutelage, the school chums learn to look out for themselves. According to Paul, Kat has a "remarkable nose for dirty weather, good food, and soft jobs." A cobbler before the war, Kat finds ways to cobble together a more comfortable life for himself and his comrades. Although Kat is of the older generation, the knowledge that he passes on to the younger men directly contrasts the useless lessons taught by Kantorek, Himmelstoss, and the men still at home. Kat's information can save lives; he knows when a barrage is about to start and he can tell the caliber gun by the sound it makes. As Christine R. Barker and R. W. Last write, "Significantly, Kat's qualities are vastly different from those of the group's parents and other figures of authority: he is admired for his ability to survive in a cruel environment and to care for the needs of his comrades." Kat's death near the end of the book leaves Paul alone. Without Kat's caretaking, Paul himself soon falls.

Although Kat is the most important character at the front, the importance of Albert Kropp to the story becomes apparent in retrospect. Paul calls his old school friend "the clearest thinker among us." His ability as a thinker is stressed throughout the early pages of the book. When Muller presses the men about their plans after the war, it is Kropp alone who understands how difficult their homecoming will be: " 'The war has ruined us for everything,'" he says. When Paul and Albert are wounded, they travel together to the army hospital for recovery. Albert's wounds are far more serious than Paul's and he loses his leg. At the end of their hospital stay, Paul reports, "Albert's stump heals well. The wound is almost closed. In a few weeks he should go off to an institution for artificial limbs. He continues not to talk much, and is much more solemn than formerly. He often breaks off his speech and stares in front of him. If he were not here with us he would have shot himself long ago." Kropp's prediction that the war has ruined them for everything seems certain to come true. If all that has kept him alive are his comrades, what will happen when he is separated from them?

When Kropp is sent home and Paul returns to the front, Kropp's significance becomes clear. Because the book ends with the report of Paul's death, we are forced to reconsider the preface Remarque provides at the very beginning at the book. In this brief paragraph, Remarque writes that his book " ... will try simply to tell of a generation of men who, even though they may have escaped its shells, were destroyed by the war." With this reconsideration, we suddenly realize that *All Quiet on the Western Front* is not Paul's story at all, but rather is the story of men like Kropp, survivors destroyed by the war. Paul, like so many others, ends face down in a field in France, oblivious to the world he leaves. Kropp, however, and the men like him, return shattered to face a world forever changed. According to Remarque, these broken men are the true tragedies of the war, and it is the story of these men that the author promises to tell.

Source: Diane Henningfeld in an essay for *Novels for Students*, Gale, 1998.

T. S. Matthews

In the following review, Matthews praises All Quiet on the Western Front *as a gritty, true-to-life treatment of modern warfare and its effects upon humanity.*

If a man has been in prison twenty years, and is then released, we should most of us agree that his life has been ruined. Not only have twenty years been taken away from him, but the bitterness of a special and futile knowledge will overshadow the rest of his days. But time, as we know (though none of us knows why), goes fast or slow according to what we are doing and where we find ourselves, and who shall say whether a few years in the trenches of the latest war might not have been the equivalent of at least twenty years in a peaceful jail?

In all the writing about the War which has the stamp of truth on it we find this feeling of the ghastly slowness of time. In *All Quiet on the Western Front* it is the first thing that strikes us. It is as if the War had been going on forever, and was creeping forward into an endless succession of to-morrows. "We are at rest five miles behind the front. Yesterday we were relieved, and now our bellies are full of beef and haricot beans. We are satisfied and at peace." The present moment is all that can possibly exist. Neither the past nor the future will bear thinking about.

This is a book about something that nobody likes to talk of too much. It is about what happens to men in war. It has nothing whatever to do with the politenesses, the nobilities, or any of the sometimes pretty and sometimes ridiculous notions to which the world has once again settled down. The hero is a boy nineteen years old, a private in a German infantry regiment; his friends are mostly the same age. But it is hardly accurate to call them boys; as the author says of them: "We are forlorn like children, and experienced like old men, we are crude and sorrowful and superficial—I believe we are lost."

Some of them have volunteered; more have been drafted. The War, though they do not know it, has passed its peak: the slow decline of attrition has set in. The vague sense of fatality that we are made to feel in the opening pages gradually becomes a realization of approaching defeat. The new recruits come to the front younger and younger— so that even these boy-veterans of nineteen feel aged and protective. This is how the new recruits look when they are dead:

Their sharp, downy faces have the awful expressionlessness of dead children.

It brings a lump into the throat to see how they go over, and run and fall. A man would like to spank them, they are so stupid, and to take them by the arm and lead them away from here where they have no business to be. They wear grey coats and boots, but

for most of them the uniform is far too big, it hangs on their limbs, their shoulders are too narrow, their bodies too slight; no uniform was ever made to these childish measurements.

The steady, unhurrying narrative picks its way from one desolation to another, following the fortunes of these precocious professionals, who have learned how to be soldiers and nothing else. They have their sprees and their moments of happiness, as when the indefatigable Tjaden spots an unlucky pig-pen or poultry-yard; they have their wind-falls, of women and extra rations; they even have their vacations. But it was not always a pleasant change, in Germany of the last war years, to go from the comparative ease of a rest-camp to the evident starvation of home. And between the civilians and the soldiers returned from the front was a gulf impossible to bridge.

They talk to me too much. They have worries, aims, desires, that I cannot comprehend. I often sit with one of them in the little beer-garden and try to explain to him that this is really the only thing: just to sit quietly, like this.

And behind all the momentary reprieves lies the inescapable reality of the life to which they are all doomed: "bombardments, barrage, curtain-fire, mines, gas, tanks, machine-guns, hand-grenades— words, words, but they hold the horror of the world."

These youngsters whom the War is swiftly making unfit for civilian life (though many of them will not have to make the change) have cast aside, of necessity, all that they have been taught. They have had to become soldiers, and they are nothing else. They believe in the present moment; it is not enough, but it is all they can be sure of. Love they have not known, patriotism and all the other abstract virtues and vices have vanished away in their first drum-fire; but something human they must cling to. They cling to their friends—not literally, and not even in words: when their friends are killed, there is nothing to be said. But what keeps them going in man's machine-made hell is the bodily presence of the friends around them.

They are more to me than life, these voices, they are more than motherliness and more than fear; they are the strongest, most comforting thing there is anywhere: they are the voices of my comrades.

I have said nothing in criticism of this book, and there is little I will say. It is written with simplicity and candor, and reads as if it had been well translated. There is nothing mawkish about it, and nothing "literary"—it is not the artful construction of fancy, but the sincere record of a man's suffering. Unlike the experimental artist, the author has nothing new to say; but he says it so honestly and so well that it is like news to us, though it is bad news.

> I am young, I am twenty years old; yet I know nothing of life but despair, death, fear, and fatuous superficiality cast over an abyss of sorrow. I see how peoples are set against one another, and in silence, unknowingly, foolishly, obediently, innocently slay one another. I see that the keenest brains of the world invent weapons and words to make it yet more refined and enduring. And all men of my age, here and over there, throughout the whole world, see these things; all my generation is experiencing these things with me. What would our fathers do if we suddenly stood up and came before them and proffered our account? What do they expect of us if a time ever comes when the war is over? Through the years our business has been killing—it was our first calling in life. Our knowledge of life is limited to death. What will happen afterwards? And what shall come out of us?

Another country has been heard from. We know by now that the victor nations got nothing but evil from the War; had we expected, then, that the Germans had derived some virtue from defeat? No, the War did no good to anybody. Those of its generation whom it did not kill, it crippled, wasted, or used up. We hear hopes expressed that another generation may be wiser. Let us pray rather, that it will not have to learn such costly wisdom.

Source: T. S. Matthews, "Bad News," in *The New Republic,* Vol. LIX, No. 759, June 19, 1929, p. 130.

Sources

Christine Barker and R. W. Last, *Erich Maria Remarque,* Oswald Wolff (London) and Barnes and Noble (New York), 1979.

Louis Kronenberger, "War's Horror as a German Private Saw It," in the *New York Times Book Review,* June 2, 1929, p. 5.

Joseph Wood Krutch, "Glorious War," in the *Nation,* Vol. 129, No. 3340, July 10, 1929, p. 43.

Brian R. Rowley, "Journalism into Fiction: *Im Westen nichts Neues,*" in *The First World War in Fiction: A Collection of Critical Essays,* edited by Holger Klein, Macmillan, 1976, pp. 101-12.

Hans Wagener, *Understanding Erich Maria Remarque,* University of South Carolina Press, 1991.

For Further Study

Modris Eksteins, "*All Quiet on the Western Front* and the Fate of a War," in *The Journal of Contemporary History,* Vol. 15, No. 2, April, 1980, pp. 345-65.
> This critic argues that *All Quiet on the Western Front* became a success because it accurately portrayed public sentiment about war in 1929.

Hildegarde Emmel, *History of the German Novel,* trans. Ellen Summerfield, Wayne State University Press, 1984.
> This book places Remarque's story in the context of other German war novels.

Richard Arthur Firda, All Quiet on the Western Front: *Literary Analysis and Cultural Context,* Twayne, 1993.
> An excellent general introduction to the themes, structure, style, and history of *All Quiet on the Western Front.*

Richard Arthur Firda, *Erich Maria Remarque: A Thematic Analysis of His Novels,* Peter Lang (Amsterdam), 1988.
> This book examines the themes of Remarque's books and refers to his temperament as "meditative and post-Romantic."

Paul Fussell, *The Great War and Modern Memory,* Oxford University Press, 1975.
> The classic study of the intersection of literature and real life in the literature of the First World War.

Frank Ernest Hill, "Destroyed By the War," in the *New York Herald Tribune Book Review,* June 2, 1929, pp. 1-2.
> An early review that comments on Remarque's spare style and suggests the is book is "surprisingly un-national."

Charles W. Hoffman, "Erich Maria Remarque," in *Dictionary of Literary Biography: German Fiction Writers 1914-1945,* edited by James Hardin, Vol. 56, Gale Research, 1987, pp. 222-241.
> An excellent starting place for any student; the volume provides an overview of Remarque's life as well as critical commentary.

C.R. Owen, *Erich Maria Remarque: A Critical Bio-Bibliography,* Rodopi, 1984.
> Although not always easy to use, this bibliography provides most notably a good selection of interviews with Remarque.

Wilfred Owen, "Dulce Et Decorum Est," in *The Collected Poems of Wilfred Owen,* edited and with an introduction by C. Day Lewis, New Directions, 1963, pp. 55-6.
> Owen's famous poem of World War I.

Harley U. Taylor, *Erich Maria Remarque: A Literary and Film Biography,* Peter Lang, 1989.
> Useful source for information on the movie versions of Remarque's novels.

Ceremony

Leslie Marmon Silko
1977

As if their near extinction, compulsory attendance at boarding schools, and constant violation of treaty rights by the U.S. Government were not enough, Native Americans were encouraged to leave the reservations for the big city during the 1950s and 1960s. Many did, but precious few were successful in large urban areas. In order to provide needed support and offer hope to these individuals, they formed political groups (Red Power, ARM, AIM, et al.). These organizations encouraged them to reject any sense of shame of their culture and assisted individuals as they waged battles in court, in federal parks, and in towns across America for their rights.

More importantly, these actions coincided with a return of the people to their traditions. Native American activists inspired young people to learn as many of the old ways as they could. A Laguna woman who was part of this cultural renaissance became its most celebrated author.

Already highly regarded for her poetry collection, *Laguna Woman* (1974), Leslie Marmon Silko became the first female Native American novelist with *Ceremony* (1977). The story illustrates the importance of recovering the old stories and merging them with modern reality to create a stronger culture. In the novel, a young man named Tayo, from the Laguna Reservation, returns from fighting in the Pacific. He is suffering from a battle fatigue that white medicine cannot cure. Through his struggle back to health, we learn that the way to heal the self, the land, and the people, is to rediscover

the neglected traditional ceremonies and our relationship to the earth. Noted technically for her non-chronological narrative and ability to blend poetry with prose, Silko has been praised as a master novelist.

Author Biography

Silko grew up on the Laguna Reservation in New Mexico and is a Pueblo Indian of mixed ancestry—Cherokee, German, Northern Plains Indian, English, Mexican, and Pueblo. She reflects her diverse heritage in her writing (from the biographical notes for *Laguna Woman*):

"I suppose at the core of my writing is the attempt to identify what it is to be a half-breed, or mixed blooded person; what it is to grow up neither white nor fully traditional Indian. It is for this reason that I hesitate to say that I am representative of Indian poets or Indian people. I am only one human being, one Laguna woman."

She was born in Albuquerque, New Mexico, in March of 1948. Her father, Lee H. Marmon, helped at his parents' grocery store and was a photographer for the U.S. Army. Her mother, Virginia, also worked. Left with her two sisters in the care of the village, Silko chose to spend her time with her great-grandmother, Maria Anaya, who lived next door. Other influences included Grandma Lillie Stagner, a Ford Model A mechanic, and Aunt Susie, a scholar and storyteller. The older women taught her Pueblo traditions and stories.

When she was 6, her father was elected Tribal Treasurer and he brought home the tensions of the Laguna people: violated treaty rights; questions of identity and blood quantum; and the problems of poverty. But more importantly, Silko overheard discussions about a lawsuit the Laguna people had lodged against the state of New Mexico. They alleged that the state had stolen six million acres of land. The lawyers, witnesses, and archeologists involved in the case met at the Marmon house. She also was present as the elders told their stories of the land and the people.

The lawsuit convinced Silko to seek justice as a lawyer. In pursuit of this goal, she attended the University of New Mexico where she majored in English. There, her short stories won her a discovery grant from the National Endowment for the Arts. The lawsuit, started when she was six, was settled by the time of her graduation. The U.S. Court of Indian Claims found in favor of the La-

Leslie Marmon Silko

guna people. However, the Claims Court never gives land back; they order compensation in nineteenth-century prices. In this case, the court ordered payment of 25 cents an acre—and the legal fees of the case amounted to $2 million.

Silko dropped out of the American Indian Law School Fellowship Program after three semesters. She decided that American law was inherently unjust after studying a 1949 Supreme Court refusal to stop the execution of a retarded black man. She left believing that storytelling could change things. After teaching on the Navajo Reservation at Chinle, she moved with her husband, John Silko, and two boys (Robert and Cazimir) to Ketchikan, Alaska, where she wrote *Ceremony*.

In 1976, Silko returned to the Southwest as a single parent. Since 1978, she has occupied a teaching position at the University of Arizona, produced another novel, several essays, and one film. Currently she is working on a screenplay.

Plot Summary

Leslie Marmon Silko's *Ceremony* tells the story of Tayo, a mixed-blood Native American from the Laguna Pueblo reservation who is severely traumatized by his unstable childhood and combat experiences during World War II. As the novel progresses, Tayo attempts to recover from these deep psychological wounds by drawing on various Native American cultural traditions.

His journey toward psychological wellness is made long and difficult, however, because his people's traditional healing ceremonies must be adapted to cure the new modern illnesses that he suffers from such as alcoholism and the psychological shocks caused by modern warfare. In addition, Silko uses a complex, fragmented, non-linear plot to represent Tayo's psychological struggles. While this initially makes the story somewhat confusing, the story becomes easier to understand once the reader recognizes how Tayo's psychological journey structures the novel's complex development. The novel frequently moves between poetry and prose and jumps across historical time and space, but its general trajectory follows Tayo's complex path toward psychological recovery.

Tayo's Alienation

After a brief introductory poem which describes the power of Native American ritual ceremonies, the novel begins revealing Tayo's troubled psyche through a series of chaotic, fragmented scenes. He has nightmares, confusing dreams in multiple languages, flashbacks to traumatic events, and a wide assortment of psychological illnesses ranging from anxiety to depression.

Initially, the novel presents these various psychological disorders as stemming primarily from Tayo's experiences during World War II. In particular, Tayo is deeply disturbed when he is ordered to kill a Japanese soldier but refuses to do it because he thinks that the soldier is actually his Uncle Josiah. Even after his cousin, Rocky, logically explains that this Japanese soldier cannot be Josiah, Tayo refuses to accept Rocky's factual logic. Instead, Tayo feels that there are deeper spiritual relationships that intimately connect all beings within a single spiritual web. This sensitivity to spiritual connections also makes Tayo feel responsible for causing a prolonged drought among his people when he cursed the jungle rains in Japan during the war, and he feels additional guilt because he could not prevent his cousin Rocky from being killed in the war.

Like many veterans, Tayo continues to re-experience these psychological traumas even after returning home, and his problems are only compounded by his friends, Harley and Leroy, who encourage him to use alcohol as a way to escape from life. Unlike his friends, however, Tayo has a deeper spiritual side. He never feels completely comfortable just getting drunk, picking up women, and bragging about his war heroics. Instead, Tayo longs to reconnect with the natural landscape and the Native American traditions that used to provide the foundation for a more harmonious lifestyle for his people. Because of this deeper spirituality, Tayo is frustrated by his friends' self-destructive behavior.

When Emo, another Native American veteran, begins bragging about how much he enjoyed killing people during the war, Tayo's uneasiness finally erupts into violent anger, and he attacks Emo. Luckily, Tayo's friends stop his violent outburst before he succeeds in killing Emo, but Tayo is arrested and sent away to an army psychiatric hospital in Los Angeles. This attempt to fight violence with violence only aggravates instead of relieves Tayo's psychological alienation.

Tayo's Visits to the Medicine Men

Eventually, a sympathetic doctor lets Tayo return to the reservation where his aunt and grandmother try to heal what the psychiatric hospital was unable to cure. When Tayo's suffering continues, however, his grandmother suggests that he see Ku'oosh, a medicine man. Ku'oosh tries to cure him with traditional healing rituals, but these rituals are only partially effective because they were created centuries before the more complex disorders of the modern world came into existence. Consequently, the traditional healing ceremony performed by Ku'oosh eases Tayo's pain, but it does not end it altogether. A stronger magic is needed to combat the more powerful modern forms of evil—modern Ck'o'yo magic.

To make matters even worse, the novel also begins to reveal how Tayo's problems extend back further before his war experiences to his unstable childhood. Tayo's mother, Laura, got pregnant out of wedlock to a white man who did not stay with her to help raise him; she was herself a wildly irresponsible parent. She spent her nights sleeping around with various men either for money or fun, and generally drank away what little money she made. Consequently, Tayo spent much of his early childhood being neglected until his mother finally left him to be raised by her mother and sister. While this move gave Tayo a more stable home life, it created other psychological burdens because his new caretakers frequently shamed him for his mother's past.

When Ku'oosh begins to realize how deep-rooted and complex Tayo's psychological problems are, he suggests that Tayo visit another mixed-blood medicine man in Gallop named Betonie who specializes in healing war veterans. Tayo's uncle takes him to visit Betonie, but Tayo is initially suspicious and nervous when he sees Betonie's eclectic modes of operation. Betonie lives in a bad section of town, and his house is filled with all kinds of clutter. There are innumerable telephone books, empty coke bottles, and old calendars mixed among prayer sticks, bags of herbs, and medicine bags. Betonie uses all of these objects to create new rituals that combine symbols from multiple cultures.

Tayo never becomes fully comfortable with Betonie's unorthodox multicultural brand of shamanism, but he stays and allows Betonie to work his magic. After performing an elaborate healing ceremony, Betonie explains to Tayo that he must complete his own healing because modern disorders are too complex. Before Tayo leaves, however, Betonie reveals to him several signs that will be part of his healing process: a constellation of stars, some spotted cattle, a mountain, and a woman.

Tayo's Recovery

When Tayo returns home this time, he is even more determined to avoid his old friends and their self-destructive behavior. He gets sick of hanging out with them in bars, so he heads into the mountains to look for his uncle Josiah's lost cattle and a new way of life. While looking for the cattle, he finds a woman named Ts'eh Montano who has sex with him and begins to teach him about the traditions he has lost. She rejuvenates his spirit, helps him find the constellation of stars that Betonie had drawn for him at the conclusion of his healing ceremony, and leads him toward Josiah's lost cattle.

However, the cattle have been stolen by a rancher named Floyd Lee who is guarding them behind a wolf-proof fence patrolled by his cowboys. Tayo cuts through the fence and eventually finds the cattle only to be caught by two of Floyd's cowboys. They start to take him back to town to arrest him, but then they lose interest in this plan when they become preoccupied by an opportunity to hunt a mountain lion. With a little more help from Ts'eh and her husband, who seem to appear out of nowhere and suddenly disappear again like mythical beings, Tayo is able to free the cattle from Floyd Lee's land and return them back to the reservation. Ts'eh teaches him more about cattle raising and

other cultural traditions and then mysteriously leaves again.

Just when it seems that Tayo has finally reestablished himself in his people's traditional way of life and reconnected himself to their cultural traditions, Emo begins spreading false rumors about Tayo having gone crazy again. Emo gets several of Tayo's friends and the local authorities involved in a manhunt to capture Tayo and send him back to the army psychiatric hospital. After a couple close calls, Tayo finally escapes Emo's vigilante posse and returns home, while his pursuers end up meeting various disastrous conclusions instead. Harley and Leroy die in a terrible auto accident, and Emo kills Pinkie, another one of his vigilantes. The novel concludes with a final ritual poem which announces the victory of good over evil but reminds the reader that such victories are always tentative, so we must remain vigilant in avoiding the continual temptations of evil Ck'o'yo magic.

Characters

Auntie

As a Christian, Auntie represents a break with the traditional ways and beliefs. In addition, she is a martyr in her own mind. As she says in the novel: "I've spent all my life defending this family … It doesn't bother me but this hurts Grandma so much." She reminds every member of the family how she has to deal with the gossip about them—especially the talk about Little Sister and Josiah. Due to this concern about what people think of her family, Tayo "knew she wouldn't send him away to a veteran's hospital" when she saw that he was sick.

When Tayo returns from war, "Auntie stares at him the way she always had, teaching inside him with her eyes, calling up the past as if it were his future too, as if things would always by the same for him." She considers him as just another burden in her life-and then reminds everyone about what she had done for him. At the end, Tayo's success frees him from Auntie but she still has "an edge of accusation about to surface between her words." It takes old man Ku'oosh's clear acknowledgement of Tayo's new place in society to quiet her.

Bear Boy
See Shush

Betonie

Chosen from birth to learn the traditions of medicine, Betonie is revered for his success at curing people. He stays in his Hogan—built long before the town of Gallup existed—so that he can keep an eye on the people. In particular, he looks for those of his people afflicted with alcoholism who might want to come back to the traditional ways.

Betonie mixes old and new in his medicine: "At one time, the ceremonies as they had been performed were enough for the way the world was then. But after the white people came, elements in this world began to shift; and it became necessary to create new ceremonies. I have made changes in the rituals. The people mistrust this greatly, but only this growth keeps the ceremonies strong … That's what the witchery is counting on; that we will cling to the ceremonies the way they were, and then their power will triumph, and the people will be no more."

Tayo confides to Betonie about his dreams, the war, and his concerns about the cattle. Betonie listens, then tells him what signs to look for; he also insists that he must retrieve the cattle. After a vision ceremony, he sends Tayo on his way.

Emo

Emo, "always with a GI haircut," represents the witchery of the story world. He represents evil. He rejects the ways of the past, favoring manipulation and deception to have his way with the people.

Envious of white society, Emo wants his stories of scoring with white women and having white things to replace the traditional stories. He denigrates the traditional ways to keep those around him thinking Indians are no good. In doing so, he simulates the mythical Ck'o'yo gambler, "Look what is here for us. Look. Here's the Indians' mother earth! Old dried-up thing!" With such sayings he aims to obscure the people's relationship to the earth. Instead he encourages an easier way—a prescription of drink and violence: "What we need is what they got. I'll take San Diego … they've got *everything* … They took our land, they took everything! So let's get our hands on white women!"

Tayo's effort to cure himself and remember the traditions of the people is a threat to Emo's manipulative ways. Tayo disrupts Emo's ceremony at the bar by delivering a rendition of the national anthem. He then tells a story about some Indians going off to war and returning as just plain Indians.

Emo wants them to forget this story and remember the killing they did. He rattles a bag of human teeth while bragging about his exploits in the Army. Eventually, Emo kills his followers (because Tayo did not try and kill him) by manipulation. He is banished from the Laguna Reservation but, as witchery, he still exists.

Grandma

Grandma lets things happen around her until she must intervene. For instance, Tayo stays in bed for some time before she comes to comfort him in his nightmare. She cries with him saying, "Those white doctors haven't helped you at all." Ignoring Auntie, she sends for the traditional medicine man, old man Ku'oosh. This is the beginning of Tayo's journey back from being white smoke. By sending for the medicine man, Grandma has started her family on its path to healing and in a small way helped to heal the whole village. At the end, Grandma asks Tayo to replenish her heating oil. This is a sign that Tayo is an adult member of the family.

Harley

Harley is a clownish character who represents the bacchanal spirits. He prescribes alcohol for all occasions. When Rocky, Tayo, and Harley were childhood friends, they tracked an old drunk and stole his hidden alcohol for their first drink. Harley also served in the war and brags to Helen Jean about his heroism.

At the start of the novel, he arrives at the ranch to help Tayo. He also wants to revive the good days of the war when they were soldiers on leave. To this end, Harley proposes a quixotic journey—the longest donkey ride ever for a cold beer. At the bar, Harley's intentions are good—if Tayo drinks he will be happy. "Liquor was medicine for the anger that made them hurt, for the pain of the loss, medicine for tight bellies and choked-up throats."

But when the ceremony is winding down, it is Harley who finds Tayo for Emo. Tayo drinks in honor of his friend and in the process almost falls prey to witchery. He realizes Harley's betrayal and eludes them. In the end, it is Harley who suffers instead of Tayo. Manipulated to betray his friend, Harley pays with his life.

Helen Jean

Helen represents the women, like Tayo's mother, who have been taught to hate their own people and to flee the reservation. She winds up like too many other women—dependant on generous war veterans and drinking themselves to death. Like many others, she started out full of good intentions. She was going to move to the city, get a job, and assimilate into white society. Instead, she is headed for the slums of Gallup.

Josiah

Josiah, the brother of Auntie and Little Sister, is the father figure for Tayo. He possesses knowledge about raising cattle and shares it with Tayo. His scheme places him among Tayo's teachers—like Old man Ku'oosh and Betonie—who are mixing new ways with the old. Along with practical life lessons like how to ride a horse, Josiah offers Tayo many insights. "Josiah said that only humans had to endure anything, because only humans resisted what they saw outside themselves."

Josiah has a mistress named Night Swan. Tayo sleeps with her and she tells him things that fit into his ceremony.

Ku'oosh

When Grandma decides that white medicine has done enough damage, she calls for the traditional medicine man, Ku'oosh. However, Ku'oosh knows that in the present day the traditional and unchanged methods no longer have the same power. He knows where to send Tayo—to Betonie. Ku'oosh, although he sticks to the old ways, is open to hearing the new stories. He ensures that Tayo is brought into the kiva and accepted once and for all.

Leroy

Another war buddy, Leroy represents the veterans that return from the war with alcohol problems. Moreover, in his purchase of the truck he represents the "gypped" Indian. Leroy thinks he fooled the white man by signing for a truck he did not have to pay for. They joke that they have to catch him for the money.

Helen and Tayo want to laugh for other reasons. Helen says the truck is worth very little. Tayo believes that "the white people sold junk pickups to Indians so they could drive around until they asphyxiated themselves." Leroy is easy prey for Emo, and eventually helps him to find Tayo.

Little Sister

Little Sister is Tayo's mother. As a young woman, she ran around with white men, Mexican men, and anyone who was not from the Laguna Reservation. She sought an escape from her heritage but wound up in Gallup. The family took Tayo and she vanished into the slums.

Night Swan

Night Swan is suspected of being a prostitute because she is single, lives above a bar, and dances for the men. When Josiah's truck is parked night after night at the bar, the women of the town are relieved that he, not their husbands, is upstairs.

A half-breed like Tayo, she reassures Tayo about their mixed race. She tells him the others blame him so that they do not have to face themselves.

Pinkie

When the Apache boy who watches their sheep leaves for California, the family is forced to hire cousin Pinkie. During a dust storm, six sheep disappear. Suspiciously, Pinkie is wearing a new shirt and wielding a new harmonica. To his credit, he stays a week longer than he was supposed to but then heads up the line towards Gallup. He is Emo's assistant in the pursuit of Tayo and helps to dispose of Harley and Leroy. Emo accidentally shoots him in the back of the head.

Robert

Auntie's husband, Robert, takes over complete control of the family's business when Josiah dies. He welcomes Tayo's offer of help but knows that Tayo must get well first. He is a quiet man who works hard. He shows he cares for Tayo when he uncharacteristically speaks out about what Emo is doing and what people are saying. He warns Tayo that he needs to come back home and face Emo.

Rocky

Rocky was a star athlete who had to win. He desired one thing, to leave the Reservation and be successful in the world. He believed what the teachers told him, "Nothing can stop you now except one thing: don't let the people at home hold you back." He is killed in the war but others like him, says Betonie, can be found in Gallup.

Shush

Shush is Betonie's helper and symbolizes the power of mixed elements. He is a mix of the human and the supernatural.

Tayo

The main character in the novel is Tayo, a Laguna Pueblo and a veteran of World War II. At the opening, he feels like white smoke, like a ghost. He is suffering from post-traumatic stress syndrome (battle fatigue) and the army doctors cannot help him.

Tayo knows that white medicine—a medicine that looks at one symptom, not the entire system—will not be effective. His sickness is a result of carrying the sins of his mother physically and mentally. He is a half-breed and as a youth was psychologically abused by Auntie. Further stress comes from being a member of an oppressed people. Tayo is very hard on himself; when Rocky dies on a death march in the Pacific, Tayo blames himself. While at war, Josiah dies and again Tayo blames himself.

The most harmful stress, however, is that while he was carrying Rocky he cursed the rain, and when the flies were everywhere he cursed the flies. Because of these two acts, he feels responsible for the drought and the neglect of the Corn alter.

All these stresses become his sickness; it keeps him in the hospital and then keeps him bedridden. Finally, Grandma sends for the traditional medicine man. But the medicine man is not as powerful as he once was. A new ceremony is needed to heal the community of the destruction brought by the whites, and it is determined that the ceremony must start with the war vets, with Tayo. The new ceremonial cure is to be found in the mixed blood of the old and the new—in Old Betonie's ceremony and in Tayo's completion of it. Then the rain will return.

Through Betonie, Tayo realizes that being a mixed blood enables him to facilitate an embracing cure for his people. But he must first destroy the manipulator, the witch Emo. Like the mythical Sun Father, he allows the witch to destroy himself. Tayo succeeds because he trusts in the greater community and draws strength from the stories. As a result, witchery eats itself and Tayo is able to bring the story to the elders. "The ear for the story and the eye for the pattern were theirs; the feeling was theirs: we came out of this land we are hers."

Tayo, with Betonie, has created a new ceremony and reestablished contact with certain elements in the Pueblo tradition: the ceremonial plants he was told to gather; the rock face painting that has not been renewed since the war; and the woman of the mountains who has chosen him as a messenger. As a result, Tayo has merged his identity with his people and become well. He has entered the story reality where the people exist. He now has a place in the society's ceremony and he has brought home the cattle to replenish his family's economy. Auntie can no longer begrudge him, Grandma is proud, and the elders recognize him as

a fly who carried the message which lead to the return of the rain.

Ts'eh

The personification of his ceremony is Ts'eh. She is the Montano—the Mountain woman, the earth. Her function is to help Tayo remember traditions that have been forgotten as well as add a new one—the gathering of the purple root. In a sense, as the embodiment of Corn Woman, she is pleased with Tayo's efforts. Accordingly she helps him by corralling the cattle and showing him the site of the she-elk painting. These things, along with the purple root, are the elements that most interest the old men in the Kiva.

Themes

Evil

The Pueblo concept of reciprocity did not allow for evil. They believed that because all things were interconnected, they simply had to keep up their end of the bargain. For example, when a hunter takes a deer, he sprinkles cornmeal to the spirits. If the dances and ceremonies are done, the crops will be plentiful.

However, the Pueblos gradually found they needed an explanation for those evils which violated this theory of reciprocity. They did not alter their cosmology by adding a devil. Instead, they attributed evil to witchery or the manipulation of life's elements to selfish and violent ends. Furthermore, Native American people out of touch with the stories of the people or wanting to replace those stories are the ones that use witchery and, therefore, only Native American medicine and story can undo witchery. One story about witches explains that Native Americans wear the skins of other animals in order to become that animal for a time.

In the novel, witchery is at work before the war when the young men were convinced they had to enlist in order to prove themselves patriotic Americans. Then, the uniforms-like skins-provided a taste of life as a white American. But the uniforms were taken back. Rather than return to their people and renew contact with the earth, they sit in the bar and tell stories about the witchery—about how much better it was chasing white women and killing "Japs." Thus their connection with the Corn Woman remains broken. Emo embodies witchery as he encourages them in their storytelling. He ma-

Woman of the Laguna Pueblo.

nipulates his friends to hate Reservation life, to remain angry and drown in alcohol.

Tradition

The central theme of Silko's novel is the relationship of the individual to the story of the community. For Tayo to be cured of the war witchery, he must remember his people's story and renew his connection with the land and its governing deities. In one specific instance, he is shown a cliff face painting of A'moo'ooh. T'seh explains, "Nobody has come to paint it since the war. But as long as you remember what you have seen, then nothing is gone. As long as you remember, it is part of this story we have together."

Religion

The three central figures in the Pueblo cosmology are Thought-Woman, Corn Mother, and Sun Father. They are interrelated and interdependent. Thought-Woman opens the novel and is considered responsible for the story. Thought-Woman created the universe by speech. She made the fifth world (the earth) and the four worlds below where the spirits of the dead go. She appears throughout Pueblo mythology and throughout the story. Tayo must make contact with her, with the people's story, in order to bring a story to the elders inside the kiva. He tells them he has seen her. "They started crying/the old men started crying…."

Corn Woman is perhaps the most important deity because corn is essential to the people's economy. Corn Woman is interchangeable with mother earth. She represents growth, life, and the feminine powers of reproduction. She is honored by prayer sticks and offerings of blue and yellow pollen (Tayo fills animal tracks with yellow pollen). Dances in her honor are done in a zigzag or lightning pattern. Large dances include everyone but only men perform small dances. The Corn dance is done to bring rain, to assure abundant crops, and to increase fertility. The female powers support and grant according to his performance. A male protagonist as a sacrificial intermediary performs the small dance in the novel—Tayo is the fly. Throughout the novel, from the entrance of Harley and the weaving journey astride a donkey, Tayo performs a series of ziz-zags. He also finds zig-zags on the supportive T'seh's blanket.

The story about Corn Woman involves an evil Ck'o'yo magician. The moral of this story is that if the Corn Alter is neglected and offerings are not given, the life processes supporting the people will not function. This story brings us to the last deity-Sun Father. He is a creative force unleashed by Thought-Woman to interact with Corn Woman. He represents masculine powers and light and it is his job to awaken the rain clouds. The offering to Sun Father is corn meal—a product of Corn Woman. Tayo's link with the Sun Father occurs when Old Ku'oosh brings him blue cornmeal. Auntie feeds him, and he is able to keep it in his stomach. Tayo's ceremony mimics the story of the Sun Father but rather than bring back the rain clouds he must bring back the cattle, thereby bringing prosperity back to the family.

Racism

One of the most divisive questions facing Native Americans today is: who is Native American? This question might seem odd, but because there is so much at stake—Native American Tribes are explicitly mentioned in the U.S. Constitution as sovereign nations, and the U.S. Congress must negotiate treaties as they do with any sovereign nation—the United States government has kept the question confused.

By recognizing only those persons with a certain quantum of a specific Nation's blood as tribal members, the notion of ancestry became a significant issue in the Native American community. In the late 1960s ancestry almost replaced the notion

Topics For Further Study

- Silko refers to some of the environmental problems facing the Laguna Reservation after World War II. How do these problems affect the people's culture? How do they affect Tayo's ceremony? How does Silko illuminate these problems without documenting them and, then, how are they resolved, if at all?

- Write an essay about the Pueblo theory of witchery. What types of behavior both in the story and in reality could be considered witchery? How does this theory help to spread responsibility while suggesting a solution to problems of greed, pollution, and hunger?

- Silko suggests that the neglected Pueblo ceremonial traditions are not only useful but also essential to future survival. Think of some other religious traditions that are either out of use or corrupted. What value might they have, if any, once rejuvenated?

- Without exception, the Native American people prophesied that the white man was coming. Those same prophecies also say that all things European will disappear. What do you think that means? Is it coming to pass?

- Some cultures have definite patterns of recognition and 'rites of passage.' For example, the Plains Indians have a Vision Quest wherein a young person is 'put out' on a hilltop, or laid in a shallow grave, with 4 days of water. This allows the adolescent to have a vision or receive a message about his future role in the community. Jews, on the other hand, acknowledge their adolescents with a Bar Mitzvah celebration. Modern secular culture has no such thing. In *Ceremony,* the young men saw enlistment in the Army as a rite of passage into white society. Research the cultural function of 'rites of passage.'

- Are they needed? If so, what sort of ceremony could you envisage for celebrating the attainment of maturity in America?

- While the rest of the nation has seen a drop in violent crime (by 22%), Native American reservations are experiencing a crime wave (up by 87%). The baby boom on the reservation of the 1980s has translated into a large number of youths, and these kids and young adults are just beginning to imitate urban gangs in terms of culture, violence, and drugs. The United States Congress and President Clinton are proposing to spend additional millions on new prisons and law enforcement on the Native American land. Thinking about *Ceremony,* argue for an alternative solution to the infant gang problem. Then, do some research into alternative programs for Native American offenders: why are they underfunded and ignored?

- Gather a number of brief accounts (cultural, historical, and archaeological) of the Pueblo Indians. Placing them next to each other, compare the ways in which the Native Americans of the Southwest are presented. Oftentimes these descriptions will include suggestions on when to visit reservations to see them dance. Given what you now know about Gallup, consider the ethics of this tourism. Is it ethical to encourage recreational gawking at Native Americans? What does this say about our culture in the 1990s?

- The Mayans were one of three civilizations to invent the mathematical concept of zero. The Pueblo People developed several strains of corn. What other knowledge and resources did the Native Americans possess that were either stolen or buried (hint: research calendars, the material used for tires, and medical procedures)?

---

of race as the determining factor for census purposes. This would have greatly diminished the racial wrangling that has perplexed America. Doing so would also have allowed Native Americans

to realize they were not a handful but a group of some 30 million—an incredible electoral force.

Be that as it may, because blood quantum notions are so strict, the U.S. government counts very few Native Americans. So, a person who is one quarter Irish, one quarter Mohawk, one quarter Ibo, and one quarter Lakota—but raised as 100% Pueblo—is not a Native American. Furthermore, the U.S. government has only recently recognized some tribes. For example, though Tucson was built around the Yaqui village of Pasqua, it was only in 1973 that Congress recognized the Yaqui as Native Americans.

This tension is everywhere in the novel. Tayo is a half-breed (his biological father was white) who was given up by his mother to be raised by his Auntie. Emo constantly reminds him of this because Emo wanted to be white (so did Rocky). But Tayo reminds him of the truth, "Don't lie. You knew right away. The war was over, the uniform was gone. All of a sudden that man at the store waits on you last, makes you wait until all the white people bought what they wanted." But even though they all know it, even though Tayo is a Native American despite what the government might say, there is too much self-hatred. This is the result of the boarding schools that taught them that Native Americans were savage people. "They never thought to blame white people for any of it; they wanted white people for their friends. They never saw that it was the white people who gave them that feeling and it was white people who took it away again when the war was over."

Night Swan adds to this complexity when she tells Tayo that mixed breeds are scapegoats. People always blame the ones who look different. "That way they don't have to think about what has happened inside themselves." Emo and Auntie's dislike of miscegenation runs counter to the custom of the Pueblo who judge by actions not appearance. As the end of the novel suggests, the people's survival depends on these mixed breeds like Tayo and Betonie who are able, by force of circumstance, to blend the old and new to tell a more relevant story.

Style

Narrative

Silko once explained the Pueblo linguistic theory to an audience (found in *Yello Woman and a Beauty of the Spirit*) and that theory explains the narrative technique of her novel.

"For those of you accustomed to being taken from point A to point B to point C, this presentation may be somewhat difficult to follow. Pueblo expression resembles something like a spider's web—with many little threads radiating from the center, crisscrossing one another. As with the web, the structure emerges as it is made, and you must simply listen and trust, as the Pueblo people do, that meaning will be made."

Not knowing the above theory, critics have lauded *Ceremony*'s non-chronological narrative. Silko's purpose in using this technique for her story is to mimic, once again, the zig-zag pattern of the corn dance as well as to stay true to Thought-Woman. That is, the whole of the novel is a ceremony that the reader performs with every new reading. It is intended to blur the distinction between real time and story time in such a way that the reader is better able to empathize with the perspective of a traditional Pueblo like Grandma: "It seems like I already heard these stories before … only thing is, the names sound different."

Additionally, the narrative is told in third person mixed with traditional narrative. The stories of Thought–Woman, the Gambler, and the witches provide context for the saga of Tayo within the larger context of the Pueblo story. The Pueblos see themselves as their language, as a story. "I will tell you something about stories/ … / They aren't just entertainment./ Don't be fooled./ They are all we have … / all we have to fight off/ illness and death. As such, there are no boundaries between the present ceremony Tayo performs and the whole ceremony the people perform to stay in balance with their belief system. "You don't have anything/if you don't have the stories."

Realism

Along with praise for her narrative technique, Silko is applauded for her close observation of human behavior. She remains true to life without idealizing her characters or setting. Her story is set in the depressed Laguna Reservation where, she says in passing, the orchards have been ruined by uranium runoff, drought is ruining crops, the Herefords are dying, and the young men are drunk. She pulls no punches in describing Gallup and she makes no effort to idealize her characters.

So a realistic picture is painted of society on the reservation after World War II. However, in doing so, she does not make the people out to be pathetic—Robert, Ku'oosh, Auntie, and Josiah are all respectable people. Nor does she make them into incredible heroes.

Silko's characters are struggling to negotiate the best route of survival in a world that they perceive as being dominated by destructive forces. Finally, as a result of their trials and tribulations, these people have a wisdom they would like to share with the white world if the white world would just pause to listen.

Style

An apocryphal story has it that when an Indian was praised for his poetry, he said, "In my tribe we have no poets. Everyone talks in poetry." There is no clear distinction between prose and poetry among people who have an oral tradition and a pictographic literature called codices (none but a handful of the codices remain). Silko took advantage of this and of her English language education to invent a written Pueblo style. By using the page itself, she mimics a pictograph in her opening quatrains. The blend of prose and poetry throughout the novel enable her to weave new events with old stories.

Silko's style also allows her to save the old stories by spreading them. The affinity she creates between herself and Thought–Woman, as well as Tayo and various story figures, allows her to tell many stories in one novel. The result is that many readers who know nothing about the Laguna Reservation feel like an old friend to the characters in the novel.

Stereotype

Stereotypes are employed throughout the novel, such as the archetype of the drunken Indian. But the novel uses these stereotypes about Native Americans to tell a powerful and potentially subversive story. The figure of the drunken Indian is used to illustrate how negative images of Native American have become ingrained in the American consciousness. In another instance, by making use of the clownish vets, she can warn America that not only are the Native Americans not defeated but they are making a comeback. All of this is done within the Pueblo style because, in fact, clowns are a big part of Pueblo ceremonies.

Part of the Pueblo technique of storytelling is the belief that the story exists in the listeners. This cuts both ways; part of the reason the novel succeeds is that white society expects Native Americans to include myth and ceremony in their explanations for the world. So while Silko can offer a solution for veterans, for example, she can also speak to mainstream whites because she is telling a Native American story. Even her accusations of white America are done in a Native American way—by a story about witches. Lastly, in an almost harmless way, Silko is telling Americans beforehand that Native Americans will get justice—all in good time.

Historical Context

Pueblo Indians

The people of the Anasazi tradition inhabit the area of what is now the Southwestern United States (from Taos, New Mexico, to the Hopi mesas in Arizona). They are named Pueblo, meaning "village Indians" in Spanish. They live in concentrated villages of buildings constructed from adobe local clay, and stone. These buildings are entered from the top floor. The buildings, often reaching to five stories, surround a plaza with a central kiva—a ceremonial place dug into the ground.

Of these people, the western Keres Tribe inhabits Acoma and Laguna. Acoma, perched atop a 400-foot mesa, has been continuously inhabited since at least 1075 AD. Laguna was established more recently. The Pueblo economy centered on a sophisticated system of dry farming and seed cultivation. The matrilineal culture had its labor division: men farmed and performed the ceremonial dances; women made intricate basketry, exquisite pottery, and built the houses. Government was carried on by consensus; warfare was avoided; and trade took place with the Plains tribes to the north and the empires to the south.

Around the time the novel was written, two tragedies struck the Laguna-Acoma communities in the 1970s. First, a teenage suicide pact led to funerals for a number of boys and girls in 1973. Second, a man murdered and dismembered two friends. The murderer then bullied another friend to borrow a car from which he scattered the parts. He later said that he found the ax irresistible.

Colonialism

Spanish rule began with Don Francisco Vasquez de Cornado in 1540. Soon thereafter, the tribes and their lands were recognized as subject to the King of Spain. This recognition is important to this day as it supersedes, by international law, the claims of Mexico and then the United States. It was this charter that Silko heard discussed when Tribal officials charged New Mexico with land theft. The Spanish conquest brought Christianity, missionaries, and death to the Pueblos. To survive, they accepted baptism and Christianity as an extension to their religion.

The Mexican authorities came in the early 1800s. They demanded that the people speak Span-

American POWs on the Bataan Death March, Philippines, c. May, 1942.

ish, live in rectangular houses, adopt a representational government, enroll their children in Mexican schools, and, more drastically, accept individual land holdings owned by the male head of household. On the positive side, Catholicism was not as rigorously imposed and so indigenous religion regained some of its popularity.

The United States took over in 1848 when the Treaty of Guadeloupe–Hidalgo ended the Mexican-American War. The Americans substituted English for Spanish and added the choice of Protestantism as a religion for the Pueblo people. The Americans also demanded that the people farm like Americans—who farmed like Europeans. This style of

agriculture, however, depends on European or Eastern seaboard rainfall. The Pueblo crescent receives an annual rainfall of 13 inches (a proper amount for a desert). It was not long before the region was ruined economically. Since then, the Pueblo cities have been declared reservations and surrounded by white society.

World War II

By the start of World War II, every Native American group had been relegated to reservations for at least 40 years. That was enough time for the boarding schools and missionaries to have broken many spirits and fostered a sense, among some, of patriotism for the United States. When war broke out, many young men saw enlisting as an opportunity to gain entrance into mainstream white society. The United States also saw a need for Native Americans. They became invaluable, cheap, and immediate code talkers. From the Pacific Theater to the European Theater the Native American languages of the Lakota, Comanche, Navajo, Kiowa, and many others were heard over the airwaves. Strangely, it is difficult to know how many Native Americans fought in World War II because only the code talkers were 'racially' identified.

In addition to their language, the Native Americans possessed other resources. Vast amounts of plutonium, uranium, gold, oil, and other valuable deposits lie beneath the barren reservations of South Dakota, Oklahoma, and the Pueblo Crescent. On the Laguna reservation they dug up the materials needed for the research being done at Los Alamos, a mere 70 miles away. Trinity—test site for the A-bomb—was also close to the Pueblo reservation.

The Indigenous Revival

From N. Scott Momaday's Pulitzer Prize to the seizure of Alcatraz Island, Native Americans were on the move in 1969 and showed no signs of slowing. In 1970, the Cherokee nation formed a new constitution and took the first steps toward rejecting the American notion of race. Their constitution allowed membership in the tribal roles by virtue of ancestry. In 1970, they reclaimed the lands illegally stolen from them after they were removed to Oklahoma. Activists from the Cherokee nation were joined by hundreds of other Native Americans in their walk retracing the Trail of Tears. In 1975, the Passamaquoddy and Penobscot tribes filed a claim for nearly the entire state of Maine.

The most notorious, feared, and militant group came from Minneapolis in the 1960s. AIM (American Indian Movement) led a caravan to DC in 1972. When the Nixon administration refused to meet with them, they took over the Bureau of Indian Affairs building. Yielding to the threat of force, they absconded with tons of records. These records were given to their lawyers and used in lawsuits against the FBI.

The tension that resulted led to the showdown at Wounded Knee. There the United States military surrounded AIM activists for 71 days. AIM won. The media presence kept fatalities to one. AIM also brought its one concern—the Laramie Treaty of 1858—to public awareness. The tie-ups in court, unfortunately, slowed down the Native American

activists by the late 1970s. By then the whole world was aware of the civil rights violations committed against Native Americans. This awareness was all the greater because of a march on the UN Conference on Indigenous Peoples held in Geneva in 1977. Prominent leaders from Canada, the Iroquois nation, Mexico, South America, and the Hopi nation were joined by AIM and paraded in under drum and song. There they made their speeches and met with world leaders. The American press corps boycotted the event.

Critical Overview

Silko's reputation was established immediately when critical reception of *Ceremony* in 1977 was not only positive but appeared in big magazine—no small accomplishment for the first female Native American novelist in the late 1970s. Critical acclaim has been even more laudatory as the novel has become required reading across the nation. One facet of the novel particularly applauded was the success with which the novel challenges the reader to merge cultural frameworks.

However, the criticism also revealed cultural gaps. Critics tried to lump Silko's novel into prefabricated genres of American literature. There seemed to be great discomfort with viewing the novel as challenging and good on its own merits. Instead, the story is often patronizingly viewed as an effort to preserve Native American legend. Surprisingly, not one reviewer commented on the fact that the novel was set in the period of World War II when the problem of 1977 was the phenomenon of the Native American Vietnam Vets (there were more than 43,000 nationwide).

In his review for *The Washington Post*, Charles Larson makes an unqualified statement that "the war becomes an incredibly enlightening experience for Tayo—as it did for so many American Indians." He later comments that Tayo's story might fit in with fiction about World War II except that the novel is "strongly rooted within the author's own tribal background." That rootedness, for Larson, is the novel's value.

Hayden Carruth is not any more helpful in Harper's Magazine. She attempts to link Tayo with Taoist philosophy because Tayo is seeking his "way." Unfortunately, Carruth continues her review to say that the narrative repeats the old tale of the man returning rain and bounty to the people. This is done, she says, with the novelty of "native

[sic] American songs, legends, parables, a religio-cultural mythology in the fullest sense...."

Carruth also has two negative criticisms of the novel. First, the story might bother some whites because they might feel blamed, and some Native Americans because it does "not soften either the disagreements in the Indian community." Second, the novel "is flawed," she says, "by narrative devices that seem too contrived and by occasional stylistic inconsistencies."

Writing a review called, "Ghost Stories," Ruth Mathewson was less forgiving and more confused—but she liked the story. She described Silko as a "saver" whose "determination to preserve so much ... makes great demands on the reader, who must exercise a selectivity the author has not provided." That is, Silko has not succeeded in blending the roles of curator and scribe.

Mathewson also brings her understanding of ceremony to bear on the novel when she says that the hero's effort to heal the people "calls for a slow, meditative response." However, Silko also "exploits popular fictional elements, raising expectations of speed and suspense that she does not satisfy." Mathewson admits many of the "interrupting" poems "fell flat for me." Finally, she says Silko's prose style is "reminiscent of long-forgotten novels of the '20s" and achieves a "gratuitous realism."

Frank MacShane, in *The New York Times Book Review,* asserts: 'the literature of the American Indian is ritualistic." Furthermore, he views the purpose of this literary tradition as the establishment of "a sense of unity between the individual and his surroundings ... [and] ... Silko's first novel, aptly titled 'Ceremony,' fits into this tradition." Although offering a favorable assessment of the novel, his comments often sound like he is talking about a work of nonfiction instead of the first novel by a Native American woman who is trying to bind her oral traditions with the demands of print culture.

Peter G. Beidler, in *American Indian Quarterly,* places Silko with other distinguished Native American authors such as N. Scott Momaday and James Welch. Here the developing similarities of Native American literature are explored—the male Native American begins confused but reorients himself to his tribal identity. He also discusses the historical consciousness evident in the stories. He does offer some negative criticism, however, when he faults Silko for not developing her women characters.

Elaine Jahner offered considerate insight into the novel in the *Prairie Schooner* by acknowledging Silko as a novelist. She said,

> "it is ... Silko's profound and efficient understanding of the relationship between the tribal sense of order that is perpetuated through oral storytelling and those other models of narrative order—the novel and the short story that makes her a writer whose works enable Indian and non-Indian alike to understand that the traditional written genres can perpetuates some of the creative impulses that were formerly limited to the oral mode of transmission."

More recent criticism has followed Jahner. James Ruppert, for example, wrote in 1988 that Silko fuses "contemporary American Fiction with Native American storytelling." By the time of Ruppert's review, however, *Ceremony* had almost reached the status of canonical work in college syllabi across the nation. It remains a favorite book for people of all backgrounds who are slightly disillusioned with America and who want to understand how to construct a new identity. With that motivation, there are many people actively identifying with Tayo as a new American hero.

Unfortunately, as Silko recently told Thomas Irmer during an *Alt-X* interview, her critical reputation as a writer has been influenced by her more political and very anti-capitalist 1991 novel, *Almanac of the Dead.*

Criticism

Robert Bennett

Bennett is a graduate student in English at the University of California at Santa Barbara. In the following essay, he analyzes how Leslie Marmon Silko's novel, Ceremony, *uses Native American cultural traditions and an environmentalist land ethic to create a revisionist critique of American politics and history.*

The central conflict of Leslie Marmon Silko's *Ceremony* is Tayo's struggle to gain psychological wholeness in the face of various traumatic experiences, ranging from a troubled childhood to cultural marginalization and combat experiences during World War II. Throughout the novel, the key to Tayo's psychological recovery is his rediscovery of Native American cultural practices.

Most of the crucial turning points in the novel occur when Tayo listens to, takes part in, or learns more about Native American cultural traditions. He

What Do I Read Next?

- St. Andrew's "Healing The Witchery: Medicine in Silko's *Ceremony*," printed in Arizona Quarterly, Vol. 44, No 1, discusses the Pueblo cosmology in greater detail. This is a good article for further investigating the underlying religious and cultural themes of the novel.

- After ten years of work, Silko published her second novel, *Almanac of the Dead*. This novel is more overtly political and reflects the hysteria surrounding illegal immigration, drug running, the CIA, and other phenomena of the 1980s. Like *Ceremony*, legends are interwoven with the present day as an ancient book is pieced back together after being smuggled out of the clutches of the book burning Spanish.

- Silko corrects some mistakes about her own biography and gives insights into her work in a book of essays, *Yello Woman and a Beauty of the Spirit* (1996). In this collection, she tells of her fascination with photography, the ancient codices, and some of the historical events which influenced her novels.

- N. Scott Momaday's *House Made of Dawn* was published in 1968 and won a Pulitzer Prize in 1969. It was published at the start of a Native American cultural renaissance and in the midst of a new assertion of political rights, the novel tells the story of a man returning to his Kiowa Pueblo from World War II.

- A decade before Dee Brown and the general reconsideration of Native Americans that occurred in the early 1970s, William Brandon presented a general survey of Native American history for The American Heritage Library. The book was appropriately titled, *Indians,* and was published in 1961. The work, though brief, is quite remarkable for its scope and objectivity.

- Ward Churchill's *A Little Matter of Genocide: Holocaust and Denial in the Americas 1492 to the Present* published in 1998, is his latest work documenting the history of his people. A Cherokee himself, Churchill has been an avid chronicler of the attempt to eradicate the Native Americans from the planet. In this work, he focuses on the attempt to cover up the story of genocide.

- A record of Native American political activism in the 1970s has been compiled by Troy Johnson, Joane Nagel, and Duane Champagne, entitled, *American Indian Activism: Alcatraz to the Longest Walk.*

- A Lumbee Indian named David E. Wilkins charted the way in which the US Supreme Court has curtailed the rights of Native Americans. The result was his 1977 work, *American Indian Sovereignty and the U.S. Supreme Court: The Masking of Justice,* where he examines fifteen landmark cases for their implications on Indians as well as all minority groups.

---

progresses towards recovery when he visits medicine men, returns to traditional customs and practices, or develops an intimate relationship with someone like Ts'eh who lives according to traditional ways. As he develops an increased understanding of native cultural practices and ritual ceremonies he finds psychological peace, which he quickly loses whenever he seeks other sources of healing—whether he seeks them in the glories of war, the pleasures of alcohol, or the medical practices of the army psychiatric hospital.

The novel's opening poem describes the incredible powers that language, stories, and rituals have in Native American cultures: ceremonies are the only cure for human and cultural ailments, and stories and language have the power to create worlds. As the novel progresses, it demonstrates this power by showing how rituals are more effective than anything else in helping Tayo heal.

Moreover, Tayo's struggle to return to indigenous cultural traditions parallels Silko's own struggle as a writer who wants to integrate Native American traditions into the structure of her novel. Instead of simply following the literary conventions used by other American and European writers, Silko develops new literary conventions that draw upon Native American cultural traditions. For example, her narrative plot follows a cyclical sense of time, like that found in Native American myths and legends, instead of a western linear sense of time. It is also open to non-rational spiritual experiences instead of limiting itself to scientific logic and reason. In addition, her general focus is more on the community as a whole and Tayo's relationship to that community than it is on Tayo's personal individuality.

Even more importantly, she structures the entire novel itself as a sacred ritual or ceremony. Throughout the novel, she repeatedly switches back and forth between the main plot and a series of interconnected poems based on various Native American legends.

These interspersed poems create a second mythic narrative that runs parallel to the realistic narrative about Tayo. Even though these mythical poems take up less space than the realistic narrative, they are equally, if not more, important than the realistic narrative. They provide additional insight into Tayo's various struggles, they outline the pattern for his recovery, and they are placed at both the beginning and the end of the novel. In addition, Betonie's healing ceremony encapsulates the central themes and struggles developed throughout the novel, and it marks the central turning point in Tayo's recovery.

By making these mythic poems and ritual ceremonies such a significant part of the novel, Silko extends her authorial voice beyond first-person and third-person narration to include the ritualistic voice of a shaman or storyteller. Thus, Silko expresses the Native American belief that ritual healing and art are intimately connected because stories and rituals have the power to heal.

Nevertheless, both Silko's description of Native American healing ceremonies and her own artistic use of Native American narrative forms are unorthodox. For example, Ku'oosh's traditional rituals partially cure Tayo, but Betonie's new complex, hybrid ceremonies are even more effective. By making Betonie's rituals more potent than Ku'oosh's, Silko suggests that recovering one's cultural roots does not always mean being stuck in the past and endlessly repeating only what has been done before. Instead, Silko argues that even traditional cultures need to evolve and change, modify-

ing to meet new circumstances and enlarging to create a broader dialogue with other cultural traditions. In this sense, Silko's sense of ritual is not narrowly Native American but broadly multicultural.

Native American traditions make up an essential part of that multicultural mosaic, but they are not the whole of it. This multicultural sensibility is further demonstrated by Silko's frequent attempts to develop connections between different cultures within her novel. In particular, Silko develops several relationships between Native American and Japanese cultures. Tayo believes that the Japanese soldier is his Native American uncle because he has a spiritual sensitivity to the interconnectedness of all peoples and cultures. Tayo cannot stand Emo's hatred toward the Japanese because he realizes that violence toward any part of this multicultural mosaic inevitably hurts everyone. In fact, Tayo eventually realizes that even his own anger toward Emo must be overcome because violence cannot be prevented with more violence.

The novel's conclusion makes this connection between Native Americans and the Japanese even clearer because both Native Americans and the Japanese were victims of World War II. Native American lands were destroyed through uranium mining in order to destroy the Japanese with bombs built from the mines on native reservations. Thus, Silko demonstrates that there are more connections between cultures than one might recognize at first glance. While this multicultural vision derives from traditional Native American beliefs about the interconnectedness of all beings, it extends beyond Native American cultures to include all of the world's many cultures.

In addition, *Ceremony* also links Native American cultural traditions to the land and people's relationship to it. The novel is full of beautiful descriptions of the natural landscape, philosophical discussions about the essential nature of land, and ritual ceremonies connected to the landscape.

In particular, Silko's sense of the land functions in two ways. First, the ceremonies heal Tayo by reconnecting him to the land. They orient him according to sacred geographies, they teach him the importance and meaning of particular places, and they endow the earth with spiritual significance. Throughout the novel, Silko repeatedly reminds the reader that Native American cultures see the land and ceremonial rituals as inseparably connected and mutually reinforcing sources of spiritual well being. Drawing closer to the land helps Tayo better understand Native American ritual ceremonies, just as participating in these ceremonies helps Tayo reconnect himself to the land. These are two sides of the same coin.

In addition, Silko also uses Native American beliefs about the land to address a wide variety of contemporary political and cultural issues such as environmentalism, colonialism, and the sovereignty of Native American peoples. In this sense, Silko's sense of the land involves not only a native spiritual worldview but also a comprehensive political critique.

By drawing attention to the relationships between colonialism and economic inequality, between private property and racial divisions, and between mining and nuclear destruction, Silko calls into question western civilization's economic and legal interpretations of the land. America's claim to the land of America is revealed as a hypocritical mask for colonial conquest, just as raping the environment through mining is revealed as part of a larger industrial-military complex whose ultimate goal is to produce weapons of mass destruction.

An excellent example of these kinds of connections can be seen when Silko exposes that the real purpose behind Floyd Lee's wolf-proof fence is to keep Indians and Mexicans out. With this image of the wolf-Indian-Mexican fence, Silko shows the relationship between western civilization's hostility toward the natural environment (wolves), its economic ideology of private property (fences), and racial divisions between the dominant Anglo-American culture and other minority cultures (Native American and Mexican).

The irony that Mr. Lee's fence enables him to steal Tayo's cattle in addition to protecting his own cattle only further emphasizes how Silko politicizes this image. Legal and political boundaries not only divide mine from yours, but they also enable me to steal what is yours, like they enabled the stealing of native lands.

Throughout the novel, Silko combines images like Mr. Lee's wolf-Indian-Mexican fence with images of international wars and mining and nuclear testing on Native American lands. In the end, it is the Trinity test site that prompts Tayo's climactic epiphany of how the divisions between cultures are created by western civilization's war against nature in the name of private property. This war against nature ends up turning the creative powers of nature against themselves to produce weapons of mass destruction. This, in turn, escalates into a war against us as neighbors turn against neighbors and

nations turn against nations justified by the boundaries legitimized by the ideology of land ownership.

Land ownership becomes the central issue, however, not only because it negates a sacred understanding of the land as a living being shared by all but also because the test site is specifically land taken from Native American peoples. Like Mr. Lee's fence, the test site simultaneously represents both the destructiveness of western economic development and the hypocrisy of what whites have done to the American continent in the name of building and defending the nation. Ultimately, Tayo rejects white civilization for a deeper spiritual understanding of a world without boundaries, without divisions, and without private property.

In this sense, Silko's novel is not just a story about one Native American veteran trying to piece his life back together after returning from World War II. In a much deeper sense, it is an allegory about America as a whole and about how Tayo and other Native Americans fit into the broader mosaic of American history. In particular, Silko's novel rewrites American history so that Native Americans like Tayo are no longer pushed into the margins and ignored. She shows that they have contributed to and continue to contribute to American history by providing the land on which it happens, by fighting for America in international conflicts, and by contributing to America's economic development.

Even more importantly, however, she shows that Native American cultural traditions also provide an alternative, and in Silko's opinion, superior view of what America's future could look like if it will chose to be more spiritually sensitive, multiculturally respectful, and environmentally responsible. In this sense, *Ceremony* adds an important and potentially healing voice to the on-going debate of what it means to be an American.

Source: Robert Bennett, in an essay for *Novels for Students,* Gale, 1998.

Elizabeth N. Evasdaugher

In Evasdaughter's analysis of Silko's use of humor in Ceremony, *the critic points out the jokes, gentle teasing, and irony that lighten the tale and confirm Silko as a "true comic novelist."*

In *Ceremony*, Leslie Silko brilliantly crosses racial styles of humor in order to cure the foolish delusions readers may have, if we think we are superior to Indians or inferior to whites, or perhaps superior to whites or inferior to Indians. Silko plays off affectionate Pueblo humor against the black humor so prominent in 20th-century white culture. This comic strategy has the end-result of opening our eyes to our general foolishness, and also to the possibility of combining the merits of all races. Joseph Campbell wrote in *The Inner Reaches of Outer Space* of the change in mythologies away from the local and tribal toward a mythology that will arise from "this unified earth as of one harmonious being." *Ceremony* is a work that changes local mythologies in that more inclusive spirit.

Silko is the right person to have written this book. She herself is a mixed-blood, and her experience has evidently given her access not only to a variety of problems, but also to a variety of styles of clowning and joking.... Although *Ceremony* is serious, offering a number of valuable propositions for our consideration, the narrative also spins a web of jokes in the morning sun....

The ceremony Silko narrates is that of a Navajo sing, but one not sung exactly as it would have been done before whites arrived in New Mexico, nor sung by a pure-blood Indian, nor sung on behalf of a pure-blood Indian. As is traditional, the ceremony is to be completed after the sing by the sick man, a Laguna named Tayo. His efforts to finish the ceremony by correct action form the last half of the novel, just as the first half was composed of the events which made him sick. These two series of events, taken together, make it clear that what the Veterans' Administration doctors have labelled *battle fatigue* is, in Tayo's case at least, really a struggle to make a decision about death. He tries two ways of responding to its invasion of his life that do not work—self-erasure and killing an agent of death. Finally he is able to find a way of opposing destruction which will not lead to his erasure as a force on the reservation, not allow anyone to kill him, and most important, not change him too into an agent of death.

Tayo's difficulty is grave, yet Silko jokes about it frequently. The belief among whites that Indians never laugh is contradicted continually by the sounds of Indians responding to subtle in-jokes or to a corrective kind of teasing crystallized in the work of ritual clowns. Black Elk [in *Black Elk Speaks: Being the Life Story of a Holy Man of the Oglala Sioux*] speaks of clowns appearing when people needed a good laugh. At that time, he says, the clowns based their performance on the minor frustrations of life or on our minor flaws as human

beings, such as our tendency to exaggerate our plight.... I believe that Leslie Marmon Silko is in effect a sacred clown, turning the light of laughter against evils which might otherwise weaken us all....

Human clowning of a farcical type, exposing our human flaws in a manifestly physical way, builds up Silko's philosophy. The drunk Indian veterans who had attempted to fight over Helen Jean "started pushing at each other, in a staggering circle on the dance floor. The other guys were cheering for a fight. They forgot about her." Their lack of real love for women goes with their general ineffectuality. The whole scene parodies the war, all its supposedly ardent love for motherland, all its proclaimed desire to protect wife and home forgotten in the blundering, futile rituals of fighting.

These clowning scenes become more elaborate as the novel continues. An example of this is the size and complexity of the expedition organized to capture Tayo at his most harmless. He is carefully surrounded at night by V.A. doctors in dark green government cars, Bureau of Indian Affairs police, and some of the old men of the pueblo, just as if he were insane, hostile, and armed, when we as readers know he has spent the summer outdoors looking after his skinny cattle and rediscovering the old religion, or if you like, dreaming of a beautiful Indian woman. The absurdity of this great stakeout does not cancel, but accompanies and points up the danger to Tayo. As readers, we both fear for him and half-expect the ambush will be 100% ineffectual....

[Silko] teases her readers in a gentle manner that can enlighten. When Tayo is ordered to shoot a Japanese soldier and suddenly sees him as his Uncle Josiah, everyone around him tells him that Josiah couldn't be in two places at the same time or that hallucinations are natural with malaria or battle fatigue.... Actually the vision, which I would call a projection of Tayo's or Josiah's mind, illustrates for Tayo the universality of human goodness and the evil of killing. When, reading along, we finally realize this, it's natural to smile at our earlier foolish Europeanized faith in our ideas of mental illness....

Silko turns her teasing also toward younger Indians like Helen Jean, who evaluates Tayo as the least friendly male at the Y Bar, when in fact he is the only one who cares, even briefly, what is going to happen to her. As for half-breeds like Tayo, Silko repeatedly exposes his gullibility toward erroneous white beliefs. His difficulty in believing that someone other than an Indian will steal, much less that a white man will steal, is typical of Indian jokes about oppression [as Joseph Bruchac said in *Parabola,* Winter, 1987.]

Silko does not exclude herself from being teased either. At the end of her innovative portrayal of evil, she allows Tayo's grandmother, the archetypal storyteller, to indicate her boredom at the story of Emo's downfall:

> Old Grandma shook her head slowly, and closed her cloudy eyes again. 'I guess I must be getting old,' she said, 'because these goings-on around Laguna don't get me excited any more.' She sighed, and laid her head back on the chair. 'It seems like I already heard these stories before … only thing is, the names sound different.'

This narrative irony is a little joke at all of us —Silko for feeling she had written an original work about evil, any Indians who might have been worrying about her modernization of the stories, any whites who might have believed the test of art is originality, or maybe entertainment, rather than spiritual power. The serious effectiveness of Silko's tale is indicated by the passage which follows: "Whirling darkness/has come back on itself.… It is dead for now."

All the instances of Indian humor in *Ceremony* have been overlooked by some of the white readers I have talked with, possibly because of lack of contact with non-European communities or culture. Indian irony can be "either so subtle or so keyed to an understanding from within of what is funny to a people that an outsider would fail to recognize it [*Parabola,* Winter, 1987.]" Such outsiders tend to take many light passages in *Ceremony* as solemn or tense, and wear themselves out before the real crisis comes. Yet Silko has given non-Indian readers enough clues to enjoy her inside jokes.…

Tayo at times carries irony as far as black humor. When other barflies buzz about their equality with whites, Tayo tells a more truthful, and by contrast, more ironic narrative about their status. When Emo repeatedly brings up how whites have taken everything the Indians had, Tayo wisecracks to himself, "Maybe Emo was wrong; maybe white people didn't have everything. Only Indians had droughts." This private shot of wry acknowledges both white injustice and Emo's dishonesty, thus mentally challenging blackness, not just learning to endure it.…

Emo mocks traditional Indian values, despises everything living, and spends his time spreading contempt, resentment, idleness, pleasure in the hu-

> " *…I believe that Leslie Marmon Silko is in effect a sacred clown, turning the light of laughter against evils which might otherwise weaken us all.…*"

miliation and suffering of other people—in short, hatred. His first diatribe in *Ceremony* is against reservation ranchlands: "Look what is here for us. Look. Here's the Indians' mother earth! Old dried-up thing!" By breaking the law of reverence, his sarcasms raise loud laughter. By speaking only of white women, he gets his fellow veterans, except Tayo, to laugh and cheer at stories about bringing women down. By referring to Japanese soldiers always and only as Japs, as officers, as enemies, he tricks the others into rejoicing at the smashing of fellow people of color. They are fooled because Emo's jokes resemble jokes made "not to take our minds off our troubles, but to point out ways to survive and even laugh" [as Bruchac noted]. Unfortunately, Emo's references to troubles do not carry hints about survival or corrections of faults. Not noticing the difference, Emo's bar buddies, most of them, commit themselves by every laugh to discard a little more of Indian tradition, their only possible road to a satisfying life.…

Silko sees through Emo's descriptions and can see where his black philosophy must end. To acknowledge evil and study it, has not made a convert of her, however. She plays a worse trick on Emo than he wanted to play on Tayo; as a true comic novelist always does, she thwarts evil and establishes the good in a new and more complete harmony. Hers is the laughter that rises in the spirit, when the preachers of inferiority and inevitable doom have been disproved and defeated. What is finest in her, I believe, is the wisdom of her method of bringing the good out of its trials safely. Her wisdom is that of choosing love.…

Although the last scenes of *Ceremony* have a number of surprises, they have been prepared for. Tayo's refusal to be caught up in the dynamics of mutual destruction is comical because it seems cowardly, as whites judge bravery, even disloyal, by Army standards. In truth, his hiding behind the rock is his least white, least hateful action, even, perhaps, a sort of yellow humor, to go with his Asian connection.

Not only does Silko as novelist arrange for the defeat of Emo's plan either to sacrifice or to corrupt Tayo. She also plots a punishment for the villain which is more appropriate and funnier than the one he has planned for Tayo. In the outcome, Silko, and readers who side with her, laugh, perhaps silently, but also happily at Emo's final defeat, hearts lifting because "he got his." In this way, as a comic novelist, Silko has brought in a third type of black humorist, the one who steals the tricks of the blackest jokers and uses them against their owners. I have found that Anglo or anglicized readers easily miss Silko's punishment of Emo, thinking he has gotten away scot-free. That's because she outfoxes him as Tayo did, aikido style, without violence. He might have died, but the old men of the pueblo only exile him, and he chooses to go to California, the epitome of all that he admires. The joke of it is seen by the now gentle Tayo: "'California,' Tayo repeated softly, 'that's a good place for him'." This brief and quiet comment scores off evil more aptly than Emo ever scored off good. Emo will be in harmony with California; the apex of his desires is as bad as he is. This joke mocks the White Lie, the delusion that whites are superior, for in it Silko is using the most prosperous part of her region, a proud achievement of white culture in this country, as the most severe punishment she can assign, far worse than mutilation, an early death, or life in Gallup. Emo's exile is a joke, too, about the self-proclaimed superiority of white institutions. If the old men were to bring charges against Emo, government courts would probably either discredit Tayo's testimony or execute Emo. None of their methods would stop Emo's impact on the pueblo. The Laguna answer to capital punishment is more intelligent, avoids imitating murderers, and punishes them less mercifully.

Whites with some appreciation for Indian culture sometimes express a surprising certitude that "this once great culture is being lost or replaced by an Anglo culture that does not have the same respect for nature … and is in some ways morally inferior to it" [according to Edith Blicksilver in *Southwest Review*, 1979]. The celestial laughter Silko calls forth by her *Ceremony* shows that Indian civilization is living and has the potential to transform anglo culture. As she said in a 1978 in-terview [in *American Studies in Scandinavian*, 1981], "These things will only die if we neglect to tell the stories. So I am telling the stories." Moreover she has turned the quietest laugh against the loudest. With the help of Indian humor, even if we do not entirely get her jokes, she purifies us of our illusions about white culture, and those about Indian culture as well. Ultimately she demonstrates that combining our cultures, as her narrative does, has the power to civilize both.

Source: Elizabeth N. Evasdaugher, "Leslie Marmon Silko's *Ceremony*: Healing Ethnic Hatred by Mixed-Breed Laughter" in *MELUS,* Vol. 15, No. 1, Spring, 1988, pp. 83–95.

Kristin Herzog

Herzog focuses on Silko's depiction of two aspects of gender portrayal in a Native American novel that transcends Western stereotypes—that of a male protagonist as a "feeling man" and that of a female divinity as a "thinking woman."

Feminist literary criticism of the past decades has often pointed to powerful women figures in American literature. From Hawthorne's Hester Prynne to Alice Walker's Meridian one can find many images which counter the stereotype of the clinging, submissive, and self-sacrificing woman. By contrast, these powerful women are courageous, independent of judgment, and as intelligent as any man, without becoming egocentric or losing their sense of interpersonal relationships. Little attention has been paid, however, to male figures who are sensitive instead of ruthless, gentle instead of heroic, community-conscious instead of individualistic. It is especially important to find such images in Native American literature because in the popular imagination the American Indian male is still either a savage killer, a degenerate drunkard, or nature's stoic, noble man.

I would like to concentrate here on two aspects of gender portrayal in a Native American novel: the holistic depiction of a male protagonist, a "feeling man," and the mythological background of such a character portrayal, a female divinity who is a "thinking woman." Both are transcending Western stereotypes of gender portrayal.

Leslie Marmon Silko's novel *Ceremony* centers on Tayo, a young man of the Southwestern Laguna tribe, who fought in the Pacific islands during World War II. His cousin, with whom he grew up like a brother, is killed by the Japanese. Tayo is driven insane by this loss as well as by seeing the image of his beloved uncle and stepfather, Josiah, in the face of one of the Japanese he is supposed to shoot.

When Tayo returns to the United States, he is placed in a mental hospital in Los Angeles and drugged into senselessness by doctors who are unable to understand his inner turmoil. On his release and return to the Laguna reservation he suffers from horrible nightmares, nausea, and a feeling of total failure. He accuses himself of having cursed the jungle rain which contributed to the death of his cousin and thereby having caused the drought which is ruining the Laguna people. Only after undergoing an ancient healing ritual (a bear cure involving sand-painting) is Tayo able to find sanity, to understand the complexities of individual, social, and "cosmic" sin—here called "witchery"—and to rediscover his strong ties to the land and his people.

The style of the novel superbly expresses the essence of the story. It is often as fragmentary as Tayo's mental condition and as disjointed as the tribe's position between cultural persistence and assimilation. Past and future are telescoped into the present. Flashbacks and dream visions contribute to the reader's feeling of disruption as well as of a continual challenge to do what Tayo instinctively tries to do, that is, weave together the fragments, struggle to find a pattern of meaning. What differentiates Silko's style from that of most Anglo-American novelists is her use of oral traditions which are intricately woven into the narrative in the form of poems, ritual prayers, stories, and tribal rumors....

The point of the novel is that Tayo finds his identity by rediscovering in himself and in all of creation what traditionally has been called the "feminine." His true manhood had been violated when he was supposed to kill people, especially since they looked like his kin. Being forced as a soldier to suppress his *anima,* he was driven insane. But the memory of childhood experiences and tribal stories reawakens his sensitivity and his nurturing instincts which, in the end, make him more, not less, of a man.

From earliest infancy, Tayo has learned to live by instinct and sensuous perception. His Laguna mother is driven from her tribe because Tayo is an illegitimate child, fathered by a Mexican. She survives for only a few years, living with other outcasts in a slum area. The neglected child orients himself by smells, sounds, and sights, whether sensing the arrival of his perfumed mother and her beer-smelling lovers or detecting morsels of food in refuse piles. When at the age of four he is taken by his aunt and uncle into their ranch home, he learns the smells of animals and the sights and sounds of mountains, winds, and rivers. It is the memory of these sensations which helps him to recover from his war trauma and to feel deep joy when he is alone with nature:

> He breathed deeply, and each breath had a distinct smell of snow from the north, of ponderosa pine on the rimrock above; finally he smelled horses from the direction of the corral, and he smiled. Being alive was all right then.... He squatted down by the pool and watched the dawn spreading across the sky like yellow wings. The mare jingled the steel shanks of the bit with her grazing, and he remembered the sound of the bells in late November.

Tayo has been shown by his uncle Josiah—another male figure who is gentle and caring—that violence is senseless. When, as a young boy, he kills many flies because his white teacher has taught the children that flies carry disease, Josiah lovingly reprimands him and explains that in immemorial times when the people were starving because they had behaved badly, it was a fly which went to Mother Earth to ask forgiveness for the people. Since then the grateful people do not kill flies.

When Tayo shoots his first deer, he carefully observes the ritual of the conscientious hunter who would never kill for sport. After he has undergone the healing ceremony, he is responsive to nature in its smallest manifestations, imitating the gentleness of the bees in pollinating flowers with a small feather or saving a tree from an early winter storm by carefully shaking the snow from its branches.

Tayo lives out of dreams—whether nightmares or beautiful visions. Compared to the other war veterans who are noisy, bragging drunkards, he is shy and often silent. But he is no coward or weakling. When one of the young men, Emo, speaks insultingly of his own people as well as of Tayo's mixed ancestry, Tayo is so enraged that, like Billy Budd, he becomes violent in his inability to express his feelings. On this occasion he comes close to killing Emo.

An important part of Tayo's story is his encounter with Ts'eh, the mysterious woman who is also—on the mythological level—a goddess or mountain spirit.... He learns how to use herbs and to gather plant seeds with great care. "Ts'eh Montano, or 'Water Mountain,' seems a coded and composite reference to the spirit-woman who returns vitality to the arid desert for Indians, Mexicans, and whites alike, all embodied in Tayo, all sharing in

> "*The point of the novel is that Tayo finds his identity by rediscovering in himself and in all of creation what traditionally has been called the 'feminine.' His true manhood had been violated when he was supposed to kill people ...*"

the sickness and health of one another, many as one with the land" [Kenneth Lincoln, *Native American Renaissance,* 1983].

There are other male figures in the novel who are "feeling" men: old Ku'oosh, a wise Laguna medicine man; Robert, the kind uncle and stepfather; and especially Betonie, the Navaho-Mexican medicine man who patiently counsels Tayo and brings about his healing by guiding him through the ceremony....

Non-Indian readers are likely to find the role of Ts'eh in Tayo's recovery ambiguous. A superficial reader might simply consider the relationship between her and Tayo a sexual-romantic interlude to be expected in any contemporary novel. Moreover, feminist readers might see in Ts'eh the stereotype of a woman who offers her body to the hero. The basic problem involved here is the bi-cultural perspective. Images, concepts, and patterns of belief are difficult to merge in a novel on American Indian life to be read by a predominantly white, Western audience....

Ts'eh reawakens Tayo's belief in a balanced world which he dimly remembers from tribal stories. She is representative of earth, rain, wind, and sky, but also of the thought power that controls the elements. Her "storm-pattern blanket" indicates her ordered strength. At times Tayo feels that Ts'eh is just an apparition or superstition, that she "meant nothing at all; it was all in his own head." Her lineage or family seem to be unknown. Her voice can be as unreal as an echo. On another level, however, she is very real: "He had not dreamed her; she was there as certainly as the sparrows had been there, leaving spindly scratches in the mud."

This double vision on a physical and a metaphysical level is alien to Western readers. They find it difficult to comprehend that a real crawling spider coming up after the rain is, seen from another aspect, Spider-Woman, the divine creatrix; that Tayo's mother, the long-dead prostitute, can mythologically and poetically merge into Mother Earth or Mother Corn; that Ts'eh, the woman that Tayo makes love to, is a manifestation of Thought-Woman, the balance of the universe. Silko may not have fully succeeded in portraying Ts'eh in terms of this double vision, but her intention is certainly to visualize Tayo's ability to overcome the split between body and mind, which Westerners had trained into him, by having him experience Spider-Woman's wholeness through Ts'eh. The Laguna people are "woman-dominant; they're a woman-centered people." Their images of gender can help us overcome Western stereotypes of excessively rational, power-wielding men as well as of women who are mindless childbearers. Each gender attains wholeness and vitality only if it includes traits usually ascribed to its opposite....

Silko's novel is in keeping with recent anthropological findings about the social complexity of gender identification. Tayo's self-understanding as a male is not just biologically determined; it changes with the influence of his environment. His story and that of his comrades show that gender identity has to be nurtured. The assumption that in all "primary" cultures of the world males basically dominate while females are the submissive sex, that men always represent culture and women nature, is an untenable Western assumption....

For American Indians, spirit ties all human beings to each other and to the whole cosmos; therefore it also unifies the genders. Spirit does not dissolve gender distinctions, but it renders certain gender traits interchangeable. When Tayo and his comrades have to fight in the Pacific jungles, spirit is trained and drained out of them, making them fit to kill blindly. Being cut off from their physical and spiritual roots, some of them, like Emo, become perverted. But Tayo is able to keep Spider-Woman's love for all of creation alive in his manhood, because some gentle men, like Josiah, Robert, Ku'oosh, and Betonie, had nurtured him in this love. After the trauma of the war, he had to experience a reenactment of Spider-Woman's spirit to recover his wholeness. A dearth of spirit hardens gender roles.

Source: Kristin Herzog, "Thinking Woman and Feeling Man: Gender in Silko's Ceremony" in *MELUS,* Vol. 12, No. 1, Spring, 1985, pp. 25–36.

Sources

Peter G. Beidler, in a review in *Native American Quarterly,* Vol. 3, No. 4, Winter, 1977-1978, pp. 357-58.

Hayden Carruth, "Harmonies in Time and Space," in *Harper's Magazine,* Vol. 254, No. 1525, June, 1977, pp. 80-2.

Elaine Jahner, "All the World's a Story" in *Prairie Schooner,* Vol. 51, No. 4, Winter, 1977-1978, pp. 415-16.

Charles R. Larson, "The Jungles of the Mind," in *Book World-The Washington Post,* April 24, 1977, p. E4.

Frank MacShane, "American Indians, Peruvian Jews: 'Ceremony'," in *The New York Times Book Review,* June 12, 1977, pp. 15, 33.

Ruth Mathewson, "Ghost Stories," in *The New Leader,* Vol. LX, No. 12, June 6, 1977, pp. 14-15.

James Ruppert, "The Reader's Lessons in *'Ceremony',*" in *Arizona Quarterly,* Vol. 44, No. 1, Spring, 1988, pp. 78-85.

Leslie Marmon Silko, "Language and Literature from a Pueblo Indian Perspective" in *Yellow Woman and a Beauty of the Spirit,* Simon & Schuster, 1996, pp. 48-59.

For Further Study

Thomas Berger, *Little Big Man,* Fawcett, 1964.
  Written by a man known for his probing satire about America, the novel is the life story of Jack Crab—the only living survivor of Custer's Last Stand. The novel and the film (with Dustin Hoffman, 1970), were part of a general redress of the image of the Indian. Custer, in this version, is not the Hollywood hero but the more historically accurate eccentric who lost all his men and himself in a battle with the Lakota lead by Crazy Horse.

Dee Brown, *Bury My Heart at Wounded Knee: an Indian History of the American West,* Holt, 1970.
  History books were being rewritten both as a reaction to the rise in minority consciousness caused by the era of Civil Rights and as a further catalyst to political activism. This volume tells a story very different from the more patriotic story 'how the West was won.' For example, such battles as the 1890 Wounded Knee event, is revealed to be the massacre of Big Foot's band of 300 old men, women, and children.

Arthur S. Flemming, *Indian Tribes: A Continuing Quest for Survival,* a Report by the US Commission on Civil Rights, 1981.
  Eight years after the siege at Wounded Knee, a long overdue report was issued by the US Commission on Civil Rights. It found that most violations of Native American rights are the direct result of public ignorance and misinformation (e.g. though "an entire volume of the US Code is devoted to Indian Law" it is a rare Law School that notices even the oversight). Furthermore, the report found that greed—not racism—accounts for the backlash which erupts whenever treaty rights are asserted or upheld in court.

Tom Holm, *Strong Hearts, Wounded Souls: Native American Veterans of the Vietnam War,* University of Texas Press, 1996.
  Some 43,000 Native Americans served in the Vietnam War but their contributions went undocumented until Tom Holm began his interviews. He reflects on those interviews to explore the role of war and warrior, how their tribal customs sustained them in war, and what happened to them when they returned. Fortunately, many Native American Vietnam Vets had different experiences from their white counterparts because many Tribes were ready with ceremonies to heal the trauma of the "white path of peace."

Gertrude Simmons Bonin, "Impressions of an Indian Childhood," in *The Norton Anthology of American Literature,* Vol. II, 1989.
  The woman who could arguably have been the first Native American novelist, had not circumstances prevented her, was Gertrude Simmons Bonin (a.k.a. Zitkala-Sa, 1876-1938). Those circumstances were, quite simply, the needs of her people. She was a violinist, short story writer, progressive reformer, labor rights advocate, and secretary of the Society of American Indians (the first all-Indian run organization agitating for Indian rights). Her autobiographical pieces are a fascinating read.

The Chosen

Chaim Potok

1967

While Chaim Potok's central characters in *The Chosen* struggle between the spiritual obligations of Orthodox Judaism and secular American life, they also reflect universal conflicts between fathers and sons. The novel, Potok's first, was published in 1967 and enjoyed a wide readership, as well as critical acclaim. Potok received the Edward Lewis Wallant Award and a nomination for the National Book Award for *The Chosen*. The novel focuses on its two main characters, Danny Saunders and Reuven Malter, and covers their high school and college years, the period in their lives when they struggle for self-realization. Both are sons of religious fathers, but while Reuven's is orthodox and secularized, Danny's father is the head of an ultra-orthodox and mystical sect of Jews called Hasids. Rabbi Isaac Saunders, Danny's father, fully expects Danny to inherit his role as the spiritual leader of his congregation, but Danny is more interested in modern psychology. Reuven's father, David Malter, is a Hebrew scholar. The story begins with a baseball game between Reuven's and Danny's school teams. They both attend rival yeshivas, Jewish religious schools. Reuven and his classmates wear ordinary clothes and are coached by a gym teacher who is an avid baseball fan. Danny's team is coached by a religious Hasid who wears the black garments, skull cap, and earlocks traditional to his sect. Danny's team is not expected to win, but they have the reputation of being fierce. They do win the game and in the process, Danny breaks Reuven's glasses and sends him to the hospital with

glass in his eye. After an initial meeting in the hospital when Danny tries to apologize for the injury, the two boys become friends. The novel explores the relationship each boy has with his own father and the relationship each develops with the other boy's father.

Author Biography

Two life experiences have been major influences on the work of Chaim Potok. They are the world of Orthodox Judaism in which he was raised and the larger world he experienced when he served as an army chaplain during the Korean War. His war experience made him realize that growing up in a strict Jewish community had limited his aspirations to become a writer. Artistic endeavors were not considered the proper pursuit for Jewish boys. Instead, they were expected to study the Talmud, the combined body of writings on Jewish traditions.

Potok was born on February 17, 1929, and was raised in the Bronx, New York. His parents, Benjamin Max and Mollie, had fled persecution in their native Poland. As a young boy, Potok studied in a parochial Jewish school, called a yeshiva. While his early training was in the Hasidic tradition (a sect originating in eighteenth-century Poland that emerged as a reaction to growing Jewish formalism), he later became a conservative rabbi.

The young Potok had a keen interest in artistic pursuits, an interest that was piqued after his parochial school hired an instructor one summer to teach the class painting. Potok's father and teachers discouraged the boy from pursuing such interests because Hasids see the arts as frivolous and even rebellious towards God. Nevertheless, Potok's parents indulged him enough to allow their son to write short stories. Potok also liked to read books that were outside those assigned to him in class. Two of the most influential of these were James Joyce's *Portrait of the Artist as a Young Man* and Evelyn Waugh's *Brideshead Revisited.* Joyce's book appealed to Potok for its portrayal of the iconoclast, the person willing to go against social norms, and how this rebellious person sees the hypocrisy of those around him. But it was Waugh's novel that convinced Potok to become a writer himself, for he admired Waugh's ability to create whole worlds on paper, and he was fascinated by her portrayal of an upper-class British society that was so outside his personal experience.

Chaim Potok

Deciding that he was interested in religious and secular societies, Potok learned about both. He studied English literature at Yeshiva University, graduating summa cum laude in 1950, and then he attended the Jewish Theological Seminary, being ordained and receiving an M.H.L. in 1954. Completing his formal education in 1965, Potok earned his doctorate in philosophy from the University of Pennsylvania. During all these studies, he married Adena Sara Mosevitzky in 1958, and the family now includes two daughters, Rena and Naama. As for work, Potok found several positions at seminaries and did writing and editing for various Jewish publications.

Potok's desire to become a writer was also intensified after his Korean experience (he was a chaplain in the army from 1956–57). For the first time, he was thrust into a world where the values of Judaism had little meaning. The conflict of loyalty to parental values and the desire to study outside the prescribed texts and forms of Hasidic Judaism became the central theme in his first novel, *The Chosen,* which was published in 1967.

Potok has written eight novels, all of them dealing with the conflicts his characters feel between their family values and the values of the larger society. Although his books are written in the first person, he denies that his novels are autobiographical. Potok has also written numerous short stories and articles for periodicals and served as an editor for *Conservative Judaism* and the Jewish Publication Society. His teaching experience includes visiting professorships at the University of Pennsylvania and Bryn Mawr College, the Teachers' Institute of the Jewish Theological Seminary, and the University of Judaism in Los Angeles. Also well known for his nonfiction work *Wanderings: Chaim Potok's History of the Jews,* Potok has published many books that have been widely reviewed. He generally receives praise for the universal themes he develops, for his ability to bring to life the details of Jewish ghetto life in America, and for the struggles confronting his characters. Potok has, however, been criticized for contrived endings to his stories and what some reviewers consider a pretentious style.

Plot Summary

Book One

The Chosen explores the friendship between Jewish Reuven Malter and Hasidic (Jewish Orthodox) Danny Saunders. In Brooklyn during World War II, Danny hits Reuven in the face with a baseball, giving him a concussion. Reuven undergoes an operation to remove a piece of glass from his eye. In the hospital, he meets former boxer Tony Savo and Billy Merrit, a young boy blinded in a car accident. Danny visits Reuven and confides that his father expects him to become a rabbi, though he wants to be a psychologist. He also explains that his father disapproves of apikorsim (Jews who are not extremely orthodox) such as Reuven. Reuven's father, David Malter, urges Reuven to become friends with Danny because the Talmud (the book of Jewish holy law) says the two things one should acquire in life are a teacher and a close friend. When Danny calls again, the boys talk about religion and reading. Danny regularly visits the library to read books recommended to him by an old man who turns out to be Reuven's father. Danny explains that his father is a tzaddik (a Jewish spiritual leader), and that after his father dies he will be obliged to become tzaddik, too, for "if the son doesn't take the father's place, the dynasty falls apart." Danny comments on the irony of being forced to become a rabbi while Reuven freely chooses the same fate. Reuven's eye is healing, and his father arrives at the hospital that afternoon to take him home in time for Shabbat (sabbath).

Book Two

When Reuven returns home, everything seems sharper and clearer to him, as if he were seeing the world around him for the first time. Rav Malter narrates a brief history of Hasidism so Reuven can understand Danny's background. Reb Saunders, Danny's father, is a great Talmudist and a great tzaddik, with a reputation for brilliance and compassion. Danny reminds Reuven's father of a brilliant scholar who rebelled against the traditions of Hasidism. Danny's grandfather was a well-known Hasidic rabbi in Russia. Danny's father inherited the position of tzaddik, and led his Jewish community from Russia to America after World War I. Reuven meets Reb Saunders at his synagogue, and after he notes a mistake in Reb Saunders' gematriya (the Jewish theory that each letter of the Hebrew alphabet corresponds with a number), Reb Saunders gives his approval to the boys' friendship. Danny and Reuven both plan to attend the Samson Raphael Hirsch Seminary before becoming ordained rabbis.

Reuven meets Danny at the library after school. After becoming disturbed by reading negative views about Hasidism, Danny begins studying Sigmund Freud's books. Rav Malter worries about Reb Saunders' reaction to Danny's reading but realizes that Reb Saunders cannot stop it. Reuven visits Danny on Shabbat afternoon, and they review the Talmud with Reb Saunders. When Danny leaves the room, Reb Saunders demands that Reuven tell him about Danny's reading. He then asks Reuven to promise that he and his father will be a good influence on Danny. Danny mentions that he and his father "don't talk anymore, except when we study Talmud…. My father believes in silence. When I was ten or eleven years old, I complained to him about something, and he told me to close my mouth and look into my soul. He told me to stop running to him every time I had a problem."

Reuven's eye heals, and he studies for his final exams. When he calls the Merrit household, he learns that Billy Merrit's operation was unsuccessful, and he is severely depressed by the news. Danny and Reuven spend the summer talking, studying Talmud, and following the war news. Danny becomes increasingly disturbed by his study of Freud. When school begins, they meet only on Shabbat afternoons. In April, President Roosevelt dies and the country mourns. When the war in Europe ends in May, everyone is horrified by news of the German concentration camps. While Reb Saunders believes they were the will of God, Rav Malter refuses to accept this viewpoint. Rav Malter suffers a heart attack, and until he recovers Reuven lives with Danny's family. Reb Saunders speaks to Danny only during their arguments over Talmud.

Reuven's father insists that Palestine must become the Jewish homeland, an idea with which Reb Saunders violently disagrees. Danny comments that his father is suffering for the six million Jews who died. Though he doesn't understand the silence, Danny admires, respects, and trusts his father. However, he feels trapped by the expectation he must become tzaddik so as not to break the dynasty. The war ends in August, and in September Danny and Reuven enter Hirsch College. Both are older and slightly more mature. Reuven has started shaving, and Danny is wearing eyeglasses.

Book Three

Danny becomes upset when he discovers he must study experimental psychology rather than psychoanalysis in college. After talking with his psychology professor, he learns Professor Appleman objects more to Freud's methodology than his conclusions. Rav Malter becomes increasingly involved with Zionist activities. Zionism is prevalent at the college, and tensions build between the Hasidim (followers of Hasidism) and the Revisionists (who support the Irgun, or Palestinian terrorists). Reuven joins a religious Zionist youth group. Danny joins none of the groups but sympathizes with the Zionists.

After Rav Malter's speech at a Zionist rally, Reb Saunders excommunicates the Malters from the Saunders family. Reuven's school work deteriorates because of his anger towards Reb Saunders.

> For the rest of that semester, Danny and I ate in the same lunchroom, attended the same classes, studied in the same school synagogue, and often rode in the same trolley car—and never said a single word to each other. Our eyes met frequently, but our lips exchanged nothing. I lost all direct contact with him. It was an agony to sit in the same class with him, to pass him in the hallway, to see him in a trolley, to come in and out of the school building with him— and not to say a word. I grew to hate Reb Saunders with a venomous passion that frightened me at times, and I consoled myself with wild fantasies of what I would do to him if he ever fell into my hands.

The United Nations votes to create a Jewish state. As violence between Arabs and Jews escalates in Israel, the anti-Zionist tensions in school cease. Reuven's father suffers a second heart attack. Reuven studies Talmud using the scientific method and explains a particularly difficult passage

in class. Later, he explains his theory to Talmud teacher Rav Gershenson, who reveres his explanation but asks Reuven never to use this heretical method during class.

Rav Malter recovers, and Reuven and Danny, forbidden to talk to one another, communicate with their eyes, nods, and hand gestures. The college students become reconciled to Israel after a graduate is killed in the fighting around Jerusalem. A year later, Reb Saunders allows the boys to resume their friendship. Danny and Reuven dominate their Talmud class. Danny tells Reuven he plans to obtain a doctorate in clinical psychology and will tell his father on the day he receives his smicha (rabbinic ordination).

The last year of college begins. Danny realizes that "you can listen to silence and learn from it … sometimes it cries, and you can hear the pain of the world in it." When Danny's brother Levi becomes ill, Danny panics. Reuven believes Danny's fears relate to his worries about destroying the dynasty if he doesn't become tzaddik. But Levi recovers. Danny applies to Harvard, Berkeley, and Columbia for graduate study. Reb Saunders repeatedly asks Reuven to visit, and Rav Malter insists that he go.

Reuven visits Danny's home on the first day of Passover (the Festival of Freedom). Reb Saunders has aged. When Reuven announces his plan to become a rabbi, Reb Saunders says he knows of Danny's plans and explains his long silence. He considered Danny's brilliance a curse because it overwhelmed his soul and eliminated the compassion he would need as tzaddik. He comments, "I had to make certain his soul would be the soul of a tzaddik no matter what he did with his life…. In the silence between us, he began to hear the world crying." He accepts Danny's decision to become a psychologist because Danny now has the soul of a tzaddik. He then speaks Danny's name, and adds: "Today my Daniel is free." The tzaddikate is inherited by Levi. Reuven and Danny graduate *summa cum laude* from college. Danny and his father now speak to each other. When Rav Malter asks him whether he will raise his son in silence, Danny answers yes—if he cannot find another way.

Characters

Abba

See Mr. David Malter

Media Adaptations

- *The Chosen* was adapted for film by Edwin Gordon and featured Rod Steiger as Reb Saunders, Maximilian Schell as David Malter, Robby Benson as Danny Saunders, Barry Miller as Reuven Malter, and Ron Rifkin as the baseball coach. It was directed by Jeremy Paul Kagan and produced by Contemporary in 1982; available from FoxVideo.

- The book was also produced on sound cassettes, with Eli Wallach reading the text; produced by Warner Audio, 1985.

- A short-lived musical adaptation of *The Chosen* opened on Broadway in January, 1988, with music by Philip Springer and lyrics by Mitchell Bernard.

Professor Nathan Appleman

Danny Saunder's experimental psychology professor at Hirsch College is Professor Nathan Appleman. Danny is in conflict with the professor and the content of the class because it is too mathematical and at odds with Freudian psychology. His friend Reuven defends the professor and the methods of experimental psychology.

Davey Cantor

One of the players on Reuven Malter's baseball team is Davey Cantor. Davey provides Reuven with information about the fierceness of the Hasidic team they are playing. Davey calls the other team "murderers."

Mrs. Carpenter

Mrs. Carpenter is the nurse who is in charge of Reuven, Tony Savo, and Billy Merritt while they are in the hospital.

Mr. Galanter

Mr. Galanter is the coach of Reuven Malter's high school baseball team. He is a dedicated instructor who teaches in public school and coaches Reuven's yeshiva team on the side.

Rav Gershenson

Danny Saunders' and Reuven Malter's Talmud teacher at Hirsch College is Rav Gershenson. He is considered a fine scholar and a warm person. Reuven considers him an exciting teacher. Danny often has long discussions with the professor in class which Reuven resents. Later Reuven learns that Rav Gershenson has great respect for Mr. Malter's scholarship. Rav Gershenson cannot openly condone Mr. Malter's methods in class because they question the accuracy of Orthodox interpretations of the Talmud.

Sidney Goldberg

Sidney Goldberg is the shortstop on Reuven Malter's baseball team. The interplay between Reuven and Sidney during the game between the rival yeshivas heightens the tension of the game.

Dr. Grossman

Dr. Grossman is the physician who attends David Malter, Reuven's father. Mr. Malter suffers a heart attack brought on by his overwork in the Zionist movement, which was pressing for a Jewish homeland after World War II. Mr. Malter ignores Dr. Grossman's warning to get more rest.

Killer

See Tony Savo

Bobby Malter

See Reuven Malter

David Malter

David Malter, a respected scholar of the Talmud, is Reuven Malter's father. Mr. Malter's relationship with his son is one of respect, warmth, and kindness. In the story, the relationship between the Malter father and son contrasts with Danny Saunders and his affectionless relationship with his father. By accident, Mr. Malter meets Danny one day in the library and begins to tutor him in secular subjects. Reuven only learns later about this relationship. As the story of the friendship between Reuven and Danny progresses from their high school to their college days, the specter of history affects the life of David Malter. He is a staunch Zionist. After World War II, when the survivors of the Holocaust struggle to establish a homeland in Palestine, Mr. Malter works avidly for this cause to the detriment of his health. He has a heart attack from which he does, however, recover.

Reuven Malter

Reuven is the son of an Orthodox Jewish Talmud scholar. His relationship with his father is one of mutual respect and open affection. They communicate about world problems, as well as personal ones. Reuven is exposed to Talmudic studies by his father, but he is also encouraged to study secular subjects. He is taught by his father not to take things for granted, but to analyze them with a critical eye. Although he is exposed to logic, mathematics, and philosophy, by the end of the book Reuven decides he wants to become a rabbi. Reuven is the narrator of *The Chosen,* therefore the reader sees the story through his eyes.

Reuven is the pitcher of his yeshiva at the baseball game where his eye is injured by Danny Saunders. This event begins a relationship that takes the two boys through their high school years into college, where they study the same subjects. Each boy decides on a direction that is in contrast to his upbringing. While the reader expects Danny to rebel against the strictness of what he has been taught, the expectation that Reuven will follow in his father's footsteps is ever present. The period in which Reuven matures to young adulthood is a turbulent one. World War II, the Holocaust, and the struggle for a Jewish homeland in Palestine serves as the background for many conversations on the social and political issues connected to the period. As the narrator of the book, Reuven uses the other characters to explain details about various Orthodox sects and how they view important issues like the Jewish state of Israel.

Robert Malter

See Reuven Malter

Manya

The Malters' Russian housekeeper is named Manya. David Malter is a widower and Manya takes the role of a substitute mother, cooking and cleaning for father and son. Manya expresses a great deal of affection for Reuven and his father, caring for them both with a display of strong emotion when Reuven is injured and when his father has a heart attack.

Billy Merritt

Billy Merrit is the blind boy Reuven meets at the hospital when he is taken there to have glass removed from his eye. Billy is waiting to have an operation in the hope that his eyesight will be restored after a car accident blinded him. After a visit to his doctor, Reuven calls Billy's family to find out how the operation turned out and is disappointed to learn that it was not successful.

Jack Rose

Jack Rose is a boyhood friend of David Malter's from Russia. Mr. Rose is now a wealthy furrier who gives large donations to Mr. Malter's Zionist causes. Reuven and his father express a fundamental difference in viewpoint in their discussion of Mr. Rose. Reuven disapproves of Rose's motives for donating money, as well his joining a synagogue for the sake of his grandchildren and not out of any religious conviction. Reuven's father defends his old friend's actions and the importance of retaining friends even when you disagree with them.

Danny Saunders

Danny is the son of a Hasidic rabbi. According to tradition, as the oldest son he is expected to take his father's place as the spiritual leader of his congregation. Danny is also a brilliant student of the Talmud, exhibiting a photographic memory for details. But Danny is passionately interested in secular subjects, too, particularly Freudian psychology. His relationship with his father revolves around the study of the Talmud. Outside of discourses on this subject, his father maintains silence with Danny. In his yearning to learn more about secular subjects, Danny goes to the library, where he meets Reuven's father, David Malter. Unknown to his father or to Reuven, who later becomes his friend, Danny is guided in his secular studies by Mr. Malter.

In the opening pages of *The Chosen,* Danny and Reuven are playing baseball on opposing teams. After Danny causes an eye injury that sends Reuven to the hospital, he goes to see him to apologize. He is first rebuffed by Reuven, but after Reuven's father scolds him for his behavior, Reuven allows Danny to apologize and their friendship begins. It is through this friendship that both boys become transformed during their high school and college years. As the story opens, Reuven expects to become a professor of mathematics and Danny wants to take his father's place as "tzaddik" (righteous one). By the time the book ends, it is clear that Reuven will become a rabbi and that Danny will become a psychoanalyst. Danny and Reuven are contrasted as two young men seeking different professional careers. Their relationship with their fathers is a key element of the story, as well. While both reject what is initially expected of them in the area of a career, it is clear that the author uses these two young men to explore the universal theme of parental rejection. While both move in opposite directions than expected, each finds a way to retain a relationship with his respective father.

Levi Saunders

Danny's younger brother is Levi Saunders. When Reuven encounters him at Danny's home he appears to be unhappy. He often cries unexpectedly and leaves the room, behavior that frightens and bewilders Reuven. Levi becomes ill the day after his bar mitzvah (a coming of age ritual) and is hospitalized. Levi's illness makes Danny's decision to pursue psychology even more difficult and adds to his guilt about disappointing his father. Reb Saunders does accept Danny's decision to go into psychology, and Levi, frail though he is, will inherit his father's role as spiritual leader.

Reb Saunders

The personality of Reb Saunders infuses *The Chosen* with tension. As the spiritual leader of a Hasidic group, he follows strict observances and demands the same from Danny. While Danny's gift of intelligence and a photographic memory satisfy his father during their study of the Talmud, the silence of their relationship baffles Danny. Reb Saunders believes that the silence between them will strengthen Danny spiritually. He knows his son will suffer and he believes that through suffering he will be able to accept his role as "tzaddik." This role would involve acting as an intermediary between the rabbi's followers and God.

Danny brings Reuven Malter to his home to meet his father. Reuven is accepted and frequently attends services with Danny, but he develops a resentment towards Reb Saunders and his harsh, inflexible methods. Reb Saunders likes to test the boys by deliberately making mistakes in the text. When Danny or Reuven catches his error, he is pleased. The warm, open relationship Reuven has with his father sharply contrasts with the wall of silence that Reb Saunders has imposed on Danny. When Reuven complains about Reb Saunders to his own father, David Malter defends the rabbi. Mr. Malter explains to Reuven that devout Hasidim kept Judaism alive for hundreds of years in eastern Europe during centuries of persecution. Reb Saunders does ultimately accept Danny's decision to study psychology, just as Mr. Malter accepts Reuven's decision to become a rabbi.

Tony Savo

Tony Savo is an ex-boxer who has lost an eye. He shares a room with Reuven when he is hospitalized to have the glass removed from his eye. Tony is a cheerful character who tries to keep everyone's spirits up, especially the children in the hospital.

Schwartzie

Schwartzie is the pitcher on Reuven's team during the baseball game between the competing yeshivas. Schwartzie complains to Reuven about the way Danny bats the ball.

Dr. Snydman

Dr. Snydman is the attending doctor when Reuven goes to the hospital to have the glass taken from his eye.

Themes

Friendship

The themes of *The Chosen* unfold through the friendship of Danny Saunders and Reuven Malter. They first meet in the contest of a baseball game between their rival yeshivas (Jewish religious schools). Reuven is hit in the eye by a baseball that Danny has hit, breaking his glasses and cutting his eye. At the hospital he at first refuses to let Danny apologize, but after his father rebukes him, he relents. Much to his surprise, he finds Danny a compelling personality. Reuven is attracted to his intellectual brilliance and is also fascinated by the differences in their personal and religious upbringing. Potok uses this friendship as the basis for exploring conflict between fathers and sons, a theme which transcends the particular setting of a Brooklyn Orthodox Jewish neighborhood where both boys live. The differences in their religious upbringing is explored in great detail as the two develop their friendship and get to know one another's fathers. Their friendship is tested by Reuven's antagonism toward Reb Saunders and the way he relates to Danny. It is put to a critical test when Danny is forbidden to talk to Reuven. Reb Saunders disagrees with Mr. Malter's outspoken views on the establishment of a Zionist state in Palestine after World War II. It was the belief of Hasidic Jews at the time that it was wrong to establish a Jewish state. They must wait for the Messiah before the Jews can have a homeland. The friendship between the two young men at the end of the novel has ripened with their maturity. They see the irony of the fact that Reuven was expected to have an intellectual career as a professor and Danny was expected to follow in his father's footsteps. Instead Reuven will become a rabbi and Danny a psychologist. There is the sense in their friendship that by viewing one another's lives, they were better able to formulate their own futures. Each has been enriched by his ability to explore their thoughts and feelings together, and each has been enriched from experiences with the other's father.

Coming of Age

Closely related to the theme of friendship is "coming of age." The novel opens when the two principal characters, Danny Saunders and Reuven Malter, are fifteen-year-old high school students. Grappling with their respective ambitions, which conflict with their father's plans, they do not realize their goals until the end of the book when they complete college. In the process of determining their careers they must exam their father's lives. Danny has to take the difficult step of disappointing his father by not following in his footsteps as a religious leader. His decision seems frightening because of the fanaticism of his father's beliefs, but the book ends happily when Reb Saunders resigns himself to his son's decision. He recognizes that Danny has been helped by Mr. Malter and that he has helped Reuven choose his career. As Chaim Potok presents this perennial conflict, his message seems to be that fathers, as well as sons, share in the coming-of-age experience. When it happens, fathers need to make the adjustment of letting their sons find their own paths in life.

Identity

Throughout the novel, the reader wonders how far Danny will break from his father's strict observance of Judaism. While he eventually must reject many of the outward appearances of a Hasidic Jew, he remains committed to Judaism. As a young boy, he grew earlocks (uncut sideburns) and wore the traditional black clothing of his sect. As a young man, he grew a beard that was never to be cut. When he is about to enter Columbia University as a psychology student, we see Danny for the first time clean-shaven and with trimmed sideburns. He must change his outward appearance to assume his professional role, but it is apparent that inside Danny is still a devoted Jew and has respect for his father. When Reuven asks him how he will raise

Topics for Further Study

- Research the reasons Orthodox Jews settled in Hebron and how their settlement there has made it difficult for Israel to withdraw from Hebron and return the city to Palestinian control.

- Compare two different religious groups and discuss where they agree and where they diverge on important spiritual issues and ritual observances.

- Describe several relationships between fathers and sons or mothers and daughters among your friends.

his son, Danny says the same way his father did, unless he can find another way. This suggests that the impact of his upbringing has been powerful and he must carry it with him even as he changes on the surface. Although Reuven is taking up a religious career, it is evident that he will continue to follow his father's approach to life. The reader expects him to be compassionate and to remain unafraid of examining ideas closely.

Politics

The political background of *The Chosen* is important to Chaim Potok's writing. World War II is a topic of discussion in the early section of the novel. The escape from Nazi persecution and the Holocaust are also important subjects. Later events, like the struggle for a Jewish homeland after the war, becomes a major subject that Reuven discusses with his father. David Malter becomes an ardent spokesperson for the Zionist cause in Palestine. His views are abhorred by Danny Saunders' father, and this causes a break in the friendship of the two young men. Throughout the book many discussions between the characters revolve around important events that helped to shape Jewish beliefs and migrations to avoid persecution. The struggles of the new state of Israel colors much of the background material in the last section of the book.

From the movie The Chosen, *starring Maximilan Schell, Rod Steiger, Robbie Benson, and Barry Miller.*

Style

Point of View

Reuven Malter is the narrator of *The Chosen,* which is written in the first person (the narrator refers to himself as "I"). Potok makes it possible for readers unfamiliar with Orthodox Judaism to identify with the conflicts in the story by having it told from Reuven's perspective. Since he is a secularized Jew, his outer appearance is the same as any young man's in American society. The opening scene of the baseball game also adds to the everyday American atmosphere. It is against Reuven's character that much of the conflict resounds. His antagonism toward Reb Saunders casts the latter in a negative light. The reader hopes then that the rabbi's son Danny will rebel and find a life of his own. On the other hand, Mr. Malter is portrayed sympathetically, especially in his warm relationship with Reuven. When his father's outspoken views on Zionism get Reuven in trouble at school, he is subjected to taunting. Because the Malters are both sympathetic characters and Reuven is the narrator, the reader is inclined to side with them whenever a conflict occurs in the novel. In this way, Potok has structured his novel to present his own point of view on controversial political and religious issues.

Setting

The Chosen is set in the Crown Heights section of Brooklyn during World War II and the period shortly after when Jews were struggling to establish a homeland in Palestine (Israel). The neighborhood is an Orthodox Jewish one in which a number of different sects reside side-by-side. Even though Danny Saunders and Reuven Malter lived for the first fifteen years of their lives only five blocks from one another, they did not meet until their rival yeshivas competed in a baseball game. The opening scene of the baseball game sets the mood for the whole novel. It is the conflicting demands between religion and secular interests that provide the dramatic tension of the story. At no time in the novel do any of the characters leave Brooklyn while they are engaged with one another. Mr. Malter does make a speech at Madison Square Garden, but it is only talked about in the book. Besides the scenes at the ball field, most events take place at Danny or Reuven's house, in the library, or in class. Several scenes are also set in the hospital after Reuven is hurt and David Malter has a heart attack. In this way, Potok has been able to devote a good portion of the novel to educating the reader about Jewish history and religion. Since the different views of Mr. Malter and Reb Saunders about Judaism are at the heart of the conflicts in the novel, keeping the characters indoors is an appropriate setting for their conversations.

Symbols

The fierceness with which Danny's team plays baseball is a mirror image of the way Reb Saunders practices his religion. He cannot tolerate other views. The baseball game becomes a symbol of the battle ahead between the two fathers and their sons and between the two world views of David Malter and Reb Saunders. It is also a symbol of the conflict within Jewish culture.

Another important image is the eye. Reuven's eye is cut when the baseball smashes his eyeglasses. The little boy in the hospital does not regain his eyesight and Tony Savo has lost one eye. The image of blindness suggests that Reb Saunders is blind to any ideas that he does not embrace. Danny and Reuven suffer from a symbolic blindness of youth, until they come of age and realize the paths they must take to reach their goals.

There are two silences in the book. Reb Saunders has a silent relationship with Danny, only speaking to him during their studies of the Talmud. When Mr. Malter makes his Madison Square Garden speech, Danny is forbidden to speak to Reuven. They maintain a silence between them for two years. The silences symbolize the inability of the sects within Orthodox Judaism to communicate with one another.

The war of liberation in Israel becomes a symbol for Danny's liberation from his obligation to follow in his father's footsteps. There is some symbolism in Danny's brother Levi inheriting his father's role as *tzaddik*. Levi is sickly, which suggests that the leadership of Hasidism is weakened when the tradition of inheritance is abandoned. The title of the book also has symbolic meaning. The Jewish people are referred to as "the chosen people." Danny was chosen by birth to become a spiritual leader, but he chooses another course. Reuven was not chosen for the role he will assume as a rabbi. Instead, he chooses that role.

The book ends with a hidden symbol. The final chapter is number eighteen. In Hebrew, this number means life, *chai*. It is a positive symbol with which Potok leaves his characters and readers. Earlier in the novel, Reb Saunders used *gematriya*, a numerology system that assigns each letter of the alphabet to a number. Since eighteen is life, Reb Saunders contends that nine, which is the difference between "this world" and "the world to come," is half of life and that people are only half alive in this world.

Historical Context

The Holocaust

Persecution by the Nazis in Germany before World War II led to the dispersal of European Jews to the United States, Palestine, and other countries. When the full extent of the annihilation of Jews in the gas chambers of Nazi Germany was revealed (six million had been exterminated), a resurgence of interest in establishing a Jewish homeland was ignited. During the 1930s, Jews in Germany began to lose their civil rights and eventually they lost their property and were relocated to the work and death camps that the Nazis established in parts of eastern Europe. Those Jews who left Germany before World War II were the first wave during the middle of the twentieth century to settle outside Europe. After the war, some 200,000 concentration camp survivors came to America. Many of them were Orthodox Jews, and they tended to settle into the type of neighborhood described by Chaim Potok in *The Chosen*. By the 1950s, the children and grandchildren of earlier Jewish immigrants from Eastern European countries tended to be assimilated into the larger American culture. Many were Reformed or Conservative Jews and had attended public schools. The influx of a new population of Jews who were religious ignited a new interest in Judaism. In Potok's story, David Malter becomes the spokesperson for ardent followers of Judaism. After the Holocaust, there was a widespread feeling within the Jewish community in America that the fervor of religious Jews like the Hasids had helped Judaism survive centuries of persecution. The feeling was that Jews would only be safe from persecution when they had their own country. This became the impetus for the widespread support among both religious and secularized Jews for the establishment of the State of Israel.

Zionism

While Zionism is regarded as a nineteenth-century movement for Jews to return to their original homeland in the Middle East, efforts to return to Zion date back to the beginning of the Jewish Diaspora in the sixth century B.C. During the Diaspora, when the Jews were exiled from Jerusalem, a leader (a false messiah) would appear, claim to be the messiah, and promise to return the Jewish people to Zion. Notable among them was Sabbatai Zevi (1626–1676), also known as Sabbatai Zebi, who led a large band of European Jews to Constantinople, but, after he was imprisoned, he converted to Islam to save himself from execution. In the sixteenth cen-

Compare
&
Contrast

- **1940s:** Anti-Semitism was widespread in the Western world in spite of the Nazi Holocaust against the Jews.

  1960s: The consciousness-raising of Americans during the Civil Rights movement helped fuel positive feelings among all ethnic groups, including Jews.

  Today: Discrimination toward minorities no longer has official sanction in the United States and other countries, but ethnic conflicts still persist in parts of the world. Hate groups in the United States continue to express racial and anti-Semitic views.

- **1940s:** The State of Israel was still a dream although many settlers had come during the 1930s to escape Nazi persecution.

  1960s: Israel was holding its own against attacks by its Arab neighbors. The Middle East became a battleground for the Cold War, with the West siding with Israel and the Soviet Union with the Arabs.

  Today: Israel has signed peace agreements with several of its Arab neighbors and has begun the process of turning control of Palestine back to the Palestinians.

- **1940s:** Jewish education was conducted primarily after the regular secular schooling of American Jewish children.

  1960s: Jewish day schools began to spring up in areas where there were sizable Jewish populations. They offered elementary and high school religious and secular education to both girls and boys.

  Today: Jewish education in the United States has been expanded to include courses for adults, similar to continuing education courses that are given in community colleges.

- **1940s:** Many countries and many parts of the world were engaged in World War II. The United States was unified in its willingness to participate in combat.

  1960s: The United States was the only Western country to fight in the Vietnam War. The country was divided over our participation in a war that was perceived as not being winnable or honorable.

  Today: Along with other members of the United Nations, the United States has supplied peacekeeping forces in areas like Bosnia, where ethnic conflict raged for several years.

---

tury, a Jewish Italian family asked the Turks, who controlled the region then, to allow them to establish a Jewish settlement in Galilee. It was not until the late nineteenth century, though, that European Jews had enough freedom of movement and financial resources to begin settling in Palestine. In 1897 the Herzl World Zionist Congress established a worldwide movement. In 1917 the British government established a homeland in Palestine with the Balfour Declaration. It was supported in 1922 by the League of Nations. In 1948 the State of Israel was established after Palestine was partitioned. Support for a Jewish state has not been universal among Jews. The Hasids and other fundamentalist Jewish groups felt strongly that Jews had to wait for the Messiah before returning to Israel. Many Jews who had assimilated, particularly in the United States, felt that an Israeli state in the Middle East would not be viable, that the antagonism of the Arabs would lead to another Jewish annihilation. In the latter part of *The Chosen,* the Jewish state is being established. Reb Saunders represents the Hasidic view that Jews must wait for the Messiah before returning to the homeland. Mr. Malter represents the Zionist view that a homeland was necessary for the survival of the Jewish people.

Hasidism

Hasidism began in the late eighteenth century in a region along the Russian and Polish border. Its leader was Israel Ben Eliezer. The traditional Orthodox approach to the study of the Talmud was based on the oral laws that Moses had been given by God on Mount Sinai and their interpretations over the centuries. Ben Eliezer emphasized spirituality and its fervent expression. His praying was characterized by ecstasy and trances, while traditional prayer was restrained. His followers continued his forms of worship and the movement spread throughout Eastern Europe. The leader of each group was considered a "righteous one" (*tzaddik*). The tzaddik acted as an intermediary between his followers and God, not unlike the relationship between a Catholic priest and his parishioners. Throughout their history, the Hasids dressed in plain dark clothing. The men were forbidden to shave their beards or their sidelocks and they wore fur-trimmed hats. They have been compared to the Amish of Pennsylvania in their dress. While the Hasids represent a small proportion of the Jewish population in the world today, they are credited with stemming the tide of assimilation during the late nineteenth and early twentieth centuries.

Young men performing a Hasidic dance at the Western Wall in Jerusalem.

Critical Overview

Chaim Potok's first novel *The Chosen,* written when he was nearly forty, was warmly received by the public. The hardcover edition sold several hundred thousand copies and several million were sold in paperback. Reviews of the book were generally favorable, though there was some mild criticism. Critics found Potok's storytelling skills compelling and praised him for his ability to present complex ideas to his readers. His presentation of Jewish history and theological ideas within his stories is a particular area for which Potok is often commended. His ability to present the religious conflicts within Judaism to both Jewish and non-Jewish readers has earned him high praise. The book "broadens the reader's understanding of the wide spectrum of Judaism," commented Beverly J. Matiko in *Masterplots.* "It is invaluable in providing all readers, particularly young ones, with [the] social, political, and religious history" of Orthodox Jews during World War II. Potok receive the Atheneum Award for *The Promise,* a sequel to *The Chosen,* published several years later. He was awarded the Edward Lewis Wallant Award for *The Chosen,* which also was nominated for a National Book Award.

Regarding the author's narrative style, Dan Barnett in a *Critical Survey of Long Fiction* ob-

served that "his sentences are simple and reportorial…. The stories develop chronologically." Barnett compares Potok's writing to Ernest Hemingway's, and other reviewers have mentioned the influence of Evelyn Waugh on his work. Lillian Kremer, writing in the *Dictionary of Literary Biography,* compared Potok's *The Book of Lights* to Waugh's *Brideshead Revisited.* Like Waugh, Potok explores religious commitment in his characters within the framework of secularized society. Waugh's book is about a dysfunctional English Catholic family. Potok was inspired by it to become a writer. Kremer also compared Potok's style to John Dos Passos' journalistic approach when he writes about the Holocaust. The impact of newspaper pictures after World War II depicted the atrocities of the Nazi death camps. This became the inspiration for Potok's use of newspaper-type headlines in his novel *In the Beginning,* which was published in 1975. A *Times Literary Supplement* reviewer found the "narrative … [in *The Promise*] rigorously and beautifully straightforward." The author's handling of issues facing Jewish women in his 1985 novel *Davita's Harp* was well received. Lisa Schwarzbaum, writing in the *Detroit News* credited Potok with sensitivity. The book, she said, "is a warm, decent, generous and patient exploration of important issues…." This is a noteworthy achievement when seen in comparison to *The Chosen*. None of the women in Potok's first novel is portrayed with any depth or has a significant role. Women are seen only in the role of shadowy wife, nurse, teasing sister, or compassionate housekeeper.

The major areas of negative criticism for all of Potok's writing are that it is too sentimental, lacks drama, and that the outcomes of his stories are somewhat contrived. Sam Bluefarb, writing in the *College Language Association Journal*, remarked that Reb Saunders' "resignation to Danny's break with Hassidism … [is] too mechanical … with Danny … going off to become a clinical or behavioral psychologist." Bluefarb found the dialogue in this climax of the book weak, but he considered it a "minor flaw in a larger pattern: that of tolerance against intolerance, empty ritual against the vital deed, rote learning against eager wonder." While reviewer Philip Toynbee in the *New Republic* applauded the "perennial theme" of the conflict between sons and fathers, he found the characters too intellectual. He also criticized Potok for sentimentality. "He can be dreadfully wet at times." In writing his review, Toynbee compared Potok's book to a contemporary book written by Herbert Gold called *Fathers*. He found Gold's characters "larger than life" and more memorable. He did, nonetheless, acknowledge that he would "not quickly forget the strange Hasidic community which Mr. Potok has painted with so much impressionistic skill."

The Gates of November: Chronicles of the Slepak Family was published by Mr. Potok in 1996. It tells the true story of Russian Jews who became refusniks during Soviet repression in the decade before the collapse of the Soviet Union. As with *The Chosen,* this book also recounts a rift between a father and son. Felicity Barringer, writing in the *New York Times Book Review* criticized the book for an "ungainly mixture of the personal and the political … [that is] short on insight in the minds and hearts of the father and son…." The book, she claimed, has too many voices for coherence, but she still found the story fascinating and the struggle of its characters heroic. David Shribman maintained in his *Wall Street Journal* review of *The Gates of November* that Potok "brings a sharp ear, a sharp eye and a soft heart" to the chronicle. In comparison with other Jewish American writers, Chaim Potok is unique in his warm affirmation of the Jewish experience in America and in his deep sympathy for those who struggle to retain spirituality in a secu-

lar world. While Potok is the author of nearly a dozen fiction and nonfiction books, *The Chosen* remains his most popular work.

Criticism

Ann Hibert Alton

In the following essay, Alton, an honorary research associate at the University of Sydney, provides an overview discussion of Potok's novel.

Chaim Potok's *The Chosen* focuses on the contrasts between extreme ends of Orthodox Judaism. Despite criticisms that Potok is overly optimistic—Reuven regains his sight, Danny renounces the tzaddikate without being ostracized by his father, Danny and Reuven resolve many of the conflicts they feel between the secular world and Orthodox Judaism—Potok's novel provides us with valuable insights into American Orthodox Jewish life during and after World War II. The novel explores in detail the lives and traditions of Hasidic and Orthodox Jews, and creates an apparently realistic portrait of both cultures. *The Chosen* attempts to explore the place of Judaism in a secular society, provides insights into tensions between faith and scholarship, and suggests Judaism's need to create a new philosophy for the modern world.

The setting is Brooklyn in the 1940s. Reuven's detailed descriptions of his and Danny's homes and Reb Saunders' synagogue appear as set-pieces in the novel. This focuses our attention on plot and theme. This self-contained Jewish world, completely separate from the secular world, suggests the conflict between Hasidic existence and secular life—a theme which is repeated throughout the novel.

Reuven Malter's first-person narrative encourages our strong identification with him. Like him, we are bewildered by Reb Saunders' silence, and are furious when Reb Saunders excommunicates him. The dialogue is direct, uncomplicated, and convincing, though relatively flat. The strong focus on plot and theme results in little richness of tone: as Sheldon Grebstein comments, the novel's "overall color is gray."

An understanding of Judaism is crucial to interpreting *The Chosen,* which focuses on the opposite poles of Orthodoxy and Hasidism. Hasidism originated in eastern Europe in the 18th century, and its followers immediately came into conflict with the Mitnagdim (opponents), or established religious authorities. The Mitnagdim focused on scholarship and formal prayer, while the Hasidim (pious ones) believed that studying Talmud (the book of Jewish law and ritual) was not as important as making every aspect of their lives holy. By the 20th century Hasidism's focus had changed substantially to value studying Talmud and eliminating anything from the secular world. Hasidism's leaders were called tzaddikim (righteous ones), and were regarded as superhuman links between God and the community. The Hasidim believed that the only correct form of worship was to approach God through their tzaddik, rather than individually as Orthodox Jews did. Non-Hasidic Jews were considered apikorsim (Jews who denied the basic tenets of their faith), and were shunned. This conflict appears during the baseball game between Reuven's Orthodox team and Danny's Hasidic team, which takes on overtones of a holy war.

Two significant historical contexts are World War II and the Zionist movement. Reuven mentions the D-Day invasion in France, the Battle of the Bulge, the death of President Roosevelt, the Germans' surrender in May 1945, and the destruction of Hiroshima and Nagasaki. The war serves as a reminder of the secular world. No one is immune to its effects, as we see in the different reactions of the Hasidic and Orthodox communities to news of the German concentration camps. Reb Saunders believes these camps were God's will, and speaks of Europe's Jewish communities having disappeared "into heaps of bones and ashes." In contrast, Rav Malter believes that Jews can wait no longer for God or the Messiah, insisting: "'If we do not rebuild Jewry in America, we will die as a people.'" He becomes an outspoken supporter of the Zionists, who believe that the American Jews must make Palestine into a Jewish homeland. The Zionists' opponents, of which Reb Saunders is one, believe this would corrupt the Holy Land. Eventually, the United Nations votes to create the Jewish state of Israel. After escalating violence between Arabs and Jews, the Zionist and Hasidic communities feel more unity. These historical contexts suggest the tension between the different sects of Judaism, and more specifically between the Malters' Orthodoxy and Reb Saunders' extreme Hasidism.

The central imagery of *The Chosen* appears in metaphors of vision. Reuven's eye trouble leads him into another world, one which forces him to leave the pieces of his old identity behind "alongside the shattered lens of my glasses." His new identity incorporates his friendship with Danny

What Do I Read Next?

- *The Promise* (1969) is Potok's sequel to *The Chosen*. In this book, Reuven prepares to become a rabbi but runs into an obstacle in the form of apostate scholar Abraham Gordon; at the same time, Danny, now a psychologist, treats Gordon's disturbed son.

- *Fathers* (1966) by Herbert Gold also concerns the relationship between a son and a father. Gold presents an irreligious father who is a shopkeeper and a son who feels he can cross the abyss between them in spite of their generational differences.

- *Call It Sleep* (1934) by Henry Roth. Considered an American classic, this novel depicts the relationship between a young boy and the father who terrifies him. While Gold depicts an affectionate father, the father in Roth's novel has an openly hostile relationship with his son. The story is set in the Lower East Side of Manhattan in the early years of the twentieth century.

- *Fathers and Sons* (1862) by Ivan Turgenev, the nineteenth-century Russian novelist. The novel depicts the struggle of two generations. The protagonist, Bazarov, is a nihilist and wants to destroy the old order (honor, patriotism, love, beauty) represented by the fathers (Kirsanov) and to establish a new order based on rational science.

along with a much wider view of the world. Danny begins wearing glasses just before he enters Hirsch College. His eye problems suggest his limitations: although he is intellectually curious, he lacks compassion, and doesn't see the wider view of the world that Reuven sees. Once Danny learns empathy, "there was a light in his eyes that was almost blinding."

The novel's main relationships are between narrator Reuven Malter, Danny Saunders, Reuven's father Rabbi David Malter, and Danny's father Reb Saunders. Reuven—whose name in Hebrew means "behold a son"—loves mathematics, but wants to become a rabbi like his father. He is a good scholar, with an open mind, and a compassionate young man. Danny—Hebrew for "God is my judge"—is heir to the tzaddikate, but wants to become a psychologist. Despite his brilliant mind, he lacks compassion, which we see in his feelings of murderous rage during the baseball game, and in his cool appreciation of Hemingway's artistry in describing ants being roasted alive on a burning log. Danny is terribly torn between the demands of his intellect and the traditions of the tzaddikate dynasty. He dreads the thought of becoming tzaddik, for he fears losing his contact with the secular world. Despite this, he already thinks of himself as tzaddik, and feels pride in the respect he's given as heir.

Like Reuven and Danny, their fathers represent opposite philosophical and religious poles. Rabbi Malter, Reuven's father, is tremendously understanding: despite his broad knowledge of Talmud, he is open to ideas from the secular world. His passionate support of the Zionist movement arises from his desire for a meaningful life. Reb Saunders, Danny's father, is tzaddik to his community. He is both a great Talmudist (scholar of Talmud) and a great tzaddik with a reputation for both brilliance and compassion. However, he is also a tyrant, absolute ruler of his household and his community. He cannot accept any idea coming from the "contaminated" or secular world; in his eyes, the Zionist movement is sacrilege and a violation of the Torah. Danny pities his father because he's intellectually trapped in his Hasidic traditions and therefore has an extremely narrow view of the world.

Minor characters include Tony Savo and Billy Merrit, whom Reuven meets while in hospital. These two characters suggest the importance of faith in a world which is often incomprehensible. Professor Appleman, Chair of the Psychology department at Hirsch College, reconciles Danny to studying experimental psychology. Rav Gershenson, the Talmud instructor, cannot allow secular methods of analysis in his class despite his sympathy for them. Danny's brother Levi—whose name in Hebrew means "joined in harmony"—is a "delicate miniature" of his father, and eventually inherits the position of tzaddik. Female characters are virtually non-existent. Only Manya, the Malters' Russian housemaid who "babbles" in Ukrainian, has a name. Reuven's mother is dead, Danny's mother is alive but practically invisible, and Danny's sister disappears into an arranged Hasidic

marriage. This lack of women significantly weakens the novel's realism and leads to a lack of balance.

The theme of father-son relationships is central to the novel's underlying conflicts. Reuven's strong relationship with his father is open and affectionate: they can—and do—talk about anything. Rav Malter teaches Reuven compassion, forgiveness, and tolerance. He encourages Reuven to become friends with Danny, and tries to teach Reuven about Danny's Hasidic heritage so that Reuven will understand Danny. Even when Reb Saunders excommunicates Reuven, Rav Malter forbids Reuven to slander him, insisting that it was just this sort of fanaticism which kept the Jews alive through two thousand years of exile. In the end, it is largely because of Rav Malter's attitudes that Reuven chooses to preserve his culture and religion by becoming a rabbi. In contrast, Danny has extremely mixed feelings about his father. Although he fears his father's temper and dreads his continued silence, he believes that his father is "'a great man.'" However, he dreads being trapped the way his father is: "'I want to be able to breathe, to think what I want to think, to say the things I want to say.'" When Danny realizes he cannot become tzaddik, he becomes terrified about telling his father, because "if the son doesn't take the father's place, the dynasty falls apart." However, Reb Saunders realizes Danny's intentions and acknowledges him as a man. His acceptance of Danny's decision is influenced by three factors. First, he has come to respect his son's soul as well as his mind, and knows Danny intends to continue to observe Jewish law. Second, he feels Danny now has the soul of a tzaddik, and that "'All his life he will be a tzaddik. He will be a tzaddik for the world. And the world needs a tzaddik.'" Finally, he realizes the dynasty will not be destroyed: since "the tzaddikate was inherited, and the charisma went automatically from father to son—all sons," Levi will become tzaddik in Danny's place. Despite this happy resolution, Reb Saunders' insistence on the strict traditions of Hasidism at the expense of the secular world have the effect of driving Danny away from his tzaddikate heritage and into his study of psychoanalysis.

Another theme arises from the Talmud's direction that the two things one should do are to choose a friend and to acquire a teacher. After their initial antagonism towards each other, Reuven and Danny find many common aspects of their lives. Despite their different heritages and opinions, they become fast friends. Certainly they illustrate Reuven's father's comment that "'Honest differences of opinion should never be permitted to destroy a friendship.'" Their friendship survives various crises, including a year of enforced silence, as well as major differences of opinion about the value of experimental psychology, mathematics, Freudian thought, and even Reb Saunders.

Both boys have teachers in their fathers. Reb Saunders chooses the traditional method of teaching Danny through public quizzes on his Talmud sermons. Later, both Danny and Reuven review Talmud with Reb Saunders, and through vehement arguments they learn the meanings of various passages. However, Reb Saunders isn't an ideal teacher because his exclusively Hasidic viewpoint completely excludes secular considerations. In contrast, Rav Malter teaches Reuven the heretical "scientific method" for studying Talmud, which includes the use of sources outside Orthodox Jewish tradition. When Reuven successfully uses this method to analyze a difficult passage, Rav Gershenson reveres the explanation but forbids him to use this method in class. Reuven then realizes his father is regarded as an heretic because of his methods and opinions. He also realizes that one can hold heretical notions, as perhaps Rav Gershenson does, and still be a rabbi.

Both boys are serious about their studies, and Danny is committed to extensive reading of secular works. In addition to knowing *Ivanhoe,* Danny reads Darwin, Huxley, and Hemingway before becoming intrigued with the writings of Freud. It is during his study of Freud that Danny begins to question many of the aspects of Hasidism. He realizes that he can approach Freud in the same way as he approaches Talmud, suggesting his temporary conversion to Freud as a religion. Just as he became upset by various interpretations of Hasidism, Danny becomes increasingly upset by Freud. However, he can't stop reading Freud because of his uncanny insights into nature of man. Here we come to one of the most significant aspects of the book: the tension between faith and scholarship. Danny cannot stop thinking about Freud and his analysis of the psyche of man, and the more he thinks about it the less he believes he can conform completely to Hasidism.

Finally, the theme of silence dominates *The Chosen.* Danny and his father don't talk, except when they study Talmud. This silence is Reb Saunders' attempt to teach Danny compassion. As a child, Danny recounted a story about terrible suffering to his father to demonstrate his excellent memory, displaying no compassion for the story's victims. Reb Saunders concluded that despite Danny's brilliance he lacked a soul. By enforcing silence between them, he believed that Danny would learn to know pain and suffering. Since a tzaddik must suffer his people's pain, Reb Saunders justifies his actions: "'I had to make certain his soul would be the soul of a tzaddik no matter what he did with his life.'" In the end, this silence is the price he's willing to pay for Danny's soul.

Two central metaphors suggest *The Chosen's* meaning. The first is the fly that Reuven gently frees from the spider's web. The fly represents Danny, who is caught in the almost invisible web of history, the rigidity of Hasidic tradition, and his father's silence. Reuven is the outsider from the secular world who sees Danny's predicament, and whose gentle influence frees Danny from his oppressive trap without destroying either the tzaddikate dynasty or Danny's relationship with his father. The second metaphor is the novel's title: The Chosen. Its most obvious meaning suggests the Hasidim themselves, who believe they are God's chosen ones. However, the chosen also refers to the vocations chosen by Danny and Reuven: psychoanalysis and the rabbinate respectively. Finally, Danny himself is the chosen, in the sense that his father chooses to raise him in silence so that he develops the soul of a tzaddik. This fate is the final choice—one which Danny was powerless to make, but for which he suffers the consequences—becoming tzaddik not for his Hasidic community, but instead for the world.

Source: Ann Hibert Alton, in an essay for *Novels for Students,* Gale, 1998.

Deanna Evans

Evans, a professor of English at Bemidji State University, discusses the friendship between Danny and Reuven and its importance within the context of the novel in the following essay.

When Chaim Potok published his first novel, *The Chosen,* in 1967, it hardly seemed destined for widespread popularity. After all, the novel contains no sex or obscenity, only a trace of violence, and its two principal characters are Jewish school boys who excel academically and enjoy engaging in theological debates with their fathers. Even so, *The Chosen,* continues to attract a large and diverse body of readers in the United States and abroad. Surely one reason for its popularity is that it presents a compelling story of friendship, a subject of universal appeal.

The novel's plot line at its most basic resembles the folktale type of "The Two Brothers," a recurring type of narrative recognized and named by the great nineteenth-century philologist Jacob Grimm. It is the pattern underlying the biblical narrative of David and Jonathan found in *I Samuel* in the Bible, which is alluded to in the novel. The typical plot of a friendship narrative usually contains the following elements: two young men become friends and grow as close as brothers, and after some kind of crisis in which one perhaps rescues the other, both become better and wiser. All of these elements are present in *The Chosen*, but Potok complicates the basic pattern by weaving into it the roles of two supporting characters, the boys' fathers. The fathers have been the principal teachers of their sons and continue to exert a strong influence throughout the novel. Hence, the fathers affect the course of the friendship and, at one point, nearly destroy it.

The Chosen, set in Brooklyn during World War II and the years immediately following, is narrated in the first person by Reuven Malter, one of the main characters. The other, Danny Saunders, is named in the opening sentence where it is also made clear that the ensuing story will be their story: "For the first fifteen years of our lives, Danny and I lived within five blocks of each other and neither of us knew of the other's existence." The reason becomes clear as the story begins to unfold. Although Reuven and Danny have much in common, even age, since they were born only two days apart in the same hospital, they live in very different worlds shaped by the religious beliefs of their fathers, who represent polar extremes of Orthodox Judaism.

David Malter, Reuven's father, is a teacher in a yeshiva (a Jewish high school); he is also a writer of controversial religious articles in which he takes a rational and scientific approach to sacred texts. He is widowed, and Reuven is his only child, so Malter enjoys an especially close and warm relationship with his son. Malter often expresses pride in Reuven's achievements and openly shows his affection. Ever the teacher, Malter encourages his son's intellectual curiosity and wants him to be fully cognizant of the world. For example, when Reuven is in the hospital and unable to read, Malter brings him a radio so that he can listen to news reports about the war. Danny, on the other hand, has been brought up to shun the world in the strict and conservative environment of Hasidism. Potok clearly does not expect readers to be familiar with this conservative type of Judaism, for within the dialogue of the novel he uses characters, especially Danny and David Malter, to explain it.

Danny's father is Reb Saunders, a "tzaddik" within his Hasidic sect. This means, as Danny explains, that Saunders is regarded as "a kind of messenger of God, a bridge between his followers and God." As the elder son, Danny is expected to follow in his father's footsteps and inherit his position. The elder Saunders has attempted to prepare Danny for this "chosen" role by training him in a very harsh way, imposing upon him the discipline of silence. Late in the novel, Saunders explains why he has done this. He realized when Danny was only four that he was a gifted child with a photographic memory, and Saunders became afraid that Danny would grow into a cold intellectual instead of a sympathetic and compassionate leader. Thus Saunders turned to the old European method of teaching by silence. Accordingly, he refuses to speak directly to Danny, except when they are engaged in religious debate. Saunders understands that his silence causes his son pain, but he believes the pain will save his son's soul and also will prepare Danny for his role of tzaddik.

The boys first meet when they participate in a baseball game between their respective yeshivas. When Reuven attempts to initiate conversation with Danny, he is asked if he is the son of the writer David Malter. Learning that he is, Danny insults him: "I told my team we're going to kill you apikorsim this afternoon." (Apikorsim is an insulting Hebrew word meaning "sinners"). Reuven retaliates, telling Danny to go rub his "tzitzit" for luck, referring to the fringes of Danny's religious garment. Then, at a climactic moment, Danny compresses his hostile feelings into a powerful swing of the bat and hits the ball directly at Reuven who stubbornly refuses to jump out of the way. The ball pounds into Reuven's glasses, causing the left lens to shatter and cut his eye.

Danny comes to the hospital to apologize to Reuven, who is not sure if his eye will heal. Reuven rudely refuses to accept the apology, but Danny tries again. This time the boys develop an admiration for each other and the seeds of friendship are planted. So it is at the hospital, a place associated with healing, that the two are healed of their hostile feelings toward each another. In addition, this hospital is where both were born. How appropriate that their friendship also comes to life here. The hospital is also the place where the boys begin to mature. Although his vision is impaired, Reuven begins to "see" while in the hospital. He becomes acquainted with fellow patients, people who are not Jewish, and he learns that he shares common interests with them. He also learns about the suffering of others. The man in the bed next to his, a professional fighter, loses an eye he injured in a fight. Billy, the boy in the bed on the other side of Reuven, is blind and is in the hospital awaiting surgery to cure his blindness. But, as Reuven will later learn, Billy's surgery is not successful. Reuven begins to "see" when he lies in the darkness of his hospital room, closes his unbandaged eye, and tries to imagine what the world is like for Billy. When he returns home five days after the accident, his familiar world looks different: "I felt I had crossed into another world, that little pieces of my old self had been left behind on the black asphalt floor of the school yard alongside the shattered lens of my glasses." To a lesser degree, Danny also begins to see more clearly when he visits Reuven in the hospital. There he discovers that David Malter is none other than the kind man who had become his mentor at the public library. Danny also comes to recognize his own dark side, for he confesses to Reuven that at the baseball game he had felt the urge to kill.

From its beginning, the friendship of the boys is affected by their fathers. David Malter, in fact, acts as catalyst, for he encourages his son to become Danny's friend. He reminds Reuven that the Talmud teaches "that a person should do two things for himself." One of these is "to acquire a teacher," and, of course, both Reuven and Danny have found teachers in their fathers. The other is to choose a friend. Malter also explains the nature of true friendship to his son: "A Greek philosopher said that two people who are true friends are like two bodies with one soul." Malter's words prove prophetic.

As the novel progresses, Reuven and Danny become good friends. Reuven wins the approval of Reb Saunders, who demands that he come with Danny to Friday services and then subjects the visiting boy to a grueling debate over a religious lesson. During the boys' last year of high school, Reuven's father suffers a heart attack. While Malter is in the hospital, Reuven is invited to live in the Saunders' home, and so the boys have the opportunity to live as brothers. They share a room and also begin to share their deepest secrets, including Danny's confession that he wants to become a psychoanalyst and reject his "chosen" role. Both boys graduate at the top of their respective classes and then attend the same rabbinical college. During their first year at college, they continue to live as brothers and are very happy.

But the joy of their friendship will be tested by conflict and crisis, and, not surprisingly, the cri-

sis is brought about by their fathers. After the war, David Malter adopts a strong Zionist position and becomes a leader in the local movement. Reb Saunders continues to hold to his conservative beliefs that a new Israel can be founded only by the Messiah, and thus he rejects Zionism. Eventually, Saunders forbids Danny to associate with Reuven, who has adopted his father's cause. Danny, although now a grown man, follows the tradition he has been reared in and obeys his father. However, his physical appearance indicates that he mourns the loss of the friendship. Reuven, as narrator, describes his suffering, particularly his feelings of loneliness and alienation when his father is hospitalized with a second heart attack. For nearly two years the young men do not speak to each other, even though they continue to attend the same college. Their suffering proves that the friendship is not dead, and on one occasion Reuven is comforted momentarily by the touch of Danny's hand. Reb Saunders lifts his ban on the friendship after Israel becomes a nation. Both Danny and Reuven are happy to be friends again and discuss the pain they had experienced. Nevertheless, the separation has helped them mature. By the end of the novel it is evident that the friendship has been essential in helping them become the compassionate men that they now are. Because of their friendship, both Reuven and Danny have come to a better understanding of themselves and of others. They have become independent of their fathers and are able to make sound life choices for themselves.

Source: Deanna Evans, in an essay for *Novels for Students,* Gale, 1998.

Sam Bluefarb

In the following excerpt, Bluefarb examines the main conflicts in The Chosen: *those caused by religious beliefs, by differences in generations, and by the split between the head and the heart.*

The conflict in Chaim Potok's novel *The Chosen* functions at several levels. These are: the generational conflict; the temperamental; the conflict between head and heart; the opposition between a petrified fanaticism and a humane tolerance; and, finally, the split between two visions of God and man's relationship to Him. Of all of these, however, it is the opposition between the head and the heart which predominates.

The locale of the story is the Crown Heights section of Williamsburg in Brooklyn from the Depression years to the founding of the State of Israel. Although much of the story's direction is determined by the conflict between Hassidic and Misnagdic traditions in Judaism (as respectively represented by the Saunders and Malter families), it is the conflict between two generations and the Hawthornesque split between the obsessions of the head and the impulses of the heart that carry the major thrust of *The Chosen.*

The Hassidic view originated as a revolt against the arid intellectual concerns of 18th century scholastic (i.e., Misnagdic) Judaism with its tortuous explications in Talmudic *pilpul* and its aristocratic disdain for the poor and illiterate Jew. This resulted in the Hassidic heresy (according to the Vilna Gaon) toward the stress on joy and the intuitions. Yet in its turn (especially as portrayed in *The Chosen*) Hassidism itself evolved into the very thing it had attacked. The distance between the *Ba'al Shem Tov* (or the *Besht,* as he was affectionately called by his followers) and his latter-day followers is relatively short, as history goes: a mere two hundred years or so; but the distance between the gentle piety of the founder of Hassidism and the fanaticism of his later followers qualitatively spans a greater distance than time alone can account for. Indeed, Reb Saunders, the Hassidic leader in *The Chosen,* has really reverted to the earlier arid scholasticism which Hassidism in its own beginnings had set itself up in opposition to.

However, in *The Chosen,* the quarrel between the Hassidim and the Misnagdim (these days, roughly those practicing Jews who are not Hassidim) though decreasing in intensity and bitterness after the slaughter of six million in the Nazi Holocaust, still makes up a substantial aspect of this novel. It is to this group—the Misnagdim (or, to acknowledge Potok's Sephardic, dialectual usage, Mitnagdim)—to which Reuven Malter, the young protagonist, belongs. We must of course remember that many Hassidim consider most Jews beyond their own circle *apikorsim* (heretics). While it is true that the Misnagdim in *The Chosen* did not actively oppose the Hassidim, the baseball game between the Misnagdic and the Hassidic schools on which the novel opens, not only triggers the conflict but determines the direction the novel will take. In a sense, *The Chosen* is a kind of exercise in the "Hegelian" dialectic which the Hassidim and the Misnagdim have engaged in for the last two and a half centuries; however, in doing so, they have articulated their respective visions toward life and God, and, in a sense, have managed to exert some beneficial influence on each other.

One of the central problems in *The Chosen* is communication—or lack of it. Part of this is de-liberate and "chosen." Reb Saunders, in his oddly "Talmudic" way, believes that he can best teach his son the language and wisdom of the heart by forbidding or discouraging, what he considers "frivolous" discourse—what most of us might think of as the minimal conversational civilities. Thus Reb Saunders denies Danny what Mr. Malter the yeshiva teacher freely gives to his son Reuven: warmth, communication, and understanding. On those rare occasions when Reb Saunders permits himself to address Danny, these exchanges take place during the periodic quizzes on Talmud which the *rebbe* subjects Danny to—or when he blows up in exasperation at his son's passivity in the face of his own religious (near violent) commitments.

On the other hand, the relationship between Reuven and *his* father is a tender one, made all the more trusting by the easy and affectionate exchange of confidences that go on between them. They, at least, can do what Danny and his father seem unable to do: communicate. In the instance of Reb Saunders it is an admixture of pride and fanatic pietism that prevents any intimacy between himself and his son (rationalized by the elder Saunders' commitment to the Talmudic *A word is worth one coin; silence is worth two*). In Danny's case it is simply fear of his father that prevents any viable relationship between the two. Conceivably, Mr. Malter, the yeshiva teacher, and Reb Saunders, the Hassidic Talmudist, are of a common generation, if not of a common age; yet it is Reb Saunders' rigidity, and his stiff-necked pride, that give the illusion that he is much older than Mr. Malter—even as Hassidism itself *appears* to be rooted in an older tradition than its Misnagdic counterpart.

The difference between Mr. Malter and Reb Saunders expresses itself most forcefully in their respective visions toward the Holocaust: Reb Saunders can do little more than shed (very real) tears for the martyred Jews of Europe. " 'How the world drinks our blood.... [But] It is the will of God. We must accept the will of God.' "... Reuven's more Westernized father, on the other hand, attempts to counter the existential nullity of the "world" by becoming ever more active in a resuscitated Zionist movement. Reb Saunders, to the contrary, in conformance with orthodox Hassidism, is bound by the Messianic belief—that only with the coming of the Messiah will Jews achieve the millennial dream, the ingathering of the exiles, the return to Eretz Yisroel.

What we find in *The Chosen* is a kind of *doppelgänger* effect—minus the *doppelgänger* itself. For Reuven and Danny are symbolically two halves of a single (perhaps ideal? Jewish?) personality, each half searching for its complement, which we already know can never be found in an imperfect world (*Siz a falsher velt!*—It's a hypocritical world! says a Yiddish Koheleth.). In short, no perfection is to be attained, except in unity. But that is precisely the problem of the characters in *The Chosen:* theirs is a search for that elusive (or illusory) goal. For neither of these two boys growing into manhood can really be said to exist at their fullest potential unless they retain some sort of relationship with each other, which on one occasion is suspended when Reb Saunders forbids Danny any association with Reuven for an interval of about a year, making the two boys doubly miserable.

Reuven, whose father allows his son forays into symbolic logic, the mathematics of Bertrand Russell, ends up a rabbi! Danny, who throughout the novel is coerced into following Hassidic tradition, and is expected to succeed Reb to the leadership of the sect on his father's death, ultimately breaks away. Danny, for want of a better word— the word has been overly used and abused, though it applies here—has been alienated—from his father, from Hassidism, and finally from the Hassidic community itself. In a sense Danny is recapitulating (suffering through) the transitions and adjustments so traumatically demanded by the exodus from the Old World to the New, adjustments required of his father and his followers, "pilgrims" who came to America from the East European *shtetle* one step ahead of Hitler's kill-squads.

The American Diaspora has also given Danny, Freud and Behaviorist psychology (though initially he has mixed feelings about the latter); but after reading Graetz's *History of the Jews,* he has found that "Freud had clearly upset him in a fundamental way—had thrown him off-balance".

More significant than the conflict of belief in *The Chosen* is the conflict between the generations—each of which is so often collateral with the other. The novel itself could as easily, if not originally, have been called *Fathers and Sons.* For it is as much about the old split between the fathers and their offsprings as it is about the conflicts between religious views and personalities. The sons have been molded by the fathers, though in the case of Danny that influence is a negative one. For Reb Saunders is a fanatic, or at least has those propensities; he represents the archetypal, God-intoxicated Hassid. And it is he who has caused Danny to grow into a tense, coldly introverted personality. Reuven's father, on the other hand, is the tolerant (albeit religious) humanist, opposed both in

mind and in heart to the cold scholasticism of the Saunderses.

In the growing estrangement between Danny and his father, the conflict of generations and of visions toward life surfaces. And it is America that is catalyst: the old East European ambiance is gone (unless one accepts Williamsburg as a pale substitute milieu for the vanished *shtetle*); and in the second instance the old ghetto traditions have become influenced, perhaps eroded—the old acculturation-assimilation story—by the pressures of urbanism and secular intellectualism.

The relationship between Reuven Malter and his father is rooted organically, not in principle—self or externally imposed—but in tolerance and mutual respect. Mr. Malter is a yeshiva teacher, yet he can comfortably discuss the secular philosophers with Reuven as Danny's father, the Hassidic Reb Saunders, never can with him. Mr. Malter tells Reuven, " 'the point about mathematizing hypotheses was made by Kant. It is one of the programs of the Vienna Circle logical positivists.' " Yet with all his easy familiarity with philosophical schools and systems, his acumen in grasping them, Reuven's father allows his son to seek truth in his own way (possibly because of his own exposure to the rationalist winds of Western philosophy). Where Danny is coerced into the study of a specific mode of religious thought, Reuven is allowed by his father to roam free through the country of ideas. This seemingly minor approach to pedagogical technique—both fathers are teachers in their own ways—will determine the direction each of the boys will later take as young men.

Reuven's father hopes his son will become a rabbi—but would not coerce him into it. The elder Saunders not only expects Danny to take his place in the rabbinic dynasty when his own time comes (as Hassidic custom requires), but can hardly imagine an alternative. On the other hand fanaticism and intolerance go to form the iron bond that binds Danny to his father. What is important here, though, is that Danny becomes an object, manipulated by his father, rather than a person one relates to. This determines Danny's ultimate hostility toward Hassidism itself, so that when he rebels, he not only rebels against a religious movement but against his father, who is its representative. The worship of God gives way, in the first flush of enthusiasm, to his admiration, if not worship, of a substitute god, Sigmund Freud.

As the novel progresses, Danny the intellectual wizard, *Wunderkind,* finds himself increasingly boxed in by the restrictive ghetto mentality of the Hassidim. He sees that his father "'Intellectually … was born trapped. I don't ever want to be trapped the way he's trapped.'"

Ultimately, though, *The Chosen* is a paradigm of two visions that have not only sundered Judaism but have affected other areas of life—the split between head and heart. The Saunderses seem to have an excess of head in their (paradoxical streak of zealousness and emotional) makeup; but the Malters have heart *and* head: they are in balance. For Reuven is not only an outstanding student of Talmud but be "has a head" for mathematics and symbolic logic. Like his father, he also has a spark of tolerance which illuminates his own knowledge of human essences as opposed to ritualistic forms.

Reuven's studies are "brain" disciplines—logic, mathematics, philosophy—yet it is he who finally turns out to have more "heart" than the brilliant son of a Hassid. Danny, on the other hand, having been raised in the tradition of the *Ba'al Shem,* should have been a "heart-and-joy specialist." Yet it is he who is all brain. And this produces a keen irony, since Hassidism, a movement that was originally a revolt against arid scholasticism became (as portrayed in *The Chosen*) transformed into its opposite. Piety, joy, even learning (a latecomer to Hassidism) becomes pietism, role learning, memorization.

In this split between head and heart, Danny Saunders shows a brilliant flare for Talmudic explication. Yet Reb Saunders, addressing Reuven Malter in Danny's presence, complains, "'the Master of the Universe blessed me with a brilliant son. And He cursed me with all the problems of raising him. Ah, what it is to have a brilliant son! … [But] There was no soul in my … Daniel, there was only his mind. He was a mind in a body without a soul.'" Too late: Danny has already "chosen" his own path, and Reb Saunders—plausibly or not—realizes at last that it is impossible to turn back now and give his son the love (or heart) he might once have given him, an act which may well have tempered Danny's mind.

Reuven is not exactly a *graubbe yung*, a moron, himself. For in one of the terminal scenes, he proves himself a master of many Talmudic brain twisters—and this, ironically, even when he *cannot* answer one difficult proposition which the teacher himself is unable to resolve! There is enough sanity in Reuven, though—presumably the heritage his father has passed on to him—to bring him to the realization that words themselves have little meaning unless they are rooted in life. If necessary, Reuven will show that he is capable of proving a formidable rival to Danny's father in his ability to untie knotty Talmudic propositions. Yet he also knows that this hardly makes a Jew, much less a compassionate human being. For brilliance, whether in Talmud or in other mental acrobatics, may as often blind the brilliant with their own brilliance as enlighten. The major irony, then, is that Hassidism—the brand portrayed in Potok's novel—though presumably a religious movement of the heart, has become transformed into its opposite.

I should like to say a few words about the symbolic symmetry of *The Chosen*. Potok seems to have extended himself beyond plausibility here. For the conclusion of this otherwise fine and sensitive work is marred by contrivance. Perhaps this can be ascribed to a symmetry which, while possible in life, somehow doesn't ring true when placed in fictional context. In this symmetry Danny escapes the confines of the Hassidic sect while Reuven stays within the wider boundaries of a more tolerant form of Judaism. Further, in this kind of resolution, Potok unintentionally (and unfortunately) reveals his intentions long before the novel ends. It takes no great effort, to guess, even early in the novel, that Danny will rebel, while Reuven, the "nice Jewish boy," will become a rabbi.

Reb Saunders' "conversion"—his resignation to Danny's break with Hassidism—doesn't convince. The novel is too mechanical in this sense—with Danny, who was to have inherited his father's leadership going off to become a clinical or behavioral psychologist, while Reuven turns to the rabbinate.

The climax of the novel is illustrated by the following exchange the two young men engage in: Danny tells Reuven: "'I can't get over your becoming a rabbi.'" Whereupon Reuven answers: "'I can't get over your becoming a psychologist.'" Even the dialogue is weak here, betraying the Procrustean ending; it is virtually the antithesis to the brilliant verbal fencing—stychomythia—that the great dramatists from Shakespeare to Shaw were such virtuosos at. In this instance, the dialogue verges on the cliché.

Thus, as Reuven moves closer to Misnagdic—non-Hassidic—Judaism, so Danny moves away from its Hassidic counterpart, giving the novel this mechanical symmetry. The saving feature in spite of the contrived ending is that the choices of the two young men are as much determined by motive and character (or lack of it) as by superimposed plot strictures.

The almost explicit theme of *The Chosen,* then, is that the more repression one is forced to knuckle under to (no matter the noble intentions), the greater will be the rebellion against the source of that repression; it's the old postulate of an opposite and equal reaction for every action. In other words, the contrivance of the rebellious son against the father and the father's resignation to the son's rebellion—"'You will remain an observer of the Commandments?'" he pathetically asks Danny—are developments which make it all the more difficult to believe in Reb Saunders as a strong, if stubborn, man.

Still—and this I mean to stress—the "contrivance of symmetry" with which the novel ends is a minor flaw in a larger pattern: that of tolerance against intolerance, empty ritual against the vital deed, rote learning against eager wonder. In any effective fiction it is the process rather than the outcome that is more important. This is especially true in *The Chosen.* For in this novel Chaim Potok gives us as keen an insight into the split between head and heart, tolerance and fanaticism, the strictures of tradition against the impulses of *rachmonis* (pity) as has appeared in the Jewish-American novel in a long time.

Source: Sam Bluefarb, "The Head, the Heart, and the Conflict of Generations in Chaim Potok's *The Chosen,*" in *CLA Journal,* Vol. XIV, No. 4, June 1971, pp. 402–9.

Sources

"Back to the Fold," review in the *Times Literary Supplement,* March 5, 1970, p. 241.

Dan Barnet, essay in *Critical Survey of Long Fiction,* edited by Frank N. Magill, Salem Press, 1991, pp. 2659-67.

Felicity Barringer, review in the *New York Times Book Review,* December 1, 1996, p. 33.

Sam Bluefarb, "The Head, the Heart, and the Conflict of Generations in Chaim Potok's *The Chosen,*" in *College Language Association Journal,* June, 1971, pp. 402-409.

S. Lillian Kremer, "Chaim Potok," in *Dictionary of Literary Biography,* Vol. 152: *American Novelists since World War II, Fourth Series,* Gale Research, 1984, pp. 232-43.

Beverly J. Matiko, an analysis and critical evaluation of *The Chosen* in *Masterplots,* New York: Harper, 1969, pp. 1121-24.

Lisa Schwarzbaum, review in the *Detroit News,* March 17, 1985, p. 5.

David M. Shribman, review in the *Wall Street Journal,* December 12, 1996, p. A10.

Philip Toynbee, review in the *New Republic,* June 17, 1967, pp. 21-22.

For Further Study

Edward A. Abramson, *Chaim Potok,* Twayne, 1994.
A book-length study presenting biographical information about the author and an overview of all of his writings to date. Chapter 2 provides a valuable commentary of *The Chosen.*

Arthur A. Cohen, "Why I Choose to be a Jew," in *Breakthrough A Treasury of Contemporary American-Jewish Literature,* edited by Irving Malin and Irwin Stark, The Jewish Publication Society of America, 1964, pp. 367-76.
Cohen explains that, until recently, Jews could not choose *not* to remain a Jew, and then he discusses his own religious choices.

Michael Gilmore, "A Fading Promise," in *Midstream,* January, 1970, pp. 76-79.
Gilmore disagrees with the view of the Jewish community found in Potok's novels.

Sheldon Grebstein, "The Phenomenon of the Really Jewish Best Seller: Potok's *The Chosen"* in *Studies in American Jewish Literature,* Spring, 1975, pp. 23-31.
A helpful analysis of the novel, which includes a discussion Potok's style and of the American Dream.

Granville Hicks, "Good Fathers and Good Sons," in *Saturday Review,* April 29, 1967, pp. 25-56.
In this early review Hicks tries to understand how Potok's "good boys"—and their fathers—are interesting as well as meaningful to a multitude of readers.

Baruch Hochman, review of *The Chosen,* in *Commentary,* September, 1967, p. 108.
In this early review, Hochman praises the psychological tension Potok creates as he explores the conflict of generations, but he criticizes the novel's conclusion as belonging to a fairy tale.

Irving Howe, "Introduction to Yiddish Literature," in *Breakthrough A Treasury of Contemporary American-Jewish Literature,* edited by Irving Malin and Irwin Stark, The Jewish Publication Society of America, 1964, pp. 278-300.
Howe's difficult essay analyzes the linguistic, historical, religious, cultural, and literary backdrops against which Yiddish literature is created.

Faye Leeper, "What Is in the Name?" in *English Journal,* Vol. 59, no. 1, January, 1970, pp. 63-64.
Leeper argues that the novel is engrossing for high school students who understand Jewish religious practices. She cites the multiple meanings of the novel's title as evidence.

Curt Leviant, "The Hasid as American Hero," in *Midstream,* November, 1967, pp. 76-80.

An analysis which criticizes the writing style in *The Chosen.*

Daphne Merkin, "Why Potok is Popular," in *Commentary,* February, 1976, pp. 73-75.

Merkin criticizes Potok's style as "amateurish," his characters as "paper thin," and his moral scheme as "black and white." She suggests that his popularity coincides with a "rediscovery of ethnic consciousness" on the part of his public.

Hugh Nissenson, "The Spark and the Shell," in *New York Times Book Review,* May 7, 1967, pp. 4-5, 34.

In this early review of the novel, Nissenson critiques Potok's prose, but praises the novel's structure and themes. He particularly admires Potok's treatment of Rabbi Saunders' silence, which is dramatically portrayed against a backdrop of God's silence.

Sanford Pinsker, "The Crucifixion of Chaim Potok/The Excommunication of Asher Lev: Art and the Hasidic World," in *Studies in American Jewish Literature,* no. 4: *The World of Chaim Potok,* edited by Daniel Walden, State University of New York Press, 1985, pp. 39-51.

Pinsker explores Potok's treatment of "sensitive" heroes who are trapped between "rival authoritarian figures." Most of the discussion centers around *My Name is Asher Lev.*

Chaim Potok, "Cultural Confrontation in Urban America: A Writer's Beginnings," in *Literature and the Urban Experience: Essays on the City and Literature,* edited by M. C. Jay and A. C. Watts, Rutgers University Press, 1981, pp. 161–67.

Potok's description of the expansion of the world of his Brooklyn Jewish childhood.

Chaim Potok, "Reply to a Semi-Sympathetic Critic," in *Studies in American Jewish Literature,* Spring, 1976, pp. 30-34.

The author's response to Sheldon Grebstein's article; Potok defends his language and style in *The Chosen*

and explains how the subject of the novel is "culture war."

Chaim Potok, *Wanderings: Chaim Potok's History of the Jews.* Knopf, 1978.

A broad view of the survival of the Jewish people in a variety of "umbrella" civilizations.

Harold Ribalow, "A Conversation with Chaim Potok," in *The Tie That Binds: Conversations with Jewish Writers,* A.S. Barnes & Co., 1980, pp. 111-37.

Potok, who calls himself a "freak," discusses his efforts to dramatizes clashes that occur between the Jewish tradition and what he calls Western secular humanism.

Karl Shapiro, "The Necessary People," in *Book Week,* April 23, 1967.

A positive view of *The Chosen* as an allegory.

Judah Stampfer, "The Tension of Piety" in *Judaism,* Fall, 1967, pp. 494-98.

Stampfer critiques Potok's portrayal of Hasidim, but praises the book for its detailed documentation of Yeshiva life.

David Stern, review in *Commentary,* October, 1972, p. 102. *My Name Is Asher Lev,* Potok's third novel, is reviewed. Stern analyses the main theme Potok explores in his novels, which is trying to live in both a religious and secular world.

Daniel Walden, ed., *Studies in American Jewish Literature,* no. 4: *The World of Chaim Potok,* State University of New York Press, 1985.

A collection of valuable essays about and interviews of Chaim Potok.

Mark Zborowski, *Life Is with People: The Culture of the Shtetl,* Schocken Books, 1995.

A flawed, over-romanticized but thorough description of the Eastern European Jewish culture which is used as model by contemporary strict Orthodox Jews and some Hasidic sects.

Go Tell It on the Mountain

James Baldwin
1953

James Baldwin was one of the most versatile and influential artists of the post-World War II generation, creating memorable short stories, novels, plays, essays and children's books. *Go Tell It on the Mountain* was his first published novel, and many critics feel that it is has stood as his best. It is a traditional bildungsroman, a novel tracing the psychological and spiritual development of its central character, John Grimes.

In the first chapter, John's family life, ruled by anger, poverty and guilt, is explored, leading to the fifth chapter, when, after night's religious service, John is accepted into his church's community because he has undergone a seizure-like conversion, writhing on the floor and speaking in foreign tongues. The middle chapters give the background stories of his aunt, his father, and his mother, who migrated to New York from the South and endured various difficulties that are reflected in John's life.

There is a strong autobiographical aspect to the novel, as many of the details in John's life mirror those in Baldwin's life, including his impoverished upbringing in Harlem, his angry vitriolic father, his fascination with an older male church member and his religious conversion at age fourteen. Explaining how writing his first novel helped him come to terms with the troubled he faced growing up, Baldwin said, "*Mountain* was the book I had to write if I was ever going to write anything else."

Author Biography

James Baldwin was born in 1924 in Harlem, New York City. Many of the details in the life of John, the main character in *Go Tell It on the Mountain,* parallel facts in Baldwin's own life. He was an awkward, gangly boy who suffered the abuse of his stepfather, a laborer and storefront preacher who had moved to New York from New Orleans. In contrast to the squalor and anger that he experienced at home, Baldwin was a resounding success at Public School 24 and at Frederick Douglass Junior High School, where his teachers recognized his brilliance and verbal skills. At age fourteen, he, like John, experienced a religious conversion during the service at his church, the Mount Calvary of the Pentecostal Faith Church.

After that, Baldwin became a preacher himself, and throughout high school he addressed the congregation at the local storefront church at least once each week. After high school he worked briefly in New Jersey, and then moved to Greenwich Village, the section of New York City that was a famous gathering place for artists. For five years he worked menial jobs and published short pieces in intellectual magazines such as *The Nation, The Partisan Review, The New Leader,* and *Commentary.*

With the help of famed African-American author Richard Wright, Baldwin received the Eugene F. Saxton Memorial Trust Award for financial help while writing his first novel. In November 1948 he sailed to France, and he never lived in America again, although he traveled here frequently on speaking engagements. He felt that America was too socially oppressive, both because he was black and because he was homosexual.

Go Tell It on the Mountain, his first novel, was published in 1953, and it gained immediate popularity among American intellectuals, establishing Baldwin as one of the keenest observers of the American racial situation. None of the other seven novels he wrote is considered to have been as successful, possibly because they sublimated storytelling to their message. From the early 1940s to his death in 1987, Baldwin was recognized as a master of the personal essay. Several of his pieces, compiled in such collections as *Notes of a Native Son* (1955), *The Fire Next Time* (1963) and *The Price of the Ticket: Collected Nonfiction 1948-1985* have created a lasting effect on American social life, particularly in the area of race relations. James Baldwin died of cancer in 1987, at his home in the south of France.

James Baldwin

Plot Summary

Part I

James Baldwin's *Go Tell It on the Mountain* chronicles the experiences of its young narrator, John Grimes, in Harlem in 1935. The novel opens on the morning of John's fourteenth birthday and centers on the events that lead up to his spiritual conversion later that evening. The narrative also provides a history of his family, of his stepfather Gabriel, a preacher in Temple of the Fire Baptized; of his aunt Florence, Gabriel's sister; and of his mother Elizabeth. All of these stories add poignancy and context to John's efforts to come to terms with his present and his future.

On that morning as he is lying in bed, John thinks about his family's expectations that he will follow in his father's footsteps into "the holy life" but wonders if that is the path he wants for himself. His lack of devotion to the church angers his father. John remembers one Sunday morning when Father James, another preacher in the church, warns Elisha and Ella Mae, two young church members, that "disorderly walking" together could lead to them "straying from the truth." This public warning shames them and so they stop meeting. John acknowledges the same sexual stirrings in himself and masturbates while in bed. Afterwards, feeling as if he has just sinned, he decides he will not devote his life to the church. He notes that he has been singled out in school for his intelligence as early as the age of five. At that point he knew he had "power other people lacked," which helped him withstand his father's beatings and his lonely childhood. John admits his hatred for his father. Since his father was "God's minister" and he knew that he would have to first bow down to his father before he could bow down to God, his heart is also "hardened against the Lord."

Later that morning his mother gives him money for his birthday and predicts that he will turn into a fine man. She tells him she knows "there's a whole lot of things you don't understand" but that God will help him find his way. John feels overwhelming love for her. After finishing his chores, he walks to Central Park, thinking about his options: church, the "narrow way," full of poverty and hard work; and the city, with its white world of riches and sin. His father has told him that all whites are "wicked," that God will punish them, and that they will never accept him into their world because he is black. On 42nd street he watches a movie about a white "evil" woman making a "glorious" fall from grace. John decides that like her, he wants to make others suffer as he has. Yet as she faces damnation on her death bed, he thinks of Hell and struggles to find a compromise for himself.

When John returns home, he discovers that his brother Roy has been stabbed while "looking for trouble" in a white neighborhood. John notes his father's love for his brother but not for him. After wiping the blood off Roy's face, Gabriel turns on his mother, insisting that she should have kept Roy out of harm's way. When she tries to defend herself, he slaps her. Roy then curses his father, who beats him severely with a belt. Elizabeth and Roy cling to each other after Aunt Florence pulls his father off of him. That night, as John cleans the church before the evening service, he wonders if Elisha still thinks about sinning and meditates again about his own confusion. Later that evening, his mother, father, and aunt arrive for the service.

Part II

In this section, Florence, Gabriel, and Elizabeth take over the narrative one at a time as they pray. Florence starts to sing a song her mother used to sing. Fighting her pride, and trying to humble herself before God, she admits she has forgotten how to pray. She is filled with hatred and bitterness but also the fear of death. While struggling to pray, she sees a vision of her dead mother and

Gabriel cursing her. Florence then thinks back to her family and growing up in Maryland. Desperate to escape from home where her mother focused only on her brother, Florence moved to New York City at the age of twenty-six, leaving Gabriel to care for their dying mother.

Florence remembers her husband Frank, who left her after ten years of marriage and later died in France during the war. She also remembers getting a letter from Deborah, her neighbor in Maryland who eventually moved to New York and married Gabriel. The letter reveals Deborah's suspicions that Gabriel fathered a child with another woman. Florence determines to use the letter some day to humiliate Gabriel. Returning to the present, she feels that she will not be saved and that everyone is laughing at her attempts.

Gabriel also recalls the past, beginning with his "redemption," which occurred when he was a young man. After a night of drinking and sex, the burden of his sin became too great and he asked God to save him. He felt that this "was the beginning of his life as a man." His first major test as a preacher came at the Twenty-four Elders Revival Meeting, where he delivered a rousing and well-received sermon on sin and redemption. Recognizing Deborah's confidence in him and deciding that the two of them were among God's chosen, he married her. Yet dreams warned him of temptation. His thoughts turn back to the present as he thinks about his family. Since he is not John's birth parent, he wants Roy, his son by Elizabeth, to be the son God promised him would carry on his name in the church.

Gabriel recalls the child he fathered with Esther while he was married to Deborah. He remembers his struggle over his desire for Esther and his growing hatred for Deborah and their passionless, barren marriage. When Gabriel discovered the pregnancy, he stole money from Deborah so Esther could have their baby elsewhere in order to spare both of them the shame of an illegitimate child. After Esther died, his son Royal returned and was raised without knowing his father. The narrative then abruptly shifts to the present and to John who, while attempting to pray, hears a voice telling him "salvation is real." He believes that if he were saved, he would be his father's equal and thus could love him, but he decides that he wants to continue to hate him and hopes his father will die.

Gabriel takes back the narrative and returns to the morning Royal died. When Deborah told Gabriel the news, he cried. Deborah then confirmed her suspicions about Royal and asked Gabriel why he didn't offer Esther more support. She insisted that she would have helped him raise Royal. Gabriel's thoughts then jump into the future when, after Deborah died, he married Elizabeth and promised to help her raise her son John. Gabriel saw this act as his last chance to redeem himself in the eyes of God. Returning to the present, he gazes into John's eyes and sees Satan and the eyes of all who have rebuked him. Gabriel feels the urge to hit John, but restrains himself and orders him to kneel down before God.

Elizabeth prays for John's deliverance. When her thoughts return to the past, she remembers her three "disasters"—when her mother died, she was taken away from the father she loved and was forced to live with her aunt. At eighteen, she met "wild unhappy" Richard, John's father, a man she loved deeply. After he was falsely accused and arrested for robbery, Richard was savagely beaten by white officers. The night he was released, he slit his wrists. Elizabeth blamed herself for his suicide, speculating that the knowledge of her pregnancy might have saved him. A few years later, Florence introduced her to Gabriel who had moved to Harlem after Deborah died. Gabriel soon asked Elizabeth to marry him, promising to take care of her and her son. Trusting his word, she agreed. When the narrative returns to the present, John is writhing on the threshing floor.

Part III

John, filled with "anguish," faces his sin and lies helpless and afraid on the floor of the church. During this torment, he has a vision of Hell. As he struggles to raise himself out of the darkness, he asks God to have mercy on him and to help him. He then becomes filled with joy. As the family walks home, Florence shows Gabriel Deborah's letter and tells him he needs to look at his own sin, and then he can accept John as his son. She warns him that she will show others the letter unless Gabriel changes. John, walking next to Elisha, acknowledges him as his brother and protector. As they reach their home, John looks at his father who stares back coldly at him. The novel closes with John declaring, "I'm ready. I'm coming. I'm on my way."

Characters

Elisha

Seventeen years old and recently arrived in Harlem from Georgia, Elisha is the nephew of the pastor of the Temple of the Fire of the Baptized. He has been publicly chastised in front of the congregation for "walking disorderly" with Ella Mae Washington, meaning that they had been walking without supervision and might have given in to temptation and had sex.

John is infatuated with Elisha. At Sunday school, "John stared at Elisha all during the lesson, admiring the timbre of Elisha's voice, much deeper and manlier than his own, admiring the leanness, and grace, and darkness of Elisha in his Sunday suit, and wondering if he would ever be holy as Elisha was holy." While clearing the church to prepare for the Saturday evening tarry meeting, John and Elisha wrestle: He saw the veins rise on Elisha's forehead and in his neck … and John, watching these manifestations of his power, became wild with delight."

John's spiritual possession follows Elisha's, both in style and in time, raising the question of whether it is a true religious experience or just an imitation. At the end of the novel Elisha kisses John on the forehead and tells him, "Run on, little brother. Don't you get weary. God won't forget you. You won't forget."

Elizabeth

Early in the novel, as the Grimes family goes about their Saturday morning chores, Elizabeth, the mother, appears to be an apologist for her husband's brutality, explaining to her children that Gabriel works hard to provide for them. She is kind to John; she is the only one in the family to remember his birthday, and she tries to distract the family with prayer when, after Gabriel has slapped her, Roy curses his father and tells him to leave her alone. It is not until much later in the novel that the reasons for her meekness appear.

Like the other characters, her childhood was a difficult one. Her mother, a cold woman that Elizabeth did not love, died when she was young, and her aunt, who thought Elizabeth was snobbish, took custody of her so she would not be raised by her father, who ran a house of prostitution. Elizabeth was devastated, because she loved her father dearly. When she was eighteen she met Richard at the local store and fell in love with him. When he moved to New York, she did too, but to keep up her reputation she lived with a "respectable" relative of her aunt, who was actually a spiritualist who conducted seances on Saturday nights. Elizabeth and Richard both worked in the same hotel and were planning to marry when he had enough money saved. He killed himself, though, before Elizabeth could tell him about her pregnancy.

When the baby was born, she withdrew from society, and despaired that the child, John, would never have a father. At work, she became acquainted with Florence, and through her met Gabriel. Gabriel took an interest in her son, and when he proposed to Elizabeth he told her he would "love John just like my own," a promise clearly broken in the favoritism he shows for Roy.

Ella Mae

The granddaughter of Praying Mother Washington, she was called before the congregation early in the novel for spending time with Elisha without an escort. After John has undergone his spiritual transformation, Ella Mae is noticeably absent: "She had a bad cold, said Praying Mother Washington, and needed to have her rest."

Florence

In the novel, Florence has two secrets. One is that she is dying, and this is why, to John's surprise, she shows a sudden interest in going to church. The second is that she knows, through a letter sent her thirty years earlier by Gabriel's first wife, that her brother had fathered a child out of wedlock with one of the local girls. "For she had always thought of this letter as an instrument in her hands which could be used to complete her brother's destruction. When he was completely cast down she would prevent him from ever rising again by holding before him the evidence of his blood-guilt."

At the end of the novel, the day he is "completely cast down" turns out to be the day his step-son John enters the religious community. The letter is from Deborah, a friend from a neighboring farm when they were growing up. As children, Florence and Deborah each had experiences that made them angry and frustrated. Deborah was gang-raped by white men and shunned by the black community because of it, and Florence lost her chance to go to school, have new clothes or even eat a hearty meal when her mother gave all privileges to Gabriel because he was a boy. Florence left home at age twenty-six and Deborah later married Gabriel.

Florence moved to Harlem where she met Frank, who was a kind, good-natured man but was foolish with money. Florence dreamed of owning a home, but Frank wasted his paychecks on ugly presents for her and on drinking with his friends. When she last saw him, they were in the middle

Media Adaptations

- *James Baldwin, Author,* a videocassette from the Black Americans of Achievement collection, available from Schlessinger Video, 1994.

- *James Baldwin: The Price of the Ticket,* a videocassette, available from California Newsreel, 1990.

- *My Childhood: Hubert Humphrey and James Baldwin.* Videocassette of a 1964 motion picture from Benchmark Films, 1989.

- *The View From Here: A National Press Club Address by James Baldwin.* Audio cassette available from Spoken Arts, 1988.

- *James Baldwin: An Interview with Kay Bonetti* is an audio cassette available from American Audio Prose Library, 1984.

- *James Baldwin,* an audio cassette from Tapes for Readers, 1979.

- *The Struggle,* by James Baldwin. This is a record album from Buddha Records, #BDS2004, 1960.

of an argument and he said, "All right, baby. I guess you don't never want to see me no more, not a miserable, black sinner like me." He walked out of the door and never came back. Years later, the woman he had lived with most recently informed Florence that he had died in France during World War I.

Frank

Florence's husband Frank was a good-natured but weak man, always spending money foolishly instead of saving it, inviting his drunken friends over and constantly apologizing to Florence. One day, during an argument, he walked out, and though she expected him to return that night, or the next morning, he never came back. She found out that he had died in France during the war from the woman that he had lived with for a few years after he had left her.

Absinnian Baptist Church, New York City, May 11, 1959.

Gabriel

John's father is a deacon at the local church in Harlem, and he had a successful career as a preacher when he was young, but he started life as a troubled boy who broke church laws by drinking, gambling and having sex with women. Gabriel's mother was harsh with him, trying to correct his behavior with spanking and forcing religion on him: "And, after the beating, with his pants still down around his knees and his face wet with tears and mucus, Gabriel was made to kneel down while his mother prayed."

His behavior did not change, though, until he was twenty-one, when his sister Florence left home and Gabriel was left to care for his aging, sick mother by himself. Faced with the silent watchfulness of his once-fiery mother, he begged God with prayers that he would be able to leave his evil ways and follow a religious life. One day, as he was to repeatedly tell the story, his prayers were answered: "I opened my mouth to the Lord that day and Hell won't make me change my mind."

Soon after this he began preaching, and made such a name for himself that he was invited to be one of twenty-four preachers on the bill for a "monster revival meeting." Disgusted with the crude remarks the older preachers made about a neighbor girl, Deborah, who had been gang-raped by whites

when she was young, Gabriel soon married her, confirming his religious sincerity to himself. But it was an unhappy marriage, and when one of the other employees where he worked showed an interest he ended up sleeping with her. The affair with Esther lasted nine days. Gabriel was cold to her in breaking it off and even colder in refusing to help when she told him she was pregnant. "She put out her hands to reach him, but he moved away"—with that gesture of rejection and denial his life became a web of deceit that ruined his early promise as a preacher.

Esther died in childbirth, naming the infant Royal to spite Gabriel, who had wanted a son named Royal "because the line of the faithful is a Royal line." The boy was raised by his grandparents and died in a knife fight in Chicago, never knowing that he was Gabriel's son. After Deborah died, Gabriel moved to Harlem, and at the time of the novel he is married to Elizabeth and raising John, who she had before she met him; Roy, the new Royal, who should be the start of his Royal line but who drinks and fights as Gabriel did as a young man; and two girls, Sarah and Ruth.

Deborah Grimes

Deborah grew up as a neighbor to Gabriel and Florence. When they were young, a gang of white men raped Deborah, and when her father went to threaten them for what they had done, they beat him and left him for dead. Deborah and Florence were friends growing up, and when Florence left to live in the North, Deborah became close to Rachel, Florence's mother. Eventually Gabriel married Deborah, but they had a cold marriage: she did not talk with him, possibly because she was in awe of his religious authority, and he was secretive about his feelings. When Gabriel cried upon hearing that his son Royal had been killed, Deborah told him that she had known about this son all along, and would have been willing to raise it as her own if he had asked her to.

John Grimes

One of the first things to cross John's mind when he wakes up at the novel's beginning is "that it was his fourteenth birthday and that he has sinned." The particular sin he refers to appears to be a combination of homosexuality and masturbation, as he had "sinned with his hands" while in the bathroom at school, "thinking of the boys, older, bigger, braver, who made bets with each other as to whose urine could arch higher." It soon becomes apparent, though, that John is likely to feel like a sinner no matter what he does—his stepfather, a Deacon of the Temple of the Fire Baptized, has physically and verbally abused John all his life, showing favor to John's younger brother Roy.

Gabriel Grimes married John's mother when John was young, and he does not know that he and Roy are of different fathers. As a result of the abuse he suffers, John harbors a hatred of shocking intensity toward his stepfather: "He lived for the day his father would be dying and he, John, would curse him on his deathbed." In balance to Gabriel's destruction of his self-esteem is John's secret satisfaction that he has been chosen for something better in life. He is a shy, awkward boy, but "he apprehended totally, without belief or understanding, that he had within himself a power that other people lacked; that he could use this to save himself; and that, perhaps, with this power he might one day win the love which he longed for."

When it appears to him that his family has forgotten his birthday, John bitterly tells himself that it is all right, that they have done it before and he deserves no better, but his mother gives him money to buy a present and he is grateful to her. He goes to a movie in Times Square and finds himself sympathizing with the villainess, a "violent and unhappy woman," because "nothing tamed or broke her, nothing touched her, neither kindness, nor scorn, nor hatred, nor love."

The one person in the book that John respects and admires is Elisha, a boy at the church who is just a little older than him. They joke around in a tender, sparring way while setting up for the Saturday evening service, then they wrestle. In the novel's climax in Part Three John's spirituality is confirmed to the church members when he falls to the "threshing-floor" in a fit of religious ecstasy, flailing about and talking in unknown languages. The elders of the church (Sister McCandless, Sister Price and Praying Mother Washington) are delighted that he has "got religion," and Elisha takes responsibility for him as a "little brother."

His stepfather is hesitant to believe in John's spiritual conversion and points out that "it ain't all in the singing and the shouting—the way of holiness is a hard way," reflecting his own inability to lead a good life. John himself seems skeptical that what happened to him was a meaningful, lasting religious conversion, but he is glad for the way that it gains him social status and binds him to Elisha.

Rachel Grimes

Gabriel and Florence's mother, who had been a slave before the Civil War.

Roy Grimes

John's younger half-brother, Roy is actually the second son named Royal to be fathered by Gabriel—the first died in a knife fight before Gabriel moved to New York and married Elizabeth. As his only son, Gabriel favors Roy, even though Gabriel thinks of himself as a man of God and Roy is wild, skipping Sunday school and arguing with his mother and hanging out in the streets with a gang.

On the Saturday in 1935 that this novel takes place, Roy comes home with a knife cut across his face, having been in a fight. His father is unable to accept Roy's wild ways, so he turns the situation on meek, churchgoing John, telling him that he should learn a lesson from this. When Elizabeth reminds Gabriel of the fate of the first Royal by telling him to discipline Roy "before somebody puts another knife in him and puts him in his grave," Gabriel slaps her. Roy shouts with incredible daring at the abusive man: "You slap her again, you black bastard, and I swear to God I'll kill you."

Sister McCandless

One of the women who attends tarry services on Saturday night at the Temple of the Fire Baptized.

Esther McDonald

Gabriel had given up sinning and married Deborah when he met Esther, and before long he was having an affair with her. The affair only lasted for nine days before he ended it, but Esther came to him weeks later and told him she was pregnant. When Gabriel refused to leave Deborah and marry her, Esther decided not to blackmail him with public disclosure of her pregnancy. Showing a religious fervor that he could never get her to feel with his preaching, she said, "I shamed before my *God*—to make somebody make me cheap, like you done." She moved North with money Gabriel gave her and died while giving birth to Royal.

Royal McDonald

Gabriel's first son, Royal was raised by his grandparents in the town that Gabriel lived in, but he never found out who his father was. Deborah befriended Royal's parents and gave Gabriel periodic updates on the boy's life. The last time Gabriel saw Royal, there had been a racial incident in town, and white men were looking for any black man they could abuse. Gabriel thought of revealing his identity, but the fear of being caught in the street talking made him mutter a weak warning to Royal and hurry away. Two years later word came that Royal had been killed in a knife fight in Chicago.

Sister Price

One of the women who attends tarry services on Saturday night at the Temple of the Fire Baptized.

Richard

Richard was John's father, Elizabeth's true love. She had moved to New York to be with him, and they planned to be married, but one night after dropping her at her doorstep, while waiting on the subway platform, Richard was arrested. Three black robbers, escaping the police, had run past him, and the police had assumed he was with them and arrested him, held him in jail and tortured him to confess. He was released for lack of evidence, but the night of his release he slit his wrists, having never found out that Elizabeth was pregnant.

Praying Mother Washington

One of the women who attends tarry services on Saturday night at the Temple of the Fire Baptized.

Madame Williams

Elizabeth's aunt that she lived with when she moved to Harlem. Madame Williams is a spiritualist, conducting seances in her apartment on Saturday nights.

Themes

Identity (Search For Self)

Go Tell It on the Mountain is primarily about John Grimes' quest to find out who he really is, to distinguish the values of those around him from the ones that he holds. It is no coincidence that the novel takes place on his birthday, which is the day representing a step forward into maturity, or that it is his fourteenth, marking the boundary between childhood and young adulthood because it implies the start of puberty. The point of growing up is discovering one's own identity.

John comes from a family that is involved in his life, but, because of his father's thoughtlessness and bullying tendencies, he cannot accept that his role in this family is who he really is. Even without knowing that Gabriel Grimes is not his real father, John holds him at a distance. This could be explained as a result of Gabriel's harshness, while Roy's wild ways, which reflect the childhood Gabriel had, might be the result of his father's narcissistic pampering.

The identity that John prefers is that of "Great Leader of his People," a fantasy clearly derived from his education in the Bible. With hope, he sees glimmers of this identity being possible in the praise he receives at school, but unfortunately his family's values are deeply ingrained and he views himself as a sinner. Looking at his features in a mirror, John does not know what to think of himself, "for the principle of their unity was indiscernible, and he could not tell what he most persistently desired to know: whether his face was ugly or not."

To settle the question of his identity, John goes beyond the features of his own personality and attaches his interests to someone outside of the family, Elisha. The loud, showy religious experience he has in the end is satisfying to his identity in several ways: it allows him to be like Elisha by having a seizure similar to his; it makes the strongly religious side of his family pleased by "converting" John into their religious life; and it satisfies his youthful ego by being loud and exotic and drawing everyone's attention to him.

Duty and Responsibility

In the middle of the novel comes a moment where Gabriel refuses to face his duty squarely, and the results of his action reverberate across time and end up affecting all of the members of the Grimes family. In this pivotal episode, Gabriel convinces himself that his responsibility to Deborah and to the people who value his preaching would be betrayed if he admitted to getting Esther pregnant. So he backs away from her, avoiding the touch of her hand, as if pretending that he is not responsible for the child could change his moral obligation.

As a result of his action, Esther left town to give birth, which probably causes the strain that made her die during labor. If his father had raised him, Royal would not have been spoiled the way his grandparents spoiled him, and his life would not have headed "towards the disaster that had been waiting for him from the moment he had been conceived." Florence might have been able to give up on the sibling rivalry of her childhood and concentrate on preserving her marriage if she had not received the letter that told her Gabriel had been unfaithful to her friend Deborah. If he had shared Royal's life, Gabriel would not have fooled himself and Elizabeth into thinking that he was willing to accept the duty of raising her child John, and they would therefore never have been married.

The novel certainly does not present responsibility as a pleasant thing, as seen in the way that John, feeling responsible for his family, feels like a sinner, while his brother Roy, who causes the family nothing but grief, sails along merrily with a clear conscience. In this book, where consequences carry on from one generation to the next, responsibility is treated seriously.

God and Religion

Although this book's main setting is a storefront church, and the strongest character, Gabriel, was once a successful preacher, and the main character, John, has a religious experience that helps him calm his greatest worries, it would be inaccurate to call this a book about religion. The truly devout characters, Elizabeth and Elisha, keep their religious feelings to themselves and only discuss them when asked. To Gabriel and John, religion is a matter of posturing, of behaving in certain accepted ways for the benefit of those watching. Gabriel's abuse of his family members indicates that he is aware of a difference between public and private life. He seems to have no more faith in God's omnipotent power than Richard, who told Elizabeth, when she mentioned the love of Jesus:

Topics for Further Study

- The adult characters in this book have moved to New York from the South, a move that was common among blacks in the early decades of the twentieth century. Choose a major northern industrial town, such as Chicago, Detroit, Pittsburgh, or New York, and research the migration patterns of blacks to that city. Explain such details as how many people came from what states and how their arrival affected the city's political structure.

- Storefront evangelical churches like the Temple of the Fire Baptized portrayed are a staple of American religion. Find out about one and report on its history, its structure, its membership, etc. If you live in a place that does not have any small churches like this one, do your report on a television ministry or one that is conducted over the internet.

- While spiritual hymns represent an important part of church life in this novel, the greatest musical influence seems to be when John, as an infant, is transfixed by the blues music that is playing in the hall of Florence's building. Explain the historical relationship between gospel music and blues, showing the evolution of each.

"You can tell that puking bastard to kiss my big black ass." Richard was at least sincere in his disdain for God, while Gabriel as a result of his difficult childhood, has learned to say things that people want to hear, just like the Twenty-Four Elders he joined, who he thought of as "circus performers, each with his own special dazzling gift."

Race

The fact that the characters in this book are black is undeniably significant, but, because they seldom interact with white characters, this cannot be considered a book that pretends to deal with race relations. The presence of racism and bigotry is felt throughout the story: in the rape of Deborah and the subsequent beating of her father; in Gabriel's nervousness about talking to Royal in the street; in

John's belief in his own special gift because a white teacher showed interest in him; in the treatment of Elizabeth and Richard by white policemen. Functionally, race is used here as a tool to highlight characteristics that are already present: the meek seem meeker and the bold seem bolder when they let their personalities show in front of white people. There are very few positive white characters shown here, but Baldwin is not trying to portray reality, he is trying to show how things look from within this closed community. Blacks and whites seldom have any reason to interact here unless there is trouble.

Style

Setting

The setting of this novel—the impoverished part of New York known as Harlem, and more specifically the storefront church within the Harlem community—was undoubtedly a key reason for the book's popularity upon its first publication, giving intellectuals an inside look at a world not many of them had known. This setting may be the reason some people read *Go Tell It on the Mountain* today, even with the inner city well documented by television cameras. The important thing about this setting, though, is that it is integral to the personality of the characters, affecting them and being formed by who they are.

The adult members of the Grimes family, for instance, all came to New York for different reasons. Florence came first, thirty years earlier, rebelling against the limitations put on her as a woman; Gabriel to escape the deaths of his illegitimate son and his barren wife; and Elizabeth came with hope and love for Richard. The fact that three such diverse characters end up in the same small section of town says much about how narrowed opportunities for African-Americans were. Similarly, the fact that they all attend the Temple of the Fire Baptized despite their different reasons (Florence in despair, Gabriel to control and Elizabeth with true religious devotion) helps define the narrowness of the options each character has.

John is a true son of New York. He goes to Central Park to feel triumphant while looking out over the powerful metropolis and goes to a seedy theater in Times Square to experience the lower side of life. But he can also connect with his country roots at the local church, which is itself urban enough to have a busy hospital across the street.

Flashback

The novel starts on a specific Saturday morning in 1935, but it intermingles stories from the family that go back in time to 1876, and it refers to times even earlier—back to the time of John's grandmother Rachel on the plantation before the end of the Civil War in 1865. Technically, a flashback occurs within the mind of the person that it happens to, and it happens "in scene"—that is, the narrative travels to the specific place and time of the flashback and does not just summarize what happened then. The scene where Rachel learned that the slaves were free is not a flashback because it is presented in Florence's memory as something her mother told her; Richard's death is not rendered in flashback because the action is not described as it occurred, only the evidence that his landlady found the next day that he had slit his wrists. The sermon that Gabriel gave at the Twenty-Four Elders Revival Meeting *is* rendered as a flashback, presented in his memory with actual details. The "Prayers of the Saints" section of this book is told mostly in flashback, but returns periodically to the real setting of the story, John's fourteenth birthday.

Stream of Consciousness

Much of the final chapter of the book, "The Threshing-Floor," applies a form of the stream-of-consciousness technique. Thoughts are presented as they pass through John's mind without reason or order, imitating the ecstatic experience that he is having on the floor of the church. John's thoughts are not recorded directly, but are filtered through the third-person narrator, who interprets what John is thinking—it is, for instance, unlikely that John would use the words "malicious" and "ironic" to describe the voice inside of his head.

Historical Context

The Rise of Harlem

The Harlem area of New York City, where the Grimes family resides, is internationally famous as a predominantly African-American neighborhood with a rich cultural history spanning back to the beginning of the twentieth century. The first great wave of blacks started migrating to New York in the 1890s. Like Gabriel and Florence, this was the generation that had been born after slavery ended in 1865, the children of freed slaves in the South— a generation with a greater sense of freedom than

125th and Lenox Ave., Harlem, 1950.

any before them. Between 1890 and 1910, the black population in New York City tripled.

At first Harlem was planned as an upscale neighborhood for wealthy blacks, but an economic depression in 1904–1905 cut off money for investment and development. Huge apartments that were meant for wealthy families were cut up with makeshift walls or rented to several families to live in together. Blacks arriving in New York City almost always ended up in Harlem, where they were allowed a degree of peace they were not given anywhere else. They migrated from the South, where Jim Crow laws made it legal to keep blacks at economic disadvantage and where violence against blacks was left unpunished. They arrived from Panama, where thousands of workers from the West Indies had been transplanted to build the Panama Canal and then left without jobs when the canal was completed in 1914. They also came from the Armed Forces, since a great number of the 370,000 blacks who had served in World War I had seen racial tolerance in the rest of the world, particularly France, and found it hard to go back to their small-minded home towns.

By the 1920s, Harlem was a vibrant community, the center of the African-American world. The Harlem Renaissance is the term used for the intellectual and artistic community that flourished in Harlem in the 1920s. Harlem nightclubs, such as the famous Cotton Club, were popular with affluent white New Yorkers, so that black entertainers could earn more in a week in Harlem than they made in a month on the road, battling travel conditions and racism. As Harlem's fame grew, more people arrived.

But then in 1929, the stock market crashed, and in the months that followed the country sank into the worst financial depression in its history. No one had money for entertainers and the artists scattered to find jobs. Racist employment practices gave preference to unemployed whites over unemployed blacks. The Depression ruined Harlem: the thriving neighborhood became an overcrowded slum, where the lucky residents had menial jobs and the unlucky residents were unemployed. By 1935, the year this novel takes place, the former center of culture was well on its way to becoming an international symbol for poverty and urban blight.

Civil Rights

Go Tell It on the Mountain was published just as the Civil Rights movement in America was starting to show results, bringing greater social justice than there had been since the Civil War ended almost a century earlier. After the slaves were freed,

Compare & Contrast

- **1935:** America was, like most of the world, in the midst of a long economic depression, which began with the collapse of the stock market on October 29, 1929 and lingered into the early 1940s.

  1953: The United States economy finally absorbed the returning veterans from World War II, reaching the lowest unemployment rate since the war ended in 1945.

  Today: The stock market reaches new highs every month, which keeps production high and unemployment low.

- **1935:** Adolph Hitler, having become the chancellor of Germany two years earlier, began exercising the dictatorial control that would eventually lead to the extermination of millions of Jews as part of his government's "Final Solution."

  1953: Josef Stalin died. He had ruled the Soviet Union since 1928, and there are unconfirmed estimates that his government killed as many millions of citizens as were killed during the Nazi Holocaust.

  Today: Mass murders by governments against various ethnic groups continues, including 250,000 killed in Bosnia in 1995 and 150,000 Tutsi civilians killed in Rwanda.

- **1935:** Crime syndicates that established their power during Prohibition (1920 to 1933) continued to do battle with the government, making legends out of criminals such as Al Capone, John Dillinger and Dutch Schultz.

  1953: America was in the middle of the Cold War, with citizens suspected of belonging to the Communist party or associating with anyone who did could be blacklisted and lose their jobs.

  Today: With the collapse of the Soviet Union in 1991, the country no longer fears Communist influences; although alcohol is legal, the government wages a continuing "war on drugs."

- **1935:** The Social Security Act was passed in order to offer government aid to senior citizens.

  1953: During the post-war prosperity, the country experienced a huge swell in the birth rate, creating the "Baby Boom" generation of those born between 1947 and 1961.

  Today: Government economists predict that unless the system is restructured the Social Security system will be driven to bankruptcy when the baby boomers start retiring in the year 2012.

---

black Americans were still not accorded equal social status. In the North, they were not held back by specific laws so much as by covert actions that were not talked about in public. In the South there were laws passed that prevented black citizens from advancing. Blacks were kept from gaining political power by voter registration laws, which put restrictions on voters that favored whites. Some places required land ownership in order to vote, even though blacks had never been able to earn high enough wages to buy property; another favored trick was the I.Q. requirement, which allowed election judges to ask increasingly diffi-cult questions of blacks until they failed to answer one, at which point they were rejected as voters.

In 1896 the Supreme Court approved the legality of segregation in America as long as both races were offered facilities that were "separate but equal." This led to a two-tiered society that seldom practiced equality. Throughout the South, blacks ate at different restaurants, slept at different motels, drank from different water fountains, rode on different train cars, etc. Although the accommodations for blacks were usually shabby, people of any race could be arrested for crossing the color line.

In the mid-1950s, due in part to writings by authors like Baldwin, blacks and whites both became less tolerant of discrimination. The Supreme Court of 1954 ruled that the idea of "separate but equal" was impossible, that one side would always be left with substandard facilities, and so they ordered that public schools had to be open to people of all races. In 1955, one of the modern heroes of race relations, Rosa Parks, was arrested in Montgomery, Alabama, when she refused to give up her seat on a bus to a white man—the resulting year-long boycott of the bus system, which made officials realize that they needed their black passengers as well as the white ones, brought international attention to the boycott's leader, Dr. Martin Luther King.

In 1957, Orval Faubus, Governor of Arkansas, stood with protesters in front of a high school in Little Rock and refused to let nine black students enter; the President sent National Guard troops to protect the students, showing that the federal government would protect equality even if they had to act against the state government.

Critical Overview

Critical praise for the success of *Go Tell It on the Mountain* has not faded since 1953, when the book was first published. One of the earliest reviews, by J. Saunders Redding in *The New York Herald Tribune Book Review* told potential readers that the book was more than just entertaining, and that "even the most insensitive of readers will put the book down with a troubled feeling of having 'looked on beauty bare.' "

While even the most insensitive of critics has recognized Baldwin's great achievement of having vividly recreated the life and times of a young African-American boy in Harlem, the problem facing critics has been in analyzing the book's significance. Early examinations, in keeping with the prevalence of racial segregation in the early 1950s, showed a fascination with the depiction of Harlem, and therefore early reviewers tended to group it with other novels by blacks at the time. An example is the review written by Granville Hicks in 1953 in the *New Leader* that mentioned that "[t]he other talented Negro artists, Ralph Ellison and Richard Wright, have recently written about Negroes without writing novels of protest." Hicks' review maintained that Baldwin's book was not primarily about race, but yet he categorized Baldwin with Wright and Ellison, viewing him as a black writer at the same time he tried to play down race.

The technique of bringing race up while denying that race is an issue provided the lead for Richard K. Barksdale's 1953 essay "Temple of the Fire Baptized," which began, "James Baldwin has written a very fine first novel. It is a story by a Negro, about Negroes, set in a predominantly Negro environment; and yet it is not essentially a 'Negro' novel." By 1958, the country had come face-to-face with the fact that segregation caused an unjust society: the Supreme Court had found segregation of public schools unconstitutional; Dr. King had led the boycott of the Montgomery bus system; and the President had sent federal troops to Arkansas to overrule state troops who were trying to obstruct integration. Critics stopped being concerned about which novels by black authors could rightly be considered "novels of protest" because protest was out in the open and no longer hidden in the pages of literature.

Robert Bone's 1958 essay "James Baldwin," revised when it was included in his 1965 book *The Negro Novel In America,* unquestionably found race to be the most significant factor in *Go Tell It on the Mountain:* "The overwhelming fact of Baldwin's childhood was his victimization by the white power structure," he wrote, reflecting the times, using a phrase ("white power structure") that would not have been available to the novel's first reviewers.

As the 1960s progressed, race relations became even more of a topic for front pages, and, consequently, less fertile territory for reviewers. Analyses of *Go Tell It on the Mountain* tended to look at its less obvious themes, such as the Freudian relationship between John and Gabriel and the homoerotic one between John and Elisha, or the subculture of the evangelical church in Harlem. Edward Margolies traced the objective distance gained by the passage of fifteen years since the novel's publication: "This is in a sense Baldwin's most ambitious book, in that he endeavors here not only to interconnect the lives and psychology of all the characters but also to relate the Southern Negro experience and the consequent of urban slum living."

In the 1970s Shirley S. Allen dismisses the earlier critics who had overemphasized the cultural significance of the novel: it deserved, she said, "a higher place in critical esteem than it generally has been accorded. Although critics have recognized its widespread appeal, often asserting that it is Baldwin's best work, and although teachers of literature have incorporated it into the standard literature, they assume that the work is primarily important as an interpretation of 'the black experience,' comparing it with *Invisible Man, Native Son* and Baldwin's own essays." Those essays, written mostly in the 1950s, 1960s, and 1970s, may be what eventually drew readers away from looking at it as a novel about race, because the author showed so much awareness of race in his nonfiction writing, leaving literary critics to examine instead areas like psychology and religion, where they might hope to turn up new ideas.

Criticism

Wendy Perkins

Perkins is an Assistant Professor of English at Prince George's Community College in Maryland and has written numerous critical articles for essay collections, journals, and educational publishers. In the following essay she explores how the variety of narrative voices in Go Tell It on the Mountain *illustrate how psychological and social forces can impede the search for self.*

In his first novel, *Go Tell It on the Mountain,* James Baldwin divides his narrative into three distinct parts. The first section, "The Seventh Day," sets the novel's central action, what Shirley S. Allen, in "Religious Symbolism and Psychic Reality in Baldwin's 'Go Tell It on the Mountain,'" calls John's "initiation into manhood." John completes that initiation and discovers a sense of self in the closing section, "The Threshing Floor."

Between these two sections comes "The Prayers of the Saints," which is broken into three narratives that focus on the history of John's family: his stepfather Gabriel, his mother Elizabeth, and his Aunt Florence. Marcus Klein in "James Baldwin: A Question of Identity," argues that the different narrative voices in this section produce "a technical fault" in the novel since "John doesn't really know the lives of his aunt, his stepfather, and his mother. Only the reader does." Yet Baldwin's juxtaposition of these family stories with John's own contextualizes his struggles to find his identity. The histories of his stepfather, his aunt, and his mother illuminate the same choices and obstacles John faces on his journey to selfhood.

The first section of the novel reveals John's confusion over his future. "The Seventh Day" opens with John lying in bed on the morning of his fourteenth birthday, considering his family's ex-

pectations that he will become a preacher like his father. He acknowledges, though, his lack of devotion to the church and his inability to feel the "joy" others feel in service to God.

The primary impediment to John's acceptance of "the holy life" lies in his destructive relationship with his father. Gabriel has severely beaten John throughout his childhood and has never been able to accept him as his own son. John, unaware that Gabriel is not his biological father, cannot understand his father's coldness and brutality. When he sees his father's tender concern over Roy's injuries, John is forced to admit that his father loves his brother but not him.

At this point, John voices his hatred for his father, admitting that "he lived for the day when his father would be dying and he … would curse him on his deathbed." This hatred prompts his decision not to follow in his father's path. Since his father was "God's minister" and he knew that he would have to first bow down to his father before he could bow down to God, his heart also becomes "hardened against the Lord."

John's second option is to devote himself to the world of the city, where, as some have insisted, he "might become a Great Leader of His People." John admits little interest in leading his people, but life outside of the church tempts him, offering a world "where he would eat good food, and wear fine clothes, and go to the movies as often as he wished." Many have recognized his superior intelligence, which gives him a sense of "power that other people lacked," a power that might some day enable him to become successful in the world outside the church and to gain the love and recognition that he longs for.

John often escapes the bleakness of his neighborhood and walks downtown where he observes fine shops and beautiful women. Here he decides that devoting one's life to the church is the "narrow way," full of poverty and hard work. Yet, his father has told him that he will never be accepted into the city world because of the color of his skin. The issue of racism adds to John's suffering and thus becomes another impetus for his struggle to find salvation.

His father has also taught him that this life is filled with sin, which John sees illustrated during that afternoon in a movie about a white "evil" woman making a "glorious" fall from grace. While John admires her independence, as she faces damnation on her deathbed, his fear of a similar end resurfaces. Just that morning, after masturbat-

What Do I Read Next?

- Nobel Prize-winning author Toni Morrison's 1992 novel *Jazz* takes place in Harlem in the 1920s and gives a stylized sense of how the community felt and operated.

- James Baldwin is even more respected as one of the great essayists of his time than for his fiction. The comprehensive collection *The Price of the Ticket: Collected Nonfiction, 1948-1985,* offers the best of Baldwin's works in one huge volume.

- In December 1971, Baldwin appeared on the television show "Soul" with young rising poet Nikki Giovanni, known then for her militant stand on racial issues. The transcript of their conversation about the state of race relations in America was published as a book in 1973 titled *A Dialog.* A similarly interesting conversation, also transcribed to book form in 1971, is *A Rap On Race,* which renders the exchange between Baldwin and white anthropologist Margaret Mead.

- In 1989, after James Baldwin's death, Simon & Schuster published a collection of essays, poems, and memoirs about him from writers whose life he had touched. The collection, *James Bald-win: The Legacy,* contains short works by such well-known authors as Toni Morrison, Amiri Baraka, William Styron, Chinua Achebe, Mary McCarthy and more, collectively giving a picture of Baldwin's gentle intelligence.

- *Giovanni's Room,* Baldwin's second novel, published in 1956, is generally not considered a masterpiece in the same realm as *Go Tell It on the Mountain,* but it is highly regarded nonetheless. It is the story of David, an American student in France, and the torrid relationship that develops between him and a local barkeep, Giovanni. Many of the same social themes from the first novel are explored here, without the backdrop of American social mores.

- Of the dozens of biographies written about Baldwin, two stand out: *James Baldwin: Artist on Fire,* by W.J. Weatherby, published in 1989, and *Talking At the Gates: A Life of James Baldwin,* by James Campbell (1991). Campbell's book is more sympathetic to Baldwin, since the author was an acquaintance of Baldwin's, while Weatherby is more academic. Both books, published soon after Baldwin's death, are heavily supported with interviews from people who knew him well.

---

ing in his bed, John had felt "the darkness of his sin" and a "wickedness" in his heart. The conflicting urges to gain salvation, to flee his father's control and brutality, and to enjoy success and comforts in the outside world produce confusion and prevent a clear vision of his future.

In the second section, members of John's family attempt to pray for comfort, salvation and a sense of communal identity as they, like John, assess their past and present conflicts and look to their future. All four suffer the same obstacles of racism, poverty, and failed relationships that have impeded their search for selfhood. John's own tortured struggle interrupts each narrative, forcing the reader to return the focus to him and to recognize the similarities among the histories.

Florence's prayer begins the novel's second section and traces her battle against the same impediments that John faces. She, like John, tries to fight her pride and humble herself before God but fails. As she recalls her past, she reveals how Gabriel had dominated her life but in a different sense than he does John's. When Florence was a child, her mother put all her energies into raising and providing for Gabriel while Florence's needs were ignored. She also remembers incidents that illustrated the racism that Gabriel warns will prevent John from enjoying a life outside of the church. She recounts the devastating effects the rape had on

Deborah and suggests that differences in their skin tone helped break up her marriage to Frank.

As a result of her family problems and experiences with racism, she, like John, is filled with hatred and bitterness but also the fear of death. Florence's prayer complicates John's quest, though, when she asks God why she "who had only sought to walk upright" was going to die "alone and in poverty, in a dirty, furnished room." The fact of her unrelieved suffering suggests John's religion might not save nor grant him a clear sense of self.

In his prayer, Gabriel provides another example of one who has been unable to find peace through devotion to the church. His faith fails to help him assuage his feelings of guilt over his affair with Esther and the birth of his illegitimate child, Royal. He notes that even after his conversion, he is plagued by dreams of temptation that produce frustration and doubt over his religious commitment. The insecurities that result from the racism he has experienced and his own capacity for sin prompt his abusive behavior toward his family and his especially harsh treatment of John. By refusing to acknowledge the illegitimate John as his son, Gabriel, in effect, refuses to acknowledge his own illegitimate son, Royal, and to confront the guilt associated with his birth.

Elizabeth's prayer begins with a focus on John. As she sits in the church, she weeps for John's deliverance, "that he might be carried, past wrath unspeakable, into a state of grace." She then recounts a life filled with pain and loss. Like John, she has suffered from the absence of love, first when she is separated from her father and then when the injustice of the "white world" takes Richard from her. Her dream of providing a happy home for John crumbles under Gabriel's stern hand.

She has, however, been able to renew and find comfort in her faith, believing that "only God could establish order in this chaos; to Him the soul must turn to be delivered." Her belief in God's grace and in John's abilities and her love for him provides comfort for John. She tells him she knows "there's a whole lot of things you don't understand," but that God will help him find his way, and she predicts that he will turn into a "fine man."

Elizabeth's prayer is brought to an abrupt close when she hears John's cries as he writhes on the threshing floor. John's anguish over his relationship with his father and his inability to find a sense of selfhood combine with his fear of damnation and produce visions of torment. At this point, John reaches out to God, determining that a devotion to the church is the only route to salvation. After John's conversion in the church, Elisha, another character that Baldwin includes in the novel to provide a context for John's struggle to achieve identity, promises to serve as his brother and protector.

In the novel's first section, John notes that Elisha has experienced the same sexual stirrings as does John, and that Elisha, after being reprimanded by the preacher, reasserted his devotion to his religion and stopped his "disorderly walking" with Ella Mae. Elisha's support throughout the novel, and especially at the close as the family walks home after church, prompts John's closing declaration, "I'm ready. I'm coming. I'm on my way." John thus appears to have found his place in his commitment to God and the church.

However, narrative elements in the novel's final section, as well as in the prayers of his family, suggest that John's resolution may be tenuous. His conversion has not settled the conflict with his father or gained John his love and respect, as evidenced by Gabriel's cold response to his son's newfound joy. Gabriel's conversation with his sister as they are trailing behind John and Elisha reveals his persistent inability to face his past failures and to accept John as his son. Gabriel's continued rejection and the peripheral threat of racism and poverty remain, and thus threaten to weaken John's sense of self and his devotion to his religion.

Baldwin's juxtaposition of narrative voice in *Go Tell It on the Mountain* provides no easy answers for John as he struggles to rise above racism, poverty, and family tensions in order to define himself and his place in his world. In his successful merging of structure and thematic import, Baldwin illustrates the difficulties inherent in the quest for selfhood.

Source: Wendy Perkins, in an essay for *Novels for Students,* Gale, 1998

Bruce Bawer

In the following excerpt, Bawer discusses some of the religious aspects of Go Tell It on the Mountain.

Baldwin's own most valiant attempt to capture the "ambiguity and irony of Negro life" was his first novel, *Go Tell It on the Mountain* (1953), which centers on a Harlem family not unlike his own. Like the Trinitarian God, the book is divided into three parts: John, who is the focus of the first and third parts (and who, like Baldwin, is known as "Frog Eyes"), is the stepson of Gabriel, a preacher who believes "that all white people [are] wicked, and that

God [is] going to bring them low," and who feels that God has promised him a son to carry on his holy work; the second part, itself divided in three and consisting largely of flashbacks, outlines the earlier lives of Gabriel (who many years ago, we learn, had a mistress and an illegitimate son, both of whom died as a consequence of his refusal to acknowledge them), of Gabriel's sister Florence, and of his second wife, Elizabeth (whose ill-fated and fervently atheistic first lover, John's father, loved art as much as Gabriel loves God). Baldwin renders this family's inner history—the details of which John will probably never know, though it has profoundly influenced his own life—with both the tenderest sympathy and the harshest insight; he sees the life of faith from both inside and out, and by exploring the past through these several pairs of eyes not only conveys something of the richness and mystery of a family's life but reminds us that to understand is to forgive. And he does a remarkably vivid job of capturing the streets of New York as seen by a boy raised on Pentecostal sermons:

> And certainly perdition sucked at the feet of the people who walked there; and cried in the lights, in the gigantic towers; the marks of Satan could be found in the faces of the people who waited at the doors of movie houses; his words were printed on the great movie posters that invited people to sin. It was the roar of the damned that filled Broadway, where motor cars and buses and the hurrying people disputed every inch with death. *Broadway:* the way that led to death was broad, and many could be found thereon; but narrow was the way that led to life eternal, and few there were who found it.

The novel, whose style has something of the stateliness of the King James Bible and the music of black vernacular, splendidly evokes Harlem's sights and sounds, its frustrations and hypocrisies. Baldwin excels at small descriptive touches, as when Gabriel observes the "distant and angry compassion" in his illegitimate son's face. This is, as Campbell says, [in his *Talking at the Gates: A Life of James Baldwin*] "Baldwin's most accomplished novel, technically, and his most disciplined," free of the "idealizations, the sentimentality, the jarring tones and overlong conversations, even the moral fervour, which, separately or all at once, were to mar, in part or whole, his later novels."

Yet Campbell is also right to call *Go Tell It on the Mountain* "somewhat stiff and formal." Though Baldwin aims for a natural-seeming lyricism (and though the novel does rise to beautiful lyrical heights), there is too often an air of contrivance about it. Like a sermon in a black church, the prose is sometimes poetic and inspired, sometimes

> *But at John's conversion the novel's very title is rendered ironic. John has no voice to speak to his mother or the other saints ... 'Salvation' has meant learning the truth about his own heart and it is a truth so horrifying that he knows 'he could never tell it,' because it would be blasphemous."*

windy, repetitious, bombastic. Baldwin hammers us relentlessly with biblical verses—and with good reason, for his purpose is to impress upon us the ubiquity of religion in John's family and his sense of being bound inextricably to God—but it doesn't take long before we're weary of it all and the verses seem like mere gimmickry. Many of the novel's more protracted sentences, too, which should sound fresh and musical—like hymns, say, with long melodic lines—strike one as rather too self-consciously constructed; and the frequent flashbacks—which were to become a familiar device in Baldwin's work, as if to suggest the immense history that lies behind even the most seemingly negligible occurence in black America—are less dramatically effective than they are confusing.

Source: Bruce Bawer, "Race and Art: James Baldwin" in *The Aspect of Eternity: Essays by Bruce Bawer*, Graywolf Press, 1993, pp. 17–35.

Maria K. Mootry,

A review of Go Tell It on the Mountain *which focuses on Baldwin's use of irony.*

Critics have complained that the point of view in James Baldwin's first novel is problematical. Very early in the novel we are told of the adolescent protagonist's religious doubts and we are led to trust a narrator who seems to state his case unambiguously. We are told in an opening church scene that John Grimes has no real belief, but it is the faith of his family and fellow church members that make the concept of faith real to him. Later, at the novel's end, during John's conversion, (when the reader would expect John's religious conflicts to end), no real resolution is offered. The reader is left with the question: Has John been converted (or saved) or not? The question remains because of Baldwin's use of an ironic voice during the conversion scene and his resort to heavy situational or dramatic irony.

At the moment of his "salvation," when John is knocked to the floor by the power of the Holy Ghost, he hears a "malicious, ironic voice which insist(s), that he rise—and, at once, … leave this temple and go out into the world." The ironic voice tells John to get up and take charge of his life. It urges John to be in awe of no one; least of all his father (who is also John's Pastor and who, ironically, stands over him with an accusatory air during his "conversion"). To the voice, John's father, and by implication, God-the-Father, are judgmental forces that should be defied: "Get up, John," the voice says, "Get up, boy. Don't let him keep you there. You got everything your Daddy got."

Yet, when the ironic voice leaves, John hears another voice which tells him to "Go through." Shortly after this voice is heard, John experiences his "conversion": "And a sweetness filled John as he heard this voice, and heard the sound of singing: The singing was for him … the light and the darkness had kissed each other, and were married now, forever, in the life and the vision of John's soul." The ironic voice, it seems, has been banished forever.

Yet, immediately after John has "come through," Baldwin shifts from narrative to dramatic irony. At the very moment when his mother's face should be a welcome sight (as a fellow saint), John feels total estrangement. The converted's first impulse is to tell everyone how he's "got over"—to "go tell it on the mountain." But at John's conversion the novel's very title is rendered ironic. John has no voice to speak to his mother or the other saints; "no language, no second sight, no power to see into the heart of any other." "Salvation" has meant learning the truth about his own heart and it is a truth so horrifying that he knows "he could never tell it," because it would be blasphemous.

When John leaves the stone front church with his fellow "saints," the Harlem streets are appropriately still quite filthy. Gutter cats (emblematic of nightly sexual jaunts) slink by. The uncomprehending saints rejoice at having recovered one "lost sheep" and equally rejoice when sirens wail, indicating another sinner "struck down."

Thus, on this day of rebirth, one day after his natural birthday, John is neither purged nor "washed whiter than snow." If he saw his face darkly in the household mirror before, there is more profound darkness to come:

> He would weep again, his heart insisted, for now his weeping had begun; he would rage again, said the shifting air, for the lions of rage had been unloosed; he would be in darkness again, in fire again, now that he had seen the fire and the darkness. He was free—whom the Son sets free is free indeed—he had only to stand fast in his liberty. He was in battle no longer, this unfolding Lord's day, with this avenue, these houses, the sleeping, staring, shouting people, but had entered into battle with Jacob's angel, with the princes and the powers of the air."

Perhaps John's abiding sense of evil comes from his burgeoning homosexuality. The joy John feels at being "converted" is rooted in the wellspring of despair relieved only by the loving arm of his fellow "saint," Elijah, which hangs *heavily* on John's shoulder as they walk away from the church.

It is Elijah who seals John's "deliverance" with a "holy kiss." But how holy is this kiss when John has felt such unambiguous infatuation for his virile, handsome friend? Thus the irony of John's "conversion" is tripled: it leaves him with a deeper sense of mankind's innate evil; it frees him, not from sin, but from the tyranny of his father's authoritarian control by replacing his father with another more supportive male presence; finally it liberates him from "closet" feelings and brings into the light his homoerotic needs.

When John says "I'm coming … I'm on my way" at the novel's end, the reader cannot be sure which "Promised Land" he refers to.

Through ironic voices and situational irony, Baldwin distances himself from his protagonist and casts doubt upon the meaning of John's salvation, leaving it to the reader to wrest his own interpretation from the multiple directions of the text.

Source: Maria K. Mootry, A review of *Go Tell It on the Mountain*," in *The Explicator*, Vol. 43, No. 2, Winter, 1985, pp. 50–52.

Shirley S. Allen

In the following excerpt, Allen explores Baldwin's use of irony in Go Tell It on the Mountain *as a means for answering various questions raised while interpreting the novel.*

A number of questions raised in critical interpretations of James Baldwin's first novel, *Go Tell It on the Mountain,* can be answered by studying his use of irony. Such questions include Baldwin's artistic distance from the characters, his attitude toward their religious beliefs, the identity of the ironic voice in Part Three, and the meaning of the novel's denouement. Although there are at least three different kinds of irony in the novel, they are closely related because they result from the narrative technique Baldwin employs, an internal and subjective point of view limited to the thoughts, feelings, and perceptions of the main character. In order to transcend the limitations of this point of view, Baldwin uses irony in the narrator's diction, irony of statement and event in the action, and an ironic voice as a character.

In the major action of the novel, which is the struggle of young John Grimes to leave childhood and achieve maturity with a sense of his own identity, the narrator is limited to John's internal point of view. Although he speaks in the third person, this point of view is strictly maintained, so that even the physical appearance of the hero is described subjectively through comments he hears from others and the images he sees in the mirror.

The point of view is further limited by confinement in time. Although the narrator uses the past tense, he recounts events as they happen, unedited by the perspective of time. We follow John Grimes through the course of his fourteenth birthday as if we were experiencing the events with him. Careful use of adverbs denoting present time, such as "now" and "still," maintain this sense of contemporary action. So does a scrupulous use of tenses, particularly the past-perfect for every event occurring even recently before the moment of the present action and frequent use of "would" to express future time in the past tense. A few sentences taken from the episode of Roy's injury illustrate Baldwin's use of tenses:

> His mother leaned over and looked into Roy's face with a sad, sympathetic murmur. Yet, John felt, she had seen instantly the extent of the danger to Roy's eye and to his life, and was beyond that worry now. Now she was merely marking time, as it were, and preparing herself against the moment when her husband's anger would turn, full force, against her.

The effect of this narrative style is immediacy and directness like the first-person, present tense point of view, but it avoids the literary awkwardness of that form. Although such a narrator is not uncommon in modern fiction, Baldwin's use is remarkable for consistency and suppleness. He also exploits fully the freedom of a third-person narrator to use whatever diction the author chooses without limitation to language characteristic of the

> *When John's malicious irony is swept away, he faces the psychic realities of his subconscious, and then only fear is left—the fear of being an adult, unprotected by parental love and responsible for his own life."*

protagonist. Baldwin's excellent command of language (improved over his earliest short stories) and his talent for almost poetic expression are used to present the thoughts of a Harlem schoolboy without restriction to his grammar and vocabulary.

In fact, the contrast between the narrator's diction and the dialogue of the characters emphasizes both the universality of their inner conflicts and the particular circumstances of their lives as Negroes in America. Baldwin's ear for language and his skill at representing it in print are nowhere better displayed than in the dialogue of *Go Tell It on the Mountain* where the dialect is conveyed with such subtlety and economy that the rhythms, accent, and colloquialisms of Harlem speech do not blur the individuality and dignity of the speakers. Contrasted with the dialogue is the educated and highly literate voice of the internal narrator, compelling the reader's understanding and sympathy beyond suggestions of race or class.

The separation between the subjective narrator and the character that is implied by use of the third-person form is also useful in this novel because in Part Two, "The Prayers of the Saints," the narrator enters the minds of three other characters serially, maintaining the same point of view in relation to each as his relation to John in Part One and Part Three. The narrator becomes in thoughts, feelings, and perceptions John's aunt, then his stepfather, then his mother; but his diction remains his own. This device is important for preserving the continuity of the novel, which has few external indications of continuity.

Having set up this type of narrator, with immediate and intimate knowledge of the character,

Baldwin partially overcomes his limitation to a single, internal point of view by introducing verbal irony into his diction. Sometimes he merely uses a word with connotations opposite to the values assumed by the character, as when he describes the great preaching mission that Gabriel regards as the most important of his career as "a monster revival meeting" and his more venerable colleagues as "war horses." Sometimes he simply lifts out of its churchly context a word used with religious conviction by the characters, as when he speaks of the saints doing their housecleaning or refers to Praying Mother Washington as "the praying mother." Several times he describes obviously human motives in terms of divine providence with such naiveté that the statement becomes ironic:

> Tarry service officially began at eight, but it could begin at any time, whenever the Lord moved one of the saints to enter the church and pray. It was seldom, however, that anyone arrived before eight thirty, the Spirit of the Lord being sufficiently tolerant to allow the saints time to do their Saturday-night shopping, clean their houses, and put their children to bed.

He also uses biblical language to describe an action contrary to the spirit of biblical precept and thus reveals hypocrisy in the pious:

> The ministers were being served alone in the upper room of the lodge hall—the less-specialized workers in Christ's vineyard were being fed at a table downstairs.

Although much of the irony is related to the religious views and practices of the characters, some is purely secular:

> Elizabeth found herself in an ugly back room in Harlem in the home of her aunt's relative, a woman whose respectability was immediately evident from the incense she burned in her rooms and the spiritualist séances she held every Saturday night.

The ironic detachment of the narrator is subtly suggested by Baldwin's careful use of the past tense to express a timeless conviction: "For the rebirth of the soul was perpetual; only rebirth every hour could stay the hand of Satan."

Such irony in the narrator's voice runs the risk of leading the reader's sympathy away from the characters and breaking the illusion of intimacy. Indeed, Wallace Graves has charged Baldwin with "literary cuteness" and lack of "moral energy" (honesty) in his treatment of John's mother and natural father, Elizabeth and Richard, because of the narrator's verbal irony in "Elizabeth's Prayer," where he finds a "shift in technique" from the "highly serious narrator elsewhere in the book." The narrator's irony, however, is not limited to one

section of the novel, and it avoids literary cuteness by its subtlety and sparseness. The ironic voice that speaks occasionally through the narrator's diction merely reminds us that there are other points of view from which the ideas and actions might be regarded. Moreover, in many cases the character whose thoughts are being presented may actually share this double view, consciously or unconsciously. A good example is the description of Sister McCandless, seen through John's mind but infused with the narrator's irony:

> There were times—whenever, in fact, the Lord had shown His favor by working through her—when whatever Sister McCandless said sounded like a threat. Tonight she was still very much under the influence of the sermon she had preached the night before. She was an enormous woman, one of the biggest and blackest God had ever made, and He had blessed her with a mighty voice with which to sing and preach.

Similar ambiguity is found in Elizabeth's view of her aunt's threat to move heaven and earth:

> Without, however, so much as looking at Heaven, and without troubling any more of the earth than that part of it which held the court house, she won the day.

Since both John and Elizabeth have serious reservations about the accepted view of the character being described, the irony may reflect their own feelings expressed in the more sophisticated language of the narrator.

The narrator's sophistication and detachment are balanced by his serious tone and poetic intensity of expression in describing important events or psychological perceptions in the lives of his major characters, so that his occasional irony is more like a wry smile than ridicule. The touch of humor in an otherwise passionately serious work relieves tension and gives the complexity of view needed to avoid sentimentality in so closely autobiographical a novel.

Baldwin also uses other kinds of irony to escape from the limitations of the subjective narrator in *Go Tell It on the Mountain*. Most obvious is the dramatic irony made possible by the three long flashbacks, which give the reader information unknown to other characters. For example, when Gabriel is thinking over the events in his life, the reader already knows, because of Florence's revelations, that Gabriel's wife is aware of his infidelity; and therefore the reader finds much irony in his account of scenes between them. Baldwin also uses irony of event to give the reader a corrective viewpoint. So Gabriel's two chance meetings with his bastard son occur under circumstances that emphasize sexual potency and thus contradict the purely paternal relationship Gabriel assumes.

But the most important and pervasive kind of irony in this novel is developed through the use of biblical texts and Christian doctrine to comment upon the attitudes and actions of the characters. Critics disagree about Baldwin's attitude toward the religious faith he ascribes to the characters in *Go Tell It on the Mountain,* often citing statements from Baldwin's subsequent essays to bolster their arguments. The question is important for understanding the novel, since its main action is the conversion of the hero to that faith and the reader must know whether this resolution is tragic or victorious. Aside from other evidence, unrelated to the subject of irony, which I believe points to the latter interpretation, a cogent argument can be found in Baldwin's use of this religious faith to pronounce judgment on his characters by irony of statement.

For example, Gabriel is ironically judged by his own quotations from the Bible and doctrines of the church. Under the title "Gabriel's Prayer" is an epigraph taken from a Negro spiritual, which asserts, "I ain't no stranger now." This expresses Gabriel's conviction that he is "saved," the fundamental tenet of his religious faith and the basis for his holier-than-thou attitude. If this assumption were allowed to stand uncorrected, the reader would condemn that faith as illusory and deplore John's conversion to it, since Gabriel is revealed as more devilish than saintly. But Baldwin carefully shows the irony of Gabriel's assumption by contrasting it with his own preaching. We learn early in the novel that he has taught his sons that they are in more danger of damnation than African savages precisely because they are not strangers to the gospel. In one of his sermons, he stresses the need for humility and consciousness of sin before God: "When we cease to tremble before him we have turned out of the way." In his thoughts about the tarry service, he remembers that "the rebirth of the soul is perpetual." Gabriel, the preacher and expositor of the faith, thus passes ironic judgment on his own self-righteousness.

Baldwin makes ironic Gabriel's favorite text, which is Isaiah's message to Hezekiah: "Set thine house in order, for thou shalt die and not live"—a quotation Gabriel uses both to terrify his children and to assert his own righteousness. The first mention of this text is ironically placed just after the breakfast scene, which has shown how disordered Gabriel's house is in its family relationships. A second mention during Florence's prayer suggests the further irony that Gabriel is unaware of his own approaching death, or at least of the inevitability of death. But more significantly, the text is used to make ironic Gabriel's unshakeable confidence in the "sign" he believes he received from God. He seizes upon the advent of Elizabeth and her bastard as the sign that God has forgiven him after he has ignored a sign that the reader recognizes as similar to that given Hezekiah the moment after Esther told him of her pregnancy, when the sun stood still and the earth was startled beneath his feet.

In another instance Gabriel's belief that God speaks aloud to men, sometimes through thunder, is turned ironically against his assumption of righteousness. First mentioned early in the novel, this belief becomes important during Deborah's confrontation of Gabriel with his mistreatment of Esther. He justifies his action as God's will: " 'The Lord He held me back,' he said, hearing the thunder, watching the lightning. 'He put out His hand and held me back.' " To make certain that the reader sees the irony, Baldwin has Gabriel repeat his belief about the thunder: " 'Listen. God is talking.' " Gabriel is thus contradicted by the voice of his own God. The final irony on this theme occurs in the conversation between Gabriel and Florence at the end of the novel:

> "I been listening many a nighttime long," said Florence, then, "and He ain't never spoke to me."
>
> "He ain't never spoke," said Gabriel, "because you ain't never wanted to hear. You just wanted Him to tell you your way was right."

Although Gabriel is the character most often ironically judged by his own religious convictions, Florence and Elizabeth also unwittingly pronounce judgment on themselves. Florence recites the conditions for successful prayer and then fails to meet them in her cry for salvation. Elizabeth tells herself that she is on her way up the steep side of the mountain, and then contracts a loveless marriage as "a hiding-place hewn in the side of the mountain."

By using the tenets of their faith for ironic comment upon the characters' actions and attitudes, Baldwin transcends the limitations of his subjective narrator and at the same time establishes as trustworthy the religious faith they profess, even when they misinterpret it. Within the novel the universe works according to the principles of the Hebrew-Christian tradition, and therefore John's conversion is the opening of his eyes to truth—a giant step on his way up the mountain.

In Part Three, "The Threshing Floor," Baldwin introduces an ironic voice that speaks to John during the early stages of his internal struggle. Critics disagree about the identity of this anonymous internal speaker. David Noble asserts that it is the voice of Gabriel, because it expresses Gabriel's wish that John would get up off the threshing floor. In order to accept this identification the reader must see Gabriel as a conscious hypocrite who could encourage John to rebel against his authority to prevent John's salvation, but Baldwin carefully shows Gabriel as an unconscious hypocrite, never capable of overt double-dealing. Other critics have taken the ironic voice as John's own common sense, fighting a losing battle against his weakness for hysterical religion. If the voice is common sense, then John's conversion is a tragedy and his joyful faith an illusion; and this interpretation is contradicted by the tone of the last few pages, by the meaning of the book's title and supporting epigraph, and by the serious attitude toward religious faith implied by Baldwin's use of it for ironic comment. Moreover, John's struggle on the threshing floor is described in terms of birth imagery, and the accomplished delivery sets him free from the womb of childhood. After his conversion he stands up to his father on the equal footing of adulthood, refuting Gabriel's scornful doubts, openly recognizing the enmity between them, and refusing to obey his command. Obedience to the urging of the ironic voice would have prevented this deliverance and left John in his state of childish rebellion, a prisoner to his longing for parental love and his feeling of sexual guilt.

In terms of the novel, we see the ironic voice as an enemy who presses John to do what Gabriel secretly hopes he will do, what Florence did when she rejected her brother's church and her brother's God. The narrator describes it as malicious: "He wanted to rise—a malicious, ironic voice insisted that he rise—and, at once, to leave this temple and go out into the world." The voice comes from within John, expressing his own wishes, and its main attack is against any belief in this religion, which it attempts to discredit by associating it with "niggers" and by ridiculing the Bible's story of Noah's curse on Ham. The voice, then, is the voice of unbelief within John, which Baldwin describes as predominant in his state of mind before his conversion. At the beginning of the tarry service he is scornful of the praying women and replies to a kindly, though pious, remark by Sister Price with "a smile that, despite the shy gratitude it was meant to convey, did not escape being ironic, or even malicious." Like Florence, who prays, "Lord, help my unbelief," he is not a believer. His unbelief and hidden scorn are expressed by the ironic voice in the first stages of his struggle on the threshing floor.

The voice also expresses his rebellion against his father, his father's religion, and his father's social status. It labels the tarry service as a practice of "niggers," with the implication that John is above that level, and its spurs him to resist his father's authority:

> Then the ironic voice spoke again, saying: "Get up, John. Get up, boy. Don't let him keep you here. You got everything your daddy got."

This explicit connection of his sexual maturity with his father's enmity brings him to the brink of understanding, but it is not until the ironic voice leaves him that John is able to penetrate the mystery:

> But now he knew, for irony had left him, that he was searching something, hidden in the darkness, that must be found. He would die if it was not found.

When he has rid himself of malice, he is free to search the subconscious depths of his mind until he grasps the true relationship of father and son—the Oedipal situation common to all human experience or, in Baldwin's interpretation, original sin.

Ridding oneself of malice is a necessary condition to salvation. Florence, unable to escape her hatred of Gabriel, founders on this rock, just as Gabriel's pride prevents him from reaching true understanding of the Oedipal situation. When John's malicious irony is swept away, he faces the psychic realities of his subconscious, and then only fear is left—the fear of being an adult, unprotected by parental love and responsible for his own life. Overcoming this fear is the final step—the step Elizabeth has not yet been able to take, and John makes it with Elisha's help. The ironic voice of unbelief, of the devil, of childish rebellion is replaced with the humble voice of faith, of God's angel, of mature self-acceptance, saying, "Yes, go through."

Perhaps Baldwin is suggesting that all irony is in a sense malicious, that human problems cannot be solved by sophisticated detachment or even common sense reasonableness. Certainly the ironic voice of the narrator is lost in the passionate seriousness of John's religious experience, which is the climax and resolution of his conflict.

Source: Shirley S. Allen, "*The Ironic Voice in* Baldwin's Go Tell It on the Mountain," in *James Baldwin: A Critical Evaluation,* edited by Therman B. O'Daniel, Howard University Press, 1977, pp. 30–37.

Sources

Shirley Allen, "Religious Symbolism and Psychic Reality in Baldwin's *Go Tell It On The Mountain*," in *CLA Journal*, Vol. XIX, No. 2, December, 1975, pp. 173-99.

Richard K. Barksdale, "Temple of the Fire Baptized," in *Phylon*, Vol. 14, 1953, pp. 326-27.

Robert Bone, "James Baldwin," in *The Negro Novel in America*, rev. ed., Yale University Press, 1965, pp. 215-39.

Granville Hicks, "Go Tell It On the Mountain," in *Literary Horizons: A Quarter Century of American Fiction*, New York University Press, 1970, pp. 87-90.

James de Jongh, *Vicious Modernism: Black Harlem and the Literary Imagination*, Cambridge University Press, 1990, pp. 5-33.

Edward Margolies, "The Negro Church: James Baldwin and the Christian Vision," in *Native Sons: A Critical Study of Twentieth-Century Negro American Authors*, J. B. Lippincott Company, 1968, pp. 102-26.

J. Saunders Redding, "Go Tell It On the Mountain," in *New York Herald Tribune Book Review*, May 17, 1953, p. 5.

For Further Study

Robert A. Bone, "The Novels of James Baldwin," in *Tri-Quarterly*, Winter, 1965, pp. 3-20.

Bone suggests that in *Go Tell It on the Mountain* Baldwin "approaches the very essence of Negro experience" and presents a "psychic drama" of religious conversion.

Arna Bontemps, *100 Years of Negro Freedom*, Dodd, Mead & Co., 1961.

At first glance, this book appears to be a primer for grade school children, but the author, Bontemps, was one of the most respected intellectuals of the Harlem Renaissance. This book is clear and straightforward, covering history lessons that are not touched by mainstream reading lists.

Jane Campbell, "Retreat into the Self: Ralph Ellison's 'Invisible Man' and James Baldwin's 'Go Tell It on the Mountain,'" in *Mythic Black Fiction: The Transformation of History*, University of Tennessee Press, 1986, pp. 87-110.

Compares confessional elements in both novels.

Richard Courage, "James Baldwin's 'Go Tell It on the Mountain': Voices of a People," in *CLA Journal*, Vol. 32, No. 4, June, 1989, pp. 131-42.

Courage argues that the novel "highlights the role of the black church in maintaining a sense of communal identity."

Michael Fabre, "Fathers and Sons in James Baldwin's *Go Tell It On The Mountain*," in *James Baldwin: A Collection of Critical Essays*, edited by Keneth Kinnamon, Prentice Hall, Inc., 1974, pp. 120-38.

Explores the religious and psychological symbolism of the novel.

Neil Fligstein, *Going North: Migration of Blacks and Whites From the South, 1900-1950*, Academic Press, 1981.

Fligstein, a sociologist, wrote this work for other professors, and it is filled with statistics and tables, but the average student should be able to get a good view of the abstract social dynamics that control the characters in Baldwin's novel.

David E. Foster, "'Cause My House Fell Down': The Theme of the Fall in Baldwin's Novels," in *Critique*, Vol. 13, No. 2, 1971, pp. 50-62.

This article explores the fall from grace in many of Baldwin's novels including *Go Tell It on the Mountain*.

James R. Giles, "Religious Alienation and 'Homosexual Consciousness' in 'City of the Night' and 'Go Tell It on the Mountain,'" in *CLA Journal*, Vol. 7, No. 3, March, 1964, pp. 369-80.

Discusses themes of religion and homosexuality in John Rechy's *City of the Night* and Baldwin's *Go Tell It on the Mountain*.

Howard M. Harper, Jr., "James Baldwin: Art or Propaganda?" in *Desperate Faith: A Study of Bellow, Salinger, Mailer, Baldwin, and Updike*, University of North Carolina Press, 1967, pp. 137-61.

Explores the fall from grace in many of Baldwin's novels including *Go Tell It on the Mountain*.

Marcus Klein, "James Baldwin: A Question of Identity," in *After Alienation: American Novels in Mid-Century*, World Publishing Company, 1962, pp. 147-95.

Examines the link between maturation and identity in *Go Tell It on the Mountain*.

Nicholas Lemann, *The Promised Land: The Great Black Migration and How It Changed Society*, Alfred A. Knopf, 1991.

Covering a period later than the one portrayed in the novel—from the 1940s to the 1960s—Lemann explores the effect of the population shift on three specific cities: Chicago, Washington, and Clarksdale, Mississippi. The relevance of this book to Baldwin's novel is slightly abstract, but it is still helpful for understanding the social situation that the Grimes family faces in Harlem.

John R. May, "Images of Apocalypse in the Black Novel," in *Renascence*, Vol. 23, No. 1, Autumn, 1970, pp. 31-45.

This article includes an exploration of images of apocalypse in *Go Tell It on the Mountain*.

Therman B. O'Daniel, "James Baldwin: An Interpretive Study," in *CLA Journal*, Vol. 8, No. 1, pp. 37-47.

Analyzes the themes of homosexuality and racism in Baldwin's novels including *Go Tell It on the Mountain*.

Horace A. Porter, *Stealing Fire: The Art and Protest of James Baldwin*, Wesleyan University Press, 1989.

This book holds Baldwin to a high standard and is not at all shy about criticizing his flaws, but it is just as free with its praise. The well-researched portrait of Baldwin that emerges here is that of a man of contradictions, who learned from the best of white tradition and kept his sympathies rooted on black culture.

Great Expectations

Charles Dickens

1861

This was Dickens' second-to-last complete novel. It was first published as a weekly series in 1860 and in book form in 1861. Early critics had mixed reviews, disliking Dickens' tendency to exaggerate both plot and characters, but readers were so enthusiastic that the 1861 edition required five printings. Similar to Dickens' memories of his own childhood, in his early years the young Pip seems powerless to stand against injustice or to ever realize his dreams for a better life. However, as he grows into a useful worker and then an educated young man he reaches an important realization: grand schemes and dreams are never what they first seem to be. Pip himself is not always honest, and careful readers can catch him in several obvious contradictions between his truth and fantasies. Victorian-era audiences were more likely to have appreciated the melodramatic scenes and the revised, more hopeful ending. However, modern critics have little but praise for Dickens' brilliant development of timeless themes: fear and fun, loneliness and luck, classism and social justice, humiliation and honor. Some still puzzle over Dickens' revision that ends the novel with sudden optimism, and they suggest that the sales of Dickens' magazine *All the Year Round,* in which the series first appeared, was assured by gluing on a happy ending that hints Pip and Estella will unite at last. Some critics point out that the original ending is better because it is more realistic since Pip must earn the self-knowledge that can only come from giving up his obsession with Estella. However, Victorian au-

diences eagerly followed the story of Pip, episode by episode, assuming that the protagonist's love and patience would win out in the end. Modern editions contain both denouements for the reader to choose a preference.

Author Biography

From the time he was twenty-one, Charles Dickens knew he would not be the great actor he had imagined, nor even the journalist he next attempted to be. Instead, he felt he was destined to become a great novelist. He not only had experiences with the same joys and tragedies his characters would have, but he also had the great talent to make his readers feel and see all these experiences in detail. The second of eight children of John and Elizabeth Dickens, Charles was born on February 7, 1812, in Portsmouth, England. His early childhood was a happy one. Though plagued by frequent illnesses, his first years were also filled with exciting stories told to him by his parents and his nurse.

However, when Dickens was twelve, his family moved to London, where his father was imprisoned for debts he could not pay. Charles was forced to go to work pasting labels on bottles at a bootblack factory. Although this job lasted less than a year, he often felt hungry and abandoned, especially compared to his sister Frances, who continued studying at the Royal Academy of Music, where she was winning awards. For Dickens, the injustice was almost more than he could stand, and his suffering was multiplied by his mother's delight about the job that he always remembered with hatred.

Although his critics are the first to say that *Great Expectations* is not directly autobiographical, Dickens' own words tell us that he resented having to work in the factory, where he dreamed of the better life he felt he deserved, much as Pip is eager to leave Joe's forge. Also, Dickens' essay "Travelling Abroad" describes a small boy who rides in a coach with Dickens past his grand house, Gad's Hill. Although the boy in the essay does not know Dickens or that this is the great author's house, he remarks that his father has told him that hard work will earn him this house, which Dickens had also admired for years before finally being able to afford it in 1856. Dickens' familiarity with youthful expectations and later-life remembrances of them are clear in this reflection.

Charles Dickens

Likewise, Dickens' first love for Maria Beadnell so impressed him by its horrible failure that even years later he could barely speak of it to his friend and biographer, John Forster. All that Dickens had written about her he later burned. He believed that Maria had rejected him because of social class differences, since Dickens had not yet established his writing career at the time and Maria's father was a banker. Decades later, his character Miss Havisham would burn, shooting up flames twice her size, in compensation for her cold heart.

Dickens' marriage to Catherine (Kate) Hogarth, the daughter of a newspaper editor, in 1836 produced ten children. Their union ended in separation in 1858, however. By the time *Great Expectations* was published in 1860, Dickens had known his mistress Ellen Ternan—an actress he had met when he became interested in the stage— for several years, and he established a separate household in which he lived with Ternan. It would not be until after the author's death, however, that Dickens' daughter would make the affair public. Ternan was twenty-seven years younger than Dickens, a fact that resembles the age difference between the happy, later-life couple Joe and Biddy in *Great Expectations*. Dickens protected his privacy because he was worried about his reputation as a respected writer and the editor of *Household Words,* a family magazine. Such turmoil and ecstasy in Dickens' intimate relationships have since been compared to the misery and bliss of couples in his novels.

If anything, Dickens' descriptions of suffering were and still are his chief endearing quality to readers who find them both realistic and empathetic. Beginning with *Bleak House* in 1852, Dickens is widely acknowledged to have entered a "Dark Period" of writing. Yet he seemed to enjoy his continuing popularity with readers and to ignore his critics' remarks that his stories were too melodramatic. While readers have long accepted that tendency, they have also warmed to Dickens' love of humor.

Critics suggest that the part of Dickens' life that is most reflected in *A Tale of Two Cities* is his personal relationships with his wife and Ellen Ternan. In 1855, he reestablished contact with his childhood sweetheart Maria Beadnell, but he was very disappointed with their meeting and depicted his disillusionment in the 1857 novel *Little Dorrit.* A quarrel with his publishers Bradbury & Evans over his mistress's reputation led Dickens to turn to a new publishing house, Chapman & Hall, to publish *A Tale of Two Cities.* Some critics suggest that Dickens' depiction of Lucie Manette in *A Tale of Two Cities* and the behavior of the two principal characters, Sydney Carton and Charles Darnay, toward her, reflects his own attitude toward Ternan.

Dickens died of a brain aneurysm in June 1870. Although he had expressly wished to be buried at his country home, Gad's Hill, his request was disregarded, apparently owing to his fame. Instead, he was buried in the Poets' Corner of Westminster Abbey, London.

Plot Summary

The First Stage of Pip's Expectations

Charles Dickens' *Great Expectations* opens as seven-year-old Philip Pirrip, known as "Pip," visits the graves of his parents down in the marshes near his home on Christmas Eve. Here he encounters a threatening escaped convict, who frightens Pip and makes him promise to steal food and a file for him. Pip steals some food from his brother-in-law, the blacksmith Joe Gargery, and his cruel sister "Mrs. Joe," with whom he lives, and takes it to the convict the next day. The convict is soon caught

and returned to the "Hulks," the prison ships from which he had escaped.

Pip is invited to visit the wealthy Miss Havisham, and to play with her adopted daughter, Estella. Miss Havisham lives in the gloomy Satis House, and Pip discovers her to be an extremely eccentric woman. Having been abandoned on her wedding day many years earlier, Miss Havisham has never changed out of her wedding dress since that time, and nothing in the house, including the rotting wedding cake covered with spider webs, has been touched since she discovered that her fiance had left her and had cheated her out of a great deal of money. Miss Havisham has raised Estella to be a cold and heartless woman who will avenge her adopted mother by breaking the hearts of men.

Pip continues to visit Satis House to play with Estella, and he begins to fall in love with her, despite the fact that she is rude and condescending to him. Because of Miss Havisham's interest in him, Pip's family and friends speculate on his future prospects, and Pip attempts to improve those prospects by asking his friend, the orphaned Biddy, to tutor him. Eventually, Miss Havisham gives Pip some money, tells him his services are no longer needed, and that it is time for him to be apprenticed to his brother-in-law, Joe. Pip is disappointed.

One day Pip learns that someone has broken into his home and that his sister, Mrs. Joe, has been injured with a great blow to the back of the head. Biddy moves in to help take care of her and the household and continues to tutor Pip, with whom she is falling in love. Biddy believes that it was Orlick, a contemptuous employee of Joe's, who injured Mrs. Joe. Biddy also fears that Orlick is falling in love with her. Pip continues to work for Joe, visiting Miss Havisham every year on his birthday, and constantly regretting his desire for a more comfortable lifestyle and his infatuation with Estella.

Some time later a stranger visits Pip and informs him that an anonymous benefactor would like to transform him into a gentleman. The stranger, a lawyer named Jaggers, will administer Pip's new income and suggests that Pip move to London and take a man named Matthew Pocket as his tutor, who happens to be a relative of Miss Havisham. Pip assumes that Miss Havisham is his mysterious benefactor. Pip buys himself some new clothes and bidding his family farewell, slips out of town on his own, embarrassed to be seen in his new outfit with Joe.

The Second Stage of Pip's Expectations

In London, Pip lodges with Pocket's son Herbert. Pip also becomes friends with John Wemmick, Jaggers' clerk, and learns that Jaggers is a famous lawyer who is noted for his work in defending prisoners and thieves who face execution. Wemmick takes Pip home to dinner one night, and Pip is intrigued by his house, which resembles a tiny castle, complete with drawbridge and moat, where Wemmick lives with his elderly and stone-deaf father, whom he calls "the Aged P." Pip is also invited to dine at Jaggers' house, where he meets Jaggers' sullen housekeeper, Molly.

Joe comes to London to bring a message to Pip, who is embarrassed to have Joe visit him. The message is from Miss Havisham, who invites Pip to come to see Estella, who is visiting her mother. Going to Satis House at once, Pip is surprised to find that Orlick is now Miss Havisham's watchman, and he tells Jaggers that the man should be dismissed. Not long after this, Pip learns that his sister has died, and he returns home for her funeral. While he is there, he promises Biddy that he will visit Joe often in the future, but Biddy expresses her doubt that he actually will do so:

"I am not going to leave poor Joe alone."

Biddy said never a single word.

"Biddy, don't you hear me?"

"Yes, Mr. Pip."

"Not to mention your calling me Mr. Pip—which appears to me to be in bad taste, Biddy—what do you mean?"

"What do I mean?" asked Biddy, timidly.

"Biddy," said I, in a virtuously self-asserting manner, "I must request to know what you mean by this?"

"By this?" said Biddy.

"Now don't echo," I retorted. "You used not to echo, Biddy."

"Used not!" said Biddy. "O Mr. Pip! Used!" …

… "Biddy," said I, "I made a remark respecting my coming down here often, to see Joe, which you received with a marked silence. Have the goodness, Biddy, to tell me why."

"Are you quite sure, then, that you WILL come to see him often?" asked Biddy, stopping in the narrow garden walk, and looking at me under the stars with a clear and honest eye.

"Oh dear me!" said I, as if I found myself compelled to give up Biddy in despair. "This really is a very bad side of human nature! Don't say any more, if you please, Biddy. This shocks me very much."

The Third Stage of Pip's Expectations

One day Pip is visited by a stranger, and soon recognizes him to be the convict to whom he had brought food years ago. The convict, Abel Magwitch, has made a fortune as a sheep farmer in New South Wales, Australia, and he has prided himself on having used his money to make a gentleman out of the little boy who had helped him long ago. Pip is shocked and embarrassed to learn that it is the convict who has given him his "great expectations" and not Miss Havisham.

Magwitch tells him of his history, and how he became involved with another more gentlemanly criminal who got him into trouble, and yet was punished less severely when they were both caught. Pip and Herbert deduce that this criminal is Compeyson, the man who schemed with his partner, Arthur, to swindle Miss Havisham of her money. Arthur was supposed to marry Miss Havisham to get her money, but his conscience caused him to abandon her at the alter when he couldn't go through with the plan. Because Magwitch faces certain death if he is discovered in England, Pip and Herbert concoct a plan for helping him escape unnoticed.

Planning to leave the country with Magwitch, Pip pays Miss Havisham a call. The old lady admits that she allowed Pip to believe that she was his benefactress, and Pip asks her to help him with a plan he has to set Herbert up in business anonymously. Pip is shocked to learn that Estella plans to marry his doltish acquaintance Bentley Drummle. Dining one night with Jaggers, Pip learns more about the housekeeper Molly's history. Having been accused of killing another woman involved with her husband and having threatened to murder her own daughter, Molly was successfully defended by Jaggers. Recognizing her face and hands, Pip realizes with astonishment that Molly is the mother of Estella.

Pip is summoned to Miss Havisham's again, where the old lady begs Pip to forgive her. After leaving her, Pip is disturbed and decides to return to the house to look in on her. He finds the poor old woman ablaze, having sat too close to the fire, and he is burned while trying to put out the flames. Later Pip learns of Miss Havisham's death, and that she has left money to Herbert, as he had requested. Returning to London, he learns the story of Magwitch's wife, and deduces that Magwitch was married to Molly, and therefore is Estella's father.

Summoned back to the marshes near his old home by a mysterious note, Pip narrowly escapes death when he is attacked by a vengeful Orlick and rescued just in time by some local villagers. He returns to London where he and Herbert carry out their plan to sneak Magwitch onto a steamer on the Thames. Their plans fail, however. They are attacked by another boat, and Magwitch is severely wounded. As the kind old Magwitch is dying, Pip tells him of his daughter Estella.

After being nursed out of a serious illness by the devoted Joe, Pip joins the business partnership he has established for Herbert in the East. After eleven years, he returns to England and visits Joe and Biddy, who have married and have a family. He also meets Estella, who has left her husband, on the property of the now demolished Satis House. This time, Pip says that "I saw no shadow of another parting from her."

In Dickens' original version, Pip and Estella part with the understanding that they will probably never see each other again, but in the revised version, Dickens' makes the ending more optimistic by implying that they will, indeed, have a future together someday.

Characters

Arthur

Arthur, Miss Havisham's suitor who once jilted her, has fallen in with the villainous Compeyson and his schemes. However, unlike Compeyson, Arthur has a conscience; he dreams of Miss Havisham dressed in white at his bedside and dies of fright. He and Compeyson had once schemed to get Miss Havisham's fortune, but at the last moment, with the wedding cake on the table and Miss Havisham dressed in her bridal finery, Arthur jilted her, presumably on an attempt at her fortune that he could not carry through.

Biddy

The gentle, loving, soft-spoken, wise, and efficient Biddy is Pip's tutor before Mrs. Joe is injured and Biddy moves into the Gargery home to take care of the house. After Mrs. Joe dies, she and Joe Gargery marry. Pip, who at one point tells Biddy that he might be interested in marrying her if it weren't for her lowly social status, later comes to realize that Biddy's true worth as a person far outshines any artificial class distinctions.

Compeyson

Compeyson is the scoundrel who arranges Miss Havisham's affair with Arthur. He also testifies in court against Magwitch in an earlier scheme that failed, after which Magwitch is banished from England and exiled to Australia. A coward, he breaks the old rule of "honor among thieves." Compeyson is the second escaped convict that is out on the marsh the night that Pip first meets Magwitch, and he eventually dies fighting with Magwitch during their second capture.

Bentley Drummle

Pip's fellow member of the Finches of the Grove in London, Bentley Drummle is no gentleman but a rude and lazy man who teases Pip about Estella's apparent preference for Drummle. Jaggers recognizes a ruthless streak in Drummle and refers to him as the Spider (presumably because he catches all the flies, i.e. anything he wants). A parallel character to Arthur, Drummle becomes engaged to and then marries Estella, whom he barely knows but whose fortune he stands to gain. However, he does not survive her.

Estella

Adopted by Miss Havisham at the age of "two or three," Estella is taught from then on to reject all who love her. This is Miss Havisham's vengeance in reaction to her romantic disappointment by Arthur. About the same age as Pip, Estella acts much older than he does and snubs or insults him more often than merely ignoring his attempts at friendship or love. In this, she is quite honest with Pip, for she has been raised to be cruel, to tolerate or to brush off love, and to reject it later in order to watch the man suffer. Miss Havisham's success in raising a cold-hearted beauty is too much for her, however, for Estella can feel no love for the old woman either. Thus, Estella cannot help but to refuse to give Pip any hope of marriage whenever he confesses his love. Instead, she tells him that she will ruin the man she does marry—and why not, when she cares for no one? When she becomes engaged to Bentley Drummle, Pip cannot talk her out of marrying such a brutal man. In the novel's revised ending, when Estella meets Pip years later she has had a daughter (also named Estella) by Drummle, who has died. Estella has survived, but she has been "bent and broken" by the doomed marriage. She has never found out who her biological parents were because Miss Havisham has led her to assume that they were dead. More tragically, Estella has never learned to care about anyone's happiness, not even her own.

Media Adaptations

- *Great Expectations* was first adapted by film in the silent movie version in 1917, released by Paramount Pictures, on five reels, Famous Players Film Company, 3 January 1917, and presented by David Frohman.

- A 1934 remake, poorly directed by Stuart Walker, starred Jane Wyatt as Estella and Phillip Holmes as Pip, but the public thought their performances were lackluster. Universal released this film on eleven reels.

- A British production of the novel on film was made in Great Britain in 1946, directed by David Lean and available from Rank/Cineguild. This most acclaimed of the film versions of Dickens' novel stars John Mills as Pip, Valerie Hobson as Estella, and Alec Guiness as Herbert Pocket, Jr., and it won two Oscars in 1947. According to critic Robert Murphy, it was "one of the finest of all film adaptations of Dickens."

- Two critical adaptations of the novel were captured on film in 1962 dealing with (1) setting, character, and themes and (2) critical interpretation. Each of these two films were produced for a high school or early college audience by the Encyclopedia Brittannica Corporation, and each are 35 minutes in length.

- In 1973, the University of Michigan produced a dramatization of Dickens' attack in *Great Expectations* on the upper class of British society, with a senior high to college level audience in mind. Available on the Dickens' World Series from the University of Michigan, this film runs 29 minutes.

- A 1974 version by Scotia-Barber/ITC was released in 1974 in Great Britain. Joseph Hardy directed.

- Produced by the BBC. the first close-captioned version of *Great Expectations* was made in 1981 and released in the US in August 1988 by CBS/Fox Video. Starring Gerry Sundquist, Stratford Johns, and Joan Hudson, it was directed by Julian Aymes and runs for 300 minutes (also available on two cassettes in Great Britain from BBC/International Historic Films, Inc., #R249).

- *Great Expectations: The Untold Story* was adapted for viewers from Magwitch's point of view. Featuring John Stanton, Sigrid Thornton, and Robert Coleby, and directed by Tim Burstall, this video was released by Facets Multimedia, Inc. in 1987.

- *Great Expectations* was filmed for prime time television by Primetime/Harlech Television in both Great Britain and the US in 1989. This was a made-for-TV presentation in 1989.

- Walt Disney Home Video also has a 1989 version of the novel on video, starring Jean Simmons and Anthony Hopkins, directed by Kevin Connor, and running 325 minutes.

- Two 1978 animated versions of *Great Expectations* represent Dickens' tale of Pip. One is close-captioned, directed by Jean Tych and produced by Burbank Films for Live Home Video, and the other is available from Library Video Company, both running 72 minutes.

- Selected readings from *Great Expectations* is available on audio tape from Time Warner. The 1994 tape, accompanied by a study guide, runs 72 minutes and is narrated by Michael York.

- A 1987 unabridged sound recording on eleven cassettes (approximately 16 hours running time) includes both endings to the novel. The narrator is Frank Muller, and the set is available from Recorded Books in Charlotte Hall, MD.

- A 1981 abridged version, two cassettes running 180 minutes, is read by Anton Rodgers, available from Listen for Pleasure, Downsview, Ontario. Both endings are included.

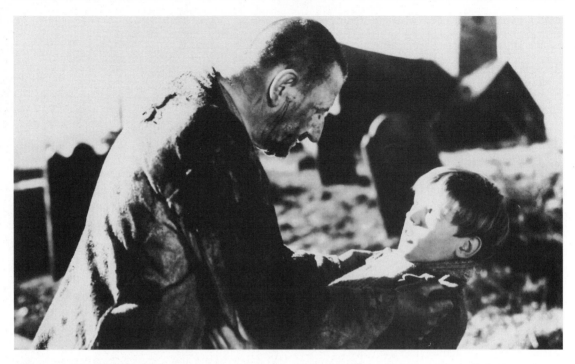

Still from the 1946 film Great Expectations, *starring Anthony Wager (right) as Pip and Finlay Currie (left) as Magwitch.*

Joe Gargery

Joe is Pip's uncle and surrogate father, but also a fellow-sufferer from his wife's nasty temper and violent behavior. He is a rough, strong working man who generally keeps his emotions to himself. According to Joe, whenever he had tried to protect young Pip from his sister's abuse, she not only hit Joe too but hurt Pip the "heavier for it." Joe gladly takes Pip on as his apprentice at the forge and misses him terribly when Pip leaves for London; however, he will not stand in the way of Pip's good fortune. After Mrs. Joe is attacked, he nurses her with the help of Biddy, whom he marries after Mrs. Joe dies. He also gently and lovingly nurses Pip back to health in London. An uneducated man, he learns enough about writing from Biddy to leave Pip a letter to say goodbye, misspelling his own name "Jo" as Pip had done as a child. Of all of the characters in the novel, Joe is one who does not change, remaining tough yet childlike in love. If he has a weakness, it is a tendency to look on the bright side when there isn't one, which seemed a bit foolish to Pip as a teenager. Yet in spite of Joe's hard life, he remains "good-natured," "easy-going," and unfailingly devoted to Pip and Biddy.

Mrs. Joe Gargery

A large, menacing woman, Mrs. Joe prides herself on raising Pip "by hand," which is a sorry pun on the way she is hitting the child and her husband whenever she is not verbally attacking them. Her favorite instrument, "The Tickler," is a stick that is "worn smooth" from caning Pip, regardless of his behavior. The bodice of her apron is stuck through with pins and needles, a true metaphor for her character. Only one man stands up to her, the evil Orlick, and she never completely recovers from his savage attack. She spends her last days in the tender care of Joe and Biddy, no longer physically or verbally vicious but in a state of childlike happiness.

Handel

See Pip

Miss Havisham

Always dressed in the wedding gown in which she had once planned to be married, Miss Havisham is colorless, from her hair to her faded white shoes, of which she wears only one. She wants Pip to play with Estella to act out her love-turned-hatred for the man who jilted her on their wedding day. She has left the house as it was then, even the items on her dressing table. The great room across from her chamber is likewise untouched; the cake, now eerily covered with spiders and dusty cobwebs, is in the middle of the long dining table. It is her wish that this table be cleared only when she is dead so that she may be laid on it for her wake. By arranging for repeated contact between the children, Miss Havisham intends that Pip will fall in love with the frosty Estella, and she constantly reminds Pip to "love her, love her, love her!" She rewards Pip's visits with coins and does not contradict him when Pip is sure that she is his anonymous benefactor. When Pip continues to visit them from London, Miss Havisham is still anxious for him to admire Estella. However, when Estella makes plans to marry Bentley Drummle, Miss Havisham finds that she has done too well in teaching Estella to be a cold, cruel lover. Estella plans to leave her and will not, and probably cannot, express any love for Miss Havisham. When the old lady's clothing accidentally catches on fire, she is saved by Pip who rolls her in the tablecloth from the great room. Her doctor orders her bed to be brought in and arranged on the table, fulfilling her wish to be laid in state where her wedding feast had once been. Before she dies, she honors Pip's request for money for his friend, Herbert Pocket, amazed that Pip wants nothing for himself. She also suffers from nightmares of dying without forgiveness, as well as from her burns. Even so, she dies with Pip's kiss of forgiveness on her wrinkled forehead.

Mr. Jaggers

All of the Londoners on the wrong side of the law know Mr. Jaggers is the lawyer with the best chance of keeping them out of Newgate Prison. Jaggers is never wrong. His reputation is so great that his clients know that Jaggers won't take a case he can't win and will tell them so. They also know that they will be refused if they cannot pay his fee. His reputation for courtroom drama is equally well-known, for he has moved many a judge and jury to tears. Outside of court, his speech is guarded so that he cannot be misinterpreted. It seems barely human that he never lets down that guard. Since he is Miss Havisham's lawyer and he is also bound by Pip's mysterious benefactor's desire to remain unknown, Jaggers bolsters Pip's belief that Miss Havisham is his benefactor. However, Jaggers has many clients, all with secrets to be kept. A cold calculator of his own financial gain, Jaggers is the sort of person one can respect but can never call "friend." Even so, he invites Pip to dinner occa-

sionally and once tells Pip to bring his classmates. While Jaggers might seem to favor Pip this way at times, he is more appreciative of Pip's schoolmate, Bentley Drummle, whom Jaggers nicknames "The Spider." He sees in Drummle the shrewd and ruthless qualities that he believes are necessary for getting ahead in the world.

Mrs. Joe

See Mrs. Joe Gargery

Abel Magwitch

In trouble from the day he was born, Abel Magwitch is an orphan like Pip but without Joe or any loving family member to befriend him. All he can recall of his early days is his name. In and out of trouble with the law all his life, he is banished to Australia, where he tends sheep and saves his money to one day make "an English gentleman" out of the little boy named Pip who once was kind to him while he was running from the police on the marshes. When he reenters Pip's life in London, Magwitch holds the key to many mysteries, but if he is recaptured he will not be sent back to Australia but sentenced to death. He calls himself "Provis" to avoid recognition and spends many happy hours with Pip, in spite of Pip's discomfort at learning that his benefactor has not been Miss Havisham but a criminal. However, Pip learns a great deal more from Magwitch than his identity, for Magwitch is the link between more characters in the novel than anyone but Pip himself. In spite of their caution, Magwitch is recaptured, injured, and sentenced to death. However, he is already dying of his wounds. Even so, he has lived out his dream of creating in Pip the respectable man that Magwitch himself could never be, as well as assuring that his former crime partner and arch-enemy Compeyson drowns. In his last days, Magwitch reveals to Pip the confidence scheme that he was drawn into with Arthur and Compeyson. However, it is only after Magwitch's death that Pip discovers that Magwitch was also Estella's father.

Molly

Jaggers' maid who serves dinner to Pip has strange scars on her wrists, as though she were once shackled. Indeed, she has known hard times before Jaggers has "tamed her," and Jaggers openly refers to her "gypsy blood." As her lawyer, Jaggers once saved her from being sent to Newgate Prison, and he shames her in front of Pip to remind her of her old life, her reform, and her alternative to serving in his house. At another dinner with Mr. Jaggers,

Pip is fascinated by Molly's hands for another reason. He has seen them somewhere before. Eventually, Pip notices other resemblances between Molly and Estella and forces a stilted admission out of Jaggers that Molly was once married to a convict and that their child, a little girl, was adopted by a rich woman with no children of her own, and that Jaggers arranged such an adoption. Put together with Magwitch's story and Jaggers' hypothetical sketch, it is obvious that Molly was Magwitch's wife and Estella's mother. With Magwitch in jail, Molly had no other means of support and had been caught thieving. Jaggers had arranged for her release on her promise to serve at his table and to stay out of trouble or else he would turn her back over to the police. Molly does not know Estella or Miss Havisham, only that her child has been cared for by someone with great wealth.

Orlick

One of the characters in the novel with no apparent redeeming qualities, Orlick is a big, unhappy clod who works at Joe's forge until he insults Mrs. Joe and is fired. Orlick also bears a grudge against Pip for having Joe's favor and a benefactor. When Orlick first threatens Mrs. Joe, it is the one time that Joe stands up and tolerates no nonsense from Orlick. Years later, however, Orlick lures Pip to the limekiln out on the marshes and ties Pip up with the intention of killing him. Meanwhile, Orlick tells Pip of the scene of his attack on Mrs. Joe's skull with a convict's (Magwitch's) leg irons that he had found on the marsh. Since it is Pip who was responsible for getting a file to Magwitch to remove his shackles, Orlick's deed may be only the delayed result of Pip's childhood "crime" of having once helped a convict. However, right wins out when help arrives and Orlick is arrested before Pip is harmed.

Philip Pirrip

See Pip

Pip

Pip is someone who is shaped by his changing circumstances. He is an orphan who never knew his dead parents or brothers. He is raised by his sister and Joe Gargery at Joe's forge on the marshes near a country village at some distance from London. For a child who perpetually fears punishment, Pip learns to lie quite convincingly. A self-proclaimed "sensitive" boy, he is frequently beaten or starved and verbally abused by his sister, although he keeps only one secret from his gentle uncle, Joe

Gargery. Threatened by an escaped convict Pip meets in the church cemetery, he steals food and a file, a "crime" he is certain will be his doom. Pip is equally intimidated by the hideous Miss Havisham and the lovely Estella. Even though Estella is his own age, Pip feels dominated by the girl and obeys Miss Havisham's order to "love her!" When Pip learns that he has an anonymous benefactor who will provide for his education in London, he eagerly leaves his apprenticeship with Joe behind, certain that his patron is Miss Havisham who is preparing him to become a gentleman worthy of marrying Estella. His hunch is supported by his long-standing belief that he is better than he has been treated and that he deserves more in life than becoming a blacksmith like Joe. Furthermore, the lawyer who pays Pip's allowance is also Miss Havisham's lawyer. However, in London, Pip's tutor, Mr. Herbert Pocket Sr., turns out to be ineffectual, and Pip finds himself without adequate training for any profession to fit his new social class. He further discovers that all of his old "expectations" have been wrong-headed. Even so, learning this seems to be his best education. For Pip, who spends much of his life either daydreaming or defending himself, such a change of heart seems heroic enough to set things right again. However, except for risking his own life to save Miss Havisham, Pip is less like a hero than like someone who expects to win the lottery any day now but has little idea what he will do with the money except to spend it. In the end, he redeems himself by realizing who his true friends are when all of his "expectations" and money are gone. He is reunited with Joe and Biddy, and his kindness to Herbert Pocket, Jr., is repaid.

Pip's convict

See Abel Magwitch

Herbert Pocket Jr.

Pip's roommate in London, Herbert Pocket, Jr., is also his best friend. Herbert nicknames Pip "Handel" because it is the name of a famous man (a compliment to Pip). Easygoing and not particularly bright, Herbert is nonetheless loyal and persevering. While they are students together, Herbert tries to help Pip figure out where all of their money is going. Later, he invites Pip to share in his sudden fortune, before finding out that Pip is the reason for it. Herbert is the receiver of Pip's only request of Miss Havisham for money. Tolerant and kind, even to the irritating alcoholic and gout-ridden Mr. Barley, Herbert falls in love with and marries the equally kind and patient daughter Clara

Barley. Also, he is trusted with helping Pip try to get Magwitch out of England. Herbert's most heroic hour is finding Orlick's letter that Pip had dropped and rushing off to save Pip at the moment that Orlick would have surely killed him. At last, Herbert provides a job for Pip when all of his fortune is gone. In the original ending, Herbert names his son "Pip."

Herbert Pocket Sr.

Unable to control his own "tumbling" family, Mr. Pocket is also an inadequate tutor to the students in his house. Pip reads and makes friends there but learns little from Mr. Pocket, Sr., that is useful. Not surprisingly, Pocket only teaches in order to keep Mrs. Pocket, who feels that she has married beneath her class for him, and their brood of children fed. Also, it is doubtful that he can do anything else for a living. However, no one seems to complain, for the Pockets' house is a place for young gentlemen to gather to meet one another if not to learn.

Provis

See Abel Magwitch

Uncle Pumblechook

Uncle Pumblechook is held in high esteem by Mrs. Joe because he is from a slightly higher social rank in the village than she is on the marsh. However, he is little more than a stereotype of a snob who takes every opportunity to poke fun at Pip when he is poor or to befriend Pip when Pip has money.

Spider

See Bentley Drummle

John Wemmick

A true friend to Pip in London, Wemmick is a dual personality. In London, where he is a chief clerk at Jaggers's law office, Wemmick is as coldly business-minded as his employer is. However, he takes a liking to Pip and invites him to his house, a miniature castle complete with a tiny moat, drawbridge, and a cannon that Wemmick fires each evening because it delights his deaf father. In his own odd household, Wemmick becomes close friends with Pip, who grows to value their relationship tremendously. Wemmick keeps one ear open at all times at the office to determine the best time to get Magwitch out of the country, and Wemmick sends word to Pip when he thinks the London underworld is unaware. Also, Wemmick thinks so much of Pip that Pip is the only wedding guest at the marriage of Wemmick and Miss Skiffins. Even so, whenever Pip sees Wemmick at the office, Wemmick is curt and businesslike again. It is Wemmick's practice to keep both of his worlds separate from each other.

Wemmick's Aged Parent

Another stereotype, the Aged Parent is old and deaf, and he responds to almost all conversation by smiling and yelling, "All right, John!" Combined with the odd house and landscape, the Aged Parent is relaxation and comic relief for Pip, who enjoys visiting Wemmick's place as a world apart from the threats of London.

Mr. Wopsle

After accompanying Pip and Joe across the marsh the night the police first catch the escaped convicts, Wopsle has seen both Magwitch and Compeyson. This is important when, after Mr. Wopsle has left the country for London to act in the theater, he recognizes the second convict, Compeyson, sitting behind Pip in the audience. With that knowledge, Pip knows that Compeyson is still alive and that he must get Magwitch out of the country as soon as possible before Compeyson finds him again.

Themes

Alienation and Loneliness

Beneath the Dickens' major theme of a great respect for wealth is an analysis of the fate of the outsider. At least four known orphans—Mrs. Joe, Magwitch, Estella, and Pip himself—have suffered loneliness, but each character reacts differently. Pip begins his story as a child standing in a gloomy cemetery at the grave site of his family, so pitifully alone that he can do no more than imagine his mother as the "wife of the above," which he can only interpret as directions to his mother's current address in heaven. Pip himself is often threatened with death by his sister and again by his convict, Magwitch. Even Orlick, the town lout, tries to kill an adult Pip. Joe Gargery is Pip's only friend on the marshes, and even after Pip is introduced to city life friends are few compared to the number of those who are coldly uncaring or dangerous. On the other hand, Estella's odd childhood, in the wrinkled hands of an old woman with a twisted mind, teaches her to reject all affection or friendships. Es-

Topics for Further Study

- Research the history and 1850-60 social climate of Australia as an English penal colony, where Magwitch had been living, when Queensland was becoming a separate colony from New South Wales.

- Investigate U.S. social conditions in 1842 when Dickens visited the United States, and compare this to conditions seen in 1868 when he returned to America on a reading tour. Keep in mind Dickens' themes of class distinction and real life versus expectation of changes he would have been likely to see in the American people. Consider the Gold Rush; the Emancipation Proclamation; John Brown's 1859 raid on Harper's Ferry, Virginia; the 1857 Dred Scott Decision; etc.

- Investigate child labor in England before the 1875-80 movement to legally limit work-hours and to improve dangerous factory conditions. Dickens' arousal of public sentiment against industry's inhuman treatment of minors and disenfranchised citizens in his novels contributed to this reform.

tella plays with Pip like a cat toys with a mouse, certainly not like an equal or playmate, for that is not Miss Havisham's intention. Likewise, as Magwitch confesses to Pip, his childhood on the streets of London was such a nightmare that he cannot even remember how he once learned his own name, and it is no wonder he has had to turn to a life of crime. Mrs. Joe is another character who is antisocial. She lives on the marshes among rough, working class men and has no friends but Joe and no female acquaintances whatever. Pip's guardian and Joe's wife, she is so rude, antagonistic, and violent that she drives away those who would otherwise love her. As Pip's sister, Mrs. Joe shares the same loss of their family, but her means of coping with loneliness is quite different from Pip's attempts to get along with people and to stay out of trouble. Indeed, Mrs. Joe causes most of the problems in

her life and everyone else's at the forge. Aside from these obvious loners, each struggling to find his or her place in the world, Jaggers also stands alone, an upholder of the law but to an inhuman degree. He never lets down his guard, as though he were likely to be sued if he relaxed, misspoke, or reacted at all with emotion. No matter how openly Pip offers friendship, Jaggers maintains a distant attitude and instead admires the wealthy but evil Bentley Drummle for knowing what he wants and getting it. While Pip has the greatest number of friends of these alienated characters, even he is strangely hesitant to leave London to rejoin Joe and Biddy or to accept Herbert Pocket's offer of a position in his firm. Only when Pip has exhausted his expectations and has no other direction to turn does he realize that he is quite lucky to have two good friends who love him for himself and can forget about his social status. By doing this, Pip is the one character who works his way out of alienation and loneliness into a socially active life that is enriched by love shared with friends. Although this hard-earned knowledge was not one of his original "expectations," Pip finds that this is far greater wealth than any benefactor's inheritance.

Identity: Search for Self

As a child, Pip is small for his age and quite weak, physically and temperamentally. An orphan living with his sister in near poverty, he dreams of great wealth. Meanwhile, finding ways to avoid abuse from his sister becomes his daily lesson. He submits to the insults of Mrs. Joe, Uncle Pumblechook, Mr. Wopsle, Estella and Miss Havisham's relatives. Pip is terrified of Miss Havisham when she first orders him to play a game as she watches him and he realizes that he is too miserable to play at anything. Later, he is anxious and delighted to escape that life and go to the city where he can establish a new identity as a gentleman in his own right. Indeed, from his first day in London he is addressed as "Mr. Pip" and treated well. He finds, however, that he has little to back up that esteem except money that he has not earned and only squanders on expensive clothes, decorations for his apartment, and a servant boy he calls "The Avenger." What is Pip avenging but the poverty to which he was born? Yet when Joe comes to London, Pip is ashamed of him, embarrassed that Joe now calls him "Sir" yet distressed by Joe's low-brow speech and country clothes. Pip is likewise mortified by Magwitch. Even after learning that the convict is responsible for Pip's rise in status and his great allowance, Pip does not want to be seen with the old man because Magwitch does not fit into Pip's new identity. That Magwitch has risked his life to come back to England to see Pip does not influence Pip's decision to get rid of Magwitch as soon as possible. Pip frequently returns to the village to visit Miss Havisham and Estella, and to enjoy a gentleman's treatment from the shopkeeper Trabb and Trabb's boy who once sneered at Pip. However, Pip neither returns to the humble forge to visit Joe nor sends any message to him. In time, Pip is ashamed of that and apologizes to both Magwitch and Joe. Also, he forgives Miss Havisham for her early cruelty with a kiss on her deathbed. But this cannot happen until he has endured greater suffering and pangs of conscience than he ever knew as a weakling boy on the marsh. Miss Havisham also rises above her reputation as a tight-fisted and heartless old woman by granting Pip's request for money to set up Herbert Pocket in a business, and by begging Pip's forgiveness before she dies. Once cruel, she ends by suffering from the realization that she has wasted her life on hatred and vengeance, yet it is too late for her to enjoy her change of heart. Pip adds this to his lessons on gaining respect and peace in his own life. Another good model comes from Wemmick, who adores his old father and shares care of the Aged Parent with Pip on at least one occasion when, ironically, Pip is avoiding contact with Magwitch. Nevertheless, Pip attends Magwitch in his last days as tenderly as Wemmick tends his own father and as lovingly as Joe nurses Pip back from death. When Pip finally returns to the marsh to propose marriage to Biddy and to thank Joe, he finds them already married. Pip asks Joe's forgiveness before he joins Herbert Pocket, Jr. to earn his way in the world and to repay Joe for covering some of his bills. Pip finally takes charge of his future and enjoys the love of his family and friends, realizing that they are his most precious wealth. Having been first a pauper, then a man of the leisure class, and finally a middle-class worker, Pip is finally certain of his place in the world by knowing true contentment and self-worth.

Victim and Victimization

In the endless struggle for power, the winners are the ruthless, thinks Jaggers. He has yet to learn that such power is not equal to the strength of being true to one's convictions, as Pip learns. Even though Jaggers deals with victims and victimizers daily, he is less informed than Pip is as a victim himself. Mrs. Joe Gargery prides herself on having brought up Pip "by hand," meaning with no help

but also with the idea that sparing the rod spoils the child. Yet Pip has not been spared numerous encounters with "The Tickler," his sister's cane. But if one who lives by the cane dies by it, so does Mrs. Joe suffer a violent beating before her death. Similarly, other victimizers become victims before their final chance to repent. Magwitch, once a thug on the streets of London, is stalked by his former accomplice. While his childhood in the underworld taught him to eat or be eaten, Magwitch risks all to return to England so that he can see for himself Pip's success and to settle his score with the villainous Compeyson. Also, Molly is "tamed" by Jaggers. A gypsy by birth, a criminal by necessity, and now bound to his household, she neither roams nor breaks the law anymore. But she is a powerless victim who never learns the fate of her daughter except that the child has been adopted into a wealthy household where she will receive the food and shelter Molly cannot provide. While Pip worries that Drummle will harm Estella, it is she who must endure a loveless marriage to outlive her cruel husband. A victim of Miss Havisham's icy character instead of enjoying the love of a mother, Estella is first the abused and then the abuser of both Pip and Miss Havisham. She then becomes the abused wife of the rotten Drummle. Yet, finally, at least in the original ending, Estella is a potentially better mother to her daughter than either her own mother or Miss Havisham ever were to her. Even in the revised ending, she breaks the abuse cycle by reconciling with Pip as his equal. And a lesser character, Trabb's boy, insults Pip and his first good suit of clothes. It is the only way that this poor fellow has of getting back at someone who has had better luck than he has had, for Trabb's boy was humiliated when his employer ordered him to be polite to the new young master Pip. In this way, Trabb's boy is both the victim of class distinction in his society and a victimizer of the upper class in the only way he can be. Through his unobserved and therefore unpunishable rudeness to Pip, he defends himself and strikes a blow at a social class that he has no hope of ever joining. Pip himself must realize that he has victimized people by treating them as lesser creatures. He realizes that he broke Joe's heart when he left the forge and again when he stayed out of contact for eleven years. He hurts Biddy by telling her that he could never love her, even though he returns intending to ask her to marry him after he has lost all of his money. Finding her already married to Joe is Pip's final lesson that power is not related to happiness and that one can only be a victim by permitting it. Trabb's boy is not Pip's only example. Jaggers is also feared by those who are not on his side. Yet Pip doubts that Jaggers has much to enjoy when he goes home at the end of the day. For all of these characters, the pleasure of power as victimizer is short-lived and/or unsatisfying.

Guilt and Innocence

With the law as a backdrop for much of the action, Pip finds that guilt and innocence are much more complex than he first thought. Having helped a convict to escape weighs heavily on his young mind, and he is sure that greater powers will catch up to punish him in time. When they do, they are much different than Pip first supposed, for he must first deal with his own conscience outside of the English courts. Underlying all of the characters' actions and outcomes is this theme: the guilty are punished by a power higher than any king's. Everyone who acts unjustly in the novel is made to either suffer and repent or to die without forgiveness. Likewise, those few who have nothing to regret are begged for mercy. While Pip is owed an apology by Mrs. Joe, her cruelty to him is avenged by her pitiful and helpless last days. The same could be said of Miss Havisham, who dies powerless, alone, and begging Pip's forgiveness. And while Pip owes Joe his life and feels great guilt for the times he wished not to know Joe, he has often abused their friendship. Pip pays for his carelessness by suffering and nearly dying, and by falling from great wealth back into poverty. His early innocence is the innocence to which he must return for forgiveness, a prodigal son who remembers the simple truth. Estella is too late to reconcile with Miss Havisham, but she finally treats Pip as an equal in both endings to the novel. Estella has also learned the truth about power. While the law is not kind to Magwitch, he accepts it. The fairness of that is left to the reader to decide since Magwitch has had few chances to be anything in life but a convict. That he is Pip's own convict is his redeeming quality, and in turn Magwitch has saved Pip's humility by revealing that a criminal, not a lady, is providing the money to fulfill Pip's grand expectations of joining the upper class. Magwitch has earned that money by the sweat of his brow, working as a common sheep rancher in Australia and not by any criminal activity. He could have easily spent the money on himself instead of Pip. These truths are Pip's salvation from a worthless, lazy, and arrogant life like Drummle. Less obvious are those who have never learned what Pip has found. Uncle Pumblechook and Miss Havisham's relatives will continue to curse others' luck and their own lack of fortune. Guilty of not listening to his heart, Jaggers will live out his days by guarding his words and emotions. While hopelessly self-involved characters such as Drummle and Compeyson are condemned to die without acknowledging their own guilt, others such as Magwitch, Molly, and Estella will be forgiven for misdeeds that are either justifiable or beyond their ability to avoid. Told through Pip's voice, the story shows that the power of forgiveness is great, for it is by mercy to others that one is forgiven. The law of the land that Pip once feared has little to do with real justice, for only by admitting his own guilt can he find happiness. As Pip concludes about himself by remembering Herbert Pocket, Jr., "I was one day enlightened by the reflection, that perhaps the inaptitude had never been in him at all, but had been in me." Or as Estella says to Pip upon meeting him again, "I am greatly changed. I wonder you know me."

Style

Point of View

The first-person narrator of Dickens' *Great Expectations* is an adult Pip who tells the story in his own voice and from his own memory. What is distinctive about that voice is that it can so intimately recall the many small details of a little boy's fear and misery, as well as the voices and dialects of others—from the rough country speech of Magwitch and Orlick to the deaf Aged Parent's loud repetitions or the mechanically predictable things Jaggers says. Yet other details seem to be forgotten. Pip tells almost nothing of his beatings from Mrs. Joe, but a great deal about his fear of them, using adult vocabulary and concepts in these reflections. The opening scene with little Pip in the cemetery recalls the tombstones as looking like "lozenges," soothing the throat of this mature narrator. This way, the adult Pip not only evaluates events as he remembers them but also adds a deeper insight than he would have had as a child. The story unfolds chronologically from Pip's earliest memories to his most recent experiences. And while some critics justify Dickens' revised ending, Pip's development is most believable for modern readers if he parts from Estella with the final realization that he could never have been happy with her and her man-hating legacy from Miss Havisham.

Bildungsroman

In *Great Expectations,* Pip must not only work out his problems but also sort out reality from his childhood dreams. Realistically, the only way that he can do this is by trial and error and learning from his mistakes. First comes his education, demonstrating that becoming a gentleman means more than having material wealth. Pip may read as many fine books as he can, but the most important lessons come not from them (he does not quote from them) but from his analysis of real people and events in his society. While Drummle is financially wealthier than Herbert Pocket or Startop, among Pip's London friends, Drummle has no redeeming qualities nor does he value his friends, which Pip learns is the most important thing in his own life. In his development, Pip discovers that Miss Havisham has not been his kindly benefactor as he had assumed. Even so, he is able to both save her life and help her to find a little left of her soul before she dies. By helping someone who only appears to be better off than he is, he finds honor in his own name, as humble as that may be. It is ironic that the criminal Magwitch had insisted, as a condition of Pip's allowance, that he keep his boyhood name "Pip" rather than "Phillip." He finds that the requirements of maturity are taking responsibility for one's actions, and this is what Pip must do by the end of the novel. He admits that he has at times been ashamed of his country life and friends. Pip also reveals that while he once enjoyed being treated royally by Uncle Pumblechook and Tragg in town, he sees now that this was a false honor. The true nobility is in his homecoming, which is similar to the biblical prodigal son's return. Pip confesses to Joe and Biddy that he has been too proud to appreciate their unfailing love until he finally comes back to them with his new knowledge.

Comic Relief

With so many serious things to think about and the ever-present dangers that appear, Pip is always glad to slip away to Wemmick's miniature castle, complete with a tiny moat and cannon, where all good things seem possible again in this stronghold against the evil of the outer world. One of the best features of the place is the stereotypical character of Wemmick's father, the laughable Aged Parent. Good-natured, deaf, dependent, and weakened by age, the old man is no threat to Pip or to anyone. Instead, he requires the protection of those who have power in the world, that is to say Wemmick and Pip. Wemmick's devotion to his old father seems to Pip to be a wonderful thing, especially in a society that constantly seeks out the weak to take advantage of them. However, the fragility of the situation makes Wemmick's house seem all the more magical. As close as it is to the unforgiving city life of London, it is a world apart—something about which Wemmick constantly cautions Pip. It is not to be mentioned to Jaggers or to anyone outside of this rare and delightfully protected environment. Pip is rewarded for honoring Wemmick's trust and friendship by being allowed to cook and watch over the Aged Parent, as well as being honored as Wemmick's only wedding guest who is not kin. Pip soon becomes as fiercely protective as Wemmick is of this place where evil dare not enter.

Setting

The distinctions between the city, the town, and the country are the most apparent shifts in Pip's story. Although all of them harbor dangerous elements, all of them also carry the forces of good. The difference is that the marsh folk are more obvious in their desires. Orlick is the example of a man without a soul, and Pip recognizes this from the beginning. It is no surprise when it is revealed that he was Mrs. Joe's savage attacker. The fact that he would also kill Pip points out Orlick's lack of distinction between those who deserve his vengeance and those who do not. He readily attacks anyone who gets in his way. However, in town Tragg's boy makes Pip the laughingstock of all who have more in life than he will ever have, thus showing humor and a knowledge of the world that Orlick does not have. Even so, Orlick believes he has power over others who may be better off than he is, which he tries to prove. By contrast, along London's sooty streets are those who know Jaggers. They both fear and respect him as someone with the education and social power to help them. He is as impersonal as the buildings around him, but if he cannot save their lives they are certain that they could not have been saved by anyone. That kind of blind trust is not found in the village—where even Tragg's boy dares to mock Pip—or on the marshes where brute strength may means survival. Of the three, the city is least likely to recognize individuality, which Pip indicates by noticing the overall dirtiness and decay of it as soon as he arrives there. A person may hide on the marshes or outside of the city, whereas the city has too many eyes to cover up anyone or any deed for long. Even Pip must escape to the suburbs (Wemmick's) for a time to avoid those eyes.

Compare
&
Contrast

- **Early 1800s:** Workhouses were set up so that the poor and those who owed money had an alternative to debtors' prison from which there was no escape without paying the debt; this was almost impossible if the debtor were unable to work.

  Today: The poor are being urged off of social welfare programs and into "workfare," low-paying jobs that teach skills but do not pay a living wage.

- **Early 1800s:** Child labor was used and abused by industry with long hours and unsafe conditions in the workplace, especially the mines. If children got sick, there was no medical care for them except from charities, such as London's Hospital for Sick Children begun in 1852 and supported by Charles Dickens.

  Today: Child labor laws are strictly enforced, and medical care for the poor is widely available since social reform laws were enacted in the United States in the mid-1960s.

- **Early 1800s:** Since most of England heated homes and industry with coal and peat, air pollution was visible and lung problems were widespread. Pip notices the grime and soot on everything in his first impression of the city and wonders how people could choose to live in such a dirty place.

  Today: Air pollution, although not always visible in PCBs and ozone-depleting chemicals, is now one of our greatest global concerns. Continual research explores new methods of cleaner heat, from solar power to natural gas.

- **Early 1800s:** Dickens supported and campaigned for public backing for the so-called "Ragged Schools" where poor children could receive some education. Despite their horrible conditions these schools were arguably better than complete neglect.

  Today: A modern belief in public education for all children owes much to such early reformers as Dickenssince that education has shown to improve society for all citizens.

Historical Context

Industrialization

Nineteenth century England had flourishing cities and emerging industries. Machines made it possible for those with money to invest to earn great profits, especially with an abundance of poor people who were willing to work long hours at hard or repetitive jobs for little pay. By contrast, the rural system included landlords, farmers, and common laborers who owned no land. In this rural system that had existed for centuries, those without land had no hope of bettering their lives: once in poverty, always in poverty. These hopeless poor moved to the city on the dream of making their own fortunes; it was usual for working class families to send young children off to the factories for twelve- to fourteen-hour shifts or longer. Child labor laws would not be enacted until the 1860s.

Meanwhile, children and women were ideal workers because they did not form labor unions, and were easily intimidated, beaten, or fired if they protested against an employer's mistreatment. School attendance was a luxury reserved for the children of parents who could afford to pay private tutors in addition to the family's loss of income from a child's labor. The first publicly funded elementary schools were not established until the 1870s, when the demand for skilled laborers increased. The idea of high schools did not receive England's public support until the turn of the century, after Dickens' death. Meanwhile, the labor-saving machines that were to make a few people's fortunes earned many others little more than bad health or early graves.

The new money caused new needs. Prior to the nineteenth century, banking had been left to businesses and was fairly informal, by reputation. Since there had been little money to exchange, except by a well-known few, there had been little need for that service. The Bank of England had been established in 1694, but it dealt mainly with government projects. Industrialization changed that, and banking houses became more numerous as a middle class emerged. New businesses needed to borrow money, and the rapid production of goods for a growing economy promised new wealth for both borrowers and lenders. That is how Pip found employment for his friend, Herbert Pocket, who later hired Pip.

Obviously, not all who turned to the city for fortune found it. There were workhouses and debtors' prisons for those who failed to achieve their dreams of advancement. Those shut out from that promise lived in misery and often turned to crime. Since money was made in the city, the rise in criminal activity appeared there. As the number of jobless residents increased, so did the number of smugglers, pickpockets, thieves, and swindlers. Those with enough money to escape the soot and dangers of London, began to build up the towns, as we see in Wemmick's choice of address. Only the outlying country folk stayed much the same as they had for centuries, and we see Pip's travel is either by stagecoach or on foot. That was normal until the 1860s when the railroad finally connected the country to the city and the past to the new age of the machine.

Critical Overview

Charles Dickens was often faulted by his early critics for writing with more melodrama or realism than suited his readers' tastes. In 1861, E. S. Dallas suggested that this was part of Dickens' charm: "Faults there are in abundance, but who is going to find fault when the very essence of the fun is to commit faults?" Yet Lady Carlisle once delicately commented, "I know there are such unfortunate beings as pickpockets and streetwalkers ... but I own I do not much wish to hear what they say to one another." Likewise, in 1862 Mrs. Margaret Oliphant found the novel "feeble, fatigued, and colorless," yet defended Miss Havisham as "a very harmless and rather amiable old woman," suggesting that among Dickens' readers were the Miss Havishams of that era. At the same time, other early critics viewed this book as a happy change of pace from Dickens' so-called "Dark Period" of writing due to the novel. According to John Moore Capes

Illustration by Frederic W. Pailthorpe, from Charles Dickens' Great Expectations.

and J.E.E.D. Acton's 1862 review, "We should be puzzled to name Mr. Dickens' equal in the perception of the purely farcical, ludicrous, and preposterously funny."

As Humphrey House later reflected, "The whole [Victorian] class drift was upwards and there was no reason to suppose that it would ever stop being so," meaning that in any age or economy people believe in whatever they hope for themselves. Other modern critics, however, tend to look on the novel as an example of Dickens' "brilliant study of guilt." In any case, it is story-telling at its best. As Angus Calder comments in his introduction to the 1965 Penguin Books edition, "The densely detailed surroundings, the strange life of these creatures, make the dialogue tense and convincing." It is a hard book to put down because we believe in Pip and want to see him win out in the end.

Yet even twentieth-century critics disagree with each other. While E. M. Forster faults Dickens for creating "two-dimensional" characters, George Orwell praises him by pointing out that "Dickens' imagination overwhelms everything, like a weed." Dorothy Van Ghent notes Dickens' accuracy in describing "the complex inner life which we know men and women have." And Angus Calder notices that "Pip does not merely see what has been there all the time; in the cases of Miss Havisham and Magwitch, he actively helps them to become better people near the end of their lives." This is the theme and ethic of redemption, but not only for Pip. As Calder concludes, "The book begins with a beast-like man so hungry that he thinks of eating a little boy ..., haunted, like the rest of Dickens' fiction, by jails and images of prisons.... [while] what makes men grow is fellowship." Connecting and interacting with one another is Dickens' timeless purpose for telling this story with all of its humorous twists and heart-wrenching turns. Considering all of the new discussion about the novel each year, Dickens seems to continue to achieve his purpose—and amazingly well. By 1987, Bert G. Hornback had claimed the existence of "more than two hundred adaptations of his [Dickens'] novels for the stage, and more than fifty versions produced as films for television."

Criticism

Arnold A. Markley

In the following essay, Markley, an assistant professor of English at Pennsylvania State University, explains how the fact that Dickens' novel was originally published serially had a profound effect on the creation of the story's plot and characters. Markley also discusses the novel as representative of Dickens' social concerns, which are a common feature in his novels.

In the Victorian era, reading fiction was an extremely favorite pastime, and new novels were commonly published in serial format in periodicals. Many writers such as Charles Dickens became quite popular and developed huge followings that dutifully bought the periodicals in which they were published month after month, hooked by the entertaining and suspenseful stories. Dickens began *Great Expectations* in the fall of 1860, publishing it in weekly installments that began in December of that year in his popular periodical *All the Year Round*. Many of Dickens' earlier novels had been published serially as well, but usually in twenty installments in a periodical issued only once a month. Because a weekly serial was necessarily shorter than one that came out only once a month, the installments of *Great Expectations* needed to be much more concise, a publishing requirement that had a great effect on the ultimate structure of the novel, which is indeed more concise than many of Dickens' earlier novels.

The fact that Victorian novels were published in installments had a great effect on the characteristics and style of those novels. For example, each installment characteristically ended with a "cliffhanger" much like a soap opera on television; that is, a suspenseful ending designed to tease the reader into buying the next issue in order to find out what happens to the characters. Novelists also frequently created their characters with certain "character tags," peculiar and often comic aspects of their physical appearances or way of talking in order to help readers remember each character from month to month. This was especially important for the minor characters. Finally, such novels characteristically included fantastic and extremely complex plots, all of the many strands of which were miraculously tied together in the final installments, as is the case with Pip's gradual discovery not only of the identity of his benefactor, but also of Estella's real parents. In *Great Expectations,* all of the major characters have been introduced by the end of "The First Stage of Pip's Expectations," and all of the major strands of the plot have begun; Dickens continues to manipulate them throughout the next two thirds of the novel before tying them all together at the end.

The serial format of the novel also allowed for the peculiar situation of the ending of *Great Expectations*. In Dickens' original ending, Pip meets Estella in London many years after the events in the main part of the narrative, and hears of her troubles with Bentley Drummle and of her plans to marry again. The two characters part, and there is no suggestion that they will ever marry, or even that they will ever meet again. But when Dickens' friend and fellow author Edward Bulwer-Lytton read the manuscript for this ending, he convinced Dickens to give the novel a happier ending, believing that the reading public would be much more satisfied if he at least hinted that Pip and Estella will be free to marry at the end of the story.

In the case of installments in weekly periodicals as opposed to monthly ones, many publishers and readers felt that autobiographical stories were more appropriate for publication. Autobiographical stories, which were reputedly "true," generally managed to grip the reader emotionally much more quickly than a fictional story. Some scholars today, such as Janice Carlisle, believe that this may have contributed to Dickens' decision to write *Great Expectations* as if it were an autobiography, with a first person narrator, Pip, telling the story of his life. One of the most consistently praised aspects of the novel, and one of the things that makes it such an extraordinary achievement, is Dickens' masterful depiction of Pip's personality. The entire story is presented to us through this main character's eyes, which allows the reader a great deal of insight into Pip's psychology. Because of this, readers through the years have tended to see Pip as a much more successful and more realistic characterization than many others of Dickens' major characters. Some scholars have attributed the success of Pip as a character to the relationship of many of the situations and events in the novel to Dickens' own life. Dickens himself came from a poor background, and he was forced to work in a shoe blacking company as a child. And, like Pip, he managed to improve his own "expectations" considerably with his phenomenal success years later as a novelist.

The fact that Dickens so effectively invites his readers into the mind of his narrator and main character, Pip, also gives great impact to the development of the novel's themes. The main action of the novel involves Pip's expectations to improve his lot in life, and the three "stages" of his transformation from a poor boy living in a small town into a gentleman successful in the world of Victorian commerce. Initially believing his benefactor to be the wealthy Miss Havisham, Pip becomes a snob, and gradually becomes more and more embarrassed by his past, by his home, and particularly by his loyal and true friend, the humble blacksmith Joe. Upon learning the true identity of his benefactor, however, Pip's mistaken assumptions and his future expectations are dashed when he is forced to confront the fact that the man who has turned him into a gentleman is none other than an uneducated and uncouth criminal. The reader who becomes caught up in Pip's outlook, sharing his assumptions with him, experiences, like Pip, a surprise and an important lesson when those assumptions are shattered.

The lesson that Pip learns comes in his gradually growing to see the goodness and humanity of Magwitch, truly a noble soul despite his past involvement in crime. Such a realization allows Pip, and the reader, to see the wrongness of a class structure that implies that wealth and a high station in life are equal to high moral virtue. After all, Magwitch is portrayed as having a gentle and noble spirit, while the more suave and gentlemanly Compeyson is a vicious and unfeeling criminal. Miss Havisham, too, who represents a wealthier class than that of Pip's family, is not his benefactor, but knowingly allows Pip to believe that she is as she involves him in her own schemes. Moreover, in

What Do I Read Next?

- Dickens' *Oliver Twist* is the story of an orphan who overcomes his humble beginnings to prove himself worthy of the virtuous Nancy's love for him, and to overcome all of his notorious enemies.

- William Thackeray's *Vanity Fair* is from the same period as Dickens' *Great Expectations.* Like it, the novel makes statements against social class distinction and snobbery. However, Thackeray's hero is a girl who inherits money and work to win the credibility and love of her readers.

- Likewise, Wilkie Collins' *The Woman in White* has the theme of virtue overcoming adversity. Laura endures an unhappy marriage and the loss of her wealth to end by marrying her true love and giving birth to their son. Although Dickensian elements of plot twists and social themes occur, his humor may seem to be missing.

looking back over the story line, the reader sees at the end that it was Pip's simple act of stealing food as a small boy to help the escaped Magwitch that led to his "great expectations," and not his appeal to Miss Havisham as a future mate for Estella, as he had convinced himself throughout the early part of the novel. Through the stages of his personal and psychological development, Pip experiences a change of heart, and learns the value of a true friend, finally seeing Joe and Biddy, the humble friends of his youth, as the loyal friends who have always stood by him despite his aspirations to rise above them in class.

By charting Pip's gradual change throughout the novel, Dickens manages to illustrate an important aspect of the socio-economic context of his times. As the Industrial Revolution continued to change the nature of commerce in England and beyond throughout the nineteenth century, a middle class gradually emerged where before there had been only the aristocrats who were born wealthy, and the lower classes. In many ways Pip represents the kind of middle class "gentleman" that was quite common during this time; that is, a gentleman who had established himself in a successful business and a comfortable lifestyle despite the fact that he had been born into poorer circumstances. If he had been born a century earlier, Pip would not have so easily found the means to rise out of his social station and enter a higher one through Magwitch's and his own success in business ventures.

This kind of social commentary is common in Dickens' works. Often he took the opportunity to criticize aspects of contemporary British culture that troubled him, like Victorian standards of education, the legal system, or crime and British prisons, which indeed he takes the opportunity to examine even in *Great Expectations* when Pip visits the notorious Newgate Prison in London. Before *Great Expectations*, many readers had begun to feel that the novels that Dickens wrote in the 1850s, such as *Bleak House* and *Hard Times*, had become too dark, gloomy, and depressing, and they missed the humor and the appealing characterizations of such popular earlier novels as *Oliver Twist, The Old Curiosity Shop*, and *David Copperfield*. Such readers were much pleased by *Great Expectations*, because, despite Dickens' occasional lapses into social criticism, they found such figures as the self-important Uncle Pumblechook, the would-be actor Mr. Wopsle, and the comic family of the Pockets worthy of comparison with the humorous caricatures that made the earlier novels so popular.

In addition to the character of Pip, *Great Expectations* offers many characters that add a rich texture to any interpretation of the novel. Some critics have found an unusual opportunity for understanding the place of women in Victorian culture and their role in Victorian fiction by studying the women in this novel: the kind Biddy, who is able to guess the identity of Mrs. Joe's attacker, and who sees more clearly than anyone the painful effects of Pip's selfish aspirations, and Molly, the mysterious woman who had been unwilling to suffer the degradation of her husband Magwitch's infidelity without a fight. Of particular interest is the peculiar and memorable case of Miss Havisham and her adopted daughter Estella. Miss Havisham embodies the wrath of a woman who has been cheated and abandoned by a reputed lover, and as a result she is a woman who has refused to accept the passage of time. The clocks in her house were stopped forever when she learned of her lover's duplicity, and the shoe she was in the process of putting on when she heard the news remains off of her foot. Her rotting wedding dress and cake represent the spoiled hopes that are turned into hatred as she plots her revenge by raising a heartless child to break the hearts of men. Far from the generous benefactor she appears to be to Pip, she lures him into her plans to make Estella into a cold and condescending young lady. And the outcome of Miss Havisham's plans offer the reader a lesson as well; she comes to find that she herself can expect no affection from a child she has raised without affection, and the vindictive life that she raised Estella to live becomes a sham and a tragedy when Estella enters a bad marriage with the abusive Bentley Drummle.

Other characters, such as the gentle blacksmith Joe, the lawyer Jaggers with his scores of grateful clients, and Jaggers' clerk Wemmick also contribute to the indelible impression of *Great Expectations* on the reader. Wemmick, particularly, is one of Dickens' most idiosyncratic and endearing characters, with his clearly delineated private side in which he serves Jaggers with the utmost professional discretion, and his diametrically opposed personal side in which he takes care of his stone deaf father, "the Aged P," in their impenetrable suburban cottage built to resemble a castle complete with cannon, moat and drawbridge. It is characters like Wemmick, and Joe, and Miss Havisham, in addition to the remarkably realistic characterization of Pip, that make *Great Expectations* one of Dickens' greatest works, and indeed one of the finest achievements of the Victorian novel. Like the Victorian readers who hurried to buy the latest issue of the magazine to read the latest in Pip's adventures, readers through the years have continued to find the experience of reading *Great Expectations* to be compelling and endlessly entertaining.

Source: Arnold A. Markley, in an essay for *Novels for Students,* Gale, 1998.

Lucille P. Shores

In the excerpt below, Shores argues that the character of Estella, often regarded as cold and cruel, acts with genuine affection and honesty in her relationship with Pip.

A close inspection of the speeches and gestures which Dickens gives to Estella can easily give credit to the notion that she has a great deal of respect and affection for Pip, but Dickens never actually has Pip put this forth as a revelation, simply because Pip continues to remain ignorant of it. He does not even give the retrospective "if-I-knew-then-what-I-know-now" analysis of this situation that he does in the cases of Joe and Magwitch. We are probably not accustomed to this much subtlety in Dickens; we are used to having him spell out his meanings for us very clearly. But the possibility of Estella's sincere affection for Pip should not be dismissed simply because Dickens does not give it the heavy underlining he usually gives; for this is an area of emotion in which Dickens the man had a customary reticence.

Although Estella has been trained by Miss Havisham to be instinctively proud and insulting, it can be seen that as a woman she is consistently gentle with Pip—in her own way, of course. She has a deep-rooted dislike of all the Pockets, from her awareness of their malicious envy of her, and Pip early wins her favor by being her champion against them. Even as a child, she rewards him with a kiss when he bests Herbert Pocket in their senseless (but very believable) fisticuffs. And as an adult, she states clearly and unequivocally that the Pockets' ill-opinion of him only strengthens her favorable opinion of Pip and that she derives bitter pleasure from the fact that he is above their petty meannesses. Even at the height of his unjustified snobbishness, Pip never comes close to the pretentiousness, intolerance, and avariciousness of the Pocket clan (Herbert and Matthew of course excepted). It is Pip's enduring decency and essential simplicity that cause Estella to regard him, albeit rather grudgingly at times, as her hero; he is undoubtedly a refreshing contrast to all she has been used to.

But besides this rather abstract respect which Estella has for Pip, we can also infer that she is attracted to him as a man. The scene where Pip and Estella first meet as adults is handled with a restraint characteristic of Victorian fiction in general and Dickens in particular, but nevertheless it can give a remarkably clear impression, if attention is paid to it.

> "Is *he* changed?" Miss Havisham asked her.
>
> "Very much," said Estella, looking at me.
>
> "Less coarse and common?" said Miss Havisham, playing with Estella's hair.
>
> Estella laughed, and looked at the shoe in her hand, and laughed again, and looked at me, and put the shoe down. She treated me as a boy still, but she lured me on.

The shoe, of course, is a symbolic shoe (reminding us of Miss Havisham's bridal slippers), but it is also a very right detail in this scene. Dickens has intuitively been able to capture here the exact behavior of a young woman who is sexually attracted to a man and embarrassed by her feelings. Estella has long schooled herself in "perfect com-

posure," but she is unable to conceal completely her physical awareness; Pip takes this reaction, in a quite typically male way, as an enticement. It is her unexpected womanliness that causes him to retreat to boyishness.

Any post-Freudian reader should be able to discern that Estella's notorious pride is only a defense against her feelings of inadequacy. Even though she is not aware that she is in fact the daughter of such "low" characters as Magwitch and Molly, she knows all too well that she is only Miss Havisham's adopted daughter and that she has quite arbitrarily been placed in a position of gentility. It is probably this very defensiveness about the precariousness of her own genteel situation that makes her as a child chide Pip for his coarseness and commonness. She has been continually beset by Miss Havisham's relatives, who resent her as the heiress of fortunes that could be theirs; she has been made to feel like an usurper. And when the artificiality of her upbringing becomes contrasted with the naturalness of Pip's, she seems to become all the more resentful of this life that she has had forced on her without her consent. As a woman, she knows that Miss Havisham has warped her personality beyond repair, and she is ashamed of what she has become. But with an admirable matter-of-factness she accepts her own limitations, and quite unselfishly she refuses to burden Pip with them. Again and again she sincerely warns him away from her; there is nothing coy about her manner of doing so.

> "Oh! I have a heart to be stabbed in or shot in, I have no doubt," said Estella, "and, of course, if it ceased to beat I should cease to be. But you know what I mean. I have no softness there, no—sympathy—sentiment—nonsense."

She asserts that she cannot love, and in the conventional sense she is probably right. Just as with Pip, conventional notions do not apply to her. Pip's love is a strongly emotional and uncontrollable sensation; he knows it must appear absurd to other people, but he cannot help it. But Pip has repeatedly shown himself to be first a boy and then a young man given to extravagance and hyperbole. It is natural for him to behave as he does—for him to have an exaggerated love and to display it in an exaggerated way. It is equally natural for Estella, who from her babyhood on has had all her personality channeled into artificial restraints, to behave in the muted, subdued, tightly controlled way she does. She has been taught by Miss Havisham not to love, but then to Miss Havisham real love consists of "blind devotion, unquestioning self-humiliation, utter submission, trust and belief against yourself and against the whole world, giving up your whole heart and soul to the smiter." It is small wonder that Estella is not able to recognize her feeling for Pip as love.

Estella is only instinctively aware that Pip is different from all other people and that he somehow deserves a different and better treatment. Her rejection of Pip, which is almost universally condemned by critics as showing her pitilessness, is actually a very laudable sort of nobility and altruism. She knows that she cannot make Pip happy (Bernard Shaw is quite right in saying that Estella's character is not conducive to providing connubial happiness), and she has too much affection for him to link her unhappy life with his. When Pip reproaches her for flinging herself away on a brute like Bentley Drummle, her reply is incisive and illuminating.

> "On whom should I fling myself away?" she retorted with a smile. "Should I fling myself away upon the man who would the soonest feel (if people do feel such things) that I took nothing to him? There! It is done. I shall do well enough, and so will my husband. As to leading me into what you call this fatal step, Miss Havisham would have had me wait, and not marry yet; but I am tired of the life I have led, which has had very few charms for me, and I am willing enough to change it. Say no more. We shall never understand each other."

> "Such a mean brute, such a stupid brute!" I urged in despair.

> "Don't be afraid of my being a blessing to him," said Estella; "I shall not be that. Come! Here is my hand. Do we part on this, you visionary boy—or man?"

Several things should become obvious upon inspection of this passage. One is that Estella is certainly not marrying Drummle for his money, as most critics blithely state in their summaries of the novel's plot. She is also not acting mechanically as an instrument of Miss Havisham; she is, in fact, defying Miss Havisham and seeking escape from the life her foster mother has subjected her to. But more importantly, she is surely marrying Drummle because she feels herself to be unworthy of Pip; she has chosen Drummle precisely because he has nothing to recommend him and she feels he is the only sort of husband to whom she can do no harm. And again her attraction to Pip should be clear just in a phrase like "you visionary boy—or man"; this is a charmingly revealing kind of thing that a woman would say to a man whose quixoticism she regards with affectionate humor.

Up to the very end, Dickens has her maintain this reserve with Pip—and it is a reserve rather than an actual coldness. She has been willing through all these years not to see Pip, and even when they meet again she has not sought him out; she gave him up thoroughly, even though the passing of years has evidently made it harder rather than easier for her to forget him. The last dialogue she is given to say is a declaration that even though now they have forgiven each other old wrongs and agreed to be friends, they must continue apart. Even now, she does not trust herself with Pip's happiness.

But of course the point is that Pip does not really want to be happy—again, in the conventional sense. He has said repeatedly that he is not happy with Estella, but even less happy without her. And the fact that all these people who condemn the "happy ending" miss is that it is not happy at all. Pip and Estella come together quite by accident; neither has determined to redeem his life by seeking out the other. Each has been shattered by many disillusioning and trying experiences. And Dickens leaves the actual conditions of their reunion quite ambiguous. "I saw no shadow of another parting from her." There is no reason, except maudlin sentimentality, to suppose that this means that they got married and lived happily ever after. It should simply mean that Pip no longer feels threatened by a separation from her, in his old desperate way. At any rate, it should be clear that if Pip and Estella do at last come together, it is only because now finally they can understand each other (as Estella supposed they never could) and admit their mutual need, which has grown more subtle but not less urgent with age.

It is often dismissed as mere sloppiness on Dickens' part that he did not go back and revise Pip's early observations of Estella if, in fact, eventually he is to win and marry her, as the new ending seems to suggest. But Dickens was almost never a sloppy writer, and certainly not in *Great Expectations.* An author who would be careful enough to change a preposition in Biddy's letter would certainly not let something as crucial as a major inconsistency of tone slip by him. If he left the strain of melancholy in Pip's retrospective remarks about Estella, it was surely because he felt that this tone continued to be appropriate, even with the revised ending. Pip's and Estella's meeting is not a joyous reunion and a promise that now everything will be all right; it is the somber and solemn merger of two people who realize resignedly that each is the other's fate.

The years and her harsh experiences have only rendered Estella more humble in her regard for Pip.

Because now she has had ample time to think about her feelings for him and to realize consciously what she only sensed instinctively before: that he has always been for her, in his own bumbling way, a hero. A woman who can speak with quiet restraint of "the remembrance of what I had thrown away when I was quite ignorant of its worth" shows no traces of Edwin Charles's wilful girl who finally triumphs by bringing Pip to her feet.

The name Estella of course means "star," and much has been made of the symbolism of Estella both as a star and as a jewel. One of Pip's first remarks about Estella is that "her light came along the dark passage like a star." There are occasions when Pip regards the stars as being cold and distant and perhaps even hostile, and they provide a contrast to the heat and brightness of the light of Joe's forge. But even though a star may seem cold and distant, it is always accepted as a reliable beacon and guide; and Estella, for all her reserve, is never false to Pip—never, in fact, anything but perfectly candid and also sound in her assessments of human nature. She says to Pip in the end, "I have been bent and broken, but—I hope—into a better shape." She has passed through the homely blacksmith's fire, just as Pip has, and she no longer possesses the same sort of lofty removal from things as she had in her reflected, starry light.

This is not a fairy-tale sort of happiness that Dickens is presenting us with. It is the very real sort of compromise that men and women make to each other, when life inexplicably but inevitably thrusts them together. Bulwer Lytton was probably reacting with basic human sympathy when he insisted that Pip and Estella should be reunited; there is nothing forced or contrived about such a circumstance. Dickens created in Estella a character who could not be denied her rights as an individual. If we react to what Dickens actually shows us of Estella's character, then we cannot make facile judgments of her as a heartless she-monster who will make Pip's life wretched and whose union with him is therefore inappropriate. Dickens has succeeded, almost in spite of himself, in portraying an honest and attractive woman who deserves the hero Pip proves himself to be.

Source: Lucille P. Shores, "The Character of Estella in *Great Expectations*," in *Massachusetts Studies in English*, Fall, 1972, pp. 91-99.

Robert Barnard

In the following excerpt, Barnard describes Dickens' symbolic use of prison and animal imagery to suggest the transference of guilt from one character to another.

It becomes clear through a variety of subtle means in the early chapters of *Great Expectations* that the young Pip soaks up guilt like a sponge. From the moment he knows he has to rob the larder, everything around him takes on an accusatory or revengeful air. The very coals in the household fire seem to him "avenging," he dreams of pirates who summon him to be hanged, the boards on the staircase cry "Stop thief," the cattle (especially one with a clerical air) accuse him, and even the gates and dykes run at him as if they were pursuers. The whole picture of a guilty and terrified childish mind is remarkably vivid, so much so that the reader is never tempted to stop and ask himself whether the depravity Pip feels in himself is commensurate with the offense he has committed. He has deprived himself of a piece of bread and butter, and stolen random items of food from the family larder-no very enormous sins in the mind of the average child. Even granting the distorted vision of a terrified boy, it would seem that Pip is exaggerating his crime.

But of course the guilt he feels on the score of this minor theft is only part of a larger guilt—congenital, as it were, since it seems to have been generally regarded as criminally stupid in him to allow himself to be born at all—fostered in him by his sister, his sister's friends, and his surroundings. To Mrs. Joe he is not just a burden; he is a delinquent, to be treated as such. As a suitable topic for conversation during that most appallingly unmerry Christmas dinner which follows the second meeting with the convict, she regales the company with a catalogue of "all the illnesses I had been guilty of, and all the acts of sleeplessness I had committed, and all the high places I had tumbled from, and all the low places I had tumbled into, and all the injuries I had done myself, and all the times she had wished me in my grave, and I had contumaciously refused to go there." When, after the convict-hunt, he is sleepy, she removes him as "a slumbrous offence to the company's eyesight." The very food she allows him is given "a mortifying and penitential character." The rest of the company follows suit. It is Pip's misfortune, both in childhood and in adulthood, to be brought into contact with overbearing characters whose most usual method of conducting a conversation is inquisitorial. His position vis-à-vis Pumblechook and Jaggers is at best that of a slippery witness, at worst that of a criminal in the dock. Whether it is Pumblechook sticking the point of the conversation into him as if he were "an unfortunate little bull in a Spanish arena," or Jaggers, gnawing his forefinger and throwing it at him, Pip's position is as abject as that of any nineteenth-century delinquent, before the court on a trivial but capital charge.

The notion that Pip's fallen condition requires constant repentance and moral "touching up" is metaphorically expressed through the clothes he is forced into. They, like his diet, are of a "penitential" character:

> As to me, I think my sister must have had some general idea that I was a young offender whom an Accoucheur Policeman had taken up (on my birthday) and delivered over to her, to be dealt with according to the outraged majesty of the law. I was always treated as though I had insisted on being born in opposition to the dictates of reason, religion, and morality, and against the dissuading arguments of my best friends. Even when I was taken to have a new suit of clothes, the tailor had orders to make them like a kind of Reformatory, and on no account to let me have the free use of my limbs.

The intensive concentration on Pip's feelings of guilt and delinquency culminate in the extraordinary suggestion that he himself is in some way responsible for the attack on his sister. Orlick, the real attacker, puts it bluntly during the scene in the sluice-house by the lime kiln: "It was you as did for your shrew sister." The more conventional Pip of those days replies: "It was you, villain." The younger Pip would have had a more ambiguous reaction. The attack occurs after two scenes in which the imaginary guilt is very obviously laid on Pip's shoulders. First we have the scene where he is "bound" to Joe, and treated as a criminal by court, family, and by-standers alike—especially by Pumblechook, who held him "as if we had looked in on our way to the scaffold." Then the reading of *George Barnwell* fixes on him, in his own eyes as well as Wopsle's and Pumblechook's, the role of ungrateful and murderous apprentice. The feeling that he had "had some hand in the attack upon my sister" is intensified when the weapon is found to be the convict's leg-iron, the symbol of Pip's "criminal" connection with the convict.

In all these ways, some with comic overtones, some completely serious, a degree of uncertainty is given to the question of guilt and innocence in this novel. With the exception of Joe, who is still in a paradisaic state of grace and innocence, the guilt of one character tinges the other characters, just as the moral regeneration of one character tinges the others. Thus all the characters participate in the fallen state of the others, and participate in their redemption too. Sin and crime are complex, both in their causes and in their consequences. In this novel the involved coincidences and connections, the gradual revelation of past wrongs which provide guilty links between disparate characters—in short the creaky machinery of a Dickens novel, so clumsily handled in *Little Dorrit,* for example—have an artistic purpose which totally justifies them. Magwitch, Miss Havisham, Pip, and Estella are connected by chains of guilt and corruption, and their roles as betrayers and betrayed, corruptors and corrupted, are deliberately allowed to become ambiguous. Miss Havisham, betrayed by Magwitch's associate, herself corrupts both Pip and Estella; Pip's childish pity for the convict starts a process of regeneration in him which itself contributes materially to the process of corruption in Pip. Guilt is infectious: Jaggers compulsively washes it off with scented soap; Pip feels contaminated by Newgate; when Magwitch is spied on after his return, it isPip who gets the "haunting idea" of being watched, and who feels that, if the convict is caught, he, Pip, will in some way be his murderer. In this matter of guilt and crime the characters are members one of another.

This fact, of course, explains why Newgate Prison has so often been felt by readers to have an importance in the novel quite incommensurate with the space devoted to it. Corruption spreads outwards from there, and almost all the major characters are affected by that corruption. In addition, a real prison is necessary to reinforce the many "images" of prison in the novel. Prison is no mere "overspill" theme from Dickens' previous novels; it is an inevitable concomitant of the main theme. Miss Havisham's crazy self-immolation is no mere repetition with variations of Mrs. Clennam's grim voluntary imprisonment in *Little Dorrit;* it is a still more powerful symbol of man's propensity to cherish his emotional wounds, distort them to mere theatricality, use them as an excuse to pervert others. In all the scenes involving Satis House, strong emphasis is placed on keys, bars, chains, and blocked windows. And throughout the novel the windows of rooms Pip is in give no view of the world outside: they are shuttered, dirty, damp, "patched like a broken head." One comes down "like a guillotine" and nearly beheads him as he tries to look through. Everywhere he goes Pip feels shut in, "caged and threatened" as he describes himself in the little causeway inn on the Thames. Innocence provides no escape from the prisons; indeed, the only way Wemmick can keep his innocence free from the contamination of Newgate is by shutting himself off from the world in his miniature castle at Walworth. Prisons, then, permeate the book, though not quite so completely as in *Little Dorrit.*

And, unlike *Little Dorrit,* the novel is also saturated with other aspects of punishment and legal repression, used symbolically. For example, Pip's "guilty" connection with the convict leads to his metaphorically bearing his leg-iron as well. The bread and butter he secretes becomes a "load on my leg," and that "made me think … of the man with the load on *his* leg." The cold morning earth rivets itself to the young Pip's feet "as iron was riveted to the leg of the man." The convict, and his messenger at the Jolly Bargemen who "rubs his leg," never appear but that we are reminded again of the iron and the associations it has for Pip.

Chains, too, pervade the novel: on a literal level, obviously enough, on the door of Satis House and attached to Jaggers' watch, sign of his mastery of the underworld characters he deals with. The symbolic use is more interesting. In a Dickens novel we usually have a symbol of "destiny," the complex interweaving of people, events, and past actions which provides the plot of the novel and makes the characters what they are. Often this symbol is quite a conventional one: in *Little Dorrit* it is a road; in this novel we have the river and the ships on it, which are several times identified with Miss Havisham and Pip's delusions concerning his expectations from her. But Pip's real destiny is connected with a chain:

> Think for a moment of the long chain of iron or gold, of thorns or flowers, that would never have bound you, but for the formation of the first link on one memorable day.

The significance of the symbol becomes more explicit when Magwitch returns. Now he is no longer a man, to be pitied, but an object: "what I was chained to." When Pip comes to contemplate the realities of his situation, as opposed to the rosy vision of a calm sea and prosperous voyage with which he had been deluding himself, he realizes that Magwitch has been "loading me with his wretched gold and silver chains."

Similarly the "traps" which have sealed Magwitch's destiny catch Pip as well. The traps are set both by the law and Compeyson. Early in the novel the convicts are described as game "trapped in a circle"; Compeyson's criminal activities involve the entrapping of others: "All sorts of traps as Compeyson could set with his hand and keep his legs out of … was Compeyson's business." Magwitch sees these traps as an occupational hazard of his kind: "I'm an old bird now, as had dared all man-

ner of traps since he was fledged." Pip is less adept at keeping out of them; indeed, he makes his own. Jaggers is compared to a man who sets a trap— "Suddenly—click—you're caught"—and Pip is a victim of his legalistic equivocations. The sluice-house is described as a trap, which indeed it is, set by Orlick. But his delusions concerning Estella are at least partly of his own construction: "You made your own snares," says Miss Havisham.

Perhaps the most subtle way Dickens suggests the transference of guilt from one character to another is by his use of the image of the dog. In chapter iii, while Pip, with the pity for his desolation which is to have such momentous consequences, is watching the convict eating the food he has brought him, a comparison occurs to his mind which is to reverberate through the novel:

> I had often watched a large dog of ours eating his food; and I now noticed a decided similarity betwen the dog's way of eating, and the man's. The man took strong sharp sudden bites, just like the dog. He swallowed, or rather snapped up, every mouthful, too soon and too fast; and he looked sideways here and there while he ate, as if he thought there was danger in every direction of somebody's coming to take the pie away. He was altogether too unsettled in his mind over it, to appreciate it comfortably, I thought, or to have anybody to dine with him, without making a chop with his jaws at the visitor. In all of which particulars he was very like the dog.

It is a comparison which has been hinted at on the convict's first appearance in the churchyard— "a man … who limped and shivered, and glared and growled"—and which is maintained throughout the early chapters in which he appears. The soldiers growl at the captured pair "as if to dogs," as Pip is to remember when he travels home from London in the company of the two other convicts. It is, indeed, an identification which Magwitch himself accepts, using it as a description of himself only less frequently than his favorite "warmint." When he hears of the existence of the escaped convict Compeyson he vows to "pull him down like a bloodhound." When he reappears to reveal to Pip the source of his expectations, he refers to himself as "that there hunted dunghill dog wot you kep life in." At this time, in spite of his resolution to keep "a genteel muzzle on," he disgusts Pip not only by his low talk, but by his eating:

> He ate in a ravenous way that was very disagreeable, and all his actions were uncouth, noisy and greedy. Some of his teeth had failed him since I saw him eat on the marshes, and as he turned his food in his mouth, and turned his head sideways to bring his

strongest fangs to bear upon it, he looked terribly like a hungry old dog.

Though the novel is full of animal imagery, the identification of the convict with a dog, by implication a miserable, starved cur, is interesting because no other character, except perhaps Pumblechook, is so surely and continuously identified with any one species. The comparison is not a particularly surprising or unusual one, but what makes it especially significant is that it spills over onto the young Pip. The convict himself calls him "young dog" and "fierce young hound," and this last phrase is remembered with anguish by Pip when he fears that the convict will imagine it was he who betrayed him. But it is later in the book, when Pip himself is in the position of the despised outcast, that the comparison comes through most clearly. Curiously enough, it comes in a scene in which he is being fed:

> She came back, with some bread and meat and a little mug of beer. She put the mug down on the stones of the yard, and gave me the bread and meat without looking at me, as insolently as if I were a dog in disgrace. I was so humiliated, hurt, spurned, offended, angry, sorry—I cannot hit the right name for the smart—God knows what its name was—that tears started to my eyes.

It is through his treatment by Estella, so different from the spirit in which he himself watched the convict, that he comes to find himself in the position of the hunted convict whom he had feared and compassionated: a spurned outcast, despised, almost beneath contempt, his humanity degraded or denied, reduced to the level of a beast.

It is through the use of this image that we see most clearly that, as Pip takes over the same metaphor as the convict, he assumes his share in his guilt and emotionally comprehends his position in society. The child can both pity the convict and put himself imaginatively in his position. The young man with "expectations" and a horror of crime can do neither, which makes doubly ironical Magwitch's part in bringing about this change in character.

Source: Robert Barnard, "Imagery and Theme in *Great Expectations*," in *Dickens Studies Annual,* 1970, pp. 238-51.

Sources

Angus Calder, Introduction to *Great Expectations,* Penguin, 1981.

Janice Carlisle, editor, *"Great Expectations" by Charles Dickens,* Bedford Books of St. Martin's Press, 1996.

Bert G. Hornback, *'Great Expectations': A Novel of Friendship,* Twayne, 1987.

Humphrey House, *The Dickens World,* 2nd edition, Oxford University Press, 1942.

For Further Study

Robert Barnard, *Imagery and Theme in the Novels of Dickens,* Humanities Press, 1974.
    Includes valuable discussions of the images and themes that Dickens pursues in his novels, including *Great Expectations.*

Mary Lamberton Becker, *Introducing Charles Dickens,* Dodd, 1940.
    This biography contains the story of Dickens' late-life encounter with a boy who, like himself in his youth, holds dreams of someday becoming the master of Gad's Hill.

Jerome Hamilton Buckley, *Season of Youth: The Bildungsroman from Dickens to Golding,* Harvard University Press, 1974.
    Provides an important discussion of *Great Expectations* in the tradition of the *bildungsroman,* a type of novel that focuses on the coming of age of a major character.

G. K. Chesterton, *Charles Dickens,* 22nd edition, Methuen, 1949.
    Besides "The Boyhood of Dickens" in Chapter 2, an excellent commentary on the lowbrow character of some highbred gentlemen (168) and "The Alleged Optimism of Dickens" in Chapter 11.

William Ross Clark, editor, *Discussions of Charles Dickens,* Heath, 1961.
    An anthology of criticism from the late nineteenth century into the twentieth, including Gissing, Bush, Orwell, House, Stange, Moynahan, and Miller.

Philip Collins, editor, *Dickens: The Critical Heritage,* Barnes, 1971.
    A collection of contemporary responses, reviews, and critical interpretations of Dickens' works.

Steven Connor, *Charles Dickens,* Basil Blackwell, 1985.
    Groups discussions of Dickens' novels according to theme; the essay on *Great Expectations* is found under the category of "Self and System."

Archibald C. Coolidge, *Charles Dickens as a Serial Novelist,* University of Iowa Press, 1967.
    A valuable study of the manner in which Dickens wrote his novels for publication in periodicals in installments, and the effects that this manner of publication had on the development of his works.

Mamie Dickens, *My Father as I Recall Him,* Dutton, n.d.
    Dickens' love of Gads Hill and his intensity in living with the characters he created.

K. J. Fielding, *Charles Dickens: A Critical Introduction,* David McKay Co., 1958.

An influential study of Dickens' works in which the author emphasizes, among other things, the fact that the novels can be interpreted in a variety of ways.

K. J. Fielding, editor, *The Speeches of Charles Dickens,* Oxford University Press, 1960.
Dickens addresses the need for more and better schools for lower class children.

George H. Ford, "Charles Dickens," in *Dictionary of Literary Biography, Volume 21: Victorian Novelists Before 1885,* edited by Ira B. Nadel and William E. Fredeman, Gale, 1983, pp. 89-124.
Dickens' biography, criticism, and themes, interwoven as *Bildungsroman* in the author's life and work.

John Forster, "Great Expectations," in *The Life of Charles Dickens,* Scribners, 1904, pp. 355-61.
Dickens plans *Great Expectations* as an autobiography similar to David Copperfield's.

John A. Garraty and Peter Gay, editors, "From Liberalism to Democracy," *The Columbia History of the World,* Harper, 1972, pp. 871-83.
General background on the socio-economic influences of the time, including the force of democracy versus the fear of rule by the many illiterate.

Robin Gilmour, *The Idea of the Gentleman in the Victorian Novel,* Allen, 1981.
A study of the cultural and political significance of "gentleman" as a recurring theme in Victorian novels; includes a discussion of Pip's desire to better his lot in life and to become a gentleman in the context of other works of Victorian literature.

Bernard D. Grebanier, Samuel Middlebrook, Stith Thompson, and William Watts, editors, *English Literature and Its Backgrounds, Volume Two: From the Forerunners of Romanticism to the Present,* 2nd edition, Holt, 1949.
A comprehensive timeline of British literature, 1550-1940, and an illustrated chapter on "The Victorian Age" (417-48).

Philip Hobsbaum, *A Reader's Guide to Charles Dickens,* Thames & Hudson, 1972.
Provides a wealth of background information on Dickens' life, Dickens' England, and Dickens' novels.

Rewey Belle Inglis, Alice Cecilia Cooper, Marion A. Sturdevant, and William Rose Benet, editors, *Adventures in English Literature,* Harcourt, 1938.
A timeline of British Victorian authors (671) and a reprint of the chapter on Dickens' childhood from G. K. Chesterton's *Charles Dickens,* published in 1906 (1090-99).

Fred Kaplan, *Dickens: A Biography,* Morrow, 1988.
A comprehensive biography of the author that provides much insight into Dickens' life and into the composition of his novels.

Charles Kent, *Charles Dickens as a Reader,* Lippincott, 1872.
A personal view of Dickens by one who knew him and his lasting love of theater and audience.

F. R. and Q. D. Leavis, *Dickens the Novelist,* Pantheon, 1970.

Includes Q. D. Leavis' insightful essay "How We Must Read 'Great Expectations,'" a useful introduction to interpreting the novel.

J. Hillis Miller, *Charles Dickens: The World of His Novels,* Indiana University Press, 1969.
Includes an influential essay in which the author interprets the major themes of *Great Expectations.*

Harland S. Nelson, *Charles Dickens,* Twayne, 1981.
Covers detailed information on the background, audience, and serialization of Dickens' works; also includes summaries of the novels.

Norman Page, *A Dickens Companion,* Schocken Books, 1984.
An invaluable resource with information on such topics as the composition, serialization, publication, and reception of Dickens' works.

J. B. Priestley, *Charles Dickens and His World,* Viking Press, 1969.
A detailed study of the England of Dickens' day; useful for gaining a better understanding of the setting of his novels.

Anny Sandrin, *Great Expectations,* Unwin Hyman, 1988.
A collection of Dickens' criticism and biography, including the story he told of meeting a young boy who reminded him of himself as a child with dreams of becoming master of Gads Hill.

Michael Slater, *Dickens on America and the Americans,* University of Texas Press, 1978.
Dickens notes distinct differences between American and English factory wage slaves.

Michael Slater, editor, *Dickens 1970: Centenary Essays,* Stein, 1970.
Comedy, social change, and children's issues are addressed, among others.

Graham Storey and Kathleen Tillotson, editors, *The Letters of Charles Dickens, Vol. Eight,* Clarendon Press, 1995.
Notable primarily for Dickens' 1858 admission of his failed marriage and his protection of the woman purported to be his mistress, closely followed by his will in which only his family is mentioned.

Adolphus William Ward, *Dickens,* Harper, 1882.
A generally positive review with attention to Dicken's revised ending as one that is less than expected.

Edmund Wilson, *The Wound and the Bow: Seven Studies in Literature,* Oxford University Press, 1947.
In the essay "Dickens: The Two Scrooges," Wilson became one of the first critics to focus on Dickens as an artist, and to attribute much of the darker themes in his novels to his personality and background.

Angus Wilson, *The World of Charles Dickens,* Viking, 1970.
Many illustrations and easy-to-understand text, including a description and illustration of the "Ragged Schools" (228-29).

George J. Worth, *Great Expectations: An Annotated Bibliography,* Garland, 1986.
An invaluable resource that will direct the student to a variety of published material on *Great Expectations* for the study of this novel.

The Handmaid's Tale

Margaret Atwood

1985

By the time *The Handmaid's Tale* was published in 1985, Margaret Atwood had already been an internationally recognized figure in literature for twenty years. Her work has been characterized as having a "feminist" focus, and this novel certainly fit into that simple understanding; the story describes a society where dehumanization of women is not just a custom but actually the law.

What keeps the novel from being only a work of propaganda for feminist ideology is the complexity and roundness of all of the characters. Among the male characters, one is willing to fight with the underground against the oppressive government and another, who is at the top of this male-oriented social order, feels trapped by it and secretly breaks the laws in order to indulge himself in simple, meaningless pleasure. The female characters may be oppressed, but they are not portrayed as powerless victims. The novel's harshest judgements are applied to the Handmaid-in-training who sells out her own integrity by declaring her own guilt for being raped as a child, and to the narrator herself for lacking the nerve to help the underground resistance movement.

The Handmaid's Tale was a best seller at the time of its publication. It is possible that Atwood's reputation and the appeal of reading about contemporary social issues such as toxic waste, abortion and pornography helped its initial rise to fame, but its continuing popularity surely rests on its seamless, chillingly believable blending of modern religious fundamentalist attitudes with the histori-

Margaret Atwood

cally proven methods of almost all totalitarian governments.

Author Biography

Margaret Atwood is one of the best-known Canadian writers of our day. She is certainly one of the most prolific authors in North America, having produced over twenty volumes of poetry and just as many books of fiction (including novels and short story collections), as well as important essays, dramas and children's books. Recognition for her work has included winning the Governor-General's Award twice, as well as the Coles Book of the Year Award, the Arthur C. Clarke Award, and the Harvard University Centennial Medal.

She was born in Ottawa in 1939 and grew up in suburban Toronto. Her father was an entomologist, and during her childhood, Atwood, showing as much ability in science as she did in writing, believed that she would follow in his footsteps in the field of biology. Her talent as a writer became apparent early: in high school, she contributed poetry, short stories and cartoons to the school newspaper. Her first volume of poetry was published the same year that she graduated from Victoria College, University of Toronto, and five years later her second book of poetry was given one of Canada's most coveted prizes, the Governor-General's Award. Since the 1960's she has taught at several Canadian and American universities, usually through honorary guest fellowships, and she has produced a tremendous body of work.

Throughout her writing career, critics have often categorized Atwood's works as "feminist," a label that she has avoided because it often applied to any work written by a woman with leading female characters. She has been one of the foremost spokespersons for the previously under-examined tradition of Canadian literature and wrote one of the most important and widely-read books about the subject, *Survival: A Thematic Guide to Canadian Literature,* indicating that gender identity is no more important in her work than national identity.

Plot Summary

Part I

In Margaret Atwood's *The Handmaid's Tale,* Offred, the main character, recounts her experiences as a Handmaid in the Republic of Gilead, a twenty-first-century authoritarian society run by radical Christian fundamentalists. In this American dystopia, women have been reduced to the status of breeders. As Offred chronicles her days as a Handmaid, she gradually pieces together for readers the horrors of the totalitarian regime and her struggle for survival.

Offred begins her story with a flashback to her time at the Rachel and Leah Center, where she and other Handmaids received their training. She remembers the Aunts, who guarded and taught them, patrolling at night with electric cattle prods and leather belts. The Handmaids-in-training were confined to what used to be a gymnasium, except for twice daily walks within the chain-link, barbed-wire fence. During the long nights the women communicated with each other in the dark by lip reading silent whispers and by touching hands.

The Commander's home, where she has served for five weeks, consists of five other people: two Marthas, Rita and Cora; Nick the chauffeur; the Commander; and the Commander's Wife. Offred recognizes the Commander's Wife as Serena Joy, a performer on a television program she had watched as a child. One of Offred's tasks is to purchase the household food during daily trips to the local stores. Every day she walks with Ofglen, another Handmaid, through guarded checkpoints. While shopping they see a pregnant Handmaid, and Offred recognizes her as an acquaintance from the Center named Janine. On the way home they walk past the prison wall where six bodies of "war criminals" hang. She explains that they were probably doctors or scientists who were executed for past "crimes" against society.

Part II

One afternoon she inspects her room and finds the indecipherable message "Nolite te bastardes carborundorum" scratched into the floor. Later during her monthly checkup at the gynecologist, her doctor offers personally to help her become pregnant. She is afraid of getting caught but acknowledges that a pregnancy will lead to her salvation.

While resting in her room she thinks back to the first time she saw her friend, Moira, at the Center; she had obviously been beaten. She also recalls Janine "testifying" about her gang rape and subsequent abortion, and, spurred on by jeering women, admitting full responsibility for these actions. Offred explains that the Aunts encouraged these testifying sessions as a "good example" for the others. Returning to the present, she dreams of her husband Luke and painful memories of trying and failing to escape with him and her daughter across the border.

That night she comes downstairs for the Ceremony, a required monthly ritual. The Ceremony begins with the Commander reading aloud a passage about procreation from the Bible. Then Offred lies on Serena's bed between her legs while the Commander tries to impregnate her. She senses his detachment and Serena's anger. Back in her room, she rubs the butter she has saved from dinner on her face to keep her skin soft, since Handmaids are not allowed any lotion. Later that night she creeps downstairs, thinking she will steal something. Nick discovers her and they kiss and touch. He later tells her the Commander wants to see her tomorrow in his study.

Part III

The next morning Offred aids in the delivery of Janine's baby. When a baby girl is born, all are happy except Janine who cries "burnt-out miserable tears." Offred notes she will be allowed to nurse the baby only for a few months when she will be transferred to another Commander's home. That night Offred sneaks downstairs to meet the Commander in his book-lined private study where she

plays Scrabble with him and, as he requests, gives him a kiss goodnight. She visits the Commander two or three nights a week after getting a signal from Nick. The Commander allows her to read forbidden books and magazines and brings her hand lotion that she applies while he watches. Both are embarrassed a few weeks later during the Ceremony since they now know each other.

During a trip to the store Ofglen identifies herself as part of the underground and tells her "you can join us." As they walk home a black van with the white-winged Eye on the side stops in front of them. Two Eyes jump out and grab an ordinary man walking in front of them, assault him and throw him into the back of the van and move on.

Later in her room she thinks back to the past, when her world changed. The new Republic began when someone shot the President and the members of Congress, the army subsequently declared a state of emergency, and the group that took over suspended the Constitution. People stayed at home for weeks, "looking for some direction" as newspapers were censored and roadblocks prevented passage without the proper passes. Offred notes that these changes met with little resistance. One day during this period she was denied access to her bank account and lost her job transferring books onto disks at a library. She soon discovered that the new rulers had made it illegal for women to work or have money.

That night in the study, she asks the Commander what "Nolite te bastardes carborundorum" means, and he tells her "Don't let the bastards grind you down." He informs her that the Handmaid who scratched that message in the floor hanged herself in her room. When he admits that he wants her life to be "bearable," and so asks her what she would like, she answers "to know what's going on!"

Part IV

One day while shopping, Ofglen tells her the secret password of the underground: "mayday." When she returns home, Serena suggests she try to get pregnant with Nick since she hasn't yet with her husband. Offred notes the risk, but agrees. Serena tells her she will try to get her a picture of her little girl and gives her a cigarette. Offred gets a match from Rita and goes up to her room, thinking that she may save the match and burn down the house and escape.

Another day Offred goes to the Prayvaganza, an event attended by all the women in the district. There she sees Janine looking pale and learns her baby was a "shredder"—deformed as many babies were by the polluted environment—and so was destroyed. After the Commander in charge of the service gives a speech about victory and sacrifice, twenty Angels returned from the front are wed to twenty girls, some as young as fourteen. On the way back Ofglen tells her they know she is seeing the Commander in secret and asks her to find out anything she can.

That night the Commander has her put on a skimpy, flashy costume and takes her to Jezebel's, a brothel. She sees Moira there who tells her that after her escape from the Center, she tried to cross the border but was caught, tortured, and sent to work as a prostitute at Jezebel's. Offred is distressed that Moira seems to have given up, and notes that this was the last time she would see her. When the Commander takes her up to one of the rooms and they have sex, she tells herself to try to fake enthusiasm.

Later that night she meets Nick in his garage apartment. She acknowledges that their subsequent sexual encounter was an act of love and thus feels she has betrayed Luke. After that night, she returns often to Nick's room, admitting that she is getting reckless and taking too many chances. She talks less with Ofglen who continues to press her for information from the Commander, but her interest lies only with Nick and their time together. She thinks she may be pregnant and thus no longer wants to leave, which makes her ashamed.

Part V

One morning she attends a district Salvaging, for women only. Two Handmaids and one Wife are salvaged—hung for unknown crimes. When a Guardian who has been accused of rape is brought out, the Handmaids form a circle around him and beat him to death. During this ceremony, Ofglen kicks the Guardian savagely in the head, later explaining to Offred that he was "one of them," and so she quickly put him out of his misery.

While shopping that afternoon, she discovers that Ofglen has been replaced with a new Handmaid. She tells her Ofglen hanged herself when she saw the black van coming for her. Offred, relieved that she was not caught, decides to repent and not break any more rules. That night the black van comes for her. Nick arrives with the Guardians and tells her that she should go with them and trust that she will be saved. They escort her out, telling Serena and the Commander that she is being arrested for "violation of state secrets." They both worry

about their own fates. The narrative ends with Offred stepping into the van.

Part VI

The last section, called "Historical Notes," jumps ahead to the year 2195 to a university conference session on Gileadean Studies. There the speaker tells his audience that what he just read—a transcript of Offred's story—was found recorded on tapes in a house in Massachusetts. He admits he does not know Offred's true identity or whether she successfully made it across the border. He then speculates about the identity of the Commander who, he suggests, played an important part in setting up the Republic of Gilead, which has now fallen.

Characters

The Commander

The Commander is a powerful figure in the Gileadean government. He is apparently sterile, although this is not confirmed because, according to law, only women are tested for being fruitful or barren.

The first time the Commander is seen breaking the strict social structure is when he sends for the handmaiden to come to his office alone at night: it is arranged like a sexual rendezvous, but she finds to her amusement that he shyly asks her to play Scrabble. As her night visits to the office increase, she becomes increasingly informal with him, sometimes even correcting him, as when she tells him "Don't ever do that again," after he nearly becomes affectionate during the impregnation ceremony.

He acts amused when she shows strength. The gifts he offers her show that he underestimates her intelligence: skin lotion, glances through magazines, and a secret trip to a house of prostitution. These are all presented with the expectation that she will be delighted, with no recognition that she only accepts them because her life is so empty of stimuli.

At the house of prostitution, the Commander does finally force himself upon her sexually, mindlessly responding to the environment of degrading sexuality. His attempts to win the handmaid's approval are contrasted to the fear he has for his wife. In the end, when the their secret relationship has been found out, she sees him sitting behind the

Media Adaptations

- *The Handmaid's Tale* was adapted as a film by Volker Schlondorff, starring Natasha Richardson, Faye Dunaway, Aidan Quinn and Robert Duvall, screenplay by Harold Pinter, Cinecom Entertainment group, 1990.

- The author is interviewed on "Margaret Atwood," which is a videotape from the Roland Collection of Films on Art/ICA Video of Northbrook, Illinois. 1989.

- Another video about the author is "Margaret Atwood: Once In August," distributed by Brighton Video if New York, NY, 1989.

- "Margaret Atwood" is the name of a short, 1978 video recording from the Poetry Archive of San Francisco State University.

- Atwood is featured in the educational film "Poem as Image: Progressive Insanities of a Pioneer," from the "A Sense of Poetry" series produced by Cinematics Canada and Learning Corporation of America.

- This book is available on audio cassette as "Margaret Atwood Reads from *The Handmaid's Tale*," by American Audio Prose Library of Columbia, Missouri, 1988. It is #17 in the "A Moveable Feast" series.

- Actress Julie Christie reads *The Handmaid's Tale* on a two-cassette audio tape recording available from Durkin Hayes Publishers in 1987. Order #DHP7214.

- Another audio tape recording of *The Handmaid's Tale* is the eight-cassette collection produced by Recorded Books of Charlotte Hall, Maryland, in 1988. Order #88060.

- "Margaret Atwood: An Interview with Jean Castro" is an audio cassette produced by American Audio Prose Library of Columbia, Missouri, in 1983. Order #3012.

---

wife, looking harried and gray: "No doubt they're having a fight, about me," the narrator asserts. "No doubt she's giving him hell."

The Commander's Wife

The Commander's Wife was once Serena Joy, the lead soprano on the *Growing Souls Gospel Hour,* a television program devoted to telling Bible stories to children. Throughout the story, Offred refers to The Commander's Wife as Serena Joy, although none of the other characters do.

Like 99 of 100 women in Gilead, the Commander's Wife has been found to be sterile. On account of her husband's high government rank, she is supposed to receive Offred's baby as soon as it is born. During the traditional fertilization ceremony, she holds the handmaiden between her legs while the Commander attempts to impregnate her. She cannot help being jealous, despite all of the rules built into the ceremony to make the relationship between her husband and the handmaid impersonal; when the ceremony is over, Serena Joy curtly tells the handmaid to leave, even though standing and walking will diminish the odds of fertilization.

In the end, she finds evidence that the Commander has taken the handmaid out of the house in makeup and frilly clothes, and the handmaid finds that her predecessor, the last Offred, hanged herself because Serena Joy found out about a similar arrangement. "Behind my back?" Serena Joy tells her. "You could have left me something," which raises the question of whether there was love in the cold relationship between the Commander and his wife after all. When the handmaid is taken away by uniformed guards, Serena Joy is angry but also panicky, afraid that the government will find out about illegal actions around the house.

Cora

Cora is a Martha, the housekeeper in the Commander's household.

Aunt Elizabeth

At the Red Center, Aunt Elizabeth is in charge of the less spiritual aspects of the training of the handmaids: she teaches gynecology and oversees discipline. When Moira escapes, it is Aunt Elizabeth that she ties up and strips of her clothes.

Janine

The handmaid who narrates this story refers to this character as "that whiney bitch Janine," and she is shown throughout this story to be annoying and pathetic. At the Red Center, when Janine tells the other handmaids-in-training about being gang-raped at age fourteen, they chant that it was her fault, that she led the boys on. The next week Janine announces that this rape was her fault. For the rest of the story she behaves as the model handmaid, is trusted as Aunt Lydia's spy when Moira escapes, and gives her baby up immediately after the delivery is over. Her compliance is achieved at the cost of her sanity: when the handmaids tear a man apart with their hands during the ritual called the Salvaging, Janine wanders around with blood smeared on her cheek and a clump of hair in her hand. Clearly delusional, she babbles cheerfully: "Hi there," "How are you doing?" "You have a nice day."

Luke

Luke was the husband of the narrator before the time in which this novel takes place. They had a daughter together. They were caught trying to escape from Gilead, and, while she was put into the handmaid program because of her ability to have children, she never finds out his fate. Their daughter's name is never mentioned, but the narrator does get to see a current photograph of her in exchange for agreeing to go along with Serena Joy's plan to get her pregnant.

Aunt Lydia

Aunt Lydia is responsible for teaching enslaved women how to be handmaids. She wears a khaki dress and lectures about what behaviors are decent and which are inappropriate, filling the women with disgust for the dangers of outlawed practices, such as pornography and abortion, while encouraging admiration that borders on awe toward pregnancy. "There's more than one kind of freedom," she tells them. "Freedom to and freedom from. In the days of anarchy, it was freedom to. Now you are being given freedom from. Don't underestimate it."

Still from the movie A Handmaid's Tale, *starring Faye Dunaway.*

Moira

An old friend who knew the narrator well before the events of this novel take place, at least since college, Moira surfaces several times throughout the story as an emblem of resistance to the misogynistic, totalitarian state. She also is used to contrast the government's repressive attitude toward sexuality.

In college, Moira once hosted an exotic lingerie party, selling the sort of items that were sold at the Pornomarts before they were outlawed by the state. Later, after the narrator has been at the teaching center for handmaids for a few weeks, Moira shows up, having been arrested for "gender treachery," or homosexuality. She tries to escape from the Red Center by feigning illness, hoping to bribe the guards in the ambulance with sex. When they cannot be bribed she shows up back at the center with her feet mutilated, causing the narrator to remember that an official has told them, "for our purposes, your hands and feet are not essential." Her second escape is successful: she makes a weapon from a part of the toilet mechanism and threatens the guard, Aunt Elizabeth, then takes Aunt Elizabeth's clothes and pass and walks out of the Center's front gate.

After eight or nine months underground, she is caught, and the narrator later meets her in Jezebel's, the house of prostitution. Moira is dressed in a tattered, lewd bunny costume. Despite the realization that prostitutes are often put to death in three or four years, Moira claims to like being at Jezebel's. She only works nights, and can drink and take drugs, and is allowed to have sex with other women. She compares it to the only other option—working with toxic waste in the Colonies until her body rotted away. Since the life of prostitution, symbolized by her ridiculous costume, is so completely the opposite of what she had stood for, her enthusiasm for working at Jezebel's can be seen as a blend of wishful thinking and potent brain washing.

The Mother

"I don't want a man around, what use are they except for ten seconds' worth of half-babies," the narrator's mother once told her, explaining why she never married. "A man is just a woman's strategy for making other women." With her view of sex as good only for procreation and her activism against pornography, her views are similar in ways to those supported by the Gileadean government, although to them she would be considered an "Unwoman," too strong-willed to have a place in society.

Nick

Nick is the commander's chauffeur. He is an attractive young man about the narrator's age. He is not allowed to associate with the handmaid, but they defy the rules and start a physical relationship. On the night after the impregnation Ceremony, the narrator goes downstairs to the sitting room of the house because she feel like stealing something. Nick finds her there, and in the silence they kiss and touch each other.

Nick functions as a messenger throughout the her series of clandestine meetings with the Commander. When he wears his hat sideways, she knows that she is to go see the Commander that night. Later, the Commander's wife arranges for the narrator to get to Nick's room safely at night in order to become pregnant by him, since it appears that the Commander is sterile. She keeps her affair with Nick going, sneaking to his room over the garage even without the approval of the Commander's wife.

Eventually Nick provides an escape from her enslavement. It is revealed that he is a member of the Mayday resistance group and takes her to safety.

Offred

We never learn the real name of the narrator of this story, although she reveals it to several other characters whom she trusts. She is officially known as "Offred": the name means that she is the possession "of" the Commander, "Fred", as "Ofwarren" and "Ofglen" belong to Warren and Glen. This name can also be read as "off-red," indicating that she is not well-suited to her role as a red-uniformed handmaid trained at the Red Center.

When the novel begins, the narrator is already a handmaid, and has been "posted" at the Commander's house for five weeks. She is not supposed to express her individuality in any way; she cannot sing, ask questions, or in any way express unhappiness with her situation. Her mission is to become pregnant by the Commander, so that he and his wife will have a baby to raise as their own.

Her history comes out as the novel progresses: she had a husband and a child and worked as a librarian before the government was overthrown by right-wing fanatics and the rights of women were limited, supposedly for their own protection. Attempting to escape the country, she and her husband and child were captured by government troops, and she never saw them again, although she thinks of them often throughout the novel. In the Republic of Gilead, she is intimidated, afraid to talk openly to the other handmaid, Ofglen, who is her companion, and is certainly afraid of confiding in any of the other members of her household.

When the Commander summons her illegally to his office at night, she goes, even though she assumes that his purpose is to have sex with her, because she feels that she has no option: it is amusing to her that all he wants to do is play word games and read magazines, which are as illegal for a Commander as they are for a handmaid, indicating that he feels as enslaved as she is. Their relationship grows, so that she can express herself more freely as time goes on, but she is always aware of the legal control he has over her.

When the Commander's Wife arranges for her to have sex with Nick, the chauffeur, in order to become pregnant and complete her mission in the house, she continues sleeping with him for weeks, even though it will be fatal for her if she is caught. She feels unfaithful to her husband, Luke, but she is so desperate for affection that she cannot help herself. But when Ofglen confides in her about the resistance movement and asks her to help, she cannot overcome her fear of the consequences. The "Historical Notes on *The Handmaid's Tale*" at the end of the book say that the narrative was recorded on a series of cassette tapes and found in a safe place along the Underground Femaleroad, indicating that she did escape from Gilead in the end.

Ofglen

The woman referred to as "Ofglen" in this story is just one of a succession: the narrator knew an Ofglen before her, and at the end of the novel another Ofglen shows up in her place.

When she first shows up in the novel, the narrator says, "she is my spy, as I am hers." They are mutually distrustful, carefully keeping conversation to officially-sanctioned topics, each unsure if the other will turn them in to the authorities as a subversive if they mention forbidden topics. As the novel progresses, Ofglen turns out to be connected to the revolutionary group called "Mayday," a fact that she first hints at by commenting on the weather: "It's a beautiful May day."

Later, she speaks openly to the narrator about the underground movement, and reveals mysteriously that she knows about Offred's evening meetings in the Commander's office. She asks her to look through his paperwork and find anything that could help them fight against the government. When the handmaids attend a Salvaging, at which they are to beat a man to death with their hands for allegedly raping a pregnant woman, Ofglen rushes out in front and knocks him unconscious with kicks to the head. She later explains that he was not a rapist but a Mayday activist, and she was putting him out of his misery. The next day a new Ofglen shows up, explaining that the old one hanged herself when government agents were coming to take her away.

Ofwarren

See Janine

Rita

Rita is a Martha, the cook in the Commander's household.

Serena Joy

See The Commander's Wife

Themes

Sex Roles

The roles that are assigned to the two genders in this novel are exaggerations of the roles tradi-

Topics for Further Study

- Research the techniques used by the government of Nazi Germany to oppress people, such as blacks, Jews, homosexuals and Gypsies in the 1930's and 40's, and compare them to the methods the Gileadean government uses to oppress women.

- What sort of images would this totalitarian government use to reinforce its control? Design several posters that might be hung in Gilead to remind women of what sort of behavior is expected of them, or write a song that handmaids and Marthas might be required to sing every morning.

- The abortion issue has been a continuing controversy in the United States, but it was a particularly important political issue in the mid-1980's, when this novel was published. Read about a prominent figure from that time who was either strongly pro-choice or strongly pro-life. Report on that person's background, what they are doing today, and what you think they would say about the Republic of Gilead.

- Find an academic history—similar to the "Historical Notes" at the end of his novel—of the Underground Railroad that was used to free American slaves in the early and mid-1800's. Write a fictional first-person account, based on details from that work, that explains what the experience might have been like for a slave trying to escape.

tionally played: women here are responsible for domestic duties and men in Gilead run the government functions (since this is a totalitarian state, business and military concerns are part of the government). To most of the people of Gilead, the strict assignment of these roles seems reasonable, a natural outcome of the physical traits that define males and females.

Industrial pollution has caused sterility in ninety-nine percent of the female population and countless numbers of the males, creating a crisis for the ability of the human race to survive into the future. From this the government had claimed the right to require any fertile females to participate in government-supervised child-bearing programs. This has caused a need to keep all non-fertile females in structured domestic roles, in order to assure the passivity and cooperation of the fertile females; and this in turn has caused the requirement that males make political decisions and enforce them with military rule. All of these steps require more than a social policy, they require an almost religious faith in order to assure the participation of the greatest number of people. Training centers like the Rachel and Leah Re-education Center become necessary.

To the social planners of Gilead, this system might seem a reasonable response to the threat of extinction. To people of the modern world and to the futuristic society of Professor Piexoto who view it from the year 2175, it seems rash, twisted, and naive, rooted more in the greed of men than in the common good.

In the name of preserving the lives of the citizens, executions become common; in order to offer women "freedom from" they must give up their "freedom to," dressing in government-assigned uniforms and suffering intellectual starvation as the only offered alternatives to rape and exploitation. Men like the Commander dictate morality—men that are so corrupt that they break the laws against sex and contraband that they themselves have established.

The roles of the two sexes in this novel are extremes of traditional roles, and that serves to raise the question of whether they are derived from nature or if men are working hard to keep oppressive traditions alive after their usefulness to society is spent. From the shocking contradictions that Gileadean society is forced to accept, the latter appears to be the case.

Free Will

Any dystopian novel, which means a novel that describes a society that is a terrible place to live in—such as George Orwell's *1984* and Aldous Huxley's *Brave New World*—raises the question of free will: to what degree, readers are asked, are the people in the novel forced to participate in a government that violates their basic ethical beliefs?

The same question dominated the Nuremberg trials after World War II, when Nazis who had participated in the Holocaust justified the murder of thousands of innocent, anonymous victims because they were "just following orders." Through this novel's structure, we are introduced to the different ways society uses to intimidate its citizens: the lack of personal possessions or identity, the cattle prods, the armed guards, the dangerous gossip, the subversives hung to death as public spectacle, etc.

It is only gradually, as the narrator recalls being trained to behave like a good housemaid, that the government's ability to control one's thoughts presents itself. The narrator behaves as she is supposed to, despite (or because of) the despair she feels, but when she describes Janine's behavior, she is disgusted as she imagines the conversation the Commander's wives would probably have about what a good handmaid Janine is. Looking at her life from the outside, the narrator can accept her own behavior as being prudent for survival, but seeing how proud Janine is of her pregnancy keeps her from accepting government-sanctioned ideas as her own.

The novel complicates the question of whether free will is absolute or if it has limits by giving no clear-cut answer about the fate of the character with the strongest will, Moira: she says that she is happy working at the house of prostitution, but such happiness would strongly contradict what she has stood for before, and it conveniently fits the government's role for her. Readers are invited to wonder whether she is really thinking for herself after enduring her torture.

The narrator herself is too fearful to help the Mayday resistance movement, even after they have reached out to her and after the Commander has shown his weakness. When the Ofglen that she knows to be part of the resistance disappears, she is fearful that she will be arrested: so strong is the government's hold over her mind that she is afraid even though she has done nothing wrong. On the other hand, she carries on her illegal affair with Nick, risking arrest and death to go to his room night after night, telling him her true name. Her love for him neutralizes her intense fear of punishment, raising the issue of her free will again, never answering whether love is freedom or a way to mentally flee worse fates.

Guilt and Innocence

For a situation that causes such misery, none of the characters in this novel is presented as evil or specifically guilty. Aunt Lydia seems to believe that her brainwashing will help her students stay safe from assault, Janine is mercilessly pressured by her peers into compliance, and even the Commander, who comes closest among all of the characters to wielding control, is such a pawn of the situation that he takes risks just to talk with the narrator, listen to her, and play games with her. None of these characters is particularly admirable, but none can be pointed to as a specific example of what has caused the problem in Gilead.

This shows Atwood to be a fair, even-handed writer, willing to examine bad behavior and negative results without losing empathy or creating a two-dimensional villain. It also gives a more accurate depiction of a totalitarian society. A society that relies upon citizens to be responsible for intimidation and oppression would leave itself vulnerable to attacks of conscience, but a society that only asks each person to compromise a little, without turning anyone into an obviously guilty party, can reach further into the homes of otherwise good people and can justify its existence for a long time.

Style

Narration

The events in this novel take place at different points in the life of the narrator, but the primary setting, the present tense of the novel, is Gilead, where she has been a handmaid in the Commander's house for five weeks. The reader is introduced to new characters that she meets from this point forward, such as the doctor and the new Ofglen, while others that she is already familiar with—Rita and Cora for example—are taken for granted and woven into the narration without explanation.

Because the narrator's life had been designed by the government to be uneventful and to not require independent thought, the tone of the novel is drab, flat, desensitized. Information about how her life came to be this way is conveyed through flashbacks, most of them drawn from two sections of time in her past: her memories of the Rachel and Leah Re-education Center inform readers about how she came to be the way she is, and her memories of the time between the government's fall and her capture at the border explain how society came to be the way that it is.

Structure

In the first few pages, the first section called "Night" is told in flashback, establishing the fact that this book takes place at a time when army blankets that say "U.S." are notably old, in a place

where women sleep in a gymnasium surrounded by barbed wire. This sets a tone of danger for the following present-tense episodes, to contrast the passivity of the bland life described there.

The chapters of the novel alternate, with the even-numbered ones naming some place in town that the narrator goes to and the odd-numbered ones named "Night" (with the exception of "Nap" in Chapter V). This emphasized the distinction between the times when the handmaid's brain is allowed to be active and when it is supposed to be shut down in sleep; ironically, her life becomes more active and colorful during the "Night" sections, usually because she uses her private time to remember, and later to carry on her affair with Nick. It is significant that the trip to Jezebel's is not placed in a "Night" section, even though it occurs after dark and is a supposedly covert action, indicating that it could still be considered mainstream because it poses no threat to the power structure.

At the end of the novel, the "Historical Notes" section offers a lecture given in the year 2195 by the Director of Twentieth-and Twenty-first Century Archives at Cambridge University. This jump to almost two hundred years beyond the events of the book allows readers to put these events into a larger perspective, offering the hope that an oppressive society like Gilead is not the fate of human kind, but instead is the sort of misstep that civilization is bound to take in its development.

Point of View

Because Atwood allows each of her characters sufficient motivation to be rounded, reasonable human beings, without relying on exceptional degrees of good or evil to explain any of them, the world of this book would have a different impact if it were presented from any other point of view. If this story were told by the Commander's wife, for example, the social structure might seem necessarily harsh and even fair, while the Commander might find it slowly improving under the tinkering of social architects.

Because the narrator is a handmaid, one of the most basic contradictions in this situation is emphasized: motherhood is praised as one of the greatest achievements in this world, but mothers are stripped of possessions, dignity, identity, and, ultimately, of their children. Having one of society's most powerless members tell the story brings out the fear of social authority that all of the characters feel, and it sheds light on the injustice of it all.

If the narrator were an angrier handmaid, she might not have gained the confidences of the Commander and Serena Joy; if the character had been more complacent, the members of the resistance may never have approached her. In either case the full story would not have been covered.

Deus ex Machina

This phrase translates from Latin to mean "god from the machine," and it refers to the practice in ancient Greek drama of having a complex, twisted plot resolved in the end by suddenly having a god character descend from the sky (lowered onto the stage by a machine) to explain all mysteries, punish the bad and reward the good. This is of course a poor substitute for having a resolution that grows naturally out of the plot.

Some readers have charged that the sudden appearance of the Mayday group at the end is a case of *deus ex machina,* providing a happy ending that the situation did not prepare for. Although the appearance of Mayday is abrupt, it is not done without preparation. First, Ofglen's knowledge of the activities in the Commander's house hints halfway through the novel that the movement had a spy there. More significantly, the strength of the resistance group is never made clear throughout the novel because the narrator is kept uninformed of any real news: Mayday could rescue hundreds of people per day from Gilead, making their appearance at the end quite reasonable, but readers would not suspect this activity because it has been hidden from the narrator.

Imagery

Most of the imagery in this novel does not occur naturally, but has been planted by the government: for instance, the frightening specters of the hanged traitors; the nun-like habits that the handmaids wear; the ominous black vans that symbolize swift and unforeseeable death; the tattered bunny costume that makes Moira look like a cheap, vulgar toy.

There are also symbols that the characters in the novel see in front of them, whether they are aware of it or not: the garden that assures Serena Joy that she is concerned with life and beauty; the chauffeur's cap, symbolic of obedience to the social order, that is turned askew when the Commander and Offred are to meet as near-equals; and the fixture that was put in the ceiling to replace the chandelier that the former Offred hung herself from, symbolizing both death and also, because it looks like a breast hanging down, life.

Historical Context

International Conservatism

In the 1980s, the political climate around the globe turned toward fiscal restraint and social conservatism. In general, this shift was a response to the permissiveness and unchecked social spending that occurred in the 1970s, which were in turn the extended results of the freedoms won by the worldwide social revolutions of the 1960s.

This conservative trend appeared in different forms in different countries. In Margaret Atwood's home country of Canada, Pierre Trudeau, the Liberal Party leader who had been Prime Minister since 1968 (with an eight-month gap in 1979-80), resigned in 1984, and the voters replaced him with Progressive Conservative Brian Mulroney. Margaret Thatcher, who was elected Prime Minister of England in 1979, reversed decades of socialism by selling government-run industries to private owners. In the United States, the 1980 election of Ronald Reagan created such a turbulent reversal of previous social policy that the changes sweeping through the government during the first half of the decade came to be referred to as "the Reagan Revolution."

The Reagan administration's popularity was based on the slogan of "getting government off of people's backs," implying government regulations had become too cumbersome and expensive for the American economy to sustain. Reagan's personal popularity allowed his administration to shift the priorities of government. Military spending was increased year after year, in order to stand up to the Soviet Union, which the President openly declared an "evil empire." As a result of this spending, the United States became a debtor nation for the first time in its history, even though social programs were cut and eliminated. The benefits gained by slashing redundant programs were offset by increases in poverty and homelessness, since many of the affected programs had been established to aid the poor, and to balance financial inequalities that had become established by centuries of racist and sexist tradition.

The extreme shift toward conservatism in the United States at that time is significant to the social change that created the Republic of Gilead in Atwood's imagination. After the novel was published, she told an American interviewer that she had tried originally to set the novel in Canada, but that it just would not fit the Canadian culture. "It's not a Canadian sort of thing to do," she told Bon-

Anti-abortion demonstration.

nie Lyons in 1987. "Canadians might do it after the United States did it, in some sort of watered-down version. Our television evangelists are more paltry than yours. The States are more extreme in everything."

Religious Fundamentalism

One of the most powerful political groups to affect American politics in the 1980s was an organization called The Moral Majority. It was founded in 1979 by Jerry Falwell, an evangelist and the host of the *Old Time Gospel Hour* on television, to register voters in support of the group's fundamentalist agenda.

Millions of voters registered and identified themselves as members of the Moral Majority, giving the group a strong voice in national politics. Among the issues opposed by the Moral Majority were the Equal Rights Amendment, which would have provided a Constitutional guarantee that women would be treated equally to men; the White House Conference on the Family, which they felt gave recognition to too many varieties of family structure; and abortion. The issues supported by the Moral Majority included the saying of prayers in publicly-funded schools, tax credits for schools that taught religious doctrine, and government opposition to pornography.

The group's impact on American politics was wide-reaching, and politicians running for national and local offices lined up to pledge their support of the "family values" program that the Moral Majority used to define their agenda, knowing that they could not win election without appeasing such a well-organized bloc of voters.

Organized Fundamentalists made their mark on the structure of the American government.

The Equal Rights Amendment went unratified when it could not gather enough support. The National Endowment for the Arts came under national scrutiny and had its budget cut because some of the artists it had benefited had produced works found to offend standards of decency. Abortion, possibly the key issue of the Christian political movement, also had its federal funding eliminated, even though attempts to limit or outlaw abortion itself were fought successfully on Constitutional grounds.

Though sexually explicit publications are also protected by the Constitution, they were studied by a Presidential Commission on Pornography, which like most symbolic actions, had little tangible impact; one large convenience store chain, for example, stopped carrying pornographic magazines, but began stocking them in a few years, after the heat was off.

As the decade wore on, the pervasive influence of the Moral Majority, and of politically active religious figures in general, wore out. Some policies, such as Reverend Falwell's support of Philippine dictator Ferdinand Marcos or his opposition to South African freedom fighter Bishop Desmond Tutu, exposed the group to ridicule and charges of hypocrisy. Falwell left the organization in 1988 to take charge of *The 700 Club,* a television ministry whose leader had been forced to resign in a sex scandal. The Moral Majority disbanded the following year.

Critical Overview

Although *The Handmaid's Tale* achieved great popular success when it was published—weeks on the best seller lists, its adaptation as a major motion picture—its reception by critics has been wildly uneven. Critics generally have been positive about the book, but for many different reasons.

These reasons have been so diverse that it seems at times that reviewers were reviewing different books. Such wide disagreement is testimony to Atwood's strength as a novelist: it shows that no reviewer could dismiss *The Handmaid's Tale* lightly, that they gave the book, its subject matter, and its implications serious attention. It takes a novel with few obvious flaws and so much social relevance to bring out so many different approaches.

In general, reviewers divided their attentions toward either the book's political success or its success as a piece of literature, although there is vast disagreement about whether it works in either of these areas.

Critic Joyce Maynard, who reviewed the book for *Mademoiselle* soon after its publication in 1986, expressed her amazement and admiration for the way that Atwood put together a complete fictional world, with "not only the basic rules and structures by which Gilead operates, but a thousand small, odd, harrowing particulars too." Maynard started reading the book at ten o'clock at night and could not stop reading until she had finished the last page, after daybreak, because she was captivated by the "incredible and moving story."

In contrast, Robert Linkous was one of the very few reviewers completely unmoved by the novel: "Offred's monotonous manner of expression just drones and drones," he wrote in *San Francisco Review of Books.*

Brad Hooper, writing for *Booklist,* contrasted the book's social aims with its narrative achievement, noting that "the book is simply too obvious (in its moral agenda) to support its fictional context." Often, this debate about whether the book's thinly-veiled criticism of contemporary politics is justified by Atwood's story-telling ability has been shifted, slightly, to an analysis of how *The Handmaid's Tale* compares to similar dystopian novels, such as *1984* and *Brave New World,* which also sound the alarm against coming political calamity.

In his review for *Newsweek* in 1986, Peter Prescott wrote that *The Handmaid's Tale* was better than those other books because Atwood was a more talented novelist. "Unlike those English gentlemen, she can create a nuanced character," he wrote in a review entitled "No Balm In This Gilead." "The dystopia she imagined may be more limited than theirs, but it's fully horrifying—and achieved without recourse to special effects."

Famed author Barbara Ehrenreich, however, saw the book as being insufficiently realized, both as a novel and as a work of political speculation. "As a dystopia, this is a thinly textured one," she wrote in *The New Republic,* directly contrasting Prescott's and Maynard's views. She pointed out improbabilities in the Atwood's imaginary Gilead, such as the fact that outlawing printed matter would be unlikely if they have cars and computers that would need operating manuals, and she faults the novel's protagonist for lacking character, calling her "a sappy stand-in for (*1984*'s) Winston Smith," and Gilead "a coloring-book version of (*1984*'s) Oceana." As a sign of the narrator's vagueness and inappropriateness for telling the tale, Ehrenreich points to the fact that, given a chance to obtain forbidden information from the Commander, Offred comes up with nothing better than a weak request for "whatever there is to know … what's going on."

It is an indicator of the distance between critical perspectives that Joyce Johnson's review in *The Washington Post* cited the same quote, but she interprets it as "a classic demand for something … valuable and forbidden."

Even those reviewers who were unimpressed with Atwood's storytelling skills found enough in the issues the book raised to make it worth reading. Although Ehrenreich thought *The Handmaid's Tale* was not as good as other dystopia novels, she did express great interest in the often overlooked phenomenon that Atwood brings attention to: the similarity between religious fundamentalism and cultural feminism. She says that the book is fascinating and worth reading, despite its literary weaknesses, because of the extra dimension it adds to its mirror of our times. "We are being warned, in this tale, not only about the theocratic ambitions of the religious right, but about the repressive tendency of feminism in general," she wrote. She went on to cite evidence in the harsh treatment of pornography and the group beating of rapists as signs that Gilead is not too far from a hard-line feminist's ideal.

If this warning was what made the book worthwhile for Ehrenreich, it was not enough to keep Mary McCarthy, the novelist, engaged in the story. McCarthy called the book "very readable" in *The New York Times Review of Books,* but she went on to explain that she could not take its scary version of the future very seriously because, even though she herself was suspicious almost to the point of being paranoid about small things like credit cards being "instruments of social control," she could not see the far right of the political spectrum rising up violently to overthrow the government, which is, of course, the novel's central premise.

Criticism

Wendy Perkins

Perkins is an Assistant Professor of English at Prince George's Community College in Maryland and has written numerous critical articles for essay collections, journals, and educational publishers. In the following essay, she explores the complex interplay of dominance, submission, and rebellion in The Handmaid's Tale *through a focus on the main character's struggle for survival.*

Critics read Margaret Atwood's *The Handmaid's Tale* as a cautionary story of oppression against women as well as a critique of radical feminism. Some who focus on Offred, the narrator and main character, criticize her passivity in the face of rigid limitations on her individual freedom: Gayle Green in her article, "Choice of Evils," published in *The Women's Review of Books* insists, "Offred is no hero." Barbara Ehrenreich in her *New Republic* article, "Feminism's Phantoms," finds her to be "a sappy stand-in for [*1984*'s] Winston Smith. Even her friend Moira characterizes her as "a wimp." Yet, although Offred cannot be considered a more obvious traditional hero like Moira, an examination of her more subtle rebellion against the oppressive totalitarian regime which governs her life illustrates the indefatigable nature of the human spirit.

The Republic of Gilead is a typical totalitarian society in that it promotes terror tactics while enforcing its rigid dogmas. Amin Malak in "Margaret Atwood's 'The Handmaid's Tale' and the Dystopian Tradition," notes that Gilead "prescribes a pattern of life based on frugality, conformity, censorship, corruption, [and] fear." The novel also illuminates the intricate politics of power: leaders define acceptable roles for subordinates (in this case, the women), who are said to be unable to perform more valued functions (reasoning and governing skills). As a result subordinates often find it difficult to believe in their own ability.

Subordinates are encouraged to develop childlike characteristics—submissiveness, docility, dependency—that are pleasing to the dominant group. This group then legitimizes the unequal relationship and incorporates it into society's guiding concepts. In Gilead's power structure women are subservient to men because they are considered not as capable as men. This system involves the marginalization of women, illustrating Simone de Beauvoir's point in *The Second Sex* that a man defines

What Do I Read Next?

- Margaret Atwood followed this book with *Cat's Eye* in 1988. Some of the same concerns show up in the later book: a controversial painter returns to the city that she grew up in and runs into old friends and the memories of old friends.

- Marge Piercy has always been associated with Atwood, mostly because both write poetry and fiction from a feminist perspective. Piercy's book most like this one is *Woman on the Edge of Time,* her 1976 novel with some science fiction elements to it. The main character, confined to the psychiatric ward at Bellevue Hospital, must learn to behave the way that her oppressors expect of her, but she also travels in time to the future, to the year 2137, with a fellow inmate.

- Critics examining *The Handmaid's Tale*'s sinister view of the future often compare it to George Orwell's *1984,* which is considered the standard bearer for dystopian novels. Published in 1949, it tells the tale of a society where government surveillance techniques have been perfected, so that every move that citizens make can be monitored and regulated, and of the struggle of one man, Winston Smith, to be free.

- The other dystopian that is usually mentioned at the same time as *1984* is *Brave New World* by Aldous Huxley. Published in 1932, the futuristic society imagined by Huxley has many similarities to our own: citizens use pills to control their moods, babies are born in laboratories, the masses are distracted from disapproving from the government by "Feelies," which are like movies that entertain with sight, hearing and touch. Like Atwood's and Orwell's novels, the problem with total government control is that it interferes when the protagonist falls in love.

- *A Clockwork Orange* by Anthony Burgess, published in 1963, gives a frightening view of the future, concentrating on the lives of juvenile delinquents and speculating about which is worse: their inhuman crimes or the mind-control techniques used by the government to stop their violence.

- Carol Ann Howell's recent book on Atwood, entitled simply *Margaret Atwood* (1996), has some complex and insightful points about Atwood's works in general. The chapter "Science Fiction in the Feminine" is especially useful to students for its examination of how the female perspective puts a different slant on the science fiction tradition and how this genre is particularly useful for conveying feminist concerns.

---

a woman not as autonomous but only as relative to him. He is the Subject and she is the Other. Women in Gilead must concentrate on basic survival and so avoid direct, honest reactions to this marginalization and the terror tactics of those in power. Sometimes the women disguise their actions, appearing to accommodate the demands of this oppressive system, while subtly rebelling.

Throughout the novel, Offred proves her consistent efforts not only to survive, but also to maintain her individuality. When she begins her story with a flashback to her time at the Rachel and Leah Center, she illustrates the politics of power that characterize the novel. She notes the Aunts guarding them with electric cattle prods and leather belts, restricting their movement and interaction with each other. The Handmaids-in-training seem on the surface to submit to this treatment. At night, however, under the threat of severe beatings, they struggle to maintain contact with each other through silent communications in the dark.

Offred also risks physical harm when she steals a few minutes during bathroom breaks to speak to Moira. During these breaks the two women reminisce about past lives and voice their fears and disgust over their present reality. Offred notes, "there is something powerful in the whispering of obscenities, about those in power. There's something delightful about it, something naughty, secretive, forbidden, thrilling…. It deflates them, reduces them to the common denominator where they can be dealt with."

As Offred's thoughts turn to the teenagers who must have once populated the former gymnasium, she commits a more personal act of rebellion. The citizens of the new Republic are repeatedly warned to forget the past or to view it with contempt. Yet, throughout her narrative, Offred continually flashes back to her life before the formation of Gilead, especially with her husband Luke and their daughter. These recollections of the freedom and happiness she used to have in her friendship with Moira, in her work, and in her life with family help her to maintain crucial ties to her past life and thus to a sense of identity.

Even under the strict regulations of the Commander's home, Offred finds ways to assert her individuality as she breaks rules. In the Commander's study she heroically reads forbidden books and magazines and begins to assert her own personality in her relationship with him. One of her most courageous actions occurs when she tells the Commander that she would like to know "what's going on"—everything from what the scribbled message "Nolite te bastardes carborundorum" means to specific details about the inner workings of the Republic. When she wants to talk to the Commander instead of read, she breaks two rules: asking for "dangerous" information and forming a relationship with him. Both activities are against the law and thus acts of subversion.

Sometimes she openly disagrees with him, as when he tries to justify the dogmas of the new regime: "We've given women more than we've taken away. This way they all get a man, are protected and can fulfill their biological destinies in peace." Offred insists they overlooked love, a crucial element in the male/female relationship. Her more subtle acts of rebellion include hoarding butter from her meals to rub on her face, and saving a match that she considers using to burn down the house. Often during her nights alone in her room she tries to come to terms with what has happened to her and to decide what she can do in order to survive physically and mentally.

Her walks with Ofglen present a more overt juxtaposition of oppression, submission, and rebellion. Every day the pair observe the consequences of rebellion as they walk through machine gun guarded checkpoints, where suspected terrorists have been shot, and past the prison wall, where bodies of "war criminals" hang. When Ofglen iden-

tifies herself as part of the underground and elicits Offred's help, they both risk their lives. This fact becomes painfully apparent one day as they observe the secret police attack and whisk away a man walking in front of them. Even with this reminder that her survival depends on submission, Offred continues to gain forbidden information and will soon begin a relationship that will place her in more danger.

At first glance her relationship with Nick appears to be evidence of her desire to withdraw from the harsh realities of her world. She communicates less with Ofglen and claims little interest in discovering new information for her during nights with the Commander. Yet Offred knowingly places her life in real danger each time she meets Nick in his apartment.

Her physical relationship with Nick is also an act of subversion. In Gilead her body determines her function. As Offred notes, in her service as a Handmaid her body is no longer "an implement for the accomplishment of [her] will." Aunt Lydia has urged them at the Center to renounce themselves and become "impenetrable" and therefore pure breeding machines.

Offred regains some individual power when she takes back her body and offers it to Nick, willingly. Their sexual union and growing affection for each other prove that she has allowed herself to be "penetrated" both literally and figuratively. Although she feels ashamed when she admits to herself that she no longer wants to leave the Commander's home when she suspects she is pregnant, her desire to maintain her relationship with Nick and their child is another form of rebellion.

Atwood juxtaposes the actions of other female characters with those of Offred in order to highlight her sensibility and her courage. Offred appears to be not as strong as Moira or her mother, who was a radical feminist before the new Republic took over. She admits she feels like "a wimp" when compared to her friend Moira who continually tries to escape the confines of the Republic. Yet Moira suffers greatly for her attempts; she is beaten severely and is sent to Jezebel's, where she will have "three or four good years" before she is sent "to the boneyard."

Offred insists that she wants "gallantry from [Moira], swashbuckling heroism, single-handed combat. Something I lack." Yet Offred survives, unlike the "Incorrigibles" like Moira who are given two choices: a few years as either a prostitute at Jezebel's or a worker in the Colonies cleaning up toxic waste dumps and then death. Offred's mother, another more traditional hero, was sent to the Colonies. Before the new Republic took over, she had staged demonstrations against oppressive treatment of women and rallies to "Take Back the Night" from male predators. Yet Offred has "taken back the night" in her own personal way during her nightly meetings with Nick. Offred's heroism is more subtle, but no less dangerous, and it helps keep her alive.

Atwood also juxtaposes Offred's behavior with that of the pregnant Handmaid, Janine who "testifies" about her gang rape and subsequent abortion, and, spurred on by jeering women, admits full responsibility for these actions, thus setting a "good example" for the others. Janine gives in completely to the Republic and its dogma and as a result often slips into a trance-like state and loses all sense of reality and her own identity.

Throughout *The Handmaid's Tale* Atwood traces her heroine's efforts to cope, endure, and survive her nightmare world. Offred's account of her life in Gilead presents a fascinating portrait of the politics of power and the strength of the individual will in its struggle to preserve a sense of self.

Source: Wendy Perkins, in an essay for *Novels for Students,* Gale, 1998.

Diane S. Wood

In the following essay, Wood compares Fahrenheit 451 *with Margaret Atwood's* The Handmaid's Tale, *focusing on their historical context and respective treatment of conformity and institutionalized repression.*

Ray Bradbury's *Fahrenheit 451* and Margaret Atwood's *The Handmaid's Tale* depict the rational decision to go into exile, to leave one's native land, that is, the pre-exile condition. These novels present horrifying views of the near future where societal pressures enforce rigid limitations on individual freedom. Their alienated characters find their circumstances repugnant. Justice and freedom are denied them, along with the possibility for enriching their lives through intellectual pursuits. These speculative novels like Orwell's *1984* are dystopian in nature, showing how precarious are today's constitutional rights and how necessary it is to preserve these liberties for future generations. They depict ordinary people, caught in circumstances that they cannot control, people who resist oppression at the risk of their lives and who choose exile because it *has* to be better than their present, unbearable circumstances. Voluntary exile neces-

sitates a journey into the unknown as an alternative to the certain repression of the present.

Both novels offer a bleak possible future for the United States. Bradbury, writing in the McCarthy era of the 1950s, envisions a time when people choose to sit by the hour watching television programs and where owning books is a crime. Atwood, in the 1980s, foresees a time when, in the wake of changes begun during the Reagan Administration, women are denied even the most basic rights of working and owning property. Both novels thus present "political" stances in the widest sense of the word....

The novels by Bradbury and Atwood examine the personal response of an individual who is in conflict with the majority in his society and whose occupation is abhorrent to him.... Atwood's novel recounts the story of a protagonist caught up in the rapid transition of her society. Dehumanized, stripped of her personal name and individual identity, and referred to only by the name of the man to whose household she is assigned, Offred (or Of-Fred), a handmaid, experiences firsthand an upheaval in the social order ending in limited personal freedom. The new oligarchy uses Old Testament injunctions to justify extreme repression. Like the shock troops to which they are compared, handmaids are in the *avant garde* of the social reform and they undergo brutal re-education at the Rachel & Leah Re-Education Centers, after which, like soldiers, they are "posted" to a commander's household. Even more than Montag, Offred's life is determined by her social role. As a fertile woman in a nearly sterile society, her function is to produce viable offspring and her entire life is regulated by her reproductive duties. She describes herself and her fellow handmaids as "two-legged wombs, that's all: sacred vessels, ambulatory chalices." There is nothing erotic about the handmaids, their mission is strictly biological: "We are for breeding purposes: we aren't concubines, geisha girls, courtesans." From the beginning of the narrative, [Offred] is literally a prisoner, watched at all times and even tattooed with a number: "Four digits and an eye, a passport in reverse. It's supposed to guarantee that I will never be able to fade, finally, into another landscape. I am too important, too scarce, for that. I am a national resoure."

In both novels the population is strictly regulated and the conduct of individuals is highly regimented. Indeed, in these repressive circumstances, it is not surprising that the protagonists would wish to flee, especially since, by the end of the novels, they have broken laws which would bring the death penalty if they were apprehended....

Discipline is less mechanized in *The Handmaid's Tale* but no less ruthless. Cadres of brutal "Aunts," "Angels," "Guardians," and "Eyes" enforce order in Atwood's imaginary Gilead. Cattleprods punish uncooperative handmaids in the rehabilitation center. For particularly bad infractions, the handmaids' hands and feet are tortured: "They used steel cables, frayed at the ends. After that the hands. They didn't care what they did to your feet or your hands, even if it was permanent. Remember, said Aunt Lydia. For our purposes your feet and your hands are not essential." Other punishments are even more severe. A woman caught reading three times merits a hand cut off. Handmaids are executed for being unchaste, attempting to kill a commander, or trying to escape. Wives die for adultery or for attempting to kill a handmaid. As in the Middle Ages, cadavers of tortured prisoners are displayed on the town wall to encourage conformity to rules. Offred describes her reaction to the cadavers hanging there:

> It's the bags over the heads that are the worst, worse than the faces themselves would be. It makes the men like dolls on which the faces have not yet been painted; like scarecrows, which in a way is what they are, since they are meant to scare. Or as if their heads are sacks, stuffed with some undifferentiated material, like flour or dough. It's the obvious heaviness of the heads, their vacancy, the way gravity pulls them down and there's no life anymore to hold them up. The heads are zeros.

Execution is a public event, called a "Salvaging." The local women are assembled to witness the execution by hanging of two handmaids and a wife. The authorities decide to depart from past procedure and not read the crimes of the condemned in order to prevent a rash of similar crimes. Offred comments on the unpopularity of this decision: "The crimes of others are a secret language among us. Through them we show ourselves what we might be capable of, after all." The assembled women are required to assent to the punishment even though they do not know the nature of the crime. As part of the audience, Offred makes the ceremonial gesture of compliance with the execution: "I ... then placed my hand on my heart to show my unity with the Salvagers and my consent, and my complicity in the death of this woman."

An even more frightening public ceremony is that of "Particicution," where handmaids act as executioners of an accused rapist. Death is the punishment set in Deuteronomy 22:23–29. Offred paints the scene in terms of bloodlust: "The air is bright with adrenaline, we are permitted anything and this is freedom." The women literally tear the accused apart with their bare hands. These brutal ceremonies serve to release violent emotion in a socially approved setting, since its normal expression is otherwise denied....

Whereas in *Fahrenheit 451* the government acted opportunistically, taking advantage of the lack of passionate readers to outlaw books, the government in *The Handmaid's Tale* actively shapes lifestyles through public policy. Atwood's protagonist recalls the governmental action that declares women may no longer own property and hold jobs. Offred is fired, along with every other woman in the country. Her money can be transferred to her husband, but she no longer may control the funds accessed by her plastic card. The government deprives women of the right to work and to own property simultaneously, to prevent a mass exodus. These freedoms were not the first to be lost, however. Offred explains the progressive loss of the women's constitutional rights, perpetrated by an ominous invisible group she identifies as "they":

> It was after the catastrophe, when *they* shot the president and machine-gunned the Congress and the army declared a state of emergency. *They* blamed it on the Islamic fanatics, at the time.... That was when *they* suspended the Constitution. *They* said it would be temporary. There wasn't even any rioting in the streets. People stayed home at night, watching television, looking for some direction. There wasn't even an enemy you could put your finger on.

Still the transition is gradual and required the complicity of the populace: "We lived, as usual, by ignoring. Ignoring isn't the same as ignorance, you have to work at it. Nothing changes instantaneously: in a gradually heating bathtub you'd be boiled to death before you knew it." The protagonist finally decides that the conditions of the military state are untenable and unsuccessfully tries to escape to freedom with her husband and child, only to find that it is too late. When captured, she is separated from her family whom she never sees again, and is forced to take her place as a handmaid.

In both novels books represent important artifacts of the past and the act of reading becomes a heroic gesture. This is not surprising since both authors are avid readers and have described the importance of books in their lives.... Allusions to being denied the right to read occur throughout *The Handmaid's Tale*. As a handmaid, Offred is forbidden to read, a hardship for a person whose former job was in a library. The only words she sees are "faith" on the petit point cushion in her room and *"Nolite te bastardes carborundorum"* (Don't let the bastards get you down) which is scratched in tiny letters near the floor of her cupboard. During the course of the novel Offred recalls reading and having access to books and regrets her former blasé attitude toward them. Because they are now denied to her, they become very precious whereas once books were commonplace and taken for granted. In the middle of the novel her Commander (the Fred of Offred) invites her to forbidden soirées in his private study. He permits her to read old women's magazines. Offred philosophically reflects on the promise that the old magazines once held:

> What was in them was promise. They dealt in transformations; they suggested an endless series of possibilities, extending like the reflections in two mirrors set facing one another, stretching on, replica after replica, to the vanishing point. They suggested one adventure after another, one wardrobe after another, one improvement after another, one man after another. They suggested rejuvenation, pain overcome and transcended, endless love. The real promise in them was immortality.

The Commander not only lets Offred read magazines but plays scrabble with her. This is the ultimate in forbidden games in a society where women are not allowed to read: "Now it's dangerous. Now it's indecent. Now it's something he can't do with his Wife. Now it's desirable. Now he's compromised himself. It's as if he's offered me drugs."

When the Commander allows Offred to read magazines, the experience is equated to the orgiastic pleasures of eating or of sex: "On these occasions I read quickly, voraciously, almost skimming, trying to get as much into my head as possible before the next long starvation. If it were eating it would be the gluttony of the famished; if it were sex it would be a swift furtive stand-up in an alley somewhere." The Commander, who watches the illicit reading, is described as a sort of pervert: "While I read, the Commander sits and watches me doing it, without speaking but also without taking his eyes off me. This watching is a curiously sexual act, and I feel undressed while he does it. I wish he would turn his back, stroll around the room, read something himself. Then perhaps I could relax more, take my time. As it is, this illicit reading of mine seems a kind of performance."

These magazines somehow escaped the government's attention, although house-to-house searches and bonfires were conducted on the orders of the oligarchy in order to remove all reading material from women. The government of Gilead denied women access to the printed word as a means of controlling them. Only the vicious Aunts are allowed to read and write as a part of their role in re-educating the handmaids. The effect of this is to silence the women, or as Atwood has said elsewhere: "The aim of all suppression is to silence *the voice,* abolish the word, so that the only voices and words left are those of the ones in power."

In her essays Atwood speaks out against suppression of reading and writing, abhoring fascism on anyone's part. This view is paralleled in the novel where Offred remembers as a young girl attending a magazine burning with her mother, who is recalled as a quintessential feminist demonstrator of the 1970s. As the pornographic material burns the image evoked is particularly poetic: "I threw the magazine into the flames. It rifled open in the wind of its burning; big flakes of paper came loose, sailed into the air, still on fire, parts of women's bodies, turning to black ash, in the air, before my eyes." Offred's views toward women's rights are much less activist in nature than her mother's. The mother/daughter relationship is fraught with tension and their opposing viewpoints brings into question some of the tactics of the women's movement including the bookburning. After attending a "Birthing," a particularly grotesque woman's ritual in Gilead, Offred ironically comments: "Mother, I think. Wherever you, may be. Can you, hear me? You wanted a women's culture. Well now there is one. It isn't what you meant, but it exists. Be thankful for small mercies." Her feminist mother probably dies a victim of the new regime, but when Gilead comes into being, there is no triumph on the part of the rightwing opponents to the woman's movement like the Commander's Wife Serena Joy. These women also find no happiness in the new society.

Despite the fact that the social order is founded on biblical references, women are not allowed to read the Bible: "The Bible is kept locked up, the way people once kept tea locked up, so the servants wouldn't steal it. It is an incendiary device: who knows what we'd make of it, if we ever got our hands on it? We can be read to from it, by him [the commander], but we cannot read." Even the familiar reading passages read by the commander hold their attraction for those hungering for the written word: "He's like a man toying with a steak, behind a restaurant window, pretending not to see the eyes watching him from hungry darkness not three feet from his elbow. We lean towards him a little, iron filings to his magnet. He has something we don't have, he has the word. How we squandered it, once." Tapes of biblical readings are an integral part of the re-education in the Rachel and

Leah Centers. The quotations, however, have been changed to further the goals of the oligarchy. Offred notices transformations in the Beatitudes: "*Blessed be the poor in spirit, for theirs is the kingdom of heaven. Blessed are the merciful. Blessed be the meek. Blessed are the silent.* I knew they made that up, I knew it was wrong, and they left things out, too, but there was no way of checking. *Blessed be those that mourn, for they shall be comforted.* Nobody said when." Her ironic comments underscore her frustration with the prohibition against reading and her resistance to indoctrination.

Just as the Beatitudes are rewritten, Marx's comments about the distribution of property are attributed to the Bible in order to justify the distribution of the precious and scarce handmaids in Gilead: "Not every Commander has a Handmaid: some of their Wives have children. *From each,* says the slogan, *according to her ability; to each according to his needs.* We recited that, three times, after dessert. It was from the Bible, or so they said. St. Paul again, in Acts."

The author's ironic use of religious terms becomes comic when she creates the franchise "Soul Scrolls" where prayers are continually spewed out on printout machines called "Holy Rollers" and paid for by pious citizens. Like the flavors in an ice cream store, there are five different prayers: "for health, wealth, a death, a birth, a sin." The state religion distortedly caricatures fundamentalist beliefs, including having a former television gospel singer as the Commander's Wife.

Each novel ends with the protagonist's escape and the beginning of his exile from repression. There is some ambiguity, however, since the alternative order is not elaborated on. In the last lines of her tale [Offred] describes her feelings as she steps into the Black Maria which has come for her: "Whether this is my end or a new beginning I have no way of knowing: I have given myself over into the hands of strangers, because it can't be helped. And so I step up, into the darkness within; or else the light." The postscript "Historical Notes on *The Handmaid's Tale*" provides information that the heroine survives to record her story on cassette tapes. She is rescued by the Mayday organization of the Underground Femaleroad. Her ultimate fate is unknown to the scholars of 2195 who, in an academic conference, comment on the handmaid's story as a historical document from the past.

The appeal of these two highly acclaimed novels stems from the main characters' difficult situation in a repressive future United States. The plau-

> *We lived, as usual, by ignoring. Ignoring isn't the same as ignorance, you have to work at it. Nothing changes instantaneously: in a gradually heating bathtub you'd be boiled to death before you knew it."*
>
> —*from* A Handmaid's Tale

sible explanations given by both Bradbury and Atwood for the ghastly turn taken by American society in the futures they portray serves as a vivid reminder that freedom must be vigilantly guarded in order to be maintained. Apathy and fear create unlivable societies from which only a few courageous souls dare escape. "Ordinary" says one of the cruel Aunts of *The Handmaid's Tale* "is what you are used to." The main characters never are able to accept the "ordinariness" of the repression which surrounds them. They are among the few who are willing to risk the difficult path of exile.

Source: Diane S. Wood, "Bradbury and Atwood: Exile as Rational Decision," in *The Literature of Emigration and Exile,* edited by James Whitlark and Wendall Aycock, Texas Tech University Press, 1992, pp. 131–42.

Amin Malak

In the following excerpt, Malak examines how Atwood infuses the conventions of the dystopian genre with her own distinctive artistry in The Handmaid's Tale.

One of [*The Handmaid's Tale*'s] successful aspects concerns the skillful portrayal of a state that in theory claims to be founded on Christian principles, yet in practice miserably lacks spirituality and benevolence. The state in Gilead prescribes a pattern of life based on frugality, conformity, censorship, corruption, fear, and terror—in short, the usual terms of existence enforced by totalitarian states, instance of which can be found in such dystopian works as Zamyatin's *We,* Huxley's *Brave New World,* and Orwell's *1984.*

What distinguishes Atwood's novel from those dystopian classics is its obvious feminist focus. Gilead is openly misogynistic, in both its theocracy and practice. The state reduces the handmaids to the slavery status of being mere "breeders." ... The handmaid's situation lucidly illustrates Simone de Beauvoir's assertion in *The Second Sex* [Knopf, 1971] about man defining woman not as an autonomous being but as simply what he decrees to be relative to him: "For him she is sex—absolute sex, no less. She is defined and differentiated with reference to man and not with reference to her; she is the incidental, as opposed to the essential. He is the Subject, he is the Absolute—she is the Other." This view of man's marginalization of woman corroborates Foucault's earlier observation about the power-sex correlative; since man holds the sanctified reigns of power in society, he rules, assigns roles, and decrees after social, religious, and cosmic concepts convenient to his interests and desires.

However, not all the female characters in Atwood's novel are sympathetic, nor all the male ones demonic. The Aunts, a vicious elite of collaborators who conduct torture lectures, are among the church-state's staunchest supporters; these renegades turn into zealous converts, appropriating male values at the expense of their feminine instincts. One of them, Aunt Lydia, functions, ironically, as the spokesperson of antifeminism; she urges the handmaids to renounce themselves and become non-persons: "Modesty is invisibility, said Aunt Lydia. Never forget it. To be seen—to be *seen*—is to be—her voice trembled—penetrated. What you must be, girls, is impenetrable. She called us girls." On the other hand, Nick, the Commander's chauffeur, is involved with the underground network, of men and women, that aims at rescuing women and conducting sabotage. Besides, Atwood's heroine constantly yearns for her former marriage life with Luke, presently presumed dead. Accordingly, while Atwood poignantly condemns the misogynous mentality that can cause a heavy toll of human suffering, she refrains from convicting a gender in its entirety as the perpetrator of the nightmare that is Gilead. Indeed, we witness very few of the male characters acting with stark cruelty; the narrative reports most of the violent acts after the fact, sparing the reader gory scenes. Even the Commander appears more pathetic than sinister, baffled than manipulative, almost, at times, a Fool.

Some may interpret Atwood's position here as a non-feminist stance, approving of women's status-quo. In a review for the *Times Literary Supplement,* [March 21, 1986] Lorna Sage describes *The Handmaid's Tale* as Atwood's "revisionist look at her more visionary self," and as "a novel in praise of the present, for which, perhaps, you

have to have the perspective of dystopia." It is really difficult to conceive Atwood's praising the present, because, like Orwell who in *1984* extrapolated specific ominous events and tendencies in twentieth-century politics, she tries to caution against right-wing fundamentalism, rigid dogmas, and misogynous theosophies that may be currently gaining a deceptive popularity. The novel's mimetic impulse then aims at wresting an imperfect present from a horror-ridden future: it appeals for vigilance, and an appreciation of the mature values of tolerance, compassion, and, above all, for women's unique identity.

The novel's thematics operate by positing polarized extremes: a decadent present, which Aunt Lydia cynically describes as "a society dying ... of too much choice," and a totalitarian future that prohibits choice. Naturally, while rejecting the indulgent decadence and chaos of an anarchic society, the reader condemns the Gilead regime for its intolerant, prescriptive set of values that projects a tunnel vision on reality and eliminates human volition: "There is more than one kind of freedom, said Aunt Lydia. Freedom to and freedom from. In the days of anarchy, it was freedom to. Now you are being given freedom from. Don't underrate it." As illustrated by the fears and agonies that Offred endures, when human beings are not free to aspire toward whatever they wish, when choices become so severely constrained that, to quote from Dostoyevsky's *The Possessed,* "only the necessary is necessary," life turns into a painfully prolonged prison term. Interestingly, the victimization process does not involve Offred and the handmaids alone, but extends to the oppressors as well. Everyone ruled by the Gilead regime suffers the deprivation of having no choice, except what the church-state decrees; even the Commander is compelled to perform his sexual assignment with Offred as a matter of obligation: "This is no recreation, even for the Commander. This is serious business. The Commander, too, is doing his duty."

Since the inhabitants of Gilead lead the precarious existence befitting victims, most try in varied ways to cope, endure, and survive. This situation of being a victim and trying to survive dramatizes Atwood's major thesis in her critical work *Survival: A Thematic Guide to Canadian Literature,* [Anansi, 1973] in which she suggests that Canada, metaphorically still a colony or an oppressed minority, is "a collective victim," and that "the central symbol for Canada ... is undoubtedly Survival, *la Survivance.*" Atwood, furthermore, enumerates what she labels "basic victim positions," whereby a victim may choose any of four possible options, one of which is to acknowledge being a victim but refuse "to accept the assumption that the role is inevitable." This position fully explains Offred's role as the protagonist-narrator of *The Handmaid's Tale*. Offred's progress as a maturing consciousness is indexed by an evolving awareness of herself as a victimized woman, and then a gradual development toward initiating risky but assertive schemes that break the slavery syndrome. Her double-crossing the Commander and his Wife, her choice to hazard a sexual affair with Nick, and her association with the underground network, all point to the shift from being a helpless victim to being a sly, subversive survivor. This impulse to survive, together with the occasional flashes of warmth and concern among the handmaids, transmits reassuring signs of hope and humanity in an otherwise chilling and depressing tale.

What makes Atwood's book such a moving tale is its clever technique in presenting the heroine initially as a voice, almost like a sleepwalker conceiving disjointed perceptions of its surroundings, as well as flashing reminiscences about a bygone life. As the scenes gather more details, the heroine's voice is steadily and imperceptively, yet convincingly, transfigured into a full-roundedness that parallels her maturing comprehension of what is happening around her. Thus the victim, manipulated and coerced, is metamorphosed into a determined conniver who daringly violates the perverted canons of Gilead. Moreover, Atwood skilfully manipulates the time sequence between the heroine's past (pre-Gilead life) and the present: those shifting reminiscences offer glimpses of a life, though not ideal, still filled with energy, creativity, humaneness, and a sense of selfhood, a life that sharply contrasts with the alienation, slavery, and suffering under totalitarianism. By the end of the novel, the reader is effectively and conclusively shown how the misogynous regime functions on the basis of power, not choice; coercion, not volition; fear, not desire. In other words, Atwood administers in doses the assaulting shocks to our sensibilities of a grim dystopian nightmare: initially, the narrative voice, distant and almost diffidently void of any emotions, emphasizes those aspects of frugality and solemnity imposed by the state, then progressively tyranny and corruption begin to unfold piecemeal. As the novel concludes, as the horror reaches a climax, the narrative voice assumes a fully engaged emotional tone that cleverly keeps us in suspense about the heroine's fate. This method of measured, well-punctuated revelations about

Gilead connects symbolically with the novel's central meaning: misogynous dogmas, no matter how seemingly innocuous and trustworthy they may appear at their initial conception, are bound, when allowed access to power, to reveal their ruthlessly tyrannical nature.

Regardless of the novel's dystopian essence, it nevertheless avoids being solemn; on the contrary, it sustains an ironic texture throughout. We do not find too many frightening images that may compare with Oceana's torture chambers: the few graphic horror scenes are crisply and snappily presented, sparing us a blood-curdling impact. (Some may criticize this restraint as undermining the novel's integrity and emotional validity.) As in all dystopias, Atwood's aim is to encourage the reader to adopt a rational stance that avoids *total* "suspension of disbelief." This rational stance dislocates full emotional involvement in order to create a Brechtian type of alienation that, in turn, generates an ironic charge. This rational stance too should not be total, because Atwood does want us to care sympathetically about her heroine's fate; hence the emotional distance between reader and character must allow for closeness, but up to a point. Furthermore, Atwood is equally keen on preserving the ironic flair intact. No wonder then that she concludes *The Handmaid's Tale* with a climactic moment of irony: she exposes, in a hilarious epilogue, the absurdity and futility of certain academic writings that engage in dull, clinically sceptic analysis of irrelevancies and inanities, yet miss the vital issues…. The entire "Historical Notes" at the end of the novel represents a satire on critics who spin out theories about literary or historical texts without genuinely recognizing or experiencing the pathos expressed in them: they circumvent issues, classify data, construct clever hypotheses garbed in ritualistic, fashionable jargon, but no spirited illumination ever comes out of their endeavours. Atwood soberly demonstrates that when a critic or scholar (and by extension a reader) avoids, under the guise of scholarly objectivity, taking a moral or political stand about an issue of crucial magnitude such as totalitarianism, he or she will necessarily become an apologist for evil; more significantly, the applause the speaker receives gives us a further compelling glimpse into a distant future that still harbours strong misogynous tendencies.

While the major dystopian features can clearly be located in *The Handmaid's Tale,* the novel offers two distinct additional features: feminism and irony. Dramatizing the interrelationship between power and sex, the book's feminism, despite condemning male misogynous mentality, upholds and cherishes a man-woman axis; here, feminism functions inclusively rather than exclusively, poignantly rather than stridently, humanely rather than cynically. The novel's ironic tone, on the other hand, betokens a confident narrative strategy that aims at treating a depressing material gently and gradually, yet firmly, openly, and conclusively, thus skilfully succeeding in securing the reader's sympathy and interest. The novel shows Atwood's strengths both as an engaging story-teller and a creator of a sympathetic heroine, and as an articulate crafts-woman of a theme that is both current and controversial. As the novel signifies a landmark in the maturing process of Atwood's creative career, her self-assured depiction of the grim dystopian world gives an energetic and meaningful impetus to the genre....

Source: Amin Malak, "Margaret Atwood's 'The Handmaid's Tale' and the Dystopian Tradition," in *Canadian Literature,* No. 112, Spring, 1987, pp. 9–16.

Sources

Barbara Ehrenreich, "Feminism's Phantoms," in *The New Republic,* Vol. 194, No. 11, March 17, 1986, pp. 33-5.

Joyce Johnson, "Margaret Atwood's Brave New World," in *Book World.*

Robert Linkous, "Margaret Atwood's *The Handmaid's Tale.*" in *San Francisco Review of Books,* Fall, 1986, p. 6.

Amin Malak, "Margaret Atwood's *The Handmaid's Tale* and the Dystopian Tradition," in *Canadian Literature,* Vol. 112, Spring, 1987, pp. 9-16.

Joyce Maynard, "Briefing for a Descent Into Hell," in *Mademoiselle,* March, 1986, p. 114.

Mary McCarthy, "Breeders, Wives and Unwomen," in *The New York Times Book Review,* February 9, 1986, p. 1.

Peter Prescott, "No Balm in Gilead," in *Newsweek,* Vol. CVII, No. 7, February 17, 1986, p. 70.

For Further Study

Arnold E. Davidson, "Future Tense: Making History in *The Handmaid's Tale,*" in *Margaret Atwood: Visions and Forms,* edited by Kathryn van Spanckeren and Jan Garden Castro, Southern Illinois University Press, 1988, pp. 113-21.
  Examines how the imaginary country of Gilead is more of a reflection of a state of mind than a political reality. Also included in this book is an autobiographical forward by Margaret Atwood.

Barbara Ehrenreich, "Feminism's Phantoms" in *The New Republic,* Vol. 194, No. 11, March 17, 1986, pp. 33-5.
  Interprets the novel as a warning about feminism's repressive tendencies.

Mark Evans, "Versions of History: 'The Handmaid's Tale' and Its Dedicatees, in *Margaret Atwood: Writing and Subjectivity,"* edited by Colin Nicholson, St. Martin's, 1994, pp. 177-88.
  Discusses Puritanism in the novel.

Barbara Garlick, "The Handmaid's Tale: Narrative Voice and the Primacy of the Tale," in *Twentiety-Century Fantasists: Essays on Culture, Society and Belief in Twentieth-Century Mythopoeic Literature,* edited by Kath Filmer and David Jasper, St. Martin's, 1992, pp. 161-71.
  Explores how the novel's treatment of utopia is supported by its structure.

Gayle Greene, "Choice of Evils," in *The Women's Review of Books,* Vol. 3, No. 10, July, 1986, p. 14.
  Green compares the novel with other writers of feminism by Marge Piercy and Doris Lessing. She concludes that the novel presents a critique of radical feminism.

Amin Malak, "Margaret Atwood's 'The Handmaid's Tale' and the Dystopian Tradition," in *Canadian Literature,* Vol. 112, Spring, 1987, pp. 9-16.
  Examines how Atwood's feminist focus distinguishes her novel from dystopian classics like Huxley's *Brave New World* and Orwell's *1984.*

Margaret Atwood: Language, Text and System, edited by Sherrill E. Grace and Lorainne Weir, The University of British Columbia Press, 1983.
  Published before *The Handmaid's Tale,* this book analyzes Atwood's use of language. Some of the essays here are written for a professional level, but most are informative and meticulously detailed.

Madonne Miner, "'Trust Me': Reading the Romance Plot in Margaret Atwood's 'The Handmaid's Tale,'" in *Twentieth Century Literature,* Vol. 37, No. 2, Summer 1991, pp. 148-68.
  Explores the theme of love in the novel and its link to survival.

Barbara Hill Rigney, *Madness and Sexual Politics in the Feminist,* The University of Wisconsin Press, 1978.
  Views four feminist authors—Bronte, Woolf, Lessing and Atwood—in terms of their treatment of madness in their work

Jerome H. Rosenberg, *Margaret Atwood,* Twayne Publishers, 1984.
  Traces Atwood's career up to *The Handmaid's Tale.*

Roberta Rubenstein, "Nature and Nurture in Dystopia: 'The Handmaid's Tale,'" in *Margaret Atwood: Vision and Forms,* edited by Kathryn Van Spanckeren, Jan Garden Castro, and Sandra M. Gilbert, So. Illinois Press, 1988, pp. 101-12.
  Discusses the issue of nature and nurture in the novel.

Hilde Staels, "Margaret Atwood's 'The Handmaid's Tale': Resistance through Narrating," in *English Studies,* Vol. 78, No. 5, September, 1995, pp. 455-67.
  Focuses on the narrative structure of the novel and shows how the task of narrative becomes a crucial part of the main character's resistance to oppression.

Charlotte Templin, in a review in *The Explicator,* Vol. 49, No. 4, Summer, 1991, pp. 255-56.
  Examines the relationship of setting and theme in the novel.

In Country

Bobbie Ann Mason
1985

In Country was the first novel that Bobbie Ann Mason had published. Until just a few years earlier, she had been an unknown college teacher. Her first book of fiction, *Shiloh, and Other Stories,* was a great critical success. The short story collection earned nominations for the National Book Critics Circle award, the American Book Award, and the P.E.N./Faulkner Award for fiction. Critics and readers awaited the publication of *In Country* with much anticipation.

The book, which takes place in western Kentucky, concerns a teenage girl's questions about the war in Vietnam, where her father died and her uncle served. Unlike many serious works of literature, which generally avoid current events because they will soon be outdated, the novel has constant cultural references that were fresh when it was published in 1984. The Vietnam Veterans Memorial, for instance, which is central to the story, had been dedicated as recently as 1982, and the Bruce Springsteen album that is quoted in the epigram and mentioned frequently thereafter was released in 1984.

In addition to the timely cultural references, the characters that Mason presented also helped her gain a broader audience than many novelists enjoy. These characters do not have their interests and sensibilities formed by reading literature, but, like most Americans, they know life through the references that the consumer culture has given them. McDonald's, Holiday Inn and the shopping mall are all not just abstract, but significant pieces of their lives. *In*

Bobbie Ann Mason

Country, like most of Bobbie Ann Mason's works, succeeds in using the mundane aspects of modern life in a search for greater meaning.

Author Biography

Bobbie Ann Mason was born in 1940 in Mayfield, a small town in western Kentucky, and she grew up outside of the town's limits, attending a rural school like Sam's father did in *In Country.* In 1962 Mason graduated from the University of Kentucky with her Bachelor of Arts degree. She then went to New York for a year, writing for fan magazines, such as *Movie Star, Movie Life,* and *T.V. Star Parade* before returning to school for postgraduate work. In 1966 she received her Master of Arts degree from the State University of New York, and in 1972 she was awarded a Ph.D. from University of Connecticut. Her doctoral thesis, *Nabokov's Garden: A Guide to Ada,* was published as a book in 1974, and *The Girl Sleuth: A Feminist Guide to The Bobbsey Twins, Nancy Drew, and Their Sisters* was published in 1975.

During the late 1970s, while teaching journalism at Mansfield State College in Pennsylvania,

Mason began writing short stories, developing her unique style from her observations of life. Looking back, she has expressed amusement at the arrogance that led her to send the second story she wrote to *The New Yorker,* arguably the most prestigious magazine that a writer could be published in. The polite rejection they sent her led Mason to submit another story, then another, until the magazine finally printed her twentieth submission in 1980. Other magazines printed her works, and in 1982, sixteen of her stories were collected in *Shiloh, and Other Stories,* which won rave reviews and was awarded the 1983 Ernest Hemingway Foundation Award, as well as being nominated for several other national prizes. *In Country,* her first novel, was published in 1985. She has published several novels, such as *Spence + Lila* and *Feather Crowns,* and a short story collection, *Love Life.* She currently lives in Kentucky.

Plot Summary

Part I

Bobbie Ann Mason's novel *In Country* is the story of Samantha Hughes, known as Sam, and her quest to uncover the truth of the Vietnam War. For seventeen-year-old Sam, the war has particular significance: her father died in Vietnam shortly before her own birth.

The novel is divided into three parts; the first and last parts, written in present tense, frame the middle of the novel, told in a long flashback. As the story opens, Sam, Sam's maternal uncle, Emmett, a Vietnam War veteran, and Sam's paternal grandmother, Mawmaw, are driving from their home in Kentucky to Washington D.C. to visit the Vietnam Veterans' Memorial. There is the suggestion that some crisis, reached about two weeks earlier, precipitated the cross-country trip.

Part II

In the second part of the story, the novel slips into past tense and recounts the events of the summer immediately before the trip to the Wall. We learn background information about Dwayne, Sam's father, and about Emmett's return from Vietnam. We also learn about Irene, Sam's mother, and her response to Dwayne's death. Irene has since remarried, has a new baby, and now lives in Lexington.

Sam lives with Emmett. Sam, just graduated from high school, has a boyfriend named Lonnie.

She does not know what she wants out of life. Emmett, who is unemployed and who has not worked since his return from Vietnam, cooks for the pair and spends his days trying to shore up the sagging foundation of their house. The two watch a lot of *M.A.S.H.* on television, and although Sam knows that the television show is about the Korean War, it starts her thinking about the Vietnam War, and about her father.

Sam is worried about Emmett who suffers from acne, headaches, and stomach disorders. She is convinced that he has been poisoned from Agent Orange, a defoliant used during the Vietnam War. At the same time, Sam finds herself increasingly interested in the Vietnam War. She wants to understand Emmett and she wants to know more about her father. Consequently, she begins spending time with Emmett's friends, a group of veterans who breakfast at McDonald's everyday.

Sam also worries about her future. She talks about her plans with her only girl friend, Dawn. When Dawn tells Sam that she is pregnant, Sam confronts her own situation. Although everyone assumes that she will marry Lonnie in the fall, she is not sure that this is the future she wants.

Meanwhile, the veterans plan a dance and Sam persuades Emmett to go. His old girlfriend, Anita, will be there and Sam wants to see them reunited. In addition, Sam has discovered that she is strongly attracted to one of Emmett's friends, Tom. Tom owns a garage, and has a VW Beetle Sam wants to buy.

At the dance, Sam and Tom spend the evening together and then return to Tom's apartment. Although they attempt to have sexual intercourse, Tom is impotent. Tom blames his impotence on the psychological damage inflicted by the war. Although Sam still desires Tom, he is mortified over his inability to have sex.

When Sam returns home she discovers Emmett has not returned from the dance. Three days later, Irene brings Emmett home. He showed up at her house in Lexington, drunk after the dance.

During Irene's visit, Sam asks her for more information about Dwayne. Irene suggests that she talk to her paternal grandparents and tells her that there may be a notebook there that Dwayne left. She also tells Sam that there are letters from Dwayne somewhere in Sam and Emmett's house. Before she leaves, Irene gives Sam the money to buy the Beetle.

After Irene leaves, Sam finds her father's letters and reads them. They do not provide the answers she needs and she grows increasingly confused over what she wants from life. Consequently, she breaks off her relationship with Lonnie.

Sam next visits her paternal grandparents who show her pictures of Dwayne. In addition, they also give Dwayne's diary to Sam. When Sam reads the diary and his account of finding a rotting Vietnamese corpse, Dwayne's life in Vietnam suddenly becomes real to her.

At the heart of Sam's distress is her understanding that both her father and Emmett had killed people. Worse, she also understands that her father thought of the people he killed as "gooks," not even really human. She decides that the only way she will understand how this happened is if she can somehow recreate the Vietnam War for herself. Thus, she loads up her car with camping goods and heads out to Cawood Pond, a swampy, dangerous location in the country.

Sam spends the night at Cawood Pond, immersing herself in smells, and noises of the thick swamp. In the dark, she thinks of her pregnant friend Dawn and then imagines the way soldiers kill babies. Disoriented and frightened, Sam survives the night only to hear someone approaching her in the morning. Hurriedly, Sam tries to fashion a weapon out of a can of smoked oysters, thinking she might be approached by a rapist.

However, it is not a rapist who approaches Sam, but Emmett, worried and looking for her. In the confrontation that follows, Emmett finally tells Sam what it was like for him in Vietnam. He weeps, and confesses how much he loves Sam, how he has tried to be a father to her, and how he has failed.

Part III

After the return from Cawood's Pond, Sam suffers from what she thinks of as "post-Vietnam stress syndrome," and seems to be unable to take any action at all. Emmett, however, suddenly seems to find direction. He announces that they are going to Washington, D.C., to see the Vietnam Veteran's War Memorial, and he persuades Dwayne's mother to go with them. The novel shifts back into present tense as the trio drive through Maryland into Washington.

When they reach the Wall, Emmett finds Dwayne's name in the directory and they approach the panel where his name is placed. Dwayne's name, on panel 9E is far above their heads. Sam gets a ladder from a workman, and they persuade Mawmaw to climb the ladder and touch Dwayne's name.

Sam, too, climbs the ladder and touches her father's name. She then goes back to the directory and looks up her father's name once again. Suddenly, she finds what she thinks is her own name: Sam Hughes. She rushes to panel 14E, and locates the name:

> SAM A. HUGHES. It is the first on a line. It is down low enough to touch. She touches her own name. How odd it feels, as though all the names in America have been used to decorate this wall.

As the novel closes, the final scene is of Emmett, sitting "cross-legged in front of the wall, and slowly his face bursts into a smile like flames."

Characters

Donna

The sister of Sam's father, she was just a child when Dwayne was killed in the war, and consequently she never knew him. Donna and her husband live with Mawmaw and Pap Hughes.

Dawn Goodwin

Dawn is Sam's age, her best friend, the person most like her in the novel. Together, they do things that teenaged girls do, such as piercing each other's ears, shopping at the mall, and dreaming about leaving their small town and becoming famous in music videos. When Dawn finds out that she is pregnant, though, Sam begins to worry about the approach of adulthood: she foresees Dawn marrying her boyfriend and giving up her dreams to stay at home in a cheap apartment and raise the baby. It is not a situation that Sam wants to relate to herself.

Tom Hudson

One of the veterans that Emmett hangs around with in Hopewell, Tom is tall and handsome, and Sam has a crush on him. When the car that she bought from him shows problems, she is defensive, saying that Tom assured her that it would run fine. She goes to Tom's apartment after the dance, but he is unable to perform sexually, a problem that he explains is due to the mental distress lingering from his experience in Vietnam. When Tom mentions a prosthetic pump for achieving erections that he has seen on the television, Sam, with youthful enthusiasm, becomes certain that it would be the answer to his problem, and she blames the Veterans Administration for failing to give Tom $10,000 to buy one.

Irene Hughes

See Irene Joiner

Mawmaw Hughes

The mother of Sam's father, Dwayne, she has never been away from home in her life before the trip to the Vietnam Veterans Memorial that Sam and Emmett take her on. Because she is not accustomed to travel, she is a nuisance on the trip, complaining about how much things cost and unable to sit in the car for any length of time without using the bathroom. At the Memorial, though, her sadness and determination are touching.

Pap Hughes

Sam's grandfather on her father's side, she does not know very much about him because, after her father's death, her mother took her infrequently to their house.

Sam Hughes

The protagonist of this book, Sam is obsessed with the war in Vietnam, where her father died before she was even born and her uncle Emmett served. As Emmett tells his friends, "Sam's got Nam on the brain." She recently graduated from high school and the options available to her reflect the divisions in her life. Her mother, Irene, wants her to attend the University of Kentucky, which would mean moving to Lexington and living with Irene and her husband and their infant daughter. Sam is reluctant to go, and is instead considering attending Murray State in nearby Paducah, which would allow her to stay home with Emmett and watch over him.

Part of her interest in the Vietnam War manifests itself in her feelings of responsibility for Emmett; she fears that his problems, from acne and headaches and gas to an inactive love life, are the results of exposure to Agent Orange, a chemical used during the war. She tries to get Emmett to tell her about the war, but he cannot describe what it was like, so she has to gather information about it from books about Vietnam and information about war in general from the television series *M*A*S*H*. Sam takes an interest in the small group of veterans that Emmett eats breakfast with at McDonald's every morning. She has a romantic crush on Tom Hudson, who sells her a car and who reminds her of Bruce Springsteen. The one night they spend together, Tom is unable to perform sexually, which he explains as a psychological problem caused by the war.

Much of Sam's interest in the war relates to her curiosity about the father she never knew. Her grandparents are simple country people who believe that their son never drank or smoked, but his diary from the war makes it clear that he did, so they prove to be a poor source of information. Sam's mother appears to have been deeply in love with him before he went to war, but they were just teenagers then and had only been married for a few weeks, so she has a hard time remembering any insightful information. Near the end of the book, Sam, upset with the image of her father that she has gotten from his diary and addled by a heavy concentration of flea poison, takes her camping gear and spends the night alone in a swamp, imagining what it was like in the jungles of Vietnam. When Emmett comes to find her, he is cured of his emotional paralysis and she is freed of having to be his protector, and the next day they set off on the trip to the Vietnam Veterans Memorial that starts and ends the book.

Irene Joiner

Sam's mother has disassociated herself from life in Hopewell, having moved to a different part of the state and started a new family, which includes a new baby daughter, Heather, who she can give more attention to than she was ever able to give Sam.

The early impression of Irene in the book is that she is a newly rich person who has run away from her roots because they embarrass her. As the story progresses it becomes clear that she has lived a difficult life, responsible for a baby when she was barely more than a child herself and then adding responsibility for her brother, who had been traumatized by the war. Irene bought the house in Hopewell with the insurance money she received after Sam's father, Dwayne, died, and when Emmett came back from the war he moved in with them. For a brief time, when Sam was a few years old, she ran off to Lexington with a hippie named Bob, but she returned to Hopewell because she felt that he could not be relied on to make a living.

After thirteen years of watching over Sam and Emmett, she met Larry Joiner and married him, giving Sam the choice of going to Lexington with them or staying in school in Hopewell and living with Emmett. Irene is delighted with her new baby, to such an extent that she talks baby talk and is lighthearted about bodily functions that Sam finds disgusting. In the end, it is apparent that leaving Hopewell is Irene's way of trying to recapture some of the life she had lost by becoming widowed

Media Adaptations

- *In Country* was adapted to a movie in 1989, currently available on videotape. Starring Bruce Willis and Emily Lloyd. Directed by Norman Jewison. Warner Brothers.

- *Bobbie Ann Mason interview with Kay Bonetti.* Audio cassette available from American Audio Prose Library, 1985.

- *Signiture: Contemporary Southern Writers.* Program 1: Bobbie Ann Mason. Video recording by Kentucky Educational Television. Annenburg/CPB Multimedia Collection, 1995.

---

young. The fact that she is successful in putting her difficulties behind her is reflected in the way that Emmett tells Sam, somewhat sarcastically, "Your mother is full of the joy of life."

Larry Joiner

Sam believes that her mother's new husband has "no personality," possibly because he provides his wife and child with the sort of stable environment that nobody she knows has ever had. She refers to him as "Lorenzo Jones" because a teacher in high school played the class an old radio drama by that name, and she sees Irene's life with him as being like a soap opera, melodramatic and lacking substance.

Lorenzo Jones
See Larry Joiner

Lonnie Malone

Sam's boyfriend at the beginning of the book, she finds herself increasingly disinterested in Lonnie as the story progresses. Part of her loss of interest is her growing infatuation with Tom, the older veteran, but much of it has to do with the fact that she does not feel that she fits into Lonnie's life. He is unable to understand her concern about what happened in Vietnam. He comes from a well-adjusted family that is supportive of one another and socially acceptable, and Sam feels outclassed by

From the movie In Country, *starring Bruce Willis and Emily Lloyd.*

them, which is symbolized by the fact that they expect her to buy a nice gift for the upcoming wedding of Lonnie's brother. For a long time in the middle of the novel, Sam does not see Lonnie because he is out of town for several days at a bachelor party. By the time he returns, Sam has spent the night with Tom and thought more about serious matters that Lonnie would not understand. He comes back with a plan for what he wants to do with his life: he wants to study camera repair through a correspondence course and open a shop. As an example of his immaturity, his response to the news of Dawn's pregnancy is "Hey! I knew she'd marry Ken somehow." Lonnie is confused and angry when, later in the same scene, Sam says that she does not want to date him any more.

Buddy Mangrum

Buddy never actually appears in the book, but the other veterans talk about him. In contrast to the way that Sam sees symptoms of Agent Orange poisoning in everything that is wrong with Emmett, Buddy actually does appear to have been affected by the poison. Among his symptoms are "nausea, the runs, jaundice, chloracne. His muscles twitch and he can't sleep and he's lost weight … His kid's being operated on down in Memphis. They're go-

ing to reroute her intestines to keep 'em from twisting so bad."

Emmett Smith

Sam's uncle is thirty-five years old and is barely able to function in society because of the trauma he suffered in Vietnam during the war. He is unable to hold a steady job and maintain a steady relationship. Although he has the presence of mind to joke about these as if their absence in his life is intentional, readers can tell from his financial problems and the book's positive portrayal of Anita, the former girlfriend who likes him, that Emmett is constrained by psychological problems.

He is a creature of habit, repeating simple actions and concentrating on simple tasks, such as meeting his friends for breakfast every day, making supper, worrying about fleas on his cat and digging a trench beside the house to stop up a hole that is letting water into the basement. "We're lucky this house is standing," he says at one point, prophetically. "You take a structural weakness. One thing leads to another, and then it all falls apart."

When he first returned from Vietnam, Emmett went traveling around the west, and when he returned he brought a van full of anti-war activists with him. They scandalized the town, first by being hippies in a conservative rural town and then by climbing up in the clock tower and flying a Viet Cong flag from it. He moved in with Irene and Sam, and Irene watched over him until her new husband was given a job in Lexington, 240 miles away. When she moved, Sam, by then a teenager, became responsible for Emmett. His eccentric behavior (such as deciding to wear a skirt instead of pants) makes him the subject of rumors in Hopewell.

The only thing Emmett really enjoys is bird watching, and in particular watching out for an egret, because he thinks that is the bird he saw in Vietnam. At the end of the novel, when he is finally able to talk about what the experience of war has done to him, Emmett explains the significance of bird watching to Sam: "If you can think about something like birds," he says, "you can get outside of yourself, and it doesn't hurt as much. That's the whole idea. That's the whole challenge for the human race." The fact that Emmett's psychological suffering is greatly healed is evident in the last sentence of the book, where the bird symbol becomes an image of the Phoenix, a mythical bird that arises from its own ashes: "He is sitting there cross-legged in front of [the Vietnam Veterans' Memorial], and slowly his face bursts into a smile like flames."

Pete Simms

One of the group of veterans that Emmett associates with, Pete is a bit of a braggart and a flirt. He shows Sam the map of the Jackson Purchase region of western Kentucky that is tattooed on his chest, but later, at the dance, he asks her not to mention to his wife that he had let her see it.

Irene Smith

See Irene Joiner

Anita Stevens

Emmett's old girlfriend is still interested in him and would like to go out with him again. She makes her interest in him clear. "Oh, he's so cute," she tells Sam. "He'll say something that just makes me speechless." Sam also wishes that Anita and Emmett would get back together. She finds Anita a perfect match for him, smart and pretty and kind. She is a nurse, and she helps out with the dance that the local veterans throw. Seeing how happy Emmett is with her at the dance, Sam assumes that their romance has been rekindled, and is disappointed to learn that it has not.

Themes

War and Peace

Because the novel is set eleven years after America's withdrawal from Vietnam, and it focuses on a protagonist who does not have direct experience of the conflict but knows it through her uncle and the father she never knew, it is able to examine the emotional and psychological effects of war from a unique perspective. While a war is being fought, and for the years following it, attention is given mainly to the theoretical debates about why it was fought. This holds especially true of the Vietnam War, where disagreements about America's responsibilities and America's guilt overshadowed any interest in the veterans who did the actual fighting, making them pawns in a struggle between two determined ideologies.

In Country ignores the reasons for and against the war and has Emmett supporting both sides, first by joining the Army and then by joining the anti-war hippies. He is not a very vocal supporter of either. The novel is less concerned with the causes of war than its effects. Emmett's trauma is obvious: it is the result of killing and having friends killed all around, which have a lingering psychological effect, regardless of popular movies and sto-

Topics for Further Study

- Research the controversy that surrounded the building of the Vietnam Veterans' Memorial in 1982: Which groups objected to it? What was the basis of their objections? What compromise measures were taken to satisfy those who did not like the memorial as it was originally planned?

- When considering military options in the past two decades, in Haiti or Bosnia or Iraq for example, strategists have frequently expressed their concern about involving the country in "another Vietnam." How did that war change the U.S. government approaches military policy? Is this change a new, permanent way of viewing warfare, or will it fade as memories of the Vietnam War fade?

- In the novel, Sam reflects that Quang Ngai, where her father died, is near My Lai. Research the My Lai Massacre that happened in 1968. Explain how what happened there, and the Army's reaction to it might, have affected the way that Americans treated returning veterans.

- Contact the nearest Veteran's Administration and try to arrange for a Vietnam veteran to come to your school, or at least to be interviewed. Prepare a list of questions, based upon things that you learned from reading *In Country,* that you think Americans of your generation ought to know about the experience of being in Vietnam.

ries that show tough characters shrugging off death in an instant. The war will always be with Emmett, and the fact that Vietnam veterans returned home to controversy instead of public praise makes it even harder for Emmett to live with what has been done.

For Sam, the very fact that she did not experience the war is frustrating; the thing that has affected her life most profoundly is lost to history, where she cannot touch it. In the end of Part Two, Emmett tells her, "The main thing you learn from history is that you can't learn from history," but this does not help the fact that Sam is still affected by the war. In the end, though, when she sees her own name on the Vietnam Veterans Memorial and realizes that she is not just touched by Vietnam but is part of it, she can finally know some peace.

Identity

It is natural for someone like Sam, who never had the chance to know one of her parents, to wonder about the effect that missing person had on her personality. Genetically, a person is made up of the DNA of both parents, and in a traditional family both parents' personalities blend into their child's. In Sam's case, the only thing she has from her father is his genes, and she feels a lack of identity. Emmett has some elements in common with her father—he is an older male, and he fought in Vietnam—but he also represents her mother's side of Sam's identity and, because she has to take care of him, he does not represent a very good father figure. Tom Hudson can be seen as a father figure, and Sam's infatuation with him can be seen as a traditional Freudian pattern of turning a loss into a sex drive, but his impotence, while it does not bother Sam, makes him keep his distance from her.

The only other person in the book who is like Sam is her friend Dawn, but by getting pregnant young and planning to marry a local boy Dawn is too much like Sam's mother to fulfill the missing part of her identity. The only person who can complete Sam's identity is her father, Dwayne, who died when he was just about her age. She looks for him in many different places: books about Vietnam; in his photograph; in the stories of the veterans who returned; in the memories of his parents and her mother; in the letters he sent home; and in the war journal he kept. When she finally finds his name on the Memorial, she also finds, to her surprise, her own name, and she realizes that she is not alone but is part of a community.

Order and Disorder

"I work on staying together, one day at a time," Emmett tells Sam in the novel's climatic scene. "There's no room for anything else. It takes all of my energy." One of the striking things about *In Country* is that it presents a society that is not the one traditionally talked about in books, but that is nonetheless recognizable and is run by its own rules of order. A traditional view of small-town American culture might present the home of Sam's mother as being typical: a basic family unit (father, mother, and child), with the father working and the mother raising the baby and keeping herself distracted with crafts and the news. Another household that is similarly traditional is that of Lonnie's parents, Martha and Bud. In this novel, both of these ordinary households seem repressive.

In the fictional world Sam lives in, the most stable family unit is Sam and Emmett, a niece and her nephew, with her boyfriend coming over sometimes to watch television and spend the night. Other examples include Tom, who lives by himself over his garage; Jim and Sue Ann, who are separated (she moved 250 miles away to Lexington) but are still on good terms; and Dawn and Ken, who hope to create a family. The characters in this book who have the hardest time coping are undoubtedly the ones who were in the war, indicating that training young men for destruction is a negative factor in their creating order in their lives when they return home.

Style

Setting

The setting of most of *In Country* is the small Kentucky town of Hopewell. The importance of this is that it adds to the sense of alienation that is felt by Emmett and, to a lesser degree, by Sam: anyone out of the ordinary is especially conspicuous in a small town, particularly in a small rural town, where ordinariness is actually pursued. In this setting, both Sam and Emmett feel that their neighbors look at them as "weird." "People in the town still talked about the day Emmett and the hippies flew the Vietcong flag from the courthouse tower," the story explains, even though that act is at least ten years in the past. Later, when they are trying on earrings, Sam's best friend Dawn tells her, "We're the baddest girls in Hopewell." This may not be an accurate reflection of how the people in the town feel in general, but it does convey their impression that most of the townspeople fear and mistrust them.

In addition to the particular state and town that the novel is set in, most of the action takes place in the house where Sam and Emmett live. The house is a symbolic reflection of Emmett's state of mind; he imagines that it is being overrun with fleas, which indicates his constant paranoia, and he feels that the structure is not solid, indicating that he is aware of his own instability. In this respect, it is a very good sign that he is trying to seal the cracks in the foundation, because this implies that Emmett is fighting against the further decay of his heart and mind.

Structure

Most of this novel is written in flashback, with the action happening before the "real time" that has been established for the story. The opening section, the four chapters that comprise the first twenty pages, is written with present tense verbs, explaining, for example, what Emmett "says" or how Sam "looks." The action in Part Two happened earlier in the summer, before the action in Part One, and it is conveyed in the past tense, describing what a character "said" or "did." In the third section the action continues from where it left off at the end of Part One, and the narrative voice resumes the present tense.

Structuring the book this way achieves several benefits. Letting readers know early about the trip to Washington that actually happens after most of the action in the novel helps keep their attention focused on the outcome as they move through the loosely-connected events that are presented in Part Two. Using different tenses to indicate different time frames helps readers keep a clear chart of what is happening when. And splitting the action into two time frames allows the story to have two climaxes: the climax of Part Two occurs at Cawood's Swamp, when Emmett is able to talk about his experience of the war, and the story that begins in Part One and ends in Part Three climaxes, of course, at the Memorial.

Symbolism

Of particular symbolic significance in this book is the idea of motion, especially moving away from something, or taking flight. The book begins with three characters travelling down the interstate highway, and when they stop for the night Sam puts on her running shoes and runs for a few miles. As the story develops, readers are told that Emmett's first response when he returned from the was to travel aimlessly out west, to Albuquerque, Eugene, Santa Cruz—American literature has a long-standing tradition of characters escaping their worries and heading to the west, which was the last part of the continent for civilization to reach. Sam's mother Irene escaped from Hopewell and went east to Lexington twice. The first time, with Bob the hippie, she felt a little too free, and worried that they would not be able to live up to the obligation of raising a child. She is apparently comfortable with life with her husband Larry, which enables her to care for her baby and to expand into new areas, such as her crafts group, although she still dreams of going further east, to the source of American civilization, to England.

All of this symbolism of flight is concentrated into the image of birds. Most obvious of these is Emmett's interest in seeing an egret, which is one of the few things he is able to focus his attention on. Ironically, it is a bird that he saw in Vietnam, meaning that even as he is trying to escape, to fly, he is taking himself back to the site of his trauma, to correct his problem at its source. The car that Sam yearns for so anxiously throughout the summer is called "a good little bird" by her early in the novel, because it offers her freedom to seek the answers she needs in the world beyond Hopewell, whether that entails going to the Hughes farm several miles out of town or all the way to Washington, D.C.

The Vietnam Veterans' Memorial, which is the source of spiritual healing for Sam, Emmett, and Mawmaw, is surrounded by images of flight. Sam thinks of a dream in which the memorial was a black boomerang, "whizzing toward her head"; the narrator explains that the Memorial is V-shaped, "like the wings of an abstract bird, huge and headless. Overhead, a jet plane angles, taking off." At the moment that Sam finally understands Emmett's fourteen years of grieving for the men who died around him in the war, another jet flies overhead- "Its wings are angled back too, like a bird's"; as Mawmaw explains that visiting the memorial has given her hope, "she loosens her bird-like claw grip" from Sam's arm.

Historical Context

The Vietnam War

As is usually the case when seeking the cause of any war, the roots of the Vietnam War can be traced backwards in time for decades or even centuries, to ancient injustices and insults that have boiled over into modern times. One place to start explaining the war could be the remote year of 208 BC, the year that the Han dynasty of China expanded southward declaring the region that contains modern Vietnam to be a new Chinese province. This began a cycle of Chinese invasion and local resistance that has flared up sporadically ever since.

Another source of the conflict came in 1863, when the French, in the process of colonizing the region that they called Indochina, established a protectorate over Cambodia and began the process of annexing Cochinchina (southern Vietnam), then Annam (central Vietnam), then Tonkin (northern Vietnam). French imperialism throughout the first

Vietnam Veterans' War Memorial.

decades of the twentieth century shifted the wealth of the land from the Vietnamese to the hands of the colonizers. By 1940, for instance, there were 600 rubber plantations in Vietnam, all owned by a few French companies.

During World War II, Vietnam, like many small countries in southeast Asia, was controlled by Japan, and when Japan surrendered to Allied forces in August of 1945 the Vietnamese people were left with two very different ideas of what the fate of their country should be. One side believed that the country had struggled against Japanese control in order to be independent; these people, concentrated in the north, followed the Communist leader Ho Chi Minh and joined his party, the Viet Minh, in fighting for their freedom. The other faction, mostly in the south of the country, believed that it was inevitable that French rule would return and that it was necessary for restoring order, and they feared the idea of letting the country fall into Communist hands. The Viet Minh wrote a declaration of independence and were supported by Communist China and, briefly, American advisors who had been in Vietnam during the war to help the rebels oppose Japan.

The tension in Vietnam broke out into fighting in 1946, and the country formally divided into two parts, with the Communist government based in Hanoi in the North and the French operating out of Saigon in the south. French opposition to the Viet Minh lasted from 1946 to 1954, when a peace agreement was reached and the French agreed to leave after they helped South Vietnam establish an independent, non-Communist government. As the French withdrew, the United States sent more support to South Vietnam. By 1957, Communist rebels in South Vietnam, who were called the Viet Cong, were staging attacks against U.S. bases, and they began guerilla attacks against the South Vietnamese government in 1959. The Viet Cong received ever-increasing support from the Communist government of North Vietnam, which was in turn supported by Russia and China, so American support to the South increased.

In December 1961 the first U.S. troops arrived in Saigon—400 uniformed army personnel. A year later, there were 11,200 U.S. troops in Vietnam; by the end of 1965 the number was up to 200,000. Despite increasing opposition from American citizens, the government continued to commit troops, reaching a peak in 1969, when 543,400 military personnel were stationed in Vietnam. A peace accord was reached in 1973, after 57,685 U.S. soldiers had died and 153,303 were wounded (which only reflected a fraction of the 2 million Vietnamese casualties, with 3 million wounded). In December 1974, after all of

Compare & Contrast

- **1985:** Mikhail Gorbachev became the general secretary of the Soviet Communist Party, marking the beginning of the end for the Soviet Union. Gorbachev instituted the policy of *glasnost,* emphasizing government openness and honesty. In December of 1991 the Soviet Union officially dissolved, allowing its constituent countries to elect their own representative governments.

  Today: Not faced with the threat of Communism, the United States is less likely to enter into a war like the one in Vietnam for the sake of maintaining a global balance of power.

- **1985:** The United States became a debtor nation, spending more than it had to spend, for the first time in over seventy years.

  Today: Politicians are cutting social programs in an attempt to bring federal expenditures in balance with the government's income. Schemes to balance the budget have come and gone since the 1980s, but economists say that current expectations are possible if the economy stays strong.

- **1985:** AIDS, which was then still a new and unfamiliar disease, gained international awareness when Rock Hudson, 59, a popular movie and television star, died of the disease. The public did not know that the actor was infected until he collapsed in a restaurant on July 21, and his quick death on October 2 shocked fans.

  Today: Basketball player Magic Johnson, who announced to the world in 1991 that he had HIV (the virus that causes AIDS), has kept the disease in control with medication.

- **1985:** Compact discs and compact disc players were introduced, giving improved sound quality and portability to the personal music market.

  Today: Some die-hard fans still stand by the sound quality of vinyl record albums, but few new recordings are released on vinyl any more.

---

the American troops were gone, the North Vietnamese and their allies launched a major offensive, and in April of 1975 Saigon fell to invading forces and the country was united in Communism.

The Opposition at Home

In the United States, the opposition to the Vietnam War grew in scope and intensity, to the extent that today the image of protestors is a stronger symbol of the 1960s to most Americans than the soldiers who fought in the war. Organizations such as the Students for a Democratic Society and the Young Socialists Alliance organized the struggle against the war on college campuses throughout the country. During the 1960s, there was a huge swell in college enrollments, caused by the children of veterans who had returned after World War II to find the country more stable and prosperous than it had been since the Stock Market Crash in 1929.

College students were the logical dissenters: they were the age of the boys who were being drafted into the army, their peer group; they were educated about the complexities of the Vietnam situation and were less likely than mainstream Americans to fear Communists or the Viet Cong without examining their theoretical positions; and, being young and for the most part away from home for the first time in their lives, college students were psychologically poised to rebel against authority. Using techniques that and proved successful for the Civil Rights demonstrations in the late 1950s and early 1960s (most notably, sit-ins and protest marches), the anti-war movement gained popular support.

In 1968, President Lyndon Johnson decided not to run for reelection, convinced that he would not be reelected because of his role in sending American troops to Vietnam; at that year's Democratic convention in Chicago, anti-war protestors commanded the world's attention. In 1969, the moratorium protest against the war brought 250,000 marchers to Washington, D.C., the site of the 1963

Civil Rights protest where Dr. Martin Luther King delivered his "I Have A Dream" speech to a similarly large crowd. At a rally at Kent State University in Ohio on May 4, 1970, National Guardsmen opened fire on 1000 protestors, killing four. That event changed opposition to the war symbolically, making average Americans see it less of a fight between students and the government and more like a fight of the government against its citizens.

By the time the war ended in 1973, most Americans did not care that the country had never walked away unsuccessfully from a war before, and they did not care what happened to South Vietnam; they had seen the killing in graphic living color on their televisions and had experienced social strife at home, and they were sick of it all. Returning veterans were treated as reminders of an episode in the country's history that had created misery and destruction and had yielded no real good.

Critical Overview

Critics have been impressed with Bobbie Ann Mason's works since the publication of her first book of fiction, *Shiloh, and Other Stories* in 1982. Most reviews and essays about her work concentrate on one of three areas: her use of simple, "normal" speech and her pop culture references (such as the use of franchise-store locations and television programs); her rendering of complex and inarticulate characters; and her importance as a Southern writer.

Regarding her use of ordinary people's language and artifacts, most critics, like most readers, agree that Mason has created a new and special form since her first published stories. Frank Conroy, a distinguished American author and critic, noted in his review of *Spence + Lila* (Mason's novel following *In Country*) that in her earlier works she "has shown a deft touch for the craft of narrative fiction and has charmed many readers with her ability to write dialogue, particularly the dialogue of country folk."

Nicci Gerard wrote a review in the *New Statesman & Society* that contrasted Mason's style with the somewhat similar (but actually quite different) styles used by other writers at the time. Mason's simplicity, she wrote, was "not the cool clever minimalism of her urban contemporaries, nor the 'dirty realism' that has so recently fired the dissatisfied American imagination." By making this distinction, she set Mason aside from a crowd of other

writers made their fame in the late 1970s and early 1980s by making use of mass consumerism and tightly-wound, inarticulate characters.

David Y. Todd made a similar distinction while reviewing the 1989 collection *Love Life:* "Inhibition seems endemic to (her characters') culture," he wrote, and he went on to state his wish that more of Mason's people could relate to one another better, but adds that "to do this would be false to the people she is writing about." It is, in fact, Mason's characters that critics seem to have the most problem with in the few cases where they have any problem with her writing at all. Most reviews and essays express admiration for the people that she illuminates in her stories.

For example, Richard Giannone's in-depth analysis, "Bobbie Ann Mason and the Recovery of Mystery" in *Studies in Short Fiction* credited the author for being able to see beyond her characters' situations: "She is alive to the distant, unseen dimension of life. One way into her art is to see how her characters, who are lost amid the Burger Chefs, K-Marts and television talk shows that level western Kentucky into the nondescript American landscape, find their spiritual portion in the turmoil."

Others simply appreciate the way that she treats the people that spring from her imagination, as seen in Michael Dorris' comment in his review of *Spence + Lila* for the *Chicago Tribune* that "Mason writes about her characters with respect and occasional lyricism." Frank Conroy, whose praise of Mason's writing is cited above, later in the same review captured the vague dissatisfaction that critics seem to be getting at when they review her works, even when it does not seem that they themselves do not know what is making them unhappy. "So what's wrong?" Conroy wrote. "Why does one feel increasingly uneasy as this smooth, artful writing flows by page after page? Perhaps out of the suspicion that the author has reduced the central characters down to manageable form to make them fit into the book, rather than risking the attempt to deal with fully complex characters who might represent more of a threat to the neatness of the narrative."

Most serious examinations of Mason's works have taken note of the fact that the area she writes about, western Kentucky, qualifies her as a Southern writer, and they link her to the long history of Southern fiction. In an essay from Spring, 1987, Robert H. Brinkmeyer, Jr., credited her with being the salvation of a category that was starting to face to history: "It is just possible that Mason is charting new directions for Southern fiction, a rebirth of sorts adapting patterns from the past to enrich and comprehend the disorder of contemporary experience." Although most reviewers have not pinned the future of a whole literary tradition on her, reviews generally do note that the tradition of rural storytellers shows up in Mason's works in a contemporary was.

Criticism

Diane Andrews Henningfeld

Henningfeld is a professor at Adrian College and has written for a variety of academic journal and educational publishers. In the following essay, she argues that Sam Hughes, the main character of In Country, *struggles with the issues of creating a text in her attempts to understand her father's life and the Vietnam War.*

In Country, Bobbie Ann Mason's first novel, was published in 1985. Before the publication of the novel, Mason was known primarily as a writer of short stories. Her work has often been compared to that of Raymond Carver and Anne Beattie. Much of Mason's work is set in rural Kentucky and her characters are caught between the traditions of the past and the intrusions of popular culture. Often characterized as a minimalist, Mason employs lean, spare prose peppered with brand names, television shows, and rock and roll music.

The novel generally met with praise from reviewers when it appeared in 1985. Joel Conarroe, for example, called *In Country* "a meticulously crafted novel." Not all reviewers were enamored with Mason's style, however, criticizing what they viewed as flat dialogue and cliched characters.

Nevertheless, in the years since the first publication of the novel, *In Country* has generated considerable critical interest. Nearly every collection of essays on Vietnam War literature includes at least one chapter on the novel, and articles treating *In Country* appear regularly in academic journals.

Critics choose the read the novel in several ways. Some see the novel as a *Bildungsroman,* that is, a coming-of-age story. They see it as the tale of a girl growing into womanhood and into a mature understanding of her place in the world. Robert Brinkmeyer credits Sam's growth to her confrontation with her own history and the history of the Vietnam War. Other writers choose to examine gender issues in the novel, opposing Sam's quest

for knowledge with the reticence of the vets. Certainly, at times it seems that the vets are unwilling to let women, including Sam, into the secrets of the war. Finally, others such as Barbara Ryan focus on language, texts, and truth. For Ryan, Sam serves as a model of a modernist reader, looking for authoritative truth, who grows into a postmodernist reader, able to understand that there are many truths to the Vietnam War.

Viewing Sam as a reader offers an interesting way into the story. It is possible, however, to consider Sam not only as a reader of texts, but also as a creator of texts. When we observe Sam trying to piece together the fragments of her father's life, we see her struggle with the very issues all writers face: finding reliable sources, doing adequate research, accounting for contradictory reports, and shaping a cohesive narrative out of source material that is both uncooperative and ambiguous, attractive and repellant. Further, it may be possible to attribute some of the critical interest in *In Country* to the ambiguity of the Vietnam War and to our own need to shape a cohesive and acceptable narrative that at once explains and contains the Vietnam War.

Sam's role as textual creator defines itself early on in the book. She has already demonstrated her interest in the war and in her father, and has been reading history books in an attempt to find answers to her questions. However, it is at the following moment that we realize that Sam will be required to do more than read:

> Sam took her *Collegiate Dictionary* from the shelf. It was a graduation present from her mother—a hint that she should go to college. Boys got cars for graduation, but girls usually had to buy their own cars because they were expected to get married—to guys with cars. Inside the dictionary was her only picture of her father.

Here then before her are the tools of her trade: Dwayne Hughes' picture, a wordless and lifeless portrait in two dimensions; and the dictionary. It seems especially significant that Sam has chosen to keep her father's picture in the dictionary. The dictionary is a collection of words, each word with a definition made up of yet other words. The dictionary exists not as a repository of meaning, but rather as potential for the creation of meaning. Sam's task is to string together the words that will bring her father to life. More important, perhaps, is her second task, to string the words together that will connect her to her father. At this moment, as she looks at her father's picture, and then at her own face in the mirror, she unable to "see any resemblance to him."

What Do I Read Next?

- The soldiers interviewed by Al Santoli for his 1981 book *Everything We Had: An Oral History of the Vietnam War by Thirty-Three Soldiers Who Fought It* tell the sort of short, focused, poignant tales of their experiences that the veterans in *In Country* come up with infrequently.

- One of the best writers to emerge from the Vietnam experience is Tim O'Brien. His book *The Things They Carried* was many years in the making (it was published in 1990) and it uses a new form, neither really novel nor short story collection, that reflects the uncertainty of life during war.

- Many veterans of the Vietnam war have written of their experiences, giving Americans a wide opportunity to look at what their life was like. Vince Gotera has put together a book that examines one particular genre, poetry, in his 1994 collection *Radical Visions: Poetry by Vietnam Veterans,* published by University of Georgia Press. Much of the text of this book is explanatory of the times and of the works, with proportionally few actual poems included.

- The story of combat veteran Robert Mason closely parallels the story that Emmett can only hint at. His book *Chickenhawk,* published in 1983, was hailed as one of the best of the generation of Vietnam autobiographies, and it led to 1993's *Chickenhawk: Back In The World,* about the experiences from 1966 to 1992, which may seem like a long time for him to carry the trauma of war to those who have not read *In Country.*

- While the testimonies of average people who just happened to have become involved in the war are interesting in themselves, it is also informational to see the war experience reflected by people whose job it is to capture reality. Eric James Schroder followed this idea in 1992, with the publication of *Vietnam, We've All Been There: Interviews With American Writers.* Not all of the writers in this book served in the military during the war, but all have a unique perspective to offer.

The sources that Sam assembles include books, records, television shows, Emmett, Emmett's friends, her mother, her grandparents, her father's letters, and her father's diaries. Some of her sources she rejects early on; the history books are dull, and they don't "say what it was like to be at war." She also rejects *M.A.S.H* as a source of information because she knows that it is not real.

In addition, Sam runs into problems with her research. The veterans are reluctant to talk to her. Some say that they would rather forget about it. Others tell her that they want to protect her from Vietnam and the war. And still others tell her that because she has not experienced the Vietnam War herself, she can never know anything about it. As Pete says to her, "'Stop thinking about Vietnam, Sambo. You don't know how it was, and you never will. There is no way you can ever understand. So just forget it. Unless you've been humping the boonies, you don't know.'"

It is possible, of course, to read the veteran's reluctance to talk to Sam about the war as their desire to control the story itself. After all, Sam is a loose cannon. Who knows what kind of story her research will lead her to? Who knows how each contribution will figure in the final product? Most important, who knows how Sam might appropriate the veterans' stories and make them her own?

Sam also runs into contradictory reports. Her grandparents tell her that her father was a nice boy. When Sam reads the diary that he left, she is shocked by what she finds there. Instead of the nice boy, she finds a scared, shallow kid who talks about the smell of dead "gooks." Sam finally understands that her grandparents, too, are trying to control the story of Dwayne's life. The story needs to be one that they can live with, even if it means ignoring the written record that he has left behind.

Further, the diary as source material both attracts and repels Sam. As much as she wants to know about her father, she hates what she finds, as she tells Emmett: "The way he talked about gooks and killing—I hated it…. I hate him. He was awful, the way he talked about gooks and killing."

Sam's trip to Cawood's Pond in order to recreate the soldier's experience is an exercise in contradictions. At the same time that she is trying to recreate the experience, she is also trying to separate herself from it. She imagines that women would never kill and make war the way that men do, but then she recognizes that this is not true:

> Women were practical. They would bury a dead bird when it started to stink. They wouldn't collect teeth and ears for souvenirs. They wouldn't cut notches on their machetes…. Then chills rushed over her. Soldiers murdered babies. But women did too. They ripped their own unborn babies out of themselves and flushed them away, squirming and bloody. The chills wouldn't stop.

Perhaps even more to the point, Sam begins to identify with her father, even as she rejects him. She recognizes that her own "insensitive curiosity" is identical to his. Her identification with her father grows throughout her night at Cawood's Pond. When Emmett finds her in the morning, she confronts him with what she has found in her father's diary. Emmett breaks down and tells her his worst experience in Vietnam. In addition, Emmett identifies himself with Dwayne as a soldier: "'Look here, little girl. He could have been me. All of us, it was the same.'" A few moments later, Emmett identifies himself with Dwayne as Sam's father: "'I *want* to be a father. But I can't. The closest I can come is with you. And I failed. I should never have let you go so wild. I should have taken care of you.'" Sam responds that Emmett and Dwayne went to Vietnam for her mother's sake, and for hers. With this response, the story Sam is creating now includes herself.

When Sam, Emmett, and Mamaw arrive at the Vietnam Veterans' Memorial, Sam's identification with her father, with Emmett, and with the Vietnam War is complete. She reads her own name on the Wall, understanding herself to be simultaneously a creator and a participant in the on-going narration of the War. By including herself in the story she creates for her father, she integrates herself into the Wall itself. By so doing, she creates a story in which "all the names in America have been used to decorate this wall." Distinctions of gender

and age disappear in Sam's narration, a narration that swells to include us all.

Source: Diane Andrews Henningfeld, in an essay for *Novels for Students,* Gale, 1998.

Ellen A. Blais

In the following excerpt, Bliss supports her premise that the questions raised by one family's experience of the Vietnam war cannot be understood without also addressing gender issues that form the subtext of In Country.

Clearly, *In Country*'s basic text is about the process whereby Samantha Hughes learns about the Vietnam War, her dead father's role in that war, and her Uncle Emmett's experiences there. But just as surely the novel contains a subtext dealing with the way attitudes toward gender have conditioned the characters' interpretation of that experience. I propose here to look at this aspect of *In Country* in the depiction of the world of the novel and the values of its minor characters, and particularly in Sam's development.

An examination of seemingly peripheral cultural background elements illustrates that the novel ties together the issues of gender and war throughout. The opening section demonstrates this. As the characters relax in their motel room watching television, a special about Geraldine Ferraro's presence on the 1984 Democratic Presidential ticket produces the following dialogue:

> "She won't get elected," Mamaw says. "Nobody's ready for a woman up there."
>
> Sam reminds her that Kentucky has a woman governor.
>
> "Geraldine's dynamite," Emmett says when a picture of Geraldine Ferraro appears on the screen. "I like her accent."
>
> "She wouldn't get us in a war," says Sam. "Reagan wants to go to war."

National television portrays a culture in which women are replacing men in some capacities and in which they may bring to society values very different from those of their male counterparts. Conversely, males like Boy George, mentioned several times in the novel, may achieve fame by imitating aspects of female dress and behavior. As we shall see later, the novel is full of random details of this sort, introduced casually through the characters' conversations or the ubiquitous television, ideas and ways of behaving that are suddenly "in the air" both in the larger American culture of the mid-

> *But, in coming to accept Dwayne's dealing out and suffering death, Sam accepts her own complicity in war, violence, and death itself, her own mortality as well as America's 'mortality . . .'"*

eighties and in smaller places like Hopewell, Kentucky.

Descriptions of *M*A*S*H* reruns, Emmett's and Sam's chief entertainment, provide several references to Corporal Klinger and his comic cross-dressing. When Emmett, dressed in a "long, thin Indian-print skirt with elephants and peacocks on it," cooks dinner for Sam and her boyfriend Lonnie, the latter interprets this as Emmett's imitation of Corporal Klinger, making cross-dressing acceptable for Lonnie, the stereotypically masculine type who "didn't even like Boy George...."

While Emmett imitates aspects of the feminine, Sam is associated with a variety of masculine qualities. Her very name suggests gender ambiguity. In fact, she offers it to her pregnant friend Dawn because "'Sam's an all-purpose name. It fits boys and girls both.'" Sam's name sets her off from the other, excessively feminine, characters in the novel whose names, like Dawn and Heather, Irene and Anita, would never allow for gender confusion.

Sam is frequently seen and sees herself in a masculine context. When she, Emmett, and Lonnie, after having a few beers, go to Cawood's Pond, she rides in the back of Lonnie's pickup and, slightly high on the beer, feels "like a soldier in an armored personnel carrier." As Sam looks at the only photograph she has of her father, she sees him in a "dark uniform with a cap like the one [she] had worn when she worked at the Burger Boy." These references prepare the reader for Sam's attempt to recreate her father's and Emmett's war experiences in Cawood's Pond....

Because of different gender attitudes among characters in the novel, we see generational differences occasionally lead to different assumptions about gender-appropriate behavior. Mamaw fibs about needing to stop at a gas station and take a pill because she "[doesn't] want Emmett to know she [has] to pee." She also hesitates to share a motel room with Emmett because she is not related to him by blood. Grandma Smith, Sam's maternal grandmother, thinks to explain Emmett's apparent lack of interest in women by reference to the mumps he had had as a child, which might have "fallen" and which, she says, "'affect boys in their—balls—and when they grow up they can't have children.'"...

Sam's parents' generation also has conservative attitudes toward gender. Lonnie's parents embody very traditional roles. Lonnie's mother, Martha, devotes most of her energy to decorating and cooking. Both Martha and her husband Bud find it strange that Emmett does not work, as does Emmett's father, who wants to know when he will "'get a job like everybody else and stop fooling around.'" The men work, and while the women may also work, they are still associated primarily with domestic concerns. Cindy, a veteran's wife, makes him take down his map of Vietnam because it just does not "'fit her decorating scheme.'"...

Ostensibly, people in Hopewell believe that women are to be protected and controlled. One of the veterans says of HBO, "'I wouldn't let my wife watch it.'" But there are also signs of change. When a veteran's wife leaves him to go to Lexington, it is evidently not because their relationship has broken down. Her husband says, philosophically, "'She got a job offer up at this place where she used to work.... Maybe we'll be one of those long-distance marriages.... We always tried to be modern.'"

Anita Stevens, Emmett's former girlfriend, is most interesting in terms of the novel's preoccupations with gender. Sexy and attractive in conventional ways—even just sitting at home, she wears "dark fuchsia pants with a silver belt and string-strap heels," as well as "a pale pink blouse and some silver chains"—Anita is nonetheless opposed to marriage and fancy weddings. She combines behavior that suggests feminine values with a rejection of practices the culture uses to celebrate publicly women's place within social institutions such as marriage. Although she does bake cakes, she says, "'I got Betty Crocker this time.... I like her a whole lot better than Duncan Hines. That old fool.'" She blames her failed marriage on conventional gender roles and expectations: "'He played baseball, and he was good-looking as all hell, but he didn't know what to make of me. He wanted me to be a picture. That's all I was supposed to do, just be beautiful.'" She dates but doesn't want to be possessed....

Even among Sam's peers, gender assumptions still sound more like those of the fifties than those of the eighties. Sam's friend Dawn and Dawn's boyfriend Ken, as their names suggest, appear to take their gender roles straight from Matell's Barbie. Sam finds Dawn "very pretty." ... Dawn is pregnant, but vehemently rejects Sam's suggestions that she get an abortion. Although she has played a wifely role for her father since her mother's death, she is, nonetheless, eager to leave home in the only way she seems able to imagine, marrying and starting her own family.

Sam's boyfriend, Lonnie, resembles the males Anita finds objectionable—both macho and possessive. When Lonnie attends a stag party for his brother, he wants to take a pair of Sam's underwear—"'Those black ones I like.'" While Lonnie obviously likes and admires Emmett, he also betrays some conventional fears about Emmett's behavior and thinks that Agent Orange can "'settle [in the genitals] and practically turn you into a woman.'"...

Sam sees men as the ones who are good at making things: "All the men she knew fiddled with gadgets. They were always fixing something." When she is at Cawood's Pond, she feels diminished by her inability to do what soldiers are supposed to do in her place: "She felt so stupid. She couldn't dig a foxhole even if she had to, because she didn't have the tools." Instead, she watches a mother racoon and her babies. But later she does think "that woman Mondale nominated could probably dig one." Unfortunately, Sam has difficulty with Geraldine Ferraro as any kind of role model because she does not like Ferraro's "old lady suits." Sam wants to wear hot pink tank tops, leather-look panties, *and* dig foxholes.

Part of Sam's difficulty stems from the fact that she subscribes to some of the standard conceptions about gender-appropriate behavior. She is, herself, somewhat uncomfortable with Emmett's failure to pursue the accepted male roles of worker, husband, and father. She thinks of men as makers and fixers, and she responds to her stepfather's playing with baby Heather much as her grandmothers might: "It made Sam feel strange to see a grown man playing with a baby."

In fact, the crux of Sam's ambivalence about gender is her discomfort with babies. She really wants Dawn to have an abortion, and when Dawn asks if she isn't worried about the side effects of her birth control pills, Sam replies, "'Having a baby would be a pretty big side effect.'" Although she does dream she and Tom Hudson have a baby, in the dream they puree it every night and store it in the freezer. When Irene comes to visit with baby Heather, Sam's ambivalence is even more pronounced: "Her digestion was screwed up and seeing the baby made her nervous...."

Sam's dilemma is that she is fighting both biological and cultural imperatives. In her cultural milieu, traditional roles are still very much in evidence for both men and women although there are some exceptions such as Anita Stevens. In his refusal to work and have a family, Emmett is still seen as eccentric, and Irene refers to Anita as "'on the loose'" as though Irene were just waiting for someone to catch Anita. Even though Sam has been accepted by both the University of Kentucky and Murray State for the fall, her preoccupation with Emmett and the veterans makes it hard for her to see this as an avenue of escape from the narrow confines of small-town Southern culture....

Her decision to attend the University of Kentucky rather than remain in Hopewell, working at the Burger Boy and taking care of Emmett, indicates she will probably be able to do this without slipping into conventional feminine roles.

As the novel progresses, the connections between gender and the war become more pronounced. When Sam and Lonnie have dinner with his parents and the subject turns to the Vietnam veterans, Lonnie's father, Bud, expresses regret at having been born "'between wars'" because he feels he "'missed out on something important.'" Sam catches him up: "'If there wasn't a war for fifty years and two whole generations didn't have to fight, do you mean there should have been a war for them? Is that why we have wars—so guys won't miss out?'"...

Sam approaches understanding the Vietnam experience through her father's experience there. She needs to know more than she finds from the unrevealing letters he had sent Irene, letters in which he "made marching through the jungle seem like a rare privilege" and "didn't say he was scared." But a notebook her father had kept in Vietnam tells Sam a different story. This notebook reveals to her some of the horrors of the war and precipitates her running off to Cawood's Pond, the event that shocks Emmett into acknowledging to

Sam and himself the horror of his own experience in the war.

Reading Dwayne's accounts of rotting bodies and his first kill sickens Sam, who struggles to understand by connecting what she reads with her own experiences: "She recalled the dead cat she dug up once in Grandma's garden, and she realized her own insensitive curiosity was just like her father's. She felt humiliated and disgusted." Upon returning home and finding that Emmett has set off a flea bomb in the house to rid it of his cat Moon Pie's fleas, Sam imaginatively connects this with the war.... Sam realizes Emmett, like Dwayne, must have killed: "Emmett had helped kill those Vietnamese, the same way he killed the fleas"....

However, during the night at Cawood's Pond, Sam begins revising her notions of men and war; she strives to "feel what wretches feel." Walking through the dark swamp, Sam "was walking point. The cypress knees were like land mines." Yet she holds briefly her conviction that women would behave differently, they "wouldn't collect teeth and ears for souvenirs.... Soldiers murdered babies." But even this is qualified: "[W]omen did too. They ripped their own unborn babies out of themselves and flushed them away, squirming and bloody."

Gradually, however, Sam begins to identify more and more with the soldiers and with her father. But she does this while in a curious way also identifying herself with women and their experiences of terror and violence. In the morning, hearing Emmett looking for her, she thinks she is being stalked by a rapist and prepares for an attack:

> Hurriedly, she worked to create a weapon with the sharp edge of [a] can.... The V.C. rapist-terrorist was still on the boardwalk.... A curious pleasure stole over her. This terror was what the soldiers had felt every minute.... They were completely alive, every nerve on edge.... She put herself in Moon Pie's place. In Emmett's place.... She was in her father's place, in a foxhole in the jungle.... She felt more like a cat than anything, small and fragile and alert to movement.... It was a new way of seeing.

Here Sam seems involved in the kind of imaginative identification that takes her beyond the simply male or female or indeed merely human, an identification, in fact, with basic animal nature. However, when Emmett discounts her swamp experience as merely a childish attempt to get revenge on him for running off to Lexington earlier in the novel and frightening her, she responds by retreating to her oversimplifications of war and the male experience in it: "'That's what you were doing in Vietnam. That explains what the whole country was

doing over there. The least little threat and America's got to put on its cowboy boots and stomp around and show somebody a thing or two.'"

As they leave Cawood's Pond, it is finally Emmett's passive, almost Eastern wisdom Sam and the reader are left with: "He waved at the dark swamp. 'There are some things you can never figure out.'"

As Sam approaches the Vietnam Memorial in Washington ... [she] moves beyond her preoccupation with men and war, women and war, to the essential human preoccupation with mortality.... This is the "work" Emmett has been engaged in since coming home from Vietnam. Sam has been doing this "work" throughout the novel as she searches out the details of her father's experiences and death during the war. But, in coming to accept Dwayne's dealing out and suffering death, Sam accepts her own complicity in war, violence, and death itself, her own mortality as well as America's "mortality," figured here in military defeat:

> As they drive into Washington ... Sam feels sick with apprehension. She has kept telling herself that the memorial is only a rock with names on it.... Maybe that's the point. People shouldn't make so much of death.... Sometimes in the middle of the night it struck Sam with sudden clarity that she was going to die someday.... But now, as she and Emmett and Mamaw Hughes drive into Washington, where the Vietnam Memorial bears the names of so many who died, the reality of death hits her in broad daylight.

We see Washington's monuments through Sam's eyes, perhaps through her "new way of seeing," and here the gender issues in the novel appear to merge with the war issues as the novel concludes with a series of startlingly sexual images. Sam first sees the Washington Monument, rising "up out of the earth, proud and tall. She remembers Tom's bitter comment about it—a big white prick. She once heard someone say the U.S.A. goes around fucking the world." She sees the Vietnam Memorial in a number of metaphorical ways suggesting female genitalia and death, beauty and terror. "It is ... a black gash in a hillside, like a vein of coal exposed and then polished with polyurethane.... It is like a giant grave." As she walks down into the foxhole that is also the memorial, Sam feels "something so strong, it is like a tornado moving in her, something massive and overpowering. It feels like giving birth to this wall." For Sam, this is a moment of transcendence that nullifies the simpler categories of male and female, war and peace, evil and good.

After she has found her father's name etched into the wall, Sam goes to the directory to look at his name there among the Hugheses. She finds her own as well and then rushes to see it on the wall: "SAM A HUGHES. It is the first on a line.... She touches her own name. How odd it feels, as though all the names in America have been used to decorate this wall." This experience, unlike her experience at Cawood's Pond, becomes, for Sam, a successful fusion of the contradictions within her of male and female.

Source: Ellen A. Blais, *"Gender Issues in Bobbie Ann Mason's* In Country" in *South Atlantic Review,* Vol. 56, No. 2, May, 1991, pp. 107–118.

Sandra Bonilla Durham

In the following excerpt, Durham explores Mason's young female protagonist's quest to understand why men wage war.

In an interview with Wendy Smith, Bobbie Ann Mason explains that she did not consciously choose to write about Vietnam, that she had characters and action in mind before she realized that they had anything to do with the war. She says, "I think it came out of my unconscious, the same way it's coming out of America's unconscious. It's just time for it to surface."...

Although the novel focuses on seventeen-year-old Sam Hughes' search for the meaning of the Vietnam War, particularly the death of her father, it explores the personal loss of other members of the Hughes family and the changes brought by the war to the community and the nation. *In Country* is structured around two quests. Sam, her grandmother MawMaw, and her uncle Emmett make a three-day journey by car to Washington, D.C., to see the Vietnam War Memorial. This quest is the result of another—Sam's going both literally and figuratively into the wilderness, or "in country," to test her ability to survive. "In country" is the phrase veterans use to refer to their time in Vietnam, and Cawood's pond, a dangerous swamp, is Sam's symbolic Vietnam. Mason articulates Sam's motives for facing the wilderness:

> If men went to war for women, and for unborn generations, then she was going to find out what they went through. Sam didn't think the women or the unborn babies had any say in it. If it were up to women, there wouldn't be any war. No, that was a naive thought. When women got power they were just like men. She thought of Indira Gandhi and Margaret Thatcher. She wouldn't want to meet these women out in the swamp at night.

> What would make people want to kill? If the U.S.A. sent her to a foreign country, with a rifle and a heavy backpack, could she root around in the jungle, sleep

in the mud, and shoot at strangers? How did the army get boys to do that? Why was there war?

These words convey Sam's anger and confusion about the war and its aftermath—the psychic wilderness in which she is struggling for survival. Her confusion includes questioning her role as a domesticated woman—Dawn's friend, Lonnie's lover, Irene's daughter, and Emmett's caretaker—and her role as free woman—a strong individual emotionally isolated from her culture and questing for a deeper sense of self. She thinks of herself as having "so much evil and bad stuff in her now."

The archetype of Sam's journey may be Psyche's search, Sam is, like Psyche, the feminine principle: "Psyche divinized is consciousness raised. Her journey is the feminine journey from blind, instinctual attraction to a knowing, individualized love" [Nor Hall, *The Moon and the Virgin: Reflection on the Archetypal Feminine,* 1980]. Sam moves from caring for Emmett because he is family and a real life version of the damaged veterans on television to real love for her uncle and understanding of his deep sorrow.

Sam's quest, like Psyche's, is motivated by distrust, jealousy, hatred, and fear. Her distrust of the social system, her jealousy of Irene, her hatred of the war, and her fear for Emmett's health and sanity have separated her from her family and friends and have created division within herself. Sam's going in country enables her to deal with these feelings as Psyche's solitary ordeals purge her. Like Psyche, "by attending to the self in isolation, rather than repressing its demands or seeking distractions, [Sam's] process of discovery is furthered." [Hall, 1980] ...

Emmett, like Sam, is seeking wholeness and his place. He is intelligent and amiable, but he finds work meaningless and relationships difficult. He and Sam subsist on her education benefits, and Emmett spends his time cooking for Sam, watching TV, playing video games, and birdwatching. Mason says ... "There is a certain kind of exotic bird he has been looking for." ... This bird is one of the major symbols in the novel. Emmett tells Sam the bird is an egret, a beautiful white wader he used to see in the rice paddies in Vietnam. He says, "That was a good memory. The only fucking one. That beautiful bird just going about its business with all that crazy stuff going on...." The bird represents life and beauty surviving in the midst of death and horror.

Sam's mother, Irene, always independent and adventurous, has left her former self behind and has

> *If it were up to women, there wouldn't be any war. No, that was a naive thought. When women got power they were just like men. She thought of Indira Gandhi and Margaret Thatcher. She wouldn't want to meet these women out in the swamp at night."*

remarried, moved to Lexington, where she is attending college, and has had a baby. Sam resents Irene's leaving Hopewell and is somewhat jealous of Irene's new life. Sam longs for the past when Irene made popcorn and they watched M*A*S*H together. Playing Irene's old rock records keeps Sam in touch with the past she shared with her mother and, in absentia, her father....

When Sam visits her grandparents, Grandma and Granddad Smith, Irene and Emmett's parents, she gains a clearer insight into how the war affected the family and the community.... Grandma has been talking about the younger generation's lack of faith and she adds, "Hopewell used to be the best place to bring up kids, but now it's not." Grandma does not elaborate on the loss of traditional values, but the idea is reinforced by her and Granddad's exchange about Emmett's service:

"He was raring to go over there and fight," said Granddad.

"You were all for him going!" Grandma cried angrily. "You said the army would make a man out of him. But look what it done."

"It's not too late," Granddad said. "It's not too late to pull himself up and be proud."...

A visit to MawMaw and Pap Hughes, whom Sam hasn't seen in two years, provides more insight. They live far out in the country which Sam imagines has changed little since her father had lived there. She begins to abandon her romantic view of her mother and father and their relation-

ship. "Sam had wanted to believe there was something magic between them that had created her and validated their love. But teen-age romances weren't very significant, she realized now." When they discuss the war, MawMaw says, "They wrote and told what a help he was to his country. I take comfort in that." And Sam replies, "What good did he do for the country? Everybody knows it was a stupid war, but fifty-eight thousand guys died. Emmett says they all died for nothing." MawMaw responds, "Well, Emmett can talk. He didn't die. Dwayne was fighting for a cause...."

MawMaw's idealized version of the war is destroyed when Sam reads her father's diary which MawMaw has given her. One entry describes finding a dead Vietnamese and taking his teeth as a good luck charm. Another describes getting revenge for a dead comrade by finding "gooks" and making "gook puddin'." Sam perceives the war and her father newly: "Now everything seemed ... like something rotten."

It is this feeling of corruptness which spurs Sam's going in country. At Cawood's pond Sam continues to think about the war and to look for the egret Emmett searches for. She survives the night in the swamp and is preparing to leave when she hears a noise, "a V.C. rapist-terrorist.... But this was real. A curious pleasure stole over her. This terror was what the soldiers had felt every minute.... They were completely alive, every nerve on edge.... It was a new way of seeing." At last Sam is beginning to understand why men fight. The noise is Emmett coming to find her.... He chides Sam for frightening him by running away, and her reply suggests that the war was the national equivalent of a child's running away....

Sam also tells Emmett she hates her father for "the way he talked about gooks and killing." Emmett replies, "It's the same for all of us!... You can't do what we did and then be happy about it. And nobody lets you forget it."

Emmett loses control of his emotions; he weeps and talks about Vietnam and tells Sam, "There's something wrong with me. I'm damaged. It's like something in the center of my heart is gone and I can't get it back." Sam replies, "But you cared enough about me to come out here."

It is at this point that Mason's bird symbol is used most effectively. Sam says, "I wish that bird would come," and Emmett explains, "If you can think about something like birds, you can get outside of yourself, and it doesn't hurt as much. That's the whole idea. That's the whole challenge for the human race." As Emmett walks out of the swamp, Sam observes, "He seemed to float away, above the poison ivy, like a pond skimmer, beautiful in his flight." Emmett has become the bird which they both wished to see—he is a symbol of the beauty and life to be found in human relationships.

Sam emerges from the wilderness reconciled to the reality of her father's killing and dying, and affirming Emmett's wholeness. Still, some conflicts remain to be resolved....

Emmett urges Sam, still dazed from her trip in country, to make the trip to Washington and invites MawMaw to go with them. Sam loves the freedom symbolized by being on the road, and, although she has first been intolerant of MawMaw's country ways, she realizes what a restricted life her grandmother has lived, and she sympathizes with the old woman's struggle to cope with a world she has never experienced before.

When the family arrives at the memorial each member experiences a healing....

Reading and touching Dwayne's name on the wall, MawMaw feels a greater sense of unity with him; Emmett ends his grieving for his lost comrades, and Sam accepts the inevitable tragedy of war....

Finding an answer to her questions about the war, Sam finds a new sense of self. Sam's quests have prepared her for a promising future.

Source: Sandra Bonilla Durham, "Women and War: Bobbie Ann Mason's *In Country*" in *The Southern Literary Journal,* Vol. 22, No. 2, Spring, 1990, pp. 45–52.

Sources

Robert H. Brinkmeyer, Jr., "Finding One's History: Bobbie Ann Mason and Contemporary Southern Literature," in *The Southern Literary Journal,* Vol. XIX, No. 2, Spring, 1987, pp. 20-33.

Frank Conroy, "The Family at Her Bedside," in *The New York Times Review of Books,* June 26, 1988, p. 7.

Michael Dorris, "Bonds of Love," in *Chicago Tribune—Books,* June 26, 1988, p. 6.

Nicci Gerard, "Love Among the Pumpkins," in *New Statesman & Society,* Vol. 2, No. 79, December 8, 1989, p. 34.

Richard Giannone, "Bobbie Ann Mason and the Recovery of Mystery," in *Studies in Short Fiction,* Vol. 27, No. 4, Fall, 1990, pp. 553-66.

Thomas Morrissey, "Mason's *In Country,*" in *The Explicator,* Vol. 50, No. 1, Fall, 1991, pp. 62-4.

James S. Olson and Randy Roberts, *Where The Domino Fell: America and Vietnam, 1945-1990,* St. Martin's Press, 1991.

David Y. Todd, "Love Life," in *The Bloomsbury Review,* Vol. 9, No. 3, May-June, 1989, pp. 2, 20.

Douglas Welsh, *The History of the Vietnam War,* Exeter Books, 1981.

Tom Wells, *The War Within: America's Battle Over Vietnam,* University of California Press, 1994.

For Further Study

David Booth, "Sam's Quest, Emmett's Wound: Grail Motifs in Bobbie Ann Mason's Portrait of America After Vietnam," in *The Southern Literary Journal,* Vol. 19, No. 2, Spring, 1987, pp. 98-109.
  Booth argues that elements of the Arthurian grail legend including the motif of the wasteland and the wounded king figure in *In Country.*

Joel Osler Brende and Erwin Randolph Parson, *Vietnam Veterans: The Road to Recovery,* Plenum Press, 1985.
  Published at the same time as *In Country,* this book raises some of the same concerns as Mason's novel. It is because of books like these that veterans are not shunned today as much as they were in 1985.

Robert H. Brinkmeyer, Jr., "Finding One's History: Bobbie Ann Mason and Contemporary Southern Literature," in *The Southern Literary Journal,* Vol. 19, No. 2, Spring, 1987, pp. 20-33.
  Brinkmeyer explores the how Sam's pursuit of her own history and the history of the Vietnam War ultimately lead to her own personal growth.

Joel Conarroe, "Winning Her Father's War," in *The New York Times Book Review,* September 15, 1985, p. 7.
  Conarroe reads *In Country* as a coming-of-age story in which Sam moves through traditional "rites of passage, progressing from separation to isolation … and finally to integration."

Wayne Gunn Drewey, "Initiation, Individuation, *In Country*" in *The Midwest Quarterly,* Vol. 36, No. 1, Autumn, 1996, pp. 59-73.
  Drewey argues that *In Country* uses as its structure the journey motif with a difference: in the case of Sam Hughes, the hero is a female.

James R. Ebert, *A Life In A Year: The American Infantryman in Vietnam, 1965-1972,* Presidio Press, 1993.
  Oddly, for all of the books written by and about veterans, there are few that try to capture the perspective of the "grunt" soldiers. This book does a thorough, intelligent job of mixing interviews with synopses in order to capture the experience as well as any book can.

Arthur Egendorf, *Healing From The War: Trauma and Transformation after Vietnam,* Houghton Mifflin Co., 1985.
  Another book published the same year the same year as *In Country,* this book reads like a "self-help" or "pop psychology" book; the tone may be a little

lighter than many academic studies, but that approach is necessary sometimes in order for ordinary people to understand the effects of the experience.

W. D. Ehrhart, "Who's Responsible," in *Vietnam Generation,* Vol. 4, No. 1-2, Spring, 1992, pp. 95-100.
Vietnam War poet Ehrhart discusses his contributions to *In Country* and offers a sympathetic and thorough analysis of the novel.

Michiko Kakutani, in *The New York Times,* September 4, 1985, p. C20.
The reviewer credits Mason with a sure ear for teen-aged dialogue and her clear sense of a "a young woman's craving for both knowledge and innocence."

Jeffrey P. Kimball, *To Reason Why: The Debate About the Causes of U.S. Involvement in the Vietnam War,* Temple University Press, 1990.
Not much is made in this novel about why America was involved in Vietnam at all, but this is certainly a factor that affected how servicemen were treated when they returned home, and what they thought of themselves as they grew up and began to understand the nature of politics.

Katherine Kinney, "'Humping the Boonies': Sex, Combat, and the Female in Bobbie Ann Mason's *In Country,*" in *Fourteen Landing Zones: Approaches to Vietnam War Literature,* edited by Philip K. Jason, University of Iowa Press, 1991, pp. 38-48.
Kinney discusses how Sam attempts to transcend gender differences so that she can understand the meaning of the Vietnam War.

Tom Myers, *Walking Point: American Narratives of Vietnam,* Oxford University Press, 1988.
This is not a collection of stories about the Vietnam experience, as the title suggests, but an academic examination of the narratives about the war. Chapters like "The Memoir as 'Wise Endurance'" and "The Writer as Alchemist" look objectively at the Vietnam stories as a sub-genre of literature.

Harriet Pollack, "From *Shiloh* to *In Country* to *Feather Crowns,* in *The Southern Literary Journal,* Vol. 28, No. 2, Spring, 1996, pp. 95-117.
Pollack examines the role of history in Mason's writing and particularly the role of southern women's history.

Barbara T. Ryan, "Decentered Authority in Bobbie Ann Mason's *In Country,*" in *Critique,* Vol. 31, No. 3, Spring, 1990, pp. 199-212.
Ryan examines Sam's use of available texts as a way of explaining her search for truth.

Jeffrey Walsh, *American War Literature 1914 to Vietnam,* St. Martin's Press, 1982.
This overview of literary themes that have touched war experiences and been touched by them in this century is a good reminder to readers that no piece of writing, no matter how well researched or how realistic, is ever objective.

Kim Willenson, with the correspondents of *Newsweek, The Bad War: An Oral History of Vietnam,* New American Library, 1987.
This book's shocking title, reflecting just the sort of hostility faced by Emmett and the other veterans in *In Country,* is actually a reference to a better-known book, Studs Turkel's 1985 *The Good War,* which is a collection of interviews with veterans of World War II.

Jonathan Yardley, "Bobbie Ann Mason and the Shadow of Vietnam," in *Book World—The Washington Post,* September 8, 1985, p. 3.
The reviewer faults Mason for using cliches and for failing to say anything new about the Vietnam War in her novel.

Jane Eyre

Charlotte Brontë
1847

Published in 1847, *Jane Eyre* brought almost instant fame to its obscure author, the daughter of a clergyman in a small mill town in northern England. On the surface, the novel embodies stock situations of the Gothic novel genre such as mystery, horror, and the classic medieval castle setting; many of the incidents border on (and cross over into) melodrama. The story of the young heroine is also in many ways conventional—the rise of a poor orphan girl against overwhelming odds, whose love and determination eventually redeem a tormented hero. Yet if this all there were to *Jane Eyre,* the novel would soon have been forgotten. In writing *Jane Eyre,* Charlotte Brontë did not write a mere romantic potboiler. Her book has serious things to say about a number of important subjects: the relations between men and women, women's equality, the treatment of children and of women, religious faith and religious hypocrisy (and the difference between the two), the realization of selfhood, and the nature of true love. But again, if its concerns were only topical, it would not have outlived the time in which it was written. The book is not a tract any more than it is a potboiler. It is a work of fiction with memorable characters and vivid scenes, written in a compelling prose style. In appealing to both the head and the heart, *Jane Eyre* triumphs over its flaws and remains a classic of nineteenth-century English literature and one of the most popular of all English novels.

Author Biography

Jane Eyre is subtitled *An Autobiography.* It is, however, a novel. Yet critics have discerned a number of autobiographical elements in the book.

Charlotte Brontë was born on March 31, 1816, in the village of Thornton in the West Riding of Yorkshire (now West Yorkshire), England. She was the third child in a family that soon consisted of five girls and a boy. Only seven years separated the eldest, Maria, from the youngest, Anne. Her father, the Reverend Patrick Brontë (originally Brunty), came from an impoverished Irish family; he had immigrated to England in the late 1700s and studied at Cambridge University before being ordained as a clergyman in the Church of England. Charlotte's mother, Maria Branwell, was originally from Penzance, Cornwall, at the southwest tip of England. In 1820 the family moved to Haworth, an isolated mill town on the edge of the Yorkshire moors. They took up residence in the small parsonage next to the local parish church where Reverend Brontë was minister. Mrs. Brontë died of cancer the following year.

In 1824 Reverend Brontë sent his four eldest daughters to the Clergy Daughters School at Cowan Bridge, Yorkshire, run by a Reverend Carus Wilson. Conditions at the school were strict and physically harsh. The two eldest Brontë sisters, Maria and Elizabeth, both developed tuberculosis and died the following year. More than twenty years later, Charlotte's experiences at the school would form the basis of several characters, incidents, and settings in *Jane Eyre.* Reverend Wilson became the model for the character Mr. Brocklehurst, while Maria Brontë served as the model for Helen Burns. Lowood Institution in the book was based largely on the Clergy Daughters School.

Charlotte and Emily returned to Haworth, where they remained for the next six years with their father and their surviving siblings, Branwell and Anne. During this time the children escaped into a world of imagination and creative fantasy. Charlotte and Branwell collaborated in writing romantic stories, in tiny hand-made books, about a fictional kingdom called Angria. The hero of these stories was a character known as the Duke of Zamorna—a character to whom Mr. Rochester in *Jane Eyre* bears much resemblance.

In 1831 Charlotte went away to Roe Head school. Although she remained only a year, she made two life-long friends, Ellen Nussey and Mary Taylor. The school's principal, Margaret Wooler,

Charlotte Brontë

would be the model for Ms. Temple in *Jane Eyre.* In 1839 Charlotte took her first job as a governess. She also received, and turned down, proposals of marriage from two ministers, one of whom was Ellen Nussey's brother. She was not in love with either of these men, and did not feel that she could enter into this kind of marriage. This situation was to be recounted fictionally in the relationship between Jane and Reverend St. John Rivers. Several years later Charlotte and Emily went to Brussels, Belgium, to attend a school run by Constantin Héger. Charlotte evidently formed a passionate attachment to Héger, an older, married man who did not return (and probably was not even aware of) her affection.

Returning to Haworth, Charlotte wrote poetry and was surprised to find that Emily also wrote poetry—as did Anne and Branwell. In 1846 the three women published a joint volume of their poems, using the pseudonyms Currer, Ellis, and Acton Bell. The collection, produced at their own expense, sold only two copies. Undaunted, the three women each wrote a novel, which they submitted to a London publisher, again using the same pseudonyms. Emily and Anne's manuscripts—*Wuthering Heights* and *Agnes Grey*–were accepted, but Charlotte's—*The Professor*—was turned down. Almost immediately, Charlotte began writing *Jane*

Eyre. She completed the book quickly and sent it off to the publishing firm of Smith, Elder & Co., the same company who had rejected *The Professor.* The publishers reacted with great enthusiasm, and *Jane Eyre* was published just three months later, in October, 1847. So good were the sales that within a year the book was issued in its third edition. Whereas her sisters had earned advances of fifty pounds for their novels, Charlotte received five hundred pounds for hers—a considerable sum of money at that time. However, her publisher and the reading public still knew the author only as "Currer Bell." There was even speculation that the three "Bells" were in fact a single author writing under three different pseudonyms. In July, 1848, Charlotte and Anne took the train to London to visit their publisher, who was astonished but delighted to learn that Currer Bell was a woman.

In the midst of their literary success, more tragedy struck the Brontë family. Branwell, who had become a hopeless alcoholic, died of tuberculosis in 1848, followed in December of that year by Emily. Anne died of the same disease the following year, leaving Charlotte the sole survivor among the original six Brontë children. She went on to write two further novels, *Shirley* (1849) and *Villette* (1853). In 1854 she married the Reverend Arthur Nicholls, her father's curate. Charlotte Brontë died less than a year later, apparently from complications during pregnancy. However, her reputation, and that of *Jane Eyre,* continued to grow.

Plot Summary

Volume I

Jane Eyre opens with the narrator, the adult Jane Eyre, recalling her childhood experiences growing up as an orphan at Gateshead, the home of her unfriendly aunt, Mrs. Reed. Mrs. Reed treats Jane as an outcast. On one occasion when her cousin John attacks her, Jane tries to defend herself. As a result, she finds herself being punished by being locked in the frightening "Red Room," where her uncle Reed had died many years earlier. A terrified Jane screams and faints.

Jane soon learns that Mrs. Reed plans to send her away to school. The stern Mr. Brocklehurst of the Lowood School for orphaned girls comes to visit. Having been told by Mrs. Reed that Jane is an evil child, he questions Jane about her religious beliefs and assures her that bad girls will suffer in hell. Mr. Brocklehurst agrees to enroll Jane in his

school. On the day she is to depart, only the servant Bessie rises to say good-bye to her.

The Lowood School offers Jane a very different life, as the conditions there are very poor. It is cold and drafty, the water is frozen, and the bland food the girls are given, which is often burnt, is insufficient to satisfy their hunger. On her second day at Lowood, Jane sees the cruel Miss Scatcherd punish a new friend, Helen Burns. Helen's reaction, however, is that she deserves such treatment and that she believes in Christian patience and endurance.

After three weeks Mr. Brocklehurst visits the school, ordering the long hair of the older girls to be cut off and lecturing the girls on the sin of vanity. Though trying to avoid notice, Jane drops her slate and catches Mr. Brocklehurst's attention. Ordering Jane to stand on a stool for punishment, Brocklehurst announces to the rest of the children that she is a liar and is not to be trusted. Jane is comforted by Helen and by the kind head teacher, Miss Temple.

In the spring Lowood suffers a typhus epidemic. Many of the girls die, and Jane learns that Helen has grown quite ill. One night after a doctor's visit, Jane sneaks into Helen's bed and talks with her about dying. Helen expresses no fears or regrets. Jane falls asleep, and when she awakens in the morning, she discovers that Helen had died during the night. Jane remains as a pupil at Lowood for six more years, and then becomes a teacher for two more. When her beloved Miss Temple marries and leaves Lowood, Jane has no reason to continue there, so she secretly advertises her services as a governess and soon is offered a position.

Jane travels to Thornfield, the estate where she is to begin a new career as a governess. She is greeted by Mrs. Fairfax, the woman who had hired her, who is the housekeeper for the house's owner, Mr. Edward Rochester. Jane's pupil is to be Adèle Varens, a young French girl who is Mr. Rochester's ward. While showing Jane around the spacious house, Jane hears a haunting cackle coming from a room on the third floor. Mrs. Fairfax assures her that it is Grace Poole, an eccentric woman hired to do sewing.

Jane finds life at Thornfield pleasant, but unstimulating. While walking out to mail a letter one day, she is passed by a huge dog and then a strange-looking man on horseback. After passing Jane, the horse slips on a patch of ice and the rider is thrown, spraining his foot. Jane helps the man back onto his horse, and upon returning home, she learns that the man is her employer, Mr. Rochester. Although his manner is brusque and often offensive, Jane is drawn to him. One night after talking with Mr. Rochester, Jane is awakened by the strange laugh, and leaves her room to find Mr. Rochester's bedroom in flames. She wakes him and helps him to put out the fire, but he offers no explanation concerning these events. To Jane's surprise and disappointment, Mr. Rochester leaves early the next day without saying good-bye.

Volume II

Two weeks later, Mr. Rochester returns home and holds a huge party at his house, during which time Jane witnesses his flirtatious behavior with the beautiful but cold Blanch Ingram. One night a gypsy visits Thornfield, and tells the fortunes of the guests. As the gypsy tries to learn of Jane's feelings for Rochester, she discovers that the gypsy is Rochester in disguise. Jane tells Mr. Rochester of a visitor, Mr. Mason, who had arrived at Thornfield that day. That night Jane hears noise coming from the ceiling, and running upstairs, finds that Mr. Mason has been attacked, apparently by Grace Poole.

Shortly after the Mason incident, Jane learns that her Aunt Reed is dying. Returning to Gateshead to visit her aunt, Mrs. Reed tells her that many years ago Jane's Uncle John in Madeira had tried to contact her; he was interested in making Jane the heir to his fortune. Mrs. Reed, however, had told Uncle John that Jane was dead.

Upon Mrs. Reed's death, Jane returns to Thornfield and meets Mr. Rochester one night while walking in the garden. He admits to her his plans to marry. Jane begins to cry, but she soon learns that Mr. Rochester's intention is to marry her, and not Blanche Ingram. That night lightning strikes the huge horse chestnut tree under which she and Mr. Rochester had become engaged.

The night before her wedding, Jane awakens to see a strange and frightening figure in her room, shredding her wedding veil. Rochester assures her that the figure is Grace Poole. The next morning, Mr. Rochester tries to rush the wedding ceremony along, but it is stopped ultimately by Mr. Briggs, a lawyer, and Mr. Mason, who reveal that Rochester is already married to Mr. Mason's sister. An angry Rochester then takes the entire party up to the third floor at Thornfield and reveals his insane wife, Bertha, who is attended there by Grace Poole. Against Rochester's wishes, Jane decides that she must leave Thornfield:

"Jane, do you mean to go one way in the world, and to let me go another?"

"I do."

"Jane" (bending towards and embracing me), "do you mean it now?"

"I do."

"And now?" softly kissing my forehead and cheek.

"I do—" extricating myself from restraint rapidly and completely.

"Oh, Jane, this is bitter! This—this is wicked. It would not be wicked to love me."

"It would to obey you."

A wild look raised his brows—crossed his features: he rose, but he forebore yet. I laid my hand on the back of a chair for support: I shook, I feared—but resolved.

"One instant, Jane. Give one glance to my horrible life when you are gone. All happiness will be torn away with you. What then is left? For a wife I have but the maniac up stairs: as well might you refer me to some corpse in yonder churchyard. What shall I do, Jane? Where turn for a companion, and for some hope?"

"Do as I do: trust in God and yourself. Believe in heaven. Hope to meet again there."

Volume III

Jane steals out early in the morning and boards a coach. Soon out of food and money, she desperately stumbles over the moors to a small house and begs for help. She is taken into "Moor House" by two kind young ladies, Diana and Mary, and their brother, the pious minister St. John Rivers. When she recovers her health, St. John finds Jane a position as a school mistress in a small local school. Soon news comes that the Riverses' Uncle John has died, but has left them only ten pounds each. One night St. John visits Jane, and amazingly, begins to recount for her the story of her past life. It turns out that he has discovered Jane's real name and identity, and that she and the Riverses are cousins. Moreover, their Uncle John is also Jane's Uncle John, and she has inherited her uncle's fortune of twenty thousand pounds.

St. John Rivers begins to press Jane into marrying him and wishes her to join him in his life as a missionary. One night, St. John attempts to make Jane believe that not following her destiny with him will result in her going to hell. A stunned Jane suddenly hears Mr. Rochester calling her name. Sharing her new wealth with her cousins, she leaves them and returns to Thornfield.

Jane is shocked to find Thornfield in ruins and learns that Mr. Rochester's wife started a terrible fire that took her life, destroyed the house, and crippled and blinded Rochester. Traveling to look for Rochester at his other house, Ferndean, Jane is reunited with him. When he describes his desperate calling out for her several days earlier, Jane realizes that they have had a psychic experience. She agrees to stay with Mr. Rochester and to marry him.

Characters

Bessie

A woman who is the "nurse" at Mrs. Reed's house, Gateshead Hall, Bessie helps take care of the Reed children and young Jane Eyre. Jane regards Bessie as the most sympathetic figure in the Reed household, although Bessie seems somewhat aloof. In her narrative, Jane recalls Bessie as "pretty" and "a slim young woman, with black hair, dark eyes, very nice features, and good, clear complexion." Jane also remarks on Bessie's "capricious and hasty temper, and indifferent ideas of principle or justice." Bessie helps Jane prepare for her departure to Lowood Institution. Bessie shows up again about eight years later as Jane is leaving Lowood for Thornfield Hall. She has married, and she tells Jane what has happened to the Reeds in the intervening years. She also says that Jane's uncle had come to Gateshead Hall searching for Jane but had gone back to his home on Madiera when Mrs. Reed told him that Jane was dead. Jane meets Bessie again when she (Jane) returns to Gateshead to visit the dying Mrs. Reed.

Mr. Brocklehurst

Mr. Brocklehurst is the proprietor of Lowood Institution—the boarding school for orphans that Jane Eyre attends. He is introduced in chapter 4, when he comes to Gateshead Hall (Mrs. Reed's home) to examine Jane before admitting her to Lowood. He is described as "a black pillar! The straight, narrow, sable-clad shape standing erect on the rug." Mr. Brocklehurst is one of the novel's hypocrites. Although he professes to run Lowood as a charitable institution, he is more concerned with making a profit than he is with educating the girls who live at the school. He criticizes Miss Temple for giving the girls a special lunch of bread and cheese, saying that the girls' bodies should be starved to help save their souls. He also denounces some girls for having naturally curly hair and orders it to be cut off. (However, he does not seem to object to his own daughters' elaborate curls.) When Jane drops her slate and breaks it, Mr. Brocklehurst makes her stand on a stool in front of the class as punishment. The character of Mr. Brocklehurst is based partly on William Carus Wilson, an evangelical clergyman who founded the Clergy Daughters' School at Cowan Bridge. Wilson mismanaged the school and many of the girls (including Charlotte Brontë and her sisters) suffered from the resulting poor conditions. However, Wilson was evidently well intentioned, unlike the hypocritical Brocklehurst.

Helen Burns

Helen Burns is a girl who becomes Jane Eyre's best friend at Lowood Institution—the boarding school for orphans that Jane attends. Jane meets Helen in chapter 5, during an outdoor exercise period. Jane notes that Helen is reading Samuel Johnson's *Rasselas;* the book's name strikes Jane as "strange, and consequently attractive." Jane has earlier heard "the sound of a hollow cough" but does not immediately identify Helen with this cough. (The cough foreshadows Helen's fatal bout of consumption, or tuberculosis). Four years older than Jane, the fourteen-year-old Helen helps the newly arrived orphan adjust to the school and teachers. Helen embodies the virtues of patience, forbearance, humility, forgiveness, and Christian love. She conveys the importance of these qualities to the more worldly Jane. As Helen lies dying of tuberculosis, she tells Jane that she is not afraid: she is going to a better world. Jane gets into bed with Helen; the next morning, Helen has died. The character of Helen Burns is modeled after Charlotte Brontë's eldest sister Maria, who died of tuberculosis in 1825.

Jane Eyre

The narrator, central character, and eponymous heroine of *Jane Eyre,* Jane is both a fully realized fictional creation in the novel and, in many ways, a voice for the author, Charlotte Brontë. In a book that makes use of many of the stock situations and characters of the Gothic genre, Jane stands out as a woman who runs against the Gothic stereotype of the submissive woman in distress. Physically plain and slight, Jane is acutely intelligent and fiercely independent. She is also a shrewd judge of character. Throughout the novel, she relies on her intelligence and determination to achieve self-fulfillment. Yet her strength of character does not

Media Adaptations

- *Jane Eyre* has been the subject of numerous adaptations for other media. During the silent film era, there were at least three silent movie versions. The first talking picture adaptation was released in 1934. Written by Adele Comandini (based on Charlotte Brontë's book) and directed by Christy Cabanne, it starred Virginia Bruce, Colin Clive, Beryl Mercer, Aileen Pringle, Jameson Thomas, David Torrence, and Lionel Belmore. Produced by Monogram Studios.

- The most famous film version of *Jane Eyre* was adapted by John Houseman, Aldous Huxley, and Robert Stevenson and released in 1944. Directed by Stevenson, it starred Joan Fontaine, Orson Welles, Margaret O'Brien, Sara Allgood, Agnes Moorehead, and Elizabeth Taylor.

- Franco Zeffirelli and Hugh Whitemore wrote the script for the 1996 film version of *Jane Eyre,* directed by Zeffirelli. This version starred Charlotte Gainsbourg, William Hurt, Anna Paquin, Joan Plowright, Billie Whitelaw, Elle Macpherson, Geraldine Chaplin, and John Wood.

- The first adaptation of *Jane Eyre* for television was broadcast in 1939 on the NBC network. Produced and directed by Edward Sobol, this version starred Flora Campbell, Dennis Hoey, Effie Shannon, Daisy Belmore, and Ruth Mattheson.

- While there have been other adaptations of *Jane Eyre* for television since 1939, critics have noted that the most faithful one is the BBC's television mini-series adaptation of *Jane Eyre* produced in 1983. Directed by Julian Aymes, it starred Zelah Clarke and Timothy Dalton.

- *Jane Eyre* has lent itself to numerous adaptations for the stage. A recent version included one for a 1996 regional touring production in England, adapted and directed by Charles Vance.

- The book was recorded, unabridged, in a series of four sound cassettes, read by Juliet Stevenson. Available from BBC Enterprises Ltd., New York, NY, 1994.

- An abridged recording read by Dame Wendy Hiller is available on two cassettes from Listen for Pleasure, Downsview, Ontario, Canada.

---

make her immune to suffering; on the contrary, she suffers because she is so keenly aware of the difference between how things are and how they might be. Jane believes that "we were born to strive and endure." Her nature is passionate, but she also recognizes the dangers of uncontrolled passion. Although she is rebellious when rebellion is called for, she is inherently conscious that actions must be tempered by reason. When she refuses to become Rochester's mistress, she cites a higher moral law as her justification: "Laws and principles are not for the time when there is no temptation; they are for such moments as this, when body and soul rise against their rigor…." In this action, as well as in refusing to marry St. John Rivers, she proves her unwillingness to compromise her principles. She wants to achieve her goals on the right terms, not on any terms. Utterly opposed to hypocrisy, she nonetheless is capable of recognizing that goodness exists within flawed human beings. Because she is secure in herself, she is able to give herself fully to Rochester as his equal. At the end of the novel, writing about her marriage in language reminiscent of the Song of Solomon, she says: "I hold myself supremely blest—blest beyond language can express; because I am my husband's life as fully as he is mine." Intellectual, faithful, loving, Jane Eyre is one of the most original, vivid, and significant characters in the nineteenth-century English novel.

Mrs. Fairfax

The housekeeper at Thornfield Hall, Mrs. Fairfax replies to Jane's advertisement and offers her the position of governess at Thornfield. Jane initially assumes that she is the owner of the house. An older woman, Mrs. Fairfax is a widow, and is a distant relation of Mr. Rochester by marriage. Jane finds her "a placid-tempered, kind-natured woman, of competent education and average intelligence." Although she treats Jane in a friendly manner, she cannot provide the kind of intellectual stimulation and companionship that Jane craves.

Jack

See John Reed

Blanche Ingram

Blanche Ingram is a young woman, the daughter of a local aristocrat who spends some time in the company of Mr. Rochester. Mrs. Fairfax tells Jane that Rochester is expected to marry her. Blanche is very tall but has a proud, haughty manner, a "mocking air," and a "satirical laugh." Her speech is affected, especially when she speaks to her snobbish mother, Lady Ingram. In short, Blanche is "very showy" but "not genuine." She treats Jane with extreme condescension and exhibits a "spiteful antipathy" toward Adèle. Although she herself is in love with Rochester, Jane seems to stoically accept that he will marry Blanche. Ironically, this apparent certainty makes Jane more passionate toward Rochester, who in turn reveals that he had no intention of marrying Blanche. As well as serving the plot function of bringing Jane's passion for Rochester to a head, Blanche serves as a character foil to Jane: her artificiality makes Jane's frankness all the more evident and attractive.

Lady Ingram

The mother of Blanche Ingram, Lady Ingram makes rude, condescending remarks about governesses during a social visit to Thornfield Hall. She reminds Jane of Mrs. Reed, with whom she has certain parallels.

Mr. Lloyd

An apothecary who examines and treats young Jane Eyre in chapter 3, Mr. Lloyd is a sympathetic figure. He notes that Jane is profoundly unhappy at Gateshead Hall (Mrs. Reed's home) and asks Jane if she would like to go away to school. He apparently broaches this subject with Mrs. Reed, although it is some months before Jane is sent away to Lowood Institution.

Bertha Mason

Bertha Mason, the insane wife of Edward Rochester who has been hidden away in an attic room at Thornfield Hall, is one of the more exotic figures of nineteenth-century fiction. Yet she ap-

Still from the film Jane Eyre, *starring Joan Fontaine as Jane Eyre and Orson Welles as Edward Rochester.*

pears on only a few pages of the book and never speaks. (Indeed, she is not capable of rational conversation; the noises she makes are scarcely human). She is not so much a character as a symbol, although critics do not agree on exactly what she symbolizes. She may be an embodiment of violence, unbridled sexuality, or the animal nature that lies behind the veil of civilization. She also suggests Rochester's dark side. It has been suggested, too, that she is Jane's darker double. (Indeed, Bertha's confinement in the attic may be seen as an echo of Jane's earlier confinement in a locked room at Gateshead Hall.) In more immediate terms of the plot, Bertha functions as an impediment to Jane's marriage to Rochester. Her Gothic existence is felt long before it is revealed. Shortly after her arrival at Thornfield, Jane hears a strange laughter that is attributed to Grace Poole, the woman who in fact looks after Bertha. Bertha subsequently instigates several violent acts that disrupt the calm of Thornfield, setting fire to Rochester's bed and later attacking her brother, Mr. Mason. On both occasions, Jane intervenes, respectively rescuing Rochester and tending to Mr. Mason's wounds. On both occasions, Rochester tells Jane that Grace Poole was responsible for this violence. On the eve of Jane and Rochester's intended wedding, Bertha enters Jane's room and tears Jane's wedding veil; Jane tells Rochester what she has seen, but Rochester dismisses the vision as a nightmare. Once Bertha can no longer be denied, Rochester shows her to Jane and tells Jane the sordid story of his arranged marriage, years earlier in Jamaica, to this woman whom he barely knew. Bertha ultimately dies when she sets fire to Thornfield—an act that also results in terrible injury to Rochester; but this action sets up Jane's return and Rochester's redemption.

Mr. Mason

Mr. Mason is the brother of Mrs. Rochester (Bertha Mason). Mason's sudden arrival at Thornfield Hall during Rochester's social party clearly upsets Rochester, though Jane is not aware of its significance. That night, Jane hears a horrible sound and discovers that Mason has been attacked and is bleeding badly. On Rochester's instructions, she tends to Mason, whose true identity she does not know. Mason is spirited away early the next morning. He returns to interrupt Jane and Rochester's wedding and reveals that Rochester is already married. Mason, who resides in the West Indies, is conventionally handsome, but Jane notes that his face lacks character. Rochester suggests to Jane that Mason shares the Mason family congenital feeblemindedness.

Miss Miller

An "underteacher" at Lowood Institution—the boarding school for orphans that Jane Eyre attends—Miss Miller is introduced in chapter 5 when Jane arrives at Lowood. She receives Jane and helps to orient her. Miss Miller is described as "a tall lady with dark hair, dark eyes, and a pale and large forehead." Jane's narrative also describes her as "ruddy in complexion, though of a careworn countenance; hurried in gait and action, like one who had always a multiplicity of tasks on hand." Miss Miller disapproves of Mr. Brocklehurst and of the way he runs the school, but is powerless to do anything about it. Jane notes that she looks "purple, weather-beaten, and over-worked."

Rosamond Oliver

The daughter of a wealthy landowner who lives near the home of St. John Rivers, Rosamond Oliver is very pretty, kind, and high-spirited. Jane finds her "elfin" and fairy-like. However, she is essentially vacuous. Jane initially assumes that Rosamond and St. John will marry, but St. John is un-interested in Rosamond, preferring to consider Jane as his potential wife.

Grace Poole

Grace Poole is a mysterious servant who works at Thornfield Hall. When Jane hears strange laughter coming from the attic, Mrs. Fairfax tells her that it is only Grace Poole, who occasionally works there as a seamstress. Grace is "between thirty and forty; a set, square-made figure, red-haired, and with a hard, plain face." She is also fond of alcohol. Rochester initially tells Jane that Grace is responsible for the mysterious incidents at Gateshead. Jane later learns that Grace is actually employed to look after Mrs. Rochester (Bertha Mason), who is insane and who is kept locked in the attic.

Blanche Ingram

Blanche Ingram is a young woman, the daughter of a local aristocrat who spends some time in the company of Mr. Rochester. Mrs. Fairfax tells Jane that Rochester is expected to marry her. Blanche is very tall but has a proud, haughty manner, a "mocking air," and a "satirical laugh." Her speech is affected, especially when she speaks to her snobbish mother, Lady Ingram. In short, Blanche is "very showy" but "not genuine." She treats Jane with extreme condescension and exhibits a "spiteful antipathy" toward Adèle. Although she herself is in love with Rochester, Jane seems to stoically accept that he will marry Blanche. Ironically, this apparent certainty makes Jane more passionate toward Rochester, who in turn reveals that he had no intention of marrying Blanche. As well as serving the plot function of bringing Jane's passion for Rochester to a head, Blanche serves as a character foil to Jane: her artificiality makes Jane's frankness all the more evident and attractive.

Georgiana Reed

Georgiana, Jane Eyre's cousin and the younger daughter of Mrs. Reed, is introduced early in the novel when the young orphan Jane is living at Gateshead Hall as a ward of Mrs. Reed. Young Georgiana has "pink cheeks and golden curls" as well as "a spoiled temper, an acrid spite, a capricious and insolent carriage." She is "universally indulged" by her mother. When Jane returns to Gateshead some nine years later, Georgiana has grown into a frivolous, self-centered woman. Jane eventually learns that Georgiana has married a wealthy man.

John Reed

Jane Eyre's cousin John, the son of Mrs. Reed, is introduced at the beginning of the novel when the young orphan Jane is living at Gateshead Hall as a ward of Mrs. Reed. John, or Jack, is fourteen years old at this time. He bullies and torments Jane behind his mother's back. Jane finds him "disgusting and ugly," but Mrs. Reed indulges the boy and blames Jane for causing trouble while overlooking John's sadistic behavior. Some years later, Jane hears that John has been expelled from college. When Jane is summoned to Gateshead to attend the dying Mrs. Reed, she learns that John had become even more dissolute and has committed suicide.

Mrs. Reed

Mrs. Reed is Jane Eyre's aunt, the widow of Jane's uncle Mr. Reed (who was the brother of Jane's mother and who died nine years before the novel begins). She is also the mother of John (Jack), Eliza, and Georgiana. Mrs. Reed is introduced at the beginning of the novel, when the young orphan Jane is living at Gateshead Hall as her ward. When Mr. Reed was on his deathbed, Mrs. Reed promised him that she would "rear and maintain" the orphan Jane. However, Mrs. Reed resents Jane and treats her as an unwanted burden rather than as a dependent child. She continually belittles Jane and punishes her for what she regards as Jane's rebellious nature, while overlooking the faults of her own children. She arranges for Jane to be sent away to Lowood Institution, a boarding school for orphans. In chapter 4, Jane defies Mrs. Reed and tells her what she really thinks of her. This incident is Jane's first moral victory. Jane returns to Gateshead just before Mrs. Reed dies, but is unable to effect a reconciliation.

Diana Rivers

The sister of Mary and St. John Rivers; Diana Rivers also turns out to be Jane Eyre's cousin. When Jane arrives at Moor House, hungry and penniless, seeking shelter after she has fled Thornfield Hall, Diana and Mary help restore her to health. Skilled, talented, and well-read, the Rivers sisters develop a close friendship with Jane. Like her, they are both governesses, and Brontë portrays them in a favorable light.

Mary Rivers

The sister of Diana and St. John Rivers; she also turns out to be Jane Eyre's cousin. When Jane arrives at Moor House, hungry and penniless, seeking shelter after she has fled Thornfield Hall, Mary and Diana help restore her to health. Skilled, tal-

ented, and well-read, the Rivers sisters develop a close friendship with Jane. Like her, they are both governesses, and Brontë portrays them in a favorable light.

St. John Rivers

A handsome young clergyman who is the brother of Diana and Mary Rivers; St. John also turns out to be Jane Eyre's cousin. When Jane arrives at Moor House, hungry and penniless, after she has fled Thornfield Hall, St. John offers her shelter. Although Jane becomes close friends with the Rivers sisters, she finds that St. John has "a reserved, an abstracted, and even … a brooding nature"; he is also restless and does not feel at home in England. He tells Jane that she is "intelligent" and that "human affections and sympathies have a most powerful hold on you." Listening to him preach a sermon with Calvinist overtones, she realizes that he has not found peace in his religious faith. He offers Jane the post of schoolmistress at a girls' school he is establishing. It is Rivers who reveals to Jane that they are cousins and that she has inherited a fortune of twenty thousand pounds from their mutual uncle, John Eyre. He persistently asks Jane to marry him and accompany him to India as a missionary—an offer she declines because she realizes that the marriage would be loveless. Although St. John is intelligent, he is austere and inflexible and is unable to appreciate Jane for herself; he would lead her into a life (and death) of martyrdom. In this, he is a complete contrast to the passionate Mr. Rochester.

Mr. Rochester

Mr. Rochester is the central male character and hero (or perhaps antihero) in *Jane Eyre*. He is generally considered to be one of the most memorable romantic characters in nineteenth-century English fiction. A wealthy landowner, Rochester is the master of Thornfield Hall. Jane gradually falls in love with him after she arrives at Thornfield to tutor his ward Adèle, the daughter of an earlier mistress. When Mr. Rochester is introduced, he is somewhere between age thirty-five and forty, and thus is as much as twenty years older than Jane. Jane first meets him when she is walking from Thornfield to a nearby town to mail a letter. When his horse slips on the ice he is thrown and injured slightly; Jane helps him to remount. She only learns his identity when she returns to Thornfield and finds him there. He is described as having "a dark face, with stern features and a heavy brow" and is not considered handsome. The frequent references to his supposed ugliness help to underscore the fact that he is not a conventional hero; they suggest both secret troubles and hidden strengths that are more than skin-deep. Also, by deliberately making him physically unattractive, (at least by a conventional definition of attractiveness), Brontë wants the reader to know that Jane is not attracted to him because of his looks but because she recognizes something good in his soul. Rochester may be considered a Gothic hero. He is haunted by his guilty knowledge and by a past of which he is ashamed. Like the typical Gothic hero, he is prone to bouts of depression and to seemingly irrational behavior; he also possesses a macabre sense of humor. However, he is much more complex than a stereotypical Gothic hero and has more humanity. His treatment of his insane wife may seem cruel by modern standards, but in his eyes it is the best that can be done for her and is preferable to abandoning her. Yet he also acts selfishly in wishing to keep her existence a secret. He considers himself the victim of a cruel hoax: His marriage to Bertha was an arranged one, and he was not told that insanity ran in her family. His subsequent wanderings in Europe and his taking of three successive mistresses are perhaps a stock reaction to the restrictions imposed on him by his sham marriage. His relationship with Jane springs from a different motive. He recognizes Jane for what she is, and realizes that he can find salvation in her love. However, in knowingly planning to enter into a bigamous marriage, and then suggesting that she become his mistress, he transgresses moral law. He must lose Jane and suffer punishment and penance (in the form of losing his eyesight and his right hand, as well as his home) by fire before Jane can be fully restored to him. His marriage to Jane is the meeting of true minds, a marriage without secrets or locked doors.

Mrs. Rochester

See Bertha Mason

Miss Scatcherd

A teacher at Lowood Institution—the boarding school for orphans that Jane Eyre attends—Miss Scatcherd is the most severe of the teachers. Jane's friend Helen Burns tells Jane that "you must take care not to offend her." Miss Scatherd punishes Helen for some minor infraction by flogging Helen on the neck with a bunch of twigs, and she verbally abuses Helen. However, Helen accepts her punishment meekly.

Miss Temple

The superintendent of Lowood Institution—the boarding school for orphans that Jane Eyre attends—Miss Temple is introduced in chapter 5 when Jane arrives at Lowood. Jane describes her as "tall, fair, and shapely," with "a stately air and carriage." She is also kindly, perceptive, well educated, and genuinely concerned with the welfare of her students. After the schoolgirls are fed an inedible breakfast, Miss Temple orders that they receive a special lunch of "bread and cheese." Later, she invites Jane and Helen Burns to her room, where she offers the two girls some seedcake and converses with them. She recognizes that both Helen and Jane are exceptional, and acts as their mentor. When Miss Temple eventually marries and leaves Lowood, Jane (who is by then age eighteen, and who with Miss Temple's help has become a teacher at the school) decides to leave the school herself and take a position as a governess.

Adèle Varens

Mr. Rochester's young ward, about seven or eight years old, Adèle is the daughter of a French opera-dancer with whom Mr. Rochester has had an affair. The woman had claimed that Mr. Rochester was the father, but there is some ambiguity as to whether this is really the case. Adèle has lived most of her young life in France and speaks a mixture of French and English. When her mother abandons her, Mr. Rochester has her brought to England, where he intends to raise her. On Mr. Rochester's instructions, Mrs. Fairfax hires Jane to be Adèle's governess at Thornfield. Adèle is lively and talkative and likes to sing and dance. Jane finds her somewhat coquettish behavior disconcerting, but she comes to feel affection for Adèle in spite of the girl's flaws. By contrast, Blanche Ingram regards Adèle with distaste.

Themes

Love and Passion

One of the secrets to the success of *Jane Eyre,* and the source of its strength in spite of numerous flaws, lies in the way that it touches on a number of important themes while telling a compelling story. Indeed, so lively and dramatic is the story that the reader might not be fully conscious of all the thematic strands that weave through this work. Critics have argued about what comprises the main theme of *Jane Eyre.* There can be little doubt, however, that love and passion together form a major thematic element of the novel.

On its most simple and obvious level, *Jane Eyre* is a love story. The love between the orphaned and initially impoverished Jane and the wealthy but tormented Rochester is at its heart. The obstacles to the fulfillment of this love provide the main dramatic conflict in the work. However, the novel explores other types of love as well. Helen Burns, for example, exemplifies the selfless love of a friend. We also see some of the consequences of the absence of love, as in the relationship between Jane and Mrs. Reed, in the selfish relations among the Reed children, and in the mocking marriage of Rochester and Bertha. Jane realizes that the absence of love between herself and St. John Rivers would make their marriage a living death, too.

Throughout the work, Brontë suggests that a life that is not lived passionately is not lived fully. Jane undoubtedly is the central passionate character; her nature is shot through with passion. Early on, she refuses to live by Mrs. Reed's rules, which would restrict all passion. Her defiance of Mrs. Reed is her first, but by no means her last, passionate act. Her passion for Rochester is all consuming. Significantly, however, it is not the only force that governs her life. She leaves Rochester because her moral reason tells her that it would be wrong to live with him as his mistress: "Laws and principles are not for the time when there is no temptation," she tells Rochester; "they are for such moments as this, when body and soul rise against their rigor...."

Blanche Ingram feels no passion for Rochester; she is only attracted to the landowner because of his wealth and social position. St. John Rivers is a more intelligent character than Blanche, but like her he also lacks the necessary passion that would allow him to live fully. His marriage proposal to Jane has no passion behind it; rather, he regards marriage as a business arrangement, with Jane as his potential junior partner in his missionary work. His lack of passion contrasts sharply with Rochester, who positively seethes with passion. His injury in the fire at Thornfield may be seen as a chastisement for his past passionate indiscretions and as a symbolic taming of his passionate excesses.

Independence

Jane Eyre is not only a love story: It is also a plea for the recognition of the individual's worth. Throughout the book, Jane demands to be treated

Topics for Further Study

- In her preface to the second edition of *Jane Eyre,* Charlotte Brontë wrote: "Conventionality is not morality. Self-righteousness is not religion.... Appearance should not be mistaken for truth." What are some examples of these precepts in *Jane Eyre?*

- Research the treatment of mental illness around the time of *Jane Eyre.* What ideas did doctors of Charlotte Brontë's time have about the causes of mental illness? How did society in general regard people with this kind of disease? How might someone like Bertha Mason be treated today?

- As a younger son, Rochester would not have inherited his father's estate; the estate would first have gone to Rochester's older brother. Under English law at the time of *Jane Eyre,* property passed only to the oldest son; therefore, younger sons were usually left little money and had to make their own livings. What professions did younger sons in such a family usually follow? Also, how did this custom affect the daughters in a family?

- The early twentieth-century English novelist Virginia Woolf once said that "in order for a woman to write, she must have money and a room of her own." Do you think that this maxim applies to Charlotte Brontë as an author? Also, consider the ways in which money and a "room of her own" (that is, a home) are important to the character Jane Eyre.

as an independent human being, a person with her own needs and talents. Early on, she is unjustly punished precisely for being herself—first by Mrs. Reed and John Reed, and subsequently by Mr. Brocklehurst. Her defiance of Mrs. Reed is her first active declaration of independence in the novel, but not her last. Helen Burns and Miss Temple are the first characters to acknowledge her as an individual: they love her for herself, in spite of her obscurity. Rochester too loves her for herself; the fact that she is a governess and therefore his servant does not negatively affect his perception of her. Rochester confesses that his ideal woman is intellectual, faithful, and loving—qualities that Jane embodies. Rochester's acceptance of Jane as an independent person is contrasted by Blanche and Lady Ingram's attitude toward her: they see her merely as a servant. Lady Ingram speaks disparagingly of Jane in front of her face as though Jane isn't there; to her, Jane is an inferior barely worthy of notice, and certainly not worthy of respect. St. John Rivers does not regard Jane as a full, independent person. Rather, he sees her as an instrument, an accessory that would help him to further his own plans. Jane acknowledges that his cause (missionary work) may be worthy, but she knows that to marry simply for the sake of expedience would be a fatal mistake. Her marriage to Mr. Rochester, by contrast, is the marriage of two independent beings. It is because of their independence, Brontë suggests, that they acknowledge their dependence on each other and be completely happy with one another in this situation.

God and Religion

In her preface to the second edition of *Jane Eyre,* Brontë made clear her belief that "conventionality is not morality" and "self-righteousness is not religion." She declared that "narrow human doctrines, that only tend to elate and magnify a few, should not be substituted for the world-redeeming creed of Christ." Throughout the novel, Brontë presents contrasts between characters who believe in and practice what she considers a true Christianity and those who pervert religion to further their own ends. Mr. Brocklehurst, who oversees Lowood Institution, is a hypocritical Christian. He professes charity but uses religion as a justification for punishment. For example, he cites the biblical passage "man shall not live by bread alone" to rebuke Miss Temple for having fed the girls an extra meal to compensate for their inedible breakfast of burnt porridge. He tells Miss Temple that she "may indeed feed their vile bodies, but you little think how you starve their immortal souls!" Helen Burns is a complete contrast to Brocklehurst; she follows the Christian creed of turning the other cheek and loving those who hate her. On her deathbed, Helen tells Jane that she is "going home to God, who loves her."

Jane herself cannot quite profess Helen's absolute, selfless faith. Jane does not seem to follow a particular doctrine, but she is sincerely religious in a nondoctrinaire way. (It is Jane, after all, who

places the stone with the word "Resurgam" on Helen's grave, some fifteen years after her friend's death.) Jane frequently prays and calls on God to assist her, particularly in her trouble with Rochester. She prays too that Rochester is safe. When the Rivers's housekeeper, Hannah, tries to turn the begging Jane away, Jane tells her that "if you are a Christian, you ought not consider poverty a crime." The young evangelical clergyman St. John Rivers is a more conventionally religious figure. However, Brontë portrays his religious aspect ambiguously. Jane calls him "a very good man," yet she finds him cold and forbidding. In his determination to do good deeds (in the form of missionary work in India), Rivers courts martyrdom. Moreover, he is unable to see Jane as a whole person, but views her as a helpmate in his proposed missionary work. Rochester is far less a perfect Christian. He is, indeed, a sinner: He attempts to enter into a bigamous marriage with Jane and, when that fails, tries to persuade her to become his mistress. He also confesses that he has had three previous mistresses. In the end, however, he repents his sinfulness, thanks God for returning Jane to him, and begs God to give him the strength to lead a purer life.

Atonement and Forgiveness

Much of the religious concern in *Jane Eyre* has to do with atonement and forgiveness. Rochester is tormented by his awareness of his past sins and misdeeds. He frequently confesses that he has led a life of vice, and many of his actions in the course of the novel are less than commendable. Readers may accuse him of behaving sadistically in deceiving Jane about the nature of his relationship (or rather, non-relationship) with Blanche Ingram in order to provoke Jane's jealousy. His confinement of Bertha may bespeak mixed motives. He is certainly aware that in the eyes of both religious and civil authorities, his marriage to Jane before Bertha's death would be bigamous. Yet, at the same time, he makes genuine efforts to atone for his behavior. For example, although he does not believe that he is Adèle's natural father, he adopts her as his ward and sees that she is well cared for. This adoption may well be an act of atonement for the sins he has committed. He expresses his self-disgust at having tried to console himself by having three different mistresses during his travels in Europe and begs Jane to forgive him for these past transgressions. However, Rochester can only atone completely—and be forgiven completely—after Jane has refused to be his mistress and left him.

The destruction of Thornfield by fire finally removes the stain of his past sins; the loss of his right hand and of his eyesight is the price he must pay to atone completely for his sins. Only after this purgation can he be redeemed by Jane's love.

Search for Home and Family

Without any living family that she is aware of (until well into the story), throughout the course of the novel Jane searches for a place that she can call home. Significantly, houses play a prominent part in the story. (In keeping with a long English tradition, all the houses in the book have names.) The novel's opening finds Jane living at Gateshead Hall, but this is hardly a home. Mrs. Reed and her children refuse to acknowledge her as a relation, treating her instead as an unwanted intruder and an inferior.

Shunted off to Lowood Institution, a boarding school for orphans and destitute children, Jane finds a home of sorts, although her place here is ambiguous and temporary. The school's manager, Mr. Brocklehurst, treats it more as a business than as school *in loco parentis* (in place of the parent). His emphasis on discipline and on spartan conditions at the expense of the girls' health make it the antithesis of the ideal home.

Jane subsequently believes she has found a home at Thornfield Hall. Anticipating the worst when she arrives, she is relieved when she is made to feel welcome by Mrs. Fairfax. She feels genuine affection for Adèle (who in a way is also an orphan) and is happy to serve as her governess. As her love for Rochester grows, she believes that she has found her ideal husband in spite of his eccentric manner and that they will make a home together at Thornfield. The revelation—as they are literally on the verge of marriage—that he is already legally married—brings her dream of home crashing down. Fleeing Thornfield, she literally becomes homeless and is reduced to begging for food and shelter. The opportunity of having a home presents itself when she enters Moor House, where the Rivers sisters and their brother, the Reverend St. John Rivers, are mourning the death of their father. (When the housekeeper at first shuts the door in her face, Jane has a dreadful feeling that "that anchor of home … was gone.") She soon speaks of Diana and Mary Rivers as her own sisters, and is overjoyed when she learns that they are indeed her cousins. She tells St. John Rivers that learning that she has living relations is far more important than inheriting twenty thousand pounds. (She mourns the uncle she never knew. Earlier she was dis-

heartened on learning that Mrs. Reed told her uncle that Jane had died and sent him away.) However, St. John Rivers' offer of marriage cannot sever her emotional attachment to Rochester. In an almost visionary episode, she hears Rochester's voice calling her to return to him. The last chapter begins with the famous simple declarative sentence, "Reader, I married him," and after a long series of travails Jane's search for home and family ends in a union with her ideal mate.

Style

Narrative

Jane Eyre is written in the first person, and told from the viewpoint of its main character, Jane Eyre. As part of her first-person narrative, Brontë uses one of the oldest conventions in English fiction: this novel is allegedly a memoir written by a real woman named Jane Eyre and edited by Currer Bell (Charlotte Brontë's pseudonym). (Indeed, the full title of the book is *Jane Eyre: An Autobiography*. As part of this convention, the narrator occasionally addresses the reader directly with the word "reader.") Modern readers know, of course, that this is simply a convention, and accept it as such.

Although the first-person viewpoint means that the narrative scope is somewhat restricted, at times the narrator of *Jane Eyre* seems more omniscient (aware and insightful) than a typical first-person narrator. Much of the action seems to unfold naturally. In part, this may be because the story is told in retrospect. That is, in Brontë's narrative technique, the action is not happening as it is being told, but has already happened. As in many traditional first-person narratives, the narrator in *Jane Eyre* describes other characters astutely, both their external appearance and their inner personalities. There are also passages in which the narrator offers particular observations and opinions about life—observations and opinions that sometimes seem as if they are coming from the author. Yet the novel's suspense relies on the fact that the narrator is not entirely omniscient—or at least on the fact that she does not reveal key information until the point in the chronology of events when Jane herself became aware of this information. For example, the narrative does not report that Rochester is married and that his wife is locked away upstairs until the moment in the wedding ceremony when other characters come forth with this information. Similarly,

Jane lives with the Rivers for some time before she, and the reader, learn that they are her cousins.

Setting

The action of the book takes place in northern England sometime in the early-to mid-nineteenth century, and covers a span of about a dozen years. Brontë does not give specific year-dates for the incidents in the book, nor does she refer to contemporary historical events. Scholars generally assume that Jane Eyre's "autobiography" parallels Charlotte Brontë's life at the same age. Because the narrative frequently mentions specific months and seasons, the reader is rarely in doubt as to the exact time of year a particular incident is taking place. This precision helps give the book a more realistic feeling.

Brontë uses a succession of several main settings—primarily, individual houses—for the plot's action. She describes the settings vividly, thereby creating a particular atmosphere as well as giving the illusion of realism. Moreover, setting is used in a way that gives the novel structural unity and variety. Each setting or grouping of settings corresponds with a distinct phase of Jane Eyre's life.

Among the novel's main settings are Gateshead Hall, the home of Jane's aunt (by marriage), with whom the orphaned girl is living at the beginning of the book. At the age of ten, Jane is sent to Lowood Institution, a charity school for impoverished orphans. From there, at age eighteen Jane goes to Thornfield Hall to serve as a governess. When she learns the secret of Mr. Rochester's marriage to Bertha, she flees across the moors to Moor House, where she is taken in by the Reverend St. John Rivers. Toward the end of the book she finds Mr. Rochester at his other home, Ferndean Manor—Thornfield having been destroyed in a fire set by Bertha during Jane's absence.

Brontë does not use the real names of her locations. However, scholars have identified a number of real places as models for the settings in the book. Lowood Institution is believed to be based on the Clergy Daughters' School at Cowan Bridge, in Yorkshire, which Brontë attended as a girl. Thornfield Hall may be modeled on two different manor houses with which Brontë was familiar. The first, called Norton Conyers, is near the city of Ripon in North Yorkshire. North Lees Hall, a large, forbidding-looking stone manor house in Derbyshire, also seems to fit the description of Thornfield. In 1846 Brontë spent three weeks in the village of Heathersage, in Derbyshire, visiting her old school friend Ellen Nussey. Just before Brontë left to return to her home at Haworth, Ellen's brother, the local vicar, conducted a funeral service for a man named Thomas Eyre. The Eyre family was prominent in the area, and Brontë would most likely also have seen the name on various memorials in the church. North Lees Hall is nearby. Local history books recount that the first mistress at North Lees Hall, one Agnes Ashurst, was insane and was kept locked in an upstairs room. This woman died in a fire, just as Bertha does in the novel. (There is a similar legend about Norton Conyers.) In this area, visible from the vicarage where Brontë stayed, is another manor house called Moorseats—believed to be the model for Moor House.

Regardless of the factual bases of her settings, Brontë's descriptions of these settings, and of the surrounding countryside, are always exceptionally vivid. These descriptions help the reader visualize the places where the action is taking place. They also create a particular mood and atmosphere. Brontë takes stock Gothic descriptive elements (clouds, moonlight, stormy weather, dark hallways) and gives them a particularity that transcends the limitations of the Gothic genre.

Structure

Addressing the reader at the beginning of chapter 11, Jane remarks that "a new chapter in a novel is something like a new scene in a play." *Jane Eyre* is divided into thirty-eight chapters. More significantly, however, the novel can be seen in three distinct parts. Each of these parts traces a pattern of conflict and resolution (or rather, until the work's conclusion, partial resolution); Jane is faced with particular obstacles and opportunities. Running through each of these sections is Jane's effort to find or establish a true home.

The first part (comprised of chapters 1 through 10), covers Jane's childhood and schooling. These chapters are set at Gateshead Hall and at Lowood Institution. The major characters include Mrs. Reed and her children, Mr. Brocklehurst, Helen Burns, and Miss Temple. The main conflicts and incidents include Jane's rebellion against Mrs. Reed and her friendship with the fatally ill Helen.

Chapters 10 through 27 tell of Jane's life as a governess at Thornfield Hall, where she falls in love with Edward Rochester. Apart from Jane herself, Mr. Rochester is the central character in this section. Mrs. Fairfax, Adèle, Blanche Ingram, Grace Poole, Bertha Mason, and Mr. Mason also have significant roles. The dramatic action in this section centers on Jane's growing love for Mr.

Rochester (and vice versa), Jane's fear that Rochester will marry Blanche, and a series of strange incidents that occur at Thornfield.

Finally, chapters 28 through the end of the book center of Jane's life after she has fled Thornfield. The action here takes place in the countryside and at Moor House and Moorton. The Reverend St. John Rivers is the other main character here, along with his two sisters. Although Rochester does not reappear until the end of the book, his presence remains significant in Jane's mind. Dramatic highlights in this part of the novel include Jane's attempt to find shelter, her uneasy relationship with Rivers, and her ultimate return to Mr. Rochester. Many readers and critics have found this to be the weakest, most contrived part of the book. However, the events of this section serve to test Jane's devotion to Rochester. When she returns to marry him at the end of the book, both characters (and their circumstances) have evolved and matured from what they were at the time of their planned wedding in the second section.

Gothicism

Because of its powerful writing, and because of its concern with moral and social issues beyond the immediate plot, *Jane Eyre* is not generally considered a Gothic novel as such. However, it makes use of many of the elements found in the Gothic genre popular in the late eighteenth and early nineteenth centuries, and critics sometimes place the work in the Gothic tradition. Horace Walpole's *The Castle of Otranto* (1764), Ann Radcliffe's *The Mysteries of Udolpho* (1794), and M. G. Lewis's *The Monk* (1796) are considered classic examples of this genre. Mary Shelley's *Frankenstein* (1818) also uses some Gothic elements, while Jane Austen's *Northanger Abbey* (1818) satirized the excesses of the genre.

Gothic literature and the Gothic tradition is identifiable by certain characteristics. Often written in overblown language, Gothic novels involve bizarre characters and melodramatic incidents. Menacing castles, decaying manor houses, and wild landscapes are frequently used as settings. The plots of these novels contain an element of the fantastic or the supernatural. There is usually a mood of mystery or suspense, and an innocent heroine is almost always threatened with some unspeakable horror. Additionally, unexplained events take place at night.

Another characteristic of this genre is a hero who has led an adventurous, unconventional life that makes him romantically attractive, but who also has a flaw (usually a terrible secret from his past) that cuts him off from respectable society or makes him socially unacceptable. The Gothic hero may be prone to violent outbursts, but he typically suffers from his awareness of his past actions. In real life, the British poet George Gordon, Lord Byron (1788-1824), was often considered a model of the Gothic hero. (Indeed, the term "Byronic hero" is sometimes used to describe Mr. Rochester and other Gothic heroes.) For Brontë, her brother Branwell also exhibited some of the characteristics associated with a Gothic hero.

In *Jane Eyre,* Mr. Rochester might be seen as a Gothic hero. However, Brontë has made him a rounded character, not a stereotype. His circumstances are Gothic, but Brontë imbues them with a moral significance. Thornfield Hall might seem a Gothic residence, but apart from the mysterious presence of Grace Poole (who turns out to be benign if unattractive) and Bertha, it is a comfortable house. The facts surrounding Bertha's presence at Thornfield are highly Gothic, as is Bertha herself. Again, however, she is not important in herself, but for what she represents. Other similarities to Gothic may be seen in Bertha's attacks on Messrs. Rochester and Mason and her intrusion into Jane's bedroom; the sudden interruption of Jane and Mr. Rochester's wedding; Jane's flight across the countryside; the cold-hearted Reverend St. John Rivers; the destruction of Thornfield by fire; and the supernatural intervention of Jane hearing Rochester's voice calling her back to him.

Coincidence

When critics point out the weaknesses of *Jane Eyre,* they almost always mention its use of unbelievable coincidence. Yet, by no means was Brontë the only major writer to use coincidence as a device for advancing a novel's plot. During the Victorian period, the use of coincidence for this purpose was very common, even among the greatest writers. It was an accepted literary convention of the period. The works of Charles Dickens, for example, are filled with coincidences that no one would believe today, yet Dickens's books remain great works of literature. Thomas Hardy, who wrote later in the Victorian period, also has unbelievable coincidences occur in most of his novels.

Of the coincidences in *Jane Eyre,* at least two have drawn critical comment. The first concerns the way in which Bertha's brother, Mason, finds out about Jane's impending marriage to Rochester. Mason, who lives in Jamaica, is in the wine trade.

So is Jane's uncle John Eyre, who lives on the is-land of Madeira, several thousand miles away. Ear-lier, on his way back to Jamaica after his attack by Bertha, Mason happened to stop at Madeira and stayed with John Eyre, unaware of Mr. Eyre's re-lation to Jane. When John Eyre mentions that his niece Jane is to marry a Mr. Rochester, Mason hur-ries back to England to stop the wedding. The sec-ond incredible coincidence concerns the way that Jane receives her inheritance and learns that the Ri-verses are her cousins. After Jane flees Thornfield and is penniless and on the verge of starvation, she is finally taken in by strangers—St. John Rivers and his two sisters. The Riverses nurture her back to health and provide her with lodging, friendship, and a position as a schoolmistress, but she does not tell them her real identity. One day St. John tells Jane that he has had a letter from a London attor-ney informing him that his uncle—John Eyre—has died and left a fortune to Jane Eyre. St. John de-duces that the young woman he has assisted is that very Jane, and Jane discovers that the very people who had helped her as a stranger are in fact her cousins. Both these coincidences strain the reader's credibility, yet they are necessary in order to drive important developments in the plot.

Symbolism and Imagery

Jane Eyre is filled with imagery drawn from nature and the English countryside. Brontë uses this imagery to suggest her characters' moral condition and state of mind. There are numerous references to weather and to the sky, in the form of storms, rain, clouds, and sun. At the very opening of the novel, Jane sets the scene by mentioning that "the cold winter wind" had brought with it "clouds so sombre, and a rain so penetrating." The moon, too, appears frequently. There is a full moon on the night when Bertha attacks her brother, as there is on the night when Jane flees Thornfield. Later, St. John Rivers reads his Bible in the moonlight. Tree imagery is perhaps even more significant. Critic Mark Shorer has noted that "nearly every impor-tant scene in the development of the passion of Rochester and Jane Eyre takes place among trees—in an orchard, an arbor, a woods, a 'leafy enclo-sure.'" Shortly after Jane has agreed to marry Rochester, he tells her that she looks "blooming." After their wedding is interrupted, "the woods which twelve hours since waved leafy and fragrant ... now spread, waste, wild and white as pine-forests in wintry Norway." Ferndean, the house where the blind and maimed Rochester has gone after Thornfield is destroyed, is hidden by the

"thick and dark ... timber ... of the gloomy wood about it." The house itself can scarcely be distin-guished from the trees; when Jane arrives there, she also notes that "there were no flowers, no garden-beds." On their reunion, Rochester tells Jane that "I am no better than the old lightening-struck chest-nut-tree in Thornfield orchard." Jane retorts that, on the contrary, he is "green and vigorous," and tells him that "plants will grow about your roots ... because your strength offers them so safe a prop."

Historical Context

Brontë's England: The Social Context

Jane Eyre is set in the north of England some-time in the first half of the nineteenth century. Dur-ing this period, British society was undergoing slow but significant change. Perhaps most apparent was the transition from a rural to an industrial economy. The Industrial Revolution had begun in Britain in the late 1700s, and by the time of *Jane Eyre*, it was running full steam. Although Charlotte Brontë wrote about some of the effects of the Industrial Revolution in her 1849 novel *Shirley*, she touches on three areas of social concern in *Jane Eyre*: ed-ucation, women's employment, and marriage.

Victorian attitudes toward education differed considerably from those prevalent in modern America. For one thing, the level of one's school-ing was determined by social class and also by gender. At all levels of society and in virtually all levels of the education system, boys and girls were taught separately. The children of poor or working-class families were taught in local schools, such as the one in which Jane Eyre is a schoolmistress. Such children would rarely progress beyond learn-ing basic skills; most learning was by rote. Most of these children would have left school by their early teen years to work on farms or in factories; boys would often leave to join the army or navy. Upper- and upper-middle-class families, on the other hand, sought to enroll their sons in exclusive private schools (known paradoxically as public schools). In truth, however, conditions in these schools were often as harsh as those in schools for orphans and the poor such as Lowood Institution in *Jane Eyre*. But a public school education would serve as an entree into good society; the graduates of public schools staffed the higher ranks of government and the professions. Virtually all young men who went on to university (i.e., college) first attended public schools. Women were excluded from universities

Haworth Village, home of the Brontë sisters, in the West Riding of Yorkshire (now West Yorkshire), England.

until the 1870s. The first women did not graduate from an English university until 1874, when four women received degrees from Cambridge University.

Young children in upper-class and upper-middle-class families—both boys and girls—would often receive their earliest education from governesses. Governesses were women who were hired to serve as live-in tutors; they provided their charges with ongoing lessons in a variety of subjects until the child was old enough to be sent away to school. For the most part these women were daughters of the middle classes and the professional classes who had attained a certain level of education. Although the profession of governess was not financially rewarding, it was respectable. Working conditions for governesses varied, depending upon the particular family for which a governess might work. Some parents treated their hired governess with respect, as a professional, while others considered governesses little more than servants who were expected to keep in their place.

In the traditional curriculum of the time, girls and young women did not study such "serious" subjects as mathematics, science, or classics. However, they were taught grammar, history, geography, and French. Art, music, and sewing or embroidery were also considered appropriate subjects, and young women were all expected to have a knowledge of the Bible and basic Christian teachings. These subjects were taught both by governesses and at school. Jane Eyre may not be a typical governess, but clearly she has an excellent command of most of these subjects. By the middle of the nineteenth century, some twenty-five thousand women in England worked as governesses.

Jane Eyre depicts several views of marriage. The marriage of Rochester and Bertha owes more to the Gothic imagination than to reality, while the marriage of Rochester and Jane may also have been more the exception than the norm. Perhaps the most historically accurate view of marriage in early Victorian England is suggested by those marriages in the novel that might, but do not, take place. The anticipated marriage of Rochester and Blanche Ingram, for example, would seem an appropriate one to many Victorians because the two partners come from the same social class. A marriage such as the potential one between Jane and St. John Rivers would also not have been unusual. A husband such as Rivers would secure a "helpmeet" to share his burdens, while the woman in such a marriage would be given an opportunity to establish her own home and family and to do good works.

Compare & Contrast

- **1840s:** Like other creative and intellectual pursuits, novel writing is considered a male preserve. Women such as the Brontë sisters, George Eliot (Mary Ann Evans), and in France, George Sand (Amandine-Aurore Lucille Dupin), write under male pseudonyms in order to have their work taken seriously.

  Today: Many of the leading novelists in Britain are women, and they are regarded as the equals of their male counterparts. Major British women novelists include A. S. (Antonia) Byatt, P. D. (Phyllis) James, Iris Murdoch, and Muriel Spark.

- **1840s:** Many well-to-do families employed women as governesses to educate their children at home and to supervise children's activities. By 1851, some twenty-five thousand women worked as governesses in Britain. Although being a governess was regarded as respectable, opportunites for governesses to move into other positions were limited.

  Today: Some young women take temporary jobs abroad as "au pairs," supervising a family's children in return for room, board, and wages. Although these jobs are low-paying, they allow young women to travel and gain life experience before going into another profession or continuing their education.

- **1840s:** A typical English governess or school teacher might make from fifteen to thirty pounds per year.

  Today: The standard salary for teachers in England rose to 420 pounds per week in 1995.

- **1840s:** Preschooling is virtually nonexistent.

  Today: Nearly two-thirds of three and four year olds in Britain attend nursery school.

- **1847:** College admission is limited to young men, most of whom come from the upper class.

  Today: Almost one out of every three teenagers goes on to college. Higher education is free for all students in Britain, therefore, young people do not have to work their way through college.

- **1840s:** Haworth was a small, isolated hilltop town. Textile mills provided the local industry.

  Today: Haworth thrives on tourism, with more than 250,000 tourists visiting Haworth every year. Many tourists go to the Brontë Parsonage, which houses a museum displaying original manuscripts and drawings by Charlotte Brontë and her siblings. The museum also includes other interesting items, such as Charlotte's wedding dress and her tiny gloves.

Critical Overview

When it was published in October, 1847, *Jane Eyre* attracted much attention, and the novel became an almost instant commercial success. So high was demand for the book that the publisher issued a second edition within three months, followed by a third edition in April, 1848. The influential novelist William Makepeace Thackeray was one of *Jane Eyre*'s earliest admirers. He wrote to the publisher, saying that he was "exceedingly moved & pleased" by the novel. He also asked the publisher to express his admiration to the author.

Brontë subsequently dedicated the second edition of the book to Thackeray.

Jane Eyre was reviewed in some of Britain's leading newspapers and literary journals. Most early reviewers were enthusiastic. The *Edinburgh Review* pronounced it "a book of singular fascination." The critic for the London *Times* newspaper called it "a remarkable production" and noted that the story "stand[s] boldly out from the mass." The *Westminster Review* noted that the book's characters were astonishingly lifelike. (However, a reviewer in *Spectator* took the opposite view, saying that the characters did not behave like people in real life.) *Fraser's Magazine* gave a resounding endorsement and helped to spur sales by encouraging readers to "lose not a day in sending for it."

Contrary to this general praise, a handful of reviewers professed to be shocked by the passions expressed in the novel. A writer in the *Christian Remembrancer* regarded the book as an attack on Christianity and an example of "moral Jacobinism." Elizabeth Rigby (Lady Eastlake) denounced it in her unsigned notice in the *Quarterly Review,* calling it "pre-eminently an anti-Christian composition" and an attack on the the English class system. Perhaps unconsciously echoing Mrs. Reed, she condemned the title character as "the personification of an unregenerate and undisciplined spirit." The identity of *Jane Eyre*'s author was still unknown, but Rigby commented that if it was a woman, she "had forfeited the society of her sex." However, unknown to Brontë and to the public, the book received the ultimate Victorian seal of approval: Queen Victoria privately referred to *Jane Eyre* as "that intensely interesting novel" and read it to Prince Albert.

Of Brontë's four novels, *Jane Eyre* has continued to be the most popular and has received the most attention of critics and scholars. Writing in the mid-twentieth century, the critic M. H. Scargill noted in the *University of Toronto Quarterly* that *Jane Eyre* marked a turning point in the English novel, away from external concerns and toward personal experience. Scargill called the novel "a profound, spiritual experience" in which fiction approaches the condition of poetry. Modern feminists see *Jane Eyre* as one of the first feminist novels. In her biography of Brontë, entitled *The Brontës: Charlotte Brontë and Her Family,* Rebecca Fraser remarks that it was "Charlotte's protest against the stifling convention society imposed, which never allowed true feeling to be voiced." However, Scargill notes that "*Jane Eyre* may speak for women, but it speaks also for all humanity...."

Much discussion centers on just what makes *Jane Eyre* such a compelling work. Critics have noted that the book succeeds in spite of some obvious weaknesses, particularly its episodic structure and a plot that in places defies credibility. In the hands of a less talented author than Brontë, the story might have amounted to little more than a conventional Gothic romance. What makes the work so memorable, say most modern critics, is the sharp delineation of the characters, the vivid realization of the settings, and the powerful theme of redemption through love. Mark Schorer is one critic who takes the book to task. "The action is pitted

with implausibilities, indeed, absurdities," notes Shorer, yet "somehow the whole of the novel is compelling and strong even though so much of it is composed of ... silly, feeble parts." Ultimately, however, Schorer finds that this novel has a "visionary quality" that makes it more akin to dramatic poetry than to conventional realistic fiction. Similarly, Margaret Lane, in her *Introduction to "Jane Eyre",* remarks that "It is ... this rare capacity for emotional feeling, expressed in a singularly musical, pure, and moving prose, which gives [Brontë] her unique place as a writer. Her prose is so compelling that it has at times an almost hypnotic quality; we lose touch with our surroundings and are swept along on the strong current of her imagination...." In a similar vein, Rebecca Fraser has argued that while Brontë lacked the creative scope of Dickens, George Eliot, and Tolstoy, "the incandescent power of her writing gives *Jane Eyre* ... a uniquely flavoured niche in the affections of the reading public." The novel's grip on the imagination is further confirmed by the numerous film, television, and stage adaptations that have been produced over the years. A century and a half after it was written, many readers of all ages continue to name *Jane Eyre* as one of their favorite novels.

Criticism

Arnold A. Markley

In the following essay, Markley, an assistant professor of English at Pennsylvania State University, provides an general overview of the many aspects of Jane Eyre, *portraying the novel as unique, both for its time and even for contemporary literature.*

Charlotte Brontë's *Jane Eyre* was first published in England in October, 1847, and it made a huge splash among the Victorian reading public. The novel was subtitled, "An Autobiography," and readers through the years have been charmed by the strong voice of the heroine who tells the story of her life. The narrator's habit of addressing the reader directly throughout the book, making statements such as "Gentle reader, may you never feel what I then felt," and "reader, forgive me for telling the plain truth!" are quite effective in drawing the reader into the action of the novel.

Jane Eyre is a character whose strength and individuality are remarkable for her times. As a

What Do I Read Next?

- Anne Brontë is the least well known of the three Brontë sister novelists. Written at the same time as *Jane Eyre,* her first novel, *Agnes Grey* (1847), is the story of an unhappy governess. Her second novel, *The Tenant of Wildfell Hall* (1848), is considered a more ambitious and passionate work. Charlotte Brontë was disturbed by Anne's depiction of the heroine's alcoholic husband, who was based on Branwell Brontë.

- *The Life of Charlotte Brontë,* by Elizabeth Gaskell, was comissioned by Reverend Patrick Brontë just after Charlotte's death and was originally published in 1857. Gaskell, one of the best-known English novelists of her time, had met Charlotte in 1850, and the two became close friends. Gaskell's frank biography caused some controversy and passages were cut from it in subsequent editions. However, the first edition of the work remains in print and is today considered a classic of English literary biography.

- The poetry of Charlotte Brontë is represented in a modern Everyman edition of the Brontës' *Selected Poems,* along with poems by Emily, Anne, and Branwell Brontë. Published in 1985, this edition was edited by Juliet Barker, curator and librarian of the Brontë Parsonage Museum in Haworth. Barker is also the author of a family biography, *The Brontës.*

- *The Brontës* (1969), by Phyllis Bentley, is an illustrated biography of the three Brontë sister-authors (Charlotte, Emily, and Anne) in Thames and Hudson's "Literary Lives" series. This book is especially good in depicting the conditions in which Charlotte Brontë lived, and in relating the places where she lived to her life and work.

- Readers have noted some similarities between *Jane Eyre* and Daphne du Maurier's classic 1938 romantic suspense novel *Rebecca.* A young woman recounts the early days of her marriage to a wealthy widower, Maxim de Winter. The first Mrs. de Winter—Rebecca—died mysteriously, and her memory casts a chilling spell over large English manor house where the new Mrs. de Winter has come to live.

- *Wide Sargasso Sea* (1966) is a novel by Jean Rhys that might be considered a "prequel" to *Jane Eyre.* In this novel, Rhys imagines the life of young Edward Rochester and the first Mrs. Rochester in Jamaica some years before the action of *Jane Eyre.*

- *Brontë* (1996) is a novel by Glyn Hughes, a young British writer who lives in West Yorkshire. The book is a fictional account of the inner and outer lives of the members of the Brontë family, including Charlotte.

model for women readers in the Victorian period and throughout the twentieth century to follow, Jane Eyre encouraged them to make their own choices in living their lives, to develop respect for themselves, and to become individuals. But the early readers of *Jane Eyre* were not all charmed by the heroine's bold personality. Many readers objected to the novel because they felt that it was "un-Christian," taking offense at Brontë's often bitter attacks on certain aspects of religion and the church in contemporary England. The character of Mr. Brocklehurst, for example, a deeply religious but highly hypocritical figure, was based on a well-

known clergyman alive at the time, and many readers recognized the characterization right away.

Other Victorian readers felt that the novel was "coarse" because it addresses issues and incidents that were not "proper" for a female narrator to discuss. When Edward Rochester tells Jane of his past history with women, for example, and his possible fathering of Adèle Varens, many readers found it highly improper to imagine a man speaking of such matters to a young girl of eighteen. Moreover, Mr. Rochester's plans to marry Jane even though he was married already was a rather shocking situation for a novel to explore. Many readers believed that the writer of the novel was a man, not able to imagine that a woman could possibly write such a story. Brontë's use of the pen-name, "Currer Bell" encouraged this assumption for some time. Many women writers like Brontë chose to publish under a man's name because publishers, critics, and readers were much more likely to respond well to a work by a man, and because the general belief was that it was improper for ladies to write at all.

The issue of female independence is central to *Jane Eyre.* Much of the strength of Jane's character comes directly from Brontë who was able to voice a lot of her own thoughts and feelings concerning the life of women in the nineteenth century. Additionally, Brontë based a fair amount of the material in the story on actual events from her own family's life. The Lowood School, for example, is closely based on an actual boarding school for the daughters of clergymen that Brontë and several of her sisters attended as children. Her depiction of the horrors of life in such a place is not exaggerated; the conditions were such that two of Brontë's sisters died from illnesses they contracted while living at the school.

In the nineteenth century women had far less personal freedom, and there were few options available for them to support themselves outside of choosing to marry and raise children. Jane's work as a governess represents one of the only respectable ways in which a woman could employ herself if she lacked personal wealth. Even so, governesses were typically treated only a little better than servants, as seen when Mr. Rochester brings his wealthy houseguests to Thornfield and they disdain to interact with Jane at all.

Many readers have noted the strong relationship between Jane Eyre's story and fairy tales. Her descriptions of her early life are very similar to the story of "Cinderella," for example. Her aunt, Mrs. Reed, is akin to the archetypal evil stepmother, and Jane is mistreated while the other children of the house are indulged in every way. The story of Jane's relationship with Mr. Rochester also reflects a few details of the story of "Beauty and the Beast." Mr. Rochester is, after all, described as a rather unattractive man with a gruff exterior, yet Jane gradually grows to love him despite his exterior, much as Beauty grows to love the Beast.

Despite the story's roots in traditional fairy tales, however, it is quite modern and unusual in its description of a woman's search for self and for the life of her choice. Sandra Gilbert has discussed the novel as the story of a woman's coming of age

that is accomplished through several important psychological stages. The story begins with Jane's first home, the Reeds' Gateshead, where Jane learns to stand up for herself when she is wrongfully accused of being a liar and a bad child. The story then moves to the grim setting of the Lowood School where Jane gains an education and "becomes a lady" as her old nurse Bessie declares when she visits Jane at the end of chapter 10. Here she is given the model of the saintly Miss Temple, and here she encounters the equally saintly Helen Burns, who responds to her irrational abuse at the hands of Miss Scatcherd with calm acceptance. Helen is in many ways a model Christian who always turns the other cheek, but Jane cannot respond to such treatment in the same way, and her resolve to demand fair treatment in her life is solidified by her relationship with Helen.

Jane then moves on to a new life at Thornfield, whose name suggests some degree of the troubles she will endure there before fleeing to a new chapter in her life with the Rivers family at Moor House, or Marsh End, which Gilbert sees as the end of Jane's journey to adulthood, and where she finally finds a family to replace the awful Reeds of her childhood. Finally, Jane chooses to return to Mr. Rochester, at a new place, Ferndean, hidden deep in the woods. Ferndean represents a separation from the rest of society which is appropriate, since her relationship with Mr. Rochester is to be a new kind of relationship—one between equals, and based on spiritual love, a concept of marriage quite unusual for its time.

One of the most unusual aspects of *Jane Eyre* is the depiction of Jane's relationship with Mr. Rochester. From the beginning, the novel defies contemporary conventions of the romance in its emphasis on Jane as a plain woman, lacking the physical beauty which usually characterized fictional heroines. As mentioned previously, Mr. Rochester is also described as being physically unattractive, dark, and sullen. At one point soon after their meeting, Mr. Rochester asks Jane if she finds him attractive, and she surprises him and the reader with a firm "No." Jane and Mr. Rochester's early conversations also progress in unusual ways; characteristically with his questioning her in terms of her beliefs and opinions, and her honest, if restrained, answers to his unusual questions. As the relationship progresses, Mr. Rochester tests Jane more and more. His first test is with statements desired to provoke a certain response. Then he tests her with his manipulative disguise as the old gypsy woman to try to discover her feelings for him, and with his cruel manner of proposing marriage by first allowing Jane to believe that he intends to marry Blanche Ingram. If Jane is not the typical Victorian heroine, Mr. Rochester is certainly not the typical Victorian hero.

In addition to these unusual conversations, Brontë gives readers a number of glimpses of Jane and Mr. Rochester in various positions that are unusual for literary depictions of Victorian couples. For example, we frequently see her, a small girl, giving physical support to the older and stalwart Mr. Rochester. When he falls off of his horse upon first seeing Jane, it is Jane who helps Mr. Rochester. When Mr. Rochester's bedroom is set aflame, Jane rescues him. Later, when he is shocked to learn of Mr. Mason's arrival at Thornfield after the gypsy incident, Jane is there for him. And at the end, when he is crippled and blind Rochester depends entirely on Jane to guide him. Moreover, when Mr. Rochester finally does propose marriage to her, Jane reacts with restraint and strongly refuses his wishes to give her jewels and fine new clothes.

Jane is able to gain a new perspective on her relationship with Mr. Rochester when she meets her cousin, St. John Rivers. Unlike Mr. Rochester, Rivers is a strikingly attractive man, but Jane finds his piety and coldness very unattractive. As cruel Mr. Brocklehurst tried to control Jane by telling her that bad girls go to hell, Rivers gradually begins to impose his will on Jane by using religion to subdue her, telling her that she will deny God if she does not accept his proposal of marriage and accompany him as a missionary to India. Just as she is about to break under the strain of this latest male oppressor, Jane psychically hears Mr. Rochester's voice calling her back to him.

Another fascinating aspect of *Jane Eyre* is Mr. Rochester's mad wife, Bertha Mason Rochester. Some critics, including Sandra Gilbert, interpret Bertha as a double of Jane—representing her "dark side" in psychological terms. Bertha can be said to represent Jane's anger and rage at society's attempts to control her and imprison her in a particular role. Perhaps Bertha's imprisonment at Thornfield can be related to the horrible fear of imprisonment that Jane suffered at being shut up in the terrifying red room at the Reeds' house as a child. Moreover, Bertha appears or is heard laughing at times that mark developments in the relationship between Jane and Mr. Rochester. She even acts out at least one of Jane's unconscious wishes when she comes into Jane's room on the night before Jane's wedding and rips up the wedding veil

that Jane felt uncomfortable about wearing. Many readers feel that the treatment of the pathetic Bertha in the novel undercuts any effort on the author's part to provide an encouraging story for women in presenting Jane as a woman who insists on her own independence. The novelist Jean Rhys reacted to the novel in this way, and responded by writing her own "prequel" to *Jane Eyre,* entitled *Wide Sargasso Sea* (1966), in which she develops Bertha's own personal story, and the story of her relationship with Edward Rochester before the events of *Jane Eyre.*

All in all, *Jane Eyre* is the story of an unusual woman who finds a family, who finds a lover, and who finds herself in a world that has not made her growing into adulthood an easy process in any way. Jane progresses from being an unwanted member of a cruel family of cousins who are forced to help her, to finding the ideal family of cousins in the Rivers, who *she* is able to help when she comes into her inheritance from her uncle John. It is this inheritance that gives Jane the freedom to make her own choices and to choose never to be dependent on anyone again. But the choice she makes is to return to the man she loves, who, chastened by his symbolic injuries in the burning of his old home and freed from his earlier marriage by the death of his first wife, is at last able to enter into the kind of spiritual relationship of equality that Jane desires as an independent woman and a strong woman who has always managed to remain true to herself.

Source: Arnold A. Markley, in an essay for *Novels for Students,* Gale, 1998.

Frederick L. Ashe

In the following excerpt, Ashe follows Jane's deprived childhood experiences and connects them to her relationship with Rochester later in life.

Critics have traditionally endowed the heroine and eponym of Charlotte Brontë's romantic masterwork, *Jane Eyre,* with a prodigious free will. According to various commentators, Jane draws on her knowledge either of good and evil or of her own nature in choosing between a series of conventional literary oppositions—reason and passion, absolute and relative morality, and, finally, love without marriage and marriage without love. Such a reading, however, judges the actions of Jane the young woman without allowing for the extraordinary childhood forces that largely determine her adult personality, thus essentially ignoring the first quarter of the novel. While many have celebrated Brontë's carefully wrought description of her protagonist's first eighteen years for its vivid pathos, no one has as yet accorded this childhood its deserved weight in the novel's ultimate resolution. When viewed from the vantage of modern child psychology, Jane's background—ten years spent at Gateshead barren of affection or adult encouragement, and eight years at Lowood School marked by severe physical privations, public humiliations, and exposure to the cheerless philosophy of Helen Burns—can only exempt Brontë's heroine from common standards of morality or human incentive. The Jane Eyre who emerges from this past of injustice and mental depression is an odd mixture of pride and insecurity. She is saddled with a tenacious pessimism concerning her prospects for happiness, and it is *this mentality* against which she must struggle, and *this* over which she triumphs in the end.

It is hard to imagine anyone learned enough to read *Jane Eyre* who would consider her first ten years emotionally healthful ones. Orphaned in her first year, Jane is given up to her resentful Aunt Reed, whose husband (Jane's mother's brother) also dies within the year. Jane's life to age ten is one of ostracism by the Reed family and unrelenting anxiety over the chidings of the servants, the violence of her cousin John Reed, and the punishments and beratings of Mrs. Reed. Though we as readers do not meet Jane until her tenth year, we may deduce from Mrs. Reed's deathbed admission that Jane's situation has been destitute since infancy—"I hated it the first time I set my eyes on it—a sickly, whining, pining thing"—and her declaration that her children could never bear to be friendly to Jane. The older Jane, who narrates the novel, makes a characteristically self-deprecating excuse for the Reeds' behavior, claiming, "I know that had I been a sanguine, brilliant, careless, exacting, handsome, romping child—though equally dependent and friendless—Mrs. Reed would have endured my presence more complacently." But we cannot admit this statement as "the more sober judgment of the mature Jane, that as a child she brought much of her punishment upon herself." For a child in such circumstances as Jane's at Gateshead to develop the traits that the "mature Jane" enumerates would be unimaginable.

Susan D. Bernstein, in ["Madam Mope: The Bereaved Child in Brontë's *Jane Eyre*], uses Brontë's depiction of childhood in *Jane Eyre* to illustrate the effects of grief and loss on children. Bernstein concentrates or the novel's first few chapters, which describe a typical afternoon of melancholy and exclusion for the ten-year-old Jane,

culminating in her traumatic banishment to the Red Room—which Jane has supposed to be haunted since her uncle died there years earlier—for defending herself against an attack by her John. The medical implications of the Red Room incident run perhaps even deeper than Bernstein allows, as Jane's emotional reaction provides a textbook example of mental depression. Jane in this scene quite clearly demonstrates five of the eight identifiable symptoms of adult or child depression cited by the American Psychiatric Association. First, she manifests a loss of appetite in her inability to eat either the night she is locked in the Red Room or the following day. Secondly, she is unable to sleep: "For me, the watches of that long night passed in ghastly wakefulness." Third, she displays a lack of interest in usual activities, as she is unable to muster enthusiasm over her favorite engraved dinner plate or over *Gulliver's Travels.* Fourth, Jane experiences feelings of guilt and worthlessness: "All said I was wicked, and perhaps I might be so." Finally, Jane indulges in suicidal fantasy in her thoughts of forsaking food or drink. It is now widely agreed that most childhood disorders can be traced to either a faulty relationship with the child's parents or to anxiety-provoking experiences that the child cannot understand. Aside from the antagonistic relationship with her guardian, the ghost in the Red Room constitutes for Jane a frightening experience, and as an older narrator she attributes to the incident "some fearful pangs of mental suffering."

Only hope enables human beings to endure such adverse conditions as those Jane endures at Gateshead, and it is the hope of leaving the Reeds that revives Jane's spirits following her fright in the Red Room. This initial experience with hope, however, proves a negative one; the young Jane is learning early the futility of optimism. The change that delivers her from Gateshead is a move to Lowood School, where onto her life of emotional privation is grafted one of physical hardship. At a critical stage in her development Jane is subjected to severe cold and near starvation, conditions that claim the lives of many of her classmates. Her bad luck with adults remains constant as well, as she is almost immediately singled out in front of her classmates by Mr. Brocklehurst, the school's headmaster. Brocklehurst christens Jane a deceitful child, and warns her classmates to "shun her example: if necessary, avoid her company, exclude her from your sports, and shut her out from your converse." Lowood school can be seen as Brocklehurst's project for infusing orphan girls with an ascetic abhorrence of worldly pleasures, and the fire-and-brimstone religion he imposes proves ideal for instilling in his pupils a sense of fear and guilt about happiness on earth.

At Lowood Jane also meets Helen Burns, a character whose acceptance of fate has led critics to read her as a positive model for Jane. But while Helen's calm stoicism later helps Jane to accept hardship, it does little to prepare her for human happiness. Helen lives only for death and the reunion it will bring with her savior. Her reliance on "an invisible world and a kingdom of spirits" may signify a venerable religious faith, but it also serves as a defense mechanism against the sufferings she has found life to hold for an orphan child. Jane finds "an alloy of inexpressible sadness" in Helen's stance—only as Helen dies does Jane see her happy. To Jane, Helen's death represents yet another defeat of hope, as it cuts short what would have been Jane's first real friendship. Jane longs for happiness in *this* life, and Helen Burns provides one more affirmation that such longing is for naught.

Although Jane does finally find friendship and encouragement at Lowood in the person of Miss Temple, it is not enough to counteract the effects of her gloomy childhood. Miss Temple is rarely able to abate the physical severity of the school, and nothing can erase the damage wrought by Jane's miserable first decade. The Jane of Lowood is the product of an absolute lack of love and affection, qualities critical to the healthy development of a growing child. While Brontë seemed to sense this truth, modern child psychology has codified it. A loving family atmosphere and a favorable emotional climate in the home are today widely held to be the most important factors in the healthy mental development of the growing child. Parents or adult guardians who deprive their children of warmth or affection risk having their child become withdrawn and depressed, and, like Jane, devoid of any sense of optimism or security. Moreover, such overstrictness as Jane suffers at the hands of Mrs. Reed and Mr. Brocklehurst is today seen as a major source of childhood anxiety and low self-esteem, qualities which well describe the Jane Eyre of Gateshead and Lowood.

Not only does Jane's early life provide an accurate portrayal of childhood depression, but the subsequent emotional development of Brontë's character possesses astonishing psychological verisimilitude as the natural extension of a rocky youth. John Bowlby has done extensive work in the area of childhood loss of or separation from the mother, and has determined such events to have a profound effect in later life. Bowlby claims that the most important factor in the development of mental health is the infant or young child's "warm, intimate, and continuous relationship with his mother or a permanent mother-substitute—one who steadily 'mothers' him." The effects of an unsatisfactory maternal relation, such as Jane's with her Aunt Reed, may extend to the child's later capacity to make and sustain relationships with others. Jane's pessimism is, moreover, a natural result of her maltreatment by the Reeds, who reinforced in her the notion of her own inadequacy and unlovability, a notion, says Bowlby, that may lead the child when grown to develop "a model of attachment figures as likely to be unavailable, or rejecting," and will likely "confirm in [her] the belief that any effort [she] might make to remedy [her] situation would be doomed to failure." *Jane Eyre* bears out this observation. The mature Jane's need for romantic love is matched by her assurance that such love does not exist for her.

This is not to suggest that Charlotte Brontë was versed in psychological literature, or that *Jane Eyre* is a calculated illustration of how an abnormal childhood might affect one's later development. Brontë's understanding of the Bowlby pattern was an experiential one, and, literature being the outgrowth of an author's imagination and experience, it is not surprising that Jane Eyre should follow that pattern. While the critic is well-advised to retain a degree of skepticism towards the narrative patterns necessarily imposed by biographers on the retrievable facts of their subjects' lives, and while one must be careful when using biographical evidence not to reduce imaginative art to mere mimesis, readers cannot ignore the verifiable pattern of Brontë's life in interpreting *Jane Eyre,* which was originally subtitled *An Autobiography* and was published under a pseudonym. The most basic facts of Brontë's life reveal a history of loss quite similar to Jane's, and it is safe to assume from her later correspondence that Brontë responded to her experience by developing a pessimistic attitude towards her own prospects, an attitude her biographers have characterized variously as a "lack of hope" and a "skeptical incredulity about good fortune." …

Jane's habitual mistrust of good fortune manifests itself perhaps most strongly when she finds herself developing amorous feelings toward Rochester. She refuses to succumb to her will because she cannot imagine his returning the love— she cannot allow for a happy ending. In her conviction that "sense would resist delirium: judgment would warn passion," Jane endeavors to punish her own presumptuousness by juxtaposing an idealized bust of Blanche Ingram with an unflattering portrait of herself—a constant reminder that Rochester could never love "a Governess, disconnected, poor, and plain." In this poignant scene Jane berates herself violently for her own giddy idealism. A more optimistic character with a more realistic self-image could not but read Rochester's many signs of affection, and accept his inability to love the haughty Blanche. But Jane refuses any insight that favors herself, and as a result she suffers greatly before Rochester's proposal.

The proposal again piques Jane's mistrust. After her characteristic initial response—"I was silent: I thought he mocked me"—she tempers her bliss by insisting on casting the future in the most unflattering light. Her response upon hearing pronounced for the first time the name "Jane Rochester" is consistent with her refusal to accept joy: "The feeling, the announcement sent through me, was something stronger than was consistent with joy—something that smote and stunned: it was, I think, almost fear." It is the pessimist—the product of Gateshead, where human attention meant criticism, and of Lowood, where life was taught as a struggle and where Jane's first friend died only months after they met—who says to Rochester:

> "It can never be, sir; it does not sound likely. Human beings never enjoy complete happiness in this world. I was not born for a different destiny to the rest of my species: to imagine such a lot befalling me is a fairy tale—a daydream … for a little while you will perhaps be as you are now,—a very little while; and then you will turn cool; and then you will be capricious; and then you will be stern, and I shall have much ado to please you: but when you get well used to me, you will perhaps like me again,—like me, I say, not love me. I suppose your love will effervesce in six months, or less." It is fitting that a Brontë character will not view even her opportunity to marry the man she loves as more than a new servitude.

Jane's refusal during the courtship to be pampered or flattered does not betoken pride, but instead a belief that she does not deserve to be treated well. Her incredulity is stoked both by Bertha Rochester's mysterious pre-nuptial antics and by her own portentous dreams. As she awaits Rochester's return on the night before the wedding, she muses, "I feared my hopes were too bright to be realized; and I had enjoyed so much bliss lately that I imagined my fortune had passed its meridian, and must now decline." Jane still sees happiness as a fluke, which will always be ephemeral. In this instance such does indeed prove to be the case, and when Rochester's first marriage and his technically bigamous intent are exposed, Jane is patently unsurprised. She blames herself for her shattered hopes, and instantly forgives Rochester. "Real affection, it seemed, he could not have for me; it had only been fitful passion, that was balked; he would want me no more. I should fear even to cross his path now: my view must be hateful to him. Oh, how blind had been my eyes! How weak my conduct." Her pithy declaration as she leaves Rochester, "we are born to strive and endure," sums up the philosophy that Gateshead and Lowood have fostered. Jane's every adult decision has been biased by the belief that the happiest alternative always is the least realistic.

Jane's departure from Thornfield marks a new stage in her psychic development. She exhibits a sustaining pride during her destitute wanderings on the way to Moor House, and even allows herself to believe that the horrible fate of wandering penniless and friendless through the countryside is not for her. In Diana and Mary Rivers she finally meets two people whose company she can enjoy. When a genealogical quirk brings her a large inheritance, she views it as something that will have only positive effects. It is during this year that Jane begins psychologically to outgrow the effects of her childhood—to realize that life can be at least pleasant, even for her. But she still has one obstacle to overcome.

Though Jane learns at Moor House that life can be bearable, she also realizes that it cannot be *happy* unless she spends it with Rochester. St. John Rivers' pragmatic proposal to marry Jane and take her along for missionary work in India awakens in the heroine a struggle between her natural pessimism and her deep-rooted desire for Rochester and happiness in England. We never believe that Jane would be happy in India, but her guilty sense of religious duty coupled with her doubts about happiness in England come quite close to making her accept Rivers' proposal. Towards the novel's end Jane's inner battle gathers in narrative intensity, climaxing in her famous discernment of Rochester's mystical voice in the night. This voice represents a triumph of Jane's true desires. She truly wants to be with Rochester, and she truly believes that "the best things the world has" are the "domestic endearments and household joys" that she might enjoy as Mrs. Rochester. The voice she hears convinces Jane to reject Rivers and a pessimistic sacrifice of future happiness, and to gamble on recovering Rochester and bliss. The voice represents the defeat of the pessimist in *Jane Eyre*.

By ignoring the deterministic role of Jane's childhood and her adult struggle against it, traditional criticism has in essence reduced *Jane Eyre* to the status of a clever vehicle for the restatement of conventional literary formulas. To see the adult Jane as the crippled but determined product of an unhealthy childhood is to re-establish the novel as the very plausible portrait of a full human life. Jane's happy ending must not be viewed merely as a proper or improper choice between right and wrong, but as the resolution of an intense psychological drama, wherein the degree of free will needed to make such a happy choice is finally attained.

Source: Frederick L. Ashe, "*Jane Eyre:* The Quest for Optimism," in *Studies in the Novel,* Summer, 1988, pp. 121-30.

Maria Yuen

In the following excerpt, Yuen demonstrates how Jane refuses to accept that she is socially and sexually inferior to Rochester and others because of her class situation and gender.

When Jane is emancipated from the thraldom of her aunt's family, she moves on to a larger social unit, the community of Lowood, exchanging moral oppression for the religious oppression of Mr. Brocklehurst. But Jane has by now built up her defenses: "I stood lonely enough, but to that feeling of isolation I was accustomed: it did not oppress me much." By nature antipathic to Brocklehurst's hypocritical Evangelicalism, Jane is nevertheless drawn towards two other representatives of religion at Lowood. Helen Burns represents a Christian ideal that Jane admires but does not aspire to. Jane, with her intense awareness of self and her fierce sense of justice, could never adopt Helen's attitude of resignation and forgiveness. Again, with her passionate longing for life, Jane could not subscribe to Helen's calm acceptance of death. Miss Temple, on a more human level, embodies the religion of love, goodness and kindness which provides the inspiration and motivation for Jane through her eight years at Lowood. But with the departure of Miss Temple, all Jane's old hunger for life, for experience returns in force: "I tired of the routine of eight years in one afternoon. I desired liberty; for liberty I gasped … For change, stimulus." "I longed to go where there was life and movement." Jane is formed not for religion, but for love. Her repressed nature now reasserts itself as she prepares to embark on a new adventure in life.

Jane's world is an even smaller one than Maggie's [Tulliver's in George Eliot's novel *The Mill on the Floss*]—she progresses from a barely tolerated dependent in a household of unloving relatives, through a charity child in a charity institution among similarly deprived children, to a governess of a foreign born child of questionable birth in a strange environment, Thornfield. The first two main phases of Jane's life are spent almost exclusively in the two houses or establishments—Gateshead Hall and Lowood—which form the background for her early development. Through these experiences and vicissitudes Jane's personality becomes more and more withdrawn, so that from the solitary child she grows into the "quaint, quiet, grave" young woman whose cool exterior nevertheless conceals "a heart hungering for affection [suggests Kathleen Tillotson in her book *Novels of the Eighteen-Forties,* 1956]." It is [as Eliot writes in, *The Mill on the Floss*] "this need of love, this hunger of the heart" that precipitates the emotional and moral crisis in the novel.

Jane Eyre's dilemma is very much like George Eliot's own—whether to live with Rochester as his unmarried wife or sever all relations with him—and George Eliot's strong condemnation of Jane's renunciation is understandable. Perhaps a quotation from George Eliot's own novel will throw light on her reaction to Jane's decision. Near the end of *The Mill on the Floss,* in a passage that comes nearest to George Eliot's own conception of the moral problem at the heart of the novel, we find this authorial comment: "Moral judgements must remain false and hollow unless they are checked and enlightened by a perpetual reference to the special circumstances that mark the individual lot." This is central to George Eliot's notion of morality and explains in large measure her censure of *Jane Eyre.* George Eliot obviously thinks that Jane's "special circumstances" justify a defiance of conventional morality and social laws. Her dissatisfaction arises from what she interprets as Jane's misplaced good faith and good intentions. What George Eliot fails to see is that Jane's renunciation of Rochester is made not in the interests of a law, diabolical or not, but in self-interest. And the motivation of Jane's action is not self-sacrifice, but rather self-protection.

Rochester tries to appeal to Jane's judgement of the balance of consequences:

Is it better to drive a fellow-creature to despair than to transgress a mere human law, no man being injured by the breach?—for you have neither relatives nor acquaintances whom you need fear to offend by living with me.

Jane is almost convinced as she tries to reason within herself:

> Think of his misery; think of his danger; look at his state when left alone; remember his headlong nature: consider the recklessness following on despair—soothe him; save him; love him; tell him you love him and will be his. Who in the world cares for *you?* or who will be injured by what you do?

And then comes the reply from the depths of Jane's soul: Jane is almost convinced as she tries to reason within herself:

> *I* care for myself. The more solitary, the more friendless, the more unsustained I am, the more I will respect myself.

In the crisis, she can only fall back on herself, on her sense of self-protection, on her instinct for self-survival.… If Jane is adhering to a principle, it is the principle of self-respecting personal integrity. As she said: "I still possessed my soul." Rochester in his saner moments would have understood the motivation of her decision, as is shown by his penetrating analysis of Jane's character in the guise of a gypsy woman on an earlier occasion:

> That brow professes to say—"I can live alone, if self-respect and circumstances require me so to do. I need not sell my soul to buy bliss.… Reason sits firm and holds the reins, … judgement shall have the casting vote in every decision.… I shall follow the guiding of that still small voice which interprets the dictates of conscience."

This is of course ironic in the light of later events, for it is precisely these same self-respect, reason, judgement, and conscience that combine to frustrate Rochester.

Jane Eyre's painful decision to leave Rochester is in line with her magnificent outburst in the moonlit garden on Midsummer's eve:

> Do you think, because I am poor, obscure, plain, and little, I am soulless and heartless? You think wrong!—I have as much soul as you—and full as much heart! And if God had gifted me with some beauty and much wealth, I should have made it as hard for you to leave me, as it is now for me to leave you. I am not talking to you now through the medium of custom, conventionalities, nor even of mortal flesh: it is my spirit that addresses your spirit; just as if both had passed through the grave, and we stood at God's feet, equal—as we are!

In a further demonstration of spirit before she understands Rochester's intentions, she declares proudly: "I am a free human being with an independent will, which I now exert to leave you." She might have said the same at the later crisis of emotion and event in which she actually leaves him. In this outburst of pent-up emotions, Jane is assuming for herself and her sex a position and an attitude never before granted to heroines in English fiction—equality in love. Charlotte Brontë believes that love between man and woman is an all-consuming passion shared not only physically, but mentally and spiritually—"to the finest fibre of my nature," as Jane says. What Charlotte Brontë is asking for is a recognition of the emotional needs of a woman—the right to feel, to love unreservedly. In a way, Jane is an … unconventional heroine. She claims independence and rejects subservience. She will consent only to a marriage which is the union of equals in independence. Charlotte Brontë sees the relationship between man and woman as one of mutual need, a kind of equal partnership in which the woman is not just the object of pursuit or desire, but is recognized as an active contributor—unafraid to love with all-consuming passion, willing to devote herself to the man, and yet exacting respect and a recognition of her rights as an individual. Charlotte Brontë does not advocate an absolute union, a complete merging of man and woman—this would mean the dissolution of the self. Unlike Catherine Earnshaw who declares: "I *am* Heathcliff," Jane asserts: "*I* care for myself." Instead of losing herself in some "otherness," Jane fights to preserve her own identity. The relationship between Catherine and Heathcliff involves a fusion of personalities and leads towards mutual annihilation. The relationship [as suggested by Ruth Bernard Yeazell in her essay "More True Than Real: Jane Eyre's 'Mysterious Summons'," *Nineteenth-Century Fictions,* 1974] between Jane and Rochester is grounded on the equality and integrity of two independent selves and leads towards life. In the "Eden-like" garden of Thornfield, Jane appears to have secured both love and independence (of spirit, at least); but when it turns out to be a Paradise Lost, Jane must flee temptation and her lover, in order to preserve the integrity of her self against an overwhelming passion.

In a curious passage earlier on, Charlotte Brontë expresses what could well be taken as the manifesto of the Women's Liberation Movement:

> Women are supposed to be very calm generally; but women feel just as men feel; they need exercise for their faculties, and a field for their efforts as much as their brothers do; they suffer from too rigid a restraint, too absolute a stagnation, precisely as men would suffer; and it is narrow-minded in their more privileged fellow-creatures to say that they ought to confine themselves to making puddings and knitting stockings, to playing on the piano and embroidering bags. It is thoughtless to condemn them, or laugh at

them, if they seek to do more or learn more than custom has pronounced necessary for their sex.

Charlotte Brontë's concern with the "condition of women" question in her day is revealed here. She herself has struggled for independence and equality not as an exhilaration dreamed of but as a necessity, and the feminist attitude expressed here is assumed by her heroine.... Charlotte Brontë really prepares the way for ... other "rebel" heroines by showing her heroine overcoming social and sexual inferiority with moral, emotional, and intellectual superiority. Jane first encounters Rochester not as his equal but as his subordinate. She escapes the confines of Lowood to enter into a "new servitude," a servitude not just in terms of work but also in terms of love. The relationship between Rochester and Jane is that of master and servant, just as the relationship between hero and heroine in all the other Charlotte Brontë novels is that of teacher and pupil. But the master-servant relationship between Rochester and Jane is essentially one of mutual admiration and respect. Rochester loves Jane for her superiority of mind and heart, and Jane feels "akin" to Rochester and has, in her own words, "something in my brain and heart, in my blood and nerves, that assimilate me mentally to him." F. A. C. Wilson [in an essay "The Primrose Wreath: the Heroes of the Brontë Novels," *Nineteenth-Century Fiction,* 1974] suggests that for Charlotte Brontë, the ideal relationship between man and woman is an extremely flexible one "by which both partners freely alternate between 'masculine,' or controlling, and 'feminine,' or responsive roles" and that "Jane, for her part, enjoys her sexual status as a subordinate, but this is only insofar as it is a role in a game." Jane has no feeling of inferiority at all: she is only conforming outwardly to the Victorian concept of the prescribed roles for men and women, while in reality she believes in equality between the sexes, as evidenced in her vehement assertion of equality in the garden of Thornfield, and Rochester's response "My bride is here, ... because my equal is here, and my likeness" testifies to his agreement. Her sexual status as a subordinate may be more apparent than real, but her social status as an employee makes her dependent on her master for her livelihood. Jane's sensitive feelings about her position and her strong sense of individuality and independence make her resent any attempt to encroach on her personality. Just before their marriage, when Rochester wants to shower her with fineries and to deck her out in jewels and satin and lace, Jane feels "a sense of annoyance and degradation," partly because her aesthetic sense tells her

she looks better as "plain Jane," partly because her moral taste finds such extravagance abhorrent, but mainly because she feels this is a violation of her sense of self and a reflection on her essential dependence. Refusing to play the pampered slave to Rochester's benevolent despot of a sultan, she tells him: "I will be myself" and "I only want an easy mind, sir; not crushed by crowded obligations." She prefers to be herself and to be loved for what she is. It is in a state of reaction against what she construes as Rochester's attempted violation of her sense of self that immediately after this Jane writes to inform her wealthy Uncle John in Madeira of her impending marriage with the underlying motive of perhaps obtaining what she terms an "independency," thereby bringing about the chain of events that leads to the interrupted wedding. So Jane unwittingly incurs her own unhappiness through her desire for independence, which means more than just economic and social status—independence means personal identity and self-esteem.

Source: Maria Yuen, "Two Crises of Decision in *Jane Eyre,* in *English Studies,* June, 1976, pp. 215-26.

Sources

Phyllis Bentley, *The Brontës,* Thames & Hudson, 1969.

Rebecca Fraser, *The Brontës: Charlotte Brontë and Her Family,* Crown Publishers, 1988.

Sandra Gilbert and Susan Gubar, *The Madwoman in the Attic: The Woman Writer and the Nineteenth-Century Literary Imagination,* Yale University Press, 1979.

Margaret Lane, Introduction to *Jane Eyre,* Dent/Dutton, 1969.

M. H. Scargill, "All Passion Spent: A Revaluation of 'Jane Eyre'," in *University of Toronto Quarterly,* Vol. XIX, No. 2, January, 1950, pp. 120-25.

Mark Schorer, "Jane Eyre," in *The World We Imagine: Selected Essays,* Chatto & Windus, 1969, pp. 80-96.

For Further Study

Miriam Allott, editor, *The Brontës: The Critical Heritage,* Routledge, 1974.
    An excellent resource for studying contemporary reviews and critiques of Charlotte Brontë's works.

Juliet Barker, *The Brontës,* St. Martin's Press, 1994.
    An unusually detailed and comprehensive biography with a wealth of information on Charlotte Brontë, her parents, and her brother and sisters and their writings.

Margaret Howard Blom, *Charlotte Brontë,* Twayne, 1977.
Includes sections on Brontë's life and on *Jane Eyre,* and assesses Brontë's achievement in the novel.

Miriam Allen deFord, "Charlotte Brontë" in *British Authors of the Nineteenth Century,* edited by Stanley J. Kunitz and Howard Haycraft, H. W. Wilson, 1936, pp. 74-6.
An overview survey of Brontë and her work, written in a somewhat dated prose style.

Richard J. Dunn, editor, *Jane Eyre,* Norton, 1971; updated, 1987.
Includes important background information, contemporary criticism, and useful interpretive articles on a variety of aspects of the novel.

Barbara and Gareth Lloyd Evans, *Everyman's Companion to the Brontës,* J. M. Dent and Sons, 1982.
Includes both commentaries and synopses of the Brontës' novels, including *Jane Eyre.*

Barbara Timm Gates, editor, *Critical Essays on Charlotte Brontë,* G. K. Hall, 1990.
Includes a collection of both contemporary and modern reviews of and critical responses to Brontë's novels.

Lyndall Gordon, *Charlotte Brontë: A Passionate Life,* W. W. Norton, 1995.
The definitive biography of Charlotte Brontë.

Q. D. Leavis, Introduction, in Charlotte Brontë's *Jane Eyre,* Penguin Books, 1966, pp. 7-29.
An exceptionally insightful discussion of the novel, and an important source for understanding how the novel breaks with Victorian literary tradition.

Pat MacPherson, *Reflecting on "Jane Eyre",* Routledge, 1989.
Provides some useful background for a study of the novel, including a discussion of Jane as a governess and a discussion of Jane's personal progress from one stage in her life to another.

Pauline Nestor, *Charlotte Brontë's "Jane Eyre",* St. Martin's Press, 1992.

Includes material on the historical and cultural context of the novel and an interpretation of its themes of motherhood, sexuality, and identity.

Beth Newman, editor, *"Jane Eyre", by Charlotte Brontë,* Bedford Books of St. Martin's Press, 1996.
Contains the text of the novel, an essay on its critical history, and a collection of five insightful critical essays from the perspectives of psychoanalytic, feminist, deconstruction, Marxist, and cultural critics. Includes the article by Sandra Gilbert mentioned in the essay.

Francine Prose, "The Brilliance of the Brontës," in *Victoria,* Vol. 11, No. 3, March, 1997.
Prose discusses the enduring appeal of *Jane Eyre* in the context of a general consideration of the Brontës' particular genius. Prose points out that although readers remember the vivid, melodramatic aspects of the novel, much more of the book is devoted to describing the sufferings of children and the poor.

Herbert J. Rosengarten, "Charlotte Brontë," in *Dictionary of Literary Biography: Volume 21: Victorian Novelists Before 1885,* edited by Ira B. Nadel and William E. Fredeman, Gale Research, 1983, pp. 24-54.
A comprehensive overview of Brontë's life and works.

Elaine Showalter, *A Literature of Their Own: British Women Novelists from Brontë to Lessing,* Princeton University Press, 1977.
Interprets the novel as an important document for providing a view of the female experience in the mid-nineteenth century.

Cathy Smith, "Moors and Mansions: *Jane Eyre* Country," in *Los Angeles Times,* October 20, 1996, p. L13.
Smith identifies real places in Derbyshire, England, believed to be models for some of the locations depicted in *Jane Eyre.* She also discusses the origin of the name "Eyre" and identifies a historical precedent for Bertha Mason.

July's People

Nadine Gordimer

1981

In light of the uprisings of the 1970s, Nadine Gordimer presented a very bleak and cynical prophecy to white and black South Africa. That prophecy suggested no solution to problematic race relations but foresaw an inevitable overthrow of the apartheid system of the Afrikaner Nationalists. With the declaration of independence by the neighboring nations of Angola, Mozambique, and Zimbabwe, the demise of white rule in South Africa was anticipated.

July's People takes place during a future revolution in South Africa. Amid such chaos, traditional roles are overturned and new ones must be forged. In that sense, the novel exists in Antonio Gramsci's (the source of the novel's epigraph) interregnum—between the explosion of the old but before the birth of the new.

July's People captures the mood of a South Africa expecting revolutionary violence just like that experienced by neighboring countries. Instead of writing about a revolution, however, the novel assumes such an event will happen and imagines what affect it might have on a liberal white family. In this case, the family decides to accept their servant's offer of refuge and flee to his village. There, with all the awkwardness of Friday nursing Robinson Crusoe, they hope to wait out the war. Gradually, all the family's accoutrements of civilization are given up, stolen, or proven to be completely useless. Simultaneously, the power relations of society are revealed as hollow. However, there is hope in that self-awareness and in the children's

immersion in village life as a possible route to the construction of a new South Africa.

Author Biography

Gordimer was born in Springs, an East Rand mining town outside Johannesburg in the Transvaal region of South Africa, in 1923. Springs served as the setting of her first novel, *The Lying Days* (1953). Her father was a jeweler from Latvia and her mother was of British descent. Growing up, Gordimer was often sequestered indoors because her mother feared she had a weak heart. She spent some time in convent school where, she admits in an autobiographical essay "A Bolter and the Invincible Summer" (1963), she was a habitual truant.

In response to her confinement, Gordimer began writing at the age of nine. Her first published story was "The Quest for Seen Gold," which appeared in June of 1937 in the *Johannesburg Sunday Express.* Fortunately, she maintains, the publication of her work did not lead to the smothering that one sees with those considered "gifted." Instead she was left to her own devices and, thus, began a long career of writing about life in South Africa.

Her short stories were continually published in magazines until her first book came out in 1952. It was a collection of short stories titled *The Soft Voice of the Serpent* (1952). Already, her technique was evident. Her writing had clarity, little emotion, and great control.

Gordimer lived through the system of Apartheid and fought to bring about its end. She was a member of the African National Congress (which was an illegal party until the 1980s), and she chose to stay in South Africa when many other writers and political dissidents left for school or safety in Europe and America. However, she was not a prominent dissident—like Ruth First—but she was a voice of protest. "I remain," she said, "a writer, not a public speaker: nothing I say here will be as true as my fiction." Still, many of her books were banned in South Africa from 1958 until 1991.

A prolific writer, Gordimer has written many essays on politics, censorship, writing, and other writers. Much of this work parallels her fictional work and taken together she has painted a damning picture of apartheid. She was a founding member of the Congress of South African Writers. She has won numerous awards for her writing, including the Booker prize, the Modern Literature Association Award, and the Bennett Award. Many uni-

Nadine Gordimer

versities have honored her with degrees and the French government gave her the decoration of Officier de l'Ordre des Arts et des Lettres. In 1991, she was awarded the Nobel Prize for Literature. Currently, she lives in South Africa, is the Vice President of PEN (a worldwide organization of writers), a member of the Congress of South African Writers, and she continues to write.

Plot Summary

In *July's People,* Nadine Gordimer depicts the lives of a liberal, white South African family, the Smales, forced to flee to the native village of their black servant, July. Gordimer sets her novel during a fictional civil war in which black South Africans violently overturn the system of apartheid. In order to escape the violence in Johannesburg, the Smales must accept July's charity and live a life that makes them all confront their assumptions about one another.

The novel opens the morning after an exhausting three-day trip through bush country to reach the village. July brings tea for Maureen and Bamford Smales and breakfast for their children, Victor, Gina, and Royce. After experiencing disorientation from the trip, Maureen asks her husband about their vehicle, a small truck called a bakkie. He tells her that July has hidden it.

The Smales find themselves dependent on July, and July's family questions their presence in the village. He explains the their situation, telling his mother and wife, Martha, about the violence in the country. They cannot, however, fully believe his account given their past experience with white dominance.

To do something other than listen constantly for news on his radio, Bam Smales builds a water tank for the village. Maureen tries to read a novel, since July will not let her work, but discovers that no fiction can compete with her current situation. She then recalls her girlhood days and remembers walking home from school with her family's black servant, Lydia, who carried Maureen's school case on her head. One day, a photographer took their picture. Years later, Maureen saw the picture in a *Life* photograph book and for the first time questioned why Lydia was carrying her books.

One night, after Bam unsuccessfully tries socializing with the villagers, Bam and Maureen are startled by July's departure as a passenger in the bakkie. Anxious over losing the vehicle, they argue, blaming each other for their situation. Later, while standing nude in the rain, Maureen sees the bakkie return. She falls asleep that night without telling Bam about the vehicle.

When July comes to their hut the next day, Bam greets him with the inappropriate authority of their former relationship. Apparently ignoring Bam's tone, July tells them he went to the shops for supplies. Though they could, they do not ask him for the keys to the bakkie. July begins to learn how to drive. When the they ask him what he will do if caught driving the vehicle, he says he will say he owns it.

Later, Maureen returns the bakkie's keys to July. Knowing that she does not want him to keep the keys, he makes her recall his former status as her "boy" when he kept the keys to her house. He also recalls the distrust he sensed from her at the time. Stung by his words, Maureen tries to defend her treatment of him and says their former relationship has ended, that he is no longer a servant. He then shocks her by asking if she is going to pay him this month. He offers the car keys back to her, saying he worked for her for fifteen years because his family needed him to. She then retaliates by mentioning Ellen, his mistress in Johannesburg. Though feeling a hollow victory, Maureen knows

July will never forgive her this transgression. He keeps the car keys.

Bam kills two baby wart-hogs with his small shotgun. During the hunt, he offers to let his black hunting companion, Daniel, shoot the gun sometime. Bam gives the larger wart-hog to the villagers and keeps the smaller (and more tender) one. Everyone joyfully feasts on the meat, an intoxicating delicacy, and Bam and Maureen make love for the first time since their journey.

The scene shifts to July and his family eating the meat and talking about the Smales. July discounts Martha's worries that the white family will bring trouble. Martha recalls the times without July when he, like most men with families, worked in the city. Like the seasons, the long absences of their husbands have become an expected part of black women's lives.

Gina and her friend, Nyiko, play with newborn kittens, and Maureen scolds them. Later, after they listen for news on the radio, Bam asks Maureen if she found a home for the kittens. She reveals that she has drowned them in a bucket of water.

Maureen tries working with the women in the fields, digging up leaves and roots. Afterward, she goes to see July, who is working on the bakkie. July does not want to hear about the killing on the news and hopes everything "will come back all right." Maureen asks, dumbfounded, if he really wants a return to the ways things were. July asks if hunger compels her to search for spinach with the women; she replies that she goes to pass the time. As always, she feels that the workplace language they speak hinders their ability to communicate.

When July says she should not work with the women, she asks if he fears she will tell his wife about Ellen. He angrily asserts that she can only tell Martha that he has always been a good servant. Maureen, frightened, realizes that the dignity she thought she had always conferred upon him was actually humiliating to him. He informs her that he and the Smales have been summoned to the chief's village. Though July has authority in his village, they still must ask the chief's permission to stay. Maureen struggles with her new subservience to July.

The Smales visit the chief the next morning, afraid that the chief will force them out. The chief asks them why they have come to his nation and asks about events in Johannesburg. He cannot believe that the white government is powerless and that whites are running from blacks. He says that the black revolutionaries are not from his nation and that the whites, who would never let him own a gun, will give him guns to aid in the struggle against the black attackers. He tells Bam to bring his gun and teach him how to shoot it.

Outraged by this suggestion, Bam asks if the chief really intends to kill other blacks, saying that the entire black nation is the chief's nation. After further discussion, the chief allows them to stay with Mwawate (July) and says that he will visit them to learn how to shoot Bam's gun.

On the return trip, July explains that the chief talks instead of acts. Furthermore, the chief, who never fought the whites, is too poor and defenseless to fight other blacks. Upon their return to their hut, Maureen and Bam speak in the phrases they had used in their former life, and these phrases cannot adequately describe their current predicament. Bam begins criticizing July's new confidence and his criticisms of the chief. Maureen says that July was talking about himself, that he will not fight for anyone and is risking his life by having the family there. Maureen suggests that they leave, making Bam confront what they both know: they have nowhere to go and no means by which to get there.

With the women, Maureen clumsily cuts grass for the huts. After the cutting, July criticizes Martha for placing the grass bundles in front of the Bam and Maureen's house, where their children will ruin it. They discuss July's past and his times in the city over the last fifteen years. Rejecting July's contention that his family will move to the city once the fighting ends, Martha suggests that he stay in the village. According to Daniel, they will no longer face white restrictions, and, with his city experience, July can run his own shop.

A man brings a battery-operated amplifier to the village and provides them with a night's entertainment, during which many villagers drink heavily. The Smales do not partake in the drinking but return to their hut, where they find their gun missing.

With no police to help him, Bam is impotent in the face of the theft. Maureen feels humiliated for Bam. She leaves to find July, who is by the bakkie. They realize that only Daniel was absent from the party, and Maureen says July must get the gun from him. Daniel, however, has left. After July asserts that the Smales always make trouble for him, Maureen accuses July of stealing small items from her in Johannesburg. Angered, he speaks to her in his own language, and "She understood although she knew no word. Understood everything: what he had had to be, how she had covered up to herself for him, in order for him to be her idea of him. But for himself—to be intelligent, honest, dignified for *her* was nothing; his measure as a man

was taken elsewhere and by others," his own people. July then informs her that Daniel has joined the revolution. She tells July that he abandoned Ellen and only wants the bakkie so he can feel important, but that, too, will become useless when his gas money runs out.

After Gina goes to play with Nyiko and Bam goes with Victor and Royce to fish, a helicopter with unidentifiable markings flies over the village. Maureen fervently chases the helicopter, and the novel ends with her still running toward it and its unknown occupants, who could be either "saviours or murderers."

Characters

The chief

The chief, as befits his position, is the only character who attempts to make sense of the greater picture. He has no weapons and no wealth. He asks Bam for his gun; however, Bam is shocked that the chief would kill the "good guys"—the people of Mandela and Sobukwe—for the white government. But at least the chief wants to do something even if alone and armed with one gun. He would prefer action to hiding out and waiting to be taken over again. What Bam does not want to understand is that the chief and his people have their own history which has little in common with the urban African National Congress.

Daniel

July's friend Daniel shows him how to drive the bakkie as well as fix it. He befriends the white family. Bam shows him how to shoot and Daniel accompanies the family to the chief. He disappears at the same time that Bam's gun goes missing. It is assumed he has taken the gun and gone off to join the revolutionary army.

Ellen

While July lives with the Smales, he has a mistress named Ellen. She is from Botswana and is an office cleaner. The money she earns in the city is sent to pay for her son's high school education in Soweto. While ironing July's clothes with Maureen's iron, she sometimes chats with Maureen. "[O]nce [she] had put a hand under her breasts with the gesture with which women declare themselves in conscious control of their female destiny ... I'm sterilized at the clinic."

July

July recalls the character of Friday in the eighteenth-century novel by Daniel Defoe, *Robin-*

Media Adaptations

- *July's People* was made into an audio cassette by Blackstone Audio Books in 1993.

---

son Crusoe. Benevolent masters named both characters for calendar measurements and both were trusted with their masters' lives. July appears to be "their servant, their host," but the revolution has disrupted traditional roles. He remains the white family's savior, but as time goes on they become his people. He represents all the myths and stereotypes of the black servant, but he also uses those same myths to his advantage.

Determined to remain their servant as long as he is paid, July seeks to become the master of the family. It is a revolution of roles rather than the herald of a new society. July accomplishes his objective by sequestering them and confining them to their role as his master. As such, they depend on him for everything. He also makes sure that Maureen is unable to establish relations with the other women and, therefore, she cannot fully integrate to society. Lastly, July slowly appropriates the tokens of civilization they have managed to bring with them, the most important being the bakkie.

Lydia

In a flashback, Maureen returns to her young love for a family servant named Lydia. She recalls with joy the many afternoons that she would "bump" into Lydia on the way home from school. Customarily, Lydia would take Maureen's burden onto her head with the shopping and they would go home. The relationship is one of master and servant. However, in Maureen's memory it is also that of young girl in love with an older female. From this context she is able to say that the photo, taken by the journalist to depict apartheid as a white girl next to a "black woman with the girl's school case on her head," shows a context of "affection and ignorance." The memory of Lydia reveals Maureen's blindness to her own empowered status.

Martha

The wife of July, Martha is a simple character. She represents the agrarian traditional figure that is resigned to her role. For her, "The sun rises, the moon sets; the money must come, the man must go." She does not react to the white people in her mother's house too much nor does she relate to Maureen. The women met and "something might have come of it. But not much."

Mwawate

See July

Nyiko

A girl from the village who becomes Gina's childhood intimate. They become more and more inseparable and are reminded of their origins of difference only when the adults want to know whose child Gina is minding. She is a subject of fascination for Bam and Maureen when she takes a sausage.

Bamford Smales

Descended from Boers (Dutch colonists), Bam has the privilege of the white South African in an Apartheid state. He is an architect for Caprano & Partners and husband to Maureen. He likes to boast of being a judge at conferences and of his professional abilities, like speaking French. He also name-drops. Being middle class, he hunts for sport and bought himself the yellow bakkie as a hunting vehicle. He sees himself as strong, masculine, and in control of his life. He does not mind exchanging suburban leisure for laboring on improvements about the village. In his mind this gives him an importance, but in reality he is a secondary character to his employers and to his wife.

Politically, Bam is a pacifist who empathizes with the blacks. Personally, the situation utterly emasculates him; his former servant controls the bakkie and calls the shots. He admits that he feels like "a boy with a pea-shooter." His final abdication as white man occurs when his gun is stolen. Without his gun he is of no use to the chief, he holds no symbolic power, and he is unable to uphold his economic place of provider and, therefore, has no sexual claim on Maureen.

Gina Smales

Of all the characters, only Gina represents the hope of that a new South Africa is possible. She shows the opposite characteristics of the small-minded Victor. She is the second child and shows every sign of ease with village life. She finds a best friend in Nyiko and a sense of responsibility in minding the younger children in the village. In addition, she begins to learn the local language. The beginning of a new South African person can be glimpsed in Gina—she is multilingual and the race barrier that her brother Victor depends on is not present for her. Gina insists on her difference from her siblings. Her mother notices she is "always a moody bastard" who acts like a witch to her brothers.

Maureen Hetherington Smales

The focus of the novel, Maureen is a woman from the Western Area Gold Mines who has been living in the safe environs of the suburbs. Until the revolution and the flight to July's village, she was in charge of her household and family. Her husband was a wonderfully successful architect and they both shared a liberal view of apartheid. Together they hoped that dialogue and discussion would bring about greater equality.

All of that vanishes in the flight in the yellow bakkie with her family and servant to the countryside. Leaving her suburban life behind, she attempts to manufacture a new value system within her new surroundings, but instead discovers that values are relative. Further, those values depend on personal relationships; in her new life, she discovers these relationships are not as strong as she once thought. Eventually, after a failed relationship with July, she runs off into the unknown.

In this final flight, she is finally understands that she must break free from the circularity of her traditional role. Thus by abandoning her family and being spurned by her servant, she virtually joins Daniel and merges with the social revolution.

Royce Smales

Royce is the littlest of the Smales and July's favorite. He annoys his parents with his request for a Coke. He slyly exacerbates his bother's tantrum by asking if he is really going to buy a buggy. He at once questions his brother's awakening masculinity while making light of the moment.

Victor Smales

The oldest child, Victor adamantly tries to maintain racial separation despite the liberal example of his parents. He wants to have the spoils of white rule. The character of Victor represents the idea that racism is childish. Furthermore, the pettiness of the racist is that of a spoiled child who insists on dragging out his racing-car track. This is demonstrated when Victor wants to keep the blacks away from the rain catch his father has made ("who owns the rain?" asks his mother). He is also infuriated that a black should accuse him of stealing

South African policeman, 1985.

garbage—an orange sack. Victor also shows that the anger of a racist person must be handled carefully, "[he] was angry with a white man's anger, too big for him." Yet Victor learns some manners from his black playmates, though not as many as Gina and Royce do. This occurs when he accepts a piece of fishing line from July with the typical open palm gesture of the other children.

Tsatsawani

July's mother gives up her hut for the Smales. She is apprehensive of the white people's presence in the village and resents being unable to replace the roof of her hut. She represents old age, as well as the natural rhythm of the village and its agricultural focus. She also contrasts with the image of Bam's associate who died in his own plane's crash. Grandmother, conversely, is still working and will work "bent lower and lower towards the earth until finally she sank to it—the only death she could afford."

Themes

Body

The incredible situation which the Smales find themselves in is attested to and dealt with at a very personal level. The real discomfort and disruption

Topics for Further Study

- The ending of July's People leaves a great deal to the imagination. Imitating Gordimer's style, write your own ending. Was there a helicopter or not?

- Do some research into the disease risks associated with living in the rural regions (as opposed to the wilderness) of South Africa. Given the fact of war and that July's home is an old agricultural village, how much of Maureen's worry about illness is valid? How much is simply an expression of her discomfort at not being in familiar surroundings?

- In the United States we had a similar, though milder, system of laws that institutionalized racial discrimination known as Jim Crow Laws. What were those laws and how would they compare with the system of apartheid?

- Gordimer wrote her novel at a time when a racial revolution seemed inevitable. Americans have felt this fear in the past as well (for example, at the times of The Great Sioux Uprising, Wounded Knee, Watts Riots, LA Riots). Does that fear exist in any form today, say, in immigration quotas or as hysteria over the Mexican border?

of the revolution has been displaced to a new awareness of the physical body. "For the first time in her life [Maureen] found that she smelled bad between her legs ... [she] disgustedly scrubbed." There is also a constant concern about living in the village, especially the risk of disease. However, this fear does not stop them from trying to keep up appearances. Maureen secretly washes her menstrual rags in the river because the shame of her period looms far greater than the "risk of bilharzia."

In addition to these sufferings, it is in the description of another person's body that the Smales admit their whiteness. Maureen comments on her children coughing like the black children do. She also notes that her kids look dirtier than the village children because of their white skin. It is never said

directly but it is suggested that there is something natural about black people living in primeval nature—they seem to blend in with darkness: "they could see his fingernails and his eyes." These are intentional stereotypical references. But the most certain sign that the family is realizing its fear of losing whiteness (or going native) and becoming villagers is Bam's terrifying report that he has seen Royce wipe himself with a stone—not a treasured piece of toilet paper.

Nature

Reversing roles, the blacks are now able to walk freely in the city, and Maureen feels herself confined to the hut: "Maureen could not walk out into the boundlessness." She excuses her confinement by saying she fears being spotted by a patrol; but everyone knows they are there. Disease keeps her from going to the river too often. She steers clear from July's hut while July keeps her from fraternizing with the other women. She tries to work with the women once in the field—but she feels self-conscious because of her white legs.

Before her flight into the unknown at the end of the novel, the only time she gives into nature is a secret, naked, dance in the rain. Her attitude or fear of the boundlessness is repeated in her attitude toward her own body and those bodies around her. Overcoming nature becomes Maureen's epiphany.

Sex Roles

The disruption of reality—or what Maureen has known as reality—caused by the revolution has forced her to reflect upon the nature of reality, "since that first morning she had become conscious in the hut, she had regained no established point of a continuing present from which to recognize her own sequence." Reality, in this context, had been decided upon in the mind of each individual according to their position in an economy of sex roles. Reality is dependent upon human relations that are based on a false resistance to apartheid and a position of claimed innocence. "The Humane creed ... depended on validities staked on a belief in the absolute nature of intimate relationships between human beings."

Maureen realizes her life has been gilded by a suburbia whose sterility thwarts honest intimacy. It is this realization that causes her to feel embarrassed about Ellen and about visiting July when he was ill. She also realizes that power relations in society are reflected within her family. She discovers that there is little real intimacy and begins to view her husband and children as strangers.

Furthermore, her previous conception relied on "sexual love formulated in master bedrooms" for the purposes of fulfilling a "place in the economy." From this viewpoint, her marriage to Bam becomes insupportable. Disgust grows between them in parallel to their individual disgust at their own body. She takes on the "matriarchal frown of necessity performed without question, without reasoning; the same frown she had had turned up to her by July's wife." While he "had the menacing aspect of maleness as man has before the superego has gained control of his body, come out of sleep. His penis was swollen under his rumpled trousers." Not only do bodies disgust them, but also the very physical life of the village disgusts them. Nothing is pressed; nothing is familiar.

The marital breakdown is reflected in the pronouns used toward each other but also in the sexual act. They do not have sex except for the night of the hog feast when they succumb to the influence of the meat. Bam dreams of the pig; he wakes to what he thinks is pig's blood on him when it is her menstrual blood he sees. It is a further sign that they are not in the sterility of the suburb and that their coitus rests on violence—the master bedrooms of apartheid economics.

Likewise, Maureen offers herself to July but "the death's harpy image she made of herself meant nothing to him, who had never been to a motor show complete with provocative girls." It is an awesome conjunction. Marital sex has become an act of drunken violence neither really wanted. Maureen, in her confusion over reality, desperately and pointlessly offers herself to July—the new master of the bakkie—as another possession, the final one. Having now broken all possible connections, marital and otherwise, Maureen is ready to leave.

Culture Clash

Along with natural bodily function, culture clash is a main thematic of the story. An important aspect of this is the way that Maureen and July conjure the legendary friendship of Robinson Crusoe and Friday—but replacing Friday's cheery obedience with a tense political dilemma.

The similarity is found in the careful listing and discussion of objects. In the story of Crusoe, he is incredibly lucky to have been able to recover many items from the shipwreck to assist the creation of a marooned settlement. The most important possessions for the Smales are the bakkie ("A ship that had docked in a far country"), the radio (before which Bam looks like a monkey fingering the bars of a cage), malarial pills, toilet paper, and

the gun. Conversely, July's unwanted items from the past—like the two pink glasses of the opening scene—are now employed to recreate the Bam and Maureen's home.

More ironic, however, are the items grabbed in the hectic moment of flight which serve absolutely no purpose: the race track; bundles of monetary notes which become bits of paper; ornamental clay vessels; and "a gadget for taking the dry cleaner's tags off clothes." In reference to these items, Maureen notes that they now have nothing. Then she sees her old scissors and her small knife-grinder in use around the village, realizing that July "must have filched them." It is Maureen's feeling of deprivation of discarded household items that prevents her from seeking July in his hut. "She no more wanted to have to see her cast-off trappings here, where they separated [July] from the way other people lived around him, than she did back there, where they separated him from the way she lived." But while Maureen works through the problem of possession, Bam, on the other hand, is utterly emasculated by the loss of his bakkie and his gun.

Style

Narrative

The narrative is told from a third person point of view and the tone of the narrative voice is that of dispassionate documentation. The voice reports on the activities and behavior of the characters as they adjust to their marooned state. However, the narration does not add information about the world that might explain the situation. In this way, the narrator knows only as much as the Smales know or learn from the radio. At the story's focus is Maureen, her thoughts are more often revealed. As a result, the story told is filtered through her and censored by her body of knowledge. Furthermore, the reader loses track of the political background and must consider what the basis of human relations are and what they need to be in a more just society.

Occasionally the focus shifts to Bam and there is some insight into his thought process; but this is not enough to give him any depth. Maureen and July (who is a function of her) are the only substantial characters in the novel. Maureen causes the narrative's linearity to be clouded in a way that reflects her disbelief that any of the revolution was possible or happening.

Realism

Realism is a literary technique often used to examine the mores and customs of middle-and lower-class characters. *July's People* focuses on middle-class liberal whites to examine them as they deal with a complete disruption of their society. The story asks the question, what next—what kind of role do white people have when they are overthrown? That question is the subtext of Maureen's battle with July. In fact, the climax of the story is the moment when he yells at her in his own language and she understands. She hears that her sympathies for him were an insult, that he is trapped as a servant in a society ruled by whites. But that is his morass.

The real criticism of the story is centered on Maureen. She represents the liberal who tried to prevent or ignore the growing revolutionary violence. Now, she discovers, she must do something. The focus on the hypocrisy of the liberal political stance is exposed without having to resort to a specific listing of their faults. It is exposed by a story of a symbolic family marooned among people it never really wanted to encounter (though they might have felt for them from a distance). Gordimer wants the reader to examine his or her beliefs. The novel's dramatic circumstances serve to point out that only a fantastic event, unfortunately, will wake people up.

Leitmotif

In musical composition, a leitmotif describes the technique whereby certain themes are repeated to signify emotion, announce a character, or accompany specific scenery. *July's People* is composed of an incredible series of such events whereby the novel's noise—the insects, the radio, the people, the helicopter—becomes a symphony or operatic display. Moreover, every superficial theme actually reinforces the overarching theme that a woman, Maureen, cannot simply hide from history.

There are subtle objects that instantly retell the story. For example, Manzoni's *I Promessi Sposi* is the only novel Maureen has taken with her. She never reads the famous nineteenth-century novel, but it reminds her of civilization. Like that novel, her marriage is thwarted by the overlord July—but there will be no happy ending because she rejects suburban culture with its fanciful tales of romance. Another example is found in the pink teacups and the way July supplies fruit at the end of the meal. The insistence upon living in the same manner as they once did only further points out the absurdity of that previous life.

Historical Context

South Africa

The Union of South Africa was formed in 1910 under a constitution excluding blacks from parliament. In 1912, a number of chiefs joined members of the middle class to form the opposition party, the African National Congress (ANC). ANC protests from 1912 until 1940 were within the law. When WWII broke out, South Africa fought with the Allies. After the war, there was a great influx of Africans into the cities. This shift in demographics, coupled with a rise in crime and shantytowns, created a degree of paranoia amongst the enfranchised (white) citizens. In the elections of 1948, the Afrikaner Nationalists were voted in because they promised to restore order.

The Afrikaner Nationalists began a system of apartheid, a regime based on racial discrimination that was instituted nationwide. In 1956, for example, the regime removed 60,000 mixed-blood "colored" from the voting rolls of Cape Province. In late summer, 100,000 non-whites were forcibly evicted from their homes to make room for whites. Africans were required to live in designated areas and carry "passes" or permission papers. The inability to provide an inquiring official with one's papers meant jail or fines. Generally, the system of apartheid aimed to keep the non-white people living under South African rule a disciplined pool of workers. Dissent or organization into labor unions or political parties was not tolerated. The political groups, lead by the ANC, used boycotts, strikes, and demonstrations in an effort to change the government.

On March 21, 1960, thousands of people all over South Africa responded to an ANC call of civil disobedience. The people marched without their passes and offered themselves for arrest. The government responded at Sharpeville, 40 miles south of Johannesburg, where 20,000 people had gathered. Police panicked and opened fire. Sixty-nine black people dead, 180 injured, and one week later the ANC was banned. This event forced leaders to flee underground where they formed armed groups whose aim was sabotage. One of the leaders jailed soon after was Nelson Mandela.

Soweto

Tensions increased as the strictures of apartheid tightened: every year saw the passage of laws decreasing the civil liberties of blacks. It also saw the highest incarceration rate in the world and

Children refugees pushing shopping cart near squatters' camps in South Africa.

barbaric police brutality. The opposition parties were working underground but were not invisible for long. In the 1970s, the Black Consciousness movement formed but then was destroyed by the government. Its purpose was accomplished; it raised awareness among people and made possible a new generation of black dissidence. A revolt was organized from schools where teachers and students were dissatisfied with low salaries, a crumbling education system, and a recent law that made Afrikaans the equivalent of English.

On June 16, 1976, roughly 15,000 school children turned out to demonstrate against apartheid in Soweto. The police opened fire, killing 25, and wounding dozens more. The protest spread over the country and continued through 1977. One of the organizers was soon arrested. His name was Stephen Biko and his death in jail created an international outcry. After restoring order, the government appointed the Collié Commission of Inquiry to investigate the cause of the unrest in the black residential areas.

The Commission gave its report in February of 1980 and stated that the problem stemmed from the implementation of the language policy and ensuing linguistic misunderstandings. As a result of the report, Soweto was given a new school, teachers were given a raise, and a new Education Act

made school compulsory—boycotts and protests were now illegal. What the government did not realize was that Soweto had galvanized a palpable opposition that had not been raised by Sharpeville or any of the other incidents. It is at this point, when "it seemed that all was quieting down again," that Gordimer published *July's People* and the ban on *Burger's Daughter* was lifted.

State of Emergency

The government dealt with Soweto effectively. An independent homeland scheme wherein there would be limited self-governance was masterminded by P. W. Botha and seemed to ease tensions. Meanwhile, some laws were changed and some liberties restored to blacks. White administration of the homelands was ended in 1982. But police actions simultaneously intensified throughout this period. In 1984, a new constitution was written and Botha became president. On the issue of parliaments, a compromise was brokered whereby there would be one lawmaking body but with three racially segregated chambers.

The developments at the parliamentary level translated into frustration at the street level. Youths were impatient for change—they had grown up aware of the Soweto massacre and conscious of the guerilla efforts of the ANC. On September 3, 1984,

Compare
&
Contrast

- **South Africa:** in 1991 the total population was about 30 million persons of which 5 million were white, 2.5 million were people of color, and the rest were black. The black population is expected to total 66 million by 2010 with little change in the other two racial categories.

- **USA:** the total population now exceeds 267 million persons. Approximately 11% are black. The birth rate among whites is low but among Hispanics and native Americans it is very high.

- **South Africa:** European colonialists designated 10 areas as reservations for blacks. These areas became known as homelands and were briefly independent. In 1994, the homelands were re-absorbed during the elections so that South Africa is one administrative unit without a reservation system.

- **USA:** European colonialists signed treaties with Native Americans granting them rights to homelands. This too was a reservation system. These treaties recognize the Indian Tribes as sovereign Nations but the United States has never allowed Native governments much independence.

---

the day the new Tricameral parliament was to become reality, riots broke out and South Africa entered a constant state of turmoil.

This unrest led to the declaration of a State of Emergency. The army re-enforced the police in October. Then in February 1985, the government tried to remove a squatter camp outside Cape Town called Crossroads. This had been tried before but the task of removing the 87,000 residents had not been achieved. During this attempt, 18 people were killed and international news cameras were on the scene. The whole world saw the violence and leaders around the world were furious. On March 21, 25 years after Sharpeville, the police killed 40 people gathered for a funeral of other police victims.

The End of White Rule

Since 1985, the ANC and its affiliates had become a revolutionary army with increasing tactical sophistication. They attacked government posts, police, and, by 1989, military installations. South Africa was in a state of civil war and the government was losing. The National Party changed its tactics by making F. W. de Klerk leader of the party. De Klerk was an outsider who was more receptive than his predecessors were. He was elected president in 1989. He lifted the ban on the ANC and released Nelson Mandela from jail. Throughout 1990s, exiles returned and new elections were

called for. Mandela was elected president in 1994 and incredible change swept the country.

Critical Overview

Gordimer has never had a large reading audience inside South Africa. South Africans have been dissatisfied with her work or they have been kept from it through censorship. Internationally, however, Gordimer has been the interpreter of South Africa through her short stories and novels. *July's People* was hardly different in this respect, but it is often treated not as a novel but as prophecy.

Soon after its publication, Anne Tyler praised the novel in the *New York Times Book Review*. She compared the story to Daniel Defoe's *Robinson Crusoe* and noted the strange symbols of civilization, like toilet paper. For Tyler, the novel "demonstrates with breathtaking clarity the tensions and complex interdependencies between whites and blacks in South Africa." Joan Silbur agreed in her review in the same magazine. She added that "Gordimer's novel is an intense look at a network of power relations—black to white, servant to master, male to female, child to parent—and the enormous changes wrought in all allegiances once power shifts utterly. For all the extremities of the

situation it chronicles and the suspense—drama of
its plot, it is a very subtle book—spare, careful, and
instructive."

Judith Chettle, however, was not so appreciative in *The National Review*. Understanding that
revolution has long been a possibility in the talk of
South Africa, she simply sees that Gordimer has
staged one. Chettle contends that revolutions "are
messy things to write about, so perhaps [Gordimer]
can be forgiven for being brief and somewhat vague
about the revolution itself. She prefers to tell about
a white family … [But] because her people think
more than they feel, Miss Gordimer never seems to
grapple seriously with the questions she has raised.
The situation may be revolutionary but the insights
are not." Another review in the *The Natal Witness*
described Gordimer as a difficult prophet. Evidently, the narrative structure was too problematic.

Academic studies of Gordimer have been consistently insightful. They pick up on the myths being exploited in the novel while understanding the
political play. Stephen Clingman, a fellow coun-
tryman, published *The Novels of Nadine Gordimer*
after the 1985 State of Emergency—an admittance
by the government that the nation was in a de facto
state of civil war. He, therefore, offers particularly
valuable insight. He writes:

> "in terms of the method in which its picture of rev-
> olution is presented, the novel is still candidly im-
> pressionistic. For there may be a way in which the
> novel is less interested in the future *per se* than in its
> unfolding in the present.… [thus the novel] may be
> the most deceptive, and deceptively simple, of all of
> Gordimer's novels, and perhaps less genuinely
> prophetic than, say, The Conservationist. What the
> novel is apparently doing is projecting a vision into
> the future; but what it may be doing most decisively
> is in fact the reverse. For what appears to be a pro-
> jection from the present into the future in the novel
> is from another point of view *seeing the present
> through the eyes of the future* … "

Change in South Africa, according to Clingman reading Gordimer, is inevitable but "nothing
new has been born." And that is why the ambiguity of the novel's end is fitting.

Rowland Smith, in his 1990 essay, focuses on
the frequency of impasse as a theme of Gordimer's
works and the way *July's People* shatters this dead-
lock. Instead of stalled and hesitant whites confused
about how to behave toward blacks, the whole of
white society is blown away: " … the collapse of
white military power which the novel assumes is
far less disturbing than the collapse of white moral
power which it analyses. Part of the degradation of
white suzerainty is shown to be white scruples

themselves, even the scruples of human, dissenting
whites. The paradox which epitomizes the dead-
lock of the book's ending is that only when the
black man refuses to talk the white woman's language is she able to understand 'everything.' "

Kathrin Wagner's recent book, *Rereading Nadine Gordimer,* discusses many features of the
novel. One element she focuses on is the "bildungsroman" element; that is, she watches Maureen's journey through a "heart of darkness" as one
of self-discovery. Her journey, moreover, is that of
a person in the "anguish of the only partially redeemed as history catches up with them." In such
a reading, the run towards the helicopter—sign of
civilization, technology, or the larger movements
of history—with its complimentary baptismal dip
in the river, becomes a simple reflex. Aware of the
shallowness of her former life and, therefore, feeling even more out of place in the village, she seizes
the moment and flees.

Still, according to Wagner, the novel falls
apart at the end. "In her writing," says Wagner,
"she implicitly and explicitly urges onward a historical process whose revolutionary phase must destroy the comfortable contexts within which she
writes."

Criticism

Darren Felty

*Felty is a visiting instructor at the College of
Charleston. In the following essay, he examines
Nadine Gordimer's depiction of the relationship
between her characters' social status and their self-
perceptions, which collapse after the overthrow of
white rule in South Africa.*

Nadine Gordimer's *July's People* explores the
nature of revolution, both on a political and a personal level. When the white Smales family must
flee the violence that erupts to end the caustic racial
oppression of South African apartheid, they lose
not only their economic and social status but also
any firm sense of their own identities.

The novel's title, in fact, underscores the indefinite nature of the relationships in the book. For
instance, the fact that July is the servant of the
Smales makes the family, to July's village, "July's
people." However, when the Smales must try to
adapt to living in this village, they encounter July's
other "people"—his family, as well as July's ex-

What Do I Read Next?

- Gordimer won the Booker Prize for her 1974 novel *The Conservationist*. The novel fictionalizes the consciousness of the agricultural settlers in South Africa and sets up the question being answered in *Burger's Daughter* and *July's People*. The question is, what role will whites have in the future of South Africa?

- *Burger's Daughter*, also by Gordimer (1979), won several awards but was banned in South Africa. It is the story of a woman very much the opposite of Maureen Smales. She is Rosa Burger, the daughter of Lionel Burger (a fictionalization of Abram Fischer—a very prominent leader of the South African Communist Party), whose self-liberation from familial restraints requires acceptance of her political inheritance and challenges apartheid. One of the sources for this novel was Joe Slovo's 1976 essay, "South Africa-No Middle Road".

- *July's People* has often been compared to *Waiting for the Barbarians* (1980), by J.M. Coetzee, because of similar questions about the fate of those in power. Coetzee's story is a parable about colonialism told by the magistrate of a fort. A garrison has come to help defend the fort against unseen barbarians. Eventually, the garrison retreats and things return to normal, but it's unclear whether anyone will survive the coming winter or when the barbarians will attack.

- When the crackdown on dissent came in the 1960s in the wake of the ANC ban, Ruth First was one of the first to be imprisoned. She wrote about her experience in a novel called *117 Days* (1965). She was assassinated by letter bomb in 1982 and was survived by her husband, who was living in exile, Joe Slovo.

- Gordimer's novel makes constant mention of health problems. Randall M. Pakard's 1990 work, *White Plague, Black Labor: Tuberculosis and the Political Economy of Health and Disease in South Africa (Comparative Studies of Health Systems and M),* discusses the daunting health problems of South Africa.

- G. H. L. Le May's 1995 work, *The Afrikaners: An Historical Interpretation,* attempts to put some perspective on the people known as Afrikaners and their political system known as apartheid. He does so with hindsight and from a new South Africa.

- In 1987, Universal Pictures released a film, entitled *Cry Freedom,* about the events which led South Africans to suspect that a revolution was imminent. Denzel Washington played Steve Biko and Kevin Kline played Donald Woods, the editor of the *Daily Dispatch.*

---

tended "people," black South Africans. They also find that in becoming July's responsibility in his home, their own status as his "people" makes them both dependent on him and an unwelcome burden to him.

In the process of this discovery, Maureen Smales discovers that her previous views of herself as a wife, mother, and liberal humanitarian were false since they were based on her economic and racial privileges. Her most painful realizations come during her confrontations with July, when she becomes aware of her inability to communicate with him and he forces her to recognize the true nature of their relationship. Maureen's losses culminate in her possibly suicidal rush to escape her situation at the novel's end.

Gordimer continually emphasizes the relationship between material possession and power in the book. Accustomed to a life defined in part by economic security and ownership, the Smales struggle to maintain their former sense of themselves once these material supports have been destroyed. The Smales children at first maintain this ethic of ownership, but they soon adapt themselves to their new situation, learning the village ways and redefining themselves within this context. Maureen and Bam, however, never fully adapt to their environment because their self-definitions rely on their status as possessors. Now dispossessed, politically, culturally, and economically, they cling to their few remaining belongings in order to maintain their identities.

The bakkie, in particular, becomes an object of contention for them. They fear July's appropriation of the bakkie both because he now controls their only means of escape and because his ownership of the vehicle inverts their relationship with him. In Johannesburg, they supervised his movements in the city. Now, however, July frustrates their futile attempts to maintain their independence by implicitly claiming the bakkie as his own.

Both he and the Smales recognize the consequences of his decision, as his first major confrontation with Maureen reveals. During their conversation, he insists on referring to himself as her "boy" and asserts that while she gave him the house keys in Johannesburg, she never completely trusted him to do his work. Maureen sees July's use of "boy" as a weapon, since the Smales never used the word. July views this as a rationalization and not using the word did not change the nature of their relationship. They were his employers, and he was completely dependent on them. And they treated him as such.

When Maureen contends that their relationship has now changed, July insults her by asking if she is going to pay him this month. Throughout their argument, he consistently reaffirms the economic foundations and divisions in their relationship. July keeps the keys and leaves Maureen profoundly disconcerted; he has made her recognize the economic underpinnings of her perceptions of both him and herself.

Not only material deprivation brings Maureen to the point of internal crisis. She also suffers from her inability to find a worthwhile role in either her family or the village community. She cannot fulfill a motherly role because her children adapt to village life without her assistance. And Bam ultimately becomes only the "blonde man" to her, as she becomes only "her" to him. Maureen and Bam become alienated from one another because they cannot identify with each other outside of their former domestic context, which defined them both.

Also, while Bam can perform small tasks like building a water tank and hunting with his shotgun, Maureen cannot work with the other women. She hopes to encourage a sense of feminine kinship between her and the village women, but July thwarts

her attempts by disapproving of her actions. Yet even with July's approval, the women would not welcome Maureen. She believes she can transcend their racial differences, but the black women see her not as a fellow woman sharing in their endeavors but as an incompetent white woman who cannot perform even simple tasks. She becomes frozen in a now bankrupt role: July's white "mistress" to whom others cater.

Once again, a confrontation with July underscores Maureen's predicament, since he will not allow her to improve her status to him and, thus, the other villagers. She desires an effective means of communication with him, but such communication proves impossible because of the limits of his English. The English they spoke in Johannesburg was not a problem because "it was based on orders and responses, not the exchange of ideas and feelings."

In their former roles, Maureen did not need to communicate complex ideas to July and did not need to discuss her emotional situation or his own needs. Their language proved functional and kept them at a distance from one another. Now this language is both an impediment to understanding and a means for July to maintain his distance from Maureen. For instance, when July disapproves of her desire to work with the other women, Maureen asks if he is afraid she will tell Martha "something." Angered, July responds, "—What you can tell?— … —That I'm work for you fifteen years. That you satisfy with me—." Once again, he asserts the mercantile nature of their relationship. She has no special knowledge of him that can prove valuable to her or dangerous to him. They were not friends and she did not know him. In fact, her pretense of liberal tolerance and respect actually humiliated him.

Thus, in her attempts to overcome the constraints of her current existence, Maureen actually discovers the limits of her former existence and the arrogance of her comfortable sense of personal worth. Having believed herself a woman of humane values with a secure place in the world, she now recognizes that she depended on an accepted cultural dominance over others to define her social (and familial) roles. Now at the mercy of a new cultural context, she is subject to the perceptions and definitions of others.

Maureen's fragile self-perceptions and her hopes of establishing a fruitful relationship with July are dealt a crippling blow in her final argument with him. When Bam's gun, their last possession, is stolen, Maureen tries to force July to retrieve it, desperately relying on him to salvage some sense of their former power. Instead, by declaring that she has become an unwanted burden to him and that he cannot help her, July makes Maureen feel "stampeded by a wild rush of need to destroy everything between them." She accuses him of stealing from her in Johannesburg, reasserting her property owner's right to indignation. He denies the accusation and, enraged, speaks to her in his own language. In this moment, Maureen understands him for the first time and realizes that she had perceived him as she *wanted* to perceive him, made him into her idea of him. He, however, never needed her approval but drew his sense of manhood from his family. Therefore, when the economic and social structures of white South Africa unravel, he retains crucial elements of his sense of self while hers disintegrates.

Because Maureen finally achieves an insight into July's character, the reader might think that this moment could lead to understanding between them and help forge a new, mutually beneficial relationship. Gordimer undermines such an optimistic reading, however, when Maureen confronts July with words that "sank into the broken clay walls like spilt blood." She tells him that he will profit from the losses of others, that he wants the possessions he never had before, regardless of their human cost. These possessions will make him feel important until, like the bakkie, they become inoperative and useless. Then he, too, will experience the same deprivation as the Smales, since they all draw their worth from what they own.

In an action that reveals Maureen's final, desperate association of herself with material possession, "she lurched over and posed herself, a grotesque, against the vehicle's hood," aligning herself as a sexual accoutrement to economic status. Her attempt fails, though, because "the death's harpy image she made of herself meant nothing to him, who had never been to a motor show complete with provocative girls." July does not share the cultural references from which Maureen derives her gesture of self-humiliation. Thus, she can neither fulfill a sexual role in July's domain, nor can she impress upon him that he, too, has been corrupted by greed and a complacent sense of superiority. She is left with only her comprehension of her own entrapment and powerlessness.

This comprehension may explain Maureen's ambiguous flight from the village toward an unidentified helicopter at the novel's end. Gordimer provides no direct explanation of either Maureen's motivations or the consequences of her actions, but the images she employs imply both the helicopter's threat and Maureen's internal transformation. Maureen experiences the sound of the helicopter as a sexual invasion as "her body in its rib-cage is thudded with deafening vibration, invaded by a force pumping, jigging in its monstrous orgasm," and she sees the helicopter with "its landing gear like spread legs, battling the air with whirling scythes." These images imply rape and warfare, but Maureen does not react fearfully to the helicopter, as if she is either unmoved by or actually welcomes the danger the helicopter poses. It could hold "saviours," who would presumably harken a return of white control, or "murderers," either black or white, who come to punish.

In her flight to reach the helicopter, she runs past "the man's voice and the voices of children speaking in English" and enters the river "like some member of a baptismal sect to be born again." In the end, she runs for herself alone, like an animal "existing only for their lone survival, the enemy of all that would make claims of responsibility." The distanced description of the Smales family implies Maureen's disassociation from her husband and children, and the baptismal imagery clearly evokes the possibility of a new birth. But a birth into what? Maureen appears to slough off both her familial obligations and her current internal conflicts, but Gordimer leaves open the question of exactly what she desires to transform into. Left with no ideals with which to define herself, Maureen seems to run by instinct toward some sense of closure, escaping the conditions that have proven so destructive to her, even if this escape means her death.

As Maureen realizes, the violent overthrow of apartheid entails not only a political revolt but also "an explosion of roles." She can no longer be "Maureen Smales," the middle-class Johannesburg wife and mother, because the preconceptions upon which she grounded her sense of self-worth collapse with the radical shifts in her social position. And she cannot become one of "July's people" because both she and they cannot escape the cultural definitions and prejudices that prohibit real intimacy between them. Therefore, her firm, comfortable perceptions of herself give way to utter emptiness, a vacancy inside of her to match the vacant horizons of the bush country. And fleeing this emptiness seems to be her only recourse as she, like the South Africa that Gordimer portrays, runs from a sterile past to an indefinite, ominous future.

Source: Darren Felty, in an essay for *Novels for Students,* Gale, 1998.

Nicholas Visser

Visser offers his interpretation on the ambiguous ending of July's People.

It is hardly surprising that the ending of Nadine Gordimer's *July's People* should have occasioned a fair amount of puzzlement. As Maureen Smales runs towards the helicopter, neither she nor the reader has any way of knowing 'whether it holds saviours or murderers; and—even if she were to have identified the markings—for whom.' And not knowing that, we are left uncertain what to make of the conclusion.

One impression readers may gain from the final pages of the novel is that they constitute what Russian Formalists called a 'zero ending', an ending in which the conclusion is left hanging in the air. Certainly, given Gordimer's guiding conception of the historical moment in which she was engaged in writing the novel, a zero ending would make sense. She chose as an epigraph for *July's People* a well-known formulation by Gramsci that was to become particularly significant for her: 'The old is dying and the new cannot be born; in this interregnum there arises a great diversity of morbid symptoms.' A notion of interregnum—a moment *between* two states of affairs, in which outcomes are not only unclear but cannot yet come into being—is necessarily going to make closure problematic. Nevertheless, I hope to show that, however perplexing the ending of *July's People* may be, it is not simply left hanging.

What we might think of as the polarities in interpretative responses to the ending of the novel have been outlined by Stephen Clingman and Margaret Lenta. Clingman is so far the only critic to opt for what might be thought of as the positive interpretation:

> at the end of the novel Maureen is running. The circumstances in which this occurs are ambiguous, but their significance surely is not. An unmarked helicopter has flown over near July's village and is coming down to land. No one knows whether it is manned by freedom fighters or by the South African army. But Maureen knows she must run. She is running from old structures and relationships, which have led her to this cul-de-sac; but she is also running towards her revolutionary destiny. She does not know what that destiny may be, whether it will bring death or life. All she knows is that it is the only authentic future awaiting her.

The confidence of Clingman's second sentence ('their significance surely is not') is belied by what follows. At precisely the moment we are to be informed of the significance, we are told 'she is running … towards her revolutionary destiny'. The phrase is rhetorically impressive, but it is more of an evasion than an explanation. Linking it to a generalized notion of authenticity only further obscures whatever significance the ending might be thought to have. Clingman sets out to address the problem of the ending; he ends up writing his way out of the interpretative dilemma the ending creates.

Clingman's account of the novel nowhere suggests why Gordimer would want to provide Maureen with a positive ending. Everything the novel discloses about Maureen's life 'back there', before South Africa boiled over into full-scale civil war, renders her as the very type of the white suburban liberal. Clingman himself recounts Gordimer's public break with South African liberalism in 1974, some seven years before the publication of *July's People*. To suggest, in light of that break, that such a figure moves at the conclusion of the novel towards a positive resolution of her dilemma would have to entail that Maureen has undergone some sort of conversion experience, a moment of Aristotelian anagnorisis or self-recognition. No such experience is rendered at the conclusion of the novel. Indeed, in linking her final action to her confrontation with July, Clingman has to supply Maureen with thoughts that are nowhere expressed: 'she *realizes* that this too [the reversal of roles whereby July is now dominant] is a circle she must break out of.'

Lenta takes issue with Clingman's account of the ending, discounting not only his positive interpretation but also the view, perhaps set out most clearly by Rowland Smith, that the ending is ambiguous and inconclusive. For Lenta,

> The fact that the nationality and loyalties of the crew of the plane are unknown to [Maureen], and that there has been earlier reference to several opposing South African and foreign contenders for power suggests strongly to me that Gordimer intends us to reflect on the negative meaning of her act: she is leaving, not joining. Our verdict is to be passed on the education and social conditioning of a white woman of our own day.

At first glance Lenta's suggestion that the novel prompts a critique of the social conditioning of Maureen in particular and, by extension, liberal values in general is persuasive. Such a view would certainly seem more in accord with Gordimer's reassessment of South African liberalism than Clingman's view. Somewhat less certain is what connection that might have with the ending. The critique is woven into the entire fabric of the novel; it does not have to wait for the ending to be initi-

> *It is not a question of deciding whether she is running 'towards' or running 'away from'. In any event, there is no clear support in the text for either view. She is drawn to the helicopter, by a power she does not understand, does not even reflect on."*

ated. Moreover, a critique does not imply a comprehensively negative judgement. After all, the Smaleses are not the villains of the piece, and certainly in the context of South African politics and history, not villains in any more general way either. Gordimer's critique of South African liberalism does not include the facile premise that liberals are fully the partners of white racists. The Smaleses are, to be sure, limited, and those limitations are explored at length; nevertheless, the novel does not in any straightforward way condemn the Smaleses. What it does, and does unrelentingly, is expose the intractable contradictions inherent in the lives of such people. In this respect, the novel does not seek to incriminate the Smaleses, but to lay bare the conditions of their social existence.

Clingman and Lenta are unable to provide convincing grounds for their views of the ending. Clingman assures us that its significance is obvious, but cannot say with sufficient clarity just what it is. Lenta says that Maureen's running 'suggests strongly' to her that the ending is to be construed negatively, but it is not immediately clear why the uncertainty about the helicopter's occupants or the fact of contending military forces should suggest *anything* in particular. Their claims to the contrary, within the framework of interpretation they share, the conclusion to the novel is undecidable.

That framework centres the significance of the ending on the particular action of an individual character—Maureen's running. The meaning of the ending, then, hinges on its significance within the fate of the individual. Given Gordimer's break with liberalism and commitment to an avowedly radical

position, which must at the very least imply a shift from the privileging of the individual over the collectivity to a position directly contrary to that, it becomes open to question whether any interpretation which does not shift its gaze beyond Maureen can hope to account for the ending.

One feature of the ending, unremarked by either critic, may provide a clue to what Gordimer is about. The helicopter's approach is represented in a language of aggressive sexuality. We read of the village 'cringing beneath the hoverer'; Maureen is 'invaded by a force pumping, jigging in its monstrous orgasm'; the helicopter descends with 'its landing gear like spread legs', making a 'rutting racket'. The helicopter is the figure of a rapist; Maureen moves spontaneously towards it. That might appear to lend itself to a negative interpretation of the ending, but something quite different is in fact implied, or so I believe.

What I want to suggest about the ending will doubtless seem, at least initially, unlikely to the point of being bizarre. All I can ask is that readers bear with me for a moment. My suggestion is that behind the ending of *July's People* is another text —Yeats's 'Leda and the Swan'. Copyright statutes preclude quoting the poem in full, which is unfortunate since a direct comparison would make it easier to argue my case.

What initially prompted my impression that Gordimer is invoking Yeats's poem is a series of parallel expressions embedded in the sexually charged language. Some of the parallels are fairly strongly marked; others are subtle echoes. There are at least four of the more direct parallels: Gordimer has 'A racket of blows', Yeats opens the poem with 'A sudden blow'; Gordimer has the 'shuddering of air', Yeats 'A shudder in the loins'; Gordimer has 'terrifying thing', Yeats 'terrified vague fingers'. The most persuasive parallel is Gordimer's 'the beating wings of its noise' and Yeats's 'the great wings beating still'. Since helicopters do not have wings, it would appear that the reference is retained to preserve the connection between the two texts, and to reproduce the excited atmosphere of the moment.

If the more obvious echoes and parallels led me to wonder about the possible connection between the two works, other features reinforced the case. The ending of *July's People* has some curious stylistic features. There is, for instance, an unusual use of the passive: 'A high ringing is produced in her ears, her body … is thudded with deafening vibration, invaded by a force'; and 'She is righted'. Related to this are such expressions as 'she must have screwed up her eyes: she could not have said what colour it was'. And finally, there is the shift in the final chapter to the present tense. Such stylistic devices may be seen as transformations of some of the linguistic forms and effects of 'Leda and the Swan', notably the mixing of present and past tenses, and the questions of the second quatrain and the conclusion of the poem.

What is involved in these stylistic devices is the relation established between Maureen and the helicopter on the one hand and Leda and Zeus in the form of a swan on the other. In both works, the violently possessed woman is overwhelmed by the violator. Not just physically—the very will to resist is obliterated. The stylistic features in both texts also operate to blur perspective so that descriptions made ostensibly in the voice of the speaker or narrator are given from the standpoint of, or filtered through the numbed, barely registering consciousness of, the woman. The 'racket of blows' is not just stated; it is experienced by Maureen: it 'comes down at her head', *just as the* 'sudden blow' and 'the great wings beating' are registered, if only dimly, by the consciousness of Leda. The passives in *July's People* reproduce stylistically the submission of Maureen to the 'force' of the helicopter, just as Leda is 'mastered by the brute blood of the air'.

It is never easy to demonstrate that one text functions as a source for another. The moment one attempts to set out the traces of the one work in the other, the relations between the two, for all that they seemed so obvious, suddenly seem quite tenuous. Nevertheless, I think a careful reading of the two works will persuade readers that 'Leda and the Swan' underlies Gordimer's conclusion. What is more, I think the relation between the two is crucial for our understanding of the ending of *July's People*.

The standard interpretation of Yeats's poem situates it within his reworking of Viconian notions of historical cycles. Following her rape by Zeus, Leda gives birth to Helen of Troy, whose abduction by Paris gives rise to the Trojan War. The editors of *The Norton Anthology of Poetry* provide a gloss that sets out the conventional understanding of the poem: 'Yeats saw Leda as the recipient of an annunciation that would found Greek civilization, as the Annunciation to Mary would found Christianity' [Allison, *et al.,* 1983.]

Such an 'annunciation' is what I believe is suggested in Maureen's final action. It is not a ques-

tion of deciding whether she is running 'towards' or running 'away from'. In any event, there is no clear support in the text for either view. She is *drawn* to the helicopter, by a power she does not understand, does not even reflect on. On her way, she crosses the river, undergoing what is explicitly figured as a 'baptismal' experience—a ritual cleansing—in which she is 'born again', and passes over the 'landmark of the bank she has never crossed to before'.

The imminent convergence of Maureen and the helicopter, like the convergence of Leda and the god-swan, heralds a new civilization, a new epoch for South Africa that cannot, particularly from within a moment of interregnum, be described but can only be symbolically prefigured in a prophetic gesture of revolutionary optimism. If in the interregnum, as Gramsci puts it, 'the new cannot be born', the convergence, taking the metaphor a vital step further, is a moment of insemination, from which new possibilities will emerge. The significance of Gordimer's conclusion lies not, then, in the particular fate of Maureen: it does not really matter whether we see her opened up to negative judgement or going to seek her revolutionary destiny (though the latter, in its very vagueness, comes closer to capturing what is going on at the end of the novel). Maureen has been overtaken by something far larger than herself, than her self. The ending is neither positive (in any narrow sense focussed on the vicissitudes of Maureen) nor negative; it is not even undecidable or inconclusive. At this moment of closure, *July's People* moves from a mode of future projection concerned, as Clingman notes, with 'seeing the present through the eyes of the future' to a mode of revolutionary, Utopian vision—a future projection intimating a realm of possibilities beyond interregnum.

Source: Nicholas Visser, *"Beyond the Interregnum: A Note of the Ending of* July's People" in *Rendering Things Visible: Essays on South African Literary Culture,* edited by Martin Trump, Ohio University Press, 1990, pp. 61–67.

Nancy Bailey

In this article, Bailey argues that the subject of July's People is actually "Maureen Smales' discovery that she has no substance and no self."

July's People moves to a world of the future where the fears of the whites in all Gordimer's books have become reality—the revolution has occurred, the whites are dispossessed and have no means of escape from the riots and the burning of their cities. They have no place to go—except back in time to the timelessness of the kraal, to the black primitive community of their servant July's village people. The novel's title reflects the two previously unconnected worlds which are brought together when July brings his city people, the white Smales family of Maureen and Bam and their three children, to his bush people, Martha his wife, his elderly mother and his extended family. Neither side is prepared for the other and both are dismayed by the reality that replaces their dream fantasies. Only the Smales children cross the cultural chasm, in a few weeks going back thousands of years in societal development. But since their hope lies in being absorbed by the black community, not in changing it, this hope does not alleviate the despair of the novel's epigraph: "The old is dying and the new cannot be born." …

The true subject of the novel is not the nightmare of South Africa as representative of "injustice and retribution, of betrayal and dispossession," central though this concern is. [In "The Testing Out of Tomorrow," *TLS,* 1981.] Instead, I will argue, the nightmare the novel records with tender but unflinching honesty is that of Maureen Smales' discovery that she has no substance and no self. The novel dramatizes the horrifying thesis (concerning even those of us lucky enough not to know of South Africa except through novels such as Gordimer's) that without selfhood there can be no adaptation and no miracle of new birth from suffering.

The novel's form is dictated by this inner journey. In both the beginning and the ending of the novel Gordimer raises the subject of delirium. Initially, delirium serves as Maureen's metaphor for the three-day-and-night journey hidden in the back of the truck that delivered her from the city to the bush. The novel proceeds to reflect, as in delirium or dream, memories that are both sharp in detail and yet discontinuous in time and in consciousness. Combined with an elliptical style the narrative form creates problems for the reader. But late in the novel Maureen associates the insubstantiality of time with her own disintegration.

> She was not in possession of any part of her life. One or another could only be turned up, by hazard. The background had fallen away; since that first morning she had become conscious in the hut, she had regained no established point of a continuing present from which to recognize her own sequence.

In the novel's opening, awakening in the hut that is "the prototype from which all the others had come and to which all returned," in a space "confining in its immensity," Maureen faces a return in time and in space which has the archetypal pos-

sibility of birth or death, of womb or tomb. Her consciousness opens and closes the novel and at the end "she runs" towards the helicopter of unknown origin that has landed in the forest. On the surface it appears that the reader's apprehension of death and destruction has been averted, and that a miracle has taken place. But one of the indications that the ending is not hopeful is that the vitality of language that Gordimer uses as one symbol of new life struggling to be born is replaced by the sounds of the machine. The repeated refrain "lucky to be alive" becomes increasingly ironic and tragic as Maureen experiences the truth of her belated awareness that as "one ought to have known from the sufferings of saints … miracles are horrors."

What is it that frustrates the miracles of rebirth? What is the nature of the self that the novel seeks and finds wanting? Maureen is not the only failure. Like her, July stripped of his persona is unable to discover substance, while her husband Bam rather surprisingly reveals a self that survives the loss of everything on which his "civilized" identity has been predicated. The contrast with the two males illustrates Maureen's plight. Let us turn first to July.

Maureen feels she understands July and has always been able to communicate with him better than her husband has, acting often as a translator between the white master and the black servant. Even when July becomes the master, Maureen continues to confront him and draw responses from him in a way Bam cannot. Their understanding even when expressed as mutual hostility arises, Gordimer shows, from the way the black servant and the white mistress share a common entrapment in a system from which they have gained nothing but material security. Maureen's name on July's paycheques represents the abstraction of money that his village wife translates into the concrete of goods. But Maureen comes to realize that she herself means nothing to July in any real sense.…

Because his self is a reflection of his worth in the eyes of his women, July's return to the village with his white people marks the crisis in his own self-regard. Perhaps intuitively he clung to the Smales and offered them asylum because they provided him with a sense of selfhood, but when they appear in his world as his possessions his own people fail to respond to his master/servant role. Instead of gaining prestige through his possession of this family he arouses the hostility of the matriarchy and becomes a victim of its power.…

July is further weakened by the loss of the young man, Daniel, before whom July could maintain his persona of power which the women had stripped from him. But Daniel steals the Smales's gun and returns to the city world of riot and violence, which July's own kindness prevents him from entering. The novel's first words commenting on July's action, however, connect this attribute to conditioning rather than to positive substance or virtue. "July bent at the doorway and began that day for them as his kind has always done for their kind...."

Of the three central figures, July's dispossession is the greatest, as is his innocence. His language fights against both grammatical structure and the absence of words in either English or his own dialect to describe his being and his situation as a victim of capitalism more than apartheid....

It was their possessions and their investments that kept the Smales in South Africa too long and prevented their emigration to Canada. But the loss of the possessions "back there" in the city has, Gordimer suggests, freed Bam to be fatherly and he assumes the role previously appropriated by July with the Smales children. Though Bam plays his new role with distinction, Gordimer does not romanticize the relationship, or suggest that it is a substitute for self-identity. As he leaves his son Victor behind when he goes to shoot the pigs, Bam has "a foretaste of the cold resentment that he would feel towards his son, sometime when he was a man; a presentiment of the expulsion from paradise, not of childhood but of parenthood."

The theft of the gun is a devastating blow to Bam's power and pride both in societal and psychological terms, yet it is he who recovers himself the same night to feed the children while Maureen retreats to the hut, drinking the whole of the water bottle "like an alcoholic who hides away to indulge secret addiction." Bam's adaptation is a remarkable and hopeful indication of a species characteristic essential for survival but it is not as remarkable as his response to the loss of his wife. The relations between husband and wife, Gordimer suggests, are the ones in which the most profound and far-reaching effects for the self are to be found. The sexual desire fostered and apparently dependent on the materialism of the "master bedroom" life disappears in the enforced intimacy of the squalid hut, brought to life once only by the aphrodisiac of the meal of meat. Though Bam recognizes that Maureen's gesture of baring her breasts before him "was not an intimacy but a castration of his sexuality and hers," he remains tender and protective towards her. It is Maureen's withdrawal from him that renders Bam silent, an impotence more serious than the loss of sexual desire.

The summons of the family to the chief's village makes it clear how little connection remains between the couple. The title of the only book they bring to the bush, *The Betrothed,* becomes an ironically apt reminder that the union of Bam Smales and Maureen Hetherington was a product of a world that no longer has any reality. Maureen cannot comprehend the fiction because her own life has become fictive:

> She *was* in another time, place and consciousness; it pressed in upon her and filled her as someone's breath fills a balloon's shape. She was already not what she was. No fiction could compete with what she was finding she did not know, could not have imagined or discovered through imagination. They had nothing.

The ambiguous "they" refers as much to the Smales as to the villagers.

It is Bam, however, who relates the deprivation to the loss of communication with his wife. As they prepare to face the village chief who Bam fears will expel them, he longs to share his concern with Maureen. But he recognizes that

> he did not know to whom to speak these days, when he spoke to her. Maureen. His wife. The daughter of the nice old fellow who had worked underground all his life ... The girl in leotards teaching modern dance to blacks at nightschool.... The consort clients meant when they said: And we'd so much like you and your wife to come to dinner.... The woman to whom he was "my husband"....
>
> Her. Not "Maureen." Not "his wife." The presence in the mud hut, mute with an activity of being, of sense of self he could not follow because here there were no familiar areas in which it could be visualized moving, no familiar entities that could be shaping it. With "her" there was no undersurface of recognition; only moments of finding each other out ... He had no idea how she would deal with his certainty. There was no precedent to go on, with her. And he himself. How to deal with it. How to accept, explain—to anyone: after all these days when his purpose (his male dignity put to the test by "Maureen," "his wife," Victor, Gina, Royce, who were living on mealie-meal) had been how to get away—now it was how to stay....

Although Bam survives the loss of language that accompanies loss of identity, the novel offers no assurance of his rebirth, or of the reintegration of self and community that the researches of Carl Jung suggest is essential for true individuation. [*The Collected Works,* 1970] Nevertheless Bam, alone of the three protagonists, remains in what

> *The novel dramatizes the horrifying thesis (concerning even those of us lucky enough not to know of South Africa except through novels such as Gordimer's) that without selfhood there can be no adaptation and no miracle of new birth from suffering."*

Jung suggests is the feminine mode (necessary for both males and females) of relatedness, as well as the masculine one (equally necessary for both sexes) of action and thought. [*The Collected Works,* 1970] As the novel ends, Bam's identity is focused at the most primitive level—of connection to his offspring, an ironic reversal of the roles enacted in the middle class suburb "back there" by the mother/wife, but parallel to the way July's Martha retains identity despite both the absence of her husband and his theoretical dominance. In contrast, at the end of the novel, Maureen

> runs: trusting herself with all the suppressed trust of a lifetime, alert like a solitary animal at the season when animals neither seek a mate nor take care of young, existing only for their lone survival, the enemy of all that would make claims of responsibility.

The last words of the novel are those of the simple sentence, "She runs." But is the helicopter towards which she is running the symbol of the survival she seeks and an implied authorial validation of the state of individualism without reponsibility, or conversely the final symbol of a delusion, a symbol of death rather than life? From the social/political aspect of the novel the latter seems more likely, since it is more probable that the helicopter is manned by black revolutionaries alerted to the existence of the white family by Daniel than that it represents an American *deus ex machina.* Even if it were the hoped for means of return to civilization, nothing in the novel suggests that Maureen is able to run to something new, a truly recreative or restorative world that would replace the one in which all her life she has lived without ac-

knowledging it as an exploiter of and parasite on the black. Though she may now be able to acknowledge the truth of the *Life* photograph of herself as a schoolgirl accompanied by her black friend Lydia who is bearing Maureen's case on her head, her sojourn in the bush has not shown her how to alter her condition. The "real fantasies of the bush" that she dreams of as she runs "delude more inventively than the romantic forests of Grimm and Disney," but what they invent are what she associates with the security of her lost part—"the smell of boiled potatoes … promises a kitchen, a house," and "the patches where airy knob-thorn trees stand free of the undergrowth and the grass and orderly clumps of Barberton daisies and drifts of nemesia belong to the artful nature of a public park."

What Maureen runs to is a return to the illusion of identity created by a world of privilege and possession. What she runs from is her failure to find any creative source for re-birth. Interestingly Jung suggests that in the second stage of life it is the mother who represents the symbol of the "unconscious as the creative matrix of the future." Maureen is fleeing from motherhood, and her own mother is significant by her absence in her daughter's memories—displaced entirely by the father, the miner "Boss." But unlike her father, who went below ground and lost a finger in the danger of his work with black helpers, Maureen has lost touch with the reality of the lives of those she depends upon. She enters July's rooms in the Smales's suburban yard only to minister to him when he is ill, and in the bush instead of going to July's hut she demands that July come to her.…

Maureen is forced to accept her failure in the area she had most prided herself on being superior, the area of communication based on sensation, feeling and intuition, traditionally associated with the feminine. Her access to the matriarchal realm where this often unspoken language is inextricably connected to a power of thought and action that dominates the male even while appearing subversive to him is blocked.

The only unqualified triumph of the novel belongs to the matriarchs, Martha and the mother. No matter who mans the helicopter, they will be freed of the unwanted white people, and they have sacrificed nothing of their own sense of self in the interval. Nevertheless, again (as with Bam's paternal role) Gordimer refuses to romanticize Martha and the mother, who represent the matriarchal way. It is the "old way" and for all its strength and dignity in its own time and place, there can be no turning back to it for someone who has known a different conception of human experience. Maureen can no more go back in time than can Martha go forward. As Martha tells July when he suggests that he will take her to the city with him, "Can you see me in their yard! How would I know my road, who would tell me where to go?"

But for Maureen, without access to the old way and without ability to create a new one the final image is that of "death's harpy … a grotesque against the vehicle's hood." Maureen's is the greatest tragedy of the novel for she has the closest instinctual link to the two creative forces the novel posits for which language is the symbol—the Eros of feminine relatedness and the Logos of masculine thought and action. The androgynous balance the novel supports though the demonstration of its absence in time present cannot be taken as a symbol for solution on the social/political level, but perhaps in its realization by individuals of both races lies the only hope for the future, for South Africa as a nation, and for each of us as individuals.

Source: Nancy Bailey, "Living Without the Future: Nadine Gordimer's *July's People*" in *World Literature Written in English,* autumn, 1984, Vol. 24, No. 2, pp. 215–224.

Sources

Judith Chettle, in a review in *National Review,* Vol. XXXIII, No. 25, December, 1981, p. 1561.

Stephen Clingman, "The Subject of Revolution: Burger's Daughter and July's People," in *The Novels of Nadine Gordimer: History from the Inside,* Allen & Unwin, 1986, pp. 170-204.

Joan Silber, in a review in *New York Review of Books,* August, 1981, p. 14.

Rowland Smith, "Masters and Servants Nadine Gordimer's *July's People* and the Themes of Her Fiction," in *Critical Essays on Nadine Gordimer,* edited by Rowland Smith, G. K. Hall & Co., pp. 140-52.

Anne Tyler, "South Africa After the Revolution," in *New York Review of Books,* June, 1981, p. 26.

Kathrin Wagner, *Rereading Nadine Gordimer,* Indiana University Press, 1994, pp. 41, 5.

For Further Study

Michael Atwell, *South Africa: Background to the Crisis,* Sidgwick & Jackson, 1986.

With a splendid glossary, maps, and some photos, Atwell gives a general history of South Africa beginning with its exploration by whites from 1652.

Rosemarie Bodenheimer, "The Interregnum of Ownership in *July's People,*" in *The Later Fiction of Nadine Gordimer,* edited by Bruce King, St. Martin's, 1993, pp. 108-20.

Analyzes Gordimer's portrayal of the meaning and power of ownership, which for the characters defines political consciousness and identity.

Stephen Clingman, *The Novels of Nadine Gordimer: History from the Inside,* University of Massachusetts Press, 1986.

In his thorough study of Gordimer's novels, Clingman addresses the political, economic, linguistic, and sexual revolutions in *July's People* and connects the work to the historical moment in which it was composed.

Joseph Conrad, *The Heard of Darkness,* Beckwood's, 1899.

Conrad's novella is the parable of colonial empire. It is just one of the many colonial myths referenced in Gordimer's work.

John Cooke, "'Nobody's Children': Families in Gordimer's Later Novels," in *The Later Fiction of Nadine Gordimer,* edited by Bruce King, St. Martin's, 1993, pp. 21-32.

Concentrating on three Gordimer novels, Cooke discusses children's breaks from parental authority and the political significance of these breaks.

Daniel Defoe, *The Life and Adventures of Robinson Crusoe,* edited by Angus Ross, Penguin USA, 1995.

The famous tale of a shipwrecked man who survives for decades on an island. He constructs a settlement with his man Friday and dies very rich. The story came to epitomize the saga of the settler attempting to recreate England everywhere in the world.

Stefanie Dojka, "*July's People:* She Knew No Word," in *Joinings and Disjoinings: The Significance of Marital Status in Literature,* edited by JoAnna Stephens Mink and Janet Doubler Ward, Popular, 1991, pp. 155-71.

Traces the South African revolution's effects on the Smales' marriage and on Maureen Smales' changing character.

Lars Engle, "The Political Uncanny: The Novels of Nadine Gordimer," in *The Yale Journal of Criticism,* Vol. 2, No. 2, 1989, pp. 101-27.

Engle contrasts Gordimer's vision for South African art with that of Hendrik F. Verwoerd, former Prime Minister of South Africa, and he employs Freud's concept of the "uncanny" to analyze the political elements of Gordimer's fiction.

Nadine Gordimer, *The Essential Gesture: Writing, Politics and Places,* edited by Stephen Clingman, Alfred A. Knopf, 1988.

Collection of Gordimer's essays about her life, theory of writing, and political events relevant to her work.

Jennifer Gordon, "Dreams of a Common Language: Nadine Gordimer's *July's People,*" in *African Literature Today,* Vol. 15, 1987, pp. 102-08.

Gordon analyzes Gordimer's treatment of the power and limitations of language. She contends that Gordimer implies that a "common language" will be necessary to foster understanding between white and black South Africans.

Robert Green, "From *The Lying Days* to *July's People:* The Novels of Nadine Gordimer," in *Journal of Modern Literature,* Vol. 14, No. 4, spring, 1988, pp. 543-63.
Green discusses Gordimer's artistic project, which records the changing consciousness of her time and intentionally challenges both her readers and herself.

Susan M. Greenstein, "Miranda's Story: Nadine Gordimer and the Literature of Empire," in *Novel: A Forum on Fiction,* Vol. 18, No. 3, spring, 1985, pp. 227-42.
Using the figures of Miranda and Caliban from Shakespeare's *The Tempest,* Greenstein examines two Gordimer novels and their breaks from traditional adventure literature about Africa.

Dominic Head, *Nadine Gordimer,* Cambridge University Press, 1994.
Traces major themes and issues throughout Gordimer's body of work and discusses the issues of identity in *July's People.*

Tom Lodge and Bill Nasson, *All, Here, and Now: Black Politics in South Africa in the 1980s,* Ford Foundation-Foreign Policy Association, 1991.
Explains the complex development of politics in the last decade of apartheid. Some background is given but its focus is on the events leading up to a negotiated end of white rule in South Africa.

Alan Paton, *Cry, The Beloved Country,* Twayne Publishing, 1991.
Set after World War II, the novel tells of the journey of man to the big city to find his son. The novel brought international attention to apartheid.

Sheila Roberts, "Sites of Paranoia and Taboo: Lessing's *The Grass Is Singing* and Gordimer's *July's People,*" in *Research in African Literatures,* Vol. 23, No. 3, fall, 1993, pp. 73-85.
Exploring the gothic devices in Lessing's and Gordimer's novels, Roberts views the dwellings the female protagonists inhabit as extensions of these women and, thus, "configurations of the uncanny."

Rowland Smith, "Masters and Servants: Nadine Gordimer's *July's People* and the Themes of Her Fiction," in *Critical Essays on Nadine Gordimer,* edited by Rowland Smith, Hall, 1990, pp. 140-52.
Connects *July's People* to Gordimer's earlier work, focusing on both the Smales' inability to escape their status as whites in July's village and the failures of communication between Maureen Smales and July.

Barbara Temple-Thurston, "Madam and Boy: A Relationship of Shame in Gordimer's *July's People,*" in *World Literature Written in English,* Vol. 28, No. 1, spring, 1988, pp. 51-8.
Examines the breakdown of culturally determined roles in the novel, particularly the gendered relationship of "Madam" and "boy" between Maureen and July.

Andre Viola, "Communication and Liberal Double Bind in *July's People* by Nadine Gordimer," in *Commonwealth Essays and Studies,* Vol. 9, No. 2, spring, 1987, pp. 52-8.
Referring to Paul Watzlawick's *Pragmatics of Human Communication,* Viola discusses the communication strategies that Gordimer depicts in the novel.

Nicholas Visser, "Beyond the Interregnum: A Note on the Ending of *July's People,*" in *Rendering Things Visible: Essays on South African Literary Culture,* edited by Martin Trump, Ohio University Press, 1990, pp. 61-7.
Visser explores connections between the novel's ending and W. B. Yeats's "Leda and the Swan."

Kathrin Wagner, *Rereading Nadine Gordimer,* Indiana University Press, 1994.
Examines Gordimer's political views, stereotypes, depictions of women and black South Africans, and use of landscape iconography in her novels.

The Natural

Bernard Malamud
1952

In his *Dictionary of Literary Biography* article on Bernard Malamud, Joel Salzberg notes that the author "holds a preeminence among Jewish-American writers that has consistently been reaffirmed by recent critical assessments." Malamud, however, began his career with his popular first novel, *The Natural,* influenced by his love of baseball and his fascination with stories of the mythological quest for the Holy Grail. The novel's allegorical framework blends realism and fantasy in its exploration of the theme of moral responsibility. Malamud employs forces of good and evil to complicate the choices and consequences that face his protagonist.

The novel introduces Roy Hobbs, an initially innocent young man, who strives to be "the best there ever was in the game" of baseball. As he attempts to reach that goal, his moral courage will be tested. Ultimately, this flawed hero will learn too late of the consequences of blind ambition. The novel received mixed reviews when it first appeared, due to its complex narrative structure. However, critical response grew to the point where many now consider it among Malamud's best works.

Author Biography

Malamud set *The Natural* in New York City, where he was born in 1914 and raised by his Russian Jewish immigrant parents. Growing up near

Bernard Malamud

Ebbets Field in Brooklyn, Malamud became an avid fan of the Brooklyn Dodgers and of baseball as an American pastime. In 1936 he earned a B.A. from the City College of New York, where he became interested in the Grail legend, and in 1942 a M.A. in literature from Columbia University. Other than serving as a clerk at the Census Bureau in Washington, D.C. in 1940, he devoted his life to teaching and writing. He began his teaching career in New York City high schools and from 1949 to 1961 taught literature at Oregon State University. In 1962 he accepted a position at Bennington College in Vermont where he continued to teach until his death in 1986.

Malamud published stories for his high school literary magazine, but his literary career did not begin until years later. Greatly affected by World War II and the horrors of the Holocaust, Malamud engaged in an exploration of his Jewish heritage. His first novel, *The Natural*, written while he was at Oregon State, would be one of the few works that would not center on a Jewish protagonist. The novel does, however, explore the themes of suffering and redemption that Malamud would return to in his later writings. While at Oregon State, he produced his most notable works including *The Assistant, The Magic Barrel* (1958), and *A New Life* (1961). His work gained him several awards, in-

cluding the National Book Award in fiction in 1959 for *The Magic Barrel* and in 1967 for *The Fixer,* and the Pulitzer Prize in fiction in 1967 for *The Fixer.*

Plot Summary

Part I: "Pre-game"

Bernard Malamud's novel, *The Natural* follows the career of baseball player Roy Hobbs from his first false start to his final failure. The story is divided into two parts, the first recounting an event during Roy's nineteenth year, and the second picking up the story some fifteen years later. Although the first part is considerably shorter than the second, it is nonetheless just as important to the novel as a whole.

The Natural opens on a train hurtling eastward toward Chicago. We learn that Roy is travelling with his manager Sam for a try out with the Chicago Cubs. Other passengers on the train include Harriet Bird, a beautiful woman who catches Roy's eye; Max Mercy, a curious sports writer; and Walt "The Whammer" Whambold, the leading hitter in the American League.

When the train makes an unexpected stop, the passengers leave the train and move toward a carnival at the edge of a town. Roy comes to the attention of the Whammer when he consistently wins at a baseball contest. Angered at remarks that the Whammer makes toward Roy, Sam bets the Whammer that Roy can strike him out.

In the contest that follows, Roy does strike out the Whammer; however, his last pitch hits Sam in the chest so hard that the old man dies later that night on the train. The contest also focuses Harriet Bird's attention on Roy.

Sam's death leaves Roy alone in Chicago. To his surprise, he receives a telephone call from Harriet Bird, inviting him to her hotel room. Roy is overjoyed, thinking that Harriet must intend a sexual tryst. Instead, when Roy arrives at her room, she shoots him in the gut with a silver bullet.

Part II: "Batter Up"

The second section jumps ahead fifteen years. Roy is now thirty-four, and has been signed to play with the Knights, a losing major league team managed by Pop Fisher. Now a batter rather than a pitcher, Roy still carries his handmade bat, Wonderboy, with him. Roy arrives as a man without a past; neither the reader nor the other characters know where he has been or what he has done for the past fifteen years. Consequently, Roy's arrival piques the interest of Max Mercy, who does not remember their earlier encounter on the train. Max is determined to uncover the truth behind the mystery of Roy Hobbes.

The team's best player, Bump Baily, subjects Roy to innumerable practical jokes. However, the rivalry between Roy and Bump seems to motivate the other players. Meanwhile, Roy falls in love with Pop's niece, Memo Paris, who is also Bump Baily's girlfriend.

The rivalry between Roy and Bump escalates until Bump accidentally kills himself by smashing into the outfield wall in pursuit of a fly ball. Roy then becomes the Knight's top player. He continues to pursue Memo, who rejects him.

Roy longs for Memo and begins an extended hitting streak in an attempt to win her. Finally, he decides that he needs more money in order to court her properly. Therefore, he approaches Judge Goodwill Banner, the team owner, for a raise. Rather than convincing the Judge to give him a raise, Roy finds himself responsible for the uniforms that Bump Baily destroyed.

After his unsuccessful visit with the Judge, Roy is accosted by Max Mercy. Roy accompanies Max to a nightclub where he meets bookie Gus Sands who is there with Memo. After betting unsuccessfully with Gus, Roy performs a series of astounding magic tricks. For the first time since Bump's death, Memo laughs.

Later, Memo and Roy go for a drive. When Roy kisses Memo and touches her breast, she rejects him. Pop Fisher warns Roy that Memo is no good for him. Roy enters a hitting slump. Memo continues to refuse to see Roy. Finally, during a game, a woman in a red dress stands up in the crowd. When Roy sees her, he smells a wonderful fragrance and knocks a pitch out of the ball park.

The woman is Iris Lemon and she and Roy meet after the game. They walk along the lakeshore, and eventually make love. But when Iris tells Roy that she is a grandmother, Roy rejects her, and returns to his longing for Memo.

Unbeknownst to Roy, Memo and Gus Sands plot to destroy Roy. Memo agrees to date Roy, but refuses his requests for sex. Somehow Roy's sexual hunger is transformed into physical hunger. Memo urges Roy to eat and he gorges himself. When he returns to Memo's room and drops his pants in preparation for sex, he has a sharp pain in his stomach and he passes out. Roy's gluttony nearly costs him his life.

Now in the hospital, Roy is approached first by Memo and then by the Judge who want him to throw the pennant game. At first Roy refuses. When the Judge suggests that Roy will lose Memo to someone richer, Roy agrees to throw the game for money. Memo is thrilled. When he is once again alone in his room, Roy reads a letter from Iris, in which she explains her life. However, when she once again talks about herself as a grandmother, Roy crumples up the letter and throws it away.

At the pennant game, Roy begins to keep his bargain and strikes out. Otto Zipp, a dwarf, taunts Roy, and Roy starts aiming foul hits at him. Just as he hits another foul ball, Iris Lemon stands in the crowd. The ball hits her square in the face and she collapses. Roy rushes to her side, and she begs him to win the game for her and for their son. In this way, Roy learns that Iris is pregnant with their child. Roy resolves to win the game and has renewed hope for his future. However, on his next hit, he not only fouls the ball, he also breaks his bat, Wonderboy. In spite of his renewed effort, Roy again strikes out, using another bat, and thus the Knights lose the game.

Later that night, Roy goes to the Judge's office where he finds the Judge, Memo, and Gus. Roy throws the money at the Judge and knocks out Gus. Memo goes after him with a gun, in a scene reminiscent of the earlier Harriet Bird incident. Memo screams at him, "You filthy scum, I hate your guts and always have since the day you murdered Bump." Roy takes away the gun and leaves the office, filled with self-loathing:

> Going down the tower stairs he fought his over-whelming self-hatred. In each stinking wave of it he remembered some disgusting happening of his life. He thought, I never did learn anything out of my past life, now I have to suffer again.

When Roy hits the street, he finds that Max Mercy has published an article uncovering both his past and his sellout of the Knights. In the closing lines of the novel, Roy weeps for his own failures.

Characters

Bump Baily

Like the Whammer, an arrogant, loudmouthed ball player and the leading hitter in the league. As he did with the Whammer, Roy challenges Bump's

Media Adaptations

- *The Natural* was adapted as a film by Barry Levinson, starring Robert Redford as Roy Hobbs, Robert Duvall as Max Mercy, Glenn Close as Iris Gaines, and Kim Basinger as Memo Paris, Tri-Star Pictures, 1984.

top standing in the team. Trying to maintain his reputation, Bump lunges for a ball, bangs into the outfield wall, and dies.

Goodwill Banner

Judge Banner, a "slick trader" and controlling owner of the Knights, offers Roy money to fix a game and thus lose the pennant for the team. The Judge took advantage of Pop's financial troubles and gained from him an extra 10% interest in the Knights. Since then he has tried to push Pop off the team. His forced trades have made him money but have hurt the Knights. When Roy appears in the Judge's office after he strikes out during the last pennant game, he throws the bribe money in the Judge's face. Humiliated and afraid for his safety, the Judge pulls a gun on Roy. After disarming him, Roy beats the Judge with his fists.

Harriet Bird

Harriet Bird is a mysterious, beautiful woman who appears on the train Roy takes to Chicago. Her "nyloned legs [make] Roy's pulses dance." Harriet, however, initially shows more interest in the Whammer, until Roy defeats him during a test of their athletic skills. When Roy tells her his ambition is to be the best in the game, Harriet replies, "Is that all? Isn't there something over and above earthly things—some more glorious meaning to one's life and activities?" When they arrive in Chicago, they meet in a hotel room where Harriet takes out a pistol and shoots Roy in the stomach. She then dances around his prone body, making "muted noises of triumph and despair." The narrator suggests she may be the same mysterious woman who has shot other athletes with silver bullets from a .22 caliber pistol.

Red Blow

Red is Pop's assistant and protector. Red admits, "I would give my right arm if I could get Pop the pennant."

Pop Fisher

Passionate about baseball, sixty-five year old Pop Fisher manages and is part owner of the Knights, a New York City baseball team. Depressed about the Knights' lackluster performance before Roy joins the team, he insists he "shoulda bought a farm." He pines for the old days of baseball and for players who put their heart into the game. Marked as a failure after a missed chance at a run during the World Series, he withstood his shame and played ten more years, compiling a fine record. Now, however, he considers himself jinxed, and looks to Roy to help him break it. Pop becomes a father figure to Roy and tries to keep him out of trouble, especially with his niece Memo Paris. He also serves as a role model to him. Pop admits he "would give his whole life to win the pennant," but is not ambitious or proud enough to expect to "be the best" and win the series.

Roy Hobbs

Roy Hobbs, the novel's protagonist, faces a test of his moral character. The novel opens with Roy as an innocent young man, whose ambition is to be "the best there ever was in the game." This ambition sometimes creates a callous determination in Roy, as when, during his contest with the Whammer, he "smelled the Whammer's blood and wanted it." His dream is shattered for a time, however, by Harriet Bird who shoots him in a hotel room in Chicago, before he gets a chance to play ball for the Chicago White Sox. He gets a second chance years later, when at the age of thirty-three, he signs with the New York Knights and helps propel them to the top of the league. Roy replaces Bump Baily as one of the leading hitters in the game, but is still "gnawed by a nagging impatience for more."

Red Blow, Pop Fisher's assistant, claims Roy is a "natural" at the game, but not perfect because "he sometimes hit at bad ones." Predicting Roy's eventual fall, Pop adds that he "mistrust[s] a bad hitter. They sometimes make harmful mistakes." Joel Salzberg in his *Dictionary of Literary Biography* article on Malamud, argues that Roy's failure "to transcend his own desires for merely personal gratification" causes him to agree to a bribe and fix the battle for the pennant. Salzberg continues that "despite Hobb's eventual change of heart,

Still from the movie The Natural, *starring Robert Redford.*

his inherent moral weakness and immaturity diminish his effectiveness as a baseball hero and culminate in the fracturing of Wonderboy, as Malamud's flawed hero literally and metaphorically strikes out."

The Judge

    See Goodwill Banner

Doc Knobb

    Doc is the team doctor. He tries to help the players relax during their slump through mesmerism and autosuggestion. Roy refuses to participate in the sessions. When Doc tries to hypnotize Pop, he fires him.

Iris Lemon

    Iris Lemon becomes a symbol of selfless love in the novel. Her belief in Roy's heroism helps him "regain his power" during his slump. She gives her heart to him, admitting, "I don't think you can do anything for anyone without giving up something of your own." She also tries to guide and advise Roy, explaining that he will learn from his suffering: "it brings us toward happiness. It teaches us to want the right things." Roy rejects her love and concern, however, in his pursuit of his dream to be the best and to gain Memo's love. The news that she is pregnant with his child helps Roy turn his back on Memo and the Judge's offer.

Max Mercy

    Max Mercy is a cocky sportswriter, with a "greedy, penetrating, ass kissing voice." To the tenacious reporter, "a private life is a personal insult." He trails Roy doggedly in order to dredge up personal information about him for his readers. Roy tries to avoid him, hoping he will not remember their initial meeting on the train to Chicago or discover details about his past. After Roy strikes out in his final pennant game, Max exposes him in his article, "Suspicion of Hobb's Sellout" and includes a photograph of Roy prone on the floor of the Chicago hotel room, taken after he had been shot by Harriet.

Memo Paris

    Memo, Pop's redheaded niece, is a "sad spurned lady, who sat without wifehood in the wive's box behind third base." When Bump dies, she goes "wild with grief" and tells Roy that she is "strictly a dead man's girl." Pop insists "she's unlucky and always has been" and is afraid her bad luck will rub off on Roy. He warns Roy that "she is always dissatisfied and will snarl you up in her trouble in a way that will weaken your strength."

Roy does not heed Pop's prediction and starts a relationship with her, which throws him into a slump. Memo's greed and her vindictiveness prompt her to help ensnare Roy in the plot to fix the pennant game. When he confronts her and the Judge after losing, she, like Harriet Bird, shoots him.

Gus Sands

Gus Sands is a "shifty-eyed" gambler with a "magic" glass eye that "sees everything." Gus helps set up the fix for Roy and has a shadowy relationship with Memo that is never fully explained.

Sam Simpson

Sam Simpson, an alcoholic scout for the Chicago Cubs, discovers the young Roy Hobbs and puts a great deal of faith in his abilities and future. Sam becomes a father figure to the innocent Roy, helping him plan out his every move in order to help insure his success. On the train to Chicago, his concern for Roy emerges. He escorts Roy to his first Major League chance, a position with the Chicago Cubs, but dies suddenly on the train after being injured by Roy's pitch to the Whammer.

Walter Wambold

At thirty-three, the Whammer is the leading hitter of the American League and three times winner of the Most Valuable Player award. Proud and arrogant, the Whammer meets Roy on the train to Chicago and challenges him to a test of their athletic skills during a stop at a carnival. This test gives readers their first glimpse of Roy's exceptional talent and reveals how fleeting fame can be. After Roy strikes him out, the Whammer becomes an "old man" before everyone's eyes and soon fades out of the game.

The Whammer

See Walter Wambold

Otto Zipp

A fanatically loyal Bump fan, who calls encouragement through a bullhorn. When Bump dies, he stops attending the games for a while, but then returns to harass Roy and forecast his doom.

Themes

Choices and Consequences

The novel's focus on morality incorporates the theme of choices and consequences and the related

Topics for Further Study

- Research the "Black Sox" scandal that involved eight Chicago White Sox players charged with bribery in the 1919 World Series. Compare the events surrounding the scandal with Roy's experiences in the novel.

- Research the mythological quest for the Holy Grail. What symbolic elements of this quest appear in the novel? What purpose do they serve?

- How is the American love of baseball illustrated in the novel?

- Focus on Malamud's development of Roy Hobbs as a character. Is he a static or a dynamic character? Does he gain any knowledge about himself and/or of his world by the end of the novel?

issue of responsibility. Malamud presents Roy with moral choices in the novel that require attention to his responsibilities as a father, a team member, and a human being. He must choose whether or not to form a lasting relationship with Iris and their child, and ignore his concerns about her being a grandmother. He must choose whether or not he will try to win the pennant for himself or for his team members and Pop Fisher. He also must choose whether or not he will accept a bribe and disgrace the game he loves in order satisfy his materialism and insure his financial security.

Failure

Roy's failure to make moral decisions in the novel cause his downfall. His failure reveals his devotion to the American dream of success that blinds him to the needs of others. A monomaniacal focus on being "the best there ever was in the game" prevents him from becoming a team player and putting the success of the Knights before his own. This self-involvement leads to loneliness and alienation. Another important part of the dream is money. Roy's growing materialism links him with the corrupt and greedy Memo and prompts him to accept a bribe from the Judge, which ultimately leads to his disgrace.

Growth and Development

During the course of the novel Roy does show some moral growth. His desire to win the pennant for Pop emerges alongside his own more selfish need to be the best. By the end of the novel, Roy accomplishes a self-transcendence when he decides to forget about trying to fix the game and determines to take care of Iris and their child. However, this development comes too late to save him.

Good and Evil

Throughout the novel, Roy is caught between the forces of good and evil; these forces wage a battle for his soul. Pop Fisher and Iris Lemon represent the forces of good. Pop struggles to turn Roy into a team player and to focus on community rather than individual success. Iris teaches him that through suffering we learn the important things in life, like love and self-respect. Unfortunately, the symbolically evil characters outnumber the good. Memo, the Judge, Gus Sands, and Max Mercy all try to drag Roy down into the world of corruption. Swayed by the power and success they offer, Roy realizes too late the dangerous consequences of his association with them.

Style

Allegory

The allegorical framework of *The Natural* successfully links historical, mythical, and fictional elements. Malamud borrows historical elements from the "Black Sox" scandal in 1919, when eight members of the Chicago White Sox baseball team were charged with bribery during the World Series. He acquires mythological elements from the Holy Grail legend and the wasteland myth. New York City becomes a moral wasteland in the novel, and Roy Hobbs becomes Perceval the Knight as he searches, under the guidance of Pop Fisher (the Fisher King), for truth and redemption and to restore the team by leading it to a pennant win. In Leslie A. Field and Joyce W. Field's interview with Bernard Malamud in their *Bernard Malamud: A Collection of Critical Essays,* he explains, "I became interested in myth and tried to use it, among other things, to symbolize and explicate an ethical dilemma of American life."

Realism and Fantasy

The novel's dominant style mixes realism and fantasy. Malamud grounds Roy's experiences in the world of baseball, but at the same time, he also incorporates supernatural elements. On his first day as a Knight, Roy notices that the team seems to be hexed. After Pop tells Roy to knock the cover off the ball, he literally does just that. Gus Sands "knows" how much money Roy has in his pocket and later, Roy makes a rabbit pop out of Memo's dress. Setting details also become fantastic. The landscape Roy passes through on the train to Chicago becomes an "unreal forest" with "tormented trees." Chicago appears as a "shadow-infested, street lamped jungle."

Foreshadowing

Malamud employs foreshadowing as part of the symbolic structure of the novel. Roy's defeat of the Whammer foreshadows a similar end for Bump and highlights Roy's ambition to be "the best there ever was" in the game. A street beggar, rebuffed by Roy, warns, "You'll get yours." When strip club dancers in devil costumes jab Roy, they forecast the evil "jabs" he will suffer in his dealings with the Judge and Memo.

Historical Context

The Presidential Campaign

Just as Roy Hobb's moral character undergoes a test in *The Natural,* so does the character of many other public figures in America during the 1950s. On September 23, 1952, General Eisenhower's running mate, Senator Richard Nixon, appeared on television to defend himself against charges that he took a "slush fund" of $18,000 from California businessmen. Nixon began, "I come before you tonight as a candidate for the vice presidency and as a man whose honesty and integrity have been questioned." He then denied that any of $18,000 was spent for personal use and claimed that the only gift he accepted was a cocker spaniel, named "Checkers" by his daughter Tricia. He explained, "the kids, like all kids, love the dog. Regardless of what they say about it, we are going to keep it." More than one million approving letters and telegrams poured in after this speech. During the ensuing election, Eisenhower and Nixon won 55 percent of the popular vote and 442 electoral votes. Nixon's moral integrity, however, would be questioned continually throughout his political life.

Babe Ruth

Communist "Witchhunt"

While testifying in front of the Dies Committee on May 22, 1952, playwright Lillian Hellman insisted she was not presently a "Red" but refused to admit whether she had been associated with the Communist party in the past. Hellman claimed she would not answer further questions so as not to "hurt innocent people in order to save myself." She added, "I cannot and will not cut my conscience to fit this year's fashions." Many Americans are forced to appear at government hearings and some, including movie stars and film producers, betray others or make unsubstantiated accusations about associations and/or involvement in the Communist party.

The Economy

Americans enjoyed a higher standard of living during the 1950s as a direct result of the United States's participation in World War II, which enabled the country to become the most prosperous economic power in the world. This new affluent age prompted an avid materialism in many Americans, as it did in Roy Hobbs. Goods like automobiles and suburban homes became powerful status symbols. Spending money became a popular American pastime for the rich as well as the burgeoning middle class.

The Media

The growing demand for information about famous Americans encourages reporters, like the fictional Max Mercy, to ferret out personal details for newspapers and tabloids. In 1952, Generoso Pope, Jr. takes over the *The National Enquirer* and promises to expand its emphasis on sensationalism by reporting lurid crimes, gossip about public figures, and sexual escapades. By 1975, Pope will increase his paper's circulation to over four million copies per week.

The 1952 World Series

The New York Yankees beat the Brooklyn Dodgers four games to two and win the World Series.

The "Black Sox" scandal

In 1919 eight members of the Chicago White Sox baseball team are charged with bribery during the World Series.

Critical Overview

The initial mixed response to *The Natural* focused on the novel's interplay of realism and fantasy. Harry Sylvester in his review in the *New York Times* insists the work is "an unusually fine novel…. What [Malamud] has done is to contrive a sustained and elaborate allegory in which the 'natural' player … is equated with the natural man who, left alone by, say politicians and advertising agencies, might achieve his real fulfillment." He closes his review claiming that *The Natural* is "a brilliant and unusual book."

Not all reviewers, however, found the narrative successful. J. J. Maloney's review in the *New York Herald Tribune Book Review* argues that the novel is a "troubled mixture of fantasy and realism in which the fantasy is fantastic enough, but the realism is not very real." While he appreciates the subject matter, he finds that "it is unfortunate that *The Natural,* which is a serious novel about baseball, should have been written by a man who seems to be completely a captive of the present fashionable cult of the obscure." E. J. Fitzgerald in the *Saturday Review,* offers the following review: "Bernard Malamud has taken some potentially exciting material and gone all mystical and cosmic on it with somewhat unhappy results…. Despite some sharp observation, nice sardonic touches, and

Compare & Contrast

- **1950s:** Money poured into defense spending during the 1940s helped to create a successful military-industrial complex that bolstered the economy in the 1950s. Companies produced goods that enabled them to become prosperous and hire more workers who would in turn buy more goods.

  Today: A healthy economic forecast causes the stock market to soar and pays huge dividends to investors.

- **1950s:** Critics attack Senator Richard Nixon's moral character when rumors of illegal funds surface during the 1952 presidential campaign.

  Today: Critics attack President Clinton's moral character when rumors of illegal funds, shady business dealings, and sexual improprieties surface.

- **1950s:** Baseball is America's favorite pastime. Salaries for top athletes soar into the thousands.

  Today: Frustrated by rising ticket prices, the 1994 strike, and players' salaries soaring into the millions, many fans become disillusioned with the game.

- **1950s:** The public clamors for news about the personal lives of actors and athletes.

  Today: The public clamors for news about the personal lives of actors, athletes, politicians, and royalty. Public figures hounded by the press lash out over their lack of privacy. "Average" Americans appear on nationally televised talk shows reporting sordid details of their lives.

---

an ability to write individually biting scenes, he doesn't quite bring it off." Other reviewers complained that Malamud overused symbolism in the novel.

Many critics, however, appreciated the complex nature of the narrative. While most consider *The Fixer* to be Malamud's best work, critical response to *The Natural* remains positive. Earl Wasserman's essay "The Natural: Malamud's World Ceres" cemented the novel's critical reputation. Wasserman argues that *The Natural* contains all the main themes that can be found in his subsequent fiction. In an exploration of the moral questions the novel raises, Wasserman points out the allegorical and historical connections between Roy Hobbs and Sir Perceval and Shoeless Joe Jackson. Pirjo Ahodas in *Forging a New Self: The Adamic Protagonist and the Emergence of a Jewish-American Author as Revealed through the Novels of Bernard Malamud* digs further beneath the allegorical structure of the novel where she explores Malamud's astute philosophy of composition. Her examination of the novel presents a new interpretation of Malamud's work.

Criticism

Diane Andrews Henningfeld

Henningfeld is a professor at Adrian College and has written for a variety of academic journals and educational publishers. In the following essay, she aligns the failure of main character Roy Hobbs with that of Gawain in Gawain *and the* Green Knight, *demonstrating Malamud's appropriation of popular culture and Arthurian legend to tell a story of pride, testing, and failure.*

Bernard Malamud, the son of Russian Jewish immigrants, published short stories in a variety of magazines during the 1940s and 1950s. He published his first novel, *The Natural,* in 1952. That Malamud chose to focus his first novel on baseball surprised and mystified his readers; even in his early short stories, Malamud had generally used Jewish characters, settings, and themes. The early reviews of *The Natural* illustrate the hesitation with which critics approached the novel. Many found the subject matter strange, the allegory strained, and the symbolism difficult.

What Do I Read Next?

- *Acts of King Arthur and His Noble Nights,* John Steinbeck's 1962 nonfiction work. Steinbeck retells the Arthurian legends and Grail romances.

- Jim Bouton's nonfiction best seller, *Ball Four,* published in 1990, is a funny and revealing diary of one of his seasons playing Major League ball.

- *Eight Men Out: The Black Sox and the 1919 World Series,* a nonfiction book by Eliot Asinof and Stephen Jay Gould, analyzes the events surrounding the famous baseball scandal.

- In *Shoeless Joe,* W. P. Kinsella (1996) presents the game of baseball as a metaphor for life. The novel was adapted into the film, *Field of Dreams.*

Consequently, apart from reviews, the novel received little critical attention in the first years after its publication. However, after the publication of *The Assistant* and *The Magic Barrel,* literary scholars returned their attention to Malamud's first novel, looking for patterns that would emerge in his later work.

In spite of renewed interest in the novel, however, critics generally agree that *The Natural* is Bernard Malamud's most uncharacteristic and difficult novel. In his book, *Bernard Malamud,* for example, critic Sidney Richmond calls *The Natural* "one of the most baffling novels of the 1950's."

A number of notable critics have attempted to render the novel less baffling by identifying Malamud's sources. Earl Wasserman, for example, identifies important allusions to the real world of baseball, including events from Babe Ruth's life, the White Sox scandal of 1919, and the shooting of Eddie Waitkus by an insane woman. He also discusses Malamud's use of the Arthurian Grail story, noting that the Grail story serves as "the archetypal fertility myth." In addition, Wasserman applies psychologist Carl Jung's notion of mythic arche-

types to help explain Roy's relationship with the female characters in the novel.

Indeed, connecting *The Natural* to Arthurian legend provides one of the most compelling ways to read the novel. Nevertheless, critics who make this connection generally look to Malory as Malamud's source. Certainly, the inclusion of Pop Fisher as the Fisher King and the motif of the Wasteland spring largely from Malory; however, there is another medieval Arthurian romance that seems more closely aligned with *The Natural.* "Honi soit qui mal y pense," says the Judge to Roy: Shame be to the man who has evil in his mind. This is, not coincidentally, also the closing line of *Gawain and the Green Knight,* a long poem written by an anonymous writer around 1400. A closer examination of *Gawain* may offer yet another way to read Malamud's novel.

Gawain and the Green Knight opens in the Christmas court of King Arthur. A huge Green Knight enters and challenges the knights to a game. He offers any knight the chance to strike him with his ax. In exchange, the Green Knight will strike the same knight with the ax in one year and a day. Gawain rushes to accept the challenge and knocks the head off the Green Knight.

To everyone's surprise, the blow does not kill the Green Knight. Rather, he merely picks up his head and tells Gawain to meet him in a year and a day at the Green Chapel. Keeping his bargain, Gawain sets out a year later. On the way, he visits the castle of Bercilak with whom he enters into another challenge: Bercilak will exchange anything he captures hunting with anything Gawain receives while staying in the castle.

While Bercilak hunts, Lady Bercilak attempts to seduce Gawain. She finally succeeds in persuading Gawain to take her green girdle as protection against the blow he will receive from the Green Knight. Gawain does not turn over the girdle to Bercilak, thus breaking his bargain. When Gawain meets the Green Knight, he discovers that he is actually Bercilak, and that Bercilak knows of his deception. Although Bercilak laughs and sends him on his way with his life, Gawain is mortified by his own moral failure and vows ever to wear the green girdle as a reminder of his own shame.

Just as *The Natural* is only apparently about baseball, *Gawain and the Green Knight* is only apparently an Arthurian romance. That is, while both Malamud and the *Gawain* poet use the baseball story and Arthurian romance respectively to structure their stories, they each have larger issues at stake. These writers use their genres to allegorically explore the sin of pride, the nature of testing, and the inevitability of human failure.

In order to fulfill their larger purposes, these writers appropriate cultural icons to serve in their tales of human imperfection. The *Gawain* poet chooses as his main character Gawain, a native English hero known to medieval audiences for his appearance in countless Arthurian romances. Gawain's reputation is complicated, however; although considered the best and most loyal of Arthur's knights, he is also known as a violent, rash, womanizer.

Likewise, Malamud appropriates incidents from the life of the greatest popular icon of baseball, Babe Ruth, and associates them with Roy Hobbs. Like Gawain, Ruth's reputation is complicated. His prowess on the field is uncontested; yet he is also known as a rash, sometimes violent womanizer, and a man of huge sensory appetite. By associating Ruth with Roy, Malamud offers a problematic hero, a man of great prowess, great appetites, and great potential for moral failure.

Further, both Roy Hobbs and Gawain strive to be the best in their respective games. However, it is not always clear what has more value to the characters: *being* the best, or *seeming* the best. When Harriet Bird asks the young Roy what he hopes to accomplish, he replies, "Sometimes when I walk down the street I bet people will say there goes Roy Hobbs, the best there ever was in the game." Clearly, it is the reputation that motivates Roy. Likewise, Gawain is reputed to be the greatest of all knights. When the temptress Lady Bercilak attempts to seduce Gawain, her tactic is to remind him of his reputation. The appeal to his pride leads him ever closer to his fall.

Because of their preoccupation with their reputations, neither Gawain nor Roy correctly assesses the tests to which each is put. Gawain assumes that the Green Knight tests his courage and Lady Bercilak tests his lovemaking. Roy assumes that his test is to prove himself on the field with the Knights and in bed with Memo. Neither understands that what is truly at stake is honor and truth.

Perhaps not surprisingly, each story has female characters who act falsely. As *Gawain and the Green Knight* opens, we discover that Gawain is Guinevere's champion. Just as Gawain has cultural currency outside the immediate tale, so does Guinevere. Any reader of Arthurian romance knows that she will betray Arthur by committing adultery with Lancelot and consequently will bring down the court of Camelot. Further, at Bercilak's castle, Gawain encounters both an old hag (whom we later discover is none other than Morgan la Fay, the architect of the entire Green Knight scheme) and Lady Bercilak. Although it appears to Gawain that Lady Bercilak is betraying her husband, she is rather working in concert with her husband to test Gawain.

In *The Natural*, Harriet Bird also hides her motivation for taking an interest in Roy. Many critics have identified Harriet with the testing women of Arthurian romance, or with Morgan la Fay. Certainly, Roy's infatuation with this false woman nearly costs him his life. Further, Memo's collusion with Gus Sands is reminiscent of Lady Bercilak's collusion with Lord Bercilak. Memo tempts Roy with sex and food, and finally with money. She offers him life, a life with her, if he will accept the Judge's money to throw the game. Roy accepts the money only to discover that Memo's motivation is far different from what he assumed. Her desire is to ruin him, not wed him.

In each story, the protagonist attaches himself to the false women and turns away from the true women. As Gawain prepares to leave Camelot in search of the Green Knight, he has the image of the Virgin Mary, "the high Queen of heaven," placed on the inner part of his shield. He loses sight of his true patroness, however, in the arms of Lady Bercilak. Roy finds a true woman in Iris Lemon, who miraculously rises from the crowd and seems to be the reason Roy breaks free from his batting slump. However, although Roy finds Iris to be a full and fertile woman, someone who would be true to him, he turns away from her when she speaks of her joy in mothering and grandmothering. Rather than remaining true to Iris, Roy rejects her, and renews his attachment to the false Memo.

The failures of these protagonists stem from their inability to learn from their past mistakes. Gawain's rash acceptance of the Green Knight's challenge is repeated in his rash acceptance of Lord Bercilak's game, and although he features himself a "true" knight, he finds himself a false one. Likewise, Roy nearly loses his life at the hands of a false woman early in his life, and then repeats the mistake some fifteen years later. As Malamud writes, "He thought, I never did learn anything out of my past life, now I have to suffer again."

Both Gawain and Roy suffer public humiliation at the close of their stories. Gawain confesses his cowardice and falsehood to the court, and vows to wear the green girdle as an emblem of his own failure. Roy, on the other hand, discovers that his story has been published in the newspaper for the entire community to read:

> A boy thrust a newspaper at him. He wanted to say no but had no voice. The headlines screamed, "Suspicion of Hobbs' Sellout—Max Mercy." ... And there was also a statement by the baseball commissioner. "If this alleged report is true, that is the last of Roy Hobbs in organized baseball. He will be excluded from the game and all his records forever destroyed." Roy handed the paper back to the kid. "Say it ain't true, Roy." When Roy looked into the boy's eyes he wanted to say it wasn't, but couldn't, and he lifted his hands to his face and wept many bitter tears.

By the time the *Gawain* poet wrote *Sir Gawain and the Green Knight,* Gawain, as a major hero of Arthurian romance, had already been supplanted by the French import, Sir Lancelot. Yet readers of Arthurian romance know that Lancelot, too, proved false. Although he was granted a glimpse of the Grail, Lancelot died a failure, supplanted by yet another, younger hero, Galahad. Within the *Gawain* poet's choice to use Gawain as his main character inheres a final message: heroes striving for perfection will inevitably fail, and be replaced by yet other heroes.

Likewise, Roy Hobbs' beginning is also his end. His saga begins as he replaces Walt "the Whammer" Whambold and ends with his own replacement by Herman Youngberry, the rising pitcher who strikes him out. As Richman argues, "*The Natural* concludes, therefore, on a note of total loss." The failure of Roy Hobbs (and of Gawain) is not a failure of courage, but a failure of morals. Roy becomes a kind of Everyman, who fails the tests set before him, and who ends, inevitably, flawed.

Source: Diane Andrews Henningfeld, in an essay for *Novels for Students,* Gale, 1998.

Earl R. Wasserman

Wasserman's essay, hailed as an outstanding example of Malamud's scholarship, provides a thorough analysis of myth as an integral element of The Natural.

The Doges of Venice dropped a ring into the Adriatic to renew annually its marriage to their city and to assure that the sea be propitious. The British monarch ceremonially opens the annual session of Parliament that it may undertake its care of the kingdom. In the United States the President annually sanctifies baseball by throwing the first ball of the season into the field; and, having received its presidential commission, baseball proceeds to its yearly task of working the welfare of the national spirit. The wonder is that we do not have a whole library of significant baseball fiction since so much of the American spirit has been seriously poured into the game and its codes until it has a life of its own that affects the national temperament. Just as a personal indiscretion can topple an English government, the White Sox scandal strained the collective American conscience, and Babe Ruth's bellyache was a crisis that depressed the national spirit nearly as much as the bombing of Pearl Harbor infuriated it. Like any national engagement, baseball, especially in that form that Ring Lardner called the "World Serious," has had not only its heroic victories and tragedies but also its eccentricities that express aspects of the American character and have become part of our folklore: Vance, Fewster, and Herman, all piled up on third base; Hilda (the Bell) Chester, the Dodger fan; Rabbit Maranville's penchant for crawling on window ledges, especially in the rain; Wilbert Robinson's attempt to catch a grapefruit dropped from a plane; Chuck Hostetler's historic fall between third and home when he could have won the sixth game of the '45 Series.

These are not merely like the materials of Malamud's *The Natural;* the items mentioned are among its actual stuff. For what Malamud has written is a novel that coherently organizes the rites of baseball and many of its memorable historic episodes into the epic inherent in baseball as a measure of man, as it once was inherent in Homeric battles or chivalric tournaments or the Arthurian quest for the Grail. Coming, like Babe Ruth, from an orphanage, Roy Hobbs, unknown pitcher of nineteen on his way to a try-out with the Cubs, strikes out the aging winner of the Most Valuable Player award and then, like Eddie Waitkus in 1949, is shot without apparent motive by a mad girl in her Chicago hotel room. The try-out never takes place, and the years that follow are degrading failures at everything. But at thirty-four, having switched—as Ruth did—from pitcher to fielder and prodigious batter, Roy joins a New York team and, with his miraculous bat, lifts it from the cellar into contention for the league championship. Like Ruth, too, his homerun cheers a sick boy into recovery, and a monumental bellyache sends him to a hospital, as it did Ruth in 1925, and endangers the battle for the pennant. Like the White Sox of 1919, Roy and another player sell out to Gus, an Arnold Rothstein gambler, to throw the crucial game for the pennant, and the novel ends with a heartbroken boy pleading, as legend claims one did to Shoeless

Joe Jackson of the traitorous White Sox, "Say it ain't true, Roy." In fact, nearly all the baseball story derives from real events, and to this extent the novel is a distillation of baseball history as itself the distillation of American life: its opportunities for heroism, the elevating or dispiriting influence of the hero on his community, the moral obligations thrust on him by this fact, and the corruption available to him. By drawing on memorable real events, Malamud has avoided the risk of contrived allegory that lurks in inventing a fiction in order to carry a meaning. Instead, he has rendered the lived events of the American game so as to compel it to reveal what it essentially is, the ritual whereby we express the psychological nature of American life and its moral predicament. Pageant history is alchemized into revelatory myth.

But the clean surface of this baseball story, as a number of critics have noticed, repeatedly shows beneath its translucency another myth of another culture's heroic ritual by which man once measured the moral power of his humanness—another and yet the same, so that Roy's baseball career may slip the bonds of time and place and unfold as the everlastingly crucial story of man. Harriet, mad maimer of champions, conceives of Roy's strike-out of the Whammer as a "tourney"; Roy's obscure, remote origin and clumsy ignorance have their archetypal form in the youth of Sir Perceval; the New York team he ultimately joins is the "Knights"; and one opponent, sick at the thought of pitching to him, sees him "in full armor, mounted on a black charger ... coming at him with a long lance." Of the mountain of gifts Roy receives on his Day at the ballpark one is a white Mercedes-Benz, which he drives triumphantly around the field and stops before the box of Memo, coldly disdainful lady of courtly love, to ask for a date. By subsuming the chivalric tourney and the Arthurian quest, baseball expands beyond time, and Roy's baseball career becomes, not merely representative, but symbolic of man's psychological and moral situation. Because of the *trompe-l'oeil*, Roy at bat is every quester who has had to shape his own character to fulfill his goal, whether it be the Grail or the league pennant. By drawing his material from actual baseball and yet fusing it with the Arthurian legend, Malamud sets and sustains his novel in a region that is both real and mythic, particular and universal, ludicrous melodrama and spiritual probing—Ring Lardner and Jung....

Malamud's syncretism of baseball and the Arthurian legend ... invites a further consideration of the novel in these terms: the psychological,

> *... what Malamud has written is a novel that coherently organizes the rites of baseball and many of its memorable historic episodes into the epic inherent in baseball as a measure of man ..."*

moral, and communal needs of the baseball champion—the American hero—to gain access to the "sources of Life." Roy long since had made his own bat out of a tree, a sort of Ygdresel, and named it "Wonderboy," and a miraculous bat it is, with an energy of its own. Derived from nature's life and shaped by Roy for the game in which he is determined to be the hero, it flashes in the sun, blinds his opponents with its golden splendor, and crashes the ball with thunder and lightning. It is, in other words, the modern Excalibur and Arthurian lance.... The phallic instrument is the raw vitality and fertility he has drawn from the universal "sources of Life." After Roy's fruit-full night with Memo, Bump says to him, "I hear you had a swell time, wonderboy," and during Roy's slump Wonderboy sags like a baloney.

With Wonderboy, Roy joins the dispirited last-place Knights in a remarkably dry season, and the manager, Pop Fisher, who laments, "I shoulda been a farmer" and whose heart "feels as dry as dirt," suffers, as his form of the Fisher King's affliction, athlete's foot on his hands. Even the water fountain is broken, yielding only rusty water. But when Wonderboy crashes the ball, its thunder cracks the sky, the rains leave the players ankle-deep, the brown field turns green, and Pop Fisher's affliction vanishes. When Roy first appeared and merely entered the batting cage, the flagging Knights suddenly "came to life." The Quester has brought his virility to the Waste Land, and, like Jung's mana-personality, he restores the dying father-king. Roy, the questing Knight, by access to the sources of life, has restored virility to his community and the vegetative process to nature. In the radical sense of the word, he is the "natural."

The Grail vegetation myth has been precisely translated into its modern American mode and is carefully sustained in this baseball story. The "Pre-Game" section, in which young Roy is shot, takes places in early spring, prior to the baseball season. When the story is resumed years later, Roy joins the Knights in summer, a third of the baseball season having passed; and with Roy's failure in the last crucial game the novel ends in a wintry autumn to complete the fertility cycle inherent in both the Grail Quest and the schedule of the baseball season. The traditional Arthurian dwarf who taunts the hero and beats him with a scourge takes his place in the bleachers as the dwarf Otto Zipp, who reviles Roy, honks a Harpo Marx horn at him, contributes razor blades on Roy's Day with the advice, "Here, cut your throat." This stunted growth, who also embodies a good deal of Homer's Thersites, is that portion of the community envious of and antagonistic to the hero's regenerative potency that spreads to the entire team, although Zipp had worshipped Roy's predecessor Bump, whose sterile triumphs were wholly his own while the team slumped; and Zipp exults over Roy's downfall with the empty gesture of hitting a phantom ball for a visionary homerun. Merlin the Magician and Morgan le Fay have evolved into the league of Gus the "Supreme Bookie," who plays the percentages, and Memo, Morganatic in every sense, the temptress for whom Roy sells out. Because of the complementary parts played in King Arthur's life by Morgan, who works for evil and slays knights, and the Lady of the Lake, who works for good and beneficently aids them, Arthurian scholars have claimed they were originally one. Correspondingly, of Roy's two women, red-haired Memo is customarily clad in black, and black-haired Iris, complementarily, in red; and it is Iris who knows Lake Michigan intimately and whose presence restores the power of Wonderboy, his Excalibur. Like the Grail fertility hero, Roy displaces the current hero whose power has waned. In the "Pre-Game" section, like Perceval slaying the Red Knight, he succeeds to the hero's office by striking out the thirty-three-year-old Whammer, thrice chosen the Most Valuable Player, who now knows he is, "in the truest sense of it, out" and trots off, an "old man." In the main narrative Roy gains his life-giving position with the Knights by including the death of Bump, who, although the leading league hitter, has transmitted no potency to his team. (Le Roi est mort, vive le Roy.) And at the novel's end thirty-four-year-old Roy's spiritual death is his being struck out by the young pitcher whose yearning, like Pop Fisher's, is to be a farmer, just as years before Roy had struck out the aging Whammer. Yet at one point Roy confuses the Whammer with Bump, at another sees Bump when he looks in his own mirror, and later dresses exactly like the Whammer; and when Roy succeeds the dead Bump the newspapers marvel at the identity of the two in body and manners. For in fact they are all the same fertility hero, displacing each other with each new seasonal resurgence and decline of potency. In nature, quite independently of moral failures, life and strength are forever renewed.

Besides the hero's charismatic power to restore the maimed Fisher King and bring the fertile waters to the Waste Land, Arthurians have added that the characteristics of the seasonal Grail hero are possession of a talisman, like Excalibur or Wonderboy, representing "the lightning and fecundity of the earth," and "marriage to the vegetation goddess." In every respect, then, Roy seems to fulfill his role as fecundity hero, except for the marriage, despite his yearning for Memo and his passing affair with Iris. His tragic failure therefore is linked with this omission; and the search for the reason takes us to the core of the novel, where we must seek the psychic and moral flaw within the fertility theme—which is embodied in the Arthurian Grail myth—which has been assimilated to the baseball story—which is purified out of actual events....

In the night of defeat Roy performs the ritual of psychic mourning. In the now parched earth he digs a grave for his split bat, his shattered vital power, and, wishing it could take root and become a living tree again, he hesitates over the thought of wetting the earth with water from the fountain. But he knows the futility—it would only leak through his fingers. Because Roy's failure to be the hero is his failure to accept the mature father role, it is properly a boy who ends the novel, begging hopefully in disillusionment, "Say it ain't true, Roy." More was lost by Shoeless Joe Jackson than merely the honor of the White Sox or even the honor of the national game. For in the boy is each new American generation hopefully pleading that those on whom it depends will grow mature through the difficult love that renders the life of the human community the self-sacrificing and yet self-gaining purpose of their vital resources; that they not, selfishly seeking the womb-like security of disengagement, evade the slime that human existence must deposit within, but willingly and heroically plunge into it, with all its horror, to release for others its life-giving power....

Baseball has given Malamud a ritualistic system that cuts across all our regional and social differences. The assimilation of the Arthurian myth defines the historical perspective, translating baseball into the ritual man has always been compelled to perform in one shape or another; and the Jungian psychology with which Malamud interprets the ritual locates the central human problem precisely where it must always be, in one's human use of one's human spirit.

Source: Earl R. Wasserman, "The Natural: *World Ceres*" in *Bernard Malamud and the Critics,* edited by Leslie A. Field and Joyce W. Field, New York University Press, 1970, pp. 45–65.

Frederick W. Turner III

In the following excerpt, Turner points out how Malamud's recurrent theme of the conflict between myths and the outer world appears in The Natural.

The Natural is a curiosity on two counts: first because it is one of the very few "non-Jewish" works of the author; and second because it makes use of a supposedly unadaptable subject for serious fiction—baseball. It is perhaps this latter factor which has contributed most substantially to the novel's wary critical reception. Baseball has resisted the best efforts of American writers to elevate it to a sufficient height to sustain a serious work, though several writers, notably Ring Lardner, Charles Einstein, and Mark Harris, have correctly seen it as a microcosm of American life. The uniqueness of Malamud's treatment derives from the fact that he has been able to invest this boy's game with tragi-comic qualities as opposed, say, to Lardner or Harris, who treat it in largely comic fashion.

Malamud's successful use of baseball in this novel has been commonly attributed to his use of myth, particularly the myth of the hero, and almost every critic who has troubled himself with *The Natural* has dutifully and sometimes painstakingly pointed out the various mythic parallels. Malamud, they observe, has equated the baseball hero of his novel with mythic heroes of the past so that the actions of Roy Hobbs, left fielder for the New York Knights, take on a significance far larger than that guaranteed even the most glorious of sweaty demigods.

Despite the ease with which critics have exposed the mythic underpinnings of *The Natural* (or perhaps because of it), there has persisted a sense of uneasiness about the book, as if Malamud were somehow cheating by using myths in such a fashion. So Norman Podhoretz [in *Commentary,* March, 1953]:

> All this amounts to a commendable effort to say that baseball is much more important than it seems to be. Using Homer, however, is not only too easy a way to do it, but also a misconception of what intelligence and seriousness of purpose demand from a writer.

Then too, the mythic parallels themselves seem to lead nowhere, and it has seemed almost as if the use of myth was an end in itself as indeed the critics themselves have made it: to assert the presence of myth in a literary work is not necessarily to explain *why* it is there, and this has unhappily been too often the case with recent criticism; it is as though finding buried traces of myths were but a refinement of the symbol archeology carried on in the journals for the past thirty-five years. Podhoretz and Marcus Klein can tell us what myths are being used where, but they fail to tell us to what effect. Podhoretz can even suggest that baseball has its own mythology:

> Mr. Malamud is truer to the inherent purpose of his book when he finds the elements of myth, not in ancient Greece, but in the real history of baseball.

Yet he fails to follow up this potentially valuable suggestion as have all other critics who have dealt with *The Natural.* To heed it is to be taken straight to the heart of this novel, and perhaps in some measure to the heart of Malamud's fiction as a whole.

All modern heroic myths are but redactions of the ur-myth of the hero as this has been dissected and outlined by Otto Rank, Lord Raglan, and Joseph Campbell. That myth is too well known to require reproduction here, but anyone can see, for example, that the Horatio Alger story is a form of the heroic myth and that, existing as it does in a democratic and predominantly Protestant society, the story has taken on the characteristics of that society while dropping those features of the old heroic myths which are culturally uncongenial: its aristocratic and sexual overtones. Similarly, it can be seen that the myth of the baseball hero is an amalgam of the heroic myth and its democratic offspring, the Horatio Alger story:

1) the hero is from undistinguished parentage and has a rural background;

2) the hero's father teaches him to play baseball, perhaps thereby fulfilling his own unrealized boyhood ambitions;

3) the hero is discovered in his rural haunts by a hard-working scout;

4) the hero is transported to the city where he finds life frightening and bewildering; he encounters difficulty in convincing the team "brass" that he has the necessary talent;

5) the hero finally gets his chance and displays prodigious talents (fastest fastball, longest home run);

6) the hero rises to stardom, has a "day" at the stadium and inarticulately expresses his humble thanks;

7) everything after the hero's day savors somewhat of anti-climax, his talents gradually decay, and he eventually retires.

Roy Hobbs, Malamud's hero, is one who lives and finds his meaning only within this mythology and this is his tragic weakness. He is obsessed with a sense of mission which is nothing less than to fill out the heroic proportions which the pattern casts for those who would follow it. Roy's lack of any values outside the mythology is one of the major sources of the tragicomic quality which Malamud has been able to impart to the novel: Roy's refusal to think in any terms other than those of baseball is, to begin with, comic, and he becomes the prototypical goon athlete immortalized in our literature by Lardner and James Thurber. So this passage in which Harriet Bird sizes Roy up as a future victim of her sexually-tinged desire to murder famous athletes:

Had he ever read Homer?

Try as he would he could only think of four bases and not a book. His head spun at her allusions. He found her lingo strange with all the college stuff and hoped she would stop it because he wanted to talk about baseball.

And:

"What will you hope to accomplish, Roy?"

He had already told her but after a minute remarked, "Sometimes when I walk down the street I bet people will say there goes Roy Hobbs, the best there ever was in the game."

She gazed at him with touched and troubled eyes. "Is that all?"

He tried to penetrate her question. Twice he had answered it and still she was unsatisfied. He couldn't be sure what she expected him to say. "Is that all?" he repeated. "What more is there?"

"Don't you know?" ...

"Isn't there something over and above earthly things—some more glorious meaning to one's life and activities?"

"In baseball?"

Fifteen years and worlds of agonies later Roy is still held in the grip of the mythology, still refusing to think or act outside of it. Now, however,

Roy's refusal to see outside the myth is not comic, but rather tragic. It is so because we are here witness to the spectacle of a man who has given his life for that myth, and because myth cannot be defended entirely from within; it must be defended by a hero who sees *both* inside and outside it. Still, there is another chance for Roy to save the myth through an acceptance of the love of Iris Lemon. Such an acceptance would prepare him to confront the world of objective reality while at the same time remaining true to baseball's mythology: Iris is in the real world but she still believes in heroes. Here Roy's refusal of Iris' love guarantees his inevitable (Natural) failure. This time when Roy reveals in conversation with a woman (Iris) his tragic limitation it is no longer a laughing matter; his vision has taken on a kind of Oedipal blindness:

"I wanted everything." His voice boomed out of the silence.

She waited.

"I had a lot to give to this game."

"Life?"

"Baseball. If I had started out fifteen years ago like I tried to, I'da been king of them all by now."

"The king of what?"

"The best in the game," he said impatiently.

She sighed deeply. "You're so good now."

"I'da been better. I'da broke most every record there was."

"Does that mean so much to you?"

"Sure," he answered....

"But I don't understand why you should make so much of that. Are your values so—!"

Roy's values are "so—" for this is what distinguishes the hero from ordinary people like Iris. A hero is someone who acts within and for a mythology—national, regional, occupational—even when to do so is to jeopardize his very existence. Malamud's ironic vision is that such an insulated hero cannot possibly win out.

What continually threatens the existence of the hero and of the mythology which he serves is what Wallace Stevens called the "pressure of reality." It is always clear that mythologies are in some ways divorced from the real world, though what they contain may be directives for solving the world's problems. Here the fading, sagging ball park where the Knights play their home games functions as metaphor for the other-worldly quality of mythology.... Inside the park gates one is transported to another world filled with grotesque devotees, magic bats, and super-sized demigods. The drama of the hero's story comes out of the conflict between the mythology within which the hero acts and the pressures of reality which work always to force the hero into a betrayal of his mythology.

In *The Natural* the pressure of reality is represented by the unholy alliance of Judge Goodwill Banner, the Knights' owner: Gus Sands, the Supreme Bookie; and Memo Paris, Roy's love. The sportswriter, Max Mercy (whose name like that of the Judge has its obvious irony), is their press agent. The Judge has a completely cynical, ruthless attitude toward the game. He is in it to make money and Malamud skillfully contrasts him with his co-owner, Pop Fisher, who manages the team and subscribes wholly to the mythology of the game. Similarly, Gus Sands has no reverence for the game itself. To him it is simply "action" on which to bet. Because of the death of her hero, Bump Baily, Memo Paris has disavowed her belief in the mythology and she now works with the Judge and Gus to destroy the hero.

The hero must meet the challenge to his mythology head-on, and it is one of the central ironies of the novel that Roy Hobbs meets this challenge as he lies bewildered and enfeebled in a hospital bed. The doctor has told Roy that he must quit baseball or risk a heart attack, and Memo, whom Roy covets, has made it clear that she is to be had only for the kind of money which comes to a famous athlete. Thus when Judge Banner appears at the bedside to bribe Roy into throwing the play-off game the hero is at his lowest ebb. Faced with his physical predicament and an uncertain financial future, the hero succumbs. He has at last seen outside the mythology, but in so doing he loses his grip on the mythology itself.

When in the midst of the play-off game Roy attempts to reattach himself to the mythology he cannot do so. Wonderboy, the magic bat, breaks in two, for once this hero has seen and acted outside the mythology—acted, that is, against it—he can never again act with it; his limited vision will not permit him to. Thus the gates of Roy's Eden are closed forever and there remains for him nothing to do but drag himself up the stairs to the Judge's darkened tower to collect his reward.

This final scene is the novel's best, for in it Malamud makes the reader fully aware of the tragedy of Roy's lost herohood. Divorced forever from the mythology which gave his life meaning, Roy can only beat up Gus Sands and the Judge, tear open the envelope containing the bribe money,

> *Roy Hobbs, as we have seen, is too limited a hero to assume this difficult stance; for him it is impossible to act within a mythology and at the same time see beyond it so as to defend it. For him it must be one thing or the other."*

and shower it over the Judge's head. The end for this failed hero is to enter the real world and to find it a sordid and bitter place:

> When he hit the street he was exhausted. He had not shaved, and a black beard gripped his face. He felt old and grimy.
>
> He stared into the faces of people he passed along the street but nobody recognized him.
>
> "He coulda been a king," a woman remarked to a man.

So with modern man: divorced forever from the mythologies of his past, he finds himself alone, on the street, adrift in a new and mythless world.

And yet, of course, this is not the end for the Malamud hero; it is merely the first installment. Roy Hobbs is the hero of a mythology, but ultimately he fails that mythology by his inability to see and act beyond it without destroying it for himself. The mythology of baseball is what keeps the game alive in the hearts of its fans. Without that mythology the game would disintegrate into a jumble of meaningless statistics and facts. Yet conditions change, and the mythology of baseball must be continually defended on new grounds. What this latest baseball hero *should* have done is to accept Iris Lemon's love, and, sustained by this new and vitalizing outside force, resist temptation and expose the Judge and Gus who represent the greed and corruption which now threaten baseball's mythology. In this way the hero would have remained true to his mythology while at the same time defending it against hostile forces. But Roy Hobbs, as we have seen, is too limited a hero to assume this difficult stance; for him it is impossible to act within a mythology and at the same time *see* beyond it so as to defend it. For him it must be one thing or the other.

Source: Frederick W. Turner III, "Myth Inside and Out: *The Natural*" in *Bernard Malamud and the Critics,* New York University Press, edited by Leslie A. Field and Joyce W. Field, 1970, pp. 109–119.

Sources

Pirjo Ahodas, *Forging a New Self: The Adamic Protagonist and the Emergence of a Jewish-American Author as Revealed through the Novels of Bernard Malamud,* Turun Yliopisto (Turku), 1991.

Leslie A. Field and Joyce W. Field, an interview with Bernard Malamud in *Bernard Malamud: A Collection of Critical Essays,* Prentice Hall, 1975, pp. 8-17.

J. J. Maloney, a review in *New York Herald Tribune Book Review,* August 24, 1952, p. 8.

Joel Salzberg, "Bernard Malamud," in *Dictionary of Literary Biography,* Vol. 2: *American Novelists since World War II,* Gale, 1978, pp. 107-27.

Harry Sylvester, a review in *The New York Times,* August 24, 1952, p.5.

Earl Wasserman, "'The Natural': Malamud's World Ceres," in *Centennial Review,* Vol. 9, No. 4, 1965, pp. 438-60.

For Further Study

Jonathon Baumbach, "The Economy of Love: The Novels of Bernard Malamud," in *The Kenyon Review,* Vol. 25, No. 3, summer, 1963, pp. 438-57.
    In a classic essay on Malamud's novels, Baumbach provides an excellent overview of the use of myth in *The Natural.*

Ronald V. Evans, "Malamud's 'The Natural,'" in *Explicator,* Vol. 48., No. 3, spring, 1990, pp. 224-26.
    Provides a Jungian reading of the novel.

Sheldon J. Hershinow, *Bernard Malamud,* Frederick Ungar Publishing Co., 1980.
    Reinforces the identification of *The Natural* with the Arthurian Legend, adding that the theme of the novel is the inevitable suffering of human beings.

Patric Keats, "Hall of Famer Ed Delahanty: A Source for Malamud's 'The Natural,'" in *American Literature,* Vol. 62, No. 1, March, 1990, pp. 102-04.
    Focuses on Malamud's treatment of Roy Hobbs and finds an historical parallel in the life of Edward "Big Ed" James.

Robert C. Lidston, "Malamud's 'The Natural': An Arthurian Quest in the Big Leagues" in *West Virginia University Philological Papers,* Vol. 27, 1981, pp. 75-81.
    Compares the novel to the Arthurian romance, especially in its linking of baseball and the quest theme.

James M. Mellard, "Malamud's Novels: Four Versions of Pastoral," in *Critique,* Vol. 9, No. 2, 1967, pp. 5-19.
    Contends that *The Natural* embodies "the pastoral fertility myths of dying and reviving gods, of youthful heroes replacing the aged, of the son replacing the father…." These archetypes provide the structure of the novel, according to this critic.

Ellen Pifer, "Malamud's Unnatural 'The Natural,'" in *Studies in American Jewish Literature,* Vol. 7, No. 2, fall, 1988, pp. 138-52.
    Explores the moral character of Roy Hobbs.

Norman Podhoretz, "Achilles in Left Field," in *Commentary,* Vol. 15, No. 3, March, 1953, pp. 321-26.
    Makes connections between Roy Hobbs and the Young Unknown from medieval romance as well as Achilles from the *Illiad* but concludes that Malamud's novel ultimately fails due to Roy's shallowness.

Sidney Richman, *Bernard Malamud,* Twayne Publishers, 1966.
    Provides an excellent introductory study of Malamud and his major works. In his chapter on *The Natural* he undertakes a systematic explication of the allegory, the themes, and the characters.

Joel Salzberg, *Bernard Malamud: A Reference Guide,* G. K. Hall Co., 1985.
    An extremely useful annotated bibliography of scholarship on Bernard Malamud.

Daniel Walden, "Bernard Malamud, an American Jewish Writer and His Universal Heroes," in *Studies in American Jewish Literature,* Vol. 7, No. 2, fall, 1988, pp. 153-61.
    Examines Malamud's treatment of the hero in *The Assistant, The Fixer,* and *The Natural* and shows how each is related to the Jewish experience.

Earl R. Wasserman, "*The Natural:* World Ceres," in *Bernard Malamud and the Critics,* edited by Leslie A. Field and Joyce W. Field, New York University Press, 1970, pp. 45-66.
    Wasserman connects *The Natural* with the tradition of the baseball story, the Arthurian Grail quest, and Jungian psychology, arguing that the novel "is the broad formulation of Malamud's world of meaning." Consequently, *The Natural* is a necessary starting point for any student of Malamud's fiction.

Night

Eliezer Wiesel
1956

With the encouragement of Francois Mauriac, Eliezer Wiesel broke his silence on the horror of the Holocaust to produce an 800 page memoir entitled, *Un di Velt Hot Geshvign,* in 1956. That cathartic story was reworked over two years and became the slim 1958 novella *La Nuit* which became *Night* in 1960. Wiesel's novel revealed the Holocaust in stark, evocative, detail. He had a hard time finding an audience, however, in a world that preferred the 1947 *Diary of Young Girl* written by Anne Frank. *Night* made no claim on innocence but created an aesthetic of the Holocaust to force people to face the horrible event and, hopefully, break the general silence surrounding that hell. For Wiesel, *Night* began a brilliant writing career.

Night begins in 1941 in a Hasidic Community in the town of Sighet, Transylvania. There we meet a devote young boy named Eliezer who is so fascinated by his own culture and religion that he wishes to study Jewish *cabbala*. His father, however, says he must master the Talmud before he can move on to the mystical side of the Jewish faith. Moshe the Beadle indulges the boy until the reality of World War II reaches them. The fascists come to power in Romania and foreign Jews are deported and Moshe with them. Some days later, he makes it back to town and tells them what happened. All the people presumed deported were shot. That was only the beginning, the dusk of the coming night. Within a matter of paragraphs, officers of the Nazi SS corps have arrived and the family is broken up and sent to Birkenau. The metaphor-

ical night only gets darker as Eliezer struggles to survive in the brutality and degradation of the camps.

Author Biography

No other individual is so identified with the Holocaust—its memory and its prevention—as Wiesel. He was born in 1928 in Sighet, Romania, to Shlomo (a grocer) and Sarah Wiesel. His parents were part of a Hasidic Jewish community and encouraged him in his religious studies. Growing up, young Wiesel "believed profoundly" and felt it his duty to pray. In 1944, the distant threat of Hitler invaded the community and his family was deported to a concentration camp. A few years after the war, Wiesel was reunited with surviving family members—two sisters.

At the war's close, Wiesel hoped to emigrate to Palestine which would see the declaration of the state of Israel in 1947. Being an orphan, however, placed him with other children enroute to Belgium. General Charles de Gaulle intervened and brought the train to France. Wiesel finished his teens in Normandy and won entrance to the Sorbonne in Paris. After completing his studies he became a journalist. After a decade of living in France, he moved to the United States and eventually gained American citizenship. In 1969, he married Marion Erster Rose. She is also a survivor of the camps and a writer in her own right. She became his English translator.

In 1954, while working on assignment for a Tel Aviv newspaper, he interviewed Nobel Laureate Francois Mauriac. When the discussion turned to the suffering of Jesus, Wiesel angrily burst out that nobody was speaking of the suffering just a few years before. Mauriac suggested he break the silence. The result was the first of many works, an 800 page memoir in Yiddish, *Un di Velt Hot Geshvign* (1956), which detailed his experience of losing his family and friends to the concentration camps. This work became the famous *La Nuit.* (1958) or, in English, *Night* (1960).

At the time of the book's completion, nobody wanted to be reminded of the Holocaust. In fact, the publishing world felt Anne Frank's *Diary of a Little Girl* was a sufficient memento of the horror. A tiny firm disagreed and managed to pay $250. Today, annual sales of the work in the United States exceed 300,000 copies.

Eliezer Wiesel

Despite the book's lack of commercial success, Wiesel was defined by it. He has spent his life, ever since, as a vocal champion of human rights. His eloquent moral voice has often been compared with that of Albert Camus. Wiesel hopes that his stories will prompt a reflection that leads to a more humane future. In 1986, Wiesel was awarded the Nobel Peace Prize.

For the last decade he has advised the U. S. Congress on memorials, religion, and the Middle East. He has served as chairman of the United States Holocaust Memorial Council and is the Andrew Mellon Professor of Humanities at Boston University. In May 1997, Wiesel was appointed to Head the Swiss Holocaust Fund. This was in "recognition of his extraordinary accomplishments and his respected moral guidance," said Swiss Foreign Minister Flavio Cotti.

Plot Summary

Sighet

Night opens with a description of Moshe the Beadle, a poor Jew in Sighet, who is teaching Jewish mysticism to young Eliezer. After Moshe is expelled with the other foreign-born Jews, he miraculously returns to tell the Jews of Sighet that all those who were expelled have been killed. However, none of the villagers believe him, and eventually Moshe stops telling his tale. In the spring of 1944, German troops appear in Sighet, and the occupiers issue anti-Semitic decrees and establish two Jewish ghettos. Eventually, the Jews of Sighet are told that they are going to be evacuated.

The Germans pack Eliezer and his family onto a train. Madame Schächter screams every night that she sees a fire and the others try to silence her, shaken by her insanity. It is not until they approach the camp itself, and see flames, that they realize that she has predicted their fate. They have arrived at Birkenau.

Birkenau

The guards order the man and women to separate, and Eliezer is parted from his mother and little sister forever. He and his father see little children being burned alive and Eliezer realizes that he will never forget the sight.

In the barracks, Eliezer's father asks an SS officer where the lavatories are and the man strikes him. Eliezer does nothing for fear of being struck himself, but he vows never to forgive the striking of his father. The men are then marched to Auschwitz.

Auschwitz

The men arrive at their block, where the prisoner in charge speaks the first human words they have yet heard. Later the men are tattooed and Eliezer becomes A-7713; he has been stripped even of his name.

A relative of Eliezer's, Stein, manages to find them, and Eliezer lies that Stein's wife and children are well. Stein continues to visit them occasionally, until he goes to find news of his family and Eliezer never sees him again. After three weeks, the remaining men in the block are marched to Buna, another camp.

Buna

At Buna, the men are transferred to the musicians' block and begin work at an electrical equipment warehouse. Eliezer befriends Tibbi and Yossi, two Zionist brothers with whom he talks of emigrating to Palestine after the war.

Idek, the Kapo, beats Eliezer for no apparent reason. A French girl wipes his bloodstained forehead and says a few comforting words. On another day, Idek beats Eliezer's father with an iron bar,

and instead of feeling anger towards Idek, Eliezer feels anger towards his father for not knowing how to avoid Idek's blows.

The foreman, Franek, demands Eliezer's gold crown. When Eliezer refuses, Franek begins to punish Eliezer's father for not marching properly. Finally, father and son decide to give up the crown, which is removed by a dentist to whom Eliezer must pay a ration of bread.

On a Sunday, usually a day of rest, Eliezer finds Idek in the warehouse with a girl, and Idek has Eliezer whipped twenty-five times. On another Sunday, the camp is bombed. One man crawls towards two pots of soup and all the men watch him enviously. He dies with his body poised over the soup. The camp is not destroyed by the air raid, but it gives the men hope.

A man is hanged, and the other prisoners are forced to witness it. Later, there is another hanging, this time of a child, beloved in the camp, who has been associated with the Resistance. The child dies a slow, agonizing and silent death as the men weep. Someone in the crown asks where God is, and Eliezer hears a voice inside him reply that God is on the gallows.

The men debate how to celebrate Rosh Hashanah, the Jewish New Year, but Eliezer's heart revolts at the thought of celebrating. On Rosh Hashanah, he finds his father and kisses his hand, silently, as a tear drops between them, knowing that they have never understood each other so clearly. Later, on Yom Kippur, the men debate whether or not they should fast. Eliezer eats, viewing it as an act of rebellion against God, but feels a great void in his heart nonetheless.

After Eliezer has been transferred to the building unit, a selection occurs. Eliezer is not selected for death, and Eliezer's father thinks he has also passed, but after several days they find out that his number was written down. While awaiting another, decisive selection, Eliezer's father gives his knife and spoon. The next day, everyone is kind to Eliezer, already treating him like an orphan. When the day is over, he finds that his father has escaped the second selection, and gives him back his knife and spoon.

In wintertime, Eliezer enters the hospital for an operation on his foot. While he recovers there, he hears that the camp is being evacuated. Eliezer and his father decide to evacuate with the others. We are told that those who stayed behind in the hospital were liberated by the Russians two days after the evacuation.

The men march away from the camp, then begin to run. Those who cannot keep up are shot; others are trampled to death in the crowd. Only his father's presence keeps Eliezer from succumbing to death. When the men are finally allowed to stop, Eliezer's father pushes him towards a brick factory, where they agree to take turns sleeping. Rabbi Eliahou enters the factory, looking for his son: Eliezer realizes the Rabbi's son has abandoned his father. Eliezer prays for the strength never to do what Rabbi Eliahou's son has done.

Gliewitz

The men arrive at Gliewitz, trampling each other on the way into the barracks. As Eliezer lies on a pile of men, he realizes that Juliek is playing his violin, giving a concert to dead and dying men. When he wakes up, he sees Juliek's corpse and his smashed violin beside him.

At Gliewitz, Eliezer saves his father from selection. Later, on the train, Eliezer's father does not wake, and Eliezer slaps him back to life before the men can throw him out with the corpses. At one stop, onlookers throw bread into the cars, and the men fight each other for it. Eliezer sees a son kill his father for a crust of bread and the son, in turn, killed by other men. When they reach Buchenwald, a dozen men, including Eliezer and his father, are left in the wagon out of the hundred who began the journey.

Buchenwald

At Buchenwald, Eliezer's father announces that he is ready to die, but Eliezer forces him to continue on. Later, his father develops dysentery and is unable to leave his bed. Eliezer arranges to stay near his father, but when his father begs him for water, an SS clouts him on the head, and Eliezer does not move, afraid he will also be hit. Eliezer's father's last word is his name; the next day, he is gone. Eliezer has no more tears to weep and in his weakened conscience he feels freedom.

Eliezer is transferred to the children's block, beyond all grief. Wiesel says nothing about the events of the rest of the winter. On April 10th, the Germans are going to evacuate the camp, then blow it up, but after the inmates are assembled, the Resistance rises up and takes over the camp, and American tanks arrive at Buchenwald that evening. After liberation, Eliezer nearly dies of food poisoning. When he recovers, he looks at himself in the mirror, something he has not done since he was in Sighet, and a corpse stares back at him.

Characters

A-7713

See Eliezer Wiesel

Alphonse

In the concentration camps, the best heads of the block to be under are Jews. When Elie is transferred to the musicians' block he finds himself under a German Jew named Alphonse "with an extraordinarily aged face." Whenever possible, Alphonse would organize a cauldron of soup for the weaker ones in the block.

Akiba Drumer

Akiba Drumer was a deeply religious elder whose "deep, solemn voice" sang Hasidic melodies. He would attempt to reassure those around him. He interpreted the camps as God's test for his people that they might finally dominate the Satan within. And if God "punishes us relentlessly, it's a sign that He loves us all the more." At one point he discovers a bible verse which, interpreted through numerology, predicted their deliverance to be a few weeks away.

Eventually he can no longer rationalize the horror of the camps with such logic. Finally, he is "selected"—but he was already dead. As soon as he had lost his faith, "he had wandered among us, his eyes glazed, telling everyone of his weakness … " He asks them to say the Khaddish for him in three days—the approximate time until his death. They promise to do so, but they forget.

Franek

The foreman in the electrical warehouse is a former student from Warsaw named Franek. He terrorizes Eliezer's father when Eliezer refuses to give up his gold crown. Eventually he gives in. A famous dentist takes out the crown with a rusty spoon. With the crown, Franek becomes kinder and even gives them extra soup when he can.

Hersch Genud

An elder who conversed with Akiba Drumer about the camps as a trial for the people, was Hersch Genud. He was "well versed in the cabbala [and] spoke of the end of the world and the coming Messiah."

Idek

Idek is a Kapo, a prisoner put in charge of a barracks. Under his charge is Eliezer's block and all who work in the electrical warehouse. He is

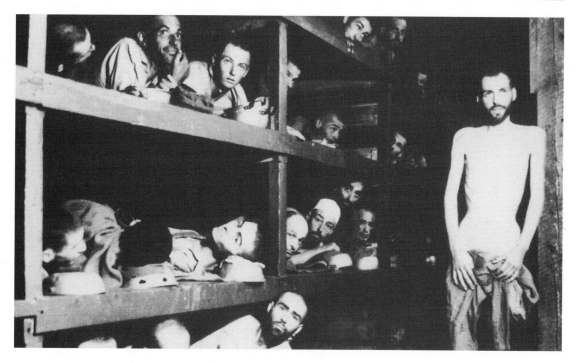

Elie Wiesel (second row from bottom, seventh person from left) and other survivors of Buchenwald concentration camp.

prone to violent fits; people try to stay out of his way. One Sunday, he takes the prisoners under his charge to the warehouse for the day so he can be with a woman. Eliezer discovers them and is whipped. Then he is warned to never reveal what he saw.

Juliek

Juliek, along with Chlomo and Moshe the Beadle, is one of the most important characters in the novel. He is "a bespectacled Pole with a cynical smile on his pale face." He kindly explains what to do and what not to do on the block, including a word of warning about the Idek, "the Kapo." Juliek is also a symbol of the artistry and talent lost in the Holocaust. He was a violinist.

When they were all run to Gleiwitz and away from the approaching Russians, they were quickly and brutally shoved into barracks, heaped in and left to struggle out of a mass of bodies. In this mess, Elie and Juliek hear each other's voice. Juliek is "OK" but he worries for his violin which he has carried with him. At this moment Elie feels himself very close to death when he hears "[t]he sound of a violin, in this dark shed, where the dead were heaped on the living. What madman could be playing the violin here, at the brink of his own grave?"

It was Juliek and he was playing Beethoven—a German composer. In the morning he was dead.

Meir Katz

A farmer who used to bring fresh vegetables to the Wiesels. He was put in charge of the wagon taking them to Buchenwald because he was the most vigorous. He saves Eliezer from strangulation. He confides to Chlomo that he can't go on. Chlomo tries to bolster him but at Buchenwald, Meir Katz does not leave the wagon with them.

Louis

Louis was a violinist from Holland who complained that "they would not let him play Beethoven: Jews were not allowed to play German music."

Moshe the Beadle

The first person we meet in the novel is the "physically awkward" Moshe the Beadle. He is poor but the community is fond of him and does not resent the generosity he needs. To Eliezer he becomes something of an uncle and tutor. He gently initiates Eliezer into the mystical side of Hasidism—something he asked his father about but he was told to stick with the Talmud. "Moshe the

Beadle, the poor barefoot of Sighet, talked to me for long hours of the revelations and mysteries of the cabbala." Moshe the Beadel is a man without means and, therefore, no investments to safeguard except the people.

When the foreign Jews are deported, Eliezer says goodbye to Moshe. A few days later, Moshe returns with a report on the massacre of those deported. The community dismisses him as a madman. They dismiss him because if he is to be believed, then they too will be as poor as he is. When the SS arrive to cordon off the Jews into a ghetto and then deport them, Moshe says he tried to warn them. Then he flees.

pipel

A pipel is a young boy servant of Oberkapo (a prisoner put in charge of several barracks) and often used as a sex slave. One pipel in particular was the servant of a beloved Oberkapo who had been killed when he was found hiding weapons for the camp resistance. The pipel refused to give information under torture. He was hanged before all the prisoners. The normal executioner refused to be involved so three SS took over. It is a horrific execution since the boy was too light to die by his own weight. He struggled for hours at the end of the rope, "That night the soup tasted of corpses."

Madame Schächter

An older woman, Madame Schächter, is huddled in a corner of the wagon with her 10 year-old son. She was a "quiet woman with tense, burning eyes." Her husband and two eldest sons had already been taken. On the first day of the journey to Auschwitz she went out of her mind. She moaned, asked where her family was, and then she became hysterical. At night she would shriek "I can see fire!" Her shrieks would come suddenly and terrify everyone. But she did see fire. The last time she shrieked and everyone looked, they saw the flames of the crematory.

Stein

Reizel Stein's husband from Antwerp seeks out Chlomo among the new arrivals at Auschwitz for news of his family. He has not seen them since 1940. Eliezer is faster than his father to recall the man as a relative. He lies and says that his mother has heard from Reizel. This gives Stein great joy. But then, after another train arrives, Stein learns the truth and stops coming round to visit.

Tibi

Representing the political opposite of the Hasidic elders who preached nonviolence and patience, were two brothers named Tibi and Yossi. They believed in the precepts of Zionism, a political pressure movement active mostly in Europe to convince the world powers to create a Jewish state of Israel in the area of Palestine. They were Jews from Czechoslovakia whose parents had been exterminated at Birkenau. "They lived body and soul for each other." They befriend Eliezer with whom they share the regret that their parents had not gone to Palestine while there was still time to do so. The two boys taught Eliezer Hebrew chants while they worked.

Chlomo Wiesel

Eliezer's father, Chlomo, is a "cultured, rather unsentimental man … more concerned with others than with his own family." He is held in great esteem by the community and symbolizes Abraham. As Abraham, however, he refuses to sacrifice his son. He lives, while in the death camps, to try and keep his son alive. Eliezer, as a representation of Isaac, also safeguards his father. This relationship is the most important of the story. The bitterest moment comes when Clomo believes himself selected and gives Eliezer his inheritance—a knife and spoon.

They have done well together until the end, when they are shipped to Gleiwitz, and then taken to Buchenwald. They are transported in open cars (despite the snow) with the result that Chlomo comes down with dysentery. Eliezer does all he can to comfort his father. He begins to resent the burden. He is tempted to take his father's ration but does not. The resentment he feels for his father haunts him. The haunting grows worse when Chlomo begins yelling to Eliezer for water. A guard silences him with a blow from a truncheon. At some point, Chlomo is taken away to the crematory still breathing. Eliezer could only stand by.

Eliezer Wiesel

The narrating survivor of the camps is Eliezer, who became A-7713. Deeply fascinated by Hasidic Judaism, he finds an indulgent teacher in Moshe the Beadle. The first cracks in his faith begin, however, when Moshe returns from deportation changed in demeanor and warning about impending doom. The cracks widen inside with every night spent in the camps. The crack is not exactly a rejection of God; it is a dismissal shouted out in anger. "Never shall I forget those moments which murdered my God and my Soul and turned my dreams to dust." But such moments passed and his argument is in keeping with Hasidism. Rather, his alteration takes this form, "I no longer accepted God's silence."

Eliezer had once believed profoundly and had lamented before God but he could no longer do so. He "felt very strong" in this realization for he "had ceased to be anything but ashes, yet I felt myself to be stronger than the Almighty." Eliezer is henceforth, except for a few moments of doubt, determined to live as a man (a being made of dust) and survive—"something within me revolted against death." Eliezer may no longer believe in the merciful and just God but he believes even less in giving into death by concentration camp madness.

Eliezer represents a truly aesthetic individual who represents the best of European civilization. He is aware of the myths of his people and their history. As such he is able to tell his tale in terms of them with references to psalms, gospel stories, and personages like Job and indirectly Abraham, Isaac, and the three children in the furnace. He is truly mystified to account for the camps both in terms of religion but also morality. Consequently, he is bent solely on survival and only his stomach takes note of time. Still he survives but merely as a corpse in a mirrored gaze just waking up from the long night.

Yossi

The brother of Tibi and friend of Elie while they all lived in the musician's block.

Themes

Death

"Someone began to recite the Khaddish, the prayer for the dead. I do not know if it has ever happened before, in the long history of the Jews, that people have ever recited the prayer for the dead for themselves."

This moment of prayer comes right after arriving at Auschwitz—"Haven't you heard about it?''—when the group is being marched "to the crematory." They will not be killed (not yet) but the terror this welcome march inflicts serves to instill despondency, melancholia, and separation of the prisoners from each other. The Germans knew this, they knew that their prisoners could not have empathy: the faster the prisoners live for themselves alone, the faster they die together. Eliezer grasps

the message of their first walk, saying, "[h]umanity is not concerned with us." There is no one to witness their death and no one to mourn them with the right prayer except themselves. Later, when Akiba Drumer is selected for death, he asks them to recite the Khaddish for him—they forget to do so because they are preoccupied with survival.

Death is a pervasive element in a story about death camps. Death is fundamental to human society—anthropologists cite burial practices as the foundation of civilization. The Nazi "slaughterhouses" and "factories of death" are antithetical to this civilized practice of death; the Final Solution is an absolute mockery of human rights and values. The effect of this madness on persons normally a part of a culture organized around a detailed belief system, is a breakdown of their social compact with each other and a fall into melancholia. The incapacitating effect of the melancholia each prisoner had—worrying only about himself—lead to the utterly gross situations of a son killing a father for a bite of bread. Finally, it is within this breakdown of empathy among the people in the camps which makes the moment of Chlomo's final gasp—his son's name—and Juliek's swan song possibly beautiful but most likely pathetic to those hearing it.

Throughout the story, men, like Reizel, say they live only because they believe their children may still be alive. Eliezer admits several times that a similar relationship exists between himself and his father. Empathy and the human need of community in the face of death, so as to mourn properly, must be put back together afterward. This is why the stories of the camps must be told and not silenced. Only madness remains if mourning occurs without empathy—only the ghastly and solitary image of one survivor seeing himself in the mirror remains. The survivors must mourn with other survivors—"let's keep together. We shall be stronger''—if they are to escape the madness of the camps and the memory.

God and Religion

The community of faith to which Eliezer belongs is Hasidic. This is a sect of Judaism that came into being during the eighteenth century and its precepts have considerable bearing upon the events of the novel. Hasidism teaches belief in a personal relationship with God. In such a system, awe of God combines with emotion toward God. One can protest, love, fear, and question God without compromising God or contradicting faith. One of Wiesel's favorite prayers may serve as a summary: "Master of the Universe, know that the children of

Topics For Further Study

- How does Elie arrive at the conclusion that he is stronger than God?

- Talking with Jason Harris for the *Tamalpais News* in 1995, Wiesel offered this parable: "A man is walking alone in the woods; he's lost and looking for a way out. Suddenly he sees another man a short distance away from him. He runs over to the man and exclaims, 'Thank God you're here! I'm saved! Surely you know the way out!' to which the man responds, 'First of all: don't go back that way—he points—'I just came from there.'"

  If one considers 'there' as the subject of *Night,* what is Wiesel suggesting about modern morality? Does it hint at a positive future?

- Consider the following passage: "The stomach alone was aware of the passage of time." What is the function of time in the novel? What mind/body problems does Elie discover in his fight for survival? Lastly, consider that after all the suffering of the camp, Elie gets food poi-

soning at the end and almost dies; what were the health challenges of saving the camp survivors?

- Do some research into the Holocaust and compare the experience of the Jews, Gypsies, Jehovah's Witness, homosexuals, and others who were imprisoned. Then compare this to the experience of Japanese-Americans and Japanese-Canadians during World War II.

- Theodore Adorno once said, "it is barbaric to continue to write poetry after Auschwitz." What did he mean? Do you agree?

- Read through some of the international treaties on human rights or consider the topic of human rights generally. What role should international bodies play in imposing the idea of human rights on other nations (for example: consider Tibet or the Serbian camps of the 1980s)? When is it proper to intervene in another country's business?

Israel are suffering too much; they deserve redemption, they need it. But if, for reasons unknown to me, You are not willing, not yet, then redeem all the other nations, but do it soon!"

With this very brief summary in mind, the disposition of the prisoners grappling with the hell they are in begins to make some sense. Neither those who doubt or question God, as does Eliezer, nor those who never doubt, betray their faith. Hasidism is antagonistic, "man questions God and God answers. But we don't understand His answers." And yet it is true that the Shoah, or Holocaust, was too much for Eliezer to immediately reconcile with his religion. He was questioning but he was growing tired of God's silence.

A key figure in this system is Job, a biblical character whose faith in God was persecuted and tested in extremity. "How I sympathized with Job!" says Eliezer, "I did not deny God's existence, but I doubted his absolute justice." Comparatively, Job

had it easy. Yet the comparison with that biblical figure undermines the tendency to conclude that Eliezer lost his faith. He lost many things but he did not lose, entirely, his faith in the morality of a social compact among men with God. This is what is important, maintaining human dignity by maintaining the empathy of society—not the question of whether or not to fast on some holy day. But it takes the telling of the story of *Night* to realize this. Meanwhile, in the death camps, Eliezer confesses that "in the depths of my heart, I felt a great void" and "we forgot to say the Khaddish" for Akiba Drumer.

Sanity and Insanity

There are many examples of madness exhibited during the novel. Two in particular stand out as representing the greater insanity of the Holocaust. The first is the hysterical Madame Schachter and the second is Idek's enthusiasm for work—being more than a simply mockery of the motto "Work is liberty!".

The first example recalls Moshe the Beadle's attempt to warn his fellow Jews of the impending doom. They brushed him off while they were still apparently safe ("You don't die of [the Yellow Star] … " said Chlomo). When they realized he was right, it was too late. Finding themselves on a hermetically sealed cattle wagon in the dead of night, they are trapped with their worst fears. Madame Schachter begins screaming out their fear: being offered as burnt sacrifice to the Nazi ideal. They physically lash her. They pity her as merely mad because they cannot believe any real harm will come of their deportation. The Germans are human after all. Even Madame Schachter as madness is silenced when her screamed hallucinations become reality and the flames of the crematorium become visible from the cattle car window.

Kapo Idek "has bouts of madness now and then, when it's best to keep out of his way." That is, he is prone to fits of violence—something neither Eliezer nor his father could avoid forever. One Sunday Idek moved "hundreds of prisoners so that he could lie with a girl! It struck me as so funny that I burst out laughing." This self-indulgence is done with forethought; it is not a fit. He moves hundreds of hungry men just so that he might have sex. It goes beyond selfishness yet oddly represents the entire death camp process—all done for ideas held by a handful of men. The general response to the Nazi challenge cannot be a loss of faith (every character in the story that loses faith dies like Meir Katz) but a reinvention of humanity. As Wiesel has said elsewhere, "in a world of absurdity, we must invent reason; we must create beauty out of nothingness."

Style

Narrative

The novella is a short piece of fiction that is based on the author's 800-page memoir of his time in the Nazi death camps. The shortened tale is told from a first person point of view. There is no attempt to enter other minds and little attempt to explain what is on the narrator's mind. The sole purpose of the book is to relate briefly and succinctly what happened. The reader's conclusions are meant to be independent although they have been lead, quite consciously, toward an abhorrence of the moral vacuum presented in the camps.

Semantics

The problem of capturing the unrepresentable, or sublime, into an art product has not been impossible since the Roman treatise on the topic by Longinus. Using examples from the Old Testament (particularly Genesis and Job), the *Iliad*, and poetry, he displayed the successful methods for capturing nature in verse, ecstasy in poetry, the abyss in myth, and supreme beings in mere names. As a result, Occidental aesthetics views nothing as beyond the ability of the well-trained artist to present it in a packaged form.

Nevertheless, the moral chaos and utter hell that was the Holocaust surpassed any previously recorded human abyss. For some, even fifty years later, it has broken the aesthetic mold of Longinus; how is it possible to comprehend, let alone represent, this most awful of all events? Not easily, yet Wiesel's methods resemble those humans who preceded him in the effort to understand the horrible and sublime by representing their experience in one form or other. It is through that artistic effort that comprehension comes.

The means of representing the unrepresentable are the techniques of the sparse and staccato. In this case, those techniques are used to keep the reader, as much as possible, in mind of how precious is the breath of air the death camp inmates survive on. Words are used sparingly and, when possible, blank space is used instead.

The terse sentences remind the reader of the necessity of conserving energy: one is meant to be bothered by the apparent waste of Eliezer's run across the camp (at the end of a workday) to check on his father. Generally, scenes are made up of few words yet loom large; the storyteller relies on the imagination of the audience, rather than on his ability. He places the dots and hints at the color, but the reader creates the image. Sentences like: "An open tomb", "Never", "The gate to the camp opened." They are fragments, scraps of evidence that remain until they are sown together into a narrative which makes sense of what happened. The narrative replaces the useless pictures the GIs took when they liberated the camps. The struggle of representing the unrepresentable horror, as Wiesel discovered, is best accomplished in the same way that Longinus felt the writers of the Talmud did—with few words and plenty of space for digestion.

Allusion

Night is full of scriptural allusions, or hints of reference to biblical passages. In fact, the very timelessness of the constant night is reminiscent of supernatural tales. Hasidic tales especially do not follow Occidental notions but develop their own time according to the message of the story. "Time," says Sibelman, "is represented as a creative force, a bridge sinking man to eternity." Within the story time are more direct allusions to particular stories. Two of the most memorable examples will suffice to demonstrate.

Immediately after realizing that the group is not marching into the death pit, there is the incantation, "Never shall I forget that night, the first night in camp …" etc. This passage is a pastiche of Psalm 150. In French (and Wiesel writes in French or Yiddish), the start of each line begins with *Jamais* (meaning never). Psalm 150 praises God for his works and deeds while the "Never" passage commits just the opposite reality to memory.

Another example of allusion is the execution of the three prisoners. One of these doomed prisoners is an innocent child, a pipel. This scene recalls the moment in the Christian Gospel when Christ is crucified. In the Gospel according to Matthew, he is accompanied by two thieves. At the point of expiration, Christ asks God why he has been forsaken. At death, the sky darkens and the onlookers murmur that this was definitely the Son of God. In contradistinction, the death of the pipel bothers the onlookers in the opposite way. There is still a look for God but this time, "[w]here is he? Here He is—He is hanging here on the gallows … "

Anti-bildungsroman

Traditionally, the bildungsroman in German literature is the story of a young, naive, man entering the world to seek adventure. He finds his adventure but it provides him with an important lesson. The denouement finds him happy, wiser, and ready for a productive life. The classic example is J.W. von Goethe's *Wilhelm Meister's Apprenticeship.*

Wiesel's novella turns this tradition on its head. He presents an educated young man forced into a hell made by human hands. There he learns more wisdom than he asked for, even when he dreamed of learning the mystical tradition. What he learns about human behavior he would rather not apply. In the end, he sees himself in the mirror, for the first time in several years, as a corpse. The result is not that he will think about being a productive worker, but about healing humanity.

Historical Context

The Eisenhower Years

Eisnehower was re-elected in 1956 to continue his leadership of an America that had emerged literally overnight as the most awesome industrial military complex the world had ever seen. At the start of WWII, while Hitler was invading Poland, there were more men employed in Henry Ford's car plants than in the Army. However, the U. S. had what nobody else on the planet did—an incredible surplus of electric power. The Grand Coulee and Bonneville Dams had just been completed with the result that immediately in 1942 the European skies were full of American planes—planes that could be instantly replaced. All this wartime manufacture was retooled for the domestic economy to produce record numbers of cars, jeeps, appliances, track housing, and a whole range of consumer items to be seen in glossy magazines like *Life* and *Playboy.* The Broadway hit about the Holocaust, *The Diary of Anne Frank,* was awarded the Pulitzer and on the television Elvis could only be shown from the waist up while singing the hit song, "Blue Suede Shoes." Real wages and the GNP were up.

Taking advantage of the opportunities offered by the military industrial strength were thousands of GI's who returned from war, went to school, and by the mid-1950s were settled in suburban housing developments. This led to new myths of domesticity. The dependence on the car was immediately born and Congress passed the Federal Highway Act authorizing the construction of 42,500 miles of roads. Along with the car, the mythological love affair with the nuclear family was born and defined. It was more of a geographical definition necessitated by the sudden separation brought by suburbia to the extended family complex. Underneath the jubilation of this prosperity there was a growing anxiety over the Soviet Union and an increasing volume of dissent from America's minorities.

Cold War

The phrase, "Cold War", was first used to describe U.S.-Soviet relations in 1947. But in 1956 there were evident signs of this war as well as a distinct development of an independent Chinese socialism. The most famous of Cold War signs became Nikita Kruschchev's welcome of Western ambassadors on November 17 when he said, "History is on our side. We will bury you!" In turn Kruschchev's repudiation of the Stalinist era opened

Compare
&
Contrast

- **1956:** The Holocaust, outside of Israel, is not discussed. The nearest approach is the reworking of Anne Frank's story for the stage.

  Today: Ignoring the rightwing extremists who deny the Holocaust ever happened, recent years have seen a number of mourning activities for Holocaust victims. Elie Wiesel was named head of the Swiss Holocaust Fund. All across Germany, memorials, art works, and peace shrines have been raised. Art has been returned and Spielberg's *Schindler's List* has been viewed by millions of people around the world. Holocaust museums have been opened in several cities and archives set up for the recording of survivor testimony.

- **1956:** The Cold War "heats" up as suburban dwellers construct bomb shelters in their backyards. At school, the kids practice air raid drills.

  Today: The Cold War has ended. The U. S. and Russia are almost partners both politically and economically. Unfortunately, little has altered in terms of nuclear targeting by either country.

- **1956:** Canada assists India with a nuclear energy program.

  Today: Both Pakistan and India have nuclear capabilities aimed at deterring the other.

- **1956:** It is a tense year in the Middle East due to disagreements over the Suez canal.

  Today: Tensions run high in the Middle East because the peace process stalls between Israel and the Palestinian Liberation Organization.

---

a rift between Soviet communism and that occurring in China. Mao Zedong reacted to Kruschchev with his speech, "On the Ten Great Relationships." There he outlined a peasant and agrarian focused structure in which the peasant would have economic consuming power. Thus, he rejected the Soviet emphasis on heavy industry.

This personal exchange was in the fall of a year that saw acceleration in the arms race. After Soviet authorities suppressed Polish and Hungarian revolts in February, the Soviets occupied Hungary and used the excuse to install intermediate ballistic missiles whose range put southern Europe on guard. Eisenhower offered asylum to all Hungarian "freedom fighters" but made no other move. The U.S. military answered the Soviet missile deployment by exploding its first airborne hydrogen bomb in May and carrying out a series of nuclear tests in the Pacific. The U.S. also developed the Polaris missile; it is a nuclear warhead that can be launched from a submarine.

Middle East

Israel accepted a UN proposed truce with Jordan that was soon followed by cease-fire agreements with Lebanon and Syria. However, the Soviets refused to allow either U.S. or British troops to patrol the cease-fire. Soviet threats were not taken too seriously. Meanwhile, an alliance formed between Saudi Arabia, Yemen and Egypt. For Israel it was a tense year but a decade of peace followed—broken by the 1967 Six Day War over the Sinai.

In early summer 1956, President Nasser of Egypt announced the Suez Canal Company's concession would not be renewed in 1968. A few weeks later, after British troops departed, he declared the company illegal and ordered its seizure. British and French nationals left Egypt while their prospective ambassadors submitted the matter of the canal to the UN. The Suez Crisis also had the delayed effect of a whole community of Jews being expelled from Egypt. In the fall of 1956, Britain, France and Israel militarily reacted to Egyptian actions. The result was a complete grounding of the Egyptian air force, occupation of the Sinai by British and French troops, and a low in Anglo-American relations. By January of 1957, however, the Suez was restored to Egypt and France was reconciled to the US.

Jewish women and children enroute to Auschwitz.

Human Political Relations

The U.S. Supreme Court outlawed racial segregation in April and, soon after, the bus boycott of Montgomery began after the insubordination of Rosa Parks. Martin Luther King accepted leadership of the boycott and the Civil Rights Movement went full speed ahead.

The Nationalist government of South Africa admitted its plan to remove 60,000 mixed-blood "colored" from the voting rolls of Cape Province. In late summer, 100,000 non-whites were forcibly evicted from their homes to make room for whites.

In China, the killings continued. From 1949 to 1960, it is estimated that 26.3 million people were killed for resisting communization.

Technology

The first successful videotape recorder is demonstrated in Redwood City, CA. Nuclear power is seen as the way of the future as well as a necessary component of a nuclear weapons arsenal. Uranium deposits found north of Saskatchewan's Lake Athabasca make that Canadian province the number one uranium producer in the world. Canada pledges to assist India with its nuclear power program so long as the plants are not used for the development of weapon grade plutonium.

Critical Overview

The reception of *Night* has remained consistent. The book did not fetch a high price and the criticism upon its publication was favorable but superficial. Reviewers were quick to empathize with the narrative but offered nothing in the way of critique or constructive engagement.

As time passed, however, critics like Simon P. Sibelman have approached the work as an ethical treatise demanding reflection. They have begun to ask Wiesel's question, "what is the state of our morality at the dawn of the next century?" Critics have also grappled with how Wiesel accomplished what many said couldn't be done—transcribe the horror of the holocaust into literary form. Thus, while Wiesel's book makes no distinguishing claim between art and life, a few critics have explored what has come to be known as the Holocaust aesthetic. Most reviews suggest the novel as compulsory for anyone concerned about civilization. Few want to accept it for what it is, a gentle voice of reason asking us to never allow the Holocaust to recur.

W. H. Hager's review for the *Christian Century* is typical of early reviews. Hager says blandly, "... it is a personal record of a child's experience.

As such it should be given a place beside Anne Frank's diary ... The worst tragedy is always the death of God in the human soul and when we see it happen to a child who has come face to face with man's evil inhumanity to man we are made to know how dark the night of the soul can be. There are unforgettable moments—like that when the Polish Juliek plays Beethoven among the corpses." Already, he was repeating what had been said in the August, 1960, issue of *Kirkus*. There the review made an "inevitable comparison with Anne Frank."

The New Yorker repeated the norm but offered a little more insight in its March 18, 1961, issue. "The author's style is precise and brief; he catches a person or a scene in a sentence. He lacks self-pity but not self-awareness." Nothing, however, was said about other semantic aspects like Wiesel's use of silence and white space.

Not all early reviews were unimaginative. Robert Alter, in "Elie Wiesel: Between Hangman and Victim," notes the role of mystical Hasidism in the story. He also declares that *Night* is only the beginning—the factual grounding—for a man whose "imaginative courage ... endows [his] factually precise writing with a hallucinated more-than-realism: [Wiesel] is able to confront the horror with a nakedly self-exposed honesty rare even among writers who went through the same ordeal."

Alter then goes on to compare Wiesel's imaginative landscape with the lyric love poetry of John Donne. This is a refreshing occurrence where one would expect to see a reference to Anne Frank. Alter perceives lyric love poetry as a likely predecessor to Wiesel's work. In his interpretation, lyric love poetry was the last time writers were so focused on the minutiae of, in their case, the lover and beloved. Alter contends that Wiesel is minutely focused on the relationship between executioners, victims, and spectators.

"Wiesel has been considered the chief novelist of the holocaust ... [because he] succeeded in blending Jewish philosophy, mythology, and historical experience," said Lothar Kahn in "Elie Wiesel: Neo-Hasidism" (1968). In the late 1970s, Wiesel's work was assessed in the 1978 book by Rosenfeld and Greenberg entitled, *Confronting the Holocaust*. Michael Berenbaum explored the trial of faith that Eliezer witnessed in his *The Vision of the Void: Theological Reflections on the Works of Elie Wiesel*.

In 1982, Ellen S. Fine published a study of the novella, *Legacy of Night; The Literary Universe of Elie Wiesel*. Keeping with Wiesel, Fine does not draw lines between life and literature. Her book is about the Holocaust, primarily Elie Wiesel's Holocaust. "The thrust of Wiesel's writing does not lie in his literary techniques and he has openly rejected the notion of art for art's sake. He is basically a storyteller with something to say." Being a storyteller has made him a good lecturer and spokesman. Fine argues that taken together, Wiesel's fiction forms a whole work with repeated and varied motifs. His work tells a continuous story of a survivor with memories.

D. L. Vanderwerken's essay explored the traditional genre of bildungsroman and its relationship to Wiesel's work. In his "Wiesel *Night* as Anti-bildungsroman," he makes comparisons with writers like Saul Bellow and Ralph Ellison to show how Eliezer is part of a new fictional hero development. This new hero is worldly to start with, discovers a more devastating wisdom, and is not even happy to be left alive at the end.

The most recent book-length analysis of Wiesel's fiction is Simon P. Sibelman's *Silence in the Novels of Elie Wiesel*. There he presents Wiesel as a *navi,* a prophet, who speaks in order to move others "to review the course of life [and, thereby,] redefine the human condition." Sibleman spends a good deal of the book showing how Wiesel's techniques work toward this end. He discusses how Wiesel uses the semantics of page layout to add to the sense-blank pages and paragraphs made up of one short sentence.

Night remains one of the most powerful literary expressions of the Holocaust. It has been responsible for sharing the Holocaust with millions of people who then register their reaction to the bleak, horrific events in the novel. The novel continues to question the role of literature in our society—a society still dealing with the memory of the Holocaust.

Criticism

Jane Elizabeth Dougherty

Dougherty is a doctoral candidate in English at Tufts University. In the following essay, she discusses themes of faith and disbelief in Night.

Elie Wiesel's *Night* was first published in an English translation in 1960; it is a slightly fictionalized account of Wiesel's experiences as a concentration camp survivor. His first attempt to write

What Do I Read Next?

- *Night* is the beginning of Wiesel's oeuvre and of a trilogy. The next two works are *L'aube* (*Dawn*, 1961) and *Le Jour* (*The Accident*, 1961) and revolve around survivors of the Holocaust and the way they deal with the memories of the camps.

- Wiesel's 1962 work, *The Town Beyond the Wall*, concerns a Holocaust survivor who returns to Hungary to confront his Nazi persecutors. Rather than find relief, the man discovers that his revenge denies and displaces moral responsibility. There is no satisfaction in revenge.

- The ever popular story of the young girl Anne Frank, *Diary of a Young Girl* (1947) tells of a group of Jews coping with the unbearable stress of hiding from the Nazis. Eventually they are discovered. The diary has been adapted brilliantly for stage and film and remains the favorite memento of the Holocaust.

- Far from the Holocaust, but contemporary with Wiesel's *Night* are the works of Saul Bellow. His *Seize the Day* was published in 1956 and deals with the father/son relationship differently than Wiesel does. Both can be read in terms of the Abraham/Isaac motif. Together, the two works are stark contrasts, yet the hero in both works is haunted by the pressure of responsibility to his father.

- Though some have difficulty with the idea that such a serious topic as the Holocaust would be treated in such a genre as the graphic novel, Art Spiegelman's 1980-1991 collection *Maus* is a brilliant synopsis of the Holocaust. With cats as Nazis, mice as Jews, and pigs as Poles, the novel exposes more of the tensions that are involved in moments of moral chaos than could be possible covered in one person's memory of the nightmare.

- The 1995 novel by Gerda Weissmann Klein called *All but My Life*, tells the story of her experience in World War II. It begins in the pre-war days of Poland and continues through her three-year stay in German work camps. The story ends happily—she marries the American lieutenant who is part of American force liberating the camp. This book is very different from other Holocaust stories because Klein writes about emotions more than about the ethics of the horror.

- Contemporary with the round up and deportation of Jews in Europe, the Japanese in the United States and Canada were also imprisoned. The story of *Obasan*, by Joy Kogawa (1981), tells the tale of how the hysterical fear of invasion by the Japanese lead to the exile of Canadian citizens with Japanese ancestry. They were forced to live in camps in the interior and were not allowed to resume life as full citizens until the early 1950s.

- One contemporary of Elie Wiesel was the poet and beatnik Allen Ginsberg. His poetry reflected much on the suffering of humanity as well as the suffering of his own people in the camps. Late in the 1950s, he brought together a collection of poems entitled *Kaddish and Other Poems*. The poem *Kaddish* itself is a personalizing of the Jewish hymn of mourning for his mother who died insane in 1956.

---

about his experiences was written in Yiddish and contained some eight hundred pages; the English translation of the French version of those experiences, *Night,* is less than a hundred and fifty pages. It is episodic in structure, with only a few key scenes in each chapter serving to illustrate the themes of the work. One of the most important of these themes is faith, and specifically Eliezer's struggle to retain his faith in God, in himself, in humanity, and in words themselves, in spite of the disbelief, degradation and destruction of the concentration camp universe.

Night opens in 1943, during a time when Hungary's Jews were still largely untouched by the horrors of the Holocaust. It begins with a description of Moshe the Beadle, who is instructing the pious young Eliezer in the mysteries of the *cabbala,* Jewish mysticism. Eliezer's education is interrupted when Moshe is deported with the other foreign-born Jews of Sighet. Moshe returns to Sighet with an almost unbelievable story: all the Jews with whom he was deported have been massacred. The villagers react with disbelief; they denounce him as a madman. As Ora Avni writes, this first episode of *Night* reminds the reader of the perils of disbelief.

Wiesel, the writer, occupies the same position as Moshe is the story: he is telling stories that are too horrible to be believed, and yet they are true. As Lucy Dawidowicz writes, "To comprehend the strange and unfamiliar, the human mind proceeds from the reality of experience by applying reason, logic, and analogy … The Jews, in their earliest encounters with the anti-Jewish policies of Hitler's Germany, saw their situation as a retro version of their history, but in their ultimate experience with the Final Solution, historical experience … failed them as explanation."

The Jews of Sighet cannot believe Moshe's stories because nothing in their experience has prepared them for the knowledge that the very fact of their existence is punishable by death. His warnings go unheeded, even after the Fascists come to power in Hungary, even after German troops appear in Sighet, even after two Jewish ghettoes are created, then rapidly liquidated, right up until the moment the last group of Jews from Sighet arrives at Birkenau. It is only as they disembark from the train, aware of the smell of burning flesh, that they recognize the consequences of their disbelief; faith in Moshe's stories might have given them the impetus to flee, to hide, or to resist before it was too late.

Night has been described as a "negative *Bildungsroman,*" a coming-of-age story in which, rather than finding his identity as a young hero would typically do, Eliezer progressively loses his identity throughout the course of the narrative. This identity-disintegration is experienced individually and collectively and symbolized in the early parts of the text by the loss of possessions. After the Jews of Sighet learn that they are to be deported, they abandon religious objects in the backyard of Eliezer's family. Later, while they are waiting to be deported, they are forced to relieve themselves on the floor of their own holy place, the synagogue.

Judaism, the shared faith in the special Jewish covenant with God which sustains Eliezer and his community, is one of the things which the villagers are forced to give up; indeed, their religion is what has marked them to be condemned. Nothing in Eliezer's religious studies has prepared him for the sight of children being burned alive in pits, a sight made all the more horrific for readers by our knowledge of his own youth and the youth of his sister Tzipora, from whom he has just been separated forever. Wiesel writes, in a now-famous passage:

> "Never shall I forget that night, the first night in camp, which has turned my life into one long night, seven times cursed and seven times sealed. Never shall I forget that smoke. Never shall I forget the little faces of the children, whose bodies I saw turned into wreaths of smoke beneath a silent blue sky. Never shall I forget those flames which consumed my faith forever. Never shall I forget that nocturnal silence which deprived me, for all eternity, of the desire to live. Never shall I forget those moments which murdered my God and my soul and turned my dreams to dust. Never shall I forget these things, even if I am condemned to live as long as God Himself. Never."

Eliezer's faith in himself, in God and in humanity has been consumed, and the horror of this annihilation is underscored by the way Wiesel structures this passage; in its repetition, it is like a prayer. Simon Sibelman writes that "Wiesel composes a new psalm, one which reflects the negativity of Auschwitz and the eclipse of God."

The religious traditions of Judaism, then, are both inadequate to comprehend the existence of Auschwitz and almost impossible to practice there. The men in the camp debate whether or not the observances of Rosh Hashanah and Yom Kippur, required of them by the Jewish covenant with God, are still required after God has betrayed them by breaking that covenant. Eliezer describes eating on Yom Kippur, traditionally a day of fasting and atonement for sins, as an act of defiance against a God in whose mercy he no longer believes. Yet he feels a great emptiness within him, as his identity, and thus his humanity, has depended on his membership in the Jewish community, a community which is being destroyed around him. He writes of meeting his father on Rosh Hashanah, the Jewish New Year, a day when his disbelief makes him feel alone in the universe:

> "I ran off to look for my father. And at the same time I was afraid of having to wish him a Happy New Year when I no longer believed it.
>
> He was standing near the wall, bowed down, his shoulders sagging as though beneath a heavy burden. I went up to him, took his hand and kissed it. A tear fell upon it. Whose was that tear? Mine? His? I said nothing. Nor did he. We had never understood each other so clearly."

In this passage, Eliezer silently shares his grief with his father; the horrors of Auschwitz have stripped their holiest holidays of all meaning and the loss is grievous to them both. Yet at other times, Wiesel suggests that faith is crucial to surviving in the concentration camp. Akiba Drumer, who had been so devout, makes the conscious decision to die after he loses his faith. Meir Katz, who had been so strong, is broken by his loss of faith and dies on the last night of the transport to Buchenwald. Wiesel has written elsewhere that "it is permissible for man to accuse God, provided it be done in the name of faith in God." In other words, Eliezer's ability to argue with God, as he learned during his study of the *cabbala,* is itself a kind of faith in God, a faith that helps him to survive the camps.

Faith is the cornerstone of a relationship with God; it is also the cornerstone of Eliezer's relationships with others, which in turn give him a sense of his own identity. It is shared faith in God which binds the Jews of Sighet together, and it is faith in each other which makes those relationships viable and strong.

The most important relationship in *Night,* and one which illustrates the power of faith and of disbelief, is Eliezer's relationship with his father. After the two are separated from the rest of their family, Eliezer's only thought is not to lose his father. Several times in the story, Eliezer saves his father's life, sometimes risking his own, as he does when he rescues his father from the line of men who have been condemned. As Ted Estess writes, "Eliezer makes only one thing necessary to him: absolute fidelity to his father. God has broken His covenant, His promises to His people; Eliezer, in contrast, determines … not to violate his covenant with his father." Yet Eliezer is haunted by a desire to abandon his father, and is filled with doubts about his own ability to keep the covenant between them. He is given contradictory advice by two veterans of Auschwitz; one tells the newly-arrived men that they must band together in order to survive, while another tells Eliezer that he is better off without worrying about anyone but himself.

Night contains many scenes where fathers and sons are separated, where the son turns on the father or abandons him. Rabbi Eliahou's faith in his son's love has kept him alive, and thus Eliezer is thankful that he has not revealed that Rabbi Eliahou's son has deliberately abandoned him. He also prays to ask for the strength never to do what Rabbi Eliahou's son has done. When Eliezer's father dies, he feels relief, yet Wiesel writes nothing of Eliezer's time in Buchenwald after the death of his father, because Eliezer feels that he himself has died. Wiesel suggests that though the guards pit loved ones against each other, wanting to impose a system of "every man for himself," the men must find the strength to have faith in each other and in their own ability to resist this almost inexorable pressure. As Ellen Fine writes, "to care for another shows the persistence of self in a system principally designed to annihilate the self."

Eliezer's silence, which occurs when his father dies, symbolizes his virtual death. Language is the underpinning of human relationships, and is itself bound up in notions of faith and disbelief. Martin Buber writes that "language … represents communion, communication, and community," and communication through language depends on faith in shared experiences and concepts. Wiesel asserts that the only word that still has meaning at Auschwitz is "furnace," because the smell of burning flesh makes it real. The other words, then, have lost their meanings, symbolized by the sign proclaiming that "Work Means Freedom."

In fact, at Auschwitz, work means a slower death than that inflicted on those who were killed immediately. A "doctor" is someone, like Dr. Mengele, who selects people for death rather than saving them from it. A "son" can kill, rather than respect, his father. Like prayer, words themselves are perverted in the concentration camp universe, and Eliezer loses faith in their ability to achieve communion with God, to communicate with others, or to bind people together in a community. His last loss of faith is his loss of faith in words themselves, which causes him to withdraw into silence and disrupts the narrative itself.

Wiesel's writings after *Night* have been attempts to reclaim faith in language, in humanity, in God, and in himself. In *Night,* faith seems an incredible burden, a hindrance to survival, and yet it remains the only way in which the Jews can survive the horrors of the Holocaust. In the context of the concentration camp universe, Wiesel suggests that the only thing more dangerous than faith is disbelief.

Source: Jane Elizabeth Dougherty, in an essay for *Novels for Students,* Gale, 1998.

Lea Hamaoui

A discussion of Wiesel's eloquent narrative as a means of understanding history and human meaning.

What follows is an attempt to study the ways in which a traumatic historical experience shapes narrative in a powerful example of this genre, Elie Wiesel's *Night*. It is my conviction that in groping toward formal and literary understanding of such texts, we move closer to the human meanings that the violent world we live in has all but erased.

To render historical horror is to render, by definition, that which exceeds rendering; it projects pain for which there is no solace, no larger consolation, no redemptive possibility. The implications, both formal and aesthetic, for such a rendering are critical. The great tragedies negotiate exactly such a balance. King Lear's terrible journey from blindness to insight brings him reunion with loyal Cordelia even as he loses her and the restoration of the Kingdom is not far behind. The young Eliezer staring into the mirror upon his liberation from Buchenwald has also gained knowledge, but this knowledge in no way justifies the sufferings that preceeded it. It is not a sign of positive spiritual development. Nor is it linked to restorative changes in the moral and political realm. *Night* is not about a moral political order violated and restored, but about the shattering of the idea of such an order.

It is clear enough that in comparing *King Lear* and Wiesel's *Night* we do violence to both. But the juxtaposition throws light on a crucial aesthetic issue. It helps us define the experience of a work like *Night* and moves our inquiry in the direction of the specific means by which the writer shapes that experience.

Lear's death is the death of an old man, flawed like ourselves, vulnerable like ourselves, a character with whom a powerful emotional transaction and bonds of identification have been established over the course of the play. In Lear's death we reexperience the tragic dimensions of our own experience. The play articulates, in symbolic form, an existential pain we could hardly afford to articulate ourselves. But it is pain that, no matter how great, is contained, since the very act of its symbolic articulation also gives form, and therefore limits or boundaries, to that pain.

Night proceeds from experience that is not universal. It does not expand from kernels of the familiar but from the unfamiliar, from data in historical reality. The deaths of Eliezer's father, of Akiva Drummer, of Juliek the violinist and of Meir Katz are different because, after all of the pain, there is nothing to be extracted by way of compensation. They are not symbolic but very real, and we experience, not a purging of feelings tapped but

> *Never shall I forget those moments which murdered my God and my soul and turned my dreams to dust. Never shall I forget these things, even if I am condemned to live as long as God Himself. Never."*
>
> —*Wiesel*

the fear of the unpredictable in life to which we, like the Jews of *Night,* are subject.

If symbol is something that stands in place of something else, the historical narrative does not stand in place of our experience, but alongside it. We experience historical narrative much the way we experience a neighbor's report of his or her visit to a place we have not ourselves visited. The report is informational—it is "adjacent" to our experience, neither interpretive nor metaphorical nor symbolic. It is "other" than our experience but also part of the same historical matrix within which we experience the flow of our own lives. *Night* threatens and disturbs in a way that symbolic narrative does not.

Night is Wiesel's attempt to bring word of the death camps back to humanity in such a form that his message, unlike that of Moshe the Beadle to Eliezer and to the Jews of Sighet, will not be rejected. The word I wish to stress here is *form.* The work, which is eyewitness account, is also much more than eyewitness account. In its rhetorical and aesthetic design, *Night* is shaped by the problematic of historical horror and by the resistances, both psychic and formal, to the knowledge Wiesel would convey.

When the narrator, Eliezer, sees a lorry filled with children who are dumped into a fiery ditch, he cannot believe what he has seen: "I pinched my face. Was I alive? Was I awake? I could not believe it. How could it be possible for them to burn people, children, and for the world to keep silent? No, none of this could be true. It was a nightmare."

Eliezer cannot believe what is before his eyes. His disbelief seems to numb him physically—he pinches his face to ascertain that the medium of that vision, his body, is alive, perceiving, present. So fundamental is the horror to which he is an eyewitness that seeing comes at the expense of his bodily awareness of himself as a vital and perceiving entity. What Eliezer witnesses contradicts psychic underpinnings of existence so thoroughly that his very awareness brings with it feelings of deadness.

It is precisely this moment, this confrontation with data that negates the human impulses and ideas that structure our lives, with which Wiesel is concerned. We cannot know that which we cannot know. In order to bring the fact of Auschwitz to us, Wiesel must deal with the inherent difficulty of assimilating the truth he would portray.

His method is simple, brilliant and depends upon a series of repetitions in which what is at stake is a breakdown of critical illusions. At this level, the experience of the reader reading the narrative is structurally parallel to his experience of life, at least as Karl Popper describes it. Life, in Popper's view,

> resembles the experience of a blind person who runs into an obstacle and thereby experiences its existence. Through the falsification of our assumptions we actually make contact with "reality." The refutation of our errors is the positive experience we gain from reality. [*Toward an Aesthetic of Reception*, 1982]

Eliezer's tale is the story of a series of shattered expectations, his and our own. The repetition of this "disappointment," of optimism proven hollow and warnings rejected, becomes the crucial aesthetic fact or condition within which we then experience the narrator's account of his experiences in Auschwitz, in Buna, in Gleiwitz, and in Buchenwald. In this way we come to experience the account of the death camps as an account cleansed of past illusion, pristine in its terrible truth.

The quest for this truth is established at the outset of the narrative in the figure of Moshe the Beadle. Eliezer is devoted to his studies of Talmud. His decision to study Kabbalah with Moshe focuses the narrative on the problematic of reality and imbues it with the spiritual longings of this quest.

> There are a thousand and one gates leading into the orchard of mystical truth. Every human being has his own gate...

> And Moshe the Beadle, the poor barefoot of Sighet, talked to me for long hours of the revelations and mysteries of the *cabbala*. It was with him that my initiation began. We would read together, ten times over, the same page of the Zohar. Not to learn it by heart, but to extract the divine essence from it.

And throughout those evenings a conviction grew in me that Moshe the Beadle would draw me with him into eternity, into that time where question and answer would become *one*.

The book, which begins with Eliezer's search for a teacher of mystical knowledge and ends with Eliezer's contemplating his image in a mirror after his liberation from Buchenwald, proposes a search for ultimate knowledge in terms that are traditional, while the knowledge it offers consists of data that is historical, radical, and subversive.

If directionality of the narrative is established early, a counter-direction makes itself felt very quickly. Following Eliezer's dream of a formal harmony, eternity and oneness toward which Moshe would take him, Eliezer's initiation into the "real" begins:

> Then one day they expelled all the foreign Jews from Sighet. And Moshe the Beadle was a foreigner.

> Crammed into cattle trains by Hungarian police, they wept bitterly. We stood on the platform and wept too.

Moshe is shot but escapes from a mass grave in one of the Galician forests of Poland near Kolomaye and returns to Sighet in order to warn the Jews there. He describes children used as targets for machine guns and the fate of a neighbor, Malka, and of Tobias the tailor.

From this point onward in the narrative, a powerful counter direction of flight away from truth, knowledge, reality, and history is set into motion. Moshe is not believed, not even by his disciple, Eliezer. The Jews of Sighet resist the news Moshe has brought them:

> I wanted to come back to Sighet to tell you the story of my death ... And see how it is, no one will listen to me ...

> And we, the Jews of Sighet, were waiting for better days, which would not be long in coming now.

> Yes, we even doubted that he [Hitler] wanted to exterminate us.

> Was he going to wipe out a whole people? Could he exterminate a population scattered throughout so many countries? So many millions! What method could he use? And in the middle of the twentieth century?

Optimism persists with the arrival of the Germans. After Sighet is divided into a big and little ghetto, Wiesel writes, "little by little life returned to normal. The barbed wire which fenced us in did not cause us any real fear."

While the narrative presses simultaneously toward and away from the "real," the real events befalling the Jews of Sighet are perceived as unreal:

On everyone's back was a pack … Here came the Rabbi, his back bent, his face shaved, his pack on his back. His mere presence among the deportees added a touch of unreality to the scene. It was like a page torn from some story book, from some historical novel about the captivity of Babylon or the Spanish Inquisition.

The intensity of the resistance peaks in the boxcar in which Eliezer and his family are taken to the death camp. Madame Schächter, distraught by the separation from her pious husband and two older sons, has visions of fire: "Jews, listen to me! I can see a fire! There are huge flames! It is a furnace!" Her words prey on nerves, fan fears, dispel illusion: "We felt that an abyss was about to open beneath our bodies." She is gagged and beaten. As her cries are silenced the chimneys of Auschwitz come into view:

> We had forgotten the existence of Madame Schächter. Suddenly we heard terrible screams: Jews, look! Look through the window! Flames! Look!

> And as the train stopped, we saw this time that flames were gushing out of a tall chimney into the black sky.

The movement toward and away from the knowledge of historical horror that Moshe the Beadle brings back from the mass grave and the violence that erupts when precious illusions are disturbed, shapes the narrative of *Night*. The portrait and analysis of the resistances to knowing help situate the reader in relation to the historical narrative and imbue the narrative with the felt historicity of the world outside the book. Eliezer's rejection of the knowledge that Moshe brings back, literally, from the grave, predicts our own rejection of that knowledge. His failure to believe the witness prepares the reader for the reception of Eliezer's own story of his experience in Auschwitz by first examining the defenses that Eliezer, and, thereby, implicitly, the reader, would bring to descriptions of Auschwitz. The rejection of Moshe strips the reader of his own deafness in advance of the arrival at Auschwitz.

Once stripped of his defenses, the reader moves from a fortified, to an open, undefended position vis-à-vis the impact of the narrative. Because the lines between narrative art and life have been erased, Wiesel brings the reader into an existential relationship to the historical experience recounted in *Night*. By virtue of that relationship, the reader is transformed into a witness. The act of witnessing is ongoing for most of the narrative, a narrative that is rife with horror and with the formal dissonances that historically experienced horror must inflict upon language.

Human extremity challenges all formal representation of it. It brings the world of language and the world outside language into the uncomfortable position of two adjacent notes on a piano keyboard that are simultaneously pressed and held. The sounds they produce jar the ear. In a work of historical horror, language and life, expression and experience are perceived as separate opaque structures, each of which is inadequate to encompass the abyss that separates them.

The most powerful passages in *Night* are those that mark Eliezer's arrival in Auschwitz. The family is separated. Eliezer and his father go through a selection and manage to stay together. Eliezer watches a truck drop living children into a ditch full of flames. He and his father conclude that this is to be Eliezer's fate as well. Eliezer decides he will run into an electrified wire fence and electrocute himself rather than face an excruciating death in the flaming ditch.

The moment is extraordinary and extreme beyond the wildest of human imaginings. Hearing his fellow Jews murmur the Kaddish, a formula of praise of the Almighty that is the traditional prayer for the dead, Eliezer revolts: "For the first time, I felt revolt rise up in me. Why should I bless His name? The Eternal Lord of the Universe, the All-Powerful and Terrible, was silent. What had I to thank Him for?" The Jews continue their march and Eliezer begins to count the steps before he will jump at the wire:

> Ten steps still. Eight. Seven. We marched slowly on, as though following a hearse at our own funeral … There it was now, right in front of us, the pit and its flames. I gathered all that was left of my strength, so that I could break from the ranks and throw myself upon the barbed wire. In the depths of my heart, I bade farewell to my father, to the whole universe.

And the words of the Kaddish, hallowed by centuries and disavowed only moments before, words of praise and of affirmation of divine oneness, spring unbidden to his lips: "and in spite of myself, the words formed themselves and issued in a whisper from my lips: *Yitgadal veyitkadach shme raba* … May His name be blessed and magnified." Eliezer does not run to the wire. The entire group turns left and enters a barracks.

The question of formal dissonance in *Night* is revealing. The narrative that would represent historical horror works, finally, against the grain of the reader and of the psychic structures that demand the acknowledgments, resolutions, closure, equivalence, and balances that are enacted in *Lear*. When Cordelia is killed in Shakespeare's play, Lear's sanity gives way and, finally, his life as well. Holding her lifeless body in his arms Lear cries out against heaven, "Howl, howl, howl! O you men of stone. / Had I your tongues and eyes, I'd use them / That heaven's vault should break." [*The Complete Works of Shakespeare,* 1238] The scene, terrible as it is, formally restores the balance disturbed by Cordelia's murder by virtue of the linguistic energies and dramatic consequences it sets in motion. Those consequences are a terrible acknowledgment of a terrible event. The adequacy of the acknowledgment reconstructs a formal balance even while taking account of the terrible in life.

The words of the Kaddish in *Night* do not express the horror to which Eliezer is a witness. They flow from an inner necessity and do not reflect but deflect that horror. They project the sacredness of life in the face of its most wrenching desecration. They affirm life at the necessary price of disaffirming the surrounding reality. The world of experience and the world of language could not, at this moment, be further apart. Experience is entirely beyond words. Words are utterly inadequate to convey experience.

The dissonance makes itself felt stylistically as well. Eliezer sums up his response to these first shattering hours of his arrival at Auschwitz in the most famous passages of *Night* and, perhaps, of all of Wiesel's writing: "Never shall I forget that night, the first night in camp, which has turned my life into one long night, seven times cursed and seven times sealed." The passage takes the form of an oath never to forget this night of his arrival. The oath, the recourse to metaphorical language ("which has turned my life into one long night"), the reference to curses and phraseology ("seven times cursed") echo the biblical language in which Eliezer was so steeped. He continues: "Never shall I forget that smoke. Never shall I forget the little faces of the children, whose bodies I saw turned into wreaths of smoke beneath a silent blue sky." The oath is an oath of protest, the "silent blue sky," an accusation: "Never shall I forget those flames which consumed my faith forever." Here and in the sentences that follow, Wiesel uses the rhythms, the verbal energy, imagery, and conventions of the Bible to challenge, accuse, and deny God:

> Never shall I forget that nocturnal silence which deprived me, for all eternity, of the desire to live. Never shall I forget those moments which murdered my God and my soul and turned my dreams to dust. Never shall I forget these things, even if I am condemned to live as long as God Himself. Never.

The elaborate oath of remembrance recalls the stern biblical admonitions of remembrance. The negative formulation of the oath and the incremental repetition of the word "never" register defiance and anger even as the eight repetitions circumscribing the passage give it rhythmic structure and ceremonial shape. Ironically, these repetitions seem to implicate mystical notions of God's covenant with the Jews, a covenant associated with the number eight because the ceremony of entrance into the covenant by way of circumcision takes place on the eighth day after birth. The passage uses the poetry and language of faith to affirm a shattering of faith.

The passage is a tour de force of contradiction, paradox, and formal dissonances that are not reconciled, but juxtaposed and held up for inspection. In a sparely written, tightly constructed narrative, it is the only extended poetic moment. It is a climactic moment, and, strangely, for a work that privileges a world outside words altogether, a rhetorical moment: a moment constructed out of words and the special effects and properties of their combinations, a moment that hovers above the abyss of human extremity in uncertain relationship to it.

Like the taste of bread to a man who has not eaten, the effect of so poetic a passage lies in what preceded it. Extremity fills words with special and different meanings. Eliezer reacts to the words of one particular SS officer: "But his clipped words made us tremble. Here the word 'furnace' was not a word empty of meaning; it floated on the air, mingling with the smoke. It was perhaps the only word which did have any real meaning here."

Wiesel's narrative changes our conventional sense of the word "night" in the course of our reading. Night, which as a metaphor for evil always projects, however subliminally, the larger rhythm and structure within which the damages of evil are mitigated, comes to stand for another possibility altogether. The word comes to be filled with the historical flames and data for which there are no metaphors, no ameliorating or sublimating structures. It acquires the almost-tactile feel of the existential, opaque world that is the world of the narrative and also the world in which we live.

Perhaps the finest tribute to *Night* is to be found in the prologue of Terrence Des Pres's book on poetry and politics, *Praises and Dispraises.* Des Pres is speaking of Czeslaw Milosz and of other poets who have lived through extremity and writes: "If we should wonder why their voices are valued so highly, it's that they are acquainted with the night, the nightmare spectacle of politics especially." [*Praises and Dispraises,* 1988] Des Pres uses the word "night" and the reader immediately understands it in exactly Wiesel's revised sense of it.

To be acquainted with the night, in this sense, and to bring that knowledge to a readership is to bring the world we live in into sharper focus. The necessary job of making a better world cannot possibly begin from anywhere else.

Source: Lea Hamaoui, "Historical Horror and the Shape of *Night,*" in *Elie Wiesel: Between Memory and Hope,* edited by Carol Rittner, New York University Press, 1990, pp. 120–29.

Karl A. Plank

In the following excerpt, Plank compares the visual text of Chagall's White Crucifixion *with Wiesel's powerful narrative.*

Around 3:00 A.M. on November 10, 1938, gaping darkness began to spew the flames that were to burn unabated for the next seven years. On this night Nazi mobs executed a well-planned "spontaneous outrage" throughout the precincts of German Jewry. Synagogues were burned, their sacred objects profaned and destroyed; Jewish dwellings were ransacked, their contents strewn and pillaged. Shattering the windows of Jewish shops, the growing swarm left businesses in ruin. Uprooting tombstones and desecrating Jewish graves, the ghoulish throng violated even the sanctuary of the dead. Humiliation accompanied physical violence: in Leipzig, Jewish residents were hurled into a small stream at the zoological park where spectators spit at them, defiled them with mud and jeered at their plight. A chilling harbinger of nights yet to come, the events of this November darkness culminated in widespread arrest of Jewish citizens and led to their transport to concentration camps. Nazi propagandists, struck by a perverse poetry, gave to this night the name by which it has endured in memory: *Kristallnacht,* the night of broken glass. Irony abounds in such a name, for in the litter of shattered windows lies more than bits of glass. *Kristallnacht* testifies to a deeper breaking of basic human continuities. Shattered windows leave faith in fragments and pierce the wholeness of the human spirit.

In that same year of 1938 the Jewish artist Marc Chagall would complete a remarkable painting titled *White Crucifixion.* Here the artist depicts a crucified Christ, skirted with a tallith and encir-

cled by a kaleidoscopic whirl of images that narrates the progress of a Jewish pogrom. The skewed, tau-shaped cross extends toward the arc of destruction and bears particular meaning in that context. Whatever the cross of Christ may mean, in 1938 it was circumscribed by the realities of Holocaust: the onrush of a weapons-bearing mob overruns houses and sets them aflame; a group of villagers seeks to flee the destruction in a crowded boat, while others crouch on the outskirts of the village; an old man wipes the tears from his eyes as he vanishes from the picture, soon to be followed by a bewildered peasant and a third man who clutches a Torah to himself as he witnesses over his shoulder a synagogue fully ablaze.

Chagall's juxtaposition of crucifixion and the immediacy of Jewish suffering creates an intense interplay of religious expectation and historical reality that challenges our facile assumptions. He does not intend to Christianize the painting, certainly not in the sense of affirming any atoning resolution of the Jewish plight. Rather, in the chaotic world of *White Crucifixion* all are unredeemed, caught in a vortex of destruction binding crucified victim and modern martyr. As the prayer shawl wraps the loins of the crucified figure, Chagall makes clear that the Christ and the Jewish sufferer are one....

We must not misunderstand Jewish appropriation of the cross in the context of Holocaust art and literature. Where used at all, the cross functions not as an answer to atrocity, but as a question, protest and critique of the assumptions we may have made about profound suffering. Emil Fackenheim puts the matter in this way:

> A good Christian suggests that perhaps Auschwitz was a divine reminder of the suffering of Christ. Should he not ask instead whether his Master himself, had He been present at Auschwitz, could have resisted degradation and dehumanization? What are the sufferings of the Cross compared to those of a mother whose child is slaughtered to the sound of laughter or the strains of a Viennese waltz? This question may sound sacrilegious to Christian ears. Yet we dare not shirk it, for we—Christians as well as Jews—must ask: at Auschwitz, did the grave win the victory after all, or, worse than the grave, did the devil himself win? [*God's Presence in History* (New York University Press, 1972) p. 75].

Questions such as these spring off Chagall's canvas and into our sensibilities. *White Crucifixion* depicts a world of unleashed terror within which no saving voice can be heard nor any redeeming signs perceived. Separated from the imperiled villagers by only his apparent passivity, Chagall's

> *... in the chaotic world of White Crucifixion all are unredeemed, caught in a vortex of destruction binding crucified victim and modern martyr. As the prayer shawl wraps the loins of the crucified figure, Chagall makes clear that the Christ and the Jewish sufferer are one...."*

Messiah, this Jew of the cross, is no rescuer, but himself hangs powerless before the chaotic fire. The portrayal of Messiah as victim threatens to sever the basic continuity we have wanted to maintain between suffering and redemption.... To have redemptive meaning, the cross must answer the victims who whirl here in torment, for, in the Holocaust, the world becomes... "one great mount of crucifixion, with thousands of severed Jewish heads strewn below like so many thieves" (Roskie, p. 268).

Yet precisely here the language of redemption seems trivial, if not obscenely blind to the sufferer's predicament. Can one speak of redemption in any way that does not trifle with the victim's cry? Before the mother's despair, words of redemption offer no consolation; instead, like the laughter and music which accompany her child's murder, such words mock her torment and deny the profundity of her suffering. The rhetoric of redemption, no matter how benevolently used, remains the ploy of oppressors even decades later. No one may invoke it for the victim in whose world it may have no place.

That world of the victim has found literary testament in the writings of Elie Wiesel, himself a survivor of Auschwitz and Buchenwald, and recently the recipient of the Nobel Peace Prize. Although his writings are prolific, few of his works have had the impact of his first narrative, the memoir *Night.* For a decade following the war—years in which he was a stateless refugee in France—Wiesel maintained a personal moratorium on his experience, a pledge of silence that would allow no word to betray the Holocaust memory. On this matter he wrote nothing and spoke nothing, but listened to the voices within himself. Then in 1956 his memories exploded into an 800-page Yiddish text, "*Un di Velt Hot Geshvign*" *(And the World Kept Silent).* Over the next two years Wiesel would live with this manuscript, paring away from its pages every letter that was not absolutely essential, every mark on the page that might divert from the intense reality of its truth. The result: the stark volume *Night,* some 120 pages that have become a landmark in Holocaust literature. *Night,* too, places the Jew on the cross. It describes the hanging of a young boy who had worked with a well-liked overseer. Both had become suspected of sabotage, and the boy is sentenced to hang, along with two prisoners found with weapons.

> One day when we came back from work, we saw three gallows rearing up in the assembly place, three black crows. Roll call. SS all around us, machine guns trained: the traditional ceremony. Three victims in chains—and one of them, the little servant, the sad-eyed angel....
>
> The three victims mounted together onto the chairs....
>
> "Where is God? Where is He?" someone behind me asked.
>
> At a sign from the head of the camp, the three chairs tipped over.
>
> Total silence throughout the camp. On the horizon, the sun was setting....
>
> Then the march past began. The two adults were no longer alive. Their tongues hung swollen, blue-tinged. But the third rope was still moving; being so light, the child was still alive....
>
> For more than half an hour he stayed there, struggling between life and death, dying in slow agony under our eyes. And we had to look him full in the face. He was still alive when I passed in front of him. His tongue was still red, his eyes not yet glazed.
>
> Behind me, I heard the same man asking:
>
> "Where is God now?"
>
> And I heard a voice within me answer him:
>
> "Where is He? Here He is—He is hanging here on this gallows ..."

Francois Mauriac, the French Catholic writer and author of the foreword to *Night,* found in this scene not only the center of Wiesel's story but also the essential question for his own appropriation of Christian faith. In 1954 Wiesel, then a young journalist, had occasion to interview Mauriac who just two years earlier had won the Nobel Prize in literature. The interview proved to be a decisive turning point for both of them: for Wiesel, Mauriac provided the compassionate challenge to tell the story of darkness; for Mauriac, Wiesel made unavoidably personal the plight of the Holocaust child. Upon reading *Night,* Mauriac wrote the following:

> And I who believe that God is love, what answer could I give my young questioner, whose dark eyes still held the reflection of that angelic sadness which had appeared one day upon the face of the hanged child? What did I say to him? Did I speak of that other Israeli, his brother, who may have resembled him—the Crucified, whose Cross has conquered the world? Did I affirm that the stumbling block to his faith was the cornerstone of mine, and that conformity between the Cross and the suffering of men was in my eyes the key to that impenetrable mystery whereon the faith of his childhood had perished? ... But I could only embrace him, weeping ["Foreword to *Night,*" pp. 10–11].

Mauriac, long a poignant witness to the connection between suffering and love, knew well that the cornerstone of his faith was at stake in Wiesel's narrative. And yet, at the point at which he might have been tempted to proclaim his gospel, he finds that the only fitting response is to embrace the victim, blessing him with tears. The reason is clear: the death of the sad-eyed angel creates a stumbling block not only for Wiesel, but for Mauriac; not only for the Jewish victim, but for the Christian onlooker who cannot interpret away the scandalous scene without trivializing its grossly unredeemed features. In Mauriac's embrace human compassion stifles theological conviction, rescuing it from becoming an oppressive utterance....

We misread the scene if we assume that the writer's tears are tied only to his perception of the victim's tragedy. The conversation between Mauriac and Wiesel begins with Mauriac's recollection of the German occupation of France, admitting his painful knowledge of the trainloads of Jewish children standing at Austerlitz station. As Wiesel responds "I was one of them." Mauriac sees himself anew as an unwitting onlooker, the bystander guilty not of acts undertaken, but of acts not taken. The indictment is not Wiesel's but Mauriac's own, born of the self-perception that not to stand with the victim is to act in complicity with his or her oppressor. Mauriac's tears signify his humble repentance, his turning away from the role of onlooker to align himself with the victim. The observer becomes witness, testifying on behalf of the victim. Crucifixion indicts, for in its shadow we are always the guilty bystander. Humility, such as Mauriac's, puts an end to any assumption of benign righteousness;

repentance denies complacency to the viewer of another's passion....

Crucifixion, be it the cross of Jesus or the nocturnal Golgotha of Auschwitz, breaks the moral continuities by which we have considered ourselves secure and whole. To mend these fragments of human experience lies outside our power. We cannot repair the broken world. Yet, as we yield these broken continuities to narrative—to memoir, to literature, to liturgy—we begin to forge a new link that binds storyteller and hearer, victim and witness. But here we must be most careful. We rush to tell the story, confident that it is ours to tell when, in fact, it is ours to hear.

Source: Karl A. Plank, "Broken Continuities: *Night* and *White Crucifixion,*" in *The Christian Century,* Vol. 104, No. 32, November 4, 1987, pp. 963–66.

Sources

Roger Alter, "Elie Wiesel: Between Hangman and Victim," in *After the Tradition,* E.P. Dutton & Co. Inc., 1962.

Ellen S. Fine, *Legacy of Night; The Literary Universe of Elie Wiesel,* State University of New York Press, 1982.

W. H. Hager, a review in *Christian Century,* January, 1961, p. 88.

Jason Harris, "Wiesel Recounts Twentieth Century" in *The Tamalpais News,* http://marin.marin.k12.ca.us/~Tamnewsl/old/LXX/tam/ads_art/wiesel.htm: 1995.

Lothar Kahn, "Elie Wiesel: Neo-Hasidism," in *Mirrors of the Jewish Mind: A Gallery of Portraits of European Jewish Writers of Our Time,* A.S. Barnes, 1963, pp. 176-93.

Kirkus, August, 1960, p. 660.

New Yorker, March, 1961, Vol. 37, p. 175.

Simon Sibelman, in *Silence in the Novels of Elie Wiesel,* New York: St. Martin's Press, 1995.

For Further Study

Ora Avni, "Beyond Psychoanalysis: Elie Wiesel's *Night* in Historical Perspective," in *Auschwitz and After: Race, Culture, and the "Jewish Question" in France,* edited by Lawrence Kritzman, Routledge, 1995, pp. 203-19.
> Explores the idea of "cognitive dissonance," i.e., the inability of the villagers in *Night* to conceive of Nazi slaughter in terms they can understand, and examines how the loss of community equals the loss of humanity in Wiesel's text.

Michael Berenbaum, *The Vision of the Void: Theological Reflections on the Works of Elie Wiesel,* Wesleyan University Press, 1979.

Analyzes the way in which the reading of the novel effects one's theology as well as the way the novel uses theology.

Alvin H. Rosenfeld and Irving Greenberg, *Confronting the Holocaust: The Legacy of Elie Wiesel,* Indiana University Press, 1978.
Includes essays exploring various themes in the works of Elie Wiesel. Several essays explore Wiesel's contributions to Jewish post-Holocaust theology.

Lucy Dawidowicz, *The War Against The Jews, 1933-1945* Holt, Rinehart and Winston, 1975.
A historical account of Nazi persecution against the Jews.

Gary A. Donaldson, *Abundance and Anxiety: America, 1945-1960,* Praeger Pub Text, 1997.
The abundance that America enjoyed after WWII was accompanied by new anxieties over the Soviet Union. The Cold War caused prosperous suburbanites to build private bomb shelters and schools to practice air raid drills. The author argues that the tension between abundance and anxiety defined the period.

Elie Wiesel: Between Memory and Hope, edited by Carol Rittner, R.S.M., New York University Press, 1990.
Presents essays that view Wiesel's works through Jewish and Christian theological perspectives.

Ted Estess, *Elie Wiesel,* Frederick Ungar Publishing, 1980.
Overviews Wiesel's life and work, with considerable attention to the historical context of the Holocaust in Hungary and to Wiesel's Hasidic background.

Ellen Fine, *Legacy of Night,* State University of New York Press, 1982.
Explores the theme of "witness" in Wiesel's works, taking *Night* as the basis for all of Wiesel's succeeding books.

Herbert Hirsch, *Genocide and the Politics of Memory: Studying Death to PreserveLife,* University of North Carolina Press, 1995.
A book-length analysis of the politics, problems, and necessity of remembering crimes against humanity. It also poses suggestions for the future preservation of human life.

Holocaust Literature: A Handbook of Critical, Historical, and Literary Writings, edited by Saul S. Friedman, Greenwood Press, 1995.

An exhaustive survey of conceptual approaches to the Holocaust, Holocaust area studies (including an essay on Hungarian Jewry), and representations of the Holocaust in education and the arts. It includes a short section on the philosophy of Elie Wiesel.

Jack Kolbert, "Elie Wiesel," in *The Contemporary Novel in France,* edited by William Thompson, University Press of Florida, 1995, pp. 217-31.
Provides an overview of Wiesel's life and major literary themes, with special attention given to his place in contemporary French literature.

Dominick LaCapra, *Representing the Holocaust: History, Theory, Trauma,* Cornell University, 1994.
Discusses issues through the lens of psychoanalytic literary theory. In particular, it deals with historical representations of the Holocaust.

Primo Levi, *Survival in Auschwitz: The Nazi Assault on Humanity,* Collier Books, 1995.
A detailed account of the famous death camp by another survivor. It is a reprint of a 1947 work.

Cynthia Ozick, *The Messiah of Stockholm: A Novel,* Vintage Books, 1988.
One of many works by this author to deal with the Holocaust. This novel positions the Holocaust as the central event in the consciousness of twentieth-century Jews.

Simon P. Sibleman, *Silence in the Novels of Elie Wiesel,* St. Martin's Press, 1995.
This volume explores the theme and practice of "silence" in Wiesel's works, arguing that "silence" represents more than the mere absence of words.

D. L. Vanderwerken, "Wiesel's *Night* As Anti-bildungsroman," in *Yiddish,* Vol. 7, No. 4, 1990, pp. 57-63.
Views Elie as the antithesis of the traditional "coming of age" hero.

Elie Wiesel, *All Rivers Run to the Sea,* Alfred A. Knopf, 1996.
This is the first volume of Wiesel's memoirs, and it expands and comments on events depicted in *Night.*

Writing and the Holocaust, edited by Berel Lang, Holmes and Meier, 1988.
The essays in this volume treat various aspects and problems in writing about the Holocaust, including the difficulty in accurately conveying the horrors of the concentration camps. Several essayists praise Wiesel's literary style as the most effective in bearing witness to the Holocaust.

The Red Badge of Courage

Stephen Crane
1895

Stephen Crane's internationally acclaimed work, *The Red Badge of Courage,* was published in 1895. Unique in style and content, the novel explores the emotions of a young Civil War recruit named Henry Fleming. What is most remarkable about this classic is that the twenty-four-year-old author had never witnessed war in his life before writing this book. Crane's story developed to some degree out of his reading of war stories by Russian novelist Leo Tolstoy and the popular memoirs of Civil War veterans, yet he also deviated from these influences in his depiction of war's horror. Critics have noted that his portrait of war is an intensely psychological one, blending elements of naturalism, impressionism, and symbolism. Indeed, he broke away from his American realist contemporaries, including his mentor William Dean Howells, in his naturalistic treatment of man as an amoral creature in a deterministic world.

For this reason, critical reactions to the *The Red Badge of Courage* in 1895 were mixed: some disapproved of Crane's use of the vernacular—the common slang of everyday folk and soldiers—and the impressionistic technique. Crane also experimented with psychological realism, and his venture into the realm of the human psyche radically changed the common perception of the novel in America. As he faces combat for the first time, Henry experiences an intense array of emotions: courage, anxiety, self-confidence, fear, and egotistic zeal. Interestingly enough, the naturalistic flavor of the work operates against this self-important

ego. The individual is not of primary importance, as is evidenced time and again in the words of Henry's mother, fellow soldiers, and officers. Henry is often referred to quite impersonally as "the youth." The men, untried and untested, are treated like scared animals against the backdrop of inimitable Nature and War. Crane also used color imagery, both vibrant and subtle, to describe war. He describes a skirmish as sounding like a "crimson roar," for example, and writes of war as "the red animal." Crane's sense of color pervades the work; note his description of the sky, which remains "fairy blue" during the day, as if to underscore the indifference of nature to the carnage taking place.

Neglected for two decades after his death, Crane's work was rediscovered in the 1920s by poets and novelists, such as Amy Lowell and Sherwood Anderson, who recognized in his experiments with new subjects, themes, and forms something of the spirit of their own literary aims. In the 1950s, critical essays focused on his religious themes. Today, Crane's novel is widely read and appreciated for its amalgamation of artistic themes and techniques.

Stephen Crane

Author Biography

The youngest of fourteen children, Stephen Crane was born November 1, 1871, in Newark, New Jersey, to a Methodist minister, Jonathan Townley Crane, and Mary Helen (Peck) Crane. His interest in writing developed in part from his parents, who wrote articles of a religious nature, and from two of his brothers, who were journalists. Crane began his higher education in 1888 at Hudson River Institute and Claverack College, a military school where he developed an interest in Civil War studies and military training. Throughout his one-year college experience, he wrote for his brother Townley's news service and began a sketch of his famous first novel, *Maggie, A Girl of the Streets* while still at Syracuse University. In 1891, he quit school to work full time as a reporter with Townley, and to live in the tenements of New York, where he gained firsthand knowledge of poverty.

In 1893, he privately published *Maggie* under a pseudonym, after several publishers rejected the work on the grounds that his description of slum realities would shock readers. He pioneered in writing naturalistic fiction and poetry: in *Maggie,* he wrote about a girl who becomes a prostitute and is driven to suicide by poverty and sweatshop labor.

In *The Red Badge of Courage,* published in 1895, Crane stressed the irony of chance and examined man's weaknesses in the midst of impersonal forces. In this novel, which brought Crane fame, he limited his point of view to a common soldier in the Civil War and dramatized the protagonist's bewilderment and fear as he eventually overcomes his initial cowardice.

Crane also published the poetry collection *The Black Riders, and Other Lines* in 1895. This volume of free verse foreshadowed the work of the Imagist poets with its concise, vivid images. The religious poems in this volume—written about the same time as *The Red Badge*—reflect the anguish of Crane's spiritual crisis and preoccupation with questions of faith. His poetry and fiction describe man's alienation in a God-abandoned world of danger and violence. During this time, Crane continued to work as a journalist, traveling throughout the American West and Mexico for a news syndicate, and later he used these experiences as the basis for fictional works. Crane wrote four volumes of short stories, which include such notable works as "The Open Boat" and "The Monster." His free-verse poems in *War is Kind* (1899) demonstrated once again how Crane was a pathfinder for present-day poets devoted to experimental reform and non-sentimentality.

In 1879 Crane met Cora Taylor, the proprietor of a hotel, nightclub, and brothel. Together as common-law husband and wife, they moved to England where Crane formed literary friendships with Joseph Conrad, H.G. Wells, and Henry James. Shortly after this move, Crane left to report on the Spanish-American War for the New York *World,* an assignment he accepted, in part, to escape financial debts. Although Crane was ill when he returned to England, he continued writing fiction to satisfy his artistic needs and to earn money to pay his debts. One of these exercises was *Active Service,* which records his experiences as a war correspondent in the Greco-Turkish War. Critics often describe it as uneven and sprawling. By 1900, Crane's health had rapidly deteriorated due to a general disregard of his physical well-being. After several respiratory attacks, he died of tuberculosis at the age of twenty-eight in Badenweiler, Germany. His young life was a prolific one, transcended by his increasing fame as more and more readers recognized Crane's brilliant work. His *Collected Works* were published from 1925 to 1926 in twelve volumes, and in the 1950s in ten volumes.

Plot Summary

The Red Badge of Courage consists of twenty-four chapters which follow the protagonist, young Henry Fleming, through his experience as a Union Army private during the American Civil War. The book can be organized into three parts: Part One, consisting of Chapters I through VI, concerns Henry's state of mind before his first battle, his initial war experiences, when he flees from battle; Part Two, consisting of Chapters VII through XIII, explores Henry's experiences away from his regiment; and Part Three, consisting of Chapters XIV through XXIV, focuses on Henry recovering his courage and returning to his regiment, his subsequent heroism, and his final sense of achieving manhood.

Part One: Chapters I through VI

Though published in 1895, *The Red Badge of Courage* takes place sometime during the American Civil War, which lasted from 1861 to 1865. The initial setting is the campsite of a regiment of the Union Army, fighting for the northern states. The soldiers can see the campfires of the Confederate Army, their enemy, which is fighting for the interests of the southern states. Most of the story is told from Henry's point of view, through his thoughts, memories, and perceptions. The scene opens with an argument about whether the regiment will finally move out after being in camp for several months. As Henry listens to this debate, he remembers his life back home, and his mother telling him how to behave on this first adventure off the farm: "Yer jest one little feller amongst a hull lot of others, and yeh've got to keep quiet and do what they tell yeh." Henry felt proud and daring when he left home to go to war, but now he wonders how he will do when confronted with the reality of battle. He seeks information from the tall soldier, Jim Conklin, who tells him that if everyone stands and fights, he will stay, but if everyone runs, he will run, too. This makes Henry feel better since he does not have to pretend to be more confident than his comrades.

When the regiment is ordered to move, Henry marches along, worrying about whether or not he will be brave. He studies his companions for clues to their feelings, but they sing and boast confidently. Henry becomes sullen and brooding, so that a loud soldier, Wilson, asks him what is troubling him. Henry cannot answer. As they draw close to the front line Henry feels curiosity about the battle-weary returning soldiers. He begins to fantasize that the officers are leading the soldiers into a trap. Henry is afraid to voice his fears and he feels deeply isolated. His regiment marches for days to get into position, sleeping and marching with no information, until one morning Henry is kicked awake by his commanding officer and hustled into battle.

Henry's regiment is positioned and repositioned without seeing battle, though they are frightened by retreating soldiers, dead bodies, and bullets whizzing overhead. Suddenly Henry sees the officers on their horses, and the enemy is upon them. He fires his rifle without thinking and suddenly breaks into a sweat, "a sensation that his eyeballs were about to crack like hot stones." He feels a "red rage" and fights boldly until the enemy is driven back. Henry feels joyful that he has stood up to the first test in battle, but when the enemy returns unexpectedly, Henry loses his nerve. When he sees others running, Henry runs, too. He loses all sense of direction and runs blindly in search of safety. As he runs he sees many different battle scenes, ending with the General who declares that the soldiers have held the enemy back. But Henry cannot share in the victory since he ran from the front lines.

Part Two: Chapters VII through XIII

Henry is full of conflicting feelings. On the one hand he feels like a criminal for running away, and on the other, he feels as though he has been cheated by fate of his glorious career as a brave soldier. He imagines how humiliated he will be if he returns to his regiment, and in a fit of rebellion and despair he sets off through the woods, away from the Union Army. He seeks solace in Nature, which he imagines to be a sympathetic woman "with a deep aversion to tragedy." As he goes deeper into the woods, Henry becomes more calm and rationalizes his escape. The deepening forest muffles the sound of the cannon.

> At length he reached a place where the high, arching boughs made a chapel. He softly pushed the green doors aside and entered. Pine needles were a gentle brown carpet. There was a religious half light.

> Near the threshold he stopped, horror-stricken at the sight of a thing.

> He was being looked at by a dead man who was seated with his back against a columnlike tree. The corpse was dressed in a uniform that once had been blue, but was now faded to a melancholy shade of green. The eyes, staring at the youth, had changed to the dull hue to be seen on the side of a dead fish. The mouth was open. Its red had changed to an appalling yellow. Over the gray skin of the face ran little ants. One was trundling some sort of a bundle along the upper lip.

> The youth gave a shriek as he confronted the thing. He was for moments turned to stone before it. He remained staring into the liquid-looking eyes. The dead man and the living man exchanged a long look.

Henry runs away, imagining that the dead man is pursuing him, and convinced that Nature has turned against him. As his wanderings bring him close to the front again, he hears a fierce battle going on and guesses that the scrimmage in which he took part earlier was just a prelude to the real battle, which is going on now. Henry encounters a line of wounded soldiers leaving the front and falls in with them, fascinated by the soldiers' stories of the fighting. But when the Tattered Soldier asks him kindly, "Where yeh hit, ol' boy," Henry has no answer and runs away. He wishes he, too, had a "red badge of courage," a wound, that would prove that he had done his share. He runs into his old friend Jim Conklin, who is badly wounded and who dies in a field where Henry and the Tattered Soldier lead him so that the artillery will not run over his body. He abandons the Tattered Soldier in the same field to die, and wrestles with the shameful secret that he is a deserter.

Henry debates with himself about whether to return to his regiment, but is both terrified of the humiliation of being recognized as a deserter, and fearful that he cannot live up to the requirements of a soldier under fire. While he broods over his dilemma, a company of retreating soldiers sweep past him, and Henry is once again terrified. As he tries to get information from them, he grabs a soldier who, also terrified, hits Henry on the head with his rifle. Henry is badly wounded, but manages to stagger on until he encounters a friendly person who walks him back to his regiment. His comrades had assumed that Henry had been killed, and now assume he has been wounded in battle, and so no explanations for his absence are necessary.

Part Three: Chapters XIV through XXIV

In the final section, Henry develops into a seasoned soldier. He is greatly relieved not to be exposed as a deserter and enters into the battle with a sincere desire to be brave. He saves the company flag from being captured by the enemy, and he exhorts his fellow soldiers to reenter the battle at a critical moment. For this he is praised by his superior officers and seen to be a valiant soldier. Henry notices that he has become tranquil about the war, and is a reassuring presence to the untried men around him. In the final chapter, Henry feels "a quiet manhood, nonassertive but of sturdy and strong blood." He proceeds into the next round of battle as "a golden ray of sun came through the hosts of leaden rain clouds."

Characters

Cheery Soldier

The Cheery Soldier, another soldier-companion known in terms of his physical traits, is Henry's unidentified, strangely lighthearted guide back to his regiment; this mysterious person has been seen by critics as an allegorical figure akin to the ancient gods and goddesses, who lent their help to the heroes of myth. It is during the climax of the book that this character appears. After Henry receives his red badge of courage, he feels lost in the maze of the forest, and is suddenly taken up by the cheery soldier. Somehow, he is able to thread "the tangled forest with a strange fortune." The stranger manages to avoid guards and patrols and, at the same time, carry on an almost incoherent monologue ("There was shootin' here an' shootin' there ...).

When they reach the campfire where Henry's regiment is resting for the night, the owner of the cheery voice bids him farewell and disappears into the night.

Jim Conklin

Basically, the characters in *The Red Badge of Courage* outside of Henry Fleming are foils (contrasts) to his character. Jim Conklin, the tall soldier, as he is described by Crane, is more realistic about war than Henry. He tells Henry: "You jest wait 'til tomorrow and you'll see one of the biggest battles ever was." Without illusions about war, Jim is not as impatient as Henry is to enter into the fray. When asked by Henry if any of the soldiers will run from battle, Jim answers that some will run, but most will stay and fight after they start shooting. If most of the company runs, says Jim, he will run too, but if most stay and fight, he will follow. Jim further points out that all the new recruits are untried in battle. Jim also enjoys being the center of attention when he spreads the rumor of troop movement and encounter with the enemy. He is mortally wounded in battle and tells Henry that the great fear he has is that he will fall down in the road and be run over by a wagon. He then races off into a field, repelling Henry's and the tattered soldier's attempts to help him. Jim dies a true hero.

Henry Fleming

Henry, the protagonist of the novel, is a naive, young farm boy from New York state whose dreams of glorious battle lead him to sign up in the Union Army against his mother's wishes. Though he gets his notion of war from books about Greek warriors, his initial confrontation with true war perplexes him. Upon entering battle and witnessing the confusion and panic of his regiment, he flees into the woods and feels like a coward. After he receives his "red badge of courage," a head wound, this shame begins to disappear, however. He realizes that there is no dishonor fleeing certain death. He becomes confident and is happy to be called a "wild cat" by the superior officer. Some critics view Henry's journey as his initiation into manhood. Others feel that he is turned away from the possibility of self-knowledge into self-serving egotism.

In terms of the first critical view, that Crane depicts a boy becoming a man, Henry's battle with the landscape mirrors his internal struggle with his vanity and immaturity. He grows in self-awareness by learning the true meaning of honor and courage,

Media Adaptations

- *The Red Badge of Courage* was adapted as a film by John Huston, starring Audie Murphy, Bill Mauldin, and Andy Devine, Universal, 1951; available from MCA/Universal Home Video.

- *The Red Badge of Courage* also appears on an educational video, with a number of different interpretations of Crane's masterpiece; produced by Thomas S. Klise Company.

- There is an abridged recording of the book, narrated by actor Richard Crenna, and published by Listen for Pleasure, Downsview, Ontario, 1985. Two audio cassettes, 120 minutes, and Dolby processed.

- The sound recording of the complete, unabridged version of *The Red Badge of Courage,* narrated by Frank Muller, is available from Recorded Books, Charlotte Hall, MD, 1981. Three audio cassettes, 270 minutes.

- A sound recording with a lecture by Warren French on *The Red Badge of Courage,* published by Everett/Edwards, Deland, FL, 1972. One audio cassette, 38 minutes.

as the novel ends with his renewed faith in life. He achieves an epiphany, as demonstrated in his instinctive desire to grab the Union flag and run with it resolutely to join his men in battle. The conclusion, thus, shows Henry as a man, aware of his maturity, his soul changed. Crane paints nature in this last scene as benevolent, with images of clover, flowers, and the clouds parting to reveal the warmth and light of the sun. As far as the second perspective is concerned, Henry is selfishly involved in his own honor and self-preservation. He does not help his fellow soldiers but is more caught up in how he looks. An example of this theory is when the young boy deserts the tattered soldier as the dying soldier answers the young boy's questions on honor and cowardice.

Still from the film Red Badge of Courage, *starring Audie Murphy (center) as the young Henry Fleming.*

What distinguishes *The Red Badge of Courage* from other war stories is the compelling chronicle of the inner emotions common to any new member of the infantry. Thus, Henry deals with doubt, fear, chaos, and confusion even during tense, death-filled moments.

Ma Fleming

The mother of Henry, simply known as Ma Fleming, offers homespun advice to her boy as he goes to war. She tells him that he will be one among many and to be quiet and do what he is told. She also adds, perhaps prophetically: "If so be a time comes when yeh have to be kilt or do a mean thing, why, Henry don't think of anything 'cept what's right …" These cautionary statements, some critics believe, underscore Henry's romantic egocentric belief in his own indestructibility. Ma Fleming is a hard-working, uneducated farm woman, who reluctantly lets her son go to war since she knows the reality of war. Fleming identifies nature as a female figure like his mother, who disapproves of the fighting and wants him to escape.

Lt. Hasbrouck

Most of the officers in this novel are viewed as arrogant and insensitive, but this lieutenant is depicted as an ideal military man encouraging his sol-diers to behave correctly in battle and praising them for their bravery. He lauds Henry's and Wilson's particular bravery and valor when they fight and seize the flag.

Loud Soldier

See Wilson

Officers

Most of the officers, including the general and colonel, in this novel are viewed as arrogant and insensitive. They refer to the recruits as "muledrivers." Lieutenant Hasbrouk differs in that he enourages his soldiers to behave correctly in battle and praises them for their bravery. He lauds Henry's and Wilson's particular bravery and valor when they fight and seize the flag.

Tall Soldier

See Jim Conklin

Veterans

The group of experienced soldiers in the book provides a contrast to the young recruits. They refer to the newcomers as "fresh fish." These veterans tell tall tales and are tattered and torn in appearance. The fact that they are not particularly distinguishable as individuals—as are most of the recruits, too—indicates the utter cruelty of an impersonal war that takes lives without concern or compassion.

Wilson

Known as the Loud Soldier, Wilson is a boastful new recruit anxious to fight and unable to admit the possibility of his cowardice in the initial confrontation with the enemy. After battle, however, he becomes strangely quiet and is no longer his usual bombastic self. He reveals his fears through his action of giving Henry a packet of letters for Wilson's family in case he does not return home. The battle clearly has a profound effect on him; he assists his fellow soldiers and takes a prominent position in later battles.

Themes

Naturalism

In *The Red Badge of Courage,* a novel about a young recruit's first encounter with real battle, Crane emphasizes the lack of free choice in human conduct. Chapter Four in particular highlights a common theme in Crane's work—the naturalistic belief in the indifference of nature. The theory of naturalism is a critical term applied to a method of literary composition that aims at a detached, scientific objectivity in the treatment of a natural man. It also holds to the theory of determinism and leans further towards pessimism, since man is controlled by his instincts or passions, or by his social and economic environment and circumstances. In any case, man is not free to choose. The theory emanates from the nineteenth-century concern for scientific thought, as exemplified in economic determinism (Karl Marx) and biological determinism (Charles Darwin). Darwinism was one of the popular social philosophies of Crane's day, and it stressed that, as in the animal world, only the stronger individuals survive.

Crane candidly reports the sordid and brutish actions of human conduct as well as the testing of human strength in the context of violence and struggle. Henry does not find solace in nature, but rather is deluded into feeling secure in an unfriendly context. As he moves deeper into the woods, away from the sounds of the guns and fighting, he comes upon a lovely spot, where the boughs of the trees form a chapel-like area with brown pine needles for the carpet. To his horror, he discovers a ghastly corpse with small ants crawling across its face,

Topics for Further Study

- Compare the attitudes of individual soldiers in Crane's battle scenes in *The Red Badge of Courage* with the attitude of individual Southern soldiers in Margaret Mitchell's *Gone With the Wind.*

- Research the literary tenets of naturalism, realism, and existentialism in books by French and Russian authors as well as American.

- Study the Battle of Chancellorsville and compare it to the fictional rendition of this battle in *The Red Badge of Courage.*

quite a shocking discovery in an otherwise sedate, peaceful scene. Henry cries out when he sees the corpse, then gazes at it intently before he gathers the strength to run away. As he flees, he is afraid that the dead man is somehow pursuing him. Finally, he stops to listen whether the corpse is calling after him. He views nature as an impersonal force able to go tranquilly on with its process like "a woman with a deep aversion to tragedy."

Coming of Age

"It is only by immersion in the flux of experience that man becomes disciplined and develops in character, conscience or soul," stated R.W. Stallman in his introduction to *The Red Badge of Courage.* The battle is where life's flux is strongest, hence the potential for change is greatest. "From the start Henry recognizes the necessity for change, but wars against it. But man must lose his soul in order to save it. The youth develops into the veteran," wrote Stallman. The book can be read as a story of the coming of age of Henry Fleming: his development from an innocent boy to a mature man. A novel that describes the development of a young character into a more aware adult is often called a *bildungsroman.* Henry encounters a hostile environment and is changed by the horror of the forest chapel, where he comes into contact with a decomposing corpse; he is also changed by the awesome death of Jim Conklin and by the patient and selfless suffering of "the tattered man." Prompted by a naive sense of patriotism and heroism to enlist, Henry is quickly disillusioned with the life of a common soldier. In the end, he grows in self-confidence and has a clearer grasp of reality.

Appearance vs. Reality

Henry Fleming has a romantic or egotistic illusion about his place in the world and about war. Crane traces the process of education by which the youth matures and changes his thoughts about reality. Man must believe that he is a rational creature whose mind can control and give significance to human conduct. Yet Crane demonstrates that man is at the mercy not only of his illusions and instincts but of superior social and cosmic forces. Rather than present to the reader the romantic, idealized notion of war, he presents its antithesis—chaotic, brutal savagery. By contrast, the book and film *Gone With the Wind* represents a romanticized version of the Civil War.

Alienation and Loneliness

In *The Red Badge of Courage*, Henry Fleming often feels alone and isolated. The woods and the smoke separate the soldiers and contribute greatly to their feelings of panic during battle. Critic Robert Shulman, writing in *American Literature,* suggested that Crane had to "test the possibilities and failures of community, an understandable interest since for him the solitary self has limited resources and God and nature are both inaccessible as sources of sustaining power." War accentuates Fleming's feeling of isolation because he faces death so often. He encounters the dead Union soldier propped against a tree and stares at him until he feels the ghastly figure is staring at him. His companions Jim Conklin and "the tattered man" both die, leaving him saddened and confused.

Style

Point of View

The book is told in third person from a young recruit's point of view and is a series of sensory impressions and dialogues between the soldiers. Henry Fleming, the main character, is anxious to understand what the other soldiers are feeling: Will they run during fire? Are they as scared as he? He misses his routine of milking the brindle cows at his family's farm. His comrades, Wilson, a vocif-

erous solider who brags about "licking" the enemy, and Jim Conklin, who warns that there will be a big battle, serve to accentuate the young man's innocence. He is impatient to see action in battle, without really knowing what it is all about. When Henry asks the loud soldier if he will run from battle if he is scared, he answers, laughing at the boy, "I'll do my share of the fightin'." The actual skirmish kills half the regiment and gives Henry a head wound, ironically, by a fellow Union soldier. He is ashamed, however, that he ran from the ferocious gunfire and fears shame when returning to the troops. When his comrades believe his pretense that his wound was inflicted in battle, he becomes a renewed person and heroically seizes the Union flag from a dead soldier and advances to his personal victory.

Symbolism

Critics acknowledge Crane as an exceptional artist, with superb skills in imagery, metaphor, similes, and irony. He has even been referred to as a Symbolist in the tradition of the French poet Mallarme and the American author Edgar Allen Poe. The red badge—a soldier's wound—is the most obvious symbol in the book and the source of its greatest irony. While it is meant to be a sign of honor and courage, gained from true action in war, Henry's red badge was given to him by accident by one of his own army and clearly not from brave battle. Henry lies about this and creates a pretense to his men that is accepted. Crane also used many nature symbols. For example, the images of flowers in bloom represent the transient, temporary nature of life. A metaphor (a figure of speech in which an object represents something else quite distinct from it) often cited by critics is the wafer-sun. Henry sees this upon his awareness of the reality of death, and it represents the communion wafer in an ecclesiastical service. It also suggests a flat, artificial "sun," glued onto a flat, imitation sky, thus diminishing Nature, eliminating Heaven, and enlarging the youth as the only observer.

Animal Imagery

Crane's novel abounds in animal imagery. The campfires of the enemy are red eyes shining in the dark, like those of predatory animals. When the battle begins, Henry fights like a "pestered animal … worried by dogs," and on the third day he plunges like "a mad horse" at the Confederate flag. Crane writes that the soldiers fight like "wild cats." Further, the regiments resemble black, serpentlike columns of regiments entering the cover of night (this imagery is known as a simile, i.e, the writer's representation of unlike objects through use of "like" or "as" comparisons). The use of animal imagery helps convey the deterministic point of view of the literary naturalist, that men are caught like animals in a world they cannot control. In the chapters where Henry runs away in fear, he does so like a creature seeking his own self-preservation. He throws a pine cone at a squirrel, which runs frightened up a tree. The squirrel "did not stand stolidly baring his furry belly to the missile…. On the contrary, he had fled as fast as his legs could carry him…." Henry feels freed since "Nature had given him a sign."

Irony

Much has been written about the novel's irony, a literary technique that demonstrates a discrepancy between the appearance and reality of a situation. Crane presents different perspectives of a situation so that the reader must put together what is really true. The book's title is the supreme irony since Henry receives his wound from a crazed soldier who hits the boy on the head with a rifle butt after Henry has fled from a skirmish. The battle is also ironic, for after Henry's great display of bravery on the third day of battle, the army retreats and all the ground won at great cost is given up. Crane makes the sacrifices of war seem futile and the suffering not worth the cost. The moral, however, is implicit, for at the end of the novel, Henry feels a sense of pride as a full-fledged man. Some critics dispute the fact that there is a moral sense at all in this book. In any case, there is a sense that Henry has undergone some transformation.

Setting

The scenario of the battle is Chancellorsville, Virginia, near Richmond, and the time is probably 1863. The Battle of Chancellorsville that pitted 130,000 Union soldiers under General Joseph Hooker against 60,000 Confederates under General Robert E. Lee eventually resulted in a large defeat for the Union troops. Hooker crossed the Rappahannock River and advanced to attack the Rebels from behind Chancellorsville. Lee and Jackson split their troops and surprised Hooker. Union casualties in the Battle included 1,606 killed and 9,762 wounded, with nearly 6,000 missing. Union generals were fired by Lincoln for not having a cohesive battle plan. In the novel, Henry Fleming runs into the woods for refuge from the fire. The woods becomes an ironic setting, since it offers neither salvation nor peace, but another look at death in the form of a partially decomposed corpse.

Historical Context

Memoirs of the Civil War

The war literature of the Civil War era glorified heroism and the courage of soldiers on both sides of the war. The numerous memoirs of war veterans influenced Crane, who had a lifelong obsession with war. He drew upon the common pattern of these chronicles for the major plot elements in *The Red Badge of Courage:* the sentimental expectation of the young recruit moved to enlist by patriotic rhetoric and heroic fantasies of war; the resistance of his parents to his enlistment; his anxiety over the apparent confusion and purposelessness of troop movements; his doubts about his personal courage; the dissipation of his heroic illusions in the first battle; his grumbling about the incompetency of generals; and other such motifs, incidents, and situations.

The editors of *Century Magazine* published *Battles and Leaders of the Civil War,* one of Crane's primary sources in writing *The Red Badge of Courage.* The editors hoped to foster mutual respect for both armies, focusing on the bonds forged by soldiers in the field rather than the horrors they endured. Crane's novel challenged these popular tales, which often featured heroes on the battlefield rewarded by the love of an awed heroine at home. In the book, Henry Fleming has similar romantic notions of warfare but they are dispelled when he encounters the grim reality of the battlefield. Crane felt that fiction should present a slice out of life. Many readers had a difficult time believing he had not yet experienced war firsthand, because he was so successful at depicting the war.

The battle he describes in *The Red Badge of Courage* is based on the Battle of Chancellorsville. Besides referring to the Rappahannock River and the city of Richmond, the author discusses the fact that Fleming's regiment passes Washington, D.C., before quartering on the Rappahannock. The setting, geographical terrain, and the references to the weather parallel historical facts. Essentially, the battle was fought in the wilderness a few miles west of Fredericksburg, Virginia. Although this provides the scenario for the book, precise identification of the battle location is clearly not a primary consideration for Crane.

A Currier and Ives engraving of the Battle of Chancellorsville, May 3, 1863, the incident upon which Stephen Crane's fictional battle is based.

The Progress of Civilization and Urban Poor

As the nineteenth century drew to a close, it was assumed that humankind was steadily progressing. Advancements in technology, rapid industrialization, and improved education made some people feel that humans—and in particular Americans—had evolved beyond the destruction and ignorance that had taken place in the past. Yet wars continued to be fought and, with the improvement of weapons technology, became bloodier and more deadly. Crane points out in his novel that though education and religion were supposed to have "civilized" men and "checked" their passions, war continued to rage, and violence had only increased. His words proved visionary when the United States engaged in an international conflict, the Spanish-American War, in 1898 (Crane covered the conflict as a war correspondent). Crane studied New York City street life, since he spent much of his early adult life living among its poor and "fringe element." He frequently kept company with prostitutes and street people, even disguising himself as a transient in order to learn how they lived and were treated by society. He was one of the first "literary bohemians," so-called because he cavorted with disreputable characters and chose unusual subjects for his fiction (many did not consider the lower classes to be a fitting topic for literary endeavors). Crane was able to use his city experiences in the novel by drawing on the grim parallels between poverty-stricken urban streets and bloody war zones. In the novel, he refers to the approaching army as a train and the soldiers as the spokes of the wheels.

The Spanish-American War

Crane was enraptured by war stories and often entered battle as a war correspondent. On February 15, 1898, the *Maine,* an American ship in Cuba, was blown up in Havana harbor, and by April, the United States was at war with Spain. Crane was working on a writing project at this time but decided to volunteer for service. He had already experienced the fear of war when he boarded a boat loaded with ammunition and arms for Cuba and escaped Spanish gunboats. Crane's ship, the *Commodore,* eventually sank off the Florida coast, but he was able to escape into a ten-foot dinghy. He fictionalized this event in his short story "The Open Boat."

There were several causes of the war. American investments in Cuba were being threatened by continual Cuban revolts against Spanish rule. The

Compare & Contrast

- **1860s:** The Southern cotton states, in a pro-secession move to protect their slave-based economy, formed The Confederate States of America. When the Civil War ended, the Industrial Revolution began in the U.S., and "King Cotton" was replaced by the growth of manufacturing in the South.

  1890s: With increased industrialization, labor strikes, such as the 1892 Homestead Steel strike and the 1894 Pullman railroad strike, erupted; a financial depression takes place between 1892 and 1894.

  Today: Labor strikes continue in transportation, civil service, and other sectors; financial insecurities exist among employees in downsizing corporations. The federal government must reduce a multibillion-dollar deficit, yet the stock market continues its strong performance.

- **1860s:** The American Civil War pits brother against brother, Southerner against Northerner. About 90,000 Confederate and 93,000 Union soldiers died, more men, in proportion to population, than the British and French lost in World War I.

  1890s: The sinking of the *Maine* ignites the Spanish-American War of 1898, which is won by the United States.

  Today: The U.S. is experiencing a period of peace and relative prosperity. The Cold War with the Soviet Union has ended, and the U.S. is not at war with any country.

- **1860s:** Cannons, rifles and revolvers, and swords and bayonets are an army's primary weapons during the Civil War.

  1890s: Naval power becomes increasingly important in warfare. Battleships and armored cruisers help the United States win the Spanish-American War.

  Today: Computers, satellites, stealth technology, and laser-guided weapons have changed the face of war. Several countries have nuclear capabilities.

Ostend Manifesto, a declaration issued by the United States, stated that if Spain refused to cede Cuba to the United States, it would be justified in taking the island by force. Also, the United States had been channeling money and munitions to aid Cuba, an act that created ill-feeling between the Spanish and American governments. The growth of anti-Spanish sentiment was fueled by "yellow journalism" tactics used during a newspaper war between Joseph Pulitzer of the New York *World* and William Randolph Hearst of the New York *Journal,* which saw the publication of many stories and pictures of the ill-fated Cuban insurrection of 1895. These stories were designed to secure newspaper readers, but they were often exaggerated accounts.

The most tangible causes of the war were the destruction of the Maine, at a cost of 260 officers and crew, and the New York *Journal's* famous masthead declaring, "Remember the Maine!", which roused the nation to action. Finally, President McKinley had to ask for a declaration of war against Spain. The war was easily won by the United States, and the Treaty of Paris in 1898 gave Cuba its independence. The United States became its protector, and the country also took possession of Guam, Puerto Rico, and the Philippine Islands. Further, the United States became a naval power and a leader in world affairs.

Critical Overview

After being serialized in magazines, *The Red Badge of Courage* was finally published in book form in the fall of 1895 to favorable reviews. George Wyndham, writing in the *New Review,* stated, "Mr. Crane has surely contrived a masterpiece." Stephen Crane's literary reputation was firmly established, and the twenty-four-year-old author's imaginative genius was hailed by critics and readers here and in England. As his letters of late 1895 and early 1896 suggest, Stephen Crane's literary situation was somewhat problematic, paradoxically because of the immense success of *The Red Badge of Courage.* It created something of a sensation in late 1895, and before the end of that year, Crane was a famous man, an international celebrity known on both sides of the Atlantic for his brilliant and uncompromisingly realistic portrayal of war. But he also spent money and suffered some notoriety as a bohemian and social radical. When the book was published, many readers disliked it, faulting its artificial style, far-fetched metaphors, and improper grammar and usage. His literary mentors, William Dean Howells and Hamlin Garland, thought the book less significant than his first novel, *Maggie, A Girl of the Streets,* which was in the realistic mode, and more in line with their style.

Crane's fame spread after his death. His work enjoyed a particular revival of interest in the 1920s, the decade of social iconoclasts. Joseph Hergesheimer, writing in *The Work of Stephen Crane,* called the work "both a novel and a narrative," adding, "I have an idea, too, that as it is poetry, lyrical as well as epic; no one, certainly, can deny that it is completely classic in its movement, its pace and return." *The Red Badge* was so original that it created many imitations of its style, and its realistic view of war.

During the 1950s, there was heavy critical emphasis on the religious themes in the novel. Crane had grown up in a deeply religious environment since his father had been a Methodist minister and his mother a devout Christian who often contributed articles to religious publications. Thus, critics equated one of Crane's characters in his book, Jim Conklin, with Christ. In particular, critic R.W. Stallman believed *The Red Badge of Courage* to be laden with religious symbols. In an introduction to *The Red Badge of Courage,* he alludes to the famous "sun-like-a-wafer" image as being particularly relevant as a religious symbol. Most of the criticism since the 1950s, however, has taken a different course, that of exploring Crane's artistic technique which blended elements of symbolism, impressionism, and naturalism.

One critic who places Crane in the Naturalistic school is Charles Child Walcutt. In his book *American Literary Naturalism: A Divided Stream,* Walcutt remarked that Crane "makes us see Henry Fleming as an emotional puppet controlled by whatever sight he sees at the moment." He added that Henry reacts "in a blind rage that turns him into an animal" without moral sense when he returns to war after receiving a wound to his head. Other critics focus on Crane's use of color imagery or impressionism (the use of light and color to describe an event or feeling). Another school of critics views Crane's depiction of Henry Fleming as an overly egocentric individual. His frequent ideas of his powers in war seem grandiose, but that is typical of one so young; it is difficult to see how he could tell his own war story otherwise. Crane himself was a young man when he wrote about Fleming, their ages just three to five years apart. This is a young man's novel about the meaning and the nature of being young. Therefore, the education of the naive, proud man is central to Crane's intent.

For the most part, critics agree that Crane disregarded plot and character delineation in his work and that he was unable to sustain longer works of fiction. However, with the proliferation of Crane scholarship during the past twenty years, his literary reputation has grown. One of the reasons why modern critics enjoy the novel is because it deals with a popular theme today: the isolated individual and his relationship to society. If human life has any meaning, man must look to it himself, Crane suggests, in a philosophy akin to today's existentialism. One critic, *American Literature* contributor Robert Shulman, observed that Crane's work shows him "responding to one of the deepest tendencies of his American society, its tendency to isolate individuals, to fragment selves and relations, and to substitute technological, contractual, and bureaucratic ties for those of human compassion and community." Critics contend that despite Crane's minor flaws, his artistry lies in his ability to convey a personal vision based on his own "quality of personal honesty" and that he pioneered a modern form of fiction that superceded the genteel realism of late nineteenth-century American literature.

Criticism

Sharon Cumberland

In the following essay, Cumberland, an assistant professor at Seattle University, provides a general overview of the novel and notes how Crane broke with Romantic traditions of the time by refusing to idealize war.

Stephen Crane's Civil War novel, *The Red Badge of Courage,* is remarkable in two ways: it is a quintessential coming-of-age story, and it is written in a style so original that many consider it to be the first modern American novel. Though written thirty years after the Civil War, in 1895, by a young man who had never seen warfare, Crane captured not only the disorientation and chaos of the battlefield, but found completely original ways to describe a foot soldier's experience. And though *The Red Badge of Courage* is part of a long tradition of war narratives, which extends from Homer's *The Iliad* to Leo Tolstoy's *War and Peace,* Crane departed from that tradition by presenting war from the point of view of a single ignorant private. No effort is made to characterize war as noble, death as glorious, or soldiers as particularly brave or admirable. Instead, *The Red Badge of Courage* is a study of the interior life of a young man, Henry Fleming, who is in turn confused, terrified, humiliated, and, ultimately, matured by his exposure to pitched battle.

Crane's strategy in *The Red Badge of Courage* is to create a sense of chaos and helplessness by withholding from the reader information that the common soldier would not have known. Henry Fleming does not know where he is at any time. It seems to the characters, as to the reader, that Fleming and his fellow soldiers are being arbitrarily moved around in mysterious patterns that suit the generals but mean nothing to the soldiers in the ranks. Scholars have determined from internal evidence, however, that Crane set his story during the Battle of Chancellorsville which took place from May 2 to May 6, 1863, near the little town of Chancellorsville, Virginia, and not far from Fredricksburg. Understanding something of that battle offers a useful perspective on Henry Fleming's odyssey to manhood, and on the settings in which each of his adventures takes place.

The Battle of Chancellorsville was fought between the Army of the Potomac, led by the Union general Joseph Hooker, and the Confederate army led by Robert E. Lee. The town was near the Rappahannock River and surrounded by a pine scrub forest called "The Wilderness." A great deal of the fighting took place in this forest, which accounts for the setting of Henry Fleming's period of desertion, and for the cathedral-like clearing in the woods where he encounters the dead soldier. Many of the skirmishes and encounters between the two armies also took place on the fields between Fredricksburg and the Wilderness. This accounts

What Do I Read Next?

- *All Quiet on the Western Front* by Erich Maria Remarque concerns a young German infantryman's experience in World War I.

- *The Catcher in the Rye* by J.D. Salinger relates in first person the story of a adolescent in New York City and his ironic, and comic, views of life.

- *Gone With the Wind* by Margaret Mitchell tells the saga of a young woman's life during the Civil War and Reconstruction periods in the South.

- *Homage to Catalonia* by George Orwell is a British soldier's firsthand account of the Spanish Civil War, during which he fought with the Republicans against fascism.

for the battle scenes in which Henry finds himself running wildly at the enemy over an open plain.

Lee's army was outnumbered by two to one, but his clever maneuvering gave the Rebel army the early advantage. Using his brilliant cavalry division, led by Stonewall Jackson, Lee forced the superior Federal troops into a desperate retreat on the first day of the battle. Henry Fleming sees these retreating soldiers as he approaches the front and fantasizes that the generals are leading them into a trap. He was not far from the truth.

Unfortunately for Lee, Stonewall Jackson received the wound that killed him in this battle, and on the second day the Federals pushed the Rebels back in one of the few bayonet charges of the war. Instead of pressing his advantage, however, General Hooker ordered the Union Army to fall back, allowing Lee to reform his line and continue the fight for another two days. The dismay and distrust that Crane represents among the Federal foot soldiers was felt in real life by the officers who served under Hooker. According to James M. McPherson in *Battle Cry of Freedom: The Civil War Era,* upon receiving orders to retreat instead of advance, one of Hooker's officers reported that he believed his commanding officer to be "a whipped man." By the end of the encounter, Lee had triumphed over the Union Army and scored one of the most resounding triumphs of the war. President Lincoln, when told of Hooker's defeat despite his tremendous advantage, exclaimed, "My God! My God! What will the country say?"

Henry Fleming, as a Union soldier being ordered here and there during one of the great fiascoes of the Civil War, is neither irrational nor cowardly for his perception of the battle as insane chaos. Nor can he be blamed for his decision to leave the front, since everything he is asked to do seems pointless. *The Red Badge of Courage* is a study in what a rational person can do in an irrational situation. Ultimately Fleming realizes that he must face his fear and reservations for the sake of his reputation and for the sake of his comrades.

Stephen Crane (1871-1900) was writing in the last decade of the century, a period that has a distinctive quality in all aspects of the arts. Romanticism had dominated literary and visual arts for the first half of the nineteenth century, and the time was ripe for new ideas as the twentieth century approached.

The Romantic movement was represented in England by Wordsworth, Coleridge, Keats, Byron, and Shelley, and in America by the Transcendentalists (Emerson, Thoreau, and Fuller, among others) and by Walt Whitman. It was a movement characterized by three attributes: 1) free and natural expression, rather than the artificial formality of the eighteenth century; 2) the elevation of the common man as a subject of literature; and 3) the use of the natural landscape to reflect human passion and expressiveness. Two schools of thought emerged in mid-century as literature developed beyond Romanticism and then reacted against these trends in writing: Realism and Impressionism.

Realism is related to Romanticism in that it draws upon the life of the common man and woman for material and inspiration. But instead of idealizing the lives of common folk, the Realists focus on the brutal and ugly aspects of lower class people and their difficult and often sordid lives. Clearly Stephen Crane is writing in the Realistic manner, since his subjects are common men presented with all their problems and flaws. A romantic telling of this story would have emphasized courage, heroism, and glorious death rather than cowardice, fear, and rotten corpses. A romantic telling of this story might also have implied that the soldiers were dy-

ing in a glorious cause of which God approved, and that their souls were going straight to heaven. Crane's realistic version of war offers the soldier no such comfort. In the realistic universe there is no God to make human folly seem sane. Henry Fleming is forced to confront the fact of death and the inevitability of his own death.

Another way in which Realism is related to but goes beyond Romanticism is in the use of nature. The Romantics projected their own imaginations onto the natural landscape, giving it magical powers. Realists, responding to Darwin's discovery of natural selection, saw nature in terms of the survival of the fittest. Part of Henry Fleming's maturing process requires that he accept the fact that predators—the enemy—are determined to kill him. He decides that it is better to be the predator and to kill his enemy than to allow the enemy to kill him.

Crane's writing style has also been described as Impressionism, a phenomenon in the literary world that responded to a corresponding impulse in the art world. French Impressionism was a school of painting that rejected Romanticism in the visual arts for the detached observation of nature. Impressionists tried to paint what they saw without adding content from their own emotions or imagination. Monet, Renoir, Cezanne, and Manet attempted to paint nature by breaking their observations down into pieces of light and showing each part independently from every other part. The same principle can be observed in *The Red Badge of Courage* because Crane describes Fleming's experiences almost as a collection of snapshots, without a coherent time sequence to give them meaning. Henry observes many things, but none of them hang together; no picture emerges that makes sense to him. Just as art critics had to learn how to understand Impressionism, Henry learns to find order in his apparently meaningless universe.

The Red Badge of Courage is a favorite text for intermediate and high school students because it is one of the great coming–of–age novels. How does a young person assume his or her place in the world of adult responsibilities? Every young person must confront the fear associated with being expected to take charge rather than to be taken care of. Sometimes the moment comes in a decision, as when Huckleberry Finn decides to help his friend Jim, even if he gets in trouble for supporting an escaped slave. Sometimes it comes in acceptance of the inevitable, as when Scarlett O'Hara in *Gone With the Wind* recognizes that many people depend upon her resourcefulness for their survival. *The Red Badge of Courage* offers a powerful text on the internal struggle of one young person to accept the great—even unreasonable—responsibilities placed upon him that will transform him from a child to an adult. This is the primary thematic approach for younger students.

For older students, the historical and stylistic themes described in the sections above give a rich context to *The Red Badge of Courage*. In addition, one can also examine Crane's text for his rich use of symbolism. Even as the "red badge" in the title represents courage, or the courage it takes to suffer a bleeding wound, so Crane uses the landscape, the other soldiers, and an array of colors and images to represent Henry Fleming's inner state. One of the most fruitful methods to use in reading *The Red Badge of Courage* is to trace Crane's descriptions of the weather, the countryside, animals, colors, sounds, or any other element one chooses, to Henry's state of mind. Crane always reflects his protagonist's feelings in some concrete object in the environment. One of the most famous images from this book, for instance, comes after Henry's friend Jim Conklin has just died: "The red sun was pasted in the sky like a wafer." The red color reflects Jim's death, while the flatness of the sun being "pasted" reflects Henry's sense of being numbed, flattened by his loss. The use of the word "wafer," however, suggests the eucharistic wafer, the body of Christ offered in communion, with all its connotations of sacrificial death and redemption.

Source: Sharon Cumberland, in an essay for *Novels for Students,* Gale, 1998.

Paul Breslin

In the following excerpt, Breslin explains how Henry, though he at first flees from battle, matures into a soldier able to accept the "inevitability of death."

The Red Badge of Courage is a familiar book, and its genre is in part familiar as well—the tale of initiation, the adventure story. Crane himself meant it to be a popular novel, a potboiler to bring in money while he worked on more serious projects. But the novel does differ, almost startlingly, from other treatments of the Civil War in the same period, not so much by what it includes as by what it leaves out. The most striking feature of *The Red Badge of Courage* is the absence of any social context in which the fighting takes place. One could almost say that Crane writes of war in the abstract. Such a treatment is sometimes met with in twentieth-century literature, but it was quite unorthodox in 1895. In particular, Crane's exclusion of the intense religious and moral atmosphere surrounding the Civil War, juxtaposed with an often-remarked abundance of religious terminology and imagery, makes *The Red Badge* point beyond itself in a way that its author perhaps did not consciously intend....

The excitement of warfare fascinated Crane, but he also seems to have understood, by the time he wrote *The Red Badge,* that impassive, matter-of-fact demeanor that had puzzled him in *Battles and Leaders of the Civil War* [edited by Robert Underwood Johnson and Clarence Clough Buel, 1887]. When one must be prepared to kill or to be killed in the course of a day's work, one cannot afford the luxury of introspection; presumably, any moral and psychological reservations about taking and risking life have been worked out beforehand, and if not, they must simply be laid aside. Like the surgeon, the soldier must disengage his imagination from what he is doing. The danger of this necessary detachment is an alienation of action from meaning. One can see this excessive detachment in the memoirs of the Civil War's most distinguished general, Ulysses S. Grant, who also had a civilian career of some importance.

Grant never wanted to enter the military in the first place, but went to West Point on his father's insistence. After his graduation, the Mexican War broke out, and his comments on it show a curious split between his private and soldierly morality:

> Generally the officers were indifferent whether the annexation was consummated or not; but not so all of them. For myself, I was bitterly opposed to the measure, and to this day regard the war as one of the most unjust ever waged by a stronger against a weaker nation. It was an instance of a republic following the bad example of European monarchies, in not considering justice in their desire to acquire additional territory.

But he fought in the Mexican War, and he describes his battles with cold lucidity, scarcely bothering to reconcile his opinion with his participation. He spent the interlude between the Mexican War and the Civil War as a civilian, then returned to service because he supported the Union cause—but not for Lincoln's reasons. He thought secession legal, and his objection was merely that the South had resisted Constitutional power instead of seceding years earlier when it had the chance. He did not believe that the country must be all slave or all free, though he changed his mind later, after the war.

Grant was an even-tempered soldier, a paragon of military professionalism. His accounts of battles read like military dispatches and, as Wilson points out, he avoids vivid descriptions of the havoc of war. The mature Henry Fleming, though not as stolid as Grant, has the same poker-faced detachment from his own feelings. It is his cowardice, rather than his aggression, that tempts him toward guilty introspection; but though the occasion is different, the response is the same. Henry must deliberately suspend the contemplative faculty. His success as a soldier depends not so much upon a moral or spiritual growth as upon a practical adjustment to the psychology of combat.

In the course of *The Red Badge of Courage,* Henry Fleming learns, essentially, what his mother had told him before his enlistment: "Don't go a-thinkin' you can lick the hull rebel army at the start, because yeh can't. Yer jest one little feller amongst a hull lot of others and yeh've got to keep quiet an' do what they tell yeh." This does not mean that he learns humility in the moral sense, but rather that he gains a practical sense of perspective which enables him to be a better soldier. His education is largely outside the realm of morality. The goal which prompted his enlistment, recognition, never changes. Even in the last charge, he is not interested in winning the battle as much as in being a hero:

> The youth had resolved not to budge whatever should happen. Some arrows of scorn that had buried themselves in his heart, had generated strange and unspeakable hatreds. It was clear to him that his final and absolute revenge was to be achieved by his dead body lying, torn and guttering, upon the field. This was to be a poignant retaliation upon the officer who had said "mule driver," and later "mud digger." For in all the wild graspings of his mind for a unit responsible for his sufferings and commotions, he always seized upon the man who had dubbed him wrongly.

Henry enlists against the advice of his mother, who "had affected to look with some contempt upon the quality of his war ardor and patriotism." We share her doubts as Henry bids farewell to his schoolmates. He was nobody; now he is suddenly special, and this is what he wants. However, the gesture of enlistment commits him to action, and the rest of the story deals with his acceptance of the less pleasant aspects of soldiership.

In camp, young Fleming seems to think the whole world is concerned with one question: will he run? It is significant that Jim Conklin echoes his mother's advice, saying, "All yeh got t'do is t'sit down an' wait as quiet as yeh kin," and "it ain't likely they'll [the regiment] lick th' hull rebel army all-to-onct th' first time." He who thinks he can lick the whole rebel army also is responsible for the whole Union defeat if he does not. Henry's egotism places an enormous burden on his shoulders. In trying to set his mind at rest, he intuitively looks in the right direction: he tries to determine what the others are feeling; but it does not occur to him that no one else is any more likely to admit self-doubt than he is.

During the regiment's advance, the thing that most troubles Henry is that he doesn't know what to expect. He cannot reason ahead. Already, there have been false rumors of battle. As the men cross the stream, he expects they will meet the enemy. They do not. His resolution is shaken, partially because he has too much "opportunity to reflect." Doubtless, the corpse which the regiment has just passed contributes to his faded spirits; it is his first encounter with death. He lingers, tempted by "the impulse of the living to try to read in dead eyes the answer to the Question." The question will be answered, most bitterly, by the eyes of another corpse in the forest "chapel."

Fleming is still decidedly puffed up with his own importance. He wants to cry out a warning to turn back, but:

> He saw that even if the men were tottering with fear, they would laugh at his warning. They would jeer him and if practicable pelt him with missiles.

That they might ignore him never enters his mind. His self-engrossment also blinds him to the situation around him, a blindness dangerous in warfare. He is so busy feeling tragically responsible that he lags behind the march.

During the battle that follows, Henry tries various conventional ways of calming himself. He belittles death and affirms his patriotic solidarity. He convinces himself that death is "nothing but rest"; and later, he has "suddenly lost concern for himself" and feels lost in a larger identity, "a regiment, an army, a cause, or a country" that is "in a crisis." Although the collective identity remains vague throughout the book, the communal sense deepens as Henry matures. Henry also begins to think of himself as a craftsman at work—he begins to acquire some military professionalism.

Once again, it is surprise that upsets Henry's delicate balance. The enemy's counterattack is unexpected. Crane compares the resentment of Henry's regiment to a rebellion against a god: "The slaves toiling in the temple of this god began to feel rebellion at his harsh tasks." Clearly, this is a pagan rather than Christian deity. Shortly afterward

Henry, seeing the first cowards depart, runs also. His fear is more intense once he runs, again because of uncertainty, for "Death about to thrust him between the shoulder blades was far more dreadful than death about to smite him between the eyes."

Fleeing into the woods to escape death, Henry finds death. Here he asks "the question," first of Nature, then of the corpse. The question may be phrased, roughly, Is there any hope of escape from death? At first, the peace of the forest and the nimble escape of the squirrel reassure him; but the animal pouncing on the fish in black water is an equally true example of natural law; and the corpse answers the question with a resounding No. It is not, in this context, a particular corpse, but the image of Henry's fate and everyone else's. It is the shrine of the war god.

Olov Fryckstedt sees in this passage a satire on "the transcendentalist and romantic view that nature could give man direct answers to his petty problems." To this one might add that the Calvinists, with their argument of design in nature, also fall in the domain of this satire. These two groups are the prime believers in the holy war, the "army of the Lord."

The real point of the scene for Henry, though, is an acceptance of the reality and inevitability of death. War, for Crane, is a heightened instance of the indifferent, Darwinistic universe which, for [Theodore] Dreiser (or the Crane of *Maggie, A Girl of the Streets*) found its symbol in the modern city. Henry, by enlisting, has committed himself to live by the laws of such a universe. When all roads lead to death, there is nothing to run from and nothing to run to. If there is no escape, one must simply make the best of the situation. When Henry's reverie is interrupted by the sound of fighting, he begins running back toward the battle.

The forest chapel scene gives Henry the laws of his reality, but it is no spur to his conscience, which alas remains impenitent. His reentry into the war is not accomplished by penitence, but by perspective:

> It suddenly occurred to the youth that the fight in which he had been was, after all, but perfunctory popping....

> Reflecting, he saw a sort of humor in the point of view of himself and his fellows during the late encounter. They had taken themselves and the enemy very seriously and had imagined that they were ... enshrining their reputations for ever in the hearts of their countrymen, while, as to fact, the affair would appear in printed reports under a meek and immaterial title.

Before Henry reaches his regiment, he falls in with the wounded, and there ensues a scene which would draw guilt from anyone with talent for that emotion. First a soldier queries him about his nonexistent wound; again he tries to escape but, as before, runs from bad to worse. He finds his old friend, Jim Conklin, dying a hideous death. Henry's reaction to all this is not guilt but anger:

> The youth turned, with sudden, livid rage, toward the battlefield. He shook his fist. He seemed about to deliver a Philippic.

> "Hell—"

> The red sun was pasted in the sky like a wafer.

Whether he shakes his fist at the battlefield, as appears, or at the sky, as Stallman claims the manuscript proves, he does not shake it at himself.

Bashed over the head with a rifle, Fleming discovers a pragmatism upon returning to his regiment. If no one can tell the difference between a drubbing and a war wound, then none exists, according to William James; and Fleming cheerfully accepts the verdict. It is important to realize that Crane does not condemn him for this, that indeed, from this point on, Henry fights as admirably as any man who did not run; and that a confession might have destroyed his confidence. Courage and conscience, as Grant's memoirs show, need not influence each other.

All the while, Henry continues to value his own standing more than victory. He says that he has "never lost his greed for a victory," but admits, "in a half-apologetic manner to his conscience," that "a defeat for the army this time might mean many favorable things for him." If everyone retreats, his own cowardice will not stand out by contrast. He has gained a certain poise when he returns. He shakes off the terrible fantasy suggested by the thought of the wounded sleeping around him at dawn. He is less easily overcome by appearances, and he ceases his railing at circumstances. Yet, as a passage deleted from the final version makes explicit, his confidence is just as self-centered as his fear:

> But he was now, in a measure, a successful man, and he could no longer tolerate in himself a spirit of fellowship for poets. He abandoned them. Their songs about black landscape were of no importance to him, since his new eyes said that his landscape was not black. People who called landscape black were idiots.

At about this time, Henry convinces himself of something which, though it puts him at ease in battle, is directly contrary to fact: that he is somehow "chosen of gods and doomed to greatness." This feeling expands to almost mystical delusions of invulnerability later on. A heightened awareness reminiscent of Farquar's in Bierce's "An Occurrence at Owl Creek Bridge" is accompanied by

> a mad enthusiasm that, it seemed, would be incapable of checking itself before granite and brass. There was the delirium that encounters despair and death, and is heedless and blind to the odds. It is a temporary but sublime absence of selfishness.

Crane obviously admires this courage, even though it does not belong to a man but merely possesses him sporadically, and even though it is grounded in illusion. The same Henry Fleming, moments after his "temporary but sublime absence of selfishness," has a tug-of-war with his companion for the regimental flag.

At the very end of the story, Henry is on the verge of guilt, but casts it out. He had run not because he was a coward, but because he was caught in "the wild mistakes and ravings of a novice who did not comprehend." Not only that, he rationalizes, his sin "would make a sobering balance. It would become a good part of him." In *The Veteran,* Crane portrays Henry Fleming as an old man still impenitent and still, to his death, genuinely courageous.

It is, I believe, Henry's impenitence, combined with a real physical courage, that is responsible for the irony of *The Red Badge of Courage.* (One feels that Crane himself was only half-conscious of the implications of his treatment, but the irony, however it came there, is in the book.) Crane's whole life testifies to his admiration for courage, and Henry Fleming unquestionably has it. But we want more from our heroes than courage: we want them to be great souls. Crane is telling us not only that courage can exist without a great soul but, further, that brave men often cannot afford great souls. We have nurtured the myth that all our wars have been fought, with great reluctance, on grounds of principle or conscience, and we do not like to be told otherwise. Crane's potboiler proves to be a more subversive book than his slum tales that shocked so many readers of the 1890s.

Source: Paul Breslin, "Courage and Convention: *The Red Badge of Courage,*" in *The Yale Review,* December, 1976, pp. 209-22.

Eric Solomon

In the following excerpt, Solomon claims that with The Red Badge of Courage, *Crane revolutionized how modern war novels would be told.*

In spite of the abundance of war novels produced by two world conflicts, *The Red Badge of Courage* is still the masterwork of war fiction. Stephen Crane's novel is the first work in English fiction of any length purely dedicated to an artistic reproduction of war, and it has rarely been approached in scope or intensity since it was published in 1895.

Any judgment of the influence of *The Red Badge of Courage* on later war fiction would of necessity be conjectural. The circumstance that Ford Madox Ford and Ernest Hemingway worshipped at the Crane shrine does not in itself prove that *No More Parades* or *A Farewell to Arms* was directly affected by Crane's book. But the novel became part of the literary heritage of the twentieth century, and whether or not a war writer consciously recalls Crane's performance, the fact remains that *The Red Badge of Courage* is a touchstone for modern war fiction. Stephen Crane gave the war novel its classic form.

Crane, however, made no great innovation in style or subject matter. Realism, irony, detail, the emotional impact of combat—all these had appeared somewhere in earlier war fiction. The contribution of Stephen Crane to the genre of war fiction was twofold. First, he defined the form in his novel that deals with war and its effect upon the sensitive individual who is inextricably involved; war is treated as neither journalism nor autobiography nor dashing romance, but as a test of mind and spirit in a situation of great tension. Crane also constructed a book that still stands as the technical masterpiece in the field....

The essential quality of Crane's novel cannot be derived from the study of one man's response to war. War has presented, among other things, a highly developed social problem ever since the days of individual combat were over. The gradation of the army system and its rigid chain of command combine with the massive troop movements of modern warfare to make combat a reflection of a special society with its own precise rules of conformity. And as Mark Schorer has pointed out [in "Foreword," *Critiques and Essays on Modern Fiction*] any novel must find a form that will encompass both the individual and social experiences.

It may not be immediately obvious that *The Red Badge of Courage* is more than the story of the young soldier who is Crane's hero and point-of-view character. The author does not try to describe his individuals fully. We do not even know the youth's whole name until Chapter Twelve. Taking Crane's novel on its own terms, we need not expect rounded figures, logically described, having past histories; neither should we overlook Henry Fleming's comrades in the war situation.

Henry comes into close contact with five other soldiers in his passage from apprenticeship to mastery. Of these, the tall soldier, Jim Conklin, is most important. Henry identifies with Conklin's calm attitude when faced with combat and attempts to accept his steadying advice. The death of Conklin has particular meaning to the hero; just as in Crane's story, *The Open Boat,* the stronger personality does not survive the test. The loud soldier, Wilson, a foil to Henry's fears at the start, undergoes a similar, and even more rapid, growth to manhood through the ordeal. The attitude of the somewhat anonymous lieutenant, Hasbrouck, reflects the hero's place in the military society. When Henry is a coward, the officer strikes at him with a sword, but when the youth is fighting well, he and the lieutenant are filled with mutual admiration.

Two more figures, shadowy ones to be sure, but still vividly realized, provide a commentary on the soldier's progress. Direct opposites, the tattered soldier whom Henry leaves wandering blindly in a field, and the cheery stranger who guides Henry back to his regiment, signify respectively betrayal and comradeship. The interaction of the hero with these five characters and the regiment as a whole furnishes the fundamental theme of *The Red Badge of Courage.* The standards by which Henry's development is measured are those of group loyalty rather than fear and courage. Although the secondary characters are typed, and meant to be so, and not sharply individualized, they are still effectively presented.

The novel opens on the large picture of the entire fighting force. "The cold passed reluctantly from the earth and the retiring fogs revealed an army stretched out on the hills, resting." As in a motion-picture opening, the scene gradually focuses on a particular group of soldiers—Conklin doing his washing, Wilson arguing violently, and then on Henry in a solitude of self-mistrust.

The key to Henry's development, and the essential meaning of war for him, comes in the flashback to his farewell from his mother. The importance of this scene is not in his mother's adjuration to do his duty bravely, nor in the general antiromantic atmosphere of cows and socks, but in her words that remind the youth of his own insignificance in the larger scheme. "'Yer jest one little feller amongst a hull lot of others, and yeh've got

to keep quiet an' do what they tell yeh. I know how you are, Henry.'" She knows, but he must learn in battle what kind of a man he is.

Henry's vanity does not allow him to be a little fellow among a whole lot of others except in the rare moments of rationalization when he comforts himself with the consideration that he is part of a vast blue demonstration. Because abstract judgment fails him in his fear, he is isolated. Crane stresses Henry's feeling of solitude. He has no one with whom to compare suspicions; he is different, "alone in space," "a mental outcast." Both the calm competence of the tall soldier and the brash assurance of the loud soldier convince Henry that his is a unique weakness.

When the regiment advances for its baptism of fire, Henry is a part of the group, albeit unwillingly. He feels himself carried along by a mob. The image Crane uses to signify Henry's attitude of helplessness is important. "...there were iron laws of tradition and law [sic] on four sides. He was in a moving box." He is doing exactly what his mother warned him against, considering himself an important individual. He hates the lieutenant and believes that only he, Henry, knows that the entire regiment is being betrayed. In other words, the youth revolts against the iron laws of the war world, the traditions of obedience and humility in the ranks. Crane plays off Henry's condition of rage against Jim Conklin's faithful acceptance of the new environment. The other soldiers are shadowy figures in Henry's mind, since his ego has denied him the comforts of military friendships. He is too wrapped up in himself to realize that others are in the same condition of doubt and fear.

A sudden shift in emphasis takes place when the battle starts, as Henry rapidly adjusts to reality. Losing concern with himself for the moment, he becomes "not a man but a member," a part of a "common personality," a "mysterious fraternity." Whereas in his isolation and doubt he was trapped in a moving box, now, by sinking his personality into the larger personality of the group, he regains control of himself. Crane describes Henry's combat activity with the same box image as before, but there is one important difference. Henry is now in charge. "He was like a carpenter who has made many boxes, making still another box...."

Crane transfers the point of view from Henry to the regiment at this juncture. In the impressionistic battle scene, the focus is on "the men," "they," "a soldier" while the regiment goes about its grim business. An integral part of Henry's development is the realization that even the regiment is not the only important participant in the battle. He understands that the fighting involves many regiments and momentarily grasps the idea of his own relative unimportance. But Crane is too acute a psychologist to conceive such a rapid character change and have Henry learn the soldier's hardest lesson easily. When the break in the combat comes, Henry reverts to his pride and considers his rather petty action to have been magnificent. He must undergo a more serious test before he can reap the full benefits of his war experience.

The second attack is too much for him. Henry cannot comprehend the rules of war that are so irrational as to impose another test so soon. He deserts the group, and by this act he breaks all the rigid rules of war. The sight of the lieutenant, angrily dabbing at him with his sword, symbolizes for Henry his new role as an outcast. The youth is no longer, in the Conradian sense, one of them. He asks himself, "What manner of men were they anyhow?" those fools who stayed behind to meet certain death.

The novel is not merely a portrait of fear; it is the portrait of a mind that learns to come to terms with itself and to live down an act of cowardice. Henry Fleming must become a man according to the rules war sets forth. Therefore, he must cast off the egoism that made him run, and gain a true perspective on his importance.

The book is often ironic, since his growth is neither particularly moral nor is it without fluctuations. Henry's failures and successes in war are those of a hero *manqué,* if we are to measure them by the usual Christian ethic. But *The Red Badge of Courage* is a war novel, and Henry Fleming should be judged by the ideals of a war world. The lesson Henry has to learn is basic to combat. The individual cannot depend on his personal reasoning powers. Henry's mind has seen the danger and he has fled, while his stupid comrades have stayed and shown courage. The beginning of wisdom comes with the comprehension that his own judgment is insufficient. He is in the position of a criminal because of his enlightened intellect. Henry feels the bitterness and rage of an outcast, a sensitive dreamer who, trapped between romance and reality, can make the best of neither world. Caught in a box of his own making, Henry faces the age-old problem of the individual at odds with society. He has not only indulged in an act of self-betrayal, he has thrown over his responsibilities to and for the others. He does not yet understand that his own salvation (physical and spiritual) must be the product

of his dedication to universal salvation. Henry's story is not tragic, because, unlike Lord Jim, the young soldier manages to compensate for his antisocial action and work his way back to the fellowship of men which, in the world of war, is represented by the regiment. But the road back is not easy.

After his dark night of the soul passed in the forest where nature appears to second war's cruelty, Henry commences his return to the battle—to life or death. The physical isolation of the youth ends when he meets a line of wounded soldiers staggering towards the rear, soldiers coming out of the active world from which Henry had fled. Henry joins the crowd, but he remains an outsider, for he has no wound. Crane reverses the symbolism of Hawthorne's *The Scarlet Letter* or "The Minister's Black Veil." Henry is distinguished by his *lack* of any mark. "He was continually casting sidelong glances to see if the men were contemplating the letters of guilt he felt burned into his brow.... He wished that he, too, had a wound, a red badge of courage." Ironically enough, he desires to be marked by the red death he had feared. Honor, or the appearance of honor, is his new goal.

As if to emphasize his sin, Henry remains with the denizens of the strange world of wounded. He meets the tattered man, one of Crane's most brilliant portraits of a nameless figure. We know nothing about the tattered man except that he is wounded, and that he is a rather naïve and gentle soul. He is the antithesis of the young soldier in every way. The tattered man has been hit; he talks proudly of his regiment and its performance; he is humble and loves the army. In other words, he stands for the simple man who has done his duty and received his mark of honor. The tattered man represents society, and to the conscience-stricken Henry the wounded soldier is a reminder of guilt. Henry cannot remain with the tattered man when he asks the probing question, "'Where yeh hit, ol' boy?',' that emphasizes the youth's isolation.

A greater shock is in store for Henry Fleming. After he leaves his tattered companion behind, he meets the spectral soldier—the tall soldier, Jim Conklin—transformed by a fatal wound. Henry's feeble wish for a little wound pales into the realm of bathos in comparison to Conklin's passion. The dying man's expression of sympathy and concern for Henry adds to the acute discomfort of the youth's position. In his walk through the valley of the shadow of death at Conklin's side, Henry's education advances. Conklin's death brings home to Henry the true nature of war, brutal and forbidding, more than the sight of an unknown corpse in the forest could do. The body of his friend stretched out before him, Henry curses the universe that allows such things to be. He shakes his fist at the battlefield and swears, but his insignificance in the larger scheme is indicated by Crane's most famous line, "The red sun was pasted in the sky like a wafer."

Despite his genuine grief at Conklin's death, Henry is unable to accept responsibility for the tattered man, who has returned to pry at Henry's guilty secret, the crime "concealed in his bosom." He deserts the tattered man a second time, and in denying him the young soldier commits his real sin. He breaks both a Christian and a military ethical rule ("Greater love hath no man...."). Like his original act of cowardice, this desertion goes unpunished. If we are to read the novel as a study in irony, there is no confusion; Henry is a sinner who succeeds in war without ever changing his ways. Crane's attitude towards his hero is ambiguous throughout the novel, however, and the betrayal of the tattered man is essential to Henry's growth to maturity. Although the tattered man himself says that "'a man's first allegiance is to number one'," Henry realizes what he has done. His later heroism is a successful attempt to wipe out his cowardice. While he eventually rationalizes his betrayal, the memory of the tattered man blocks any real return to the egocentric immaturity that marked his character at the outset of the novel.

He heads back to the "furnace" of combat, since the heat of that purgatory is clearly more desirable than the icy chill of solitude. His progress is halting. Henry is unable to throw off his romantic visions; he imagines his new self in a picturesque and sublime role as a leader of lurid charges. Once again the reality of war breaks his dreams apart, reality in the forms of physical exhaustion, thirst, and the memory of his cowardice. No longer a visionary, Henry can now make his way through the war world.

Crane's bitterness comes to the surface in this part of the novel. Henry is really worried about appearance. How can he pretend to be something he is not—a hero? It is when the self-centered youth is concerned with the difficulty of fabricating a lie effective enough to account for his disappearance that his full name is given for the first time by the author. The young soldier mentions it in apprehension of the name, "Henry Fleming," becoming a synonym for coward. Names and appearances are his only concern.

Henry Fleming's actions must be judged by the standards of war. While he is planning his lie (a sin, from a normal ethical viewpoint), fate, in the form of a hysterical soldier who clubs Henry out of the way, provides the wound that not only preserves the appearance of his integrity but also opens the way for his attainment of genuine honor. It is ironic, even cynical, for war to help Henry after he has broken the rules, and for the coward to pass as a hero. Two other points must be kept in mind, however. Crane constantly refers to his hero as "the youth," and despite his transgressions, Henry is still an innocent fumbling for the correct path, not a hardened sinner. Furthermore, he does not receive his wound in flight, but in the performance of an act of courage! Henry is struck down (by a coward) while inarticulately striving "to make a rallying speech, to sing a battle hymn." He is in a position to suffer such a wound because he has originally fled from his regiment, but he is going against the current of retreating infantry, *towards* the battle, when he gains the red badge. The wound, then, may be seen as the result of heroism, not cowardice, and the irony is vitiated. Henry has escaped from his nightmare of weakness before he is wounded. His own efforts have proved him not completely unworthy of the saving grace granted him by the fate of war.

The wounded Henry is again part of the fellowship of armed men. "The owner of the cheery voice," who plays Mr. Strongheart in Henry's progress, guides the dazed youth through the forest wasteland back to the regiment. The gratuitous support of the cheery man is in direct contrast to Henry's earlier refusal to accompany the tattered man. The first twelve chapters of the novel come to an end with Henry outlined in the reflection of his regiment's campfires. The return to the company, which in war fiction has stood for homecoming from Kipling's "The Man Who Was" to Jones's *From Here to Eternity,* marks the completion of Henry Fleming's isolation and the start of the conquest of glory for himself and the regiment.

The hero of Crane's war novel has not yet learned what the author is in a later story to call "virtue in war." His relief at the arrival back into the "low-arched hall" of the forest (a suggestion perhaps of the mead hall of the Old English epics, the symbol of the fellowship of strong warriors) is intense. He views the sleeping company with complacency because to all appearances he is one of them, since he performed his mistakes in the dark. In the second part of the novel Henry will come to understand war and his own nature. For the present, it is enough to go to sleep with his fellows. "He gave a long sigh, snuggled down into his blanket, and in a moment was like his comrades."

Source: Eric Solomon, "The Structure of *The Red Badge of Courage,* in *Modern Fiction Studies,* Autumn, 1959, pp. 220-34.

Sources

Joseph Hergesheimer, "Introduction: 'The Red Badge of Courage', 1895–1924," in *The Work of Stephen Crane, Vol. I,* edited by Wilson Follett, 1925. Reprint by Russell & Russell, 1963, pp. ix-xviii.

Donald Pizer, "Nineteenth-Century American Naturalism: An Essay in Definition," *Bucknell University Review,* Fall, 1965.

Robert Shulman, "Community, Perception, and the Development of Stephen Crane: From 'The Red Badge' to 'The Open Boat'," in *American Literature,* Vol. 50, No. 3, November, 1978, pp. 441–60.

R.W. Stallman, "Introduction" in *The Red Badge of Courage: An Episode of the American Civil War,* by Stephen Crane, The Modern Library, 1951, pp. v-xxxvii.

R.W. Stallman, *Stephen Crane, an Omnibus,* New York: 1952.

Charles Child Walcutt, "Stephen Crane: Naturalist and Impressionist," in his *American Literary Naturalism: A Divided Stream,* University of Minnesota Press, Minneapolis, 1956, pp. 66–86.

Edmund Wilson, *Patriotic Gore: Studies in the literature of the American Civil War,* 1962 New York: Norton, 1994.

George Wyndham, "A Remarkable Book," in *New Review,* Vol. XIV, No,. 80, January, 1896, pp. 30–40.

For Further Study

Maurice Bassan, editor, *Stephen Crane: A Collection of Critical Essays,* Prentice-Hall, 1967.
 This collection is notable for its reprint of essays by other famous authors of Crane's period who report on his personality ("When I Knew Stephen Crane" by Willa Cather) and the sensational effect of the publication of *The Red Badge of Courage* ("His War Book" by Joseph Conrad). This collection also contains the famous essay "Crane's Art" by poet John Berryman and many other useful discussions of Crane's place in American and world literature.

Thomas Beer, *Stephen Crane: A Study in American Letters,* Knopf, 1923.
 Beer's work was the first biography about Crane. Though later scholars have found some factual errors in the book, it is still considered an important work.

Frank Bergon, in his *Stephen Crane's Artistry,* Columbia University Press, 1975.
 Bergon analyzes the aspects of Crane's use of dreams and dream images in his literature. He offers a complete characterization of Crane's style.

John Berryman, in his *Stephen Crane: A Critical Biography,* Sloane, 1950.
 A biography of Crane notable for being written by one of the important poets of the post World War II era, whose insights into Crane and his work have not yet been superseded by more scholarly biographies.

John Berryman, *Stephen Crane: A Critical Biography,* Farrar, Straus, 1982.
 This biography examines symbolism in Crane's work, with an interesting chapter on his Freudian themes.

Harold Bloom, editor, *Modern Critical Interpretations: The Red Badge of Courage,* Chelsea House, 1987.
 A collection of critical essays containing discussions of psychology, literary impressionism, and the heroic ideal in *The Red Badge of Courage.* Sophisticated but important theory for a more contemporary, postmodern understanding of Crane's novel.

Edwin H. Cady, in his *Stephen Crane,* revised edition, Twayne, 1980.
 This is a balanced critical biography.

Richard Chase, *The Red Badge of Courage and Other Writings,* Houghton, 1960.
 A critical view of Crane's contribution as a naturalist writer. Chase contests Stallman's view that Crane is a symbolist.

James B. Colvert, "Stephen Crane," in *Concise Dictionary of American Literary Biography: Realism, Naturalism, and Local Color, 1865–1917* Gale, 1988, pp. 88-109.
 Colvert presents an in-depth survey of Crane's major works, and adds perspective to the author's similarity to Rudyard Kipling.

Lois Hill, *Poems and Songs of the Civil War,* Gramercy Books, 1990.
 A very useful collection of the popular songs and poems that common soldiers like Henry Fleming would have sung and cherished. Songs such as "Lorena," "The Vacant Chair," and "The Bonnie Blue Flag" and poems such as Whitman's "Bivoac on a Mountainside" and Melville's "Running the Batteries" give the real flavor of the war—often sentimental—that Crane was trying to capture.

James M. McPherson, *Battle Cry of Freedom: The Civil War Era,* Ballentine Books, 1988.
 This is the only one-volume treatment of the entire Civil War, and by all accounts, one of the best. It contains a detailed discussion of the Battle of Chancellorsville, which is the setting of *The Red Badge of Courage*

David Madden and Peggy Bach, *Classics of Civil War Fiction,* University Press of Mississippi, 1991.
 James Cox's essay on *The Red Badge of Courage* places it in the context of other Civil War novels such

as Mary Johnston's *The Long Roll,* Ellen Glasgow's *The Battle-Ground,* and John Peale Bishop's *Many Thousands Gone.*

Richard M. Weatherford, editor, *Stephen Crane: The Critical Heritage,* Routledge & Kegan Paul, 1973.

Contains thirty-two reviews of *The Red Badge of Courage* from 1894 through 1898, showing the critical reception of Crane's work in America and England. While some critics were slow to recognize Crane's genius, others were able to see it instantly, and to relate it to the Impressionism movement that was dominating the art world at that time.

Seize the Day

Saul Bellow

1956

Bellow's fourth novel, *Seize the Day* was published as a novella in 1956 in a volume that also included three short stories—"A Father-to-Be," "Looking for Mr. Green," and "The Gonzaga Manuscripts"—and a play, *The Wrecker*. Considered by many critics to be Bellow's finest work of fiction, the novella was immediately singled out from among its companion pieces as a major work. The powerful impact of *Seize the Day* comes from its tightly constructed plot; from Bellow's ability to control effectively in a concentrated form such enormous themes as victimization, alienation, and human connection; and from his creation of Tommy Wilhelm, one of his most moving protagonists.

Bellow's work before *Seize the Day* had attracted the attention of readers and critics, but he was particularly praised for his achievement in this fourth novel, which Baker says "demonstrates his attainment of full artistic maturity." *Seize the Day* deals with themes familiar to readers of Bellow's fiction, such as that of the father-son relationship, yet in this novella the concentrated structure enabled Bellow to render this theme more intensely.

At the heart of the action in *Seize the Day*, Tommy Wilhelm's relationship with his father revolves around Tommy's neediness and his father's disapproval of him. Tommy's problems with his father feed yet another theme of the novel and of Bellow's fiction in general: alienation from oneself and from humanity. Tommy feels cut off not only from his father and from the rest of his family—his sister, his dead mother, his estranged wife and their

two sons—but he also feels alienated from himself and from everyone he meets. Bellow's ability to treat weighty themes in *Seize the Day,* while making Tommy Wilhelm a pitiable yet sympathetic character, explains the success of this novella: it is capable of seizing both the reader's mind and heart.

Author Biography

Saul Bellow is recognized as one of the most important American writers of the twentieth century. The youngest of four children, Bellow was born in 1915 to Russian immigrant parents in Lachine, Quebec, Canada, a suburb of Montreal. Bellow's father, Abraham, had come to Canada from Russia just two years before his youngest child was born. While living in Montreal, Bellow learned English, Hebrew, Yiddish, and French. He lived with his family in Montreal's Jewish ghetto until the family moved to Chicago when he was nine.

Bellow spent a great deal of time in libraries as a child, as he loved to read. His family struggled with financial difficulties during his youth. His father wanted Bellow to go into a lucrative profession such as law or medicine, and his mother wanted him to become a scholar of Jewish law and tradition. Instead, Bellow chose to study anthropology and sociology—the sciences of man and of society—and to become a writer and a teacher of writing. Bellow's writing came to reflect his chosen educational focus, as his work examines large themes such as the value of existence and the ways that people relate to each other.

While the themes he explores in his fiction are universal, Bellow's fiction is informed by his Russian and Jewish background and by his wide reading in American and European literature, as well as by his familiarity with the modern urban landscape. His heroes—Tommy Wilhelm, for example—are typically thinking men, Jewish urban-dwellers who are in search of meaning in the world. Bellow himself, at the time he wrote *Seize the Day,* was interested in Reichianism, a sociological-psychological belief system based on the thought of Wilhelm Reich. According to Eusebio Rodrigues, Bellow's interest in Reichianism helped to shape *Seize the Day.*

Reichianism, says Rodrigues, revolves around the belief that human beings possess "a three-tiered character structure." The first tier consists of "man's natural sociality, his enjoyment of work,

Saul Bellow

and his innate capacity for love"; the second tier consists of "inhibited drives of greed, lust, envy, and sadism"; and the "outer layer is a mask of politeness, self-control, and artificial sociality." Bellow has acknowledged that during the 1950s, when *Seize the Day* was published, he and a friend were involved in Reichianism, and Rodrigues proposes that "The three layers of Tommy Wilhelm are apparent as he lives through his tragic day."

Plot Summary

Chapter 1

Saul Bellow's *Seize the Day* is the story of one day in the life of Wilhelm Adler, a.k.a. Tommy Wilhelm, a man in his mid-forties who is going through a mid-life crisis. As the book opens he is standing outside of the dining room in the residential hotel in which he lives, contemplating his troubles and working up the courage to go in to breakfast and face his father, who also lives in the Gloriana Hotel.

Wilhelm reminisces about how he left school twenty-five years ago in order to go to Hollywood to try to become a movie star. He had at first been approached by a talent scout, Maurice Venice, but even after the screen test went badly and the scout tried to discourage him, Wilhelm decided to change his name to Tommy Wilhelm and go to California. Once there he discovered that Maurice Venice was himself a failure and that a recommendation from him was a curse.

He nevertheless stayed in Hollywood for seven years, unwillingly to admit defeat. Now, twenty-five years later, he finds himself unemployed, broke, and in despair. He is separated from his wife, but she refuses to give him a divorce. He has invested his last money in the commodities market, and he fears it is all lost. And he is endlessly quarreling with his father, who refuses to help Wilhelm and who seems to be ashamed of his son.

Chapter 2

Still working up the courage to face his father at breakfast, Wilhelm collects his mail. He has received a number of bills, including some from his wife, who wants him to pay the premiums on some educational insurance plans for their two boys. He finally goes into breakfast, where his father introduces him to an elderly man named Mr. Perls. They have a quarrelsome breakfast, with Dr. Adler feeling ashamed of his unemployed and slovenly son and Wilhelm resenting his father's unwillingness to help him in any way.

Dr. Adler presses his son to tell Mr. Perls about his former job as a salesman, which he lost after quarreling with his employers. Wilhelm is disgusted with how focused on money his father and Mr. Perls are. Dr. Adler and Mr. Perls begin discussing Dr. Tamkin, another resident of the hotel and the man to whom Wilhelm had trusted to invest his last seven hundred dollars in the commodities market. The two older men feel that Tamkin is a fraud and a fool, and as he listens to them, Wilhelm again begins to worry about his money.

Chapter 3

Mr. Perls leaves and Wilhelm and his father continue to argue. Wilhelm reveals how he tried to get a divorce so that he could marry another woman, Olive, but his wife continually refused to give him the divorce. Wilhelm recites many of his problems, but his father does not sympathize, feeling that everything is the result of Wilhelm's poor choices and not wanting to be burdened with caring for his adult children in his last few years. His parting advice to Wilhelm is "Carry nobody on your back."

Chapter 4

After leaving the dining room, Wilhelm seeks out Tamkin. They head to the commodities market to see how their stocks have done. Wilhelm spends the conversation trying to figure out whether Tamkin is trustworthy or not. They discuss many philosophical matters, and Wilhelm is attracted to the doctor's ideas, especially his philosophy about living in the present and seizing the day, but he is suspicious of Tamkin nonetheless.

Chapter 5

They arrive at the commodities market and take their place next to some friends of Tamkin. Wilhelm becomes nervous about the money, and when he sees that some of their shares have risen, he wants to sell and recover at least some of their lost money. Tamkin insists that they should leave their shares alone, and he says that Wilhelm needs to learn to trust and to live in the here and now. As Tamkin tries to show him some methods for focusing on the here and now, Wilhelm wonders if the doctor is trying to hypnotize or con him.

Chapter 6

They go to lunch and discuss Wilhelm's problems with his wife and father. Wilhelm realizes that although Tamkin is probably a charlatan, he also believes that Tamkin has managed to survive for a long time, and he hopes that perhaps he can help him to survive as well. He begins to feel that he is "on Tamkin's back," trusting the other man to take the necessary steps for him.

They return to the commodities market, but before they can enter Mr. Rappaport, a very old man who was sitting next to them earlier, greets them. He demands that Wilhelm take him to the cigar store, and when Wilhelm protests that he wants to check on his commodities, Tamkin pushes him to go with Rappaport, insisting that he can learn a lot from the elderly man. When he returns from the cigar store Wilhelm finds that his commodities have dropped so far that he has lost all of his money. Tamkin is nowhere to be found.

Chapter 7

Wilhelm comes to the painful realization that it was he that had been carrying Tamkin on his back. He goes to his father to ask for help, but his father refuses him, yelling at him and telling him that he will not support his grown children. Wilhelm reminds him that there are other things besides money that a father can give a son, but his father refuses to listen. He says that he will see Wilhelm dead before he will allow his son to become a cross for him to bear.

Wilhelm goes in search of Tamkin. He receives an urgent message from his wife. Fearing that something has happened to one of his boys, he calls her. She is angry that he has sent her a post-dated check. They quarrel, and she blames him for the separation and for his unemployment. He resolves that he will find Tamkin and at least recover the two hundred dollars that the doctor owed him. He hopes that he will be able to start again with Olive, the woman he wanted to marry.

Searching for Tamkin he comes across a funeral procession, and he thinks that he sees Tamkin in the crowd. As he tries to get closer, he is swept into the church and eventually finds himself looking at the dead man in the casket. He is overwhelmed by grief at the death of the stranger. He sobs uncontrollably, and the other mourners wonder who he is and how he knew the deceased. Wilhelm only continues to sob.

Characters

Dr. Adler

Tommy Wilhelm's elderly father, Dr. Adler lives at the Hotel Gloriana in New York but "in an entirely different world from his son." Wilhelm's relationship with his father is at the center of the novel. Dr. Adler is a handsome, orderly, well-dressed man who is respected by all who know him. He has retired from his medical practice and is financially secure, but he refuses to lend money to his son, whom he continues to call by his childhood name, "Wilky." Tommy/Wilky disgusts Dr. Adler in his sloppiness, his emotional intensity, and his seeming inability to make a good decision, and Dr. Adler is impatient with his son's apparent lack of initiative.

When he talks about his son to friends and acquaintances, Dr. Adler builds up Wilky's achievements in an attempt to impress his listeners, although in truth he is not proud of his son. Although Tommy/Wilky pleads with his father to care for him—"'I expect *help!*'"—Dr. Adler is unmoved. He tells his son that if he were to help him by giving him money to cover his bills, it would only make Tommy/Wilky dependent on him. He also refuses to help his daughter, who also wants his financial assistance, explaining himself by declaring "'I want nobody on my back. Get off!'"

Media Adaptations

- *Seize the Day* was adapted in 1986 as a film featuring Robin Williams, Joseph Wiseman, Jerry Stiller, and Glenne Headly, and with a cameo appearance by Bellow; this film aired on PBS in 1987. Directed by Fielder Cook; available on VHS and Laserdisc; distributed by HBO (Canada).

Catherine

Wilhelm's younger sister, Catherine has taken "a professional name," Philippa. She is a painter and has asked Dr. Adler for money to rent a gallery for an exhibition of her work, but he refuses to support her. Neither Wilhelm nor his father thinks Catherine has talent.

Dad

See Dr. Adler

Father

See Dr. Adler

Margaret

Margaret is Tommy Wilhelm's estranged wife, whom he claims is "'killing'" him by constantly demanding money from him. Margaret will not divorce Wilhelm, and because she is raising their two boys, she refuses to get a job. Tommy sees Margaret as "unbending, remorselessly unbending."

Olive

Wilhelm's girlfriend in Roxbury, whom he used to see when he was working for the Rojax Corporation. He wanted to marry her, but their marriage was prevented by Margaret's refusal to divorce Wilhelm.

Paul

Tommy Wilhelm's younger son, Paul, is "going to be ten." He calls his father a "'hummus-potamus,'" or hippopotamus.

Mr. Perls

Another elderly resident of the Hotel Gloriana and a friend of Dr. Adler's, Mr. Perls is introduced to Wilhelm as having been a "hosiery wholesaler," but Wilhelm perceives from his appearance that he has had a difficult life. His presence at breakfast annoys Wilhelm: he sees Perls as his father's way of avoiding being alone with him. Wilhelm also despises his father's need to impress Perls by boasting about his children's accomplishments, particularly because neither one has been especially successful. Perls is eager to know the details of Wilhelm's salary and position at the Rojax Corporation, and Wilhelm is disgusted by his intense interest in money.

Philippa

See Catherine

Mr. Rappaport

Rappaport is the blind old retired chicken merchant whom Wilhelm sits near in the brokerage office. Wilhelm envies Rappaport's ability to remain calm about the fluctuating stock market; he does not have as much to lose as Wilhelm does. As Wilhelm returns to the brokerage office after leaving for lunch, Rappaport meets him outside and asks him to take him across the street to the cigar store. Wilhelm reluctantly agrees, as this errand delays his return to the market. When he does return, he learns he is ruined.

Mr. Rowland

Wilhelm sits near Mr. Rowland in the brokerage office as they watch the progress of their stocks. According to Tamkin, Rowland supports himself on his earnings from the stock market. This fact gives Wilhelm hope as he invests his last few hundred dollars.

Rubin

The well-dressed Rubin is "the man at the newsstand" in the Hotel Gloriana where Tommy Wilhelm lives. Wilhelm thinks of Rubin as "the kind of man who knew, and knew and knew."

Dr. Tamkin

The mysterious Dr. Tamkin claims to be a psychologist but turns out to be a con artist: he tricks Tommy Wilhelm into giving him his last seven hundred dollars to invest while assuring Tommy that this investment will make him wealthy. Tamkin, like Wilhelm and Dr. Adler, lives at the Hotel Gloriana, and the men know each other through a nightly card game. Wilhelm's father calls Tamkin "'cunning … an operator,'" but Wilhelm wants to believe that Tamkin can make him rich, so he makes himself trust this man with "a hypnotic power in his eyes."

Tamkin tells Wilhelm incredible stories about his work with his patients and insists that "'I have to do good wherever I can.'" He presents to Wilhelm his belief that in each human being "'there are two main [souls], the real soul and a pretender soul.'" Essentially, he is speaking about alienation from oneself, a subject that resonates with Wilhelm. In spite of his philosophical revelations, Tamkin remains a mystery to Wilhelm, who never quite comes to trust him fully. When Wilhelm realizes he has been ruined on the stock market and can't find Tamkin, who has slipped away from the brokerage office, Wilhelm is not completely surprised to understand at last that Tamkin is a fake.

Tommy

Tommy is Tommy Wilhelm's 14-year-old son, the older of his two boys.

Maurice Venice

Maurice Venice is the shady talent scout who approached the handsome young Wilhelm Adler— now Tommy Wilhelm—with the idea that he should go out to Hollywood to try to become a star. Wilhelm had a warning sense that Venice "protested too much" about his credentials. Yet he made his "first great mistake" by giving in to Venice's pressure, abandoning college, and going to Hollywood only to find when he got there that "a recommendation from Maurice Venice was the kiss of death."

Tommy Wilhelm

Middle-aged, overweight, slovenly, out of work, estranged from his wife and arguing with his father, Tommy Wilhelm is the protagonist of Bellow's novel. Emotional rather than rational, Wilhelm tends to make bad decisions. On the day portrayed in the novel, he is feeling as though all of his bad decisions are coming together to choke him; he repeatedly says things like "'I just can't catch my breath'" and that he feels "congested" and "'about to burst.'" In addition to being on the verge of financial ruin, Wilhelm feels alone in the world. He has left his wife and their two sons, although his wife will not give him a divorce and he misses his sons terribly. He is estranged from his mistress, Olive. He does not see his only sister, his mother died years ago, and although he and his father live "'under the same roof'" of the Hotel Gloriana, his father does not approve of him.

Wilhelm's conversations with his father center on Wilhelm's need for "'help,'" but while his father, Dr. Adler, interprets his pleas for help as being merely financial, Wilhelm also is asking for his father's approval and some kindness. Wilhelm is, however, down to his last few dollars and is extremely self-conscious about his lack of money. He feels bitterly that the world has "a sort of hugging relish" for money: "Everyone was supposed to have money…. They'd be ashamed not to have it." Wilhelm's inner confusion is represented in part by his confusion over which name is his true name: Wilky, his childhood name; Tommy Wilhelm, the name he chooses when he goes to Hollywod; or Velvel, the Yiddish name his old grandfather had called him.

Wilky

See Tommy Wilhelm

Themes

Alienation and Loneliness

Tommy Wilhelm's sense of estrangement not only from his own family but also from his acquaintances and the entire city of New York places the themes of alienation and loneliness at the core of the novel. From the novel's opening scene, in which Wilhelm talks briefly with "Rubin, the man at the newsstand," it is clear that these men know many things about each other, and yet "None of these could be mentioned, and the great weight of the unspoken left them little to talk about."

Wilhelm longs to connect on an emotional level with his father, but old Dr. Adler speaks to his son "with such detachment about his welfare" that Wilhelm, Adler's "one and only son, could not speak his mind or ease his heart to him." Wilhelm's sense of alienation from himself is represented by his confusion over his different names: his father calls him "Wilky," his childhood name, but Wilhelm had chosen the name "Tommy Wilhelm," dropping the name Adler, when he went to Hollywood to pursue an acting career.

When Dr. Tamkin talks to Wilhelm about his ideas on the soul, Wilhelm recognizes himself in Tamkin's description of "two main [souls], the real soul and a pretender soul." Wilhelm is "awed" by Tamkin's vision: "In Tommy he saw the pretender.

Topics for Further Study

- Research middle-class marriage in the 1950s. What roles were married men and women expected to play, and how successful was this model?

- Investigate post-World War II trends in popular psychology and self-help literature. Based on the popularity of the literature you find, can you speculate as to the kinds of advice and support Americans were looking for? What might these needs tell us about American culture at the time?

- During the years of President Eisenhower's terms of office—1952 to 1960—what was the general view of success among the middle-class? What did it mean to be successful in 1950s America?

And even Wilky might not be himself. Might the name of his true soul be the one by which his old grandfather had called him—Velvel?"

Looking outside of himself and his small circle, Wilhelm feels alienated from humanity, as represented by New York City and its inhabitants. He feels that communication with others is as difficult as learning another language: "Every other man spoke a language entirely his own, which he had figured out by private thinking … and this happened over and over and over with everyone you met. You had to translate and translate, explain and explain, back and forth, and it was the punishment of hell itself not to understand or be understood…." Wilhelm has a encompassing sense that the alienation he feels is not unique to him, but that "everybody is outcast," that the experience of loneliness is part of the human condition.

American Dream

The so-called "American Dream" has taken many shapes—streets paved with gold, a chicken in every pot—but the theme is always the same: financial success. Bellow looks at a dark side of this dream—what happens when a believer in the American Dream fails to succeed? Tommy Wilhelm feels the pressure of the American Dream. Money, or the lack of it, is an irritant to Wilhelm. His success as a salesman for the Rojax Corporation is in the past, and "Now he had to rethink the future, because of the money problem."

Wilhelm's "money problem" is that he no longer has any—he has given his last seven hundred dollars to the dubious Tamkin to invest in stocks, but in the meantime he cannot pay this month's rent, nor does he have any money to send to his estranged wife to support her and their two sons. Wilhelm looks around him and sees everywhere the expectation that he should have money: "Holy money! Beautiful money! … if you didn't have it you were a dummy, a dummy! You had to excuse yourself from the face of the earth."

Wilhelm's lack of income and his anxiety about his precarious position clearly influence his attitude about money and the American Dream. Part of this Dream is that one's children should find more success in the world than one has found, and Wilhelm is highly aware that his father, a respected doctor, amassed more wealth than Wilhelm himself will ever be able to do.

Father and Son

Wilhelm's sense of disconnection from the world seems to start with his relationship with his father. When Wilhelm tells Tamkin about his struggles with his father, Tamkin comments, "'It's the eternal same story … The elemental conflict of parent and child. It won't end, ever.'"

The theme of father and son appears in much of Bellow's fiction, and in *Seize the Day* it drives much of the plot. Wilhelm, or Wilky, as his father calls him, cannot satisfy his father, and his father refuses to help Wilhelm. "'My dad is something of a stranger to me,'" Wilhelm tells Tamkin, although he admits, "'of course I love him.'" When Wilhelm asks his father for help, Dr. Adler refuses "'to take on new burdens,'" but Wilhelm replies, "'it isn't all a question of money—there are other things a father can give a son.'" He pleads with Dr. Adler, "'I expect *help!*'" but Dr. Adler seems incapable of giving the kind of help his son needs.

Individual vs. Society

A teeming, confusing New York City provides an appropriate setting for Tommy Wilhelm's overwhelming day of alienation and ruin. Wilhelm sees himself as an outsider in his world. Although he was born and raised in this city, Wilhelm feels like a stranger here: "I don't belong in New York any more." New York takes on an apocalyptic quality for Wilhelm when he thinks about the failure of communication in such a place: "New York—the end of the world, with its complexity and machinery, bricks and tubes, wires and stones, holes and heights. And was everybody crazy here?"

Wilhelm's deepest need is for connection, for the sympathetic understanding of another person. He feels completely alone in a city that seems to assault him: "'There's too much push for me here. It works me up too much.'" He does have one transcendental moment of connection with humanity —a "blaze of love"—while passing through an underground corridor beneath Times Square: " … all of a sudden, unsought, a general love for all these imperfect and lurid-looking people burst out in Wilhelm's breast. He loved them. One and all, he passionately loved them. They were his brothers and sisters."

But this romantically sweeping sense of connection does not last and in retrospect seems to Wilhelm to have been an arbitrary event, "only another one of those subway things. Like having a hard-on at random." Finally, in the last moments of the novel, when Wilhelm weeps in a funeral parlor over the corpse of a stranger, he is able to move "toward the consummation of his heart's ultimate need" when he recognizes that mortality is the bond among human beings.

Success and Failure

Tommy Wilhelm has made a series of mistakes and bad decisions in his life, and "through such decisions somehow his life had taken form." Motivated by feeling or emotion rather than by rational thought, Wilhelm decided to go to Hollywood to try to become a "screen artist," to leave the Rojax Corporation because his territory was being divided and he was not being promoted, and to give Tamkin the last of his money. All of these decisions, made in hopes of finding some kind of success, have resulted in Wilhelm's failure. He ponders the fact that in the past "He had been slow to mature, and he had lost ground." At the nightly gin game in which he often participates, Wilhelm "had never won. Not once…. He was tired of losing."

His father, in order to preserve appearances to his friends, emphasizes Wilhelm's past success as a salesman with the Rojax Corporation when he introduces his son, but this emphasis on the past only serves to highlight what a failure Wilhelm is now. Wilhelm's father, Dr. Adler, is considered a success, not only in terms of his financial attainment or his achievements in his field prior to his retirement, but also in terms of his character: "He was idolized by everyone." In contrast to his son, Dr. Adler is controlled and self-contained and is not ruled by his emotions but is instead rational. Wilhelm's failure is connected to his lack of control and "style," while his father's success stems from his restraint and his ability to master appearances.

Style

Point of View

The third-person, limited omniscient point of view in *Seize the Day* provides a balanced view of the actions of the characters while offering some insight into the protagonist's mind. Thus Wilhelm is the central consciousness of the novel without being the narrator. The point of view of the novel recreates Wilhelm's frantic, disorderly state of mind while placing Wilhelm amongst his more orderly father and the rational Tamkin. A first-person narration by Wilhelm would prevent a balanced view of his father and other characters, as the world of the novel would be shaped by Wilhelm's internal turmoil. Yet a third-person narration that also accounts for Wilhelm's thoughts enables a controlled sequence of events while creating for sympathy for the protagonist.

Setting

New York City plays a crucial role as the setting for *Seize the Day*. The city itself, huge and teeming with infinite forms of activity, serves as a backdrop to Wilhelm's confusion and sense of isolation, but it also inhabits Wilhelm's imagination as a force that presses upon his soul and chokes him. The swarming sidewalks of New York help to create Wilhelm's sense that communication with others is impossible: he sees there "the great, great crowd, the inexhaustible current of millions of every race and kind pouring out, pressing round, of every age, of every genius, possessors of every human secret … in every face the refinement of one particular motive or essence." Wilhelm feels out of place in the city and prefers the country, his memories of which soothe his mind.

Wilhelm's home in the city, a rented room at The Hotel Gloriana, reflects his transient status in New York. In addition, "most of the guests at the Hotel … were past the age of retirement," and "a great part of New York's vast population of old men and women" lives in the neighborhood of the hotel. Thus Wilhelm, only forty-four himself, is living like an elderly person, which is indicative of his sense that his life is essentially over.

Images/Imagery

Images of water and drowning permeate *Seize the Day,* reflecting Wilhelm's feeling that he is choking and suffocating. From the opening paragraph, in which Wilhelm rides the elevator that "sank and sank," and eventually reaches the lobby where the carpet "billowed toward [his] feet," Bellow presents a series of images that suggest water and its potential threat. Wilhelm's father presses his son to stop taking so many pills and to try hydrotherapy—"'Simple water has a calming effect'"—but Wilhelm's response is "'I thought … that the water cure was for lunatics.'"

Wilhelm connects images of death by water with his sense of personal ruin: "The waters of the earth are going to roll over me." Ominously, Tamkin tells Wilhelm that his wife drowned, a suspected suicide, and Tamkin insists that for Wilhelm to understand the process of investing he had to take a risk: "'To know how it feels to be a seaweed you have to get in the water.'" In the final moments of the novel, as Wilhelm is overwhelmed by emotion at the funeral of a stranger, he hears the "heavy, sea-like music" and "[sinks] deeper than sorrow," seemingly about to drown in his own tears.

Anti-hero

While a hero is traditionally a fortunate individual of superhuman power or spirit, an anti-hero is by definition the opposite of a hero and is thus a person who is neither strong nor purposeful. An anti-hero may be portrayed as having little control over events, seeming aimless or confused, or as being out of step with society. Tommy Wilhelm is an anti-hero. He seems to drift through his life, making poor decisions that remove him farther and farther from his family and friends, and he feels like an outsider in the city of his birth. He is down on his luck in *Seize the Day,* but his bad luck is connected to the "great mistakes" he has made throughout his life.

Catharsis

Catharsis is a release of built-up emotion, and the classical definition of catharsis involves a combination of terror and pity in that release. As the images of Wilhelm's growing frustration and desperation mount, the novel creates a sense that something has to give before Wilhelm, in his own words, "bursts" or "chokes." In the final moments of the novel, the realization of his utter financial ruin dawns upon Wilhelm. He sees at the same time that Tamkin, whom he had trusted and had looked up to as a kind of spiritual advisor, has betrayed his trust. Thus two main threads of the novel—Wilhelm's fears about his financial instability and his intense desire for human connection—have simultaneously and devastatingly come to a head.

As Wilhelm goes into the street, blindly searching for Tamkin, he goes into a funeral parlor, where he suddenly finds himself beside the coffin of a stranger. In Wilhelm's thoughts as he gazes upon the corpse's face—"A man—another human creature … What'll I do? I'm stripped and kicked out…. Oh, Father, what do I ask of you? What'll I do about the kids—Tommy, Paul? My children"—all of his fears and feelings of isolation coalesce. He breaks down, "past words, past reason, past coherence…. The source of all tears had suddenly sprung open within him." This moment, when Wilhelm sinks "deeper than sorrow" and cries "with all his heart" is the catharsis of the novel.

New York City street scene.

Historical Context

Middle-Class Family Life and Suburbia in the 1950s

In the wake of World War II, middle-class life in the 1950s was relatively peaceful, though it was dominated by cultural expectations. Middle-class Americans were marrying younger and in greater numbers than previously, and many of these young married couples were moving out of the cities, building houses in the rapidly-expanding suburbs, and filling their new houses with babies. In most cases, the husband went into the city to work and the wife stayed home and took care of the house and the children.

Levittowns, developer William J. Levitt's huge suburbs on Long Island and in Pennsylvania, offered uniform houses on tiny lots and became enormously popular. Other developers imitated Levitt's mass-production methods in hopes of cashing in on the appeal of such suburbs. This appeal came from the promise of a quiet, safe life outside of the noisy cities, a life where one could belong to a community of others like oneself. Conformity in the suburbs was considered the norm. The suburbs of the 1950s were almost exclusively inhabited by whites. Many suburbs dictated that their residents could not change their yards or the exterior of their houses outside of stated parameters. Rarely did elderly, single, homosexual, or childless couples buy homes in these new suburbs: the young white family dominated the scene. The development of the suburbs also fed the automobile industry, as living in the suburbs necessitated owning a car, and public transportation became much less popular than it had been.

Away from the movie houses of the cities, families living in the suburbs watched television for entertainment. At the beginning of the decade, television was far from being the ubiquitous presence it quickly became. But television grew immensely popular in the 1950s, as more and more middle-class consumers purchased their own TV sets. Popular shows included "I Love Lucy," "Father Knows Best," "The Untouchables," and "Gunsmoke," which today's audiences can still watch in syndication.

Fear in the 1950s

Fear of communists occupied the American imagination of the 1950s. During this post-World War II decade, anti-communism grew out of a fear of Soviet aggression and led many Americans to point accusing fingers at one another. One of the most notorious finger pointers was Senator Joseph McCarthy, whose systematic pursuit of commu-

Compare & Contrast

- **1950s:** In spite of a generally positive attitude toward capitalism, American participation in the stock market was not widespread, with stock owned by just 3.5 percent of working Americans in 1956.

  Today: Through Individual Retirement Accounts, mutual funds, and retirement plans, more Americans than ever before have money invested in the stock market.

- **1950s:** America popular culture—television shows, movies, magazines—portrayed marriage as essential to happiness, and within marriage, sex roles were strictly defined, with the husband as breadwinner and the wife as housekeeper and mother. Divorce among middle-class marriages was uncommon and considered a failure.

  Today: Middle-class marriage and family life in America depend less upon cultural expectations and more upon what works for the individual family. Many middle-class married women work outside the home, divorce has become more common and accepted, and married couples often share housework, childcare, and other domestic duties.

- **1950s:** Because of the military, political, and economic triumphs of the 1940s, the U.S. experienced unprecedented prosperity in the 1950s that led Americans to believe that affluence and middle-class status were a birthright.

  Today: Many middle-class American families need more than one income just to make ends meet.

- **1950s:** Norman Vincent Peale published his best-seller *The Power of Positive Thinking* in 1952, promoting a way of thinking that he assured readers would give them "peace of mind, improved health, and a never-ceasing flow of energy" and would help them "modify or change the circumstances in which [they] now live, assuming control over them rather than continuing to be directed by them."

  Today: Best-selling authors like Stephen Covey (*Seven Habits of Highly Effective People*) and Richard Carlson (*Don't Sweat the Small Stuff* and *Don't Worry, Make Money*) claim to teach readers how to gain more satisfaction from their lives.

---

nists in American society seized the country's attention for the first half of the decade.

From early 1950 to late 1954, McCarthy and his movement—dubbed "McCarthyism"—named government officials, authors and journalists, movie actors and directors, and many others, for the stated purpose of rooting out communism in American culture. Being named by McCarthy ruined many a career during the 1950s; for instance, actors were blacklisted and could not get work after being accused of communist practices. McCarthy was extremely popular; to a nation gripped by fear, he was a powerful figure. Although McCarthy did not invent anti-communism and in fact shared the anti-communist watch with many others, he remains a symbol of the hysteria and slan-

der that characterized anti-communism in the 1950s.

Related to the fear of communists and communism was the dread of nuclear warfare in the 1950s. The bombing of Hiroshima and Nagasaki in 1945 had shown the world the destructiveness of nuclear weapons, and this knowledge, combined with widespread fear of the Soviet Union, left Americans in constant fear of being bombed. Many Americans chose to build atomic bomb shelters—underground rooms outfitted with supplies—in case of nuclear attack, and schoolchildren were drilled in what to do if a bomb were dropped on their cities. Such drills included such ineffective strategies as "duck and cover," which required children to hide under their desks and cover their heads at the first warning of a nuclear attack. Living under the constant threat of the bomb created a sense of impending doom, but also a desire to pretend that everything is all right.

Critical Overview

When *Seize the Day* was published in 1956, critics praised the novella and maintained that it followed in a natural progression from Bellow's first three novels, *Dangling Man* (1944), *The Victim* (1947), and *The Adventures of Augie March* (1954). In his 1957 *Chicago Review* assessment of *Seize the Day,* Robert Baker wrote that Bellow in all of his novels "has tried to lasso the universe, to explore the splendid, profligate diversity of human experience, and to seek the ties that bind." Baker found that in *Seize the Day,* Bellow had matured as an artist: "The growth and ripening of Bellow's attitudes have been paralleled by the perfecting of his medium of expression."

Baker alluded in his review to the three short stories that accompany *Seize the Day* in the volume entitled *Seize the Day,* but he claimed that "these stories do not match the brilliance of 'Seize the Day,' and so the less said about them the better." Baker suggested that Bellow's writing does contain flaws, particularly that he fails to "deal convincingly with women" and that "his books don't end, they just stop." However, he called Bellow "perhaps the major talent of the past decade."

Irving Malin joined Baker in his praise of *Seize the Day.* In Malin's 1969 book *Saul Bellow's Fiction,* Malin called *Seize the Day* a "'blest nouvelle,'" or blessed novel. He asserted in his book, a study of Bellow's fiction through *Herzog* (1964), that *Seize the Day* was "Bellow's greatest achievement." Harry T. Moore, in his preface to Malin's book, called *Seize the Day* and *The Victim* "two of the finest novels to come out of America since World War II." Malin's assessment of Bellow in general was that he was "probably the most important living American novelist"; Malin's judgment was based on his belief that Bellow's work was "mature, human, [and] imaginative."

Robert R. Dutton in his book *Saul Bellow* (1971) discussed *Seize the Day* mainly in terms of the theme of the novel's sources, the father-son relationship between Tommy Wilhelm and Dr. Adler, Dr. Tamkin as a "Contemporary Witch-doctor," and the novel's water and drowning imagery. Although Dutton acknowledged that it is difficult for critics to make "definitive judgments" about contemporary American literature, he admitted that "Bellow's novels represent the contemporary American novel at its best," adding that this judgment came not only from literary critics but also from more popular sources such as newspaper book reviews and weekly news magazines. In attempting to make a distinction between Bellow and his fellow American novelists, Dutton asserted that "In each of [Bellow's] novels he finds the human spirit to be quietly triumphant, quietly able to sustain itself in an alien and unfriendly world."

Superlatives have often been used to describe Bellow's work. Brigitte Scheer-Schazler in her 1972 study of Bellow's fiction, *Saul Bellow,* devoted her introduction in part to discussing Bellow's critical reputation. She describes him as "America's most important living novelist," "a 'contemporary classic,'" and asserts that "no contemporary American novelist equals Bellow in the precision, wit, and elegance of his style." Scheer-Schazler noted that *Seize the Day* "contains elements that are familiar from former works." She focused on "the open and closed forms of Bellow's novels and his vacillating between tight and loose modes of language," placing *Seize the Day* in what she called the "'restrained' category." This tension in Bellow's fiction between what Scheer-Schazler called "emotional intensity" and "artistic control" represents "two diverging aspects of his talent."

In his introduction to *Critical Essays on Saul Bellow* (1979), which he edited, Stanley Trachtenberg wrote that in the early part of his career "Bellow reflected the interests of a new generation" that had come of age during the Depression and World War II. Trachtenberg saw Bellow as having "abandoned the ironic mode of alienation adopted by the modernists in favor of a moral judgment that emerged from the attempt to allow ideas a dramatic expression." In other words, Trachtenberg suggested, Bellow examined "the look and feel of things" in order to "establish the importance of action."

Eusebio Rodrigues nodded to the philosophical underpinnings of *Seize the Day* in his 1979 article "Reichianism in *Seize the Day.*" In this article, Rodrigues discussed Bellow's early interest in the thought of Wilhelm Reich, "who combined the insights of a sociologist with those of a psychologist, [insisting] … that the vast majority of human beings suffer from … inner tensions generated by the conflict between natural human demands and the brutal pressures exerted by the world." Rodrigues stated that in *Seize the Day,* "Tommy Wilhelm is a dramatic illustration of how human character structure is molded and distorted by a society that is patriarchal, death-dealing, money-oriented and barren."

Criticism

Donna Woodford

Woodford is a doctoral candidate at Washington University and has written for a wide variety of academic journals and educational publishers. In the following essay, she discusses Wilhelm's struggle to understand his connection with others in Seize the Day.

Seize the Day is the story of one day, or more precisely the daylight hours of one day, in the life of Tommy Wilhelm, formerly Wilhelm Adler. In his mid-forties, unemployed, separated from his wife and children, and at odds with his father, Wilhelm feels alienated and alone in the world. His story is, as critics have often noted, a search for self, but it is also a search for connection with others. Ironically, he will only truly understand himself and feel connected to others when he comes to the full realization of how alone he really is, and how isolated all people truly are.

Throughout the book, Wilhelm is surrounded by the aged and dying, a fact that emphasizes his own feelings of isolation. Though only in his mid-forties, he is living in the Hotel Gloriana where "most of the guests ... were past the age of retirement," which makes him feel "out of place." At the commodities brokerage he is similarly surrounded by the aged: "Wilhelm sat between Mr. Rowland, who was elderly, and Mr. Rappaport, who was very old." Moreover his elderly companions are not wise old men who can father him and guide him; they are, rather, desperate, dying men, as helpless and alone as he is. Mr. Perls, the elderly breakfast companion of Wilhelm and his father, is dying of a progressive bone disease, and Mr. Rappaport is "nearly blind," and unable to go to the cigar store or even to see the price of the commodities without Wilhelm's help.

Only at the end of the book will Wilhelm recognize that death is his only true connection to other people. Prior to the last scene he sees it only as one more form of alienation, and he is unable or unwilling to sympathize with the dying all around him. The sight of Mr. Rappaport, who needs and relies on him, stimulates not compassion, but rather impatience and resentment in Wilhelm:

He barely crawls along, thought Wilhelm. His pants are dropping off because he hasn't got enough flesh for them to stick to. He's almost blind, and covered with spots, but this old man still makes money in the market. Is loaded with dough, probably. And I bet he doesn't give his children any. Some of them must be in their fifties. This is what keeps middle-aged men as children. He's master over the dough. Think—just think! Who controls everything? Old men of this type. Without needs. They don't need therefore they have. I need, therefore I don't have. That would be too easy.

Even when faced with an acute example of another man's need, the pathetic and dependent Mr. Rappaport, Wilhelm is incapable of sympathy. Focused only on his own need for money, he sees the overtly needy Mr. Rappaport as "without needs." He fails to recognize Mr. Rappaport's need for a guide and escort and instead focuses only on the old man's money and perceived power. Significantly, he also projects his anger at his own father onto the elderly man, assuming that all wealthy, dying men are selfish, ungenerous fathers. He does not recognize, even for a second, that he himself is being ungenerous in his refusal to offer the dying man his sympathy and respect.

It is significant that Wilhelm immediately sees Mr. Rappaport as a father unwilling to share with his children, since Wilhelm's troubled relationship with his own father is at the heart of his feelings of isolation and abandonment. Wilhelm sees his father as cold and distant, and he resents his father's cold and rational way of interacting with him: "He behaved toward his son as he had formerly done toward his patients, and it was a great grief to Wilhelm; it was almost too much to bear. Couldn't he see—couldn't he feel? Had he lost his family sense?"

Dr. Adler, of course, is cold and distant. He prides himself on being independent and on refusing to let anyone depend on him, and he advises his son to do likewise: "I want nobody on my back. Get off! And I give you the same advice, Wilky. Carry nobody on your back." Even when his son comes to him desperate for help, he refuses to budge from his rule of not lending money to his children. Wilhelm's plaintive suggestion that "it isn't all a question of money—there are other things a father can give to a son" only annoys his father more. Dr. Adler resists any suggestion that he should support his son, financially or emotionally, and when Wilhelm suggests that this means his father is "not a kind man," Dr. Adler explodes in rage: "'You want to make yourself into my cross. But I am not going to pick up a cross. I'll see you

What Do I Read Next?

- Bellow's first novel, *Dangling Man* (1944), is written as the diary of the 27-year-old protagonist, Joseph, who is left "dangling" as he waits to hear at any moment about his induction into the army. *Dangling Man* is often discussed as a stylistic predecessor of *Seize the Day*.

- *The Victim* (1947), Bellow's second novel, also anticipates *Seize the Day* stylistically; both are controlled, well-constructed narratives. *The Victim* tells the story of Asa Leventhal, a New York magazine editor, and his conflict with Kirby Allbee, a troubled former acquaintance who reenters his life for the purpose of settling old scores.

- *The Adventures of Augie March* (1953) represented a change in style and tone for Bellow. Narrator and protagonist Augie March recounts the sprawling story of his life, a series of adventures, during which he shows that he is driven by a hunger for experience but possesses no desire to put down roots.

- Bellow's 1959 novel *Henderson the Rain King* portrays the adventures of restless and dissatisfied millionaire Eugene Henderson as he leaves behind his chaotic life in America in quest of spiritual fulfillment in Africa.

- In *Herzog,* published in 1964, Bellow depicts his protagonist, Moses Herzog, as a man who is both innocent and romantic about the world, but who continually bumps up against the harsh realities of his life.

- In *The Fifties: The Way We Really Were* (1977), authors Douglas T. Miller and Marion Nowak set out to dispel the popular myths about the 1950s as a decade of universal tranquility and complacency. The authors claim that "the image of that decade conveyed by current nostalgia is badly distorted."

- *The Lonely Crowd* (1950) by David Riesman represents a significant piece of social criticism of the 1950s. In this widely-read book, Riesman presents his theory that the American character had changed from being "inner directed" to "other directed," meaning that Americans no longer were guided by an inner sense of right and wrong but instead found their values outside of themselves and felt compelled to conform to the "crowd."

- *The Organization Man* (1956) by William Hollingsworth Whyte, Jr. looks at the 1950s evolution of the work ethic in America into "a belief in the group as a source of creativity; [and] a belief in 'belongingness' as the ultimate need of the individual." Whyte's book, like Riesman's, traced a move away from traditional American self-reliance toward a reliance on the group and a need to belong.

dead, Wilky, by Christ, before I let you do that to me.'"

But while Dr. Adler is far from an ideal and loving father, the failed relationship is not entirely his fault. If Dr. Adler is an ungenerous father, Wilhelm is a self-centered son. He mourns his father's impending death not for his father's sake, but for his own: "When he dies, I'll be robbed, like. I'll have no more father." Just as he saw only his own needs and not Mr. Rappaport's, so he sees his father's death as a loss for himself and not for his father. He notes that he will be robbed of a father, but he does not consider that his father will be robbed of life. Wilhelm is, with his father as with others, unable or unwilling to sympathize. He thinks only of how their lives and deaths impact him.

His frustration with and isolation from his father lead Wilhelm to search for another father in Tamkin. He admits this substitution to himself when he thinks, "I wouldn't turn to Tamkin ... if I could turn to him. At least Tamkin sympathizes with me and tries to give a hand, whereas Dad doesn't want to be disturbed."

Once again, however, Wilhelm's mistake is in focusing too much on himself and his own needs. So wrapped up is he in his own need for advice, sympathy, and support, that he readily accepts Tamkin's apparent attempts to help him, assuming them to be trustworthy and sincere. Focused, as usual, on his own needs he fails to consider that Tamkin might have needs of his own which he is using the desperate Wilhelm to achieve. He is so anxious to make some money in the commodities market, and, at the same time, so hungry for connection with another human, that he accepts Tamkin's offers of help at face value. He does not question the fact that Tamkin puts less money into the investment, while maintaining all of the control of their joint venture. Nor does he realize that Tamkin continually tricks him into paying the bill for their meals. Even when he finally admits to himself that Tamkin is a charlatan, he continues to trust him:

> Tamkin was a charlatan, and furthermore he was desperate. And furthermore, Wilhelm had always known this about him. But he appeared to have worked it out at the back of his mind that Tamkin for thirty or forty years had gotten through many a tight place, that he would get through this crisis too and bring him, Wilhelm, to safety also. And Wilhelm realized that he was on Tamkin's back. It made him feel that he had virtually left the ground and was riding upon the other man. He was in the air. It was for Tamkin to take the steps.

So great is his desire to depend on someone else that he continues to trust Tamkin even when he knows him to be a con-artist, and so complete is his self-centered need that he cannot believe that an equally needy man will not help him. Though Wilhelm himself is seldom able to recognize other's needs, he assumes that his own needs will be as important to others as their own. His inability to recognize or sympathize with the needs of others leads him to trust Tamkin, and after they lose their money in the market, Wilhelm realizes to his horror that it was he who was carrying Tamkin, and not the other way around.

Only in the final scene of the novel is Wilhelm finally able to sympathize with another human being, and then it is with a corpse: "He sobbed loudly and his face grew distorted and hot, and the tears stung his skin. A man—another human creature, was what first went through his thoughts." His thoughts then drift to other people, and to his own problems, but the focus is different now. He is not focused on his own needs to the exclusion of others. He thinks of his children, his mistress, his father, and when his thoughts turn to himself, he is pondering not only what he himself needs, but also what he can do for them. "Oh, Father, what do I ask of you: What'll I do about the kids—Tommy, Paul? My children."

The recognition of the needs of others comes after he has been able to look at "a man—another human being" and see not his own needs, but rather his connection to the corpse. He, like the dead man in front of him, will die. That is what connects him not only to the man in the coffin, but also to his father, his sons, and all others. They all share the burden of mortality. For the first time in the book Wilhelm is able to truly think of others, and of his connection to them, rather than of how they can help him. He realizes at last that "his heart's ultimate need" is to feel connected to others, and it is finally in his mourning for a fellow human, that he is able to achieve the consummation of that need. He has seized the day in that he has finally learned the lesson of that day: to recognize his connection to others and to sympathize with them in their shared suffering and mortality.

Source: Donna Woodford, in an essay for *Novels for Students,* Gale, 1998.

Lee Siegel

In the following excerpt, Siegel lambasts an article on Seize the Day *written by Cynthia Ozick, accusing her of trying to turn Bellow into a "Jewish wisdom-writer."*

The New Criterion is the Dow Jones of cultural journals, where "high" art is always gaining, and the touchstone of literary greatness might just as well be Shakespeare's First Portfolio. Yet Cynthia Ozick's essay on Saul Bellow's 1956 *Seize the Day* in a recent issue (September 1995) made me think first not of official culture's sour exhalations but of *Beauty and the Beast.*

The story goes that Greta Garbo once gave a private screening of Jean Cocteau's *Beauty and the Beast* in her apartment. Beauty passed through her ordeal, she and the newly restored prince fell into each other's arms, the kingdom sprang back into shape. The film stopped rolling. Some seconds passed. Then, rising in a slow, silky pout from the back of the room came Garbo's unmistakable voice: "Give me back my beast."

Give me back my Bellow, Cynthia Ozick. It's bad enough that some multi-cultural commissars collapsed Bellow's lifetime of fiction into one silly attempt at epigram-making. Bellow survived his collision with a speeding culture. But will he survive Ozick? She has been stalking him for nigh unto twelve years, aiming to turn him into a Jew-

> *It's bad enough that some multi-cultural commissars collapsed Bellow's lifetime of fiction into one silly attempt at epigram-making. Bellow survived his collision with a speeding culture. But will he survive Ozick? She has been stalking him for nigh unto twelve years, aiming to turn him into a Jewish wisdom-writer who fashions his fictional worlds out of the unchanging aspects of eternity."*

ish wisdom-writer who fashions his fictional worlds out of the unchanging aspects of eternity. "The Eye of God.... is perhaps what [Bellow's] intellectual fevers have always pointed to," Ozick feverishly wrote in 1984. What she really seems to want is to build some Saul Bellow golem, a golem to vanquish all the enemies of her soul.

Seize the Day's plot is a simple one. Tommy Wilhelm is 44 years old, unemployed, broke and desperate. He is living in the same cavernous Upper West Side residence hotel as his rich elderly father, a tightfisted retired doctor who refuses to throw his son the lenderest financial line. Wilhelm quit his well-paying job as salesman (Ozick mistakenly thinks he was fired) after his boss first reneged on a promise to promote him and then gave half of Wilhelm's territory to a son-in-law. Before that, Wilhelm had dropped out of college to become an actor in Hollywood but never made it. He is separated from his wife, Margaret, and has two sons. Despite his lack of funds, Margaret is pressing him for money; the fact that he can no longer send it is driving him nuts. And he has lost the woman he loves because Margaret, who detests him, won't give him a divorce.

Wilhelm entrusts his last few hundred dollars to a super-seductive and unstable con man named Tamkin, who has promised to invest it in com-

modities and make Wilhelm solvent again. In truth, Tamkin is as broke as Wilhelm and manipulates his prey into financing his own speculations. But the market disappoints, Wilhelm loses everything and Tamkin vanishes without paying back an additional $200 that Wilhelm had loaned him. At novel's end, Wilhelm is sinking toward a breakdown, sped on by a sudden, brutal eruption from his father. Bereft of money, love, friends and hope, Wilhelm wanders into a stranger's funeral where "the heavy sea-like music came up to his ears," stops before the open coffin and begins weeping uncontrollably, "deeper than sorrow, through torn sobs and cries toward the consummation of his heart's ultimate need." The novel seems to pick you up and drop you, as Rilke once said about music, deep into the unfinished.

Of Ozick's dazzling tirades—against T.S. Eliot (anti-Semite), Isaac Babel (hung out with anti-Semites)—her meditation on *Seize the Day* has to be the weirdest. She starts out ... by advancing cautiously on the possibly philistine reader, her slingshot loaded with "higher consciousness," the "human essence," "the importance of one's own depths." These are Bellow's themes, she warns, the themes of all great literature, but nobody cares about literature anymore. When *Seize the Day* first came out, "Ah! How to describe it?" There was "hunger, public hunger ... you lived by it, you absorbed it, you took it into your system." Now, nobody reacts to literature like that, nobody writes literature like that, etc., etc.

Then we get the weirdness. "Re-entering the theater of this short novel after more than forty years, you will find the scenery hardly altered." Upper Broadway, Ozick believes, where *Seize the Day* takes place, hasn't changed in four decades. The "human essence" is immutable, you see, even if it can't find a one-bedroom for under $1,200. But most bizarre, for Ozick the fabulously timeless thing about Bellow is that he "has invented a refreshed phrenology ... is on to something few moderns would wish to believe in: the human head as characterological map." Show me what you look like and I will tell you who you are. Beauty and the Beauty, in other words.

With friends like Ozick, Bellow doesn't need Zulus. She quoted from *Seize the Day* the description of a minor character—the manager of a brokerage office—to prove that Bellow, this Jewish writer, believes in the moral equivalence of numina and noses. Here is the passage Ozick expropriates, with her ellipses:

"Silvery, cool, level, long-profiled, experienced, indifferent, observant, with unshaven refinement, he scarcely looked at Wilhelm ... The manager's face, low-colored, long-nostriled, acted as a unit of perception; his eyes merely did their reduced share. Here was a man ... who knew and knew and knew."

This is quite a flattering picture of a stockbroker for *The New Criterion*'s readers—a sort of cross between Guicciardini and Sam Shepard. Ozick comments: "And about whom there is nothing further to know." He is a prince of sang-froid, a duke of high finance, a dependable and capable man. It's all in the face.

You wouldn't know from this characterological map of a human head that the broker is a German, and that he watches the commodities board from the back of the office through a pair of small binoculars. Or that the Jewish Wilhelm is afraid of this very efficient German—the full quote is: "he scarcely looked at Wilhelm, who trembled with fearful awkwardness." We find out later that the broker could have disclosed to Wilhelm the truth about Tamkin's lies, but he didn't (he is a heart-broker). That is because in Saul Bellow's world, to know and know—to be all brain and no heart—sucks the oxygen out of reality (see the splenetic Mr. Sammler's Planet's clement last paragraph). Says Wilhelm: "Everybody seems to know something. Even fellows like Tamkin. Many people know what to do, but how many can do it?"

How many can do the felling thing, he means. For Ozick, the con man Tamkin knows and does. Ozick thinks Tamkin is ultimately the savior of Wilhelm's "thwarted expression of the higher consciousness," as she puts it. Through the medium of a universal—of money, of all the intricate processes and forms of money—Tamkin becomes, for Ozick, "the healer of self-castigation ... a doctor to Wilhelm's sorrow, a teacher of limitlessness, a snake-oil charlatan whose questionable bottles contain an ancient and legitimate cure for mortality's anxieties: seize the day."

In short, a wisdom tale. The bumbling loser gets taught about life by a shaman of the marketplace, a prophet of what is profitable. A lesson for our time. But just as important for Ozick, the novel's action takes place "the day before Yom Kippur, the Day of Atonement, comprising the most solemn hours of the Jewish liturgical calendar. Old Mr. Rappoport [misspelled in *The New Criterion*!], half-blind, whom Wilhelm encounters at the broker's, reminds him of his synagogue obligations." It is an ancient Jewish wisdom tale. Tamkin, therefore, is a figure straight out of "tra-

ditional Jewish storytelling," a force of "wisdom" or "ontology."

The commissars ignored all the beauty in Bellow; Ozick has banished the beast. She's got everything backward. For Ozick, Wilhelm is "hollow flounderer." But Bellow compares him to Buddha and to Christ. For Ozick, Tamkin's elaborate con "catch[es] and catch[es] Wilhelm's heart"; it is "garble and gobbledygook, but with a magnetism that can seduce: love, truth, tragedy, the importance of one's own depths."

Yet Tamkin is the consummate seller, and like demagogues and some sadists, he is a demon of empathy. He "catch[es] Wilhelm's heart," not with wisdom, but because he knows how to play on Wilhelm's paralyzing guilt and shame. He is Wilhelm's self-destroying alter ago. Tamkin has a "drooping" lower lip; Wilhelm has a "high upper lip." "Yes, yes, he too," says Wilhelm to himself at the novel's climax, when he realizes that Tamkin's own suffering exactly fits Tamkin's description of Wilhelm.

Wilhelm himself is an angel of empathy—he would subscribe to Tikkun if he could. "He would never willingly hurt any man's feelings," Bellow tells us. But Wilhelm's hyper-sharp sense of other people's pain keeps him from standing up to those who try to hurt him out of their own hurt. He is on one level the Holy Shlemiel in the American marketplace, a semi-satiric figure in Bellovian extremis, a wholly good person faced with the inhuman choice between making a killing and being killed.... It is the untrammeled business culture that throws down this choice, that deforms kindness into self-inflicted cruelty and offers nothing in between. "People come to the market to kill," Tamkin explains to Wilhelm. "They make a killing by fantasy." "I don't understand what you mean," says Wilhelm. "By and by, you'll get the drift," Tamkin ominously replies.

A "healer of self-castigation"? An exploiter of self-castigation. Tamkin goes on mesmerizing Wilhelm with the keenest social and psychological truths—iron truths that he mines from Wilhelm's doubts and fears and wields against him. His advice to "seize the day" clinches Wilhelm's decision to invest, and it is perverse. For Wilhelm is the only character in the novel who really has seized the day. Bellow pointedly writes that Wilhelm had "seized the feeling" to jump into a Hollywood career. Wilhelm has always seized the feeling: He dropped out of stifling college to search for a larger life; he left a rotting marriage to try to love again; he quit his job because his dignity had been crushed. What he never learned to deal with was the yellowing brick road of banana peels fate has in store for people who follow their hearts without first calculating the loss or gain in social power.

Tamkin, on the other hand, never seizes the day. What he seizes is Wilhelm, like an object. Tamkin invests, after all, in commodities, in futures. For Bellow to use carpe diem in this novel's world without bitter irony would be like Dante inscribing "Our Customers Come First" over the gates of hell. Even more ironically, Tamkin has Wilhelm investing most of his money in lard. Wilhelm is speculating in a purely animal substance, the very element in human relations that is crippling him because he can't bring himself to bite and scratch like everyone he comes in contact with. Balzac and Simmel knew, rationalizes bestiality into an accountant's headache. Bellow tells us twice that Tamkin has "deadly" brown eyes.

Tamkin in fact recalls old Mr. Rappaport, who has made his fortune in chickens. On the eve of Yom Kippur, these "most solemn hours of the Jewish liturgical calendar," Wilhelm looks at this callous and manipulative character and thinks with disgust of "a man who had grown rich by the murder of millions of animals … the slaughter … the blood filling the Gulf of Mexico … the chicken shit, acid, burning the earth." This is not the image of your average haimish kosher butcher, much less Ozick's ancient Jewish conscience. No more than Tamkin, who has Wilhelm investing in fat of the ritually unclean pig, is Ozick's disguised essence of ancient Jewish wisdom.

Deep down, against the evidence of his daring lunges toward a more meaningful existence, Wilhelm accepts the evidence of the marketplace. He believes that because he cannot "kill" his way through the obstacles arrayed against him, he is an indecisive failure. So "seize the day" strikes his heart like a gong. Tamkin teaches him the "importance of one's own depths"—and how. He literally leads the weak-willed Wilhelm to market like a chicken—if not a lamb—to the slaughter, and drowns him in Wilhelm's own depths of self-doubt. As in another great work of social protest, the business culture in *Seize the Day* exacts the *Death* (in this novel, symbolic) *of a Salesman*—a work that also ends with a funeral—as the price for a human being's efforts to wrestle his humanness beyond cash value.

Not for Ozick. Fetishizing *Seize the Day* as one of the last expressions of the "higher consciousness" and the "human essence" in the Western world, she turns the novel on its head: Seize Your Bootstraps. She ends up packaging her grand abstractions into neat little concepts the way Tamkin travesties the ancient maxim. That's what happens when the defenders of official culture, as opposed to living, breathing art, do handstands on the ramparts of respectability. (Are you listening, Saul?) Yet when I hear the words status quo, I reach for Bellow's best fiction. And for Ozick's. And for all the "great" and "high" literature I can get my hands on. Because literature is social protest simply as part of its own intangible motion into the material world.

Source: Lee Siegel, "Ozick Seizes Bellow" in *The Nation*, Feb. 26, Vol. 262, No. 8, 1996, pp. 33–4.

Cynthia Ozick

In the following excerpt, Cynthia Ozick explores Bellow's Seize the Day *as a link to higher consciousness.*

When *Seize the Day* first appeared, the old system was fully at work. Ah! How to describe it? Hunger, public hunger; and then excitement, argument, and, among writers, the wildly admiring disturbances of envy. A new book by Bellow! You lived by it, you absorbed it, you took it into your system.…

There was … another element in Bellow's prose—in the coloration of his mind—that could not be immediately detected, because it contradicted a taken-for-granted sentiment about human character: that the physical body is simply a shell for the nature hidden within, that what I look like is not what I truly am, that my disposition is masked by the configuration of my features. The American infatuation with youth tends to support this supposition: a very young face *is* a sort of mask, and will generally tell you nothing much, and may, in fact, mislead you. Bellow in a way has invented a refreshed phrenology, or theory of the humors; in any case, by the time *Seize the Day* arrived, it was clear he was on to something few moderns would wish to believe in: the human head as characterological map. But such a premise is not a retreat or a regression to an archaic psychology. It is an insight that asks us to trust the condition of art, wherein the higher consciousness can infiltrate portraiture. Disclosure is all. Human flesh has no secrets … Bellow, like every artist, is no dualist—his bodies are not bodies, they are souls. And the soul, too, is disparaged by moderns as an obscurantist archaism.

But Bellow's art escapes the judgment of the merely enlightened. The nursery-rhyme proverb may be more to his liking: my face is my fortune. If manners are small morals, as Hobbes said, then bodies and faces may be morals writ large; or what is meant by soul. Here is Dr. Tamkin, a central character of *Seize the Day*—who may not be a doctor at all:

> What a creature Tamkin was when he took off his hat! The indirect light showed the many complexities of his bald skull, his gull's nose, his rather handsome eyebrows, his vain mustache, his deceiver's brown eyes. His figure was stocky, rigid, short in the neck, so that the large ball of the occiput touched his collar. His bones were peculiarly formed, as though twisted twice where the ordinary human bone was turned only once, and his shoulders rose in two pagodalike points. At mid-body he was thick. He stood pigeon-toed, a sign perhaps that he was devious or had much to hide. The skin of his hands was aging, and his nails were moonless, concave, clawlike, and they appeared loose. His eyes were as brown as beaver fur and full of strange lines. The two large brown naked balls looked thoughtful—but were they? And honest—but was Dr. Tamkin honest?

And here is a minor character, the manager of a brokerage office, no more than a walk-on:

> Silvery, cool, level, long-profiled, experienced, indifferent, observant, with unshaven refinement, he scarcely looked at Wilhelm.... The manager's face, low-colored, long-nostriled, acted as a unit of perception; his eyes merely did their reduced share. Here was a man ... who knew and knew and knew.

And about whom there is nothing further to know. What more would the man's biography provide, how would it illuminate? Bellow's attraction to the idea of soul may or may not be derived from an old interest in Rudolf Steiner; but no one will doubt that these surpassingly shrewd, arrestingly juxtaposed particulars of physiognomy are inspired grains of what can only be called human essence.

Dr. Tamkin, curiously, is both essence and absence: which is to say he is a con man, crucially available to begin with, and then painfully evaporated. Wilhelm, strangled by his estranged wife's inflated expenses, father of two boys, runaway husband who has lost his job—salesman for a corporation that promised him advancement and then fired him in an act of nepotism—is drawn to Tamkin as a savior. Tamkin takes Wilhelm's last seven hundred dollars, introduces him (bewilderingly) to the commodities market, pledges a killing in lard, and meanwhile spills out advice on how to live: Tamkin is a philosopher and amateur poet. Wilhelm's vain and indifferent father, Dr. Adler, an elderly widower, also supplies advice, but brutally, coldly.

Much of this futile counsel takes place in the Gloriana, a residence hotel within view of the Ansonia, an ornate Stanford White-era edifice which "looks like a baroque palace from Prague or Mu-

> *Bellow's fiction hardly counts as 'moral' or instructive.... His stories look for something else altogether: call it wisdom, call it ontology, or choose it from what Tamkin in free and streaming flight lets loose: 'Creative is nature. Rapid. Lavish. Inspirational. It shapes leaves. It rolls the waters of the earth. Man is the chief of this.'"*

nich enlarged a hundred times, with towers, domes," a leftover from the socially ambitious Broadway of a former age. Despite its name, the Gloriana's glory days are well behind it; its denizens are chiefly retired old Jews like Wilhelm's fastidious father and the ailing Mr. Perls, who drags "a large built-up shoe." Wilhelm at forty-four may be the youngest tenant, and surely the healthiest— "big and fair-haired," "mountainous," with "a big round face, a wide, flourishing red mouth, stump teeth." But he is also the humblest: failed husband, failed actor still carrying a phony Hollywood name, broke, appealing to his father for the rent money, pleading with his wife not to squeeze him so hard.

Though maimed and humiliated, Wilhelm is no cynic; he is a not-so-naïve believer in search of a rescuer. And because he is hopeful and almost gullible, and definitely reckless, a burnt-out sad sack, he is aware of himself as a hapless comic figure. "Fair-haired hippopotamus!" he addresses his lumbering reflection in the lobby glass. And later, heartlessly: "Ass! Idiot! Wild boar! Dumb mule! Slave!"

Wilhelm may seem even to himself to be a fool, but there are no outright fools in Bellow's varied worlds: all his clowns are idiosyncratic seers. Wilhelm sees that his father is mesmerized by old age as death's vestibule, incapable of compassion beyond these margins: a confined soul, disappointed in his son, Dr. Adler, though affluent enough, refuses him help. "He doesn't forget death for one single second, and that's what makes him like this," Wilhelm thinks. "And not only is death on his mind but through money he forces me to think about it, too. It gives him power over me." Wilhelm may be a hollow flounderer in all other respects—work, wife, sons, father, lover, past, future, all lost—but he can *see*. And he sees a glimmering in Tamkin, a market gambler with Wilhelm's money, a fly-by-night speculator, a trickster, a kind of phantom appearing and disappearing at will, an opportunist and exploiter, plainly shady if not an out-and-out crook—he sees that Tamkin is somehow and despite everything a man in whom to put his trust. Pragmatically, this will turn out to be a whopper of a mistake; yet Wilhelm, in a passion of nihilist self-seeing, embracing his blunders, defines himself through misjudgment and miscalculation:

> ... since there were depths in Wilhelm not unsuspected by himself, he received a suggestion from some remote element in his thoughts that the business of life, the real business—to carry his peculiar burden, to feel shame and impotence, to taste these quelled tears—the only important business, the highest business was being done. Maybe the making of mistakes expressed the very purpose of his life and the essence of his being here. Maybe he was supposed to make them and suffer from them on this earth. And though he had raised himself above Mr. Perls and his father because they adored money, still they were called to act energetically and this was better than to yell and cry, pray and beg, poke and blunder and go by fits and starts and fall upon the thorns of life. And finally sink beneath that watery floor—would that be tough luck, or would it be good riddance?

And still there is hope's dim pulse:

> "Oh, God," Wilhelm prayed. "Let me out of my trouble. Let me out of my thoughts, and let me do something better with myself. For all the time I have wasted I am very sorry. Let me out of this clutch and into a different life. For I am all balled up. Have mercy."

Mercy is what Tamkin brings, even if only briefly, fitfully, almost unrecognizably; he sports "a narrow smile, friendly, calming, shrewd, and wizardlike, patronizing, secret, potent." He spins out sensational stories, difficult to credit, speaks of "love," "spiritual compensation," "the here-and-now," brags of reading Aristotle in Greek ("A friend of mine taught me when I was in Cairo"); he declares himself to be "a psychological poet." His topic is the nature of souls:

> "In here, the human bosom—mine, yours, everybody's—there isn't just one soul. There's a lot of souls. But there are two main ones, the real soul and a pretender soul. Now! Every man realizes that he

has to love something or somebody. He feels that he must go outward. 'If thou canst not love, what art thou?' Are you with me?"

"Yes, Doc, I think so," said Wilhelm, listening—a little skeptically, but nonetheless hard.

"... The interest of the pretender soul is the same as the interest of the social life, the society mechanism. This is the main tragedy of human life. Oh, it is terrible! Terrible! You are not free. Your own betrayer is inside of you and sells you out. You have to obey him like a slave. He makes you work like a horse. And for what? For who?"

"Yes, for what?" The doctor's words caught Wilhelm's heart. "I couldn't agree more," he said. "When do we get free?"

Tamkin carries on, catching and catching Wilhelm's heart: "The true soul is the one that pays the price. It suffers and gets sick, and it realizes that the pretender can't be loved. Because the pretender is a lie. The true soul loves the truth." Garble and gobbledygook, but with a magnetism that can seduce: love, truth, tragedy, the importance of one's own depths. "As a matter of fact," Tamkin winds up, "you're a profound personality with very profound creative capacities but also disturbances." Wilhelm falls for all this and at the same time doubts. Tamkin soothes, procrastinates, plunges into tangential narratives, distracts, eats, philosophizes, and finally hands Wilhelm four stanzas of semiliterate self-help verse studded with greatness, joy, beauty, ecstasy, glory, power, serenity, eternity. "What kind of mishmash, claptrap is this!" Wilhelm shouts in his thoughts. Yet Tamkin continues to lure him; at the brokerage office, where the doctor, an operator, hurries from stocks to commodities and back again, Wilhelm's breast swarms with speculations about the speculator: "Was he giving advice, gathering information, or giving it, or practicing—whatever mysterious profession he practiced? Hypnotism? Perhaps he could put people in a trance while he talked to them."

In the large and clumsy Wilhelm there is a large and clumsy shard of good will, a privately spoken, half-broken unwillingness to be driven solely by suspicion: Tamkin is right to count two disparate souls—only, for Wilhelm, which is the pretender, which the true? Is hopeful trust the true soul, and suspicious doubt the pretender? Or the other way around? For a time it hardly matters: Tamkin is a doctor to Wilhelm's sorrow, a teacher of limitlessness, a snake-oil charlatan whose questionable bottles turn out to contain an ancient and legitimate cure for mortality's anxieties: seize the day.... The effectively fatherless Wilhelm finds in Tamkin a fairy godfather—but, as might be expected in the land of wishes, one whose chariot melts to pumpkin at the end of the day. Yet again and again, swept away by one fantastic proposition or another, Wilhelm, moved, is led to respond, "This time the faker knows what he's talking about." Or: "How does he know these things? How can he be such a jerk, and even perhaps an operator, a swindler, and understand so well what gives?"

Wilhelm is absurd; sometimes he is childish, and even then, longing for pity and condemning himself for it, he muses: "It is my childish mind that thinks people are ready to give it just because you need it." In spite of a depth of self-recognition, he will burst out in infantile yells and preposterous gestures. Complaining to his father how his wife's conduct and her attitudes suffocate him, he grabs his own throat and begins to choke himself. A metaphor turns into a boy's antics. And after an argument with his wife on a public telephone—during which she accuses him of thinking "like a youngster"—he attempts to rip the telephone box off its wall. There is something of the Marx Brothers in these shenanigans, and also of low domestic farce. "I won't stand to be howled at," counters his wife, hanging up on him. But a man's howl, of anguish or rage, belongs to the Furies, and is not a joke.

Nor is the timing of these incidents. It is the day before Yom Kippur, the Day of Atonement, comprising the most solemn hours of the Jewish liturgical calendar. Old Mr. Rappoport, half-blind, whom Wilhelm encounters at the broker's, reminds him of his synagogue obligations. Wilhelm replies that he never goes; but he reflects on his mother's death, and remembers the ruined bench next to her grave. Dr. Adler, preoccupied with dying as his near destination, has no interest in religion. Wilhelm, though, is fixed on his own destiny, with or without God; and Tamkin is a fixer—a repairer—of destiny and of despair. Yet who is more farcical than Tamkin? Bellow once noted—commenting on the tone of traditional Jewish story-telling—how "laughter and trembling are so curiously intermingled that it is not easy to determine the relations of the two. At times the laughter seems simply to restore the equilibrium of sanity; at times the figures of the story, or parable, appear to invite or encourage trembling with the secret aim of overcoming it by means of laughter."

Seize the Day is such a parable; or, on second thought, perhaps not. The interplay of the comic and the melancholic is certainly there—but a parable, after all, is that manner of fable which means to point a moral, or, at the least, to invoke an instructive purpose. The "secret aim," as Bellow has it, is generally more significant than the telling or the dramatis personae. Bellow's fiction hardly counts as "moral" or instructive (though there are plenty of zealous instructors wandering through). His stories look for something else altogether: call it wisdom, call it ontology, or choose it from what Tamkin in free and streaming flight lets loose: "Creative is nature. Rapid. Lavish. Inspirational. It shapes leaves. It rolls the waters of the earth. Man is the chief of this." A tornado of made-up maxims and twisted tales, Tamkin is among the great comic characters (comedy being a corridor to wisdom, though not the only one): that he flaunts his multiple astonishments in the modest compass of a short novel is a Bellovian marvel. And he is, besides, Bellow's sentry in reverse, standing watch over an idea of fiction that refuses borders.

Source: Cynthia Ozick, "Saul Bellow's Broadway" in *The New Criterion,* September, Vol. 14, No. 1, 1995, pp. 29–36.

Bruce Bawer

In the following excerpt, Bawer explains why he finds Seize the Day *superior to other Bellow novels.*

Bellow followed his longest novel with his shortest. *Seize the Day* (1956) is Bellow's most admirable work of fiction—concise, cogent, and finely controlled. Tommy Wilhelm is in his middle forties and is residing at the Hotel Gloriana on New York's Upper West Side, which is mostly occupied by elderly people, his physician father among them. Like Augie March, Tommy Wilhelm has energy—and it's done him nothing but harm. For years he tried to be a movie actor in Hollywood, but then "his ambition or delusion had ended," and he became a salesman, and now—that pursuit having failed as well, along with his marriage—another resident of the hotel, a shady character named Dr. Tamkin, has talked him into speculating in the commodities market. "Seize the Day," Tamkin advises.

The books is unique among Bellow's works. The setting is meticulously described, and several of the characters are memorably developed. Most remarkable of all, though, is Bellow's restraint: with a few exceptions (e.g., the list of books by "Korzybski, Aristotle, Freud, W. H. Sheldon" in Dr. Tamkin's apartment), neither the narrator nor any of the characters feels obliged to drop the names of high-toned books and authors or to generalize about such matters as suffering, death, freedom, and the meaning of America—which are, nonetheless, among the themes of *Seize the Day;* and the book is all the more effective, of course, because of this avoidance of explicit theme-mongering. The novel's conclusion is especially powerful: in quick succession Wilhelm discovers that Dr. Tamkin has swindled him, is rejected by his father ("Go away from me now. It's torture for me to look at you, you slob!"), and has a painful telephone conversation with his estranged wife; he then finds himself in "the great, great crowd" on Broadway,

> the inexhaustible current of millions of every race and kind pouring out, pressing round, of every age, of every genius, possessors of every human secret, antique and future, in every face the refinement of one particular motive or essence—*I labor, I spend, I strive, I design, I love, I cling, I uphold, I give way, I envy, I long, I scorn, I die, I hide, I want.*

A moment later he is in a funeral chapel, on a slow line filing past a coffin; the dead man's meditative look strikes him with "horror," then "heartsickness," and then finally "sorrow," but he cannot leave the corpse, and is soon crying over it, his sadness at the death of "another human creature" mixed with his continuing anguish over his own problems. It is an affecting ending, as much a reminder of the ubiquity of death (and of the fact that life continues, in all its equivocality, pettiness, and pathos, in spite of death) as it is an affirmation of human connectedness. One of the special things about *Seize the Day* in fact, is that it seems more universal—less bound to its particular time and place, less concerned with facile social criticism, more sharply focused upon the eternal verities—than Bellow's other novels. Of all Bellow's endings, moreover (which are, as a rule, notorious for their inconclusiveness), the ending of *Seize the Day* is the one that feels most like a coherent, satisfactory, and earned resolutions.

Source: Bruce Bawer, "Talking Heads: The Novels of Saul Bellow" in *Diminishing Fictions: Essays on the Modern American Novel and Its Critics,* Graywolf Press, 1988, pp. 194–220.

Sources

Robert Baker, "Bellow Comes of Age," in *Chicago Review,* Vol. 11, 1957, pp. 107-10.

Robert R. Dutton, *Saul Bellow,* Twayne Publishers, Inc., 1971.

Irving Malin, *Saul Bellow's Fiction,* Southern Illinois University Press, 1969.

Harry T. Moore, "Preface," in *Saul Bellow's Fiction* by Irving Malin, Southern Illinois Press, 1969.

Eusebio Rodrigues, "Reichianism in *Seize the Day,*" in *Critical Essays on Saul Bellow,* edited by Stanley Trachtenberg, G.K. Hall & Co., 1979, pp. 89-100.

Brigitte Scheer-Schazler, *Saul Bellow,* Frederick Ungar Publishing Co., 1972.

Stanley Trachtenberg, "Introduction," in *Critical Essays on Saul Bellow,* G.K. Hall & Co., 1979.

For Further Study

Robert Baker, a review in *Chicago Review,* Vol. 11, 1957, pp. 107-10.

Asserts that *Seize the Day* demonstrates that Bellow has attained "full artistic maturity."

Richard Giannone, "Saul Bellow's Idea of Self: A Reading of *Seize the Day,*" in *Renascence: Essays on Value in Literature,* Vol. 27, 1975, pp. 193-205.

Sees Wilhelm, like all of Bellow's protagonists, on a quest to discover what makes him human and gives him dignity.

Andrew Jefchak, "Family Struggles in *Seize the Day,*'" in *Studies in Short Fiction,* Vol. 11, 1974, pp. 297-302.

An analysis of the frustrated family relations in the novel and the alienation that results.

M. A. Klug, "Saul Bellow: The Hero in the Middle," in *Dalhousie Review,* Vol. 56, 1976, pp. 462-78.

Views Bellow's work within the tradition of American literature and discusses his heroes from Joseph in *Dangling Man* through Sammler in *Mr. Sammler's Planet.* Klug believes Bellow "offers the most sustained and penetrating criticism of contemporary American life of any novelist of his generation."

Julius Rowan Raper, "The Limits of Change: Saul Bellow's *Seize the Day* and *Henderson the Rain King,*" in *Narcissus from Rubble: Competing Models of Character in Contemporary British and American Fiction,* Louisiana State University Press, 1992, pp. 12-36.

According to Raper, Bellow's novels illustrate the fact that one can only change one's state and find one's self by discovering and relying on one's inner resources.

Lee J. Richmond, "The Maladroit, the Medico, and the Magician," in *Twentieth Century Literature,* Vol. 19, 1973, pp. 15-26.

Richmond perceives Dr. Tamkin as "the nexus for the novel's artistic truth."

Philip Stevick, "The Rhetoric of Bellow's Short Fiction," in *Critical Essays on Saul Bellow,* edited by Stanley Trachtenberg, G.K. Hall & Co., 1979, pp. 73-82.

Examining Bellow's short stories, including the three stories published along with *Seize the Day* in its first edition, Stevick discusses the "uncommon power and integrity" of Bellow's short fiction.

The Sound and the Fury

William Faulkner

1929

The Sound and the Fury, published in 1929, was William Faulkner's fourth novel and is considered his first masterpiece. The story is set in the fictional county of Yoknapatawpha that Faulkner created for the setting of his third novel *Sartoris.* Faulkner set fifteen of his novels and many short stories in this geographical location that he invented, the descriptions of which mirror the area in northern Mississippi where he spent most of his life. While he is called a Southern writer, most critics praise this book and many of Faulkner's other fictional works for their universal and humanistic themes. The book was published in the year of the great stock market crash on Wall Street in 1929 and sales were meager. Faulkner did, however, gain considerable critical recognition for the work.

Before writing *The Sound and the Fury,* Faulkner found himself overly involved with the problem of selling his previous books to publishers. He decided to refocus his attention back on his writing so that he could create a finely crafted work. The result was *The Sound and the Fury.* The inspiration for the novel came from one of his short stories, "Twilight." He had created the character of Caddy in this story. In a scene where Caddy has climbed a pear tree to look into the window where her grandmother's funeral is being held, her brothers are looking up at her and they see her muddy pants. Faulkner claimed he loved the character of Caddy so much that he felt she deserved more than a short story. Thus the idea for *The Sound and the Fury* was born.

Author Biography

The oldest of four sons of Murry Cuthbert Falkner and Maud Butler Falkner, William Cuthbert Falkner was born in New Albany, Mississippi, on September 25, 1897. (He changed the spelling of his name in 1918.) When he was five years old, his family moved to Oxford, Mississippi, where Faulkner would spend much of his life. Faulkner's ancestors came to America from Scotland during the eighteenth century. William Clark Falkner, his great-grandfather, was a source of inspiration for the young Faulkner. William Clark had been a colonel in the Civil War, built railroads, and had also written a popular romance in 1881 called *The White Rose of Memphis.* He was murdered on the street by a business partner, and Faulkner re-created this event several times in his fiction. Faulkner also used his great-grandfather as the model for his fictional character Colonel John Sartoris in his 1929 novel *Sartoris.*

Faulkner did not complete his last year of high school, nor did he complete a college education, although he was admitted to the University of Mississippi as a special student. He served briefly in the Canadian branch of the Royal Air Force during World War I after being rejected by the United States Army because he did not meet the weight and height requirements. The war ended before he could participate in any action, however. After the war he worked in various clerical and building jobs until he could establish himself as a full-time writer.

Faulkner's writing career began with poems, some of which were published. A play he wrote was performed in 1921, and his first book of poems was published in 1924. In 1925 he met Sherwood Anderson, best known as the author of *Winesburg, Ohio,* who influenced him to become a fiction writer. (The pieces he wrote during the period he spent with Anderson in New Orleans were collected in 1958 under the title of *New Orleans Sketches.*) Following the trend of other American writers, Faulkner made a six-month tour of Europe in 1925. On his return to the United States, he began writing seriously. He produced his first novel in 1926 and his second in 1927. His third, *Sartoris,* in which he introduced the fictional Yoknapatawpha county, was published in 1929. That year also saw the appearance of *The Sound and the Fury,* the work which first gained him critical notice. In 1929 he also married his high-school sweetheart, Lida Estelle Oldham Franklin. They had two daughters,

William Faulkner

one of whom died in infancy. He also helped raise two stepchildren.

Except for brief periods during the early 1930s and early 1940s, when Faulkner went to Hollywood as a screenwriter and produced scripts for such films as *To Have and Have Not* and *The Big Sleep,* he spent most of his time in Oxford, Mississippi, writing stories and novels. In 1949, he received the Nobel Prize for Literature and in 1955 he received the National Book Award and the Pulitzer Prize for *A Fable,* a story of France during World War I. Already suffering from failing health, Faulkner suffered a number of injuries caused by falls from horses. After being admitted to the hospital for one such injury, he died of a heart attack on July 6, 1962. Faulkner produced a sizable body of work that includes a number of critically acclaimed masterpieces.

Plot Summary

April Seventh, 1928

Set in Mississippi during the early decades of the twentieth century, *The Sound and the Fury* tells the tumultuous story of the Compson family's gradual deterioration. The novel is divided into four sections, each told by a different narrator on a different date. The three Compson brothers, Benjy, Quentin, and Jason, each relate one of the first three sections while the fourth is told from an omniscient, third-person perspective. At the center of the novel is the brothers' sister, Caddy Compson, who, as an adult, becomes a source of obsessive love for two of her brothers, and inspires savage revenge in the third.

The first section is narrated by Benjy, a thirty-three-year-old mentally handicapped man who is unable to speak and doesn't fully comprehend the world around him. His perceptions in the present are combined with memories of childhood and adolescence and, as a result, his narrative provides a disjointed and incomplete interpretation of events. In the opening scene, Benjy is standing by a fence near a golf course where the regularly heard cry of "here, caddie" is a constant reminder of the sister who has now married and left home. He is accompanied by one of the family's servants, Luster, who is trying to find the quarter he lost so he can go to the travelling show playing in town that night. As they crawl through a broken place in the fence, Benjy snags himself on a nail and is immediately reminded of a similar experience he had with Caddy. From here, Benjy's monologue continues to shift back and forth between the present and the past.

Although the significance of many of Benjy's fragmented memories is not immediately evident, several important incidents are revealed. What is most apparent is Benjy's strong attachment to Caddy, who smells "like trees." It has been almost eighteen years since Caddy's wedding, yet Benjy continues to await her return at the fence. Besides her wedding day, other significant memories include the changing of Benjy's name from Maury, the image of Caddy's muddy drawers as she climbs the pear tree, and an incident at the fence involving a young school girl.

June Second, 1910

The novel's second section relates Quentin's final day before he commits suicide. Quentin is a student at Harvard but his obsessive thoughts about his sister's sexuality and marriage of convenience to Herbert Head far outweigh any academic aspirations. Memories of past events again intrude on the present and, as a result, Quentin's narration is not unlike Benjy's. (The technique, where thoughts interrupt each other and move back and forth, is known as "stream-of-consciousness.") However, Quentin's intense awareness of time lends his sec-

tion a more coherent structure. He wakes to the sound of his watch, a gift from his father intended to help him "forget [time] now and then," twists off its hands and, instead of attending his morning classes, prepares for his death. He packs a trunk, mails a letter to his father, and purchases some flat-iron weights.

Quentin makes his way to the train station. Once out of town, Quentin goes for a walk along a river. He recalls his attempt to prevent Caddy from marrying Herbert by proposing that they and Benjy run away someplace where nobody knows them. As he is walking, Quentin encounters a little girl whom he addresses as "sister." He buys the girl an ice cream and is attempting to help her find her way home when her brother suddenly appears and accuses Quentin of kidnapping his sister. Quentin is eventually cleared of the accusations and drives away with some friends from school. His thoughts, however, remain focused on Caddy. He reflects upon his unsuccessful attempt to confront Dalton Ames, the man who may have impregnated Caddy, and is seemingly unaware of the present moment when he strikes the boasting Gerald Bland in the car. He eventually returns to his room in town and makes the final preparations for his suicide. As he is doing so, he recalls a conversation he had with his father concerning his feelings for Caddy and his desperate attempt to prevent her marriage:

> ....and he i think you are too serious to give me any cause for alarm you wouldn't have felt driven to the expedient of telling me you had committed incest otherwise and i i wasnt lying i wasnt lying and he you wanted to sublimate a piece of natural human folly into a horror and then exorcise it with truth and i it was to isolate her out of the loud world so that it would have to flee us of necessity and then the sound of it would be as though it had never been and he did you try to make her do it and i i was afraid to i was afraid she might and then it wouldnt have done any good but if i could tell you we did it would have been so and then the others wouldnt be so and then the world would roar away and he and now this other you are not lying now either but you are still blind to what is in yourself.... you cannot bear to think that someday it will no longer hurt you like this now.

Quentin then brushes his teeth, turns out the light, and leaves the room. It is revealed in the following section that he took his own life by drowning himself.

April Sixth, 1928

The confusion and obsession which characterize the first and second sections, respectively, become anger and brutal sarcasm in the third. Jason's opening words set the tone: "Once a bitch always a bitch, what I say." He is referring to Caddy's daughter, Quentin, who has just received a warning from school concerning her frequent absences. Jason brings her to school himself and then stops by the post office and goes to his job at Earl's store. As he is going through his mail, he recalls how Quentin was first sent to live with the family after Caddy was cast off by her husband. Caddy has only seen her daughter once since that time. After her father's funeral, she paid Jason fifty dollars to see Quentin, and he drove by with Quentin in a carriage, allowing Caddy only a glimpse of the girl. The first letter Jason opens is addressed to Mrs. Compson and contains the monthly check Caddy sends to support her daughter. Jason has been keeping this money for himself as compensation for the job he was promised by Herbert but never got. He replaces the checks with fakes that he burns in front of his mother. A second letter, addressed to Quentin, contains a money order for fifty dollars. He later pressures Quentin into signing it over to him without disclosing its true value.

That afternoon, Jason catches Quentin walking past the store with a man from the show. He eventually chases them down a wagon road with his car, but they manage to give him the slip and leave him stranded by deflating one of his tires. When he finally makes his way home, he cruelly teases Luster by burning free tickets to the show that Luster desperately wants to see. He refuses to sit down to dinner until Dilsey, another of the family's servants, gets the entire family to join him at the table. Quentin and Mrs. Compson come down to dinner and Jason taunts his niece by making up a story about how, earlier that day, he lent his car to one of the show men so that he could pursue his sister's husband who was out riding with "some town woman." He interrupts himself and tells his mother that he will continue the story later because he does not "like to talk about such things before Quentin."

April Eighth, 1928

It is now Easter Sunday and, as Dilsey is serving breakfast, Jason descends from his room and accuses Luster and Benjy of breaking his bedroom window. It is only when Dilsey goes up to wake Quentin that Jason figures out what has happened. He rushes upstairs and finds Quentin's room empty and her bed undisturbed. He also discovers that the metal box he keeps hidden in his closet has been broken into. Jason calls the sheriff to report a robbery and leaves the house. A little while later, Dilsey, Luster, and Benjy attend a special Easter

service where they hear visiting preacher, Reverend Shegog, deliver a stirring sermon. Meanwhile, Jason has driven to Mottson, the next stop for the travelling show, and attempts to find Quentin and the twice-stolen money. However, his trip is unsuccessful and he is finally obliged to hire a man to bring him back home because he has a severe headache from a scuffle with one of the showmen. Upon his return to town, he crosses Luster and Benjy as they are approaching the town square in the family's surrey. Luster swings to the "wrong" side of the monument and Benjy begins to shriek in horror. Jason hurls Luster aside, sets the surrey on the "right" side of the monument and sends the two back home. Benjy finally ends his hollering when he sees that "cornice and facade flowed smoothly once more from left to right," and that "post and tree, window and doorway and signboard [were] each in its ordered place."

Characters

Dalton Ames

One of Caddy's lovers who may have made her pregnant. In his monologue, Caddy's brother Quentin remembers his failed confrontation with Dalton Ames over Caddy and tries to deny Ames's role in Caddy's life.

Sheriff Anse

Jason tries to get the sheriff to help him catch his niece Quentin after she robs him and runs away from home. The sheriff refuses to help him, saying he figures the money was probably not Jason's to begin with.

Maury L. Bascomb

Mrs. Compson's brother and an uncle to the Compson children. Benjy is named after Uncle Maury when he is born, but Mrs. Compson changes his name to Benjamin when she learns he is retarded. Uncle Maury appears in Benjy's monologue, humoring his sister's complaints. In Jason's story, Uncle Maury is shown borrowing yet another sum of money from his sister in order to pursue a dubious business deal. In his "Appendix: Compson 1699–1945," Faulkner describes Maury as a "handsome flashing swaggering workless bachelor who borrowed money from almost anyone."

Gerald Bland

One of Quentin's acquaintances at Harvard. He is spoiled by his indulgent mother, who puts on parties for him and allows him a car. When Gerald begins boasting of his success with women, a distracted Quentin tries to punch him. Gerald is a boxer, however, and bloodies Quentin without damage to himself.

Charlie

One of Caddy's boyfriends. He appears as a memory in Benjy's section. Charlie is obviously trying to make out with Caddy and she is pushing him away because Benjy is with her.

Benjamin Compson

Benjy is the youngest of the Compson brothers. He had orignally been named after his uncle Maury, but when the Compsons discover that he is retarded, they change his name to Benjamin. The first section of the book, "April Seventh, 1928," is Benjy's monologue. Benjy sees the world in terms of sights and sounds, and his narration reflects this emphasis. At the time of this section, Benjy is thirty-three years old, making him the same age as Jesus was when he was crucified. His brother Jason has despised him since childhood, when he destroyed the paper dolls Benjy and Caddy made. As head of the family, Jason has Benjy castrated when he makes advances to a young girl. After their mother dies, Jason has Benjy put into a mental hospital.

Benjy loves his sister Caddy, and his monologue mainly consists of memories of her. Caddy treats him with love and affection, unlike his mother Caroline, a complaining, dependent woman who treats him as a shameful nuisance. Benjy has never recovered from Caddy's leaving the family after her pregnancy. His thoughts reflect this loss, and his memories focus on Caddy's budding sexuality as if he knows this was the cause of her exile. His positive memories of his sister include her "smelling like trees," and his sad ones relate his bellowing whenever she shows signs of womanhood—putting on perfume or sitting with a boyfriend. At the conclusion of the novel, Benjy hears a golfer call for his "caddie" and bellows his grief once again: "it was horror; shock; agony eyeless, tongueless; just sound." Benjy can be seen as a personification of innocence in the novel.

Benjy Compson

See Benjamin Compson

Media Adaptations

- Jerry Wald produced and Martin Ritt directed a film version of *The Sound and the Fury* in 1959. Jason was played by Yul Brynner and Benjy by Jack Warden. Margaret Leighton portrayed Caddy and Joanne Woodward played her daughter, Quentin. Ethel Waters was cast in the role of Dilsey. Unavailable on video.

Caddy Compson

Caddy is the central character of the novel, even though none of the narration is seen through her eyes. In each of the three sections that represent the internal monologues of her brothers, she is of primary concern to them. The reader learns about Caddy through each of her brothers. They are all involved with her, but each in a different way. To a large extent, the brothers' characters are formed around their responses to Caddy. Benjy and Quentin love her in two distinct ways. Jason despises her as he does everything and everyone else. Caddy is the most normal of the Compson children. As the novel progresses and the pieces of her life unfold, she is seen as a young girl. She is loving in her relationships to Benjy and Quentin, but she also matures and has boyfriends. When Caddy becomes pregnant by one of them (perhaps Dalton Ames), she does the socially correct thing and marries another man, Herbert Head, who will be able to provide financially for her and her child. After her husband learns that her daughter is not his child, he turns her out. Caddy leaves her daughter, whom she has named after her dead brother Quentin, with the Compsons. She leaves the Compson home but sends money to support her daughter. In his "Appendix: Compson 1699–1945," Faulkner describes how Caddy travelled to Mexico and Paris after a second divorce and was never heard from again. According to the author, Caddy was "doomed and knew it, accepted the doom without either seeking it or fleeing it."

Still from the 1959 movie The Sound and the Fury, *starring Yul Brynner as Jason and Joanne Woodward as Quentin.*

Candace Compson
See Caddy Compson

Mrs. Carolyn Bascomb Compson

The mother of Benjy, Jason, Quentin, and Caddy. Mrs. Compson is depicted as a negligent mother. She is a self-absorbed hypochondriac and spends a great deal of time in bed. She does not show any maternal feelings for her children. Their care and nurturing are left mostly to Dilsey, the Compson's African-American housekeeper.

Jason Compson III

The father of Quentin, Jason, Benjy, and Caddy. Mr. Compson is a retired lawyer and has become an alcoholic. He is already dead at the time of the novel in 1928, and is shown in flashback during Benjy's and Jason's narrations. His deterioration accelerates after losing his oldest son Quentin to suicide and his daughter Caddy to marriage. He also loses much of his social position, because he has had to sell the last of his inherited estate in order to pay for Caddy's wedding and Quentin's tuition to Harvard. In his conversations with his children, especially Quentin, Mr. Compson is shown as cynical.

Jason Compson IV

The middle son of the Compson family. After his brother Quentin's suicide and the death of his father, Jason is the head of the family. Throughout the novel Jason is shown as a cold-blooded person. Mrs. Compson, however, sees him as the only one of her children with any common sense; in his "Appendix: Compson 1699–1945," Faulkner describes him as "the first sane Compson since before Culloden and (a childless bachelor) hence the last." Jason does seem attached to the real world more than his other siblings. He sees the necessity of succeeding in society, which he translates as the need to make money. Because of his rationality, the only person he fears and respects is Dilsey, the family's black housekeeper—"his sworn enemy since birth."

Jason is embittered by whatever seems to get in his way. He resents his parents for sending his brother Quentin to Harvard and seems eaten up by jealousy. He is angry with his sister Caddy because he believes her promiscuity caused her divorce and thus his chances of getting a job in her husband's bank. When Caddy leaves her daughter Quentin with the Compsons after her divorce, he schemes to keep the money Caddy sends for Quentin's support for himself. He further takes revenge by preventing Caddy from seeing her daughter, even briefly, and by treating the girl spitefully and with contempt. When his niece Quentin attempts to assert herself, Jason reacts cruelly and angrily. He finds her behavior a reflection of Caddy's actions, which he believed caused his present unhappy state. Quentin finally rebels and steals Jason's money and runs away—not just the $4000 he swindled from her but an additional $2800 in his own savings besides. Jason is beside himself and tries to find her and have her arrested. In terms of his anger, Jason is a man out of control, even though he is able to meet the practical demands of making a living. Although he is later seen as a moderately successful businessman, Jason is the final representation of the Compson family's downfall.

Maury Compson

See Benjamin Compson

Quentin Compson

The eldest son of the Compsons. Quentin's monologue, the second section of the book, takes place on June 2, 1910, while he is a student at Harvard. It is the day Quentin decides to commit suicide and the whole monologue details the events of this day and the events that led up to his decision

to take his life. Faulkner's themes of family pride and the changes wrought on an individual over time are played out in Quentin's character. He cannot stand the changes that have taken place in his relationship with his sister Caddy, for whom he has incestuous feelings. He is devastated when she reaches sexual maturity and obsesses over her relationships with men. But as Faulkner writes in his "Appendix: Compson 1699–1945," Quentin loves "not his sister's body but some concept of Compson honour precariously and (he knew well) only temporarily supported by the minute fragile membrane of her maidenhead."

The notion that Quentin's preoccupation with an outdated ideal of family "honor" has been much commented on by critics. The loss of the innocence that Quentin witnesses in Caddy's "fall" is something that he finds intolerable. He cannot accept his father's reassurances that in time his pain "will no longer hurt like this now," for that would make his pain meaningless. Unable to adjust, seeing no other alternative, Quentin commits suicide. As the child for whom the Compson parents sacrificed so much, his death is a terrible loss to the family. His death is also symbolic of the feeling of meaninglessness of life for the Compson family, particularly for Mr. Compson, who uses alcohol to blunt his sense of purposelessness.

Damuddy

The Compson children's grandmother. In his narration, Benjy recalls the day of her funeral, when Caddy climbs up a tree to peer in a window while her brothers and Dilsey's children watch her muddy underpants.

Deacon

An African-American porter at the train station near Harvard who hires himself out to Southern students he meets at the station. He has been "guide mentor and friend to unnumbered crops of innocent and lonely freshman," Quentin says. Deacon tells Quentin that "you and me's the same folk, come long and short." This parallels Quentin's observation that "a nigger is not a person so much as a form of behaviour" and that "the best way to take all people, black or white, is to take them for what they think they are."

Earl

Jason's supervisor at the store where he works. He puts up with Jason's lateness and rude talk, even though he suspects Jason of robbing his own mother, because he feels sorry for Mrs. Compson.

Dilsey Gibson

The Compson housekeeper, who is seen to be the most positive character in the novel. Dilsey is the person who nurtures the Compson children, since both their mother and father are incapable of displaying love and affection. Her service to the family, even as she suffers from arthritis, is in stark contrast to Mrs. Compson's neglect due to imagined illnesses. She is the only character that is able to embrace the meaning of life and accept a sense of family history. Her section is the fourth and final one and takes place on Easter Sunday, a time of resurrection. An inspiring sermon is an important part of the section and both Dilsey and Benjy, whom Dilsey has brought along to church, are spiritually moved. Dilsey's response, unlike Benjy's, is more than an emotional one. She experiences an epiphany—a sudden perception of truth—and tells her children "I seed de beginnin, en now I sees de endin." Some critics have interpreted this as a comment on the fall of the Compson family.

Through what is often called the "Dilsey" section of the novel, the author's point of view is expressed. Faulkner handles this by telling her story through the third person. It is through Dilsey's tireless caring for the elder Compsons and their children that the author expresses his belief in the enduring quality of humanity. She is portrayed as a selfless and realistic person. She understands the behavior of all the children and accepts life in all its aspects because of a faith which flows from Christian love.

Frony Gibson

Dilsey's daughter. When Dilsey, Benjy, and Frony are at church on Easter Sunday, Frony has to speak for her mother when Dilsey refuses to answer some youngsters who ask how she's doing. Frony answers for her out of a sense of common courtesy. Dilsey is shown here to have the capacity to be somewhat scornful of others, a quality that has also been attributed to the author.

Luster Gibson

Dilsey's grandson, whose primary function is as Benjy's caretaker. As Faulkner writes in the "Appendix: Compson 1699–1945," Luster is "a man, aged fourteen" who is "capable of the complete care and security of an idiot twice his age and three times his size." He is with Benjy during the opening scenes of Benjy's monologue. They pass the golf course where Benjy begins to cry upon hearing the word "caddie" called it. This reminds him of his sister Caddy. Luster sometimes teases Benjy, but for the most part he comforts and guides Benjy.

Roskus Gibson

Dilsey's husband. Roskus appears in Benjy's monologue. Benjy sees him milking the cow in the barn. Roskus is critical of the Compsons in many ways. Among other things, he disapproves of their changing Benjy's name after they realized he was retarded.

T. P. Gibson

One of Dilsey's sons, who is beginning to take jobs over from his ailing father Roskus. He appears in Benjy's section struggling to control the horse Queenie when he is told to take the reins. Mrs. Compson is uneasy about his handling the reins also. When Benjy recalls Caddy's wedding, he remembers his brother Quentin hitting young T.P. and knocking him into the pigpen. The good-natured T.P. seems to take it all in fun, and continues his care of Benjy. Later Luster is shown taking over similar tasks from T.P.

Versh Gibson

Another son of Dilsey's. Benjy likes to go to Versh's house for the smell of the fire.

Sydney Herbert Head

Called Herbert, he is Caddy's fiance and later her husband. He turns Caddy out when he discovers that he is not the father of Miss Quentin. While he is engaged to Caddy, he has a conversation with her brother Quentin about cheating that illustrates Quentin's rigid view of ethics and morality.

Uncle Maury

See Maury L. Bascomb

Miss Quentin

Caddy's daughter, whose father is uncertain but may be Dalton Ames. When Caddy's husband Herbert Head, discovers Quentin is not his, he divorces Caddy. The Compsons also disown their disgraced daughter. Unable to support Quentin, Caddy brings her daughter home to be brought up by the Compsons. She leaves but sends support money for her daughter. Jason uses the money to save for himself. When at age seventeen Quentin has had enough of Jason's mistreatment, she steals the money from his strong box—including some of his own savings—and runs away. Jason attempts to pursue her to recover his money. He has nothing but contempt for her, seeing in her a reflection of Caddy, whom he blames for all his troubles.

Reverend Shegog

The guest preacher at the Easter Sunday service Dilsey attends with Frony and Benjy. He is a fiery speaker and moves both Benjy and Dilsey to tears. His appearance, which is small and undistinguished, contrasts sharply with that of the regular preacher at Dilsey's church, who is large and impressive. Rev. Shegog's sermon, which progresses from a cold tone to a rousing, passionate plea, leaves Benjy rapt and Dilsey in tears.

Shreve

Quentin's roommate at Harvard. He is friendly and concerned for Quentin's well-being, so much so that Spoade teasingly calls Shreve Quentin's "husband." He is one of the two people for whom Quentin leaves a suicide note.

Spoade

One of Quentin's friends at Harvard. He has "cold, quizzical eyes" and teasingly calls Shreve Quentin's "husband." Although he is Quentin's friend, he is puzzled by his behavior.

St. Louis preacher

See Reverend Shegog

Topics for Further Study

- Research mental retardation and discuss the accuracy of Faulkner's portrayal of Benjy. Compare public attitudes toward mental impairment and illness today to the attitudes shown in Faulkner's novel.

- Discuss the importance of Dilsey's role in the novel. What do you think is Faulkner saying about race relations in the book and how does his portrayal compare with current depictions of African Americans in literature or the media?

- Find information about other cultures' attitude toward incest. Discuss the concept of incest as a taboo, and from both a moral and biological perspective.

- Compare Faulkner's style in *The Sound and the Fury* with James Joyce's use of the subjective point of view in *The Dubliners* or *The Portrait of the Artist as a Young Man*.

Themes

Time

The themes in *The Sound and the Fury* are so closely interwoven with the characters and structure of the novel that it is difficult to separate these elements. In all four sections of the novel, however, time is an important theme that Faulkner develops. The central characters of the four sections each cope with time in a different way. In the first section, Benjy's sense of time is defective. His thoughts move from present to past time without the ability to grasp the real meaning of events. Benjy is free from time because he cannot understand its impact on his feelings. Quentin's efforts to cope with the present are impeded by his memories. He cannot accept the changes in his life that time inevitably brings. His sense of loss over the innocence of his childhood love of Caddy is unbearable. Rather than deal with life's changes over time, he puts an end to time by committing suicide. Jason, on the other hand, lives in time present,

around which all his actions flow. By living in time present, Jason reacts to events as they occur, unlike Quentin who acts on time past. In the last section of the book, Dilsey represents another view of time. Hers is a historical view. She embraces all of her life experiences and those of the Compsons with a religious faith about the timelessness of life. Her view most closely reflects the author's viewpoint on time. By having the novel cover four days, each section representing one day, Faulkner is able to use time to give the novel a tight framework.

Pride

Pride is the undoing of the Compson family. The loss of their property and status demoralizes the elder Compsons, Caroline and Jason III, the parents of Benjy, Quentin, Jason, and Caddy. Out of their sense of family pride and their economic and social decline, they turn inward. Mr. Compson turns to alcohol in his sense of loss. Mrs. Compson retreats to her bed and self-pity. Quentin's concern over the family "honor" and how Caddy has shamed the family lead him to kill himself. The younger Jason is racked with pride and it is his undoing. With him it is both pride and jealousy. He feels cheated and feels that he deserves better. Caddy deceived him, he thinks, and he uses this to justify stealing from her. When Caddy's daughter, Quentin, steals from her uncle, Jason, he is outraged that he has been undone. Faulkner shows the tragic results of pride in the characters of these Compson family members.

Love and Passion

Natural and unnatural love among siblings, love between the sexes, and Christian love are themes that pervade *The Sound and the Fury*. Faulkner shows the love the Compson brothers have for Caddy. Benjy loves the care she gave him when they were young. When he hears the word "caddie" called out on the golf course, he moans because it sounds like her name. He misses her after she leaves home to marry. Benjy's love is the love of an innocent for someone who has shown him affection. Quentin's love for his sister Caddy is an unnatural one. He has incestuous feelings for her. He is jealous of her boyfriends and denies that she has had lovers. He fantasizes an incestuous relationship between them, although Faulkner writes in his "Appendix: Compson 1699–1945" that Quentin "loved not the idea of the incest which he would not commit, but some presbyterian concept of its eternal punishment: he, not God, could by that means cast himself and his sister both into hell, where he could guard her forever and keep her forevermore intact amid the eternal fires." Caddy, as she is presented through her brothers' monologues, seems to develop in a natural way. As a child, she shows love toward Benjy and Quentin. As a young woman, she has lovers, becomes pregnant, marries, and leaves home. Christian love is the thematic note on which the book ends. Through Dilsey, Faulkner presents the view of love that springs from religious faith, a love that endures pain and accepts reality.

Sanity and Insanity

The contrast between Benjy and Jason reflects a theme of sanity and insanity in *The Sound and the Fury*. An idiot who does not comprehend reality, Benjy displays a world in chaos through his monologue. Faulkner uses his character to explore the meaninglessness of sensory reactions to sounds, sights, and language. Quentin's suicide also can be regarded as an act of insanity because it comes from his inability to deal with reality. Mr. Compson's al-coholism can be seen as a slow suicide. It is an unnatural retreat from reality, as is Mrs. Compson's retreat to her bed. The two characters who emerge as sane in the novel are Jason and Dilsey. Dilsey's sanity is rooted in her total acceptance of the realities of life. Jason also deals with the here and now, but his sanity is perverted by his resentments.

Style

Structure

Faulkner has created an unusual structure in *The Sound and the Fury*. The story takes place over a period of four days, each of which is seen through the eyes of a different character. The first part of the book is the monologue of Benjy on April 7, 1928, the day before Easter. The second part of the book belongs to Quentin on the day of his suicide on June 2, 1910. Jason, the son, is the focus of the third section, April 6, 1928, which covers Good Friday, the day before Benjy's monologue. The fourth and final section takes place on Easter Sunday, April 8, 1928. The story is not related by a single individual, but is often referred to as Dilsey's section. In a fragmented way, the story of the Compson family and their tragedy is gradually pieced together. Each section adds bits and pieces of the history of the Compson family. Benjy's account covers a period of twenty-five years. Quentin's story ends earlier than the other two brothers, since he has committed suicide in 1910. In this section the reader learns more about the family's early relationships. Jason's section, the third in the book, reveals more of the dark side of the Compson family. This section echoes the religious events of Christ's betrayal on Good Friday. The betrayal is by young Quentin, who steals money from her Uncle Jason and runs away from home. Dilsey's section, the fourth and last, reveals Faulkner's affirmation of her enduring qualities. It is Dilsey who has cared for and tried to keep the family intact for decades. The final section contains an Easter Sunday service in an African-American church. The church service affirms Dilsey's acceptance of Christian love, an event some critics have interpreted as echoing the resurrection of Christ.

Point of View

By dividing the story into four sections, Faulkner is able to present the Compson story from four separate points of view. As he moves from Benjy's perspective to Quentin's to Jason's and finally to the voice of an omniscient, third-person narrator, the author presents the story as if it were a patchwork quilt. It is only when all the pieces are finally put together that the reader knows the tragic events of the Compson family and the extent of their decline. While this changing point of view adds to the complexity of the book, it also adds a depth of understanding to the individual characters and their story. Faulkner seemed to understand that if he told the story from only one point of view, he would not be able to delve deeply into the nature and motives for his characters' behavior. When one person tells a story, something is always left out. When many tell a story, it is never quite the same story, but the listener or reader then becomes more involved because he or she must think about it from those different perspectives. This is the effect of reading *The Sound and the Fury.* The first three sections that focus on the Compson brothers also explore their distinct perceptions of their sister Caddy. In this way she also becomes a central character, but only as she is seen by others, never from her point of view. By writing the final section in the third person, Faulkner can present his overview through Dilsey. Her perception of the Compsons and their decline reflects the author's tragic vision of the universal human struggle to find meaning in life.

Interior Monologue

Except in the last section, the narrations of *The Sound and the Fury* are interior monologues. Interior monologues are narratives in which characters' thoughts are revealed in a way that appears to be uncontrolled by the author. The chaotic thoughts of Benjy narrate the first section. He also records what is said around him without understanding it. Quentin's inner voice relates his experiences in the Compson family and details his thoughts and behavior on the day of his suicide. Jason's inner voice relates the third part of the book. By this method, Faulkner lets the reader see the nature of all three characters without describing them. Because we know what these three characters are thinking, they are clearly focused in the novel. Many of the other characters, particularly the Compson parents and Caddy, are less clearly drawn, because we always see them through the eyes of Benjy, Quentin, or Jason. Dilsey's section is not written as an interior monologue and the reader sees her character from her behavior and her dialogue.

Stream of Consciousness

"Stream of consciousness" writing is designed to give the impression of the everchanging, spontaneous, and seemingly illogical series of thoughts, emotions, images, and memories that make up real-life thought. Faulkner was influenced by the writings of Irish novelist James Joyce, who had developed the use of stream of consciousness in his novel *Ulysses.* Many writers of the period, including Faulkner, were influenced by Joyce's use of this technique. Within some of the interior monologues in *The Sound and the Fury,* Faulkner uses techniques peculiar to stream of consciousness. An absence of punctuation and capitalization characterizes stream of consciousness, as well as the repetition of words and phrases. Changes in type, such as switching to italics, can also be used effectively to portray changes in thought. While the writing of this book came early in his career, Faulkner showed a mastery of this technique. It has been largely abandoned by contemporary novelists, who still frequently use the interior monologue.

Setting

Although most of the action of *The Sound and the Fury* is communicated through the characters' inner thoughts, their physical situation also plays a significant role in the novel. Faulkner created the fictional Mississippi county of Yoknapatawpha in his third novel, *Sartoris,* and revisited it in many of his subsequent works, including *The Sound and the Fury.* This setting of the South in the 1920s figures very prominently into the character of Quentin. He is holding on to an outdated ideal of the Southern gentleman, one who upholds the family's honor and protects those in his care, especially women. His sister Caddy, who acts according to more liberated standards of behavior, forces him to realize his ideals cannot survive in the modern world. When she becomes pregnant out of wedlock, it is both a stain on the family honor and a sign that Quentin has failed to protect her. Changing ideas of race relations also figure in Quentin's narrative, which takes place in the Northeast. This contrast in setting causes Quentin to consider the difference in race relations in the North and South. From this difference he gains the insight that "the best way to take all people, black or white, is to take them for what they think they are, then leave them alone."

Historical Context

The Impact of the Civil War on the South

The loss of the Civil War in the nineteenth century had a profound impact on the psyche of the south. The region not only lost the war, but their

William Faulkner (right) with jockey Eddie Arcaro at the Kentucky Derby, 1955.

whole way of life as well. The aristocratic structure of slavery was destroyed when the South lost the war, but many of the social values remained. Whites still controlled the economic and social structure of the region. Blacks, while no longer slaves, were generally under the rule of white society. What evolved over the next hundred years in the South was a society where blacks were legally free, but socially disenfranchised from an equal education and equal economic opportunities. The relationship of the blacks to whites depicted by Faulkner in *The Sound and the Fury* reflects that social and economic divide. The blacks in the novel are servants of the Compsons. Their role as servant is expanded by Faulkner to that of spiritual caretaker, especially as he portrays the character of Dilsey.

In conjunction with the South's defeat in the Civil War was the area's lessening economic influence. During the end of the nineteenth century and beginning of the twentieth, industrial and manufacturing businesses came to dominate the U.S. economy. Agriculture, the mainstay of the Southern economy, was less profitable, especially for relatively small family farms. The economic problems of the South can be seen in the way Faulkner portrays the Compsons. Their economic decline spans several generations, each one experiencing a greater decline. By 1910, Jason's father is forced to sell the last of the family's land to pay for Caddy's wedding and Quentin's tuition. Jason, the central character of section three, is left to work in a local store to support the family. He reflects the attitude expressed by President Calvin Coolidge during the prosperity of the 1920s that "the business of America is business." Even during the boom period of the 1920s, the textile industry suffered a depression. As a cotton-producing region, the South was hurt economically. The stock market crash of 1929 came just as *The Sound and the Fury* hit the book market. The Great Depression that followed in the 1930s made it difficult for Faulkner to succeed economically with his writing.

The "Lost" Generation

A counterpoint to the bleakness that followed the 1929 stock market crash and the depression of the 1930s was the proliferation of artistic accomplishments. No other period in American history had a generation that produced so many important works in literature, music, and the arts. Beginning after World War I and up until World War II, America saw writers like Faulkner, Eugene O'Neill, Ernest Hemingway, F. Scott Fitzgerald, Thomas Wolfe, Sinclair Lewis, Dashiell Hammett, and Dorothy Parker emerge on the literary scene. Georgia O'Keeffe and Thomas Hart Benton were a few

Compare & Contrast

- **1929:** Black and white relations in the South were stratified along racial lines. Education was officially segregated, with facilities for black and white children "separate but equal."

  Today: In the urban South, many African Americans, as elsewhere in the United States, have gained economic and professional status. Poor blacks everywhere in America are experiencing poverty and poor education at record low levels. Education is supposedly integrated, but neighborhood racial patterns have worked against equalizing education.

- **1929:** While the family structure was beginning to disintegrate because of social changes in the country, most families had two parents and extended families living close together was common.

  Today: The two-parent "nuclear" family structure has been shattered by high rates of divorce and remarriage. A relatively high percentage of children in the United States live in single-parent families.

- **1929:** Creativity in the arts was flourishing in the United States. Reading novels and short stories was a major form of entertainment. Only a few writers were financially successful.

Today: Much of the literary creativity of Americans has become channeled into team efforts for television sitcoms and dramatic serials. The novel is still a significant form of recreation, but the film has superseded the novel as the primary form for written creative expression. A few novelists write best sellers which make lots of money, but writers for television and movies generally make more money than novelists or short storywriters.

- **1929:** Illegitimate pregnancy among middle class women was a social disgrace that could lead to ostracization.

  Today: There is little stigma attached to unwed motherhood, at least for older women who are financially independent. Single women who want children become pregnant deliberately, either through artificial insemination or a relationship they do not wish to make permanent.

- **1929:** Mental retardation was considered a curse and a burden that a family had to bear. Families felt ashamed and guilty when they had a retarded child.

  Today: The mentally impaired have many educational programs and opportunities to help them be productive and independent.

---

of the American artists who were productive during this period. Theaters on Broadway and other places were alive with new productions and Hollywood was grinding out new dramas and musicals every week. In December 1928 George Gershwin debuted his famous symphonic piece "An American in Paris." The Chicago Civic Opera building opened in 1929 with a 3500-seat auditorium. In popular music, 1929 was the year Guy Lombardo began his New Year's Eve radio broadcast. Songwriter Hoagy Carmichael wrote his famous "Stardust" in 1927, and "Georgia on My Mind" in 1930. America was alive with creativity. It was as if the economic downturn unleashed a volcano of cre-

ative energy that had not been seen in this country before—or since. This generation of young creative people has been called "The Lost Generation," for many of their contemporaries were killed during the Great War (World War I), which lasted from 1914 to 1918. The disillusionment inspired by the war led many creative artists to explore what it meant to be American in the modern world, and what it meant to be human.

When Faulkner accepted the Nobel Prize in 1950, he made a speech that became a famous statement of the modern world and the artist's place in it. He spoke of the threat of physical destruction to the human spirit. What he expressed was the prevalent feeling of the Lost Generation that human be-ings had lost a sense of the meaning of life. In his speech, he expressed his belief that "man will not merely endure; he will prevail. He is immortal, not because he alone among creatures has an inex-haustible voice, but because he has a soul, a spirit capable of compassion and sacrifice and endurance. The poet's, the writer's duty is to write about these things. It is his privilege to help man endure by re-minding him of the courage and honor and hope and pride and compassion and pity and sacrifice which have been the glory of the past." Old values had been shattered by the events of the first half of the twentieth century. It was not yet apparent what the new values would be.

Critical Overview

Critical reaction to *The Sound and the Fury* was by no means universally favorable when it first appeared in print in 1929. While finding the novel powerful and sincere, Frances Lamont Robbins, writing in *Outlook and Independent* commented that "the theme, dramatic and potentially moving, loses much of its force and clarity by being pre-sented, almost wholly, through subjective analysis. It takes a stronger hand than William Faulkner's to divert the stream of consciousness into channels of perfect usefulness and beauty." In the 1929 book *On William Faulkner's "The Sound and the Fury,"* however, Evelyn Scott congratulated the publish-ers for "presenting a little known writer with the dignity of recognition which his talent deserves." The critic called Faulkner's book "an important contribution to the permanent literature of fiction." "Hardly Worth While" was the title Clifton Fadi-man used in his 1930 review in the *Nation.* The main problem with Faulkner's book, Fadiman felt, was that "the intelligent reader can grasp the newer literary anarchies only by an effort of analytical at-tention so strained that it fatigues and dulls his emo-tional perception." He did praise Faulkner for his portrayal of Benjy, but ridiculed it as too much of a good thing to listen to "one hundred pages of an imbecile's simplified sense perceptions and mono-syllabic gibberings." Fadiman also thought Quentin and Jason were not interesting enough "to follow the ramifications of their minds and memories."

Since its publication, *The Sound and the Fury* has come to be recognized as one of Faulkner's mas-terpieces. *As I Lay Dying, Light in August, Absalom, Absalom!,* and *Go Down, Moses* are his other her-alded novels. Faulkner has long been considered a major American writer and many critics regard him as the most important American novelist of the twen-tieth century. Terry Heller, in a 1991 essay in the *Critical Survey of Long Fiction,* wrote that Faulkner "dramatizes in most of his novels some version of the central problem of modern man in the West," which he feels is an uncertainty about the meaning of human history. Linda W. Wagner compared Faulkner to Shakespeare, Dostoevski, Dickens, Mil-ton, and Dante for his moral point of view. Her 1981 essay in the *Dictionary of Literary Biography* com-mends the author for his inventiveness and vigor. "Faulkner faces the problematic existence of the modern world, and he insists that human beings can surmount those problems," she remarks.

The strongest praise for *The Sound and the Fury* centers around its moral message. In "Worlds in Counterpoint," Olga W. Vickery's 1964 essay, the critic praises Faulkner for his structure, themes, and characterizations. "Out of Dilsey's actions and her participation in the Easter service arise once more the simple verities of human life," writes Vickery. "The splinters of truth presented in the first three sections reverberate.... [Out] of those same events ... come Dilsey's triumph and her peace, lending significance ... to the book as a whole," Vickery concludes. "*The Sound and the Fury* is a moral book," comments Robert J. Griffin in his 1963 essay in *Essays in Modern American Litera-ture.* He continues: "Integral to its structure is the depiction of four distinct ethical points of view.... The novel is definitely a moral book, and ultimately a sort of religious book," Griffin contends. Arthur Mizener called the portrayal of Jason Compson, "Faulkner's finest portrait of a poor white." Con-tinuing in his 1967 essay in *Twelve Great Ameri-can Novels,* Mizener echoes other critics in his as-sessment of the novel for being "in a quiet way quite unlike the melodramatic religiosity of much twen-tieth-century literature." It "is a religious book," as-serts Mizener. After Faulkner received the Nobel Prize in Literature in 1949, he emerged from a pe-riod of obscurity. The Nobel Prize was the first of many other awards and his reputation grew steadily after receiving it. His books have been translated in many other languages. Few writers since William Shakespeare have had so much written about them.

Criticism

Jeffrey M. Lilburn

In the following essay, Lilburn, a teaching as-sistant at the University of Western Ontario, ana-

lyzes how each of the novel's narrations comes to focus on Caddy Compson. He notes that while a reader of The Sound and the Fury *can only learn of Caddy through the observations of her family, interpreting her character is central to understanding the novel.*

William Faulkner's fourth novel, *The Sound and the Fury* is a haunting and sometimes bewildering novel that surprises and absorbs the reader each time it is read. The novel was Faulkner's personal favorite and, along with James Joyce's novel *Ulysses* and T. S. Eliot's poem *The Waste Land,* is generally thought to be one of the greatest works of literature in English of the twentieth century. *The Sound and the Fury* also signalled the beginning of the "major period" of Faulkner's own literary creativity; four of the five novels that followed—*As I Lay Dying, Sanctuary, Light in August,* and *Absalom, Absalom!*—are, along with *The Sound and the Fury,* often regarded as the best in Faulkner's oeuvre. Not surprisingly, the novel has received an extraordinary amount of critical analysis, much of which has been devoted to explaining Faulkner's technical experimentations. Critics have also widely discussed Faulkner's treatment of issues such as race, suicide, incest, time, history, and religion. Central to any reading of the novel, however, is the character that Faulkner claimed was his source for the novel—Caddy. Richard Gray has described Caddy as the novel's "absent presence" and each of the four sections as "another attempt to know her." But to the reader, Caddy remains an elusive mystery whose enforced silence prevents her from ever being known. To her three brothers, she is a source of obsession and irritation that cannot be forgotten or overcome.

The Sound and the Fury explores the breakdown of the familial relationships that lead to the Compson family's tragic deterioration. Few readers would disagree that the family's demise is indeed tragic, but the precise reasons for the downfall are still debated. David Dowling has suggested that the tragedy of the Compsons is that they are slaves to themselves and to the past. This argument is particularly relevant to the novel's first two sections. Benjy's monologue, for example, is uttered in the present—Easter weekend, 1928—but is mainly comprised of memories from his childhood and adolescence. Most of these memories are connected to his sister, Caddy, whose departure following her marriage to Herbert Head leaves a void in Benjy's life. Because Caddy was the one family member to provide Benjy with the nurturing love

What Do I Read Next?

- A tale of incest in the Sutpen family set in the South, Faulkner's *Absalom, Absalom!* (1936) features Quentin Compson as a character.

- Truman Capote's 1948 novel *Other Voices, Other Rooms* is the story of alienated youth set in the author's usual Southern Gothic atmosphere.

- Margaret Mitchell's Pulitzer Prize-winning romantic novel *Gone with the Wind,* published in 1936, depicts the destruction of Southern culture during the Civil War.

- Robert Penn Warren's 1946 Pulitzer Prize-winning novel *All the King's Men* portrays a charismatic Southern politician who has been compared to the real politician Huey Long.

- Both of Tennessee Williams' Pulitzer Prize-winning plays *Cat on a Hot Tin Roof* (1955) and *A Streetcar Named Desire* (1947) depict the sexual frustration of his characters in the context of Southern society.

that he needed, and because, as Margaret Bauer observes, Mrs. Compson does little else but whine about being punished by God for her family's transgressions, Caddy was more of a mother figure to Benjy than Mrs. Compson was. Through his monologue, which often obscures the boundaries between present and past, Benjy reveals both a deep-seated attachment to a past inhabited by Caddy and a desperate yearning for her return. Like his companion, Luster, who is busy searching for a lost quarter, Benjy, too, hopes to find that which he has lost.

As many critics have noted, Benjy's memories are largely concerned with Caddy's sexuality. His disapproving cries after catching Caddy and Charlie on the swing provide merely one example of his preoccupation with his sister's sexual awakening. It is in the second section, however, that Caddy's sexuality emerges as the central issue of the novel. Quentin is totally obsessed by the subject and, throughout the morning, afternoon, and evening of June 2, 1910, can think of little else. His relationship with his sister is anticipated by the childhood scene at the branch where Caddy, ignoring Quentin's protests, removes her dress in front of her brothers and Versh. Quentin slaps Caddy, who then falls on her behind and muddies her drawers. This highly symbolic scene prefigures Caddy's future as a so-called "fallen woman" and shows Quentin's futile attempts to protect his sister's honor and body. Some readers also believe that the scene suggests Quentin's implication in his sister's later promiscuity, as well as his own incestuous feelings towards her.

When Caddy reaches sexual maturity, Quentin is still trying to protect her but his attempts are always unsuccessful. Just as he fails to prevent Caddy from taking off her dress at the branch, so he fails later in life when confronting Caddy's lover, Dalton Ames. His final defeat occurs on the afternoon of June 2, 1910, as he is driving with Mrs. Bland and some friends from school. One of his friends, Gerald Bland, begins "blowing off" about his many women and Quentin, who has just been thinking about the humiliating incident with Caddy's lover, automatically repeats the same question he had asked Dalton: "Did you ever have a sister?" Ironically, the beating Quentin then receives from Gerald occurs just moments after Quentin was himself accused of kidnapping a little girl. The girl's brother, Julio, threatens to kill Quentin, thereby reproducing—and mocking—Quentin's threats against Dalton.

Like Benjy, Quentin is determined to maintain—or rather recapture—some elusive ideal that, in childhood, seemed genuine and permanent. His need to protect his sister stems from an anachronistic sense of honor that derives from what Richard Gray describes as "an authoritative discourse issuing out of some epic past." That discourse, Gray explains, is based on notions of gentility traditionally attached to Southern plantation aristocracy and gives Quentin "an instinctive sense of how life should be." But unfortunately, Quentin's notions of how life should be do not, David Dowling argues, allow women any space between saint and sinner. As Diane Roberts explains, in the South, ideologies were based on hierarchies or oppositions; as a result, a person is defined not by what he or she is, but by what he or she is not. Mrs. Compson, for example, has a very rigid idea of what it means to be a lady: "I was taught that there is no halfway ground that a woman is either a lady or not." In her eyes, Caddy occupies the sec-

ond half of the virgin/whore pairing and is incontrovertibly a "fallen woman."

Quentin's section has been described as a dialogue, or debate, in which he struggles to determine the validity of these notions of honor and Southern ladyhood. As he wanders through the final day before his suicide, Quentin finds himself caught between his beliefs and the surfacing realization that his beliefs have no foundation. His main problem, Dowling and others have argued, is that he cannot bring himself to accept changes in meaning. He tries to come to terms with his sister's unconventional behavior and marriage to Herbert but the thought, suggested to him by his father, that someday his despair "will no longer hurt [him] like this now" is intolerable to him. To acknowledge such a change would mean that even Caddy "was not quite worth despair." It would mean that the "authoritative discourse" he clings to is not only outdated, but that it was never more than one fiction among many others. His suicide thus becomes symbolic of both his inability to accept the fluctuating nature of meaning and, as Kevin Railey shows, of the futility of attempting to "assert the power of a displaced class and its fading values" in the South of the twentieth century.

The third section marks a drastic shift in the novel. Whereas Quentin struggles with his inability to renounce the anachronistic values discussed above, and wishes he could maintain the relationship he and Caddy had as children, Jason feels only contempt for his family and his past. He does not mourn Caddy's absence like Benjy does; instead, Jason's thoughts of the past are accompanied by feelings of resentment and rage. The only loss he mourns is that of the job he was promised at Herbert's bank. Jason's pettiness is evident throughout his monologue, but the grudge he bears over this one lost opportunity is unparalleled. He believes that Caddy's promiscuity deprived him of the job because Herbert would not have left her had her daughter, also named Quentin, not been born too early. As a result, he views his niece Quentin as the symbol and joint cause of his present misery and acts out his revenge on Caddy through her. Not coincidentally, Quentin is now about the same age Caddy was at the time of her pregnancy, and Jason's brutal treatment of his niece may have as much to do with her own promiscuity as it does with his desire for revenge.

It is evident that Jason enjoys tormenting his niece and will go well out of his way to do so. He spends much of the Easter weekend attempting to foil Quentin's rendezvous with a man from the show and often appears preoccupied by what his niece is wearing. Diane Roberts has argued that this excessive attention paid to the young girl's body and boyfriend suggests "barely concealed desire." She even describes Jason's treatment of Quentin as "sadistic eroticism." Jason's own words appear to support this interpretation. When his mother, attempting to foster kindness towards her granddaughter, reminds Jason that the girl is his "own flesh and blood," his response suggests that his brother Quentin may not have been the only family member to harbor incestuous desires: "That's just what I was thinking of—flesh. And a little blood too, if I had my way." Whether or not Jason's desire for revenge is mingled with a sexual desire for his niece's body shall be left for the reader to decide. What is now finally clear, however, is that the Compson brothers' obsessive preoccupations with female sexuality play a significant role in the family's downfall. Benjy's disapproving cries and Quentin's psychological turmoil have become open hostility in Jason. His cruel treatment of both Caddy and her daughter in the final two sections provides what is perhaps the best view of the destructive forces operating within the Compson household.

The final section of the novel is often referred to as the "Dilsey section." But while Dilsey is one of the main characters of this section, her story, like Caddy's, is told for her, not by her. Also, much of this section is again devoted to Jason and his mad pursuit of his niece and her money. The result is a jarring contrast between Dilsey's epiphany-like experience at the Easter service and Jason's frustrating failure in Mottson. Richard Gray has noted how, in this section, Jason's pride, rage and isolation are countered by Dilsey and the Easter Day congregation's collective voice and "feelings of spiritual consummation." Other critics, however, have suggested that Dilsey's repeated refrain following the Reverend Shegog's moving sermon refers to the end of the Compson family. "I seed de beginnin, en now I sees de endin," she says, seemingly foreseeing the Compsons' final downfall.

Yet, the exact fate of the Compson family remains unknown at the novel's end. After turning the final page, readers may find themselves looking for something that isn't there: the conspicuously absent "Caddy Section." Although Faulkner did offer some additional information in the Compson Appendix that he wrote to accompany the publication of *The Portable Faulkner* in 1946, the fact remains that Caddy's voice is never heard. Why is Caddy the only Compson sibling who is not given

the opportunity to express her own story? Roberts reports that Faulkner thought Caddy "too beautiful and too moving to reduce her to telling what was going on" and felt it would be "more passionate" to represent her through the voices of others. Another explanation might be found by returning to the scene that inspired the novel. When a young Caddy climbed the pear tree to look into the parlor window, she demonstrated courage, adventurousness, and a willingness to defy authority. Her male onlookers, meanwhile, could merely stand below and watch the muddy seat of her drawers. Is it a coincidence then that, in this novel, Caddy remains imprisoned within the narratives of three brothers whose obsessions and preoccupations reveal that, in a sense, they are all still fixated on those muddy drawers? Certainly, Caddy's unchosen silence signifies more than the desire to make her seem "more passionate."

Source: Jeffrey M. Lilburn, in an essay for *Novels for Students,* Gale, 1998.

Philip Dubuisson Castille

In the following excerpt, Castille argues that the character of Dilsey is more developed than many critics have seen her. He interprets her actions after hearing the Reverend Shegog's sermon as leading her away from the Compsons and back to her family, a change that reflects the Christian idea of redemption.

The main action of William Faulkner's *The Sound and the Fury* occurs during Easter Week, 1928. Because Easter is the holiest event in the Christian calendar, and because the Passion Week serves as the book's main organizing device, many readers have sensed the presence of religious themes in this often opaque work. But over the past five decades, critical interpretations have ranged from Christian spirituality to existential nothingness. While there has been no consensus on the meaning of the novel, Faulkner scholars have agreed over the years that the structure of *The Sound and the Fury* follows the Modernist "mythical method." Much as the *Odyssey* gives form and sequence to Joyce's *Ulysses,* episodes and images from the Christian Holy Week provide an external framework to Faulkner's narrative. Members of the Compson family undergo experiences which rehearse episodes from the last days of Jesus's life. The four sections of the novel form four Compson gospels, which like the biblical originals develop and expand the story they retell. These parallels to the gospel tradition are most insistent during the

Sunday church service in the fourth section of *The Sound and the Fury*. By means of his powerful if unorthodox rendition of the Passion narrative, the Reverend Shegog wakens in Dilsey capacities for spiritual renewal. Her visionary Easter experience then rouses her to secular acts of rejection and affirmation.

Dilsey Gibson, the kindly and long-suffering domestic worker at the Compson place, is the major non-Compson character in *The Sound and the Fury*. A long-standing scholarly interpretation is that Dilsey represents a moral norm in the decadent Compson world and her actions set a standard of humane behavior. Opposing such a "religious" reading of the novel is the nihilistic view, in which Dilsey's Christianity is meaningless or irrelevant. Both approaches tend to regard Dilsey, whether noble or absurd, as static. Few critics of *The Sound and the Fury* see her as a developing character, although some describe her at the end of the novel as more devoted to the Compsons. My view is that the novel's fourth section, as well as the "Appendix: Compson," suggests the opposite—that she turns away from the Compsons after the Easter Sunday service. Her conversion is religious in that the Reverend Shegog's sermon revitalizes her faith in the Christian God. Yet her Easter experience also has practical consequences. Her life changes as she begins to distance herself from the Compsons and to reaffirm her membership in her African-American family.

Although she appears in the novel's first three sections, Dilsey figures most importantly in the fourth chapter—so much so that it is frequently called "Dilsey's section." She wakes to a cold, gray dawn on Sunday and works to warm the tomblike Compson house. It is worth noting that Easter means nothing to the Compsons (although Dilsey leads the retardate Benjy Compson uncomprehending to Sunday service). Her morning chores done, she makes the long walk to church. Dilsey, her daughter Frony, and her grandson Luster follow the wet streets of Jefferson, Mississippi, until the pavement runs out. Then they step down a dirt road to "a weathered church" outside town, where a revivalist minister from St. Louis preaches the Easter sermon. At first they are disappointed with the "shabby" little traveling minister, with his "monkey face" and "monkey body." But when his voice glides from the "level and cold" inflections of a white man into African-American intonations, they respond warmly.

However, the Reverend Shegog's use of Black English to stir his Mississippi congregation appar-

ently has led some readers to underestimate him as a thinker. His Easter sermon is an acknowledged masterpiece of style and showmanship, but it is also impressive for its artistic skill and intellectual understanding of the Christ story. The Reverend Shegog reveals himself in Faulkner's text to be a learned man whose unconventional exegesis combines material from Christian, Hebraic, and Near Eastern sources to reconstruct the Passion narrative. By advancing a renovating vision of the power of life over death, his homily prompts Dilsey to break free from the Compsons and to renounce her years of resignation and denial.

The Reverend Shegog's sermon is based on the Christian concept of divine love, the mainspring for the redemption of humankind. But at the same time it insists that God's grace and forgiveness are not boundless. When the Last Judgment comes, the Almighty sternly warns, "'I aint gwine load down heaven!'" God's mercy and the granting of salvation are presented as inherently limited and conditional. This sermon depicts an angry God who denounces those who reject goodness and deny His love. In effect He says, you have murdered my innocent Son; for that, you will be destroyed. God the Father in heaven looks down on the cross on Calvary and cries in fury, "'dey done kilt Jesus; dey done kilt my Son!'" In punishment for the crucifixion, God drowns the world. "O blind sinner! Breddren, I tells you; sistuhn, I says to you, when de Lawd did turn His mighty face, say, Aint gwine overload heaven! I can see de widowed God shet His do'; I sees de whelmin flood roll between; I sees de darkness en de death everlastin upon de generations."

As many commentators have shown, and as he insisted, Faulkner knew the Scriptures well; his fiction includes many biblical parallels as well as Christ and Adam figures, such as Joe Christmas or Isaac McCaslin. In *The Sound and the Fury* the Reverend Shegog does not merely repeat the well-known events of the Easter story. Instead, he refashions the details of the life, death, and resurrection of Jesus to develop a mythological pattern consistent with the Passion narrative.

The most significant of these scriptural rearrangements occurs when the Reverend Shegog places the destruction of the world by water *after* the crucifixion of Christ. When Jesus dies on Calvary, His Father sends down global ruin in the form of a flood, an audacious reworking of the Noah-flood story from Hebrew Scripture. Then, amid total devastation caused by the scourging waters, there arises the promise of renewal in the figure of the risen Christ. The millennium arrives all of a sudden at the darkest hour:

> "Den, lo! Breddren! Yes, breddren! Whut I see? Whut I see, O sinner? I sees de resurrection en de light; sees de meek Jesus saying Dey kilt Me dat ye shall live again; I died dat dem whut sees en believes shall never die. Breddren, O breddren! I sees de doom crack en hears de golden horns shoutin down de glory, en de arisen dead whut got de blood and de ricklickshun of de Lamb!"

In a dramatic departure from creedal orthodoxy, the Reverend Shegog's sermon abruptly asserts the power of life (the resurrection of Jesus) precisely at the moment when the power of death seems all-engulfing (the destruction of the world by flood after the crucifixion). While this account revises the orthodox Passion narrative, it has a mythic or poetic logic which recalls the classical literary form of the elegy. In "a rebound as sudden as that in 'Lycidas,' [the Reverend Shegog] makes the typical elegiac turn from universal despair to universal comfort and joy" [according to Richard P. Adams in *Faulkner: Myth and Motion*]. This ancient pre-Christian parabola of death and resurrection gives the Reverend Shegog's sermon its formal structure: borrowing from elegiac tradition, the Reverend Shegog alternates death images (such as the total darkness caused by the flood) with rebirth images (such as the breaking dawn heralded by the resurrected Jesus).

In addition to form, his resounding sermon recalls pre-Christian religious ritual and belief, which Faulkner had studied in the twenties.... In *The Golden Bough* [James] Frazer documents that the Christian Easter story is not unique in world religion. Instead, it draws upon the widespread Near Eastern springtime practice of worshipping "dying and reviving gods," from which the elegiac poetic tradition springs....

My point is that Frazer's theory of mythology and his comparative approach to religion seem to inform Faulkner's technique in section four of *The Sound and the Fury*. In the Reverend Shegog's sermon, Faulkner employs the idiomatic language of twentieth-century Southern Afro-Christianity, which he knew first-hand, to dramatize anew the ancient mystery of springtime resurrection, which he read about in Frazer.

Consistent with nature cult imagery, the Reverend Shegog's sermon portrays the Holy Land before the redemption as a dark estate, steeped in misery. The suffering falls hardest on mothers and children. The Reverend Shegog depicts a terrified Mary as she tries to shield her baby Jesus from the Roman death squads: "'Mary jump up, sees de sojer face: We gwine to kill! We gwine to kill! We gwine to kill yo little Jesus!'" Under the nightmare of oppression and deprivation, the country groans with "'de weepin en de lamentation'" as "'de long, cold years rolls away!'" Then the scene shifts to the evil hour on Calvary. The mourning women keen their "'evening lamentations'" as the apocalyptic darkness falls and the world sinks beneath the all-destroying flood. But when Jesus rises from the grave on Easter, golden cornets on high sound a new anthem of victory and freedom to mark His glorious return to the regenerated earth.

The Reverend Shegog's revisions to the Passion story serve to strengthen its message that God's life-giving love can redeem the past from apparently total defeat. Amid circumstances of overwhelming desolation, the redemptive force of His grace remains a present reality. The pattern of death and rebirth which shapes his rendition of the resurrection implies the immediate possibility of self-transcendence. "'I sees it, breddren! I sees hit. Sees de blastin, blindin sight,'" shouts the Reverend Shegog. His verbs are all in the present tense, signifying that the past is transfigured and time begins again. Existence is no longer a curse or affliction but a means of revelation and transformation....

In *The Sound and the Fury* [Faulkner] brings his "Passion Week of the heart" metaphor to fulfillment in the Easter service. According to the Reverend Shegog's sermon, the evil past can be immediately redeemed and all things made new again under the auspices of the resurrection of Jesus. That is, the mystery of rebirth calls upon us personally to rise up from deep hurt and hopelessness and to start over. But for those who lack vision in spring, who shut their eyes and harden their hearts, no salvation is possible.

The Reverend Shegog's jarring retelling of the Passion narrative, with its double emphasis on the power and the limits of love, leaves Dilsey profoundly moved. As light falls through the "dingy windows" of the church, she sits bolt upright, awed by a great sense of discovery, and cries unashamedly. There is no evidence that anyone else is deeply affected by the homily, although it is well received by the congregation. Frony is embarrassed by her mother's open emotionalism; she has not herself been touched. "'Whyn't you quit dat, mammy?'" she hisses, "'Wid all dese people lookin.'" Luster is plainly unmoved. As the crowd drifts away, nothing in the text suggests that Dilsey's spiritual awakening is shared. The churchgoers chat "easily again group to group" on their way home, much as they did before the service. But Dilsey, silent and weeping, has been granted an epiphany. Suddenly, winter has ended. The morning clouds part under "the bright noon" as she proclaims to Frony, "'I seed de beginnin, en now I sees de endin,'" with emphasis on the word *now*. According to the theologian Gabriel Vahanian [in *Wait without Idols,* 1964], Dilsey seems to mean that "the fullness of time is a possibility even within time. Eternity does not 'begin' after time; it happens within time. The resurrection does not take place after one's physical death; it is the only experience by which here and now the human reality can be transfigured, by which man can become that which he is not; it is the possibility of authentic existence."

The consequences of Dilsey's Easter conversion occur in distinct phases. In the first phase Dilsey gives up her long and fruitless effort to "save" the Compsons from themselves. Through her participation in the death and rebirth cycle traced by the Reverend Shegog, she is able to lay her past bare and see it truly. She perceives that the thankless devotion she has given the Compsons has been wasted because no love can reach them. She comes to understand that the Compsons are beyond salvation, beyond even help, because God has turned "'His mighty face'" and "'shet His do'" to them for their cruelty and hatred.

Charged with this revelation, Dilsey immediately evidences a new attitude and purpose. As she and her companions walk home from the church, Dilsey chides her grandson, "'You tend to your business en let de white folks tend to deir'n.'" This reflects a sharp alteration from her previous concern about Compson matters and her long struggle to bind them together. When Luster tries to pique her curiosity with hints of Miss Quentin's intrigues, Dilsey shows no interest; she no longer wants to know about Miss Quentin. Nor does she care to try further to protect Miss Quentin from her Uncle Jason or her grandmother. With the past at her back, she approaches the Compson place and looks at "the square, paintless house with its rotting portico," the first time in the novel that the house takes on a detailed, objective reality. This description suggests that, like the crumbling mansion they inhabit, the Compsons are beyond renovation, and Dilsey now knows it. As a result of the Reverend Shegog's sermon, she foresees the end of the Compson line.

Although at basis Dilsey's act is a renunciation, it includes an important affirmation. Years

earlier her husband Roskus had warned her that nothing but bad fortune would come from remaining on the Compson place. But she had ignored him and pursued the illusion of preserving the Compsons as a family by lavishing them with her compassion. In the second phase of Dilsey's Easter conversion, she realizes that her years of service to the Compsons have drawn her away from Roskus and her children. She gains a new perspective on her own family and moves toward reunion with them.

Dilsey eventually will leave Mississippi to reassume her matriarchal role in the Gibson family. This breakthrough apparently occurs in 1933, when Jason sells the moldering Compson house and is "able to free himself forever … from the Negro woman." The dispersal of the Compsons—anticipated by Miss Quentin's departure on Easter Sunday, 1928—is now complete: Mrs. Compson is dead, Benjy is in an asylum, and Jason is a "childless bachelor" whose twisted sexual urges are gratified only by prostitutes. Dilsey calls upon Frony, who has moved to St. Louis with her husband, a railroad porter. Frony goes "back to Memphis to make a home for her mother since Dilsey refused to go further than that." Averting the doom of the Compsons, Dilsey renews her lapsed family ties and puts the barren past behind her....

In summary, before Dilsey participates in the 1928 Easter service, she shares the doom of the Compsons. But the Reverend Shegog's sermon reinvigorates her belief in redemption. After hearing him preach, she attains a transforming vision, one which has spiritual as well as secular consequences. Her hope for salvation is rekindled as she is reminded that the Passion of Jesus is an immanent reality. In temporal terms, her "'ricklickshun of de Lamb'" leads her to remember that despite everything, the future still lies open before her. She undergoes a conversion which allows her to break free from the morbid past represented by the Compsons. She perceives that they are a dying family in a rotting house, and that her integrity as a woman, wife, and mother has been undermined by her useless devotion to them. Like the fed-up God of the Reverend Shegog's sermon, she resolves to leave them to the extinction that awaits. In time she redirects her life toward reunion with her own family.

However, as Cleanth Brooks cautioned nearly thirty years ago [in *William Faulkner: The Yoknapatawpha Country,* 1963] Faulkner makes no claim in *The Sound and the Fury* for Christianity, "one way or the other." Faulkner's religious beliefs, particularly in the early phase of his career, remain ambiguous. When Faulkner uses Christian imagery and narrative, they are organizational devices; they are not devotional. He always subjects religion or mythology to his artistic purposes. He does not relinquish control to the legends or their authority.

My feeling is that *The Sound and the Fury* uses its persistent Christian analogues not to evangelize but to stir the human need for hope and renewal. From Frazer, Faulkner found that he could appropriate the lore of Christianity without endorsing its creed. The Reverend Shegog's Easter sermon in section four of the novel sounds a triumphant note of affirmation which draws upon Christian doctrine without submitting to it. His homily, delivered to Dilsey and the reader, draws us by means of its unorthodox rendition of the Easter story into a symbolic recapitulation of the death-and-rebirth pattern. Using the comparative methodology of *The Golden Bough,* Faulkner has the Reverend Shegog revise the Christian Passion by fusing several ancient religious traditions. This technique universalizes the message of his sermon and emphasizes that the human longing for salvation is not contained by any single doctrine or tradition. As Frazer stressed, all springtime ceremonies on behalf of dead and risen deities are periodic efforts to restore a necessary faith in the future.

Christianity served Faulkner's artistic needs by providing him with a formal tradition to shape Dilsey's conversion experience. By means of his "Passion Week of the heart" metaphor, he sought to convey the message that redemption means being vulnerable to the saving moment, when time falls away and life starts again. Like Christ and many other dying and reviving deities—as well as their celebrants—Dilsey is reborn in spring. Christianity, as a religion of incarnation which stresses the transforming presence of the divine in the human, provides the specific context for Dilsey's deliverance. Her Easter conversion miraculously elevates her to an incommunicable vision of heavenly salvation. But it also leads her to forge a new secular identity independent of the Compsons and to recover an enduring family heritage of her own.

Source: Philip Dubuisson Castille, "Dilsey's Easter Conversion in Faulkner's *The Sound and the Fury,*" in *Studies in the Novel,* Vol. 24, No. 4, winter, 1992, pp. 423-33.

John L. Longley Jr.

In the following excerpt, Longley states that the novel is about "the death of a family and the corresponding decay of a society," and explores how the character of Caddy is central to the actions of all three of her brothers.

The subject-matter [of Faulkner's *The Sound and the Fury*] is the death of a family and the corresponding decay of a society. More narrowly, the novel is about the various Compson's—parents and children, brothers and sisters—and how they are able or not able to love each other, and how the failure of love destroys them all. The central focus is the beautiful and doomed Candace Compson. We never see her full-face or hear her speak in her own *persona*. She lives for us only in the tortured and highly subjective recollection of her three brothers: Benjy, the congenital idiot; Quentin, the moral abstractionist and suicide; Jason, the sociopath who lives only for money ("who to me represented pure evil. He's the most vicious character in my opinion I ever thought of.") These recollections form the first three sections of the novel. They are followed by Section Four, describing the events of Easter Sunday, 1928. This part belongs mainly to Dilsey, but is told from an outside, third-person point of view, magnificently distanced and controlled....

If the dominant theme of the novel is love—love between members of the family, and how they are able or not able to give that love freely—then the accidents of time and place [of the setting] fade in importance. The evil that the Compson children experience is conventional enough. Much of it is not evil at all, but simply the heartbreak of loss of innocence and the inevitable corruption that comes with growing up. There are evil characters in the book—Jason, certainly. But there are others who are merely weak, irresponsible, and self-serving, like the whining hypochondriac Caroline Compson and her brother Maury. Most of these people, whatever their pretentions, are examples of love defective or love perverted. Only three persons in the novel are able to give pure, whole-hearted, unselfish love: Caddy, Mr. Compson, and of course Dilsey. There are many scenes of love and affection between the children and their father, and with each other when they were younger....

Caddy's tragedy is that she will never find anyone commensurate with her own capacity to love: not father, mother, brothers or lover. Again, it is her misfortune to be born in the wrong age. The general moral climate of rural, southern, Victorian America—a religious atmosphere of morbid Calvinism gone decadent—can view Caddy's tentative sexual experience only as the ultimate horror. She has loved her father as a child and as a young woman. She has defended Benjy from Jason, and treats him always as if he were no different from other children. She is especially close to

Quentin in childhood and adolescence, until his morbid obsession with her chastity drives them apart.

At the point in her life when she is old enough to turn away from father and brother, and begin courtship, she finds she has nowhere to turn. There is literally no one to help her, certainly not among the jellybeans and town squirts of her adolescence. When she meets a man in Dalton Ames, she does not know how to resist him. Ames is the ultimate *macho:* handsome, powerful, violent, and totally amoral. When Quentin confronts him, and orders him to leave town, Ames is able to subdue him literally with one hand.

Foreshadowing the fate of her daughter, Caddy is driven to nymphomania by the hysterical posturings of her mother and the increasing pressure from Quentin. When Caddy was about fourteen, she was caught kissing a town boy. For three days Caroline Compson walks around the house wearing a black veil and declaring her daughter is dead. She attempts to spy on Caddy's movements, until Mr. Compson forbids it.

Already pregnant, Caddy accompanies her mother to the spa at French Lick. She returns, engaged to marry Herbert Head. One may only imagine the emotional process she has gone through; the forces that have pushed her into marriage with someone like Head, a man who has been expelled from Harvard for cheating at cards and on examinations. He is vulgar, loud, and falsely hearty. On Caddy's wedding day, T. P. finds the champagne for the reception stored in the basement, begins drinking it and giving it to Benjy. Benjy begins to bellow, and the result is pandemonium.

When Head discovers Caddy is pregnant, he divorces her. When her daughter is born, Caddy names her Quentin, for the brother who is now dead by his own hand. Mrs. Compson agrees that the family will take the child and raise it. With the weight of community mores heavily on her side, together with her own hysterics, she is able to impose these conditions: 1) Caddy shall never enter the house again; 2) never see her child again; 3) her name shall never be mentioned to the child.

Occasionally, Mr. Compson will violate this heartless pact by letting Caddy into the house to see her baby. After he is dead, Jason is the remaining competent male Compson, and he enforces the pact even more brutally, including the episode of the hundred dollars and the momentary look at the baby. After Quentin reaches adolescence, takes Jason's accumulated money, and runs away with the showman, Caddy's last viable link with the Compson house is gone. We have one more glimpse of her in a picture magazine, as the mistress of a Nazi *Stabsgeneral.* The librarian believes the woman in the picture is Caddy; Jason does not. Dilsey will not say. Perhaps it is; perhaps not.

This, in brief, is the life of Candace Compson. Whatever else, that life is the central definitive presence in the lives of her brothers. She is an obsession with each of them, but in different ways....

Benjy loved three things: firelight, his sister Caddy, and the pasture that was sold to pay for Quentin's year at Harvard and Caddy's fancy wedding. His mental retardation is severe; he cannot speak at all. Yet, he is sensitive to color, light and dark, heat and cold, and above all, smells. He has emotions, and responds to the slightest shift in what he is used to. He hates and fears change, and bellows with outrage and terror at any upset in his routines. He whimpers when he is unhappy. Chronology is beyond him; he cannot distinguish *then* from *now.* All time is the same to him; a sort of continuous present in which he does not know his memories are only memories. Thus he cannot "... remember his sister but only the loss of her, and firelight was the same bright shape as going to sleep, and the pasture was even better sold than before because now he and TP could not only follow timeless along the fence the motions which it did not even matter to him were human beings swinging golfsticks."

Dilsey takes care of him, and Caddy is his champion and defender when they are little. It is to Caddy and only Caddy that he looks for emotional support ("You're not a poor baby. Are you"). He relies on her to bring him the physical objects that have a quieting effect on him—the paper dolls and the box of tinsel stars. As Caddy grows up, many things become disturbing to Benjy: her interest in boys, her use of perfume, the change to long dresses....

[Eventually] Caddy goes away on her honeymoon. From here on, Benjy will not have a sister; only the loss of her to remember. What can we say of him; his child-like nature, his man's body, and his eyes empty and blue and serene? Benjy is, as Ratlift once said of another unfortunate, "... something that don't want nothing but to walk and feel the sun and wouldn't know how to hurt no man even if it would and wouldn't want to even if it could ..." Perhaps we could leave him at that, except for the powerful and violent last scene of the novel....

Quentin is clearly the most intelligent of the Compson children. He is thoughtful and sensitive. His segment of the novel is a *cri du coeur* uttered silently on the last day of his life. We go with him that day, following his apparently aimless actions, witnessing the obsessive, fugue-like images and sets of words which he repeats over and over again. We watch as he buys and then conceals the flatirons he will use to weight his body when he drowns himself. He is twenty years old and has his life before him. What has brought him to this pass?

The answer is clear but not simple. He ends his life because of what life has done to him. The world cannot be changed into what he wants it to be. He cannot change Caddy back into what she was. He is sure he cannot live knowing what he knows; his father tells him he will, and he will not risk that. *[T]hats it if people could only change one another forever that way merge like a flame swirling up for an instant then blow cleanly out along the cool eternal dark....*

Surely; surely the main thrust of [Mr. Compson's] words is to show his son that his anguish can be endured, that the pain will lessen, that he can go on, and even make something of his life. Just as surely, the advice does not have its desired effect. Quite clearly, Quentin kills himself not because he cannot stand his agony, but because he too believes it will grow less and will someday fade away.

"Once a bitch always a bitch, what I say." Jason is speaking of his niece, but it could very easily be his sister. In the way his hatred functions, he does not always clearly distinguish between the two of them. As noted earlier, Benjy and Quentin love Caddy, however twisted and self-seeking that love may be. Jason's one great sustaining passion is "... immortal hatred and study of revenge."

In the Compson Appendix, Mr. Faulkner calls Jason the first sane Compson since Culloden; "... rational contained and even a philosopher in the old stoic tradition." All the human race are Compsons; that is, predictable if essentially inexplicable, hence not to be trusted. The rest of humanity operates on the basis of emotion (pity, love, generosity, pride) which is why they are insane and Jason is not. This is the cream of the jest, because the central defining obsession in everything Jason does is the job promised to him by Herbert Head. If Jason were one-third the businessman he thinks he is, or were at all capable of rational, objective assessment, he could see what impulsive, irrational people (like you and me, or Quentin Compson) know at one glance: Herbert Head is a tinhorn blowhard, a liar,

and a cheat. How good is his promise? Who knows where his money comes from? Yet this is precisely the point. The "lost job" is Jason's crutch, his security blanket, his justification for every sadistic, criminal thing he does. *I reckon you'll know now that you cant beat me out of a job and get away with it* he says, after he has taken Caddy's hundred dollars to let her see the baby "just for a minute." *The bitch that cost me a job, the one chance I ever had to get ahead* he says to the sheriff, describing his niece....

Jason embodies the instinctive, irrational love of self; the monstrous, incestuous self-concern that leaves no room for love of others. Since we dare not admit the fear of imperfection in the self that is loved, we seek out and punish others in retaliation for any frustration or thwarting that the self encounters. Jason is paranoid and sees the world with a paranoid's logical consistency. He sees himself as a long-suffering, put-upon man, doomed to live as the only sane human in a world of irrational, incompetent fools. It seems clear that Jason does not recognize the ultimate motivation of his actions, how they grow out of his crippling inadequacy of the soul, his total inability to love.

Jason's most complex, most sensuous wound is his relation to his niece, Quentin. She is for him both the outward visible proof of Caddy's shame and the living reminder of the lost job. Thus she is both the constant focus of his hatred and the most gratifying target for his cruelty and retaliation. Probably, he does not himself realize the source of his constant neurotic anxiety over Quentin's chastity or what he is sure is the lack of it. In the monologues of his incessant inner fantasies, he can at the same time believe she is beyond redemption and still complain of the effort he is making to save her. He can assert that he does not care what she does, even when running up and down back alleys to spy on her....

Jason's day of reckoning dawns on Easter Sunday. He is sitting at breakfast, savoring his latest theft and anticipating the entire day in which to torment his family. He has begun on the topic of the broken window in his bedroom, not yet realizing its significance. He begins the ritual of refusing to eat until Quentin is up at the table. Only when he realizes that Quentin is not in her room does the edge of an apprehension, too terrible to be thought of, intrude itself. "... he stood ... as if he were listening to something much further away.... His attitude was that of one who goes through the motions of listening in order to deceive himself."...

The great sensuous wound of Jason's complex relaxation to his niece is far too precious to relinquish. He still wishes, hopes, wants to believe that he will be able to slip stealthily up to Quentin and the man with the red tie, beat them both severely, and regain every cent of the money. He is not yet ready to accept what his common sense might have told him long before. The agonizing headache that strikes him at this point does not deter him. Still full of the fictitious role he has constructed for himself, he roughs up the elderly carnival cook, who retaliates by almost splitting Jason's head with a hatchet. Rescued by the carnival owner, Jason sits in his car, blind with pain, haggling futilely with a series of Negro youths to drive him back to Jefferson. People who pass in their Easter clothes look at him, "the man sitting quietly behind the wheel of a small car, with his invisible life raveled out about him like a worn-out sock." Eventually he pays the price one of the youths is asking.

In the middle of these sordid events is the Easter service in the Negro church. It rests like a jewel in the setting of Jason's insane pursuit, Mrs. Compson's vindictive whining, the needless tormenting Dilsey is put through. Everything contrasts: all this shabby and futile materialism against the impassioned and beautiful promise of resurrection and life. Dilsey's own family, what is left of it, is with her: her daughter Frony and her grandson Luster. And of course Benjy, who can be taken to the Negro church because the white people don't want him in theirs. This congregation is surely the despised and rejected, the outcasts of the earth. The preacher is a famous black evangelist, brought in for the occasion....

Only one scene remains to be played out. Back at the house, Benjy begins moaning again. He knows, powerfully and unanswerably, that Quentin is gone, as her mother was gone before her. Dilsey tries everything to comfort and quiet him. There is only one recourse left. Much against her better judgement, Dilsey allows Luster to drive Benjy in the ancient ramshackle surry for his usual Sunday visit to the cemetery. Luster is very full of himself, bantering with the other Negroes. He notes that Jason's car is back, parked on the Square. In his self-importance, Luster drives to the wrong side of the statue of the Confederate soldier. Instantly terrified by the dislocation of tangible objects, Benjy begins his loud terrified bellowing: "There was more than astonishment in it, it was horror; shock; agony eyeless, tongueless; just sound...." Jason's apathy and resignation vanish as this old focus of his festering resentment presents itself. In Jefferson, at least, Jason will still be able to control and abuse his own family, or at least Benjy and the Negro children who depend on him for a living....

Like Dilsey, we have seen the beginning. This is the ending. No effort can explain the intricate web of all the themes of the novel, nor account for the power of this closing scene. It is all there: cruelty, hatred, race, the family, tradition, history, time, the dead and buried past that will not rise again. In the Appendix, one can learn what eventually happened to the Compsons. Jason will turn up a few times, a cotton-buyer now, who will take another heavy loss when he tries to outsmart Flem Snopes. Benjy lives on in the asylum at Jackson. Perhaps it is Caddy in the photograph, perhaps not. Dilsey, who lived long enough to see that too, will not tell us. These endured.

Source: John L. Longley Jr. , " 'Who Never Had a Sister': A Reading of *The Sound and the Fury*", in *Mosaic,* Vol. VII, No. 1, Fall, 1973, pp. 35-53.

Sources

Clifton Fadiman, "Hardly Worth While," *Nation,* January 15, 1930, pp. 74-75.

Robert J. Griffin, "Ethical Point of View in *The Sound and the Fury,*" in *Essays in Modern American Literature,* edited by Richard E. Langford, Stetson University Press, 1963, pp. 55-64.

Terry Heller, in *Critical Survey of Long Fiction,* Salem Press, 1991, pp. 1088-1110.

Arthur Mizener, "William Faulkner: *The Sound and the Fury,*" in *Twelve Great American Novels,* New American Library, 1967, pp. 120-59.

Frances Lamont Robbins, in a review in *Outlook and Independent,* Vol. 153, No. 7, October 16, 1929, pp. 268-69.

Evelyn Scott, in *On Faulkner's "The Sound and the Fury,"* Jonathan Cape and Harrison Smith, 1929.

Olga W. Vickery, "Worlds of Counterpoint" in *The Novels of William Faulkner,* Louisiana State University Press, 1959.

Linda W. Wagner, in *Dictionary of Literary Biography,* Volume 9: *American Novelists, 1910–1945,* Gale, 1981, pp. 282-302.

For Further Study

Margaret D. Bauer, "The Evolution of Caddy: An Intertextual Reading of 'The Sound and the Fury' and Ellen Gilchrist's 'The Annunciation'," in *Southern Literary Journal,* Vol. 25, No. 1, fall, 1992, pp. 40-51.

Bauer describes Caddy as both a strong woman who chooses to live according to her own value system, and as a victim who is ultimately broken down by her family. In addition to reviewing the question of incest, Bauer also discusses parental neglect and Caddy's abandonment of her daughter.

Michael H. Cowan, compiler, *Twentieth-Century Interpretations of "The Sound and the Fury": A Collection of Critical Essays,* Prentice-Hall, 1968.

This book collects important essays on the novel that were previously published in other books or journals.

David Dowling, *Macmillan Modern Novelists: William Faulkner,* Macmillan, 1989.

In his section on *The Sound and the Fury,* Dowling touches on many of the novel's major themes, including time, loss, and incest. He also suggests that the Compson parents offer two theories of language that represent the two extremes of meaningless flux and frozen meaning.

Richard Gray, *The Life of William Faulkner: A Critical Biography,* Blackwell, 1994.

Gray's discussion of *The Sound and the Fury* is largely concerned with language: language is not only the medium of the novel but also its subject. He argues that Faulkner obliges the reader to recognize "how we constitute our reality, personal and social, with the words we use."

Vernon T. Hornbeck, Jr., "The Uses of Time in Faulkner's *The Sound and the Fury,*" in *Papers on English Language and Literature,* Vol. I, No. 1, winter, 1965, pp. 50-8.

Hornbeck analyzes how Faulkner relates time in *The Sound and the Fury* to each of his central characters.

Cheryl Lester, "Racial Awareness and Arrested Development: 'The Sound and the Fury' and the Great Migration," in *The Cambridge Companion to William Faulkner,* edited by Philip M. Weinstein, Cambridge University Press, 1995, pp. 123-45.

Arguing that mainstream historiography in the post-Reconstruction South has been constructed primarily from a white Southern viewpoint, Lester focuses on the story told by African-American historiography, and in particular, the phenomenon of black migration from the South to the North.

Noel Polk, editor, *New Essays on "The Sound and the Fury,"* Cambridge University Press, 1993.

A collection of interpretations of the novels written specifically for the volume.

Kevin Railey, "Cavalier Ideology and History: The Significance of Quentin's Section in 'The Sound and the Fury'," in *Arizona Quarterly,* Vol. 48, No. 3, autumn, 1992, pp. 77-94.

Railey argues that Quentin symbolizes the ideological conflict experienced by those who felt alienated by the changing world of the New South, and that his section epitomizes the struggle of the Cavalier Ideology.

Diane Roberts, *Faulkner and Southern Womanhood,* The University of Georgia Press, 1994.

Roberts interrogates the stereotypes of the Southern woman in Faulkner's fiction. Her book includes detailed discussions of Caddy Compson and Dilsey.

Winesburg, Ohio

Sherwood Anderson

1919

Winesburg, Ohio was Sherwood Anderson's break-through work, the one that first gained widespread attention for him as an artist, although it was years before he would produce a best seller. He was forty-two when it was published, with two novels published previously that had received little interest from the reading public.

According to the story that Anderson would later relate in his *Memoirs,* the book started one night when he was living by himself in a run-down rooming house in Chicago, in 1915: it was a place full of would-be artists, and Anderson, who was supporting himself by writing advertising copy, sat down one December evening and, almost miraculously, produced the story "Hands" in one sitting. In the version he often told, the story came out exactly as he wanted it and he never changed a word, although researchers have since turned up drafts that show substantial differences.

Having found his style in this one inspired flash, he went on to develop the other stories that make up *Winesburg, Ohio* over the next few years. When the book was published in 1919, it did not sell very well, but the critical response marked the author as a man of talent and artistic integrity. Some critics lambasted it for being immoral because of its sexual themes, both hidden and blatant, such as the child molestation charge in "Hands" or the implied impotency in "Respectability."

For each critic put off by the buried subjects, though, there were two or three who appreciated Anderson's courage in examining areas previously

untouched by mainstream writers. Anderson's greatest influence on American literature has been indirect, in the ways that *Winesburg, Ohio* inspired the following generation of post-World War I writers, such as Ernest Hemingway, William Faulkner, Eudora Welty, and John Steinbeck. It was when these writers began speaking of the debt they owed to Sherwood Anderson that the book stopped being just a favorite of writers and gathered mass attention from the public.

Author Biography

Sherwood Anderson was born in 1876 in Camden, Ohio. In 1884 his family moved to Clyde, the small Ohio town that Winesburg is patterned after. After his mother's death in 1896, he moved to Chicago. He hoped to find better opportunities in the big city, but was unable to find any employment except menial, back-breaking labor; discouraged, he joined the army two years later, serving in the Spanish-American War.

After the war he finished his high school degree in Ohio and, invigorated by travel and education, he moved to Chicago again in 1900. He found employment working in the new field of advertising. In 1907, after marrying a wealthy manufacturer's daughter, he moved to Elyria, Ohio, as president of the Anderson Manufacturing Company. For five years he struggled to keep his business afloat, writing a few poems and some short stories that were of no interest to anyone until later, when he became famous.

What followed has become one of the great legends of American literature. According to Anderson's version, he simply realized, sitting at his desk one afternoon, that the business life was vapid and shallow, and so he stood up, walked out of the door, and kept on walking. According to the Cleveland hospital he checked into four days later, he had suffered a nervous breakdown. Either way, his career in business was over, and in early 1913, at age thirty-seven, he left his wife and family and returned to Chicago again. He worked for an advertising firm by day, wrote by night, and associated with other aspiring writers in the lively Chicago artistic scene whenever he had the time.

The short stories he wrote were traditional, and he was dissatisfied with his output until one day late in 1915, when, in a flash of inspiration, he sat down and wrote "Hands." After that, the other stories that comprise *Winesburg, Ohio* followed

Sherwood Anderson

slowly. He published the stories in magazines as they appeared, and at the same time published his first two novels, *Windy MacPherson's Son* and *Marching Men.*

Winesburg, Ohio was not a commercial success when it was published in 1919, but it was well received among writers. Anderson traveled and met European and American writers in Europe, who began mentioning him in interviews as an influence on their work. He was not financially comfortable enough to quit his advertising job until 1922, and did not have financial success with a novel until 1925, with *Dark Laughter.*

With his reputation established, Anderson continued to be sought as a writer up to his death in 1941, producing three volumes of autobiography, some memorable short stories (especially those in *Death In the Woods,* which some critics argue rivals *Winesburg*). Most of his time in his later years was spent writing social essays, which are seldom read anymore.

Plot Summary

Rather a single, well-defined plot, *Winesburg, Ohio* has a loosely interconnected set of stories with overlapping time frame and characters. Only when the town itself is considered the "main character" can one speak of an overall plot. In this macro-plot, the traditional small town life of nineteenth-century America comes to an end; its hard but stable community is broken into the dynamic but impersonal atoms of twentieth-century American society

The historical macro-plot is composed of twenty-four micro-plots centered on individual characters, the inhabitants of Winesburg. Some characters appear as supporting players in more than one story, and one figure appears in several: George Willard, a youth working as a reporter in Winesburg's newspaper office. Many characters are connected to George, and his departure at the end brings the whole phase of Winesburg's history to a close.

Anderson prefaces his stories with a list of the tales and a chapter entitled "The Book of the Grotesque." This chapter suggests that a grotesque character comes into being when a man or woman takes one of the many truths of life and pursues it obsessively. Anderson's stories illustrate, often in a few terse pages, how a character becomes trapped by his or her obsession with freedom, lost love, sex, innocence, age, power, money, or indecency.

The first story, "Hands," focuses on an odd-ball named Wing Biddlebaum, whose hands are always in motion. A friend of George Willard, he is about to tell the youth about his past when he breaks off in fright. Anderson's narrator, however, fills in the story. Once named Adolph Myer, Wing was a teacher in a Pennsylvania town. Much beloved by his boys, he was tender with them in turn. One boy, however, fell in love with Adolph and recounted his fantasies as if they were facts. Branded a pervert, Adolph was beaten and chased away, barely escaping being lynched. He took the name Biddlebaum from a box in a railway station and ended up in Winesburg, tormented by his hands, which in his trauma he blamed for his undeserved suffering.

"Paper Pills" sketches Doctor Reefy, who fills his pockets with bits of paper on which he jots down ideas and inspirations. The narrator connects this peculiarity to the Doctor's courtship of his wife, who visited his office with an illegitimate pregnancy and died less than a year after their marriage. He did not condemn her, and his strange thoughtful nature, represented by the wads of paper, made her love him.

"Mother" reveals the family background of George Willard. His mother Elizabeth, disappointed with her life, has come to despise her husband Tom. Her love for her son is mixed with an anxious hope to be fulfilled through him. George tells his mother that he wants to leave Winesburg, a wish he will eventually carry out after her death.

"The Philosopher" presents the shabby, idle doctor, Doctor Parcival. The doctor tells young George about his family. The doctor's father was insane and died in an asylum; his brother was run over by a train when drunk. At the end of the story, the doctor refuses to come down from his office to look at a child who has been thrown from a buggy and killed. He visits George Willard in panic, convinced that the town will be enraged at his callousness about the child. He whispers his obsessive idea to George:

> everyone in the world is Christ and they are all crucified. That's what I want to say.

"Nobody Knows" narrates George Willard's sexual adventure with Louise Trunnion, who offers herself to him in a note. When she later hesitates, he coaxes her by telling her that no one will know. Later, after he has left her, he repeats the thought, but with a different sense: she has nothing on him, no one knows.

The four-part story "Godliness" focuses on the patriarchal head of the Bentley Farm, Jesse. The first part depicts Jesse's background and his tough management of the farm after the Civil War. It introduces his biblical obsession: he imagines himself the only godly man among "Philistines." He prays to God for a son called David to help him overcome his enemies. In the second part, the ironic thwarting of his prayer is revealed: his wife had died in childbirth, giving birth to a girl, Louise. Louise is unhappily married to the banker John Hardy; their child is named David. Jesse takes the grandchild to the farm. Still biblically obsessed, however, Jesse frightens the boy with an intense prayer, and the child flees.

Part three narrates the youth of Louise, passed in the Hardy household. Mistreated by her foster sisters, she seeks to become the lover of John, her future husband. David's birth disappoints her hopes for a daughter, just as she had foiled Jesse's desire for a son. In part four, David abandons Jesse, who has tried to realize his religious designs by sacrificing a lamb. Boy and lamb flee from the knife-wielding grandfather, and when David knocks Jesse unconscious with a stone, he thinks he has killed the old man and runs away forever. Coming to in despair, Jesse believes God has cursed him for his pride.

The next three stories, "A Man of Ideas," "Adventure," and "Respectability" offer character-sketches. In the first, Joe Welling, a generally quiet man, is seized with fits of obsessive thinking, poured out in a torrent of words. In the second, Alice Hindman goes out walking naked, driven by solitude to a desperate, half-mad desire for adventure. The third, "Respectability," focuses on the gross, dirty, and misogynistic telegraph operator Wash Williams.

"The Thinker" introduces Seth Richmond, George Willard's friend and a failed candidate for the love of Helen White, who figures in several stories. Seth cannot shake his feeling of not belonging in Winesburg. This sense inhibits him from trying to win Helen's love. He leaves her to George Willard, considered the typical Winesburg insider.

In "Tandy," a drunken stranger perceives in a little girl an image of a love he will never possess. The qualities of this love he calls "Tandy," which the girl takes as her name.

"The Strength of God" depicts the Reverend Curtis Hartman, who peers through a hole in the bell-tower window at the schoolteacher Kate Smith, whose bedroom is opposite the church. Torn with guilt, the minister continues peeping until one night he sees Kate naked, beating her bed with her fists, then kneeling to pray. Believing this sight a message from God, the minister breaks the glass with his fists, destroying his post of forbidden observation.

The next story, "The Teacher," returns to these same events from another angle. The mature and experienced teacher detects something special in young George Willard, and she seeks him out to advise him about his pursuit of writing. She initiates an erotic encounter but breaks it off, beating at him with her fists, and fleeing to weep and pray in her room.

"Loneliness" portrays the aging child-man Enoch Robinson, who earlier lived in a world of make-believe in the art world of New York. In order to preserve his imaginary life, he drove off the woman who loved him, destroying his dreams as well.

In "An Awakening," George Willard is seduced by Belle Carpenter to make her real love, Ed Handby, jealous. Ed deflates George's pride by breaking in on them, knocking George around, and leaving with Belle. In the story "'Queer,'"George also gets a surprise beating. Elmer Cowley, the misfit son of a shopowner, thinks George, like all of Winesburg's inhabitants, laughs at him and thinks

him "queer." Before fleeing Winesburg on the train, Elmer calls George to the platform, tries to speak his mind, and when unable, beats George half-unconscious.

In "The Untold Lie," a middle-aged farm worker, Ray Pearson, is asked by his younger friend Hal Winters what to do about a woman Hal has made pregnant. Ray wants to advise him not to throw away his freedom, as he himself did in marrying. But he holds his tongue, realizing that anything he said would only be a lie.

A quiet boy, Tom Foster, is the central figure of "Drink." One night the boy gets drunk and visits George. Tom tells George that he drank to understand something and that he has learned from it, comparing it to how he imagines making love must be.

The last three stories conclude George's life in Winesburg. "Death" describes the circumstances of George's mother's death, including her passionate encounter with Doctor Reefy late in her life and the stash of money that will allow George to escape the town that made her suffer. "Sophistication" depicts a brief moment of silent understanding between Helen White, back from college, and George, who will soon leave for good. "Departure" presents the town's send-off of George. Winesburg fades from view as the train pulls away, changed to nothing more than "a background on which to paint the dreams of his manhood."

Characters

Jesse Bentley

He is the main character of the four-part story in the middle of the book, "Godliness." A reluctant farmer, who studied to be a minister but took over the family farm when his brothers died in the Civil War, his farm grew huge over the course of several decades. Jesse believes that the growth of his farm was God's will, and in his old age, he wants to sacrifice a lamb to God, as Abraham did in the Bible. His grandson David Bentley, who he takes along to the sacrifice, fears that the old man intends to kill him with the knife instead, and he shoots Jesse in the head with a slingshot, just as David did to Goliath in the Bible.

Wing Biddlebaum

In "Hands," the story of Wing Biddlebaum is revealed: the citizens of Winesburg know nothing of his past before he came to town because he was

A small Ohio town, 1936.

run out of his former town, were he was a school-teacher accused of touching one of his male students inappropriately.

Belle Carpenter

She spends time with George Willard, dating him casually. Her true love is Ed Handby, a bartender at the saloon, but he is too embarrassed to ask her out until he has enough money to date her in style. In "An Awakening," Ed does approach her while she is on a date with George, shoving George aside repeatedly while the lovers discuss their mutual affection.

Curtis Hartman

In "The Strength of God," Reverend Hartman, who has been finding his sermons uninspired lately, notices that he can see into the bedroom of the woman next door from his office in the bell tower, and he becomes obsessed with looking at her.

Dr. Parcival

Dr. Parcival is not really a doctor at all, but a drifter who came to town calling himself a doctor. He relishes the fact that he has had several identities in different towns and that nobody knows the true story of his past. In "The Philosopher," his delight in fooling the citizenry turns to paranoia: when

he refuses to see a child who has been killed in a horse accident, he is certain that the people of Winesburg will come to lynch him, even though they have simply gone to another doctor and forgotten him.

Dr. Reefy

The doctor is one of the few citizens of Winesburg to figure prominently in two of the stories in the book, "Paper Pills" and "Death." In "Paper Pills," the second story, he is an old man, described in the first line as having "a white beard and huge nose," while the other story, which appears near the end of the book, he is a middle-aged man: "The gray beard he later wore had not yet appeared, but on his upper lip grew a brown moustache."

"Death" concerns his relationship with Elizabeth Willard, George's mother. She was a very sick woman and therefore a frequent patient, but as she talked during her office visits, he fell in love with her. Once, they embraced, but were interrupted by a clerk from the store downstairs emptying the garbage. He did not see her again after that. "Paper Pills" tells of his marriage to a much younger woman whose name is never given. She comes to him with an illness and a relationship develops, during which she appreciates the eccentric ideas that he writes on scratch paper sheets and stuffs in wads in his pockets. Within a year of their wedding, she dies, and he is alone again.

Seth Richmond

In the story that features him, "The Thinker," Seth Richmond is presented as George Willard's friend, and of all of the citizens of Winesburg, he seems like the one that George feels most comfortable with. In many ways, Seth is similar to George in disposition, but he is a little more reserved. His father died a scandalous death when Seth was young, killed during an argument with a newspaper editor when an article alleged that the older Richmond was having an affair. After his death his family discovered he had lost all of his money in investments, showing him to be a bad husband and worse businessman, like George's father (who is seen in "The Thinker" arguing politics with his hotel guests).

Like George, Seth is an intellectual, but, he is too emotionally insecure to pursue the girl he has a crush on, perhaps made timid by the family scandal. In "Respectability" George has a conversation with Helen White where he is as awkward as Seth is in "The Thinker," but George does not leave her until he has said what he wants to tell her.

Enoch Robinson

Enoch is a member of a family that moved to Winesburg from the country and opened a small, eclectic odds-and-ends store. He is very self-conscious of how he and his family appear to the other citizens, and in the story "Queer" he confronts George Willard, who he thinks is one of the main people in town laughing at him.

Kate Swift

Kate Swift appears in "The Strength of God," as the woman that Reverend Hartman looks at and fantasizes about in his tower room, and in the following story, "The Teacher," she is George Willard's former teacher. In her excitement over teaching and expressing herself to him, she kisses him on the lips.

Louise Trunion

In "Nobody Knows," George Willard has sex with Louise after receiving a letter from her that says, "I'm yours if you want me." Rather than feel triumphant, he immediately becomes afraid that she will hold this over him, even though she gives no indication of wishing to do so.

Media Adaptations

- There are three different versions of a "Winesburg, Ohio" audio cassette available: from the Audio Bookshelf, 1995; from Recorded Books, 1995; and as an audio cassette or phonographic album from Caedmon, 1983.

- A 1977 video, "Sherwood Anderson's I'm a Fool," is available from Perspective Films, 1977.

Joe Welling

Joe Welling is an agent for the Standard Oil Company. His mind is continuously running, almost tripping over itself as he thinks up new things. "A Man of Ideas" tells the story of his falling in love with Sarah King, which could be trouble because her father and brother are violent bullies. Rather than assault Joe, they fall under the spell of his jittery enthusiasm and walk off down the street with him, engrossed in what he has to say.

Helen White

Helen White is a girl, about George Willard's age, who has the distinction of being the banker's only child and therefore coming from one of Winesburg's wealthiest families. In "The Thinker," George Willard expresses a romantic interest in Helen to his friend Seth Richmond, but he does so casually, claiming that he is working on a story about love and would like to practice being in love with her. Helen is briefly attracted to Seth when he conveys the message, but her attraction is based in part on the fact that he has claimed to be saying his final goodbye at that moment.

The other story that concerns Helen prominently is "Sophistication." In this story, George Willard's thoughts turn to her as he reaches a moment of emotional maturity. Despite the fact that she is only in town briefly, having come home from college on break with a young instructor, her thoughts are on him also: "What George felt, she in her young woman's way felt also." What they both feel is not lust, even though they temporarily confuse it for something sexual.

Anderson uses Helen's privileged background to highlight George's moment of feeling a sense of responsibility, as he sees beyond the temporary distractions of his day-to-day life in the same way that she can see the town objectively, because she is an outsider now. Although the story is about adolescent confusion and is therefore a jumble of confused emotions, the narrative sums up the feelings that both George and Helen feel: "'I have come to this lonely place and here is this other,' was the substance of the thing felt." They find out that what they want is not a physical encounter, but just a chance to act child-like again, and they chase each other down the hill, running and laughing. Helen White is not the love of George Willard's life, but she is more like him than any other character in Winesburg.

Elizabeth Willard

George's mother is featured in two of the stories in this book, the third from the beginning and the third from the end. Her existence is marked by depression and bitterness, symbolized by the unspecified illness that keeps her shut up in the boarding house and under the doctor's care. She is disappointed that her life has not had more excitement and she has a vague hope that her son's life will turn out better than hers.

"Mother" explains that she grew up in the boarding house and dated, or "walked with," the traveling men who stopped there briefly, and that when she was young she enjoyed drawing attention to herself: "Once she startled the town by putting on men's clothes and riding a bicycle down Main Street." As an adult she slinks along in the shadows of the boarding house, dreading the idea that one of the boarders will see her because her former vibrancy is gone, leaving her now ghostly and worn out.

There is a great deal of empathy between Elizabeth Willard and her son, as she recalls what it was like to grow up being aware of the world's wide greatness but having that sense of wonder held in check by narrow-minded men like the boy's father, Tom Willard. In "Mother," she braces herself to confront her husband in the boy's defense, to insist that George must be free to leave Winesburg and discover the world for himself. When George comes to her and reports that a talk with his father has convinced him to do just that, she finds herself taking a position just opposite the one she had in-

tended, mocking his ambitions when she had meant to be encouraging.

"Death" tells of a somewhat romantic relationship at the end of her life with her doctor. In his grim, dusty office, she talks freely about her life and is finally able to discuss her father's disgust with the man she chose to marry, and his warnings that the marriage would turn out miserably, which it did. Being open with Dr. Reefy leads to the closest thing she has to intimacy in her married life; for one moment, they find themselves in each other's arms, but they are interrupted and the moment never presents itself again. Elizabeth Willard has a stroke and lingers for a week before dying, never able to tell George that she has hidden eight hundred dollars for him to live his life in freedom.

George Willard

The central character in the book, it sometimes seems as if George Willard is the central character in the town: because he is the son of rooming-house owners, Anderson has put him in a position to meet travelers passing through town, while his job as a reporter for the *Winesburg Eagle* makes him known to all of the town's citizens.

Only a few of the stories in this book are explicitly concerned with events in George's life—"Mother," "Nobody Knows," "The Thinker," "The Teacher," "An Awakening," "Sophistication," and "Departure." In the other stories, the main characters generally find some reason to relate their stories to George, or he has some other connection to the action, such as when "The Untold Lie" explains to readers, "Boys like George Willard and Seth Richmond will remember the incident quite vividly …." Other examples are when Dr. Reefy of "Paper Pills" later develops a secret relationship with George's mother, or the folktale tone of "Godliness," that makes it seem as if everyone in town is familiar with what has happened. It is through the use of this structure that Anderson reveals influences that mold the young man into who he will become by the time of his departure from the town.

From the start, George is the son of an unhappy marriage, whose parents have conflicting expectations for his future. As related in "Mother," his father is an unsuccessful businessman, transferring his own ambitions to hopes for his son's future success. His mother also copes with her disappointment by living vicariously through George, but her hopes are conflicted within themselves: "Even though I die I will in some way keep defeat from you," she promises George in a prayer. Soon after that she asks God to "not let him become smart and successful either."

With his father's encouragement to be practical and his mother's hopes that he transcend his meager upbringing, George could grow up in any direction, and it is his encounters with other people in town that define his growing personality. From Wing Biddelbaum he learns the danger of being too familiar with others. Dr. Parcival's story is a warning against being too cerebral, but he also sees Joe Welling survive by staying true to his dreams. From Belle Carpenter he learns not to be too free with his sexuality, while Kate Swift's behavior shows him what happens if he suppresses it too thoroughly. There is a lesson for his life in each story, and, even if George does not seem to learn the lesson each time, the reader can absorb it as something he should learn.

In the book's climax, "Sophistication," George and his female counterpart, Helen, not only learn how to act maturely, but they also learn that behaving immaturely once in a while is necessary: after running down a hill and rolling in the grass like children, "they had for a moment taken hold of the thing that makes the mature life of men and women in the modern world possible."

Tom Willard

George Willard's father was a clerk at the boarding house in Winesburg, hoping to become a successful businessman some day. He married the daughter of the boarding-house owner, possibly because she was pregnant. In "Death," it is revealed that her father was so against her marrying Tom that he gave her eight hundred dollars cash to leave town, but she married to spite her father. Tom Willard is an unsuccessful businessman, and in his hands the boarding house is becoming shabby and decrepit. He is interested in local politics, and enjoys arguing with customers about political issues.

Wash Williams

A friend of George's, the name is considered ironic, bestowed on him because of his poor hygiene. In "Respectability," he explains to George Willard that he was once married, but that his wife was unfaithful.

Themes

Rite of Passage

The overall arc of this book is George Willard's maturation; the climax is when he finally

Topics for Further Study

- The characters in *Winesburg, Ohio* are very specific to their place and time. Write a short story that brings one of these characters forward to your town. Would they be better adjusted than they are presented in the book? Would the added burden of fast-paced modern life be too much for them? Would they find help for their problems that was not available in Winesburg?

- Research the Chicago renaissance of the 1910s and 1920s. Report on one of the writers that Anderson was acquainted with: Edgar Lee Masters, Harriet Monroe, Margaret Anderson, Francis Hackett, Ben Hecht, or Floyd Dell. Try to focus your biographical report on where the writer lived before coming to Chicago, and how moving to a major metropolitan area affected her or his writing.

- In the twentieth century, America had gone from being a principally rural country to being overwhelmingly urban and suburban. Explore the social elements that changed society during Anderson's time, when towns like Winesburg were already becoming old fashioned.

- One of the few things that is learned about George Willard's father, Tom Willard, is that he is a staunch Democrat. In "The Thinker," Tom Willard argues with a travelling salesman about the relationship between President William McKinley and Mark Hanna, the U.S. Senator from Ohio. Explore the situation that is referred to in this story and report on what it tells readers about the two men holding the argument.

leaves town. Unlike a novel that is driven along by external events and situations, this book has no specific occurrence that prompts him to leave. As a matter of fact, George appears to be the ideal citizen for Winesburg: as much as the various citizens seem to rely upon him as someone that they can tell their stories to, he seems to need them equally, to feed his curiosity.

The way that he outgrows the town is developed indirectly, through the positive and negative responses that readers have toward each character. "Hands," for instance, might be about Wing's determination to outrun his past, but a sub-theme is the small-mindedness and anger that can boil up in a small town. When George has a sexual encounter in "Nobody Knows," his main concern is that no one finds out about it. The King bullies accept Joe Welling in "A Man of Ideas" exactly because he is oblivious to the dangers that surround him in Winesburg. "The Untold Lie," which does not mention George, still raises the reader's awareness that the miseries suffered by Ray Pearson are unavoidable in a town like Winesburg.

Even as the town seems more and more like a trap for someone like George, the decision to leave does not become comfortable to him until the moment in "Sophistication" when he turns the clock back on his maturation process and for once, instead of trying to act older, he breaks from a kiss with Helen White and they both laugh, becoming "not man and woman, not boy and girl, but excited little animals." The drive toward experience and understanding leaves them, and as they run down the hill they have climbed "they played like two splendid young things in a young world." The struggle with "the young thing within" that has pulled at George in every story, through his association with disappointed older Winesburg citizens who had or had not won the struggle, is settled for him, and then it becomes time for him to leave.

Loneliness and Alienation

The main source of dramatic tension in this book is that Winesburg is a small town. This means that the citizens are familiar with one another and hold each other to certain standards of behavior, but, within this frame of familiarity, all of the people who make up the group feel that they do not belong to it. Of all of these, the most blatantly alienated might be Elizabeth Willard, the mother of the novel's central character. "Mother," the first story concerning her, establishes the fact that she had, at one time in her youth, felt a bond to the travelling men who had stayed at the Willard house and had romanced her. The story says that "They seemed to understand and sympathize with her." In maturity, though, she has no such bond with anyone, not even her husband or her son, and she hides upstairs, hoping to not be seen.

In the last years of her life, related in "Death," her alienation is pierced by the relationship she forms with Dr. Reefy, meeting him in his secluded office that is adjacent to a dusty storage room. The climax and destruction of their relationship occurs when they embrace for the first time and are interrupted by a clerk throwing an old box onto a pile of rubbish in the hall: "Doctor Reefy did not see the woman he had held in his arms again until after her death." Elizabeth Willard is so alienated that she does not get the chance to pass on the secret that she had been saving for her son—eight hundred dollars in cash, hidden within a wall.

The other glaring example of the loneliness that permeates the characters in this book is, of course, Enoch Robinson, in the story titled "Loneliness." Interestingly, the story explains that it was in New York City that Robinson withdrew from life with fellow human beings to live with the people of his imagination, and in New York that he lost his imaginary people to the girl he was involved with. Robinson is lonely in Winesburg, but the town itself has not made him that way, indicating that the alienation felt by each of Winesburg's citizens is more a condition of human experience than a result of small-town life.

Doubt and Ambiguity

Most of the characters in this book suffer from their efforts to keep their true natures hidden from other people and themselves. In cases like those of Wing Biddlebaum, Wash Williams or Dr. Parcival, the effort is to obscure shameful deeds in their past. Others, such as Reverend Hartman, Jesse Bentley, Kate Swift and Seth Richmond, feel that they have a reputation in the community that must be upheld at all costs, and so they do not allow themselves to become introspective enough to wonder what it is they really want.

In most cases, the citizens of Winesburg want desperately to be someone they are not, but their personalities are too strong to be changed, which leaves them in an ambiguous state where truth and lie mingle together freely. The problem is that they have doubts about what is real, and this often turns out to be devastating in the end, leaving the characters torn apart when they are forced to face the bare, unvarnished truth.

Style

Structure

Winesburg, Ohio is most noticeably a series of short stories, each one capable of making sense if read by itself. Reading the book as a novel requires some imagination and a willingness to be loose with one's definition of just what a novel is.

There is a main character, George Willard, but his significance is based mainly on the fact that he appears in almost all of the stories. Often, he is not central to the story's action, but is just mentioned as someone that a central character has spoken with. If the reader accepts the fact that George's appearances must be more than a coincidence, then it would follow that the whole book is one continuous piece, with each independent story defining George and moving him forward toward some final resolution. The fact that George leaves town in the last story supports this reading. It seems to provide a climax to the book in general.

There is a continuing character who comes to a resolute change at the end. Readers who are willing to agree that this is enough evidence that the book is indeed a novel will look for signs within the stories, even those with little or no mention of George, that he is growing throughout the book to be the person he is in "Departure." They will find enough evidence to see a novel's structure running throughout the collected stories.

Plot

Sherwood Anderson despised stories that existed in order to serve their plot, usually with the actions occurring one upon the next in order to lead readers in one direction, with no more purpose than to sting them with a surprise at the end. An example of such a story might run like this: a man decides to make enough money to marry the girl he loves; he works hard for years and uses inferior materials in his construction business, in order to amass his fortune; the *very day* that he is on his way to propose to her, he finds out that she has been killed in the collapse of one of the shabby buildings he put together. Anderson called such stories "poison-plot" stories because they were built upon coincidences, not character. When he was writing *Winesburg, Ohio,* poison-plot stories were practically all that mainstream magazines published—today we still have the stories of O. Henry (William Sydney Porter) as examples of the types of heavily plotted stories published at the turn of the century.

The stories in *Winesburg, Ohio* often fail to capture the interest of novice readers of literature because they are structured around character, not plot. These stories introduce readers to their central characters, show how these characters see the world, and then, at the climax, their external circumstances do not change much, even though their personalities may be changed forever.

Setting

The events of this book could happen nowhere else but in a small Ohio town. In part, this is due to definition, because the author has defined this book as happening in or around the town of Winesburg. In addition, the stories all stay close to Winesburg because they just would not make sense anywhere else. In a larger town, in another part of the country or in a different country, there would not be the social pressure toward conformity that is unique to the American Midwest. That pressure is integral to the stories, squeezing any artificial sense of comfort out of the characters, which pushes them to act, which develops their stories.

The map of downtown Winesburg in the front of the book helps to orient readers to where specific actions take place in relation to others, but Anderson could have explained such relationships within the text if they were important. More significantly, the map makes the town seem real, as if offering proof of Winesburg's existence, beyond what the fiction writer says.

Prologue

The one story that is written in a distinctly different style from the others is "The Book of the Grotesque," which mentions neither George Willard nor the town of Winesburg and uses a different narrative style, with a narrator who exists within the story. "The Book of the Grotesque" helps introduce readers to the story that follows by placing the incidents in Winesburg within the memories of a tired, disturbed old man, which helps to explain why the stories have such an indistinct, dreamy feel about them. It also introduces the idea of the grotesque, asserting that each of the characters to follow has one thing exaggerated, which helps readers of *Winesburg, Ohio* understand what makes the characters behave as they do.

Historical Context

The First World War

World War I was the first of two conflicts in this century to draw most of what is referred to as Western Civilization (generally speaking, Europe, North America and Russia) into battle. It was the first war to use submarines, aerial bombings and chemical warfare, which added a new dimension of impersonality to the usual carnage of war.

A rural farm setting, similar to the environs of Winesburg, Ohio.

It began in Europe, where the battles between ethnic groups in the Balkan nations at the end of the nineteenth century led to a balance of power between two rival military alliances: The Triple Alliance of Germany, Austria-Hungary and Italy, and the Triple Entente of Great Britain, France and Russia. Most of the smaller countries were affiliated with one of these or the other. On June 28, 1914, Austrian Archduke Franz Ferdinand was assassinated by a Serbian. When the Austrian government blamed Serbia, obligations to existing treaties pulled most of the nations into war, one at a time.

Originally, Americans were reluctant to become involved: President Woodrow Wilson was re-elected in 1916 with the campaign slogan "He Kept Us Out Of War." In early 1917, though, Germany started using submarines against ships travelling to Great Britain, and the United States, which had warned against such action, was drawn into participating. When peace was declared in 1918, thirty-two nations had been involved in the fighting, with 37 million casualties and 10 million civilian deaths.

The veterans who returned to the United States in 1918 were angry and disillusioned, having participated in destruction on a greater scale, with deadlier weapons, than the world had ever known

before. Of the one million Americans drafted and sent overseas, many came from small rural towns like Winesburg, and may never have gone beyond the county limits, much less traveled to Europe and killed people, if not for the war. The returning veterans brought back stories of their experiences, cracking the shell that secluded farm towns from the outside world. *Winesburg, Ohio* was published the year after the war ended.

The Rise of the Soviet Union

Russia's weak economy, coupled with the strain of a great number of military defeats in World War I and the subsequent high casualties, forced Russian Tsar Nicholas to abdicate his throne in March of 1917. A liberal government took control of the country briefly, but protests and riots quickly forced them from power; the moderate government that followed did no better to restore order. In October of 1917 the Bolsheviks, under the leadership of Vladimir Ilich Lenin, staged a revolution and reorganized the country under principles of Marxist socialism.

To American artists and intellectuals, the Russian Revolution stood as a symbol of hope that social progress toward equality was possible and that the market forces that disfavored creativity could be overthrown one day. Journalist John Reed,

Compare & Contrast

- **1919:** Soldiers coming back from World War I had experienced massive destruction in the age of airplanes and automation. Because American manufacturing facilities were not damaged the way those in Europe had been, the U.S. economy prospered in the 1920s.

  Today: After the military build-up of the 1980s created an economic crisis, running up unprecedented trade deficits, the American economy has stabilized and is enjoying prosperity without war.

- **1919:** F. W. Woolworth died at age 67. The Woolworth chain of five-and-dime stores started in 1879 and had over 1000 stores in small American towns by the time it was incorporated in 1911, becoming the first franchise in many rural centers like Winesburg.

  Today: The Woolworth chain closed its last stores in 1997, run out of business by huge discount stores, particularly the Wal-Mart chain, which has over 1700 stores built on the outskirts of American downtown areas.

- **1920:** The 18th Amendment, prohibiting sale and consumption of alcohol, was passed by Congress, to go into effect on January 20, 1920.

- **1933:** Prohibition was considered a failure because it did not greatly reduce alcohol consumption and it encouraged gang violence. The 21st Amendment, repealing Prohibition, became effective December 5, 1933.

  Today: Many states are lowering the amount of alcohol that the law will tolerate in the blood of a person who has been operating a motor vehicle; at the same time, a growing percentage of the population, discouraged by the feeble results of strict drug policies, is calling for legalization of drugs.

- **1919:** The 19th Amendment, allowing women to vote in the United States, was adopted by Congress and was ratified by the states the following year.

- **1972:** The Congress passed the Equal Rights Amendment, which would have guaranteed that women would be treated equally with men, but it failed to be ratified by two-thirds of the states in the next ten years and therefore did not become law.

  Today: Social groups monitor discrimination against women and offer legal support to those who have been mistreated due to gender.

- **1921:** The pogo stick was invented. Throughout the 1920s, children kept themselves amused bouncing on a spring-powered stick.

  Today: The most sought-after games for children are those with computer graphics.

- **1921:** The first nonstop transatlantic airplane flight went from Newfoundland to Ireland in 16 hours, 12 minutes.

  Today: The Concorde can fly from New York to Paris in less than four hours.

---

whose 1919 book *Ten Days That Shook The World* gave his eyewitness account of the Revolution and who founded the American Communist Labor Party, became a sought-after speaker for social events.

To American politicians, the threat of a revolution was justification for continuing the wartime censorship that had been established to protect military secrets. Charges were brought against writers and publishers who were branded as "radicals" and "freethinkers." Ordinary citizens were split: more identified themselves as "communists" or "socialists" than at any time since (their affiliation with leftist politics would come back to haunt them thirty years later, during the blacklisting that made many lose their jobs in the 1950s), but those who supported capitalism feared leftists as being not just different political parties, but as a threat.

The Chicago Renaissance

When Sherwood Anderson moved to Chicago in 1913, he found a blossoming literary environment. Among the writers that he became acquainted with, some famous and some yet-to-be, were Carl Sandburg, Edgar Lee Masters, Harriet Monroe, Ben Hecht, and Floyd Dell. Literary magazines of lasting cultural significance, such as *Poetry, Little Review,* and *Seven Arts* were new and eager to publish works by writers who were just starting to build their reputations.

Enthusiasm was high among this group for the experimental art of the post-Impressionist painters, such as Cezanne, van Gogh, and Gaugin, who stopped trying to reproduce visual images and worked instead to record their internal impressions of what they saw, reducing physical forms to abstract structures. The art exhibit at the 69th Regimented Armory in New York City from February 17 to March 15, 1913, made history as the first modern art showing in the United States. To this day, the Armory Show is referred to as a defining moment in American art. In 1914 the show traveled to Chicago, where angry students of the Art Institute were so offended that they burned an effigy of painter Henri Matisse. Anderson and his friends spent nights discussing artistic theory and determining how they could apply theories about paint to their work with words.

Critical Overview

As is the case with any groundbreaking work of art, there is a tendency to view the early critical responses to *Winesburg, Ohio* as being shortsighted and prudish, reflecting a world that was both unable to appreciate Anderson's accomplishment and much less sexually sophisticated than our own. There is some truth to this view, but much of it can be traced to the fact that the original reviewers did not, for obvious reasons, have the benefit of studying the book for eighty years, and so their analyses seem to be much simpler than those written today.

Adjusting for the modern critic's advantage of accumulated Anderson studies, the critics who commented on *Winesburg* when it was first published appear to have been quite astute in what they had to say. Only a few critics took Anderson to task for examining subjects like shame and lust in his work, like the writer for the *New York Sun* who announced to the world that the book dealt with "nau-

seous acts" in a review called "A Gutter Would Be Spoon River" (the title refers to Edgar Lee Masters' 1915 poetry collection, also about inhabitants of a small town). A few other reviewers proclaimed disgust, but they were published mostly in family papers where the main interest was not literature but sales.

Their influence was exaggerated by several sources, including Sherwood Anderson himself, who seemed to allow each negative comment to strike with ten times the impact that he allowed to praise. In his *Memoirs,* he complained that he had been portrayed "almost universally, in public prints, as a filthy-minded man and that after the book was published, for weeks and months, my mail was loaded with letters calling me 'filthy,' 'an opener of sewers,' etc." It may have been convenient for him to remember himself being martyred like this, for, as he says in the following paragraph, "We men of the time had a certain pioneering job to do ... "

A more typical response of the time would have been H. W. Boynton's generally favorable review in the August 1919 edition of *The Bookman.* Boynton recognized the depiction of life in Winesburg as being "a life of vivid feeling and ardent impulse doomed, for the most part, to be suppressed or misdirected ... ". He did not ignore the sexual content of the book, but correctly and quietly assumed that Anderson was caught up in the excitement about Sigmund Freud that was sweeping the intellectual community: "At worst he seems in this book like a man who has too freely imbibed the doctrine of psychoanalysis.... At best he seems without consciousness of self or of theory to be getting to the root of the matter—one root, at least—for all of us."

Throughout the decades, it is this lack of self-consciousness that has made *Winesburg, Ohio* a favorite among writers. The writers of the "Lost Generation," those who had been through World War I and started making their mark in the literary world in the late twenties, looked upon Anderson as a sort of father figure in a way that they never looked up to his peers, probably because his success without being too obvious appealed to their artistic senses.

The book's appeal to artists was captured by Rebecca West, whose 1922 review for *New Statesman* called *Winesburg, Ohio* an "extraordinarily good book." She went on to explain that "it is not fiction, it is poetry. It is unreasonable; it delights in places where those who are not poets could not delight ... it stands in front of things that are of no importance, infatuated with their quality, and hymns them with obstinate ecstasy...."

Waldo Frank, who in the 1910s edited *Seven Arts,* a Chicago magazine that originally published several of the Winesburg stories, remembered in a later essay that he had been thrilled with the intuitiveness of the stories. For that reason he had feared revisiting them after twenty years, not knowing if they would have the impact they had in his youth. To his delight, the stories that he had remembered as being held together by the writer's instincts actually turned out to be examples of "technical perfection."

Because Anderson was so popular with writers, he drew the attention of critics, who could not accept the strange elements of Winesburg with a sense of mysticism: it was their job, after all, to explain it. In 1960, Malcolm Cowley's famous essay that introduced the Viking Press edition of *Winesburg, Ohio,* identified the root of the book's intangible greatness in the way that Anderson worked. "He knew instinctively whether one of his stories was right or wrong, but he didn't always know why," Cowley wrote. "[I]f he wanted to improve the story he had to wait for a return of the mood that had produced it, then write it over from beginning to end ... ".

As the world has become more logical and accountable, so literary criticism also has been able to accept a successful mystery, and as *Winesburg, Ohio* has continued to hold public attention, critics have sought to identify what creates the book's unique mood. Tony Tanner's essay in his book *The Reign of Wonder: Naivete and Reality in American Literature* identified the unnamed element as "the constant inclusion of seemingly gratuitous details." James M. Mellard explained in 1968 that other critics had overlooked the fact that there was not just one structure to the stories, but many. Sam Bluefarb identified a pattern of escape that he found common in American literary works in his 1972 book *The Escape Motif in the American Novel.* A. Carl Bredahl found the book to be held together by the twin urges of sex and art in his 1986 essay "The Young Thing Within: Divided Narrative and Sherwood Anderson's *Winesburg, Ohio.*"

As these examples show, recent critical trends have pushed toward more complex explanations of the book, but admiration for Anderson's artistry have stayed fairly constant throughout the book's long history.

Criticism

Tyrus Miller

Miller is an assistant professor of Comparative Literature and English at Yale University. In the following essay, he discusses the thematic and formal significance of storytelling in Winesburg, Ohio.

From the time of its original publication as a complete book in 1919, *Winesburg, Ohio* has posed readers, reviewers, and critics with a puzzle: is it a short story collection or a novel? Already in 1916, Anderson had published sections of it as stories in the "little magazines" of the Chicago Renaissance and modernist literary movements: in Floyd Dell's *The Masses,* Margaret Anderson's *Little Review,* and Waldo Frank's *Seven Arts.* By their author's own admission, then, the individual chapters appeared to stand on their own, and early readers generally followed this lead, seeing in *Winesburg* a short story collection. Only later, after greater critical scrutiny and further experimentation in prose by innovators such as James Joyce, Gertrude Stein, William Carlos Williams, and William Faulkner, did Anderson's readers seriously consider the possible unity of *Winesburg* as a novel.

Much of the later critical discussion of *Winesburg, Ohio,* however, has been constrained by this problem of identifying its proper genre. Much ink, argument, and intelligence has been dedicated to discovering the hidden thread, narrative or thematic, binding its apparently disconnected stories. Equal effort has been spent in denying that this missing link really exists.

Winesburg's admirers praise the book's disjoined structure as poetical, lyrical, even mystical, and have valued its flashes of psychological and spiritual insight over any mere realism to be found in more conventional novels. Its detractors, cool and skeptical about "lyrical form," have found *Winesburg* too slack and intellectually murky to be a good novel, yet also lacking the compactness of incident, the quick narrative punch of a well-wrought short story.

These debates have gone round and round, largely on the same terrain, for three-quarters of a century. And the very grounds of the argument—novel or not, good one or bad one—have led to this stalemate. Without a shift of the question no satisfactory resolution is likely to be forthcoming.

Winesburg, it must be said, is a mixed work and can only be approached with finer instruments

What Do I Read Next?

- Edgar Lee Masters' 1915 collection of free-verse poems, *Spoon River Anthology,* was one of the most direct influences on *Winesburg, Ohio.* Published the year that Anderson started the book, each poem tells the story of a different citizen of a fictional town, Spoon River.

- When Anderson was writing this book, between 1915 and 1919, Chicago was experiencing a literary renaissance. Among the writers of Anderson's circle of friends in those days, Floyd Dell is considered one of the most innovative. His 1920 novel, *Moon Calf,* is like *Winesburg, Ohio* in that it draws heavily on the author's past in a farm community, applying urban sensibilities and a sense of pity that comes from sophistication.

- Although *Winesburg, Ohio* is considered Anderson's finest, most haunting work, he wrote many other novels, poems and short stories. His 1925 novel *Dark Laughter* is the most highly-regarded work of long fiction and was the most financially successful during his lifetime.

- Ernest Hemingway considered Anderson to be a friend and mentor—it was Anderson who in-troduced Hemingway to Gertrude Stein and other European writers who were to become part of the Hemingway legend. Hemingway's 1925 collection of stories, *In Our Times,* shows the influence of *Winesburg, Ohio* in the way that the separate stories all refer back to one main character and theme.

- Anderson wrote several autobiographies, but the one he had been working on for nine years before he died is considered the most important one. When it was first published, it was dramatically cut, but as Anderson's reputation as a literary figure grew, his original writing was added back in. The revised, restored version was published in 1943 as *Sherwood Anderson's Memoirs.*

- Irving Howe, one of the most respected literary critics of our century, published *Sherwood Anderson: A Biographical and Critical Study* in 1951, adding a new introduction to the 1966 edition. His explanation of Anderson and his works is not the only one, but he does give a brief, intelligent, comprehensive explanation that students can follow and understand.

---

than the crude tool kit of genre categories. The question of its nature and, eventually, its quality cannot be answered without more careful attention to its subtler design. Its patterns are not set down by a generic stamp, but rather come faintly into view in the knots of a complex weave: the multiple dimensions of storytelling employed by Anderson, ranging from narratives told or withheld by characters within individual stories, the narrational modes of the individual chapters, the explicit and implicit joins and intersections between stories, and the narrative implied by the work as a whole.

Anderson sets *Winesburg* in a transitional period in American history, the years between the Civil War and the turn of the century, when small town communities were just starting to be affected by the consolidation of wealth and the sharpening of class divisions; the shift from small farming towards banking and manufacturing; the spread of newspaper reading and the rise of a consumer culture; the flight of the young to the large cities and the stagnation of towns by-passed by new developments.

Storytelling, for Anderson, is the key index of these large-scale social tendencies, for in the changing nature and value of stories one can grasp the effects of these trends in the lives of individuals and particular communities. In an earlier epoch, stories had served as the social glue for small communities such as Winesburg, articulating a shared experience and rendering it transmissible to new candidates for membership, whether they came from outside or from the younger generations of the town. The correspondence of the story to factual truth was less important than the recognition of itself accorded by the community to a given story: a story became truth by being transmitted among its members and down to its children.

But Anderson presents a new phase in this history, a turning point at which this glue of shared experience has ceased to hold. His storytellers, by and large, fail at their craft, unable to furnish myths to the community that might become its truth. The stock of transmissible experience has been tapped down to dregs, and the community can only perceive individual eccentricities in the stories its members tell rather than recognizing its collective identity in each of them.

Stories themselves have become poorer in form and sense, less able to offer guidance to the lives of the listeners. Thus dramatizing this impoverishment of the communal economy of stories, Anderson does not simply "use" the story as a literary form. He makes it a central theme, an object of scrutiny to be held up to the reader's gaze, revolved, and interrogated. In his handling of stories as thematic matter, Anderson registers the rising skepticism about the cognitive worth of narrative itself; he depicts the loss of faith in stories, their diminished capacity to connect modern Americans.

In many cases, Anderson's concern with narrative and its ability to inform the lives of people remains implicit, though crucial. His four-part story, "Godliness," for example, seems to be primarily a set of character-sketches of the farmer-patriarch Jesse Bentley and his family. Yet two of the parts, Part II and Part IV (subtitled "Terror"), hinge on a pathological translation into real life of stories from the bible: Jesse destroys his relation to his beloved grandson David by trying to reenact the Old Testament stories through which he interprets his experience.

The other two parts, dealing with Jesse's troubled daughter Louise, are more subtly connected to the same sort of twisted reading. Her life has been tainted at its source, it is suggested, by Jesse's desire to live out the biblical succession of patriarchs and their sons. In his pursuit of this terrible dream, Jesse drives his delicate wife to exhaustion, and at the birth of Louise, she dies. As a girl-child, Louise can never fit into Jesse's story. Substituting for any more intimate human bond, his inner narrative has no place for a girl despite her bothersome presence in his outer life. Nor can she look to her mother for the tenderness she can never receive from her fa-

ther. At her very birth, the child was sacrificed to her father's destructive story.

Winesburg, Ohio is full of storytellers of different sorts. Its opening and closing stories present the most formal sort: professional writers, artists of the word. The prefacing chapter, "The Book of the Grotesque," thus depicts an old writer composing a book out of the many "grotesque" characters who populate his memory. The concluding story "Departure," a mirror-image of the opening tale seen across time, tracks the young reporter George Willard as he leaves Winesburg to become a writer.

The old writer, lying in his bed, watches "a long procession of figures" pass through his mind, while on the train taking him to the big city, George consigns his life in Winesburg to "a background on which to paint the dreams of his manhood." Though Anderson does not explicitly identify the youth and the old man, he does suggest that George may be destined to become like the old writer, while the old man seems to account for his "book of the grotesque" by including a story like "Departure," in which a younger version of himself gets free of the town that gave him his stock of memories.

Both the old writer and young George picture their life as a broad interior tableau, a novel-like prospect of the mind that differs greatly from the damaged braggarts, compulsive confessors, and tongue-tied sputterers of their old town. Their sort of storytelling is uniquely whole, able to encompass all the other forms, although it never reduces the other storytellers to mere puppets of their literary design

Of the figures of the town, Doctor Reefy in "Paper Pills" and Doctor Parcival in "The Philosopher" together offer a distorted mirror-image of these two successful writers. Reefy is a writer, but only of scraps and fragments. His words congeal into unreadable wads, rather than coalescing into an artistic whole. Parcival is also a writer, but a debilitated one. The doctor claims to have come Winesburg to write a book, and George visits him to listen to the doctor read from his manuscript. Anderson, however, clearly suggests that the doctor's book will never be completed. He is too much the traditional storyteller to limit his book to a rounded, novel-like design:

> The tales that Doctor Parcival told George Willard began nowhere and ended nowhere. Sometimes the boy thought they must all be inventions, a pack of lies. And then again he was convinced that they contained the very essence of truth.

Moreover, even the doctor's exchange of stories with George is marked by an ambiguity. When he reads to George from his *manuscript,* their relation is that of author to reader; at the same time, however, the author and reader sit face-to-face, an overlay from the older relation of storyteller to listener. In this ambiguity, Anderson subtly suggests the grounds of the doctor's failure as a writer. He has not made the break from the already obsolete world of Winesburg into the modern urban life of the city, the precondition of being a "real" writer. The writer must accept the tragic distance between the author and his anonymous readers, a distance spanned only by a silent book. One does not *come to* Winesburg to become a writer, one escapes from it. The doctor headed the wrong way on the train, and his book will never be written. He is doomed to be, at best, a storyteller in a town that no longer believes in stories.

Opposed to the synthetic vision of the old man and George and distinct from the failed doctor-writers are such town figures Joe Welling in "A Man of Ideas," Reverend Curtis Hartman in "The Strength of God," and Tom Foster in "Drink." These characters, unlike all the writers, are bound to speech. Yet each of the three founders as storyteller when he tries to capture his inner, personal experience in communicable form. Though Joe Welling tries to use narratives to illustrate his ideas, the churning motor of his overactive brain makes futile his attempt to give them narrative order. The result is stories that skirt the edge of sense, leaving his listeners baffled and dazed:

> Suppose this—suppose all of the wheat, the corn, the oats, the peas, the potatoes, were all by some miracle swept away…. There is a high fence built all around us. We'll suppose that. No one can get over the fence and all the fruits of the earth are destroyed, nothing left but these wild things, these grasses. Would we be done for?

The Reverend, similarly, bursts in one night on George to announce that he has seen God in the naked body of the schoolteacher. The reader, filled in by Anderson's narrator about the background to this strange declaration, understands it as meaningful; George, however, lacking all context, takes it as nonsense if not insanity. Tom Foster, finally, does manage to tell a story about his (imagined) love-making to Helen White, but he fails to convey to George that it is a fantasy, a metaphor seized upon to capture his inner experience of being drunk for the first time. George, who has seen Helen that same night, becomes angry, misunderstanding

Tom's flight of fancy as a slur on Helen's good character.

One final type of storytelling demands special mention: the story not told. This "negative storytelling," implying the existence of a story while refusing to tell it, is characteristic of the loneliest and most disappointed figures of the town: Wing Biddlebaum in "Hands," Alice Hindman in "Adventure," Seth Richmond in "The Thinker," and Elmer Cowley in "'Queer'."

Seth Richmond reveals that his refusal of words is not simply a lack of something to say, but a rejection of contact with those who know how to use words superficially, with the community bound by stories. His shortcoming points beyond itself toward an unconventional and more genuine form of community—akin to the silent understanding achieved by George and Helen in the late story "Sophistication." Explaining to himself his failure to express his love to Helen White, Seth concludes, "She'll be embarrassed and feel strange when I'm around…. When it comes to loving someone, it won't never be me. It'll be someone else—some fool—someone who talks a lot—someone like that George Willard."

Wing Biddlebaum, whose all-encompassing tenderness earned him the fear and hatred of the Pennsylvania town from which he fled, a community that saw perversion in a love that went beyond its narrow bounds, likewise keeps his story to himself. In all these cases of withheld storytelling, however, Anderson's narrator, implicitly a professional writer like the old man or George, steps in to allow their silence to have its word, to take its place among the stories actually pronounced.

Storytelling in *Winesburg* is not simply a formal or generic issue, a choice Anderson made before a stack of paper about whether to tell little stories about many characters or one big story about a few characters. The generic uncertainty of the work—story collection or novel?—was not the result of indecision or literary incompetence, but rather the complex outcome of Anderson's concern with the crisis of storytelling itself.

Storytelling is an invisible actor throughout the book. A character's telling a story or holding it back can itself be the crucial "plot" event in a given chapter. More than outward incident or even psychological detail, the different forms and rhythms of storytelling are the reader's main clues to the book's inner design, the primary facts calling for further thought and explanation.

Source: Tyrus Miller, in an essay for *Novels for Students*, Gale, 1998.

Sally Adair Rigsby

In the following excerpt, Rigsby argues that Anderson's Winesburg, Ohio *is concerned with the meaning of the feminine and the "relationships between the men and women of Winesburg."*

The meaning Sherwood Anderson gives to the characters of women and to the qualities of the feminine is an important source of unity in *Winesburg, Ohio.* Anderson identifies the feminine with a pervasive presence of a fragile, hidden "something" that corresponds both to the lost potential of each of the grotesques and to the secret knowledge that each story is structured to reveal. The themes most frequently identified as the unifying forces of *Winesburg, Ohio,* the failure of communication and the development of the artist, are closely related to Anderson's focus on the meaning of the feminine. In *Winesburg, Ohio* communication is blocked because of the devaluation of the feminine qualities of vulnerability and tenderness even though the artist's creativity springs from deep feelings of vitality which Anderson associates with the feminine.

Through one of Enoch Robinson's paintings in "Loneliness," Anderson creates an image that reveals his vision of a woman's condition in Winesburg and of her potential power. The painting is of a man driving down a road to Winesburg. The look on the man's face indicates that he is vaguely aware of "something hidden" behind "a clump of elders" beside the road. Enoch longs for his critics to see this hidden subject, an essence so beautiful and precious that it could not be rendered directly:

> "It's a woman and, oh, she is lovely! She is hurt and is suffering but she makes no sound. Don't you see how it is? She lies quite still, white and still, and the beauty comes out from her and spreads over everything. It is in the sky back there and all around everywhere. I didn't try to paint the woman, of course. She is too beautiful to be painted."

Enoch's painting portrays precisely the condition of the female characters who inhabit Winesburg. The women are "invisible" because their real identities are eclipsed by their social roles. The relationships between the men and women of Winesburg are corrupted and uncreative, for their acceptance of conventional sexual roles prevents them from experiencing the genuine communication that comes when relationships are equal and reciprocal. The neediness, frustration, and failure that encompass the lives of Louise Bentley, Alice Hindman, Elizabeth Willard, and Kate Swift are the result of the discrepancy between their own capacity for intimacy, affection, and creativity and the inability of others, especially the men in their lives, to "see" or to relate to who they really are. In Enoch's painting, as in Anderson's stories, the beauty and suffering of woman become visible only through art that brings to a level of conscious awareness what is unrecognized by conventional society.

It is in his characterization of Louise Bentley that Anderson shows best the suffering of women that results from the devaluation of feminine needs and aspirations. Louise is completely rejected by her father because, as a female, she is an unacceptable heir. She is ignored and unloved as a child, and her vulnerability is heightened by her instinct to value relationships intensely. As a young girl, Louise has a remarkably intelligent and mature vision of what is necessary for human intimacy. She imagines that Winesburg is a place where relationships are natural, spontaneous, and reciprocal: "... Men and women must live happily and freely, giving and taking friendship and affection as one takes the feel of a wind on the cheek." Louise turns to John Hardy in search of a friend who will understand her dream. She seeks from her husband an intimate exchange of feelings and thoughts. Hardy seems kind and patient; however, his vision of Louise's humanity is limited to his own very inadequate concept of "wife"....

To Hardy, Louise is a sexual object whose human voice he suppresses by kisses which are not a mark of affection but an unconscious means of ignoring and belittling his wife's desperate effort to be her deepest self. Louise's complete defeat in the denial of her personhood by her father and her husband is expressed in her rejection of her child: "'It is a man child and will get what it wants anyway.... Had it been a woman child there is nothing in the world I would not have done for it.'" Anderson's point is that in her surrender to marriage Louise surrenders all hope that her gift for friendship and affection will be realized.

Through the story of Alice Hindman, Anderson shows how the conventional sexual morality of Winesburg works against the fulfillment of women's needs. Alice is clearly morally superior to her lover, Ned Currie, and is capable of a much finer quality of relationship than he is. Just as Ned is contemplating inviting her to become his mistress, Alice proposes that she go to the city to live and work with him until they are sufficiently established to marry. Unable to comprehend the spirit of independence and equality Alice envisions, Ned demands that she wait for him in Winesburg, forc-

> *... Anderson identifies the feminine with a pervasive presence of a fragile, hidden "something" that corresponds both to the lost potential of each of the grotesques and to the secret knowledge that each story is structured to reveal."*

ing her into a passive dependency which denies her the sustained relationship she needs. Their brief sexual intimacy is so sacred to Alice that she feels bound to Ned in a spiritual marriage even when years of waiting prove he has abandoned her. Despite her economic and legal independence, Alice Hindman is as much imprisoned by marriage as Louise Bentley is, for she has no understanding of Anderson's concept of "the growing modern idea of a woman's owning herself and giving and taking for her own ends in life."

The tragic loss which characterizes the lives of Louise Bentley and Alice Hindman and the accompanying shriveling of their sexuality and their capacity for affection suggest that Anderson regarded the failure to find fulfillment in love as a crucial issue of female identity. The natural, reciprocal relationships which Louise Bentley and Alice Hindman envision are a reasonable expectation; however, Anderson shows that the patriarchal marriages of Winesburg preclude the possibility of achieving the intimacy of equal relationships. When they are not related to as persons, and no emotional or spiritual dimension emerges in the marriage relationship, all possibility for sexual satisfaction is completely lost to the women. The marriages of Louise Bentley and Elizabeth Willard are in no sense real to them except as a legal duty. Furthermore, the social pressure to limit feelings of intimacy to monogamous marriage denies the women of Winesburg any legitimate way of establishing the kind of relationships they need. When women are subordinates, the institution of marriage becomes a social means of controlling their natural instincts for love and self-actualization....

Once the theme of the suffering of women is identified, it becomes obvious that an emphasis on the crippled feminine dimension of life permeates *Winesburg, Ohio*. The image of Elizabeth Willard, "tall and gaunt" with her face "marked with small-pox scars," is repeated in the wounded bodies of other overworked and suffering women who hover in the background: Dr. Parcival's mother with her "red, sad-looking eyes," Joe Welling's mother, "a grey, silent woman with a peculiar ashy complexion," Tom Foster's grandmother whose worn hands look like "the dried stems of an old creeping vine." The general abuse of women is captured most vividly in "Paper Pills" when a young girl is so frightened of the lust of her suitor that she dreams "he had bitten into her body and that his jaws were dripping."...

Through the character of Elizabeth Willard, Anderson shows that the urge for creative self-expression is an extension of the basic feminine instinct for intimacy. Restless and energetic, Elizabeth dreams of becoming an actress in a big city. Her fantasy is a symbolic expression of her need to develop the full range of her personality and to achieve the artistic expression that would bring her into intimate communion with the world. Like Louise Bentley and Alice Hindman, Elizabeth's openness to life makes her open to sexual relationships. Her lovers, the traveling men who stay in her father's hotel, are her only means of touching the larger and more vital life of the cities. When she turns to marriage as the conventional solution to her restlessness, Elizabeth quickly discovers that the "secret something" growing within her is killed by her insensitive husband. Unable to extend the boundaries of her life, Elizabeth creates dramatic roles for herself in an effort to be the person she can only vaguely imagine. In "Mother," when she is determined to protect the creativity of her son from her husband's materialistic ambitions, Elizabeth uses theatrical make-up to transform herself into the powerful woman who can kill the "evil voice" of Tom Willard.

Just as Elizabeth Willard imagines, women can transform themselves through their own creative powers. In fact, Anderson suggests that the creativity of the feminine is such an energized force in these sensitive women that a moment of crisis can release deep feelings that have been suppressed for years. In these "adventures," the bodies of the women are transformed to reveal their hidden power. When Louise Bentley fears her son is lost, all of her capacities for motherly care flow out to embrace him. To David Hardy, the voice of his mother is "like rain falling on trees," and her face becomes "the most peaceful and lovely thing he had ever seen." In Alice Hindman's "adventure," the rain releases her suppressed spontaneity; the imagery of falling rain and of leaping and running reveals the potential of Alice's sexual passion and creative vitality. Kate Swift's scarred face is transformed when she walks the winter streets of Winesburg: "… Her features were as the features of a tiny goddess on a pedestal in a garden in the dim light of a summer evening." Elizabeth Willard's wild drive into the country, which she describes to Dr. Reefy in "Death," expresses the mounting tension of her desire to transcend the limitations of her life. The black clouds, the green trees, and the falling rain (symbols of the natural, reproductive processes of the earth) represent the vital, spontaneous, and creative life Elizabeth is seeking but cannot quite comprehend.

The language that describes these "adventures" links the moments of feminine self-actualization to the rich beauty of nature and to the spiritual transformation associated with creative inspiration and mystical religion. The "something" which Elizabeth Willard is seeking is a more humane life in which her sexuality, her need for intimacy, her creativity, and her spirituality, can be fully realized, harmonized, and expressed: a life in which the wholeness of her selfhood might be recognized and appreciated by some other human being. Years later, in her encounter with Dr. Reefy, Elizabeth glimpses momentarily the magnitude and significance of the emotions she has experienced. In the excitement of describing her "adventure" to her friend, she transforms herself into the gifted actress who can miraculously "project herself out of the husk" of an old, tired body into the image of "a lovely and innocent girl." Dr. Reefy is entranced by the beauty and rhythm of Elizabeth's body, the symbolic expression of her hidden capacity to move with life and to express her creative vitality. This moment of communion in "Death" is the experience of liberating, intimate understanding which all of the Winesburg characters are seeking. The intimacy is achieved because Dr. Reefy possesses the sensitivity and wisdom that enable him to see and appreciate the hidden identity of a woman: "'You dear! You lovely dear! Oh you lovely dear!'" When the moment is broken by their fear of an intruder, Elizabeth turns to death as the only lover who can receive her full identity.

Elizabeth Willard hopes that her creative drives will be expressed through her son; however, not until her death does George acquire the qual-ity of feeling necessary for the artist. The progress of his development toward that goal is revealed by the nature of his relationships with women. Early in *Winesburg, Ohio* in "Nobody Knows," George takes advantage of the subordinate position of Louise Trunnion, impersonally using her for sexual adventure. Proud, satisfied, and egotistical, George divorces himself completely from any possible affiliation with Louise, for he sees women only as objects to be used to expand his own sense of personal power. In "The Thinker," a story at the midpoint of the collection, George brags that he plans to fall in love with Helen White to get material for a story. Yet, beneath his nonchalance there is the hint of a deeper self in George which gradually emerges through a series of encounters with Kate Swift, Belle Carpenter, his mother, and Helen White.

Kate Swift is eager to share with George her love of art and her understanding of life. However, George understands Kate's earnest seriousness as evidence that she is in love with him, and his mind becomes filled with "lustful thoughts" about her. Thus, in "Teacher," when Kate comes to him ablaze with the intensity of her desire "to open the door of life," his sexual desire kindles her own, and she loses touch with the intellectual, spiritual, and creative potentials of her emotion. At last, however, George begins to perceive that there is something more to be communicated between men and women than physical encounter; he knows that he is missing something important that Kate Swift is trying to tell him.

Gradually his boyish superficiality fades, and in "An Awakening" George consciously begins his search for those truths that will give order and meaning to his life. However, the moment the thrill of a new insight comes to him, he is eager to share it with a woman, not in order to enrich a relationship but to have the pleasure of releasing physically his new surge of energy. George's spiritual experience merely heightens his grandiose egocentricity, and he plans to use his new self-confidence to win sexual mastery over a potent and challenging woman. As George walks with Belle Carpenter, unaware that they are pursued by her lover, he becomes "half drunk with the sense of masculine power." However, when he is duped by the older couple, George's sudden loss of power becomes precisely the reversal of fortunes his character needs.

Although the Winesburg stories are loosely connected and do not generally follow any logical sequence, the stories that show George Willard's growing understanding of the meaning of the feminine do progress sequentially. In the last third of the collection, George's increasing sensitivity to women is extended through his initiation into suffering. In "An Awakening" George is tricked and humiliated; in the following story, "Queer," he is knocked "half unconscious" by the force of Elmer Cowley's undirected efforts to express himself. In "Drink" George tries to defend Helen White's good name from Tom Foster's drunken fantasies but, instead, becomes deeply moved by the young man's sincere effort to understand and experience suffering. The story is a humorous, indirect, and understated preparation for "Death...."

The sensitivity that comes to George as a result of his mother's death and his vision of her spiritual beauty prepare him for his experience with Helen White in "Sophistication." "Sophistication" is a very slight story, actually a denouement of the two climactic moments in "Death " when Elizabeth Willard's true identity is recognized. However, the story is profoundly meaningful when it is read with an awareness of the thematic significance of Anderson's portrayal of the devaluation of the feminine throughout *Winesburg, Ohio*. At the end of the story Anderson describes the satisfaction Helen White and George Willard have achieved through their relationship:

> For some reason they could not have explained they had both got from their silent evening together the thing needed. Man or boy, woman or girl, they had for a moment taken hold of the thing that makes the mature life of men and women in the modern world possible.

The tone and placement of this passage make it clearly a key thematic statement; yet, there is very little clarity in the passage itself or even in the story about exactly what the "thing" is that Helen and George have experienced. The various interpretations of the passage which focus on the theme of communication are accurate enough, but the episode itself as well as Anderson's emphasis on "the mature life of men and women" certainly indicate that the focus of his concern is not just human relationships generally but the special problems of communication between men and women. It is against the background of Anderson's presentation throughout *Winesburg, Ohio* of the suffering of women and their unfulfilled relationships with men that the encounter of these two young people can best be appreciated.

The positive nature of the experience which George and Helen share is a product of their mutual treasuring of those tender, vital feelings that

Anderson associates with the feminine. Both are aware of a fragile, new self that is alive in each of them; their silent communion gives these sensitive feelings the nurturing that is needed. Despite their youth and inexperience, they momentarily share a relationship that is trusting and reciprocal, for in George and Helen, Anderson creates characters who are free of sexual role expectations. It is appropriate that Helen and George should recapture the joyful, natural spirit of childhood when males and females meet in relationships that are equal. Their release of emotions in spontaneous playfulness is integrated with their mature, brooding reflection on the transience of life. George's awareness of the reality of death and of his own finitude is his "sophistication," but he has also learned that he needs to share this new knowledge with a woman, for "he believes that a woman will be gentle, that she will understand." His acceptance of Helen as a spiritual mediator indicates that George's masculinity is balanced by the feminine qualities of tenderness and gentleness, an integration that Anderson suggests is necessary for the artist.

The conclusion of "Sophistication" suggests that *Winesburg, Ohio* is intended to be a prophetic statement about the quality of the relationships of men and women in the modern world. That prophetic tone is even more direct in "Tandy," a story that seems to have been created primarily as an invocation of the woman of the future. The drunken man who defines the meaning of Tandy expresses the view of the feminine that pervades *Winesburg, Ohio*:

> "There is a woman coming.... Perhaps of all men I alone understand.... I know about her struggles and her defeats. It is because of her defeats that she is to me the lovely one. Out of her defeats has been born a new quality in woman.... It is the quality of being strong to be loved.... Be brave enough to dare to be loved. Be something more than man or woman. Be Tandy."

The suffering of women, Anderson argues, will lead to the evolution of a new kind of woman who will insist that sexual roles be transcended and that she be loved as a human being, an event that Anderson suggests is as much needed by men as it is by women....

Throughout *Winesburg, Ohio* Anderson associates the feminine with a quality of feeling that is delicate and intangible; it is a tender nuance, a transient moment of intimacy, a creative, secret something growing within the self, a slight quiver of insight that seems to hold great promise. Anderson's mode of presentation of the feminine is as appropriate as the invisibility of the woman in Enoch Robinson's painting, for *Winesburg, Ohio* presents a microcosm of the modern world in which the potential of the feminine has not yet been realized.

Source: Sally Adair Rigsby, "The Feminine in *Winesburg, Ohio*," in *Studies in American Fiction*. Vol. 9, No. 2, autumn, 1981, pp. 233–44.

George D. Murphy

In the following essay, Murphy categorizes characters according to their "responses to sexual emotion" and follows this theme throughout the entire novel.

One of the bits of learning which students of modern literature treasure up against their examinations is the notion that Sherwood Anderson was an American equivalent of D. H. Lawrence.... Indeed, Irving Howe, the critic who has been most insistent upon Anderson's debt to Lawrence, has pointed out that even Anderson's most "sex-centered" work reveals that "for the man who wrote those novels sex was a source of deep anxiety."

Nowhere is the weight and tenor of the evidence for this anxiety quite so impressive as in *Winesburg, Ohio,* the early work on which Anderson's greatly depleted reputation now almost entirely depends. In that work he displays an extremely hesitant, almost puritanical attitude toward physical sexuality which seems to have been considerably more Platonic than Lawrencian or Freudian in its complexion. In fact, most of the major characters in *Winesburg* "may be seen as illustrating this markedly cautious attitude toward sex on the part of their creator, and ... [that] attitude exerts a controlling influence upon the form and theme of the book...."

The majority of *Winesburg*'s grotesques can be classified into four distinct types on the basis of their responses to sexual emotion: the first type consists of those who are repelled by their sexual feelings and desperately seek to avoid the fact of sex altogether. The second is devoted to those who complacently accept sex and cannot see beyond it, while the third group embraces those who, though they wistfully apprehend a state of feeling which transcends the merely sexual, are compelled by circumstance to settle for sex. Finally, there is that very important group of initiates who perceive the role of sexuality in Anderson's own terms and experience it as a prelude—a material reflection of a kind of Platonic perfection of the soul.

Familiar examples of the first type—the characters whose grotesqueness derives from their in-

ability to accept the gross fact of sex—are Wash Williams ("Respectability"), the telegrapher who went berserk when brusquely confronted with his naked wife, and Enoch Robinson ("Loneliness"), the childlike, schizoid artist who, to his pain, kept "bumping against things, against actualities like money and sex and opinion" and whose precious fantasy life was destroyed by contact with an actual woman. Another of this company is Wings Biddlebaum ("Hands"), the inspired teacher whose hands were vital to his communication and who had been accused of homosexuality on the basis of the fantasies of a half-witted student. Wings is very often cited as a victim of the low-brow's intolerance of the life of the spirit, but his real tragedy seems to me to lie in his own demoralizing recognition of the essential truth of the embattled farmers' charges. For Wings is of the homosexual persuasion, or, as Anderson puts it, "In their feelings for the boys under their charge such men are not unlike the finer sort of women in their love of men."...

Very few of the grotesques in *Winesburg* fall into [the] second classification—that is, the frankly and uncomplicatedly sexual. One of them, however, is Will Henderson, the newspaper owner and George Willard's employer, who is, as Anderson styles him, "a sensualist," and who, at the beginning of "The Philosopher," figures in as explicit a bit of moral allegory as ever Hawthorne created: one of Will's cronies is the bartender Tom Willy, whose hands are blotched by crimson birthmarks, and, as he and the newspaper owner talked of womanizing, "he grew more and more excited" and the red of his fingers deepened. "It was as though the hands had been dipped in blood that had dried and faded." This scene, which is so evocative of bloody, violent sexuality, is juxtaposed with George Willard's philosophical conversations with Parcival. Art Wilson, the butcher's son of "Awakening," is another of the sensualists whose chief use is to be employed in one of these contrapuntal tableaux, for as he sits in the pool room, spitting and talking of whores, George Willard is portrayed as wandering through the moonlit night entertaining a vision of cosmic love and order. Belle Carpenter and Ed Handby are a pair of full sublunary lovers who figure in the same story. Their love is depicted as restricted to the sensual order, condemned to sexuality for its expression, and, when George Willard unwittingly intrudes into their relationship, to violence.

Throughout *Winesburg* Anderson seems to have been establishing a connection between sexual ardor and violence. Certainly Dr. Reefy's young

> *... most of the major characters in Winesburg 'may be seen as illustrating this markedly cautious attitude toward sex on the part of their creator, and ... [that] attitude exerts a controlling influence upon the form and theme of the book....'"*

wife ("Paper Pills") made that connection subconsciously when, before her marriage, she was haunted by a nightmare in which one of her suitors "had bitten into her body and ... his jaws were dripping." She married Dr. Reefy—who figures as a kind of wise mystical *guru* to his young wife and to Elizabeth Willard—after she watched him pull a tooth from a patient, thereby exorcising, or, if you will, symbolically castrating, the ravenous sexual monster of her dreams.

George Willard's mother, Elizabeth, is the most pathetic representative of the third category of grotesques to be discovered in *Winesburg*. These are the sexually injured and insulted, those who, though they are tantalizingly aware of the possibility of a more satisfying mode of communication, confuse it at a critical time in their lives with sexuality and are condemned to an existence of dreary frustration as a consequence. In her youth George's mother had been visited by a great restlessness and a yearning for "some big definite movement to her life," and had sought relief in the specious glamour of sex with the travelling men who frequented her father's hotel and with her husband-to-be, Tom Willard. In sexuality "she felt for a time released and happy," but the satisfaction was ephemeral and, when we first encounter her in "Mother," she is broken and despondent, hoping only that her son will somehow manage to achieve the freedom of expression that she had once glimpsed....

[These] three categories of grotesques may be regarded as constituting a paradigm of the clue to the thematic unity of *Winesburg* which Anderson himself supplied in the gnomic "Book of the Grotesque" with which he prefaced the volume.

There he put it forward that spiritual deformity must result from the kind of obsessive rigidity which selects only one "truth" from the multitude which make up reality. The Wash Williamses of the world can only comprehend the "truth" that sex can be gross, violent and repulsive. The Will Hendersons can only see the "truth" that sex is a powerful, absorbing and attractive force, while the Elizabeth Willards ... dimly descry another "truth" about life but, to their cost, confuse it with sex. Although the Elizabeth Willards come close, none of these characters appreciates the point that Anderson seemed to be trying to establish, and that is that there can be many "truths" about sex, just as there can be many "truths" about life, and that the most comprehensive of these truths is that while sex can be gross, violent, and degrading, it can, when sublimated, be tremendously inspiring, lifting the personality into a higher stage of consciousness.

The *Winesburg* characters who attain to this last view of sexuality fall into the fourth and most thematically significant category... and, on the internal evidence, Anderson appears to have regarded them as constituting a sort of spiritual elite. They are Love's Elect, those who have approached the final stages of that mystical mode of communication Anderson so highly prized. Their company numbers Dr. Reefy, the Reverend Curtis Hartman ("The Strength of God"), Kate Swift ("The Teacher"), Tom Foster ("Drink"), and George Willard. In every case they are presented as being in the grip of a strong physical passion which, for one reason or another, they do not consummate. Rather, they sublimate their desire and, by avoiding the trap of a merely sensual mode of communication, are admitted to a plane of consciousness where communication operates in terms of an imaginative, mystical sympathy. These folk, at least, manage to grasp two of the paradoxical truths which Anderson sets forth in "The Book of the Grotesque"—"the truth of virginity and the truth of passion."

"You must not try to make love definite," says Dr. Reefy to Elizabeth Willard. He had loved her chastely for years, and he goes on to say, "If you try to be definite and sure about it ... the long hot day of disappointment comes swiftly...." Gentle Tom Foster of "Drink" had had an early experience of the more definite and violent aspects of love as a youngster in Cincinnati and had determined "that he would put sex altogether out of his own life." But he was human and young, and one spring he fell in love with Helen White, the banker's daughter with whom all the youth of Winesburg dallied in their fantasies. He resolved his emotional dilemma in a most peculiar and deliberate way: he neither repressed nor physically indulged his emotion, but allowed himself to "think of Helen White whenever her figure came into his mind and only concerned himself with the manner of his thoughts." The manner of his thoughts took a mystical turn, and one night, with the aid of a little alcohol, he conceived of her in terms of images of flame and wind. It was all over in one night, and, as Anderson pointedly remarks, "no one in Winesburg was any the worse for Tom's outbreak." And Tom himself was all the better for his expansion of consciousness, for, as he said to George Willard later, "I want to learn things, you see. That's why I did it."

The Reverend Curtis Hartman ("The Strength of God") had felt his life become stale and empty; he had come to dread delivering his weekly sermon and "dreamed of the day when a strong sweet new current of power would come like a great wind into his voice and his soul and the people would tremble before the spirit of God made manifest in him." Instead he is visited by an awesome lust for the teacher Kate Swift. In a bit of strenuous allegory, Anderson depicts him as seeing her in her bedroom through a chink in the stained-glass window of his church. Night after night he watched her, racked by his conscience, yet unable to repress his passion. He had almost determined to throw over his cure of souls and become a "creature of carnal lusts," declaring that man "has no right to forget he is an animal," when he noticed that Kate, who is now naked, has begun to weep and to pray. Instantly his lust is quite sublimated away, and his desire for her as a woman is replaced by a sympathy and concern for her as a person. As he tells the baffled George Willard later that night, "After ten years in this town, God has manifested himself to me in the body of a woman...."

Earlier on the same night that the Reverend Hartman was to undergo his revelation, Kate, who was "the most eagerly passionate soul" among the inhabitants of Winesburg, sets out in search of George Willard, an ex-pupil in whom "she had recognized the spark of genius." On another occasion she had been filled with a "passionate desire to have him understand the import of life," and their interview had closed with a kiss from which she broke away, declaring angrily that "it will be ten years before you begin to understand what I mean when I talk to you." But on this fateful evening she became again possessed by the impulse to communicate with George, to try again "to open

the door of life" for the boy whose potential for communication she had divined, and once again the attempted moment of epiphany was obscured by sexual excitement. "So strong was her passion that it became something physical," and she allowed George to take her into his arms, only to break away, leaving him alone, confused and "swearing furiously." It is Kate's frustration at being unable to communicate with George which precipitates the moment of despair in her bedroom. And, ironically, it is the sight of that despair that brings about the dramatic enlargement of the Reverend Hartman's understanding of humanity. George Willard, however, had managed to confuse the Reverend's exaltation with madness and Kate's compassionate concern with garden-variety lubricity, and he goes to bed that night muttering, "I have missed something." He has indeed something, but he will not have to wait ten years until he begins to understand what it is.

Several years ago, Edwin Fussell [in "*Winesburg, Ohio:* Art and Isolation," *Modern Fiction Studies,* VI (summer, 1960), pp. 106–14] addressed himself to the popular critical exercise of attempting to isolate the unifying elements which make *Winesburg* something more than a series of loosely articulated short stories. Wondering whether the simple themes of "loneliness and isolation" were really enough to account for the work's cumulative effect, Fussell argued persuasively that the real unity of the work is not to be found among the grotesques themselves, but rather in their relation to George Willard. *Winesburg,* he felt, is in the tradition of the *Bildungsroman,* and in it we may observe at work the theme of George Willard's maturation as an artist. My reading of *Winesburg* has brought it home to me that Fussell is essentially correct in his appreciation of the fact that George Willard's development as an artist is central to the meaning of the work, but it has also suggested that the *Bildungsroman* view of *Winesburg* may be enlarged to include the complementary theme of George's development from a merely passionate, dull sublunary lover to the stage of becoming an initiate of the more Platonic aspects of human love. At the book's end George too seems to have grasped the simultaneous and arcane truths of virginity and passion.

In the early episode called "Nobody Knows," we observe George Willard's conduct of his first amorous affair in concert with the obliging Louise Trunnion. His approach to Louise is marked by adolescent awe and shy terror, but, once he has had her, he comports himself like any other coarse, rustic roaring-boy, desiring to boast of his conquest while at the same time meanly assuring himself that "she hasn't got anything on me." The incident is entirely physical and egotistical with none of the expansion of consciousness and the quality of communion which Anderson so valued. A little later in the book—in the twin episodes of "The Strength of God" and "The Teacher"—we see that George still takes a most mundane view of the nature of human passion as he utterly fails to appreciate the quality of the emotions animating the Reverend Hartman and Kate Swift. It is, in fact, not until we reach the adventure which is aptly called "An Awakening" that we see any notable tendency in George to view love on any but the most basic terms. Here we discover George in the toils of a frustrated physical passion for Belle Carpenter which becomes converted into a mystical yearning for self-expression of a more abstract nature than the merely sexual. Some little time after this, George's encounter with the gentle, mystical Tom Foster is described in "Drink," and the stage is set for George's initiation into the company of Love's Elect in "Death" and "Sophistication."

A remarkable experience overtakes George at the death-bed of his mother. He has come there unwillingly, for he has had to break an appointment with Helen White to do so and, even as he stands by his mother's corpse, he is preoccupied by persistent sexual fantasies: "He closed his eyes and imagined that the red young lips of Helen White touched his own lips." So absorbing were these imaginings that his "body trembled" and "his hands shook," and then, as Anderson simply puts it, "something happened." George became convinced that it was not the corpse of his mother before him, but rather the "unspeakably lovely" body of a young and graceful living girl. Running out of the room, and "urged by some impulse outside himself," George exclaimed, "The dear, the dear, oh the lovely dear," thereby unconsciously echoing the words uttered years before by Dr. Reefy when, for a moment, he held the living Elizabeth Willard in his arms.

Although the symbolism here cannot be subjected to any very precise analysis in terms of conventional discourse, I believe that the conversion of George's sexual impulses into a vision of his mother as a young and desirable girl is more than simply Oedipal, and emphasizes instead the subtle connection which Anderson discerned between *eros* and *agapé*—between a specific, egocentric sexual desire and a generalized love and sympathy for humanity.

In any event, George's attitude toward Helen White has changed considerably in "Sophistication," *Winesburg*'s penultimate episode. Here Anderson shows us George Willard as he and Helen walk out together one evening to the deserted fair ground. This is a tender interlude, and he and Helen hold hands and kiss, but Anderson takes especial care to indicate that the nature of their relationship is now more than simply sexual, and indeed, that the physical aspect of love would constitute a profanation of the feeling that had taken hold of them, the feeling that "makes the mature life of men and women in the modern world possible." There is a sense of communion between them, but there is also the sad knowledge of the essential and inviolate loneliness that must tinge all mature affection. In describing the state of George's mind as this bittersweet emotion replaces his earlier desire, Anderson employs an almost Manichaean imagery: "In youth there are always two forces fighting in people. The warm unthinking little animal struggles against … the more sophisticated thing [that] had possession of George Willard."

Standing in the deserted fairground, George felt a "reverence for Helen. He wanted to love and to be loved by her but he did not want at the moment to be confused by her womanhood." On this note, one which is reminiscent of the arcane code of Courtly Love, George Willard may be said to have completed, in Anderson's terms, his novitiate in art, in life, and in love. An ardent candidate for experience, he has sublimated his passion and achieved, for the moment at least, the delicate equipoise between "the truth of virginity and the truth of passion."

Source: George D. Murphy, "The Theme of Sublimation in Anderson's *Winesburg, Ohio*" in *Modern Fiction Studies,* Vol. 13, No. 2, summer, 1967, pp. 237–46.

Sources

Sherwood Anderson, *Sherwood Anderson's Memoirs,* edited by Ray Lewis White, The University of North Carolina Press, 1942.

Sam Bluefarb, "George Willard: Death and Resurrection," in *The Escape Motif in the American Novel: Mark Twain to Richard Wright,* Ohio State University Press, 1972, pp. 42-58.

H. W. Boynton, "All Over The Lot," in *The Bookman,* Volume XLIX, No. 6, August, 1919, pp. 728-34.

Carl Bredahl, "'The Young Thing Within': Divided Narrative and Sherwood Anderson's *Winesburg, Ohio,*" in *The*

Midwest Quarterly, Vol. XXVII, No. 4, summer, 1986, pp. 422-37.

Malcolm Cowley, "An Introduction to *Winesburg, Ohio,*" The Viking Press, 1960, pp. 1-15.

Waldo Frank, "*Winesburg, Ohio* After Twenty Years," in *Story,* Vol. XIX, No. 91, September-October, 1941, pp. 29-33.

James M. Mellard, "Narrative Forms in *Winesburg, Ohio,*" in *PMLS,* Vol. 83, No. 5, October, 1968, pp. 1304-312.

"A Gutter Would Be Spoon River," in *New York Sun,* June 1, 1919, p. 3.

Tony Tanner, "Sherwood Anderson's Little Things," in *The Reign of Wonder: Naivete and Reality in American Literature,* Cambridge University Press, 1965, pp. 205-27.

Rebecca West, "*Winesburg, Ohio,*" in *New Statesman,* Vol. XIX, No. 484, July 22, 1922, pp. 443-44.

For Further Study

David D. Anderson, "Moments of Insight" in *Sherwood Anderson: An Introduction and Interpretation,* Barnes and Noble, 1967, pp. 37-54.

Views *Winesburg, Ohio* as a "collection of short stories and sketches" and emphasizes Anderson's focus on problems of communication. Describes Anderson's narrative mode as "character-plotting," in which changes in the character's state are more important than outward incident.

Maxwell Anderson, "A Country Town," in *Critical Essays on Sherwood Anderson,* edited by David D. Anderson, G. K. Hall & Co., 1981, pp. 32-4.

This review of *Winesburg, Ohio,* originally published in *The New Republic* in June of 1919, shows that at least some of the reviewers of the book's time "got" the ideas that Sherwood Anderson was presenting.

Sherwood Anderson, *The Writer at His Craft,* edited by Jack Salzman, David D. Anderson, and Kichinosuke Ohashi, Paul P. Appel Publisher, 1979.

A collection of Anderson's minor texts, including reviews, tributes to other writers, travel sketches, and notes on writing. A good source of background to Anderson's writing career.

Walter Benjamin, "The Storyteller," in *Illuminations,* edited by Harry Zohn, Schocken, 1968, pp. 83-109.

A brilliant essay, focused on the 19th-century Russian writer Nikolai Leskov. Benjamin establishes important distinctions between novels and storytelling in their handling of time, their relation to readers, the nature of experience, and the place of death. He sees in Leskov the remnants of a storytelling culture about

to disappear definitively with industrialization and the rise of information.

Peter Brooks, "The Storyteller," in *Psychoanalysis and Storytelling,* Blackwell, 1994, pp. 76-103.

Though not specifically about Anderson, Brooks provides ways of thinking about the meaning of storytelling in *Winesburg, Ohio.*

Irving Howe, "The Book of the Grotesque," in *Sherwood Anderson,* William Sloane Associates, 1951, pp. 91-109.

Interprets Anderson's use of the grotesque as ethically motivated. The grotesques are those who have sought the truth and been misled; grotesqueness is not merely deformity, but also the trace of deeper feeling that has been damaged or estranged.

Clarence Lindsay, "The Community in *Winesburg, Ohio:* The Rhetoric of Selfhood," in *Midamerica,* No. 15, 1988, pp. 39-47.

Challenges "romantic" readings of Anderson's characters that pit the good individual against the bad, narrow-minded community. Anderson uses subtle irony to unsettle this opposition, showing how characters use it rhetorically to justify isolating themselves and defining themselves as different.

William L. Phillips, "How Sherwood Anderson Wrote *Winesburg, Ohio,*" in *Winesburg, Ohio: Text and Criticism,* edited by John H. Ferres, Penguin, 1996, pp. 267-90.

An important study, based on manuscripts discovered in the 1940s, of the genesis of *Winesburg, Ohio.* The manuscripts reveal that Anderson had a large-scale work in mind in composing the individual chapters and that the book versions of the chapters published separately in magazines were often closer to the original drafts.

David Stouck, "Anderson's Expressionist Art," in *New Essays on Winesburg, Ohio,* edited by John W. Crowley, Cambridge University Press, 1990, pp. 27-51.

Discusses Anderson's connections with modernist painting and writing.

Wellford Dunaway Taylor, "Anderson and the Problem of Belonging," in *Sherwood Anderson: Dimensions of His Literary Art,* edited by David D. Anderson, Michigan State University Press, 1976, pp. 63-75.

Examines Anderson's status as an "outsider" in the world of literature, speculating on how that may have helped form the prevailing mood of *Winesburg, Ohio.*

Ray Lewis White, *Winesburg, Ohio: An Exploration,* Twayne Publishers, Inc., 1990.

White is one of the foremost scholars on Anderson's works, having edited all three volumes of the author's autobiography and written numerous books and articles about him. This one explores three themes: "The Youth," "The Grotesques," and "The Town and the Time."

The Women of Brewster Place

Gloria Naylor

1982

The Women of Brewster Place depicts seven courageous black women struggling to survive life's harsh realities. Since the book was first published in 1982, critics have praised Gloria Naylor's characters. They contend that her vivid portrayal of the women, their relationships, and their battles represents the same intense struggle all human beings face in their quest for long, happy lives. For example, in a review published in *Freedomways,* Loyle Hairston says that the characters " ... throb with vitality amid the shattering of their hopes and dreams." Many commentators have noted the same deft touch with the novel's supporting characters; in fact, Hairston also notes, "Other characters are ... equally well-drawn."

Most critics consider Naylor one of America's most talented contemporary African-American authors. Her success probably stems from her exploration of the African-American experience, and her desire to "... help us celebrate voraciously that which is ours," as she tells Bellinelli in the interview series, *In Black and White.* She stresses that African Americans must maintain their identity in a world dominated by whites. Hairston, however, believes Naylor sidesteps the real racial issues. In his *Freedomways* review, he says of *The Women of Brewster Place:* "Naylor's first effort seems to fall in with most of the fiction being published today, which bypasses provocative social themes to play, instead, in the shallower waters of isolated personal relationships."

Author Biography

The oldest of three girls, Naylor was born in New York City on January 25, 1950. Her family moved several times during her childhood, living at different times in a housing project in upper Bronx, a Harlem apartment building, and in Queens. When Naylor graduated from high school in 1968, she became a minister for the Jehovah's Witnesses. To fund her work as a minister, she lived with her parents and worked as a switchboard operator. In 1974, Naylor moved first to North Carolina and then to Florida to practice full-time ministry, but had to work in fast-food restaurants and as a telephone operator to help support her religious work. She left the Jehovah's Witnesses in 1975 and moved back home; shortly after returning to New York, she suffered a nervous breakdown.

Later that year, Naylor began to study nursing at Medgar Evers College, then transferred to Brooklyn College of CUNY to study English. Two years later, she read Toni Morrison's *The Bluest Eye;* it was the first time she had read a novel written by a black woman. Dismayed to learn that there were very few books written by black women about black women, she began to believe that her education in northern integrated schools had deprived her of learning about the long tradition of black history and literature. She resolved to write about her heritage—the black woman in America. She completed *The Women of Brewster Place* in 1981, the same year she received her Bachelor of Arts degree.

Naylor earned a Master of Arts degree in Afro-American Studies from Yale University in 1983. That same year, she received the American Book Award for Best First Novel, served as writer-in-residence at Cummington Community of the Arts, and was a visiting lecturer at George Washington University. Since 1983, Naylor has continued to write, lecture, and receive awards for her writing.

Naylor attributes the success of *The Women of Brewster Place* as well as her other novels to her ability to infuse her work with personal experience. While Naylor's characters are fictional, they immortalize the spirit of her own grandmother, great aunt, and mother.

Plot Summary

Gloria Naylor's *The Women of Brewster Place* is made up of seven stories of the women who live

Gloria Naylor

on Brewster Place, a dead end street cut off from the city by a wall.

Mattie Michael

Mattie's journey to Brewster Place begins in rural Tennessee, but when she becomes pregnant she leaves town to avoid her father's wrath. For a while she manages to earn just enough money to pay rent on the room she shares with her baby, Basil. One night a rat bites the baby while they are sleeping and Mattie begins to search for a better place to live. Just as she is about to give up, she meets Eva Turner, an old woman who lives with her granddaughter, Ciel. Eva invites Mattie in for dinner and offers her a place to stay. Years later when the old woman dies, Mattie has saved enough money to buy the house. Ciel's parents take her away, but Mattie stays on with Basil. She refuses to see any faults in him, and when he gets in trouble with the law she puts up her house to bail him out of jail. When he jumps bail, she loses the house she had worked thirty years to own, and her long journey from Tennessee finally ends in a small apartment on Brewster Place.

Etta Mae Johnson

Though Etta's journey starts in the same small town as Mattie's, the path she takes to Brewster

Place is very different. Discovering early on that America is not yet ready for a bold, confident, intelligent black woman, she learns to survive by attaching herself "to any promising rising black star, and when he burnt out, she found another." She joins Mattie on Brewster Place after leaving the last in a long series of men. Attending church with Mattie, she stares enviously at the "respectable" wives of the deacons and wishes that she had taken a different path. Eyeing the attractive visiting preacher, she wonders if it is not still possible for her to change her lot in life. When Reverend Woods clearly returns her interest, Etta gladly accepts his invitation to go out for coffee, though Mattie expresses her concerns about his intentions. By the end of the evening Etta realizes that Mattie was right, and she walks up Brewster Street with a broken spirit. As she climbs the stairs to the apartment, however, she hears Mattie playing Etta's "loose life" records. With pleasure she realizes that someone is waiting up for her.

Kiswana Browne

Kiswana is a young woman from a middle-class black family. Idealistic and yearning to help others, she dropped out of college and moved onto Brewster Place to live amongst other African-American people. She resents her conservative parents and their middle-class values and feels that her family has rejected their black heritage. When her mother comes to visit her they quarrel over Kiswana's choice of neighborhood and over her decision to leave school. Kiswana thinks that she is nothing like her mother, but when her mother's temper flares Kiswana has to admit that she admires her mother and that they are more alike that she had realized.

Lucielia Louise Turner

Ciel, the grandchild of Eva Turner, also ends up on Brewster Place. Her chapter begins with the return of the boyfriend who had left her eleven months before when their baby, Serena, was only a month old. She is relieved to have him back, and she is still in love with him, so she tries to ignore his irresponsible behavior and mean temper. When she becomes pregnant again, however, it becomes harder to deny the problems. He complains that he will never be able to get ahead with her and two babies to care for, and although she does not want to do it, she gets an abortion. When he leaves her anyway, she finally sees him for what he is, and only regrets that she had not had this realization before the abortion. As she is thinking this, they

hear a scream from Serena, who had stuck a fork in an electrical outlet. After the child's death, Ciel nearly dies from grief. She stops eating and refuses to take care of herself, but Mattie will not let her die and finally gets Ciel to face her grief.

Cora Lee

Cora Lee began life as a little girl who loved playing with new baby dolls. As a grown woman she continues to love the feel and smell of new babies, but once they grow into children she is frustrated with how difficult they are. She stops even trying to keep any one man around; she prefers the "shadows" who come in the night. With these anonymous men, she gets pregnant, but doesn't have to endure the beatings or disappointment intimacy might bring. To pacify Kiswana, Cora Lee agrees to take her children to a Shakespeare play in the local park. As she watches the actors on stage and her children in the audience she is filled with remorse for not having been a more responsible parent. She vows that she will start helping them with homework and walking them to school. She comes home that night filled with good intentions. She will encourage her children, and they can grow up to be important, talented people, like the actors on the stage. But when she finds another "shadow" in her bedroom, she sighs, and lets her cloths drop to the floor.

The Two

When Lorraine and Teresa first move onto Brewster street, the other women are relieved that they seem like nice girls who will not be after their husbands. But soon the neighbors start to notice the loving looks that pass between the two women, and soon the other women in the neighborhood reject Lorraine's gestures of friendship. Teresa, the bolder of the two, doesn't care what the neighbors think of them, and she doesn't understand why Lorraine does care. Feeling rejected both by her neighbors and by Teresa, Lorraine finds comfort in talking to Ben, the old alcoholic handyman of Brewster Place. Lorraine reminds Ben of his estranged daughter, and Lorraine finds in Ben a new father to replace the one who kicked her out when she refused to lie about being a lesbian. One night after an argument with Teresa, Lorraine decides to go visit Ben. As she passes through the alley near the wall, she is attacked by C.C. Baker and his friends, the teenage boys who terrorize Brewster Place. All six of the boys rape her, leaving her near death. In her delirium and pain she sees movement at the end of the alley, and she picks up a brick to protect herself from what she perceives as a possible threat. She beats the drunken and oblivious Ben to death before Mattie can reach her and stop her.

The Block Party

For a week after Ben's death it rains continuously, and although they will not admit it to each other, all the women dream of Lorraine that week. The sun comes out for the block party that Kiswana has been organizing to raise money to take the landlord to court. The party seems joyful and successful, and Ciel even returns to see Mattie. But even Ciel, who doesn't know what has happened by the wall, reports that she has been dreaming of Ben and Lorraine. The rain begins to fall again and Kiswana tries to get people to pack up, but they seem desperate to continue the party. Then Cora Lee notices that there is still blood on the bricks. In a frenzy the women begin tearing down the wall. Then suddenly Mattie awakes. It is morning and the sun is still shining; the wall is still standing, and everyone is getting ready for the block party.

Characters

Ben

Ben belongs to Brewster Place even before the seven women do. The first black on Brewster Place, he arrived in 1953, just prior to the Supreme Court's Brown vs. Topeka decision. The Mediterranean families knew him as the man who would quietly do repairs with alcohol on his breath. He bothered no one and was noticed only when he sang "Swing Low, Sweet Chariot."

As black families move onto the street, Ben remains on Brewster Place. He befriends Lorraine when no one else will. She reminds him of his daughter, and this friendship assuages the guilt he feels over his daughter's fate. When he sharecropped in the South, his crippled daughter was sexually abused by a white landowner, and Ben felt powerless to do anything about it. He lives with this pain until Lorraine mistakenly kills him in her pain and confusion after being raped.

Kiswana Browne

Kiswana grew up in Linden Hills, a "rich" neighborhood not far from Brewster Place. She leaves her middle-class family, turning her back on an upbringing that, she feels, ignored her heritage. Light-skinned, with smooth hair, Kiswana wants desperately to feel a part of the black community

Media Adaptations

- King Phoenix Entertainment produced *The Women of Brewster Place* as a made-for-TV drama in 1989. Directed by Donna Deitch, the movie starred Oprah Winfrey and Cicely Tyson.

- *The Women of Brewster Place* ran as a 30-minute weekly TV series during May and June of 1990. Oprah Winfrey starred as Mattie Michael and was the only cast member included from the original TV movie. The series was produced by Winfrey, Earl Hamner, and Donald Sipes.

- *The Women of Brewster Place* made-for-TV drama is available on home video distributed by J2 Communications.

and to help her fellow African Americans better their lives. After dropping out of college, Kiswana moves to Brewster Place to be a part of a predominantly African-American community. She becomes friends with Cora Lee and succeeds, for one night, in showing her a different life. In a ironic turn, Kiswana believes that her mother denies her heritage; during a confrontation, she is surprised when she learns that the two share a great deal.

Melanie Browne

See Kiswana Browne

Butch Fuller

Butch Fuller exudes charm. Built strong by his years as a field hand, and cinnamon skinned, Mattie finds him irresistible. Mattie's father, Samuel, despises him. He believes that Butch is worthless and warns Mattie to stay away from him. Butch succeeds in seducing Mattie and, unbeknownst to him, is the father of the baby she carries when she leaves Rock Vale, Tennessee.

Etta Mae Johnson

Etta Mae Johnson and Mattie Michael grew up together in Rock Vale, Tennessee. While they are

From the film The Women of Brewster Place, *starring Oprah Winfrey as Mattie Michael.*

complete opposites, they have remained friends throughout the years, providing comfort to one another at difficult times in their lives.

Etta Mae Johnson arrives at Brewster Place with style. Driving an apple-green Cadillac with a white vinyl top and Florida plates, Etta Mae causes quite a commotion when she arrives at Brewster Place. The children gather around the car, and the adults wait to see who will step out of it. She disappoints no one in her tight willow-green sundress and her large two-toned sunglasses.

Etta Mae has always lived a life very different from that of Mattie Michael. As a black girl growing up in a still-segregated South, Etta Mae broke

all the rules. She did not believe in being submissive to whites, and she did not want to marry, be a mother, and remain with the same man for the rest of her life. She is a woman who knows her own mind. While the rest of her friends attended church, dated, and married the kinds of men they were expected to, Etta Mae kept Rock Vale in an uproar. "Rock Vale had no place for a black woman who was not only unwilling to play by the rules, but whose spirit challenged the very right of the game to exist." Etta Mae was always looking for something that was just out of her reach, attaching herself to "… any promising rising black star, and when he burnt out, she found another." As a result,

Etta Mae spends her life moving from one man to the next, living a life about which her beloved Billie Holiday, a blues musician, sings.

Cora Lee

Cora Lee loves making and having babies, even though she does not really like men. Her story starts with a description of her happy childhood. An obedient child, Cora Lee made good grades in school and loved playing with baby dolls. When Cora Lee turned thirteen, however, her parents felt that she was too old for baby dolls and gave her a Barbie. When she discovers that sex produces babies, she starts to have sex in order to get pregnant. Cora Lee has several young children when Kiswana discovers her and decides to help Cora Lee change her life. Only when Kiswana says that "babies grow up" does Cora Lee begin to question her life; she realizes that while she does like babies, she does not know what to do with children when they grow up. For one evening, Cora Lee envisions a new life for herself and her children. Yet, when she returns to her apartment, she climbs into bed with another man.

Lorraine

See The Two

Basil Michael

Mattie names her son, Basil, for the pleasant memory of the afternoon he was conceived in a fragrant basil patch. Unfortunately, he causes Mattie nothing but heartache. He seldom works. He never helps his mother around the house. He associates with the wrong people. Much to his Mattie's dismay, he ends up in trouble and in jail. When he jumps bail, Mattie loses her house. Basil leaves Mattie without saying goodbye.

Fannie Michael

Fannie Michael is Mattie's mother. Fannie speaks her mind and often stands up to her husband, Samuel. She assures Mattie that carrying a baby is nothing to be ashamed about. She tries to protect Mattie from the brutal beating Samuel Michael gives her when she refuses to name her baby's father. Unable to stop him in any other way, Fannie cocks the shotgun against her husband's chest.

Mattie Michael

Mattie is the matriarch of Brewster Place; throughout the novel, she plays a motherly role for all of the characters. While the novel opens with Mattie as a woman in her 60s, it quickly flashes back to Mattie's teen years in Rock Vale, Tennessee, where Mattie lives a sheltered life with her over-protective father, Samuel, and her mother, Fannie. Mattie allows herself to be seduced by Butch Fuller, whom Samuel thinks is worthless. When Samuel discovers that Mattie is pregnant by Fuller, he goes into a rage and beats her. To escape her father, Mattie leaves Tennessee to stay with her friend, Etta Mae Johnson, in Asheville, North Carolina. Mattie's son, Basil, is born five months later. Etta Mae soon departs for New York, leaving Mattie to fend for herself. After a frightening episode with a rat in her apartment, Mattie looks for new housing. She meets Eva Turner and her granddaughter, Lucielia (Ciel), and moves in with them. Later, when Turner passes away, Mattie buys Turner's house but loses it when she posts bail for her derelict son. Mattie is moving into Brewster Place when the novel opens. She renews ties here with both Etta Mae and Ciel. All of the Brewster Place women respect Mattie's strength, truthfulness, and morals as well as her ability to survive the abuse, loss, and betrayal she has suffered. Critic Jill Matus, in *Black American Literature Forum,* describes Mattie as "the community's best voice and sharpest eye."

Samuel Michael

Samuel Michael, a God-fearing man, is Mattie's father. Having her in his later years and already set in his ways, he tolerates little foolishness and no disobedience. He loves Mattie very much and blames himself for her pregnancy, until she tells him that the baby is not Fred Watson's—the man he had chosen for her. He loses control and beats Mattie in an attempt to get her to name the baby's father.

The Two

"The Two" are unique amongst the Brewster Place women because of their sexual relationship, as well as their relationship with their female neighbors. The other women do not view Theresa and Lorraine as separate individuals, but refer to them as "The Two." As lesbians, Lorraine and Theresa represent everything foreign to the other women. Lorraine feels the women's hostility and longs to be accepted. Theresa, on the other hand, makes no apologies for her lifestyle and gets angry with Lorraine for wanting to fit in with the women. Theresa wants Lorraine to toughen up—to accept who she is and not try to please other people. Lorraine turns to the janitor, Ben, for friendship. Ben relates to her because she reminds him of his daughter. Later in the novel, a street gang rapes Lorraine, and she kills Ben, mistaking him for her attackers. She dies, and Theresa regrets her final words to her.

Theresa

See The Two

Ciel Turner

Ciel first appears in the story as Eva Turner's granddaughter. Early on, she lives with Turner and Mattie in North Carolina. When Mattie moves to Brewster Place, Ciel has grown up and has a child of her own. Ciel loves her husband, Eugene, even though he abuses her verbally and threatens physical harm. Her life revolves around her relationship with her husband and her desperate attempts to please him. After she aborts the child she knows Eugene does not want, she feels remorse and begins to understand the kind of person Eugene really is. Unfortunately, the realization comes too late for Ciel. She goes into a deep depression after her daughter's death, but Mattie succeeds in helping her recover.

Miss Eva Turner

Miss Eva opens her home to Mattie and her infant son, Basil. She shares her wisdom with Mattie, resulting from years of experience with men and children. Miss Eva warns Mattie to be stricter with Basil, believing that he will take advantage of her. She also encourages Mattie to save her money. When Miss Eva dies, her spirit lives on in the house that Mattie is able to buy from Miss Eva's estate.

Lucielia Turner

See Ciel Turner

Themes

Community

According to Webster, in *The Living Webster Encyclopedic Dictionary of the English Language,* the word "community" means "the state of being held in common; common possession, enjoyment, liability, etc." Naylor uses Brewster Place to provide one commonality among the women who live there. The women all share the experience of living on the dead end street that the rest of the world has forgotten. It is on Brewster Place that the women encounter everyday problems, joys, and sorrows. In her interview with Carabi, Naylor maintains that community influences one's identity. While the women were not literally born within the community of Brewster Place, the community provides the backdrop for their lives.

Female Bonding

Naylor captures the strength of ties among women. While these ties have always existed, the women's movement has brought them more recognition. According to Annie Gottlieb in *Women Together,* a review of *The Women of Brewster Place,* "... all our lives those relationships had been the backdrop, while the sexy, angry fireworks with men were the show ... the bonds between women are the abiding ones. Most men are incalculable hunters who come and go." Throughout *The Women of Brewster Place,* the women support one another, counteracting the violence of their fathers, boyfriends, husbands, and sons. For example, while Mattie Michael loses her home as a result of her son's irresponsibility, the strength she gains enables her to care for the women whom she has known either since childhood and early adulthood or through her connection to Brewster Place. She provides shelter and a sense of freedom to her old friend, Etta Mae; also, she comes to the aid of Ciel when Ciel loses her desire to live. It is the bond among the women that supports the continuity of life on Brewster Place.

Violence Against Women

The novel begins with a flashback to Mattie's life as a typical young woman. But this ordinary life is brought to an abrupt halt by her father's brutal attack on her for refusing to divulge the name of her baby's father. From that episode on, Naylor portrays men as people who take advantage of others. The men in the story exhibit cowardice, alcoholism, violence, laziness, and dishonesty. The final act of violence, the gang rape of Lorraine, underscores men's violent tendencies, emphasizing the differences between the sexes.

Alienation and Loneliness

Victims of ignorance, violence, and prejudice, all of the women in the novel are alienated from their families, other people, and God. For example, when Mattie leaves her home after her father beats her, she never again sees her parents. Then her son, for whom she gave up her life, leaves without saying goodbye. Throughout the story, Naylor creates situations that stress the loneliness of the characters. Especially poignant is Lorraine's relationship with Ben. Having been rejected by people they love

Topics For Further Study

- In the book, *Gloria Naylor: In Search Of Sanctuary,* author Virginia Fowler contends that Naylor structured *Mama Day* after Faulkner's *As I Lay Dying.* Confirm or contradict this assertion with a detailed explanation supported by examples.

- One critic has said that the protagonist of *The Women of Brewster Place* is actually the street itself. The street undergoes birth, maturation, aging, and death. Create a visual that depicts the street as the protagonist. Be prepared to explain your visual, relating the specific ways that it represents the entire story.

- Research the music of Billie Holiday. Review the lyrics of several of her songs. Why do you think Etta Mae Johnson liked her music? Support your answer with details about Etta Mae's character as well as specific lyrics from three or more songs.

- Kiswana (Melanie) Browne denounces her parents' middle-class lifestyle, adopts an African name, drops out of college, and moves to Brewster Place to be close to those to whom she refers as "my people." One critic has said that her character may be modeled after adherents of the Black Power movement of the 1960s. Research the era to discover what the movement was, who was involved, and what the goals and achievements were.

- After Ciel underwent an abortion, she had difficulty returning to the daily routine of her life. Although eventually she did mend physically, there were signs that she had not come to terms with her feelings about the abortion. Give evidence from the story that supports this notion. Research the psychological effects of abortion, and relate the evidence from the story to the information you have discovered.

- When Naylor read Morrison's *The Bluest Eye* in 1977, she was appalled to find that there were few other books written by black women about black women. See how many books you can find that were available at that time, and create a bibliography for these books. Then, locate as many as you can find that are available now, and create a second bibliography.

- Why are there now more books written by black females about black females than there were twenty years ago? Explain. Provide detailed support for your answer drawing from various perspectives, including historical or sociological.

- Why were Lorraine and Theresa, "The Two," such a threat to the women who resided at Brewster Place? Give reasons. Support your reasons with evidence from the story.

---

or want to love, Lorraine and Ben become friends. Lorraine's horrifying murder of Ben serves only to deepen the chasm of hopelessness felt at different times by all the characters in the story.

African-American Heritage

Naylor wants people to understand the richness of the black heritage. She uses the community of women she has created in *The Women of Brewster Place* to demonstrate the love, trust, and hope that have always been the strong spirit of African-American women. Based on women Naylor has

known in her life, the characters convincingly portray the struggle for survival that black women have shared throughout history. Like those before them, the women who live on Brewster Place overcome their difficulties through the support and wisdom of friends who have experienced their struggles. This bond is complex and lasting; for example, when Kiswana Browne and her mother specifically discuss their heritage, they find that while they may demonstrate their beliefs differently, they share the same pride in their race. As she explains to Bellinelli in an interview, Naylor strives in *The*

Women of Brewster Place to "help us celebrate voraciously that which is ours."

Female Sexuality

Naylor uses each woman's sexuality to help define her character. Mattie's entire life changes when she allows her desire to overcome her better judgement, resulting in pregnancy. She spends her life loving and caring for her son and denies herself adult love. Etta Mae spends her life moving from one man to the next, searching for acceptance. She believes she must have a man to be happy. Ciel keeps taking Eugene back, even though he is verbally abusive and threatens her with physical abuse. She cannot admit that she craves his physical touch as a reminder of home. Cora Lee does not necessarily like men, but she likes having sex and the babies that result. Lorraine and Theresa love each other, and their homosexuality separates them from the other women.

Style

Structure

Critics agree that one of Naylor's strongest accomplishments in *The Women of Brewster Place* is her use of the setting to frame the structure of the novel, and often compare it to Sherwood Anderson's *Winesburg, Ohio.* Naylor sets the story within Brewster Place so that she can focus on telling each woman's story in relationship to her ties to the community. According to Fowler in *Gloria Naylor: In Search of Sanctuary,* Naylor believes that "individual identity is shaped within the matrix of a community." Thus, living in Brewster Place partly defines who the women are and becomes an important part of each woman's personal history.

Point of View

Naylor created seven female characters with seven individual voices. Naylor tells each woman's story through the woman's own voice. That is, Naylor writes from the first-person point of view, but she writes from the perspective of the character on whom the story is focusing at the time. In Bonetti's, *An Interview with Gloria Naylor,* Naylor said "one character, one female protagonist, could not even attempt to represent the riches and diversity of the black female experience." This technique works for Naylor because she has used the setting to provide the unity underlying the story. Brewster Place provides the connection among the seven very unique women with stories of their own to tell.

Personification

Naylor gives Brewster Place human characteristics, using a literary technique known as personification. In this case, Brewster Place undergoes life processes. Brewster Place is born, in Naylor's words, a "bastard child," mothers three generations, and "waits to die," having "watched its last generation of children torn away from it by court orders and eviction notices … too tired and sick to help them." Naylor tells the women's stories within the framework of the street's life—between its birth and its death.

Allegory

The extended comparison between the street's "life" and the women's lives make the work an "allegory." All of the women, like the street, fully experience life with its high and low points. At the end of the story, the women continue to take care of one another and to hope for a better future, just as Brewster Place, in its final days, tries to sustain its final generations.

Symbolism

Naylor uses many symbols in *The Women of Brewster Place.* Both literally and figuratively, Brewster Place is a dead end street—that is, the street itself leads nowhere and the women who live there are trapped by their histories, hopes, and dreams. The brick wall symbolizes the differences between the residents of Brewster Place and their rich neighbors on the other side of the wall. It also stands for the oppression the women have endured in the forms of prejudice, violence, racism, shame, and sexism. Representing the drug-dealing street gangs who rape and kill without remorse, garbage litters the alley. A final symbol, in the form of toenail polish, stands for the deeper similarities that Kiswana and her mother discover.

Climax

Naylor creates two climaxes in *The Women of Brewster Place.* The first climax occurs when Mattie succeeds in her struggle to bring Ciel back to life after the death of her daughter. The scene evokes a sense of healing and rebirth, and reinforces the sense of community among the women. The second climax, as violent as Maggie's beating in the beginning of the novel, happens when Lorraine is raped. The women again pull together, overcoming their outrage over the destruction of one of their own.

Urban decay.

Flashback

Soon after Naylor introduces each of the women in their current situations at Brewster Place, she provides more information on them through the literary technique known as "flashback." In other words, she takes the characters back in time to show their backgrounds. For example, when the novel opens, Maggie smells something cooking, and it reminds her of sugar cane. At that point, Naylor returns Maggie to her teen years in Rock Vale, Tennessee, where Butch Fuller seduced her after sharing sugar cane with her.

Historical Context

The Northern States after World War II

While Naylor sets the birth of Brewster Place right after the end of World War I, she continues the story of Brewster for approximately thirty years. Many immigrants and Southern blacks arrived in New York after the War, searching for jobs. Like many of those people, Naylor's parents, Alberta McAlpin and Roosevelt Naylor, migrated to New York in 1949. Members of poor, sharecropping families, Alberta and Roosevelt felt that New

York would provide their children with better opportunities than they had had as children growing up in a still-segregated South. The Naylors were disappointed to learn that segregation also existed in the North, although it was much less obvious. They did find, though, that their children could attend schools and had access to libraries, opportunities the Naylors had not enjoyed as black children.

The Civil Rights Movement of the 1960s

The year the Naylors moved into their home in Queens stands as a significant year in the memories of most Americans. It was 1963, a turbulent year at the beginning of the Civil Rights Movement. Most Americans remember it as the year that Medgar Evers and President John F. Kennedy were assassinated. That year also marked the August March on Washington as well as the bombing of the 16th Street Baptist Church in Birmingham. Later in the decade, Martin Luther King was assassinated, the culmination of ten years of violence against blacks. Critics say that Naylor may have fashioned Kiswana's character after activists from the 60s, particularly those associated with the Black Power Movement. According to Bellinelli in *A Conversation with Gloria Naylor,* Naylor became aware of racism during the 60s: "That's when I first began to understand that I was different and that that difference meant something negative."

The Jehovah's Witnesses

Naylor was baptized into the Jehovah's Witnesses when she was eighteen years old. At that point in her life, she believed that after the turmoil of the 1960s, there was no hope for the world. Women and people of color comprise the majority of Jehovah's Witnesses, perhaps because, according to Harrison in *Visions of Glory: A History and a Memory of Jehovah's Witnesses,* "Their religion allows their voices ... to emerge ... People listen to them; they are valuable, bearers of a life-giving message." Jehovah's Witnesses spread their message through face-to-face contact with people, but more importantly, through written publications. Naylor's writing reflects her experiences with the Jehovah's Witnesses, according to Virginia Fowler in *Gloria Naylor: In Search of Sanctuary. The Women of Brewster Place* portrays a close-knit community of women, bound in sisterhood as a defense against a corrupt world. As the Jehovah's Witnesses preach destruction of the evil world, so, too, does Naylor with vivid portrayals of apocalyptic events. Two examples from *The Women of*

Brewster Place are Lorraine's rape and the rains that come after it. When Naylor speaks of her first novel, she says that the work served to "exorcise ... demons," according to Angels Carabi in *Belles Lettres 7.*

Critical Overview

Critics have praised Naylor's style since *The Women of Brewster Place* was published in 1982. They agree that Naylor's clear, yet often brash, language creates images both believable and consistent. The story's seven main characters speak to one another with undisguised affection through their humor and even their insults. Naylor places her characters in situations that evoke strong feelings, and she succeeds in making her characters come alive with realistic emotions, actions, and words. For example, Deirdre Donahue, a reviewer for the *Washington Post,* says of Naylor, "Naylor is not afraid to grapple with life's big subjects: sex, birth, love, death, grief. Her women feel deeply, and she unflinchingly transcribes their emotions ... Naylor's potency wells up from her language. With prose as rich as poetry, a passage will suddenly take off and sing like a spiritual ... Vibrating with undisguised emotion, *The Women of Brewster Place* springs from the same roots that produced the blues. Like them, her books sing of sorrows proudly borne by black women in America."

Critics also recognize Naylor's ability to make history come alive. She sets the beginning of *The Women of Brewster Place* at the end of World War I and brings it forward thirty years. The story traces the development of the civil rights movement, from a time when segregation was the norm through the beginnings of integration. The changing ethnicity of the neighborhood reflects the changing demographics of society. The women who have settled on Brewster Place exist as products of their Southern rural upbringing. Their ability to transform their lives and to stand strong against the difficulties that face them in their new environment and circumstances rings true with the spirit of black women in American today. Linda Labin asserts in *Masterpieces of Women's Literature,* "In many ways, *The Women of Brewster Place* may prove to be as significant in its way as Southern writer William Faulkner's mythic Yoknapatawpha County or Sherwood Anderson's *Winesburg, Ohio.* It provides a realistic vision of black urban women's lives and inspires readers with the courage and spirit of black women in America."

Critic Loyle Hairston readily agrees with the favorable analysis of Naylor's language, characterization, and story-telling. Yet, he remains more critical of her ability to make historical connections—to explore the depths of the human experience. In other words, he contends in a review in *Freedomways* that Naylor limits the concerns of Brewster Place to the "warts and cankers of individual personality, neglecting to delineate the origins of those social conditions which so strongly affect personality and behavior." Furthermore, he contends that he would have liked to see her provide some insight into those conditions that would enable the characters to envision hope of better times.

Hairston says that none of the characters, except for Kiswana Browne, can see beyond their current despair to brighter futures. He implies that the story has a hopeless ending. Yet other critics applaud the ending for its very reassurance that the characters will not only survive but prosper. Christine H. King asserts in *Identities and Issues in Literature,* "The ambiguity of the ending gives the story a mythic quality by stressing the continual possibility of dreams and the results of their deferral." Referring to Mattie's dream of tearing the wall down together with the women of Brewster Place, Linda Labin contends in *Masterpieces of Women's Literature:* "It is this remarkable, hope-filled ending that impresses the majority of scholars." In *Magill's Literary Annual,* Rae Stoll concurs: "Ultimately then, *The Women of Brewster Place* is an optimistic work, offering the hope for a redemptive community of love as a counterforce to isolation and violence."

While critics may have differing opinions regarding Naylor's intentions for her characters' future circumstances, they agree that Naylor successfully presents the themes of *The Women of Brewster Place.* The "community among women" stands out as the book's most obvious theme. Each of the women in the story unconditionally loves at least one other woman. This selfless love carries the women through betrayal, loss, and violence. For example, when one of the women faces the loss of a child, the others join together to offer themselves in any way that they can. This unmovable and soothing will represents the historically strong communal spirit among all women, but especially African-American women. The second theme, violence that men enact on women, connects with and strengthens the first. The men Naylor depicts in her novel are mean, cowardly, and lawless. As a result of their offenses toward the women in the

story, the women are drawn together. Many male critics complain about the negative images of black men in the story.

In summary, the general consensus of critics is that Naylor possesses a talent that is seldom seen in new writers. Critics like her style and appreciate her efforts to deal with societal issues and psychological themes. According to Stoll in *Magill's Literary Annual,* "Gloria Naylor ... is already numbered ... among the freshest and most vital voices in contemporary American literature."

Criticism

Donna Woodford

Woodford is a doctoral candidate at Washington University and has written for a wide variety of academic journals and educational publishers. In the following essay, she discusses how the dream motif in The Women of Brewster Place *connects the seven stories, forming them into a coherent novel.*

Gloria Naylor's novel, *The Women of Brewster Place,* is, as its subtitle suggests, "a novel in seven stories"; but these stories are unified by more than the street on which the characters live. The interactions of the characters and the similar struggles they live through connect the stories, as do the recurring themes and motifs. Of these unifying elements, the most notable is the dream motif, for though these women are living a nightmarish existence, they are united by their common dreams.

The novel begins with Langston Hughes's poem, "Harlem," which asks "what happens to a dream deferred?" And just as the poem suggests many answers to that question, so the novel explores many stories of deferred dreams. Each woman in the book has her own dream.

As a young, single mother, Mattie places all of her dreams on her son. She leaves her boarding house room after a rat bites him because she cannot stay "another night in that place without nightmares about things that would creep out of the walls to attack her child." She continues to protect him from harm and nightmares until he jumps bail and abandons her to her own nightmare.

Etta Mae dreams of a man who can "move her ... off of Brewster Place for good," but she, too, has her dream deferred each time that a man disappoints her.

What Do I Read Next?

- Naylor's second novel, *Linden Hills,* takes place in Linden Hills, a wealthy and privileged neighborhood; it is familiar because it is the place Kiswana Browne—a character from *The Women of Brewster Place*—left. Published by Ticknor in 1985, *Linden Hills* reminds some critics of Dante's *Inferno.* The story revolves around two young men and their observations of the effects of black aspirations in contemporary America.

- *Mama Day* is Naylor's third novel. The setting is far removed from those in the first two stories. Willow Springs, an all-black island community off the coasts of South Carolina and Georgia, is home to Cocoa and Mama Day, characters that appeared briefly in *Linden Hills.* Descendants of an African slave and sorceress, Cocoa and Mama Day lead disparate lives until Cocoa becomes desperately ill. Ticknor published *Mama Day* in 1988.

- Naylor depicts the lives of 1940s blacks living in New York City in her next novel, *Bailey's Cafe,* published by Harcourt in 1992. Set in a Brooklyn diner, the story relates the lives of the diner's varied and interesting patrons who overcome hardship to survive.

- The focus on the relationships among women in *The Women of Brewster Place* presents feminist ideals similar to those about which Amy Tan writes in *The Joy Luck Club.* Published by G. Putnam's Sons in 1989, *The Joy Luck Club* features the bonds between mothers and daughters and the strength that women share in good times and in bad.

- While love and politics link the lives of the two women in *Blood Sisters: An Examination of Conscience,* the stronger tie between them is the bond joining grandmother, mothers, and daughters. Published by St. Martin's Press, and written by Valerie Miner, this story portrays three generations of an Irish clan and the struggles among its men and women.

- Critics have compared the theme of familial and African-American women in *The Women of Brewster Place* to the same theme in *The Color Purple,* published in 1992 by Harcourt and Brace. Author Alice Walker writes a story of two sisters that vividly portrays the bonds between black women.

Kiswana, an outsider on Brewster Place, is constantly dreaming of ways in which she can organize the residents and enact social reform. Even as she looks out her window at the wall that separates Brewster Place from the heart of the city, she is daydreaming: "she placed her dreams on the back of the bird and fantasized that it would glide forever in transparent silver circles until it ascended to the center of the universe and was swallowed up." But just as the pigeon she watches fails to ascend gracefully and instead lands on a fire escape "with awkward, frantic movements," so Kiswana's dreams of a revolution will be frustrated by the grim realities of Brewster Place and the awkward, frantic movements of people who are busy merely trying to survive.

Ciel dreams of love, from her boyfriend and from her daughter and unborn child, but an unwanted abortion, the death of her daughter, and the abandonment by her boyfriend cruelly frustrates these hopes. She is left dreaming only of death, a suicidal nightmare from which only Mattie's nurturing love can awaken her.

Lorraine dreams of acceptance and a place where she doesn't "feel any different from anybody else in the world." She finds this place, temporarily, with Ben, and he finds in her a reminder of the lost daughter who haunts his own dreams. But their dreams will be ended brutally with her rape and his death, and the image of Lorraine will later haunt the dreams of all the women on Brewster Place. But perhaps the most revealing stories about dreams are those told in "Cora Lee" and "The Block Party."

Cora Lee's story opens with a quotation from Shakespeare's *A Midsummer Night's Dream:* "True, I talk of dreams, / Which are the children of an idle brain / begot of nothing but vain fantasy." The quotation is appropriate to Cora Lee's story not only because Cora and her children will attend the play but also because Cora's chapter will explore the connection between the begetting of children and the begetting of dreams. It will also examine the point at which dreams become "vain fantasy."

As a child Cora dreams of new baby dolls. When her parents refuse to give her another for her thirteenth Christmas, she is heartbroken. Her mother tries to console her by telling her that she still has all her old dolls, but Cora plaintively says, "But they don't smell and feel the same as the new ones." As an adult, she continues to prefer the smell and feel of her new babies to the trials and hassles of her growing children. Her babies "just seemed to keep coming—always welcome until they changed, and then she just didn't understand them." Once they grow beyond infancy she finds them "wild and disgusting" and she makes little attempt to understand or parent them. They no longer fit into her dream of a sweet, dependent baby who needs no one but her.

Kiswana finds one of these wild children eating out of a dumpster, and soon Kiswana and Cora become friends. Confiding to Cora, Kiswana talks about her dreams of reform and revolution. Excitedly she tells Cora, "if we really pull together, we can put pressure on [the landlord] to start fixing this place up." She is similarly convinced that it will be easy to change Cora's relationship with her children, and she eagerly invites them to her boyfriend's production of *A Midsummer Night's Dream.* Cora is skeptical, but to pacify Kiswana she agrees to go.

It is at the performance of Shakespeare's play where the dreams of the two women temporarily merge. The production, sponsored by a grant from the city, does indeed inspire Cora to dream for her older children. She imagines that her daughter Maybelline "could be doing something like this some day—standing on a stage, wearing pretty clothes and saying fine things .... Maybelline could go to college—she liked school." When she remembers with guilt that her children no longer like school and are often truant, she resolves to change her behavior in order to ensure them brighter futures:

> "Junior high; high school; college—none of them stayed little forever. And then on to good jobs in insurance companies and the post office, even doctors and lawyers. Yes, that's what would happen to her babies."

Her new dream of maternal devotion continues as they arrive home and prepare for bed. She tucks them in and the children do not question her unusual attention because it has been "a night for wonders."

At this point it seems that Cora's story is out of place in the novel, a mistake by an otherwise meticulous author. Amid Naylor's painfully accurate depictions of real women and their real struggles, Cora's instant transformation into a devoted and responsible mother seems a "vain fantasy."

In the last paragraph of Cora's story, however, we find that the fantasy has been Cora's. After kissing her children good night, she returns to her bedroom and finds one of her shadow-like lovers waiting in her bed, and she folds "her evening like gold and lavender gauze deep within the creases of her dreams" and lets her clothes drop to the floor. She will not change her actions and become a devoted mother, and her dreams for her children will be deferred. They were, after all, only fantasies, and real dreams take more than one night to achieve.

"The Block Party" tells the story of another deferred dream, this one literally dreamt by Mattie the night before the real Block Party. The chapter begins with a mention of the troubling dreams that haunt all the women and girls of Brewster Place during the week after Ben's death and Lorraine's rape. They will not talk about these dreams; only a few of them will even admit to having them, but every one of them dreams of Lorraine, finally recognizing the bond they share with the woman they had shunned as "different." Sadly, Lorraine's dream of not being "any different from anybody else in the world" is only fulfilled when her rape forces the other women to recognize the victimization and vulnerability that they share with her.

In Mattie's dream of the block party, even Ciel, who knows nothing of Lorraine, admits that she has dreamed of "a woman who was supposed to be me ... She didn't look exactly like me, but inside I felt it was me."

In a novel full of unfulfilled and constantly deferred dreams, the only the dream that is fully realized is Lorraine's dream of being recognized as "a lousy human being who's somebody's daughter or somebody's friend or even somebody's enemy." In dreaming of Lorraine the women acknowledge that she represents every one of them: she is their daughter, their friend, their enemy, and her brutal rape is the fulfillment of their own nightmares.

Mattie's dream presents an empowering response to this nightmare of disempowerment. When she dreams of the women joining together to tear down the wall that has separated them from the rest of the city, she is dreaming of a way for all of them to achieve Lorraine's dream of acceptance. They will tear down that which has separated them and made them "different" from the other inhabitants of the city. They will tear down the wall which is stained with blood, and which has come to symbolize their dead end existence on Brewster Place. As Jill Matus notes in "Dream, Deferral, and Closure in *The Women of Brewster Place*," "Tearing at the very bricks of Brewster's walls is an act of resistance against the conditions that prevail within it."

But the group effort at tearing down the wall is only a dream—Mattie's dream-and just as the rain is pouring down, baptizing the women and their dream work, the dream ends. Mattie awakes to discover that it is still morning, the wall is still standing, and the block party still looms in the future.

Nevertheless, this is not the same sort of disappointing deferral as in Cora Lee's story. Though Mattie's dream has not yet been fulfilled, there are hints that it will be. She awakes to find the sun shining for the first time in a week, just like in her dream. They are still "gonna have a party," and the rain in Mattie's dream foreshadows the "the stormy clouds that had formed on the horizon and were silently moving toward Brewster Place." Mattie's dream has not been fulfilled yet, but neither is it folded and put away like Cora's; a storm is heading toward Brewster Place, and the women are "gonna have a party."

The book ends with one final mention of dreams. In the epilogue we are told that Brewster Place is abandoned, but does not die, because the dreams of the women keep it alive:

> But the colored daughters of Brewster, spread over the canvas of time, still wake up with their dreams misted on the edge of a yawn. They get up and pin those dreams to wet laundry hung out to dry, they're mixed with a pinch of salt and thrown into pots of soup, and they're diapered around babies.

Brewster Place lives on because the women whose dreams it has been a part of live on and continue to dream. Their dreams, even those that are continually deferred, are what keep them alive, continuing to sleep, cook, and care for their children. Dreams keep the street alive as well, if only in the minds of its former inhabitants whose stories the dream motif unites into a coherent novel.

Source: Donna Woodford, in an essay for *Novels for Students,* Gale, 1998.

Jill L. Matus

In the following excerpt, Matus discusses the final chapter of The Women of Brewster Place *and the effect of deferring or postponing closure.*

After presenting a loose community of six stories, each focusing on a particular character, Gloria Naylor constructs a seventh, ostensibly designed to draw discrete elements together, to "round off" the collection. As its name suggests, "The Block Party" is a vision of community effort, everyone's story. We discover after a first reading, however, that the narrative of the party is in fact Mattie's dream vision, from which she awakens perspiring in her bed. The "real" party for which Etta is rousing her has yet to take place, and we never get to hear how it turns out. Authorial sleight of hand in offering Mattie's dream as reality is quite deliberate, since the narrative counts on the reader's credulity and encourages the reader to take as narrative "presence" the "elsewhere" of dream, thereby calling into question the apparently choric and unifying status of the last chapter. The displacement of reality into dream defers closure, even though the chapter appears shaped to make an end. Far from having had it, the last words remind us that we are still "gonna have a party."

The inconclusive last chapter opens into an epilogue that too teases the reader with the sense of an ending by appearing to be talking about the death of the street, Brewster Place. The epilogue itself is not unexpected, since the novel opens with a prologue describing the birth of the street. So why not a last word on how it died? Again, expectations are subverted and closure is subtly deferred. Although the epilogue begins with a meditation on how a street dies and tells us that Brewster Place is waiting to die, *waiting* is a present participle that never becomes past. "Dawn" (the prologue) is coupled neither with death nor darkness, but with "dusk," a condition whose half-light underscores the half-life of the street. Despite the fact that in the epilogue Brewster Place is abandoned, its daughters still get up elsewhere and go about their daily activities. In a reiteration of the domestic routines that are always carefully attended to in the novel—the making of soup, the hanging of laundry, the diapering of babies—, Brewster's death is forestalled and postponed. More importantly, the narrator emphasizes that the dreams of Brewster's inhabitants are what keep them alive. *"They get up and pin those dreams to wet laundry hung out to dry, they're mixed with a pinch of salt and thrown into pots of soup, and they're diapered around babies. They ebb and flow, ebb and flow, but never disappear."* They refers initially to the "colored daughters" but thereafter repeatedly to the dreams. The end of the novel raises questions about the relation of dreams to the persistence of life, since the capacity of Brewster's women to dream on is identified as their capacity to live on. The street continues to exist marginally, on the edge of death; it is the "end of the line" for most of its inhabitants. Like the street, the novel hovers, moving toward the end of its line, but deferring. What prolongs both the text and the lives of Brewster's inhabitants is dream; in the same way that Mattie's dream of destruction postpones the end of the novel, the narrator's last words identify dream as that which affirms and perpetuates the life of the street.

If the epilogue recalls the prologue, so the final emphasis on dreams postponed yet persistent recalls the poem by Langston Hughes with which Naylor begins the book: *"What happens to a dream deferred?"* In a catalog of similes, Hughes evokes the fate of dreams unfulfilled: They dry up like raisins in the sun, fester like sores, stink like rotten meat, crust over like syrupy sweets: They become burdensome, or possibly explosive. The poem suggests that to defer one's dreams, desires, hopes is life-denying. Images of shriveling, putrefaction, and hardening dominate the poem. Despair and destruction are the alternatives to decay. My interest here is to look at the way in which Naylor rethinks the poem in her novel's attention to dreams and desires and deferral....

The dream of the last chapter is a way of deferring closure, but this deferral is not evidence of the author's self-indulgent reluctance to make an end. Rather, it is an enactment of the novel's revision of Hughes's poem. Yet the substance of the dream itself and the significance of the dreamer raise some further questions. Why is the anger and frustration that the women feel after the rape of Lorraine displaced into dream? There are many readers who feel cheated and betrayed to discover that the apocalyptic destruction of Brewster's wall never takes place. Are we to take it that Ciel never really returns from San Francisco and Cora is not

taking an interest in the community effort to raise funds for tenants' rights? All that the dream has promised is undercut, it seems. And yet, the placement of explosion and destruction in the realm of fantasy or dream that is a "false" ending marks Naylor's suggestion that there are many ways to dream and alternative interpretations of what happens to the dream deferred....

The chapter begins with a description of the continuous rain that follows the death of Ben. Stultifying and confining, the rain prevents the inhabitants of Brewster's community from meeting to talk about the tragedy; instead they are faced with clogged gutters, debris, trapped odors in their apartments, and listless children. Men stay away from home, become aggressive, and drink too much. In their separate spaces the women dream of a tall yellow woman in a bloody green and black dress— Lorraine. Mattie's dream expresses the communal guilt, complicity, and anger that the women of Brewster Place feel about Lorraine. Ciel is present in Mattie's dream because she herself has dreamed about the ghastly rape and mutilation with such identification and urgency that she obeys the impulse to return to Brewster Place: "'And she had on a green dress with like black trimming, and there were red designs or red flowers or something on the front.' Ciel's eyes began to cloud. 'And something bad had happened to me by the wall—I mean her—something bad had happened to her'." The presence of Ciel in Mattie's dream expresses the elder woman's wish that Ciel be returned to her and the desire that Ciel's wounds and flight be redeemed. Mattie's son Basil, who has also fled from Brewster Place, is contrastingly absent. He is beyond hope, and Mattie does not dream of his return. For many of the women who have lived there, Brewster Place is an anchor as well as a confinement and a burden; it is the social network that, like a web, both sustains and entraps. Mattie's dream scripts important changes for Ciel: She works for an insurance company (good pay, independence, and status above the domestic), is ready to start another family, and is now connected to a good man. Ciel hesitantly acknowledges that he is not black. Middle-class status and a white husband offer one alternative in the vision of escape from Brewster Place; the novel does not criticize Ciel's choices so much as suggest, by implication, the difficulty of envisioning alternatives to Brewster's black world of poverty, insecurity, and male inadequacy. Yet Ciel's dream identifies her with Lorraine, whom she has never met and of whose rape she knows nothing. It is a sign that she is tied to

> *... the narrator emphasizes that the dreams of Brewster's inhabitants are what keep them alive. 'They get up and pin those dreams to wet laundry hung out to dry, they're mixed with a pinch of salt and thrown into pots of soup, and they're diapered around babies. They ebb and flow, ebb and flow, but never disappear.'"*

Brewster Place, carries it within her, and shares its tragedies....

Everyone in the community knows that this block party is significant and important because it is a way of moving forward after the terrible tragedy of Lorraine and Ben. As it begins to rain, the women continue desperately to solicit community involvement. A man who is going to buy a sandwich turns away; it is more important that he stay and eat the sandwich than that he pay for it. As the rain comes down, hopes for a community effort are scotched and frustration reaches an intolerable level. The dream of the collective party explodes in nightmarish destruction. Poking at a blood-stained brick with a popsicle stick, Cora says, "'Blood ain't got no right still being here'." Like the blood that runs down the palace walls in Blake's "London," this reminder of Ben and Lorraine blights the block party. Tearing at the very bricks of Brewster's walls is an act of resistance against the conditions that prevail within it. The more strongly each woman feels about her past in Brewster Place, the more determinedly the bricks are hurled. Ciel, for example, is not unwilling to cast the first brick and urges the rational Kiswana to join this "destruction of the temple." Kiswana cannot see the blood; there is only rain. "Does it matter?" asks Ciel. "Does it really matter?" Frustrated with perpetual pregnancy and the burdens of poverty and single parenting, Cora joins in readily, and Theresa, about to quit Brewster Place in a cab,

vents her pain at the fate of her lover and her fury with the submissiveness that breeds victimization. The women have different reasons, each her own story, but they unite in hurling bricks and breaking down boundaries. The dismal, incessant rain becomes cleansing, and the water is described as beating down in unison with the beating of the women's hearts. Despite the inclination toward overwriting here, Naylor captures the cathartic and purgative aspects of resistance and aggression. Demonic imagery, which accompanies the venting of desire that exceeds known limits, becomes apocalyptic. As the dream ends, we are left to wonder what sort of register the "actual" block party would occupy. The sun is shining when Mattie gets up: It is as if she has done the work of collective destruction in her dream, and now a sunny party can take place. But perhaps the mode of the party about to take place will be neither demonic nor apocalyptic. The close of the novel turns away from the intensity of the dream, and the satisfaction of violent protest, insisting rather on prolonged yearning and dreaming amid conditions which do not magically transform. The collective dream of the last chapter constitutes a "symbolic act" which, as Frederic Jameson puts it, enables "real social contradictions, insurmountable in their own terms, [to] find a purely formal resolution in the aesthetic realm." ...

Not only does Langston Hughes's poem speak generally about the nature of deferral and dreams unsatisfied, but in the historical context that Naylor evokes it also calls attention implicitly to the sixties' dream of racial equality and the "I have a dream" speech of Martin Luther King, Jr....

The sermon's movement is ... from disappointment, through a recognition of deferral and persistence, to a reiteration of vision and hope:

Yes, I am personally the victim of deferred dreams, of blasted hopes, but in spite of that I close today by saying I still have a dream, because, you know, you can't give up in life. If you lose hope, somehow you lose that vitality that keeps life moving, you lose that courage to be, that quality that helps you to go on in spite of all. And so today I still have a dream.

The remainder of the sermon goes on to celebrate the resurrection of the dream—"I still have a dream" is repeated some eight times in the next paragraph. Naylor's novel is not exhortatory or rousing in the same way; her response to the fracture of the collective dream is an affirmation of persistence rather than a song of culmination and apocalypse. King's sermon culminates in the language of apocalypse, a register which, as I have already suggested, Naylor's epilogue avoids: "I still have a dream today that one day every valley shall be exalted and every mountain and hill will be made low …, and the glory of the Lord shall be revealed ….” Hughes's poem and King's sermon can thus be seen as two poles between which Naylor steers. The novel recognizes the precise political and social consequences of the cracked dream in the community it deals with, but asserts the vitality and life that persist even when faith in a particular dream has been disrupted. Although remarkably similar to Dr. King's sermon in the recognition of blasted hopes and dreams deferred, *The Women of Brewster Place* does not reassert its faith in the dream of harmony and equality: It stops short of apocalypse in its affirmation of persistence. Further, Naylor suggests that the shape and content of the dream should be capable of flexibility and may change in response to changing needs and times. What the women of Brewster Place dream is not so important as that they dream.…

Brewster's women live within the failure of the sixties' dreams, and there is no doubt a dimension of the novel that reflects on the shortfall. But its reflection is subtle, achieved through the novel's concern with specific women and an individualized neighborhood and the way in which fiction, with its attention focused on the particular, can be made to reveal the play of large historical determinants and forces. There is an attempt on Naylor's part to invoke the wide context of Brewster's particular moment in time and to blend this with her focus on the individual dreams and psychologies of the women in the stories. Perhaps because her emphasis is on the timeless nature of dreams and the private mythology of each “ebony phoenix,” the specifics of history are not foregrounded. Even though the link between this neighborhood and the particular social, economic, and political realities of the sixties is muted rather than emphatic, defining characteristics are discernible. In Brewster Place there is no upward mobility; and by conventional evaluation there are no stable family structures. Brewster is a place for women who have no realistic expectations of revising their marginality, most of whom have “come down” in the world. The exception is Kiswana, from Linden Hills, who is deliberately downwardly mobile.…

As presented, Brewster Place is largely a community of women; men are mostly absent or itinerant, drifting in and out of their women's lives, and leaving behind them pregnancies and unpaid bills. It would be simple to make a case for the unflattering portrayal of men in this novel; in fact

Naylor was concerned that her work would be seen as deliberately slighting of men:

> …there was something that I was very self-conscious about with my first novel; I bent over backwards not to have a negative message come through about the men. My emotional energy was spent in creating a woman's world, telling her side of it because I knew it hadn't been done enough in literature. But I worried about whether or not the problems that were being caused by the men in the women's lives would be interpreted as some bitter statement I had to make about black men. (“Conversation”)

Bearing in mind the kind of hostile criticism that Alice Walker's *The Color Purple* evoked, one can understand Naylor's concern, since male sins in her novel are not insignificant. Mattie is a resident of Brewster partly because of the failings of the men in her life: the shiftless Butch, who is sexually irresistible; her father, whose outraged assault on her prompts his wife to pull a gun on him; and her son, whom she has spoiled to the extent that he one day jumps bail on her money, costing her her home and sending her to Brewster Place. There is also the damning portrait of a minister on the make in Etta Mae's story, the abandonment of Ciel by Eugene, and the scathing presentation of the young male rapists in “The Two.”

“The enemy wasn't Black men,” Joyce Ladner contends, “ ‘but oppressive forces in the larger society’ ” [When and Where I Enter: The Impact of Black Women on Race and Sex in America, 1984], and Naylor's presentation of men implies agreement. But while she is aware that there is nothing enviable about the pressures, incapacities, and frustrations men absorb in a system they can neither beat nor truly join, her interest lies in evoking the lives of women, not men. Their aggression, part-time presence, avoidance of commitment, and sense of dislocation renders them alien and other in the community of Brewster Place. Basil and Eugene are forever on the run; other men in the stories (Kiswana's boyfriend Abshu, Cora Lee's shadowy lovers) are narrative ciphers. Mostly marginal and spectral in Brewster Place, the men reflect the nightmarish world they inhabit by appearing as if they were characters in a dream.…

“The Block Party” is a crucial chapter of the book because it explores the attempts to experience a version of community and neighborhood. People know each other in Brewster Place, and as imperfect and damaging as their involvement with each other may be, they still represent a community. As the title suggests, this is a novel about women and place. Brewster Place names the women, houses them, and defines their underprivileged status. Although they come to it by very different routes, Brewster is a reality that they are "obliged to share" [as Smith States in "Toward a Black Feminist Criticism," *Conditions*, 1977.] *Obliged* comes from the political, social, and economic realities of post-sixties' America—a world in which the women are largely disentitled. *Share* directs emphasis to what they have in common: They are women, they are black, and they are almost invariably poor. Among the women there is both commonality and difference: *"Like an ebony phoenix, each in her own time and with her own season had a story."*

Naylor's novel does not offer itself as a definitive treatment of black women or community, but it reflects a reality that a great many black women share; it is at the same time an indictment of oppressive social forces and a celebration of courage and persistence. By considering the nature of personal and collective dreams within a context of specific social, political, and economic determinants, Naylor inscribes an ideology that affirms deferral; the capacity to defer and to dream is endorsed as life-availing. Like Martin Luther King, Naylor resists a history that seeks to impose closure on black American dreams, recording also in her deferred ending a reluctance to see "community" as a static or finished work. There are countless slum streets like Brewster; streets will continue to be condemned and to die, but there will be other streets to whose decay the women of Brewster will cling. The image of the ebony phoenix developed in the introduction to the novel is instructive: The women rise, as from the ashes, and continue to live. Although the idea of miraculous transformation associated with the phoenix is undercut by the starkness of slum and the perpetuation of poverty, the notion of regeneration also associated with the phoenix is supported by the quiet persistence of women who continue to dream on. While acknowledging the shriveling, death-bound images of Hughes's poem, Naylor invests with value the essence of deferral—it resists finality.

Source: Jill L. Matus, "Dream, Deferral, and Closure in *The Women of Brewster Place*" in *Black American Literature Forum*, spring, 1990, pp. 49–64.

Laura E. Tanner

Tanner examines the reader as voyeur and participant in the rape scene at the end of The Women of Brewster Place.

The rape scene in *The Women of Brewster Place* occurs in "The Two," one of the seven short stories that make up the novel. This story explores the relationship between Theresa and Lorraine, two lesbians who move into the run-down complex of apartments that make up "Brewster Place." Lorraine's decision to return home through the short-cut of an alley late one night leads her into an ambush in which the anger of seven teenage boys erupts into violence:

> Lorraine saw a pair of suede sneakers flying down behind the face in front of hers and they hit the cement with a dead thump.… [C.C. and the boys] had been hiding up on the wall, watching her come up that back street, and they had waited. The face pushed itself so close to hers that she could look into the flared nostrils and smell the decomposing food in its teeth.…

> [C.C.] slammed his kneecap into her spine and her body arched up, causing his nails to cut into the side of her mouth to stifle her cry. He pushed her arched body down onto the cement. Two of the boys pinned her arms, two wrenched open her legs, while C.C. knelt between them and pushed up her dress and tore at the top of her pantyhose. Lorraine's body was twisting in convulsions of fear that they mistook for resistance, and C.C. brought his fist down into her stomach.

> Better lay the fuck still, cunt, or I'll rip open your guts.

> The impact of his fist forced air into her constricted throat, and she worked her sore mouth, trying to form the one word that had been clawing inside of her—"Please." It squeezed through her paralyzed vocal cords and fell lifelessly at their feet. Lorraine clamped her eyes shut and, using all of the strength left within her, willed it to rise again.

> Please.

> The sixth boy took a dirty paper bag lying on the ground and stuffed it into her mouth. She felt a weight drop on her spread body. Then she opened her eyes and they screamed and screamed into the face above hers—the face that was pushing this tearing pain inside of her body.

In Naylor's representation of rape, the victim ceases to be an erotic object subjected to the control of the reader's gaze. Instead, that gaze, like Lorraine's, is directed outward; it is the violator upon whom the reader focuses, the violator's body that becomes detached and objectified before the reader's eyes as it is reduced to "a pair of suede sneakers," a "face" with "decomposing food in its teeth." As the look of the audience ceases to perpetuate the victimizing stance of the rapists, the subject/object locations of violator and victim are reversed. Although the reader's gaze is directed at a body that is, in Mulvey's terms, "stylised and fragmented by close-ups," the body that is dissected by that gaze is the body of the violator and not his victim.

The limitations of narrative render any disruption of the violator/spectator affiliation difficult to achieve; while sadism, in Mulvey's words, "demands a story," pain destroys narrative, shatters referential realities, and challenges the very power of language. The attempt to translate violence into narrative, therefore, very easily lapses into a choreography of bodily positions and angles of assault that serves as a transcription of the violator's story. In the case of rape, where a violator frequently co-opts not only the victim's physical form but her power of speech, the external manifestations that make up a visual narrative of violence are anything but objective. To provide an "external" perspective on rape is to represent the story that the violator has created, to ignore the resistance of the victim whose body has been appropriated within the rapist's rhythms and whose enforced silence disguises the enormity of her pain. In *The Accused,* a 1988 film in which Jody Foster gives an Oscar-winning performance as a rape victim, the problematics of transforming the victim's experience into visualizable form are addressed, at least in part, through the use of flashback; the rape on which the film centers is represented only at the end of the film, *after* the viewer has followed the trail of the victim's humiliation and pain. Because the victim's story cannot be told in the representation itself, it is told first; in the representation that follows, that story lingers in the viewer's mind, qualifying the victim's inability to express herself and providing, in essence, a counter-text to the story of violation that the camera provides.

While Naylor's novel portrays the victim's silence in its narrative of rape, it, too, probes beneath the surface of the violator's story to reveal the struggle beneath that enforced silence. Naylor represents Lorraine's silence not as a passive absence of speech but as a desperate struggle to regain the voice stolen from her through violence. "Power and violence," in Hannah Arendt's words, "are opposites; where the one rules absolutely, the other is absent" [*On Violence,* 1970]. The nicety of the polite word of social discourse that Lorraine frantically attempts to articulate—"please"—emphasizes the brute terrorism of the boys' act of rape and exposes the desperate means by which they rule. "Woman," Mulvey observes, "stands in patriarchal culture as signifier for the male other, bound by a symbolic order in which man can live out his phan-

tasies and obsessions through linguistic control by imposing them on the silent image of woman still tied to her place as bearer of meaning, not maker of meaning." In Naylor's description of Lorraine's rape "the silent image of woman" is haunted by the power of a thousand suppressed screams; that image comes to testify not to the woman's feeble acquiescence to male signification but to the brute force of the violence required to "tie" the woman to her place as "bearer of meaning."…

Rather than watching a distant action unfold from the anonymity of the darkened theater or reading about an illicit act from the safety of an armchair, Naylor's audience is thrust into the middle of a rape the representation of which subverts the very "sense of separation" upon which voyeurism depends. The "imagised, eroticized concept of the world that … makes a mockery of empirical objectivity" is here replaced by the discomforting proximity of two human faces locked in violent struggle and defined not by eroticism but by the pain inflicted by one and borne by the other:

> Then she opened her eyes and they screamed and screamed into the face above hers—the face that was pushing this tearing pain inside of her body. The screams tried to break through her corneas out into the air, but the tough rubbery flesh sent them vibrating back into her brain, first shaking lifeless the cells that nurtured her memory. Then the cells went that contained her powers of taste and smell. The last that were screamed to death were those that supplied her with the ability to love—or hate.

The gaze that in Mulvey reduces woman to erotic object is here centered within that woman herself and projected outward. The reader is locked into the victim's body, positioned *behind* Lorraine's corneas along with the screams that try to break out into the air. By manipulating the reader's placement within the scene of violence, Naylor subverts the objectifying power of the gaze; as the gaze is trapped within the erotic object, the necessary distance between the voyeur and the object of voyeuristic pleasure is collapsed. The detachment that authorizes the process of imaginative identification with the rapist is withdrawn, forcing the reader within the confines of the *victim's* world.

Situated within the margins of the violator's story of rape, the reader is able to read beneath the bodily configurations that make up its text, to experience the world-destroying violence required to appropriate the victim's body as a sign of the violator's power. Lurking beneath the image of woman as passive signifier is the fact of a body turned traitor against the consciousness that no longer rules it, a body made, by sheer virtue of physiology, to encircle and in a sense embrace its violator. In Naylor's representation, Lorraine's pain and not the rapist's body becomes the agent of violation, the force of her own destruction: "The screams tried to break through her corneas out into the air, but the tough rubbery flesh sent them vibrating back into her brain, first shaking lifeless the cells that nurtured her memory." Lorraine's inability to express her own pain forces her to absorb not only the shock of bodily violation but the sudden rupture of her mental and psychological autonomy. As the body of the victim is forced to tell the rapist's story, that body turns against Lorraine's consciousness and begins to destroy itself, cell by cell. In all physical pain, Elaine Scarry observes, "suicide and murder converge, for one feels acted upon, annihilated, by inside and outside alike." Naylor succeeds in communicating the victim's experience of rape exactly because her representation documents not only the violation of Lorraine's body from without but the resulting assault on her consciousness from within.

In order to capture the victim's pain in words, to contain it within a narrative unable to account for its intangibility, Naylor turns referentiality against itself. In her representation of violence, the victim's pain is defined only through negation, her agony experienced only in the reader's imagination:

> Lorraine was no longer conscious of the pain in her spine or stomach. She couldn't feel the skin that was rubbing off of her arms from being pressed against the rough cement. What was left of her mind was centered around the pounding motion that was ripping her insides apart. She couldn't tell when they changed places and the second weight, then the third and fourth, dropped on her—it was all one continuous hacksawing of torment that kept her eyes screaming the only word she was fated to utter again and again for the rest of her life. Please.

> Her thighs and stomach had become so slimy from her blood and their semen that the last two boys didn't want to touch her, so they turned her over, propped her head and shoulders against the wall, and took her from behind. When they had finished and stopped holding her up, her body fell over like an unstringed puppet. She didn't feel her split rectum or the patches in her skull where her hair had been torn off by grating against the bricks. Lorraine lay in that alley only screaming at the moving pain inside of her that refused to come to rest.

Recognizing that pain defies representation, Naylor invokes a referential system that focuses on the bodily manifestations of pain—skinned arms, a split rectum, a bloody skull—only to reject it as ineffective. Lorraine, we are told, "was no longer

conscious of the pain in her spine or stomach. She couldn't feel the skin that was rubbing off of her arms.... She couldn't tell when they changed places.... She didn't feel her split rectum or the patches in her skull where her hair had been torn off." Naylor piles pain upon pain—each one an experience of agony that the reader may compare to his or her own experience—only to define the total of all these experiences as insignificant, incomparable to the "pounding motion that was ripping [Lorraine's] insides apart." Naylor ... brings the reader to the edge of experience only to abandon him or her to the power of the imagination; in this case, however, the structured blanks that the novel asks the reader to fill in demand the imaginative construction of the victim's pain rather than the violator's pleasure....

As Naylor disentangles the reader from the victim's consciousness at the end of her representation, the radical dynamics of a female-gendered reader are thrown into relief by the momentary reintroduction of a distanced perspective on violence: "Lorraine lay pushed up against the wall on the cold ground with her eyes staring straight up into the sky. When the sun began to warm the air and the horizon brightened, she still lay there, her mouth crammed with paper bag, her dress pushed up under her breasts, her bloody pantyhose hanging from her thighs." In this one sentence, Naylor pushes the reader back into the safety of a world of artistic mediation and restores the reader's freedom to navigate safely through the details of the text. Under the pressure of the reader's controlling gaze, Lorraine is immediately reduced to the status of an object—part mouth, part breasts, part thighs—subject to the viewer's scrutiny. In the last sentence of the chapter, as in this culminating description of the rape, Naylor deliberately jerks the reader back into the distanced perspective that authorizes scopophilia; the final image that she leaves us with is an image not of Lorraine's pain but of "a tall yellow woman in a bloody green and black dress, scraping at the air, crying, 'Please. Please.'" This sudden shift of perspective unveils the connection between the scopophilic gaze and the objectifying force of violence. The power of the gaze to master and control is forced to its inevitable culmination as the body that was the object of erotic pleasure becomes the object of violence.... By framing her own representation of rape with an "objective" description that promotes the violator's story of rape, Naylor exposes not only the connection between violation and objectification but the ease with which the reader may be persuaded to accept both.

As the object of the reader's gaze is suddenly shifted, that reader is thrust into an understanding of the way in which his or her own look may perpetuate the violence of rape.

In that violence, the erotic object is not only transformed into the object of violence but is made to testify to the suitability of the object status projected upon it. Co-opted by the rapist's story, the victim's body—violated, damaged and discarded—is introduced as authorization for the very brutality that has destroyed it. The sudden interjection of an "objective" perspective into Naylor's representation traces that process of authorization as the narrative pulls back from the subtext of the victim's pain to focus the reader's gaze on the "object" status of the victim's body. Empowered by the distanced dynamics of a gaze that authorizes not only scopophilia but its inevitable culmination in violence, the reader who responds uncritically to the violator's story of rape comes to see the victim not as a human being, not as an object of violence, but as *the object* itself.

The "objective" picture of a battered woman scraping at the air in a bloody green and black dress is shocking exactly because it seems to have so little to do with the woman whose pain the reader has just experienced. Having recognized Lorraine as a human being who becomes a victim of violence, the reader recoils from the unfamiliar picture of a creature who seems less human than animal, less subject than object. As Naylor's representation retreats for even a moment to the distanced perspective ... the objectifying pressure of the reader's gaze allows that reader to see not the brutality of the act of violation but the brute-like characteristics of its victim. To see Lorraine scraping at the air in her bloody garment is to see not only the horror of what happened to her but the horror that *is* her. The violation of her personhood that is initiated with the rapist's objectifying look becomes a self-fulfilling prophecy borne out by the literal destruction of her body; rape reduces its victim to the status of an animal and then flaunts as authorization the very body that it has mutilated. Insofar as the reader's gaze perpetuates the process of objectification, the reader, too, becomes a violator.

Naylor's temporary restoration of the objectifying gaze only emphasizes the extent to which *her* representation of violence subverts the conventional dynamics of the reading and viewing processes. By denying the reader the freedom to observe the victim of violence from behind the wall

> *Naylor ... brings the reader to the edge of experience only to abandon him or her to the power of the imagination; in this case, however, the structured blanks that the novel asks the reader to fill in demand the imaginative construction of the victim's pain rather than the violator's pleasure....*"

of aesthetic convention, to manipulate that victim as an object of imaginative play, Naylor disrupts the connection between violator and viewer that Mulvey emphasizes in her discussion of cinematic convention.... Inviting the viewer to enter the world of violence that lurks just beyond the wall of art, Naylor traps the reader behind that wall. As the reader's gaze is centered within the victim's body, the reader, ... is stripped of the safety of aesthetic distance and the freedom of artistic response. In Naylor's representation of rape, the power of the gaze is turned against itself; the aesthetic observer is forced to watch powerlessly as the violator steps up to the wall to stare with detached pleasure at an exhibit in which the reader, as well as the victim of violence, is on display.

Source: Laura E. Tanner, "*Reading Rape:* Sanctuary *and* The Women of Brewster Place" in *American Literature,* Vol. 62, No. 4, December, 1990, pp. 559–82.

Sources

Bellinelli, director, RTSJ-Swiss Television, producer, *A Conversation with Gloria Naylor* on *In Black and White: Six Profiles of African American Authors,* (videotape), California Newsreel, 1992. http://www.newsreel.org/films/inblack.htm.

Kay Bonetti, "An Interview with Gloria Naylor" (audiotape), American Prose Library, 1988.

Angels Carabi, in an interview with Gloria Naylor, *Belles Lettres 7,* spring, 1992, pp. 36-42.

Anne Gottlieb, "Women Together," *The New York Times,* August 22, 1982, p. 11.

Loyle Hairston, a review in *Freedomways,* Vol. 23, No. 4, 1983, pp. 282-85.

Barbara Harrison, *Visions of Glory: A History and a Memory of Jehovah's Witnesses,* Simon & Schuster, 1975.

Joel Hughes, "Naylor Discusses Race Myths and Life," *Yale Daily News,* March 2, 1995. http://www.cis.yale.edu/ydn/paper.

Christine King, *Identities and Issues in Literature,* Vol. 3, edited by David Peck and Eric Howard, Salem Press, 1997, pp. 1004-5.

Linda Labin, *Masterpieces of Women's Literature,* edited by Frank Magill, HarperCollins, 1996, pp. 571-73.

The Living Webster Encyclopedic Dictionary of the English Language, The English Language Institute of America, 1975.

Jill Matus, "Dream, Deferral, and Closure in *The Women of Brewster Place." Black American Literature Forum,* Vol. 24, No. 1, spring, 1990, pp. 49-64.

Gloria Naylor, *The Women of Brewster Place,* Penguin, 1983.

Rae Stoll, *Magill's Literary Annual,* Vol. Two, edited by Frank Magill, Salem Press, 1983, pp. 918-22.

For Further Study

Michael Awkward, "Authorial Dreams of Wholeness: (Dis)Unity, (Literary) Parentage, and *The Women of Brewster Place,"* in *Gloria Naylor: Critical Perspectives Past and Present,* edited by Henry Louis Gates, Jr. and K.A. Appiah, Amistad Press, 1993, pp. 37-70.
> Discusses Naylor's literary heritage and her use of and divergence from her literary roots.

Julia Boyd, *In the Company of My Sisters: Black Women and Self Esteem,* Plume, 1997.
> Explores interracial relationships, bi-and gay sexuality in the black community, and black women's lives through a study of the roles played by both black and white families. Boyd offers guidelines for growth in a difficult world.

Children of the Night: The Best Short Stories by Black Writers, 1967 to the Present, edited by Gloria Naylor and Bill Phillips, Little Brown, 1997.
> An anthology of stories that relate to the black experience. The four sections cover such subjects as slavery, changing times, family, faith, "them and us," and the future.

The Critical Response to Gloria Naylor (Critical Responses in Arts and Letters, No. 29), edited by Sharon Felton and Michelle C. Loris, Greenwood, 1997.
> A comprehensive compilation of critical responses to Naylor's works, including: sections devoted to her novels, essays and seminal articles relating feminist perspectives, and comparisons of Naylor's novels to classical authors.

William Faulkner, *As I Lay Dying,* Cape and Smith, 1930.
> This is a story that depicts a family's struggle with grieving and community as they prepare to bury their dead mother. Faulkner uses fifteen different voices to tell the story.

Virginia C. Fowler, "'Ebony Phoenixes': *The Women of Brewster Place,"* in *Gloria Naylor: In Search of Sanctuary,* edited by Frank Day, Twayne Publishers, 1996, pp. 21-58.
> Offers a general analysis of the structure, characters, and themes of the novel.

———, *Gloria Naylor: In Search of Sanctuary,* Twayne, 1996.
> Biographical and critical study. Fowler tries to place Naylor's work within the context of African-American female writers since the 1960s.

Annie Gottlieb, a review in *The New York Times Book Review,* August 22, 1982, p. 11.
> Praises Naylor's treatment of women and relationships.

Home Girls: A Black Feminist Anthology, edited by Barbara Smith, Naiad, 1989.
> A collection of works by noted authors such as Alice Walker, June Jordan, and others. Essays, poetry, and prose on the black feminist experience.

bell hooks, *Ain't I a Woman: Black Women and Feminism,* South End, 1981.
> A nonfiction theoretical work concerning the rights of black women and the need to work for change relating to the issues of racism, sexism, and societal oppression.

Kate Rushin, *Black Back-ups,* Firebrand Books, 1993.
> The author captures the faces, voices, feelings, words, and stories of an African-American family in the neighborhood and town where she grew up.

Sapphire, *American Dreams,* Vintage, 1996.
> Through prose and poetry, the author addresses issues of family violence, urban decay, spiritual renewal, and others, yet rises above the grim realism to find hope and inspiration.

Dorothy Wickenden, a review in *The New Republic,* September 6, 1982, p. 37.
> Observes that Naylor's "knowing portrayal" of Mattie unites the seven stories that form the novel.

Glossary of Literary Terms

A

Abstract: As an adjective applied to writing or literary works, abstract refers to words or phrases that name things not knowable through the five senses.

Aestheticism: A literary and artistic movement of the nineteenth century. Followers of the movement believed that art should not be mixed with social, political, or moral teaching. The statement "art for art's sake" is a good summary of aestheticism. The movement had its roots in France, but it gained widespread importance in England in the last half of the nineteenth century, where it helped change the Victorian practice of including moral lessons in literature.

Allegory: A narrative technique in which characters representing things or abstract ideas are used to convey a message or teach a lesson. Allegory is typically used to teach moral, ethical, or religious lessons but is sometimes used for satiric or political purposes.

Allusion: A reference to a familiar literary or historical person or event, used to make an idea more easily understood.

Analogy: A comparison of two things made to explain something unfamiliar through its similarities to something familiar, or to prove one point based on the acceptedness of another. Similes and metaphors are types of analogies.

Antagonist: The major character in a narrative or drama who works against the hero or protagonist.

Anthropomorphism: The presentation of animals or objects in human shape or with human characteristics. The term is derived from the Greek word for "human form."

Antihero: A central character in a work of literature who lacks traditional heroic qualities such as courage, physical prowess, and fortitude. Antiheroes typically distrust conventional values and are unable to commit themselves to any ideals. They generally feel helpless in a world over which they have no control. Antiheroes usually accept, and often celebrate, their positions as social outcasts.

Apprenticeship Novel: See *Bildungsroman*

Archetype: The word archetype is commonly used to describe an original pattern or model from which all other things of the same kind are made. This term was introduced to literary criticism from the psychology of Carl Jung. It expresses Jung's theory that behind every person's "unconscious," or repressed memories of the past, lies the "collective unconscious" of the human race: memories of the countless typical experiences of our ancestors. These memories are said to prompt illogical associations that trigger powerful emotions in the reader. Often, the emotional process is primitive, even primordial. Archetypes are the literary images that grow out of the "collective unconscious." They appear in literature as incidents and plots that repeat basic patterns of life. They may also appear as stereotyped characters.

***Avant-garde*:** French term meaning "vanguard." It is used in literary criticism to describe new writing that rejects traditional approaches to literature in favor of innovations in style or content.

B

Beat Movement: A period featuring a group of American poets and novelists of the 1950s and 1960s—including Jack Kerouac, Allen Ginsberg, Gregory Corso, William S. Burroughs, and Lawrence Ferlinghetti—who rejected established social and literary values. Using such techniques as stream of consciousness writing and jazz-influenced free verse and focusing on unusual or abnormal states of mind—generated by religious ecstasy or the use of drugs—the Beat writers aimed to create works that were unconventional in both form and subject matter.

***Bildungsroman*:** A German word meaning "novel of development." The *bildungsroman* is a study of the maturation of a youthful character, typically brought about through a series of social or sexual encounters that lead to self-awareness. *Bildungsroman* is used interchangeably with *erziehungsroman,* a novel of initiation and education. When a *bildungsroman* is concerned with the development of an artist (as in James Joyce's *A Portrait of the Artist as a Young Man*), it is often termed a *kunstlerroman.* Also known as Apprenticeship Novel, Coming of Age Novel, *Erziehungsroman,* or *Kunstlerroman.*

Black Aesthetic Movement: A period of artistic and literary development among African Americans in the 1960s and early 1970s. This was the first major African-American artistic movement since the Harlem Renaissance and was closely paralleled by the civil rights and black power movements. The black aesthetic writers attempted to produce works of art that would be meaningful to the black masses. Key figures in black aesthetics included one of its founders, poet and playwright Amiri Baraka, formerly known as LeRoi Jones; poet and essayist Haki R. Madhubuti, formerly Don L. Lee; poet and playwright Sonia Sanchez; and dramatist Ed Bullins. Also known as Black Arts Movement.

Black Humor: Writing that places grotesque elements side by side with humorous ones in an attempt to shock the reader, forcing him or her to laugh at the horrifying reality of a disordered world. Also known as Black Comedy.

Burlesque: Any literary work that uses exaggeration to make its subject appear ridiculous, either by treating a trivial subject with profound seriousness or by treating a dignified subject frivolously. The word "burlesque" may also be used as an adjective, as in "burlesque show," to mean "striptease act."

C

Character: Broadly speaking, a person in a literary work. The actions of characters are what constitute the plot of a story, novel, or poem. There are numerous types of characters, ranging from simple, stereotypical figures to intricate, multifaceted ones. In the techniques of anthropomorphism and personification, animals—and even places or things—can assume aspects of character. "Characterization" is the process by which an author creates vivid, believable characters in a work of art. This may be done in a variety of ways, including (1) direct description of the character by the narrator; (2) the direct presentation of the speech, thoughts, or actions of the character; and (3) the responses of other characters to the character. The term "character" also refers to a form originated by the ancient Greek writer Theophrastus that later became popular in the seventeenth and eighteenth centuries. It is a short essay or sketch of a person who prominently displays a specific attribute or quality, such as miserliness or ambition.

Climax: The turning point in a narrative, the moment when the conflict is at its most intense. Typically, the structure of stories, novels, and plays is one of rising action, in which tension builds to the climax, followed by falling action, in which tension lessens as the story moves to its conclusion.

Colloquialism: A word, phrase, or form of pronunciation that is acceptable in casual conversation but not in formal, written communication. It is considered more acceptable than slang.

Coming of Age Novel: See *Bildungsroman*

Concrete: Concrete is the opposite of abstract, and refers to a thing that actually exists or a description that allows the reader to experience an object or concept with the senses.

Connotation: The impression that a word gives beyond its defined meaning. Connotations may be universally understood or may be significant only to a certain group.

Convention: Any widely accepted literary device, style, or form.

D

Denotation: The definition of a word, apart from the impressions or feelings it creates (connotations) in the reader.

Denouement: A French word meaning "the unknotting." In literary criticism, it denotes the resolution of conflict in fiction or drama. The *denouement* follows the climax and provides an outcome to the primary plot situation as well as an explanation of secondary plot complications. The *denouement* often involves a character's recognition of his or her state of mind or moral condition. Also known as Falling Action.

Description: Descriptive writing is intended to allow a reader to picture the scene or setting in which the action of a story takes place. The form this description takes often evokes an intended emotional response—a dark, spooky graveyard will evoke fear, and a peaceful, sunny meadow will evoke calmness.

Dialogue: In its widest sense, dialogue is simply conversation between people in a literary work; in its most restricted sense, it refers specifically to the speech of characters in a drama. As a specific literary genre, a "dialogue" is a composition in which characters debate an issue or idea.

Diction: The selection and arrangement of words in a literary work. Either or both may vary depending on the desired effect. There are four general types of diction: "formal," used in scholarly or lofty writing; "informal," used in relaxed but educated conversation; "colloquial," used in everyday speech; and "slang," containing newly coined words and other terms not accepted in formal usage.

Didactic: A term used to describe works of literature that aim to teach some moral, religious, political, or practical lesson. Although didactic elements are often found in artistically pleasing works, the term "didactic" usually refers to literature in which the message is more important than the form. The term may also be used to criticize a work that the critic finds "overly didactic," that is, heavy-handed in its delivery of a lesson.

Doppelganger: A literary technique by which a character is duplicated (usually in the form of an alter ego, though sometimes as a ghostly counterpart) or divided into two distinct, usually opposite personalities. The use of this character device is widespread in nineteenth- and twentieth-century literature, and indicates a growing awareness among authors that the "self" is really a composite of many "selves." Also known as The Double.

Double Entendre: A corruption of a French phrase meaning "double meaning." The term is used to indicate a word or phrase that is deliberately ambiguous, especially when one of the meanings is risqué or improper.

Dramatic Irony: Occurs when the audience of a play or the reader of a work of literature knows something that a character in the work itself does not know. The irony is in the contrast between the intended meaning of the statements or actions of a character and the additional information understood by the audience.

Dystopia: An imaginary place in a work of fiction where the characters lead dehumanized, fearful lives.

E

Edwardian: Describes cultural conventions identified with the period of the reign of Edward VII of England (1901-1910). Writers of the Edwardian Age typically displayed a strong reaction against the propriety and conservatism of the Victorian Age. Their work often exhibits distrust of authority in religion, politics, and art and expresses strong doubts about the soundness of conventional values.

Empathy: A sense of shared experience, including emotional and physical feelings, with someone or something other than oneself. Empathy is often used to describe the response of a reader to a literary character.

Enlightenment, The: An eighteenth-century philosophical movement. It began in France but had a wide impact throughout Europe and America. Thinkers of the Enlightenment valued reason and believed that both the individual and society could achieve a state of perfection. Corresponding to this essentially humanist vision was a resistance to religious authority.

Epigram: A saying that makes the speaker's point quickly and concisely. Often used to preface a novel.

Epilogue: A concluding statement or section of a literary work. In dramas, particularly those of the seventeenth and eighteenth centuries, the epilogue is a closing speech, often in verse, delivered by an actor at the end of a play and spoken directly to the audience.

Epiphany: A sudden revelation of truth inspired by a seemingly trivial incident.

Episode: An incident that forms part of a story and is significantly related to it. Episodes may be either self-contained narratives or events that depend on a larger context for their sense and importance.

Epistolary Novel: A novel in the form of letters. The form was particularly popular in the eighteenth century.

Epithet: A word or phrase, often disparaging or abusive, that expresses a character trait of someone or something.

Existentialism: A predominantly twentieth-century philosophy concerned with the nature and perception of human existence. There are two major strains of existentialist thought: atheistic and Christian. Followers of atheistic existentialism believe that the individual is alone in a godless universe and that the basic human condition is one of suffering and loneliness. Nevertheless, because there are no fixed values, individuals can create their own characters—indeed, they can shape themselves—through the exercise of free will. The atheistic strain culminates in and is popularly associated with the works of Jean-Paul Sartre. The Christian existentialists, on the other hand, believe that only in God may people find freedom from life's anguish. The two strains hold certain beliefs in common: that existence cannot be fully understood or described through empirical effort; that anguish is a universal element of life; that individuals must bear responsibility for their actions; and that there is no common standard of behavior or perception for religious and ethical matters.

Expatriates: See *Expatriatism*

Expatriatism: The practice of leaving one's country to live for an extended period in another country.

Exposition: Writing intended to explain the nature of an idea, thing, or theme. Expository writing is often combined with description, narration, or argument. In dramatic writing, the exposition is the introductory material which presents the characters, setting, and tone of the play.

Expressionism: An indistinct literary term, originally used to describe an early twentieth-century school of German painting. The term applies to almost any mode of unconventional, highly subjective writing that distorts reality in some way.

F

Fable: A prose or verse narrative intended to convey a moral. Animals or inanimate objects with human characteristics often serve as characters in fables.

Falling Action: See *Denouement*

Fantasy: A literary form related to mythology and folklore. Fantasy literature is typically set in non-existent realms and features supernatural beings.

Farce: A type of comedy characterized by broad humor, outlandish incidents, and often vulgar subject matter.

***Femme fatale*:** A French phrase with the literal translation "fatal woman." A *femme fatale* is a sensuous, alluring woman who often leads men into danger or trouble.

Fiction: Any story that is the product of imagination rather than a documentation of fact. Characters and events in such narratives may be based in real life but their ultimate form and configuration is a creation of the author.

Figurative Language: A technique in writing in which the author temporarily interrupts the order, construction, or meaning of the writing for a particular effect. This interruption takes the form of one or more figures of speech such as hyperbole, irony, or simile. Figurative language is the opposite of literal language, in which every word is truthful, accurate, and free of exaggeration or embellishment.

Figures of Speech: Writing that differs from customary conventions for construction, meaning, order, or significance for the purpose of a special meaning or effect. There are two major types of figures of speech: rhetorical figures, which do not make changes in the meaning of the words, and tropes, which do.

***Fin de siecle*:** A French term meaning "end of the century." The term is used to denote the last decade of the nineteenth century, a transition period when writers and other artists abandoned old conventions and looked for new techniques and objectives.

First Person: See *Point of View*

Flashback: A device used in literature to present action that occurred before the beginning of the story. Flashbacks are often introduced as the dreams or recollections of one or more characters.

Foil: A character in a work of literature whose physical or psychological qualities contrast strongly with, and therefore highlight, the corresponding qualities of another character.

Folklore: Traditions and myths preserved in a culture or group of people. Typically, these are passed on by word of mouth in various forms—such as legends, songs, and proverbs—or preserved in customs and ceremonies. This term was first used by W. J. Thoms in 1846.

Folktale: A story originating in oral tradition. Folktales fall into a variety of categories, including legends, ghost stories, fairy tales, fables, and anecdotes based on historical figures and events.

Foreshadowing: A device used in literature to create expectation or to set up an explanation of later developments.

Form: The pattern or construction of a work which identifies its genre and distinguishes it from other genres.

G

Genre: A category of literary work. In critical theory, genre may refer to both the content of a given work—tragedy, comedy, pastoral—and to its form, such as poetry, novel, or drama.

Gilded Age: A period in American history during the 1870s characterized by political corruption and materialism. A number of important novels of social and political criticism were written during this time.

Gothicism: In literary criticism, works characterized by a taste for the medieval or morbidly attractive. A gothic novel prominently features elements of horror, the supernatural, gloom, and violence: clanking chains, terror, charnel houses, ghosts, medieval castles, and mysteriously slamming doors. The term "gothic novel" is also applied to novels that lack elements of the traditional Gothic setting but that create a similar atmosphere of terror or dread.

Grotesque: In literary criticism, the subject matter of a work or a style of expression characterized by exaggeration, deformity, freakishness, and disorder. The grotesque often includes an element of comic absurdity.

H

Harlem Renaissance: The Harlem Renaissance of the 1920s is generally considered the first significant movement of black writers and artists in the United States. During this period, new and established black writers published more fiction and poetry than ever before, the first influential black literary journals were established, and black authors and artists received their first widespread recognition and serious critical appraisal. Among the major writers associated with this period are Claude McKay, Jean Toomer, Countee Cullen, Langston Hughes, Arna Bontemps, Nella Larsen, and Zora Neale Hurston. Also known as Negro Renaissance and New Negro Movement.

Hero/Heroine: The principal sympathetic character (male or female) in a literary work. Heroes and heroines typically exhibit admirable traits: idealism, courage, and integrity, for example.

Holocaust Literature: Literature influenced by or written about the Holocaust of World War II. Such literature includes true stories of survival in concentration camps, escape, and life after the war, as well as fictional works and poetry.

Humanism: A philosophy that places faith in the dignity of humankind and rejects the medieval perception of the individual as a weak, fallen creature. "Humanists" typically believe in the perfectibility of human nature and view reason and education as the means to that end.

Hyperbole: In literary criticism, deliberate exaggeration used to achieve an effect.

I

Idiom: A word construction or verbal expression closely associated with a given language.

Image: A concrete representation of an object or sensory experience. Typically, such a representation helps evoke the feelings associated with the object or experience itself. Images are either "literal" or "figurative." Literal images are especially concrete and involve little or no extension of the obvious meaning of the words used to express them. Figurative images do not follow the literal meaning of the words exactly. Images in literature are usually visual, but the term "image" can also refer to the representation of any sensory experience.

Imagery: The array of images in a literary work. Also, figurative language.

In medias res: A Latin term meaning "in the middle of things." It refers to the technique of beginning a story at its midpoint and then using various flashback devices to reveal previous action.

Interior Monologue: A narrative technique in which characters' thoughts are revealed in a way that appears to be uncontrolled by the author. The interior monologue typically aims to reveal the inner self of a character. It portrays emotional experiences as they occur at both a conscious and unconscious level. Images are often used to represent sensations or emotions.

Irony: In literary criticism, the effect of language in which the intended meaning is the opposite of what is stated.

J

Jargon: Language that is used or understood only by a select group of people. Jargon may refer to terminology used in a certain profession, such as computer jargon, or it may refer to any nonsensical language that is not understood by most people.

L

Leitmotiv: See *Motif*

Literal Language: An author uses literal language when he or she writes without exaggerating or embellishing the subject matter and without any tools of figurative language.

Lost Generation: A term first used by Gertrude Stein to describe the post-World War I generation of American writers: men and women haunted by a sense of betrayal and emptiness brought about by the destructiveness of the war.

M

Mannerism: Exaggerated, artificial adherence to a literary manner or style. Also, a popular style of the visual arts of late sixteenth-century Europe that was marked by elongation of the human form and by intentional spatial distortion. Literary works that are self-consciously high-toned and artistic are often said to be "mannered."

Metaphor: A figure of speech that expresses an idea through the image of another object. Metaphors suggest the essence of the first object by identifying it with certain qualities of the second object.

Modernism: Modern literary practices. Also, the principles of a literary school that lasted from roughly the beginning of the twentieth century until the end of World War II. Modernism is defined by its rejection of the literary conventions of the nineteenth century and by its opposition to conventional morality, taste, traditions, and economic values.

Mood: The prevailing emotions of a work or of the author in his or her creation of the work. The mood of a work is not always what might be expected based on its subject matter.

Motif: A theme, character type, image, metaphor, or other verbal element that recurs throughout a single work of literature or occurs in a number of different works over a period of time. Also known as *Motiv* or *Leitmotiv.*

Myth: An anonymous tale emerging from the traditional beliefs of a culture or social unit. Myths use supernatural explanations for natural phenomena. They may also explain cosmic issues like creation and death. Collections of myths, known as mythologies, are common to all cultures and nations, but the best-known myths belong to the Norse, Roman, and Greek mythologies.

N

Narration: The telling of a series of events, real or invented. A narration may be either a simple narrative, in which the events are recounted chronologically, or a narrative with a plot, in which the account is given in a style reflecting the author's artistic concept of the story. Narration is sometimes used as a synonym for "storyline."

Narrative: A verse or prose accounting of an event or sequence of events, real or invented. The term is also used as an adjective in the sense "method of narration." For example, in literary criticism, the expression "narrative technique" usually refers to the way the author structures and presents his or her story.

Narrator: The teller of a story. The narrator may be the author or a character in the story through whom the author speaks.

Naturalism: A literary movement of the late nineteenth and early twentieth centuries. The movement's major theorist, French novelist Emile Zola, envisioned a type of fiction that would examine human life with the objectivity of scientific inquiry. The Naturalists typically viewed human beings as either the products of "biological determinism," ruled by hereditary instincts and engaged in an endless struggle for survival, or as the products of "socioeconomic determinism," ruled by social and economic forces beyond their control. In their works, the Naturalists generally ignored the highest levels of society and focused on degradation: poverty, alcoholism, prostitution, insanity, and disease.

Noble Savage: The idea that primitive man is noble and good but becomes evil and corrupted as he becomes civilized. The concept of the noble savage originated in the Renaissance period but is more closely identified with such later writers as

Jean-Jacques Rousseau and Aphra Behn. See also Primitivism.

Novel of Ideas: A novel in which the examination of intellectual issues and concepts takes precedence over characterization or a traditional storyline.

Novel of Manners: A novel that examines the customs and mores of a cultural group.

Novel: A long fictional narrative written in prose, which developed from the novella and other early forms of narrative. A novel is usually organized under a plot or theme with a focus on character development and action.

Novella: An Italian term meaning "story." This term has been especially used to describe four-teenth-century Italian tales, but it also refers to modern short novels.

O

Objective Correlative: An outward set of objects, a situation, or a chain of events corresponding to an inward experience and evoking this experience in the reader. The term frequently appears in modern criticism in discussions of authors' intended effects on the emotional responses of readers.

Objectivity: A quality in writing characterized by the absence of the author's opinion or feeling about the subject matter. Objectivity is an important factor in criticism.

Oedipus Complex: A son's amorous obsession with his mother. The phrase is derived from the story of the ancient Theban hero Oedipus, who un-knowingly killed his father and married his mother.

Omniscience: See *Point of View*

Onomatopoeia: The use of words whose sounds express or suggest their meaning. In its simplest sense, onomatopoeia may be represented by words that mimic the sounds they denote such as "hiss" or "meow." At a more subtle level, the pattern and rhythm of sounds and rhymes of a line or poem may be onomatopoeic.

Oxymoron: A phrase combining two contradictory terms. Oxymorons may be intentional or uninten-tional.

P

Parable: A story intended to teach a moral lesson or answer an ethical question.

Paradox: A statement that appears illogical or con-tradictory at first, but may actually point to an un-derlying truth.

Parallelism: A method of comparison of two ideas in which each is developed in the same grammat-ical structure.

Parody: In literary criticism, this term refers to an imitation of a serious literary work or the signature style of a particular author in a ridiculous manner. A typical parody adopts the style of the original and applies it to an inappropriate subject for hu-morous effect. Parody is a form of satire and could be considered the literary equivalent of a caricature or cartoon.

Pastoral: A term derived from the Latin word "pas-tor," meaning shepherd. A pastoral is a literary composition on a rural theme. The conventions of the pastoral were originated by the third-century Greek poet Theocritus, who wrote about the expe-riences, love affairs, and pastimes of Sicilian shep-herds. In a pastoral, characters and language of a courtly nature are often placed in a simple setting. The term pastoral is also used to classify dramas, elegies, and lyrics that exhibit the use of country settings and shepherd characters.

Pen Name: See *Pseudonym*

Persona: A Latin term meaning "mask." *Personae* are the characters in a fictional work of literature. The *persona* generally functions as a mask through which the author tells a story in a voice other than his or her own. A *persona* is usually either a char-acter in a story who acts as a narrator or an "im-plied author," a voice created by the author to act as the narrator for himself or herself.

Personification: A figure of speech that gives hu-man qualities to abstract ideas, animals, and inan-imate objects. Also known as *Prosopopoeia.*

Picaresque Novel: Episodic fiction depicting the adventures of a roguish central character ("picaro" is Spanish for "rogue"). The picaresque hero is commonly a low-born but clever individual who wanders into and out of various affairs of love, dan-ger, and farcical intrigue. These involvements may take place at all social levels and typically present a humorous and wide-ranging satire of a given so-ciety.

Plagiarism: Claiming another person's written ma-terial as one's own. Plagiarism can take the form of direct, word-for-word copying or the theft of the substance or idea of the work.

Plot: In literary criticism, this term refers to the pattern of events in a narrative or drama. In its sim-plest sense, the plot guides the author in compos-ing the work and helps the reader follow the work. Typically, plots exhibit causality and unity and have a beginning, a middle, and an end. Sometimes, however, a plot may consist of a series of disconnected events, in which case it is known as an "episodic plot."

Poetic Justice: An outcome in a literary work, not necessarily a poem, in which the good are rewarded and the evil are punished, especially in ways that particularly fit their virtues or crimes.

Poetic License: Distortions of fact and literary convention made by a writer—not always a poet—for the sake of the effect gained. Poetic license is closely related to the concept of "artistic freedom."

Poetics: This term has two closely related meanings. It denotes (1) an aesthetic theory in literary criticism about the essence of poetry or (2) rules prescribing the proper methods, content, style, or diction of poetry. The term poetics may also refer to theories about literature in general, not just poetry.

Point of View: The narrative perspective from which a literary work is presented to the reader. There are four traditional points of view. The "third person omniscient" gives the reader a "godlike" perspective, unrestricted by time or place, from which to see actions and look into the minds of characters. This allows the author to comment openly on characters and events in the work. The "third person" point of view presents the events of the story from outside of any single character's perception, much like the omniscient point of view, but the reader must understand the action as it takes place and without any special insight into characters' minds or motivations. The "first person" or "personal" point of view relates events as they are perceived by a single character. The main character "tells" the story and may offer opinions about the action and characters which differ from those of the author. Much less common than omniscient, third person, and first person is the "second person" point of view, wherein the author tells the story as if it is happening to the reader.

Polemic: A work in which the author takes a stand on a controversial subject, such as abortion or religion. Such works are often extremely argumentative or provocative.

Pornography: Writing intended to provoke feelings of lust in the reader. Such works are often condemned by critics and teachers, but those which can be shown to have literary value are viewed less harshly.

Post-Aesthetic Movement: An artistic response made by African Americans to the black aesthetic movement of the 1960s and early '70s. Writers since that time have adopted a somewhat different tone in their work, with less emphasis placed on the disparity between black and white in the United States. In the words of post-aesthetic authors such as Toni Morrison, John Edgar Wideman, and Kristin Hunter, African Americans are portrayed as looking inward for answers to their own questions, rather than always looking to the outside world.

Postmodernism: Writing from the 1960s forward characterized by experimentation and continuing to apply some of the fundamentals of modernism, which included existentialism and alienation. Postmodernists have gone a step further in the rejection of tradition begun with the modernists by also rejecting traditional forms, preferring the anti-novel over the novel and the antihero over the hero.

Primitivism: The belief that primitive peoples were nobler and less flawed than civilized peoples because they had not been subjected to the tainting influence of society. See also Noble Savage.

Prologue: An introductory section of a literary work. It often contains information establishing the situation of the characters or presents information about the setting, time period, or action. In drama, the prologue is spoken by a chorus or by one of the principal characters.

Prose: A literary medium that attempts to mirror the language of everyday speech. It is distinguished from poetry by its use of unmetered, unrhymed language consisting of logically related sentences. Prose is usually grouped into paragraphs that form a cohesive whole such as an essay or a novel.

Prosopopoeia: See *Personification*

Protagonist: The central character of a story who serves as a focus for its themes and incidents and as the principal rationale for its development. The protagonist is sometimes referred to in discussions of modern literature as the hero or antihero.

Protest Fiction: Protest fiction has as its primary purpose the protesting of some social injustice, such as racism or discrimination.

Proverb: A brief, sage saying that expresses a truth about life in a striking manner.

Pseudonym: A name assumed by a writer, most often intended to prevent his or her identification as the author of a work. Two or more authors may work together under one pseudonym, or an author may use a different name for each genre he or she publishes in. Some publishing companies maintain "house pseudonyms," under which any number of authors may write installations in a series. Some authors also choose a pseudonym over their real names the way an actor may use a stage name.

Pun: A play on words that have similar sounds but different meanings.

R

Realism: A nineteenth-century European literary movement that sought to portray familiar characters, situations, and settings in a realistic manner. This was done primarily by using an objective narrative point of view and through the buildup of accurate detail. The standard for success of any realistic work depends on how faithfully it transfers common experience into fictional forms. The realistic method may be altered or extended, as in stream of consciousness writing, to record highly subjective experience.

Repartee: Conversation featuring snappy retorts and witticisms.

Resolution: The portion of a story following the climax, in which the conflict is resolved. See also *Denouement.*

Rhetoric: In literary criticism, this term denotes the art of ethical persuasion. In its strictest sense, rhetoric adheres to various principles developed since classical times for arranging facts and ideas in a clear, persuasive, appealing manner. The term is also used to refer to effective prose in general and theories of or methods for composing effective prose.

Rhetorical Question: A question intended to provoke thought, but not an expressed answer, in the reader. It is most commonly used in oratory and other persuasive genres.

Rising Action: The part of a drama where the plot becomes increasingly complicated. Rising action leads up to the climax, or turning point, of a drama.

Roman a clef: A French phrase meaning "novel with a key." It refers to a narrative in which real persons are portrayed under fictitious names.

Romance: A broad term, usually denoting a narrative with exotic, exaggerated, often idealized characters, scenes, and themes.

Romanticism: This term has two widely accepted meanings. In historical criticism, it refers to a European intellectual and artistic movement of the late eighteenth and early nineteenth centuries that sought greater freedom of personal expression than that allowed by the strict rules of literary form and logic of the eighteenth-century neoclassicists. The Romantics preferred emotional and imaginative expression to rational analysis. They considered the individual to be at the center of all experience and so placed him or her at the center of their art. The Romantics believed that the creative imagination reveals nobler truths—unique feelings and attitudes—than those that could be discovered by logic or by scientific examination. Both the natural world and the state of childhood were important sources for revelations of "eternal truths." "Romanticism" is also used as a general term to refer to a type of sensibility found in all periods of literary history and usually considered to be in opposition to the principles of classicism. In this sense, Romanticism signifies any work or philosophy in which the exotic or dreamlike figure strongly, or that is devoted to individualistic expression, self-analysis, or a pursuit of a higher realm of knowledge than can be discovered by human reason.

Romantics: See *Romanticism*

S

Satire: A work that uses ridicule, humor, and wit to criticize and provoke change in human nature and institutions. There are two major types of satire: "formal" or "direct" satire speaks directly to the reader or to a character in the work; "indirect" satire relies upon the ridiculous behavior of its characters to make its point. Formal satire is further divided into two manners: the "Horatian," which ridicules gently, and the "Juvenalian," which derides its subjects harshly and bitterly.

Science Fiction: A type of narrative about or based upon real or imagined scientific theories and technology. Science fiction is often peopled with alien creatures and set on other planets or in different dimensions.

Second Person: See *Point of View*

Setting: The time, place, and culture in which the action of a narrative takes place. The elements of setting may include geographic location, characters' physical and mental environments, prevailing cultural attitudes, or the historical time in which the action takes place.

Simile: A comparison, usually using "like" or "as", of two essentially dissimilar things, as in "coffee as cold as ice" or "He sounded like a broken record."

Slang: A type of informal verbal communication that is generally unacceptable for formal writing. Slang words and phrases are often colorful exaggerations used to emphasize the speaker's point; they may also be shortened versions of an often-used word or phrase.

Slave Narrative: Autobiographical accounts of American slave life as told by escaped slaves. These works first appeared during the abolition movement of the 1830s through the 1850s.

Socialist Realism: The Socialist Realism school of literary theory was proposed by Maxim Gorky and established as a dogma by the first Soviet Congress of Writers. It demanded adherence to a communist worldview in works of literature. Its doctrines required an objective viewpoint comprehensible to the working classes and themes of social struggle featuring strong proletarian heroes. Also known as Social Realism.

Stereotype: A stereotype was originally the name for a duplication made during the printing process; this led to its modern definition as a person or thing that is (or is assumed to be) the same as all others of its type.

Stream of Consciousness: A narrative technique for rendering the inward experience of a character. This technique is designed to give the impression of an ever-changing series of thoughts, emotions, images, and memories in the spontaneous and seemingly illogical order that they occur in life.

Structure: The form taken by a piece of literature. The structure may be made obvious for ease of understanding, as in nonfiction works, or may obscured for artistic purposes, as in some poetry or seemingly "unstructured" prose.

***Sturm und Drang*:** A German term meaning "storm and stress." It refers to a German literary movement of the 1770s and 1780s that reacted against the order and rationalism of the enlightenment, focusing instead on the intense experience of extraordinary individuals.

Style: A writer's distinctive manner of arranging words to suit his or her ideas and purpose in writing. The unique imprint of the author's personality upon his or her writing, style is the product of an author's way of arranging ideas and his or her use of diction, different sentence structures, rhythm, figures of speech, rhetorical principles, and other elements of composition.

Subjectivity: Writing that expresses the author's personal feelings about his subject, and which may or may not include factual information about the subject.

Subplot: A secondary story in a narrative. A subplot may serve as a motivating or complicating force for the main plot of the work, or it may provide emphasis for, or relief from, the main plot.

Surrealism: A term introduced to criticism by Guillaume Apollinaire and later adopted by Andre Breton. It refers to a French literary and artistic movement founded in the 1920s. The Surrealists sought to express unconscious thoughts and feelings in their works. The best-known technique used for achieving this aim was automatic writing—transcriptions of spontaneous outpourings from the unconscious. The Surrealists proposed to unify the contrary levels of conscious and unconscious, dream and reality, objectivity and subjectivity into a new level of "super-realism."

Suspense: A literary device in which the author maintains the audience's attention through the buildup of events, the outcome of which will soon be revealed.

Symbol: Something that suggests or stands for something else without losing its original identity. In literature, symbols combine their literal meaning with the suggestion of an abstract concept. Literary symbols are of two types: those that carry complex associations of meaning no matter what their contexts, and those that derive their suggestive meaning from their functions in specific literary works.

Symbolism: This term has two widely accepted meanings. In historical criticism, it denotes an early modernist literary movement initiated in France during the nineteenth century that reacted against the prevailing standards of realism. Writers in this movement aimed to evoke, indirectly and symbolically, an order of being beyond the material world of the five senses. Poetic expression of personal emotion figured strongly in the movement, typically by means of a private set of symbols uniquely identifiable with the individual poet. The principal aim of the Symbolists was to express in words the highly complex feelings that grew out of everyday contact with the world. In a broader sense, the term "symbolism" refers to the use of one object to represent another.

T

Tall Tale: A humorous tale told in a straightforward, credible tone but relating absolutely impossible events or feats of the characters. Such tales were commonly told of frontier adventures during the settlement of the west in the United States.

Theme: The main point of a work of literature. The term is used interchangeably with thesis.

Thesis: A thesis is both an essay and the point argued in the essay. Thesis novels and thesis plays share the quality of containing a thesis which is supported through the action of the story.

Third Person: See *Point of View*

Tone: The author's attitude toward his or her audience may be deduced from the tone of the work. A formal tone may create distance or convey politeness, while an informal tone may encourage a friendly, intimate, or intrusive feeling in the reader. The author's attitude toward his or her subject matter may also be deduced from the tone of the words he or she uses in discussing it.

Transcendentalism: An American philosophical and religious movement, based in New England from around 1835 until the Civil War. Transcendentalism was a form of American romanticism that had its roots abroad in the works of Thomas Carlyle, Samuel Coleridge, and Johann Wolfgang von Goethe. The Transcendentalists stressed the importance of intuition and subjective experience in communication with God. They rejected religious dogma and texts in favor of mysticism and scientific naturalism. They pursued truths that lie beyond the "colorless" realms perceived by reason and the senses and were active social reformers in public education, women's rights, and the abolition of slavery.

U

Urban Realism: A branch of realist writing that attempts to accurately reflect the often harsh facts of modern urban existence.

Utopia: A fictional perfect place, such as "paradise" or "heaven."

V

Verisimilitude: Literally, the appearance of truth. In literary criticism, the term refers to aspects of a work of literature that seem true to the reader.

Victorian: Refers broadly to the reign of Queen Victoria of England (1837-1901) and to anything with qualities typical of that era. For example, the qualities of smug narrowmindedness, bourgeois materialism, faith in social progress, and priggish morality are often considered Victorian. This stereotype is contradicted by such dramatic intellectual developments as the theories of Charles Darwin, Karl Marx, and Sigmund Freud (which stirred strong debates in England) and the critical attitudes of serious Victorian writers like Charles Dickens and George Eliot. In literature, the Victorian Period was the great age of the English novel, and the latter part of the era saw the rise of movements such as decadence and symbolism. Also known as Victorian Age and Victorian Period.

W

Weltanschauung: A German term referring to a person's worldview or philosophy.

Weltschmerz: A German term meaning "world pain." It describes a sense of anguish about the nature of existence, usually associated with a melancholy, pessimistic attitude.

Z

Zeitgeist: A German term meaning "spirit of the time." It refers to the moral and intellectual trends of a given era.

Cumulative
Author/Title Index

A

Achebe, Chinua
Things Fall Apart: V2
The Adventures of Huckleberry Finn
(Twain): V1
All Quiet on the Western Front
(Remarque): V4
Anderson, Sherwood
Winesburg, Ohio: V4
Angelou, Maya
I Know Why the Caged Bird
Sings: V2
Animal Farm (Orwell): V3
Annie John (Kincaid): V3
Atwood, Margaret
The Handmaid's Tale: V4
Austen, Jane
Pride and Prejudice: V1
The Awakening (Chopin): V3

B

Baldwin, James
Go Tell It on the Mountain: V4
The Bell Jar (Plath): V1
Bellow, Saul
Seize the Day: V4
Black Boy (Wright): V1
Blair, Eric Arthur
Animal Farm: V3
The Bluest Eye (Morrison): V1
Bradbury, Ray
Fahrenheit 451: V1
Brontë, Charlotte
Jane Eyre: V4
Brontë, Emily
Wuthering Heights: V2

C

Catch-22 (Heller): V1
The Catcher in the Rye
(Salinger): V1
Cather, Willa
My Ántonia: V2
Ceremony (Marmon Silko): V4
The Chocolate War (Cormier): V2
Chopin, Kate
The Awakening: V3
The Chosen (Potok): V4
Cisneros, Sandra
The House on Mango Street: V2
Clemens, Samuel
The Adventures of Huckleberry
Finn: V1
Conrad, Joseph
Heart of Darkness: V2
Cormier, Robert
The Chocolate War: V2
Crane, Stephen
The Red Badge of Courage: V4
Crime and Punishment
(Dostoyevsky): V3
Cry, the Beloved Country
(Paton): V3

D

Democracy (Didion): V3
Dickens, Charles
Great Expectations: V4
Didion, Joan
Democracy: V3
Dinner at the Homesick Restaurant
(Tyler): V2

Dorris, Michael
A Yellow Raft in Blue Water: V3
Dostoyevsky, Fyodor
Crime and Punishment: V3

E

Ellen Foster (Gibbons): V3
Ellison, Ralph
Invisible Man: V2

F

Fahrenheit 451 (Bradbury): V1
A Farewell to Arms
(Hemingway): V1
Faulkner, William
The Sound and the Fury: V4
Fitzgerald, F. Scott
The Great Gatsby: V2
Flowers for Algernon (Keyes): V2
Forster, E. M.
A Passage to India: V3
Frankenstein (Shelley): V1

G

García Márquez, Gabriel
Love in the Time of Cholera: V1
Gardner, John
Grendel: V3
Gibbons, Kaye
Ellen Foster: V3
The Giver (Lowry): V3
Go Tell It on the Mountain
(Baldwin): V4

Golding, William
  Lord of the Flies: V2
Gordimer, Nadine
  July's People: V4
Great Expectations (Dickens): V4
The Great Gatsby (Fitzgerald): V2
Grendel (Gardner): V3
Guest, Judith
  Ordinary People: V1

H

The Handmaid's Tale (Atwood): V4
Hardy, Thomas
  Tess of the d'Urbervilles: V3
Hawthorne, Nathaniel
  The Scarlet Letter: V1
Heart of Darkness (Conrad): V2
Heller, Joseph
  Catch-22: V1
Hemingway, Ernest
  A Farewell to Arms: V1
The House on Mango Street
  (Cisneros): V2
Hurston, Zora Neale
  *Their Eyes Were Watching
  God:* V3

I

I Know Why the Caged Bird Sings
  (Angelou): V2
In Country (Mason): V4
Invisible Man (Ellison): V2

J

Jane Eyre (Brontë): V4
The Joy Luck Club (Tan): V1
July's People (Gordimer): V4

K

Kesey, Ken
  *One Flew Over the Cuckoo's
  Nest:* V2
Keyes, Daniel
  Flowers for Algernon: V2
Kincaid, Jamaica
  Annie John: V3
Knowles, John
  A Separate Peace: V2
Kogawa, Joy
  Obasan: V3

L

Lee, Harper
  To Kill a Mockingbird: V2
Lord of the Flies (Golding): V2
Love in the Time of Cholera (García
  Márquez): V1
Lowry, Lois
  The Giver: V3

M

Malamud, Bernard
  The Natural: V4
Marmon Silko, Leslie
  Ceremony: V4
Mason, Bobbie Ann
  In Country: V4
Morrison, Toni
  The Bluest Eye: V1
My Ántonia (Cather): V2

N

The Natural (Malamud): V4
Naylor, Gloria
  The Women of Brewster Place:
  V4
Night (Wiesel): V4

O

Obasan (Kogawa): V3
O'Connor, Flannery
  Wise Blood: V3
Of Mice and Men (Steinbeck): V1
One Flew Over the Cuckoo's Nest
  (Kesey): V2
Ordinary People (Guest): V1
Orwell, George
  Animal Farm: V3

P

A Passage to India (Forster): V3
Paton, Alan
  Cry, the Beloved Country: V3
Plath, Sylvia
  The Bell Jar: V1
Potok, Chaim
  The Chosen: V4
Pride and Prejudice (Austen): V1

R

The Red Badge of Courage (Crane):
  V4

Remarque, Erich Maria
  All Quiet on the Western Front:
  V4

S

Salinger, J. D.
  The Catcher in the Rye: V1
The Scarlet Letter (Hawthorne): V1
Seize the Day (Bellow): V4
Separate Peace (Knowles): V2
Shelley, Mary
  Frankenstein: V1
Slaughterhouse-Five (Vonnegut): V3
The Sound and the Fury (Faulkner):
  V4
Steinbeck, John
  Of Mice and Men: V1

T

Tan, Amy
  The Joy Luck Club: V1
Tess of the d'Urbervilles (Hardy): V3
Their Eyes Were Watching God
  (Hurston): V3
Things Fall Apart (Achebe): V2
To Kill a Mockingbird (Lee): V2
Twain, Mark
  *The Adventures of Huckleberry
  Finn:* V1
Tyler, Anne
  *Dinner at the Homesick
  Restaurant:* V2

V

Vonnegut, Kurt, Jr.
  Slaughterhouse-Five: V3

W

Wiesel, Eliezer
  Night: V4
Winesburg, Ohio (Anderson): V4
The Women of Brewster Place
  (Naylor): V4
Wise Blood (O'Connor): V3
Wright, Richard
  Black Boy: V1
Wuthering Heights (Brontë): V2

Y

A Yellow Raft in Blue Water
  (Dorris): V3

Cumulative
Nationality/Ethnicity Index

African American

Angelou, Maya
  *I Know Why the Caged Bird
    Sings*: V2
Baldwin, James
  Go Tell It on the Mountain: V4
Ellison, Ralph
  Invisible Man: V2
Hurston, Zora Neale
  *Their Eyes Were Watching
    God*: V3
Kincaid, Jamaica
  Annie John: V3
Morrison, Toni
  The Bluest Eye: V1
Naylor, Gloria
  The Women of Brewster Place: V4
Wright, Richard
  Black Boy: V1

American

Anderson, Sherwood
  Winesburg, Ohio: V4
Angelou, Maya
  *I Know Why the Caged Bird
    Sings*: V2
Bradbury, Ray
  Fahrenheit 451: V1
Cather, Willa
  My Ántonia: V2
Chopin, Kate
  The Awakening: V3
Cisneros, Sandra
  The House on Mango Street: V2
Clemens, Mark
  *The Adventures of Huckleberry
    Finn*: V1

Cormier, Robert
  The Chocolate War: V2
Crane, Stephen
  The Red Badge of Courage: V4
Didion, Joan
  Democracy: V3
Dorris, Michael
  A Yellow Raft in Blue Water: V3
Ellison, Ralph
  Invisible Man: V2
Faulkner, William
  The Sound and the Fury: V4
Fitzgerald, F. Scott
  The Great Gatsby: V2
Gardner, John
  Grendel: V3
Gibbons, Kaye
  Ellen Foster: V3
Guest, Judith
  Ordinary People: V1
Hawthorne, Nathaniel
  The Scarlet Letter: V1
Heller, Joseph
  Catch-22: V1
Hemingway, Earnest
  A Farewell to Arms: V 1
Hurston, Zora Neale
  *Their Eyes Were Watching
    God*: V3
Kesey, Ken
  *One Flew Over the Cuckoo's
    Nest*: V2
Keyes, Daniel
  Flowers for Algernon: V2
Kincaid, Jamaica
  Annie John: V3

Knowles, John
  A Separate Peace: V2
Lee, Harper
  To Kill a Mockingbird: V2
Lowry, Lois
  The Giver: V3
Mason, Bobbie Ann
  In Country: V4
Morrison, Toni
  The Bluest Eye: V1
O'Connor, Flannery
  Wise Blood: V3
Plath, Sylvia
  The Bell Jar: V1
Potok, Chaim
  The Chosen: V4
Salinger, J. D.
  The Catcher in the Rye: V1
Steinbeck, John
  Of Mice and Men: V1
Tan, Amy
  The Joy Luck Club: V1
Twain, Mark
  *The Adventures of Huckleberry
    Finn*: V1
Tyler, Anne
  *Dinner at the Homesick
    Restaurant*: V2
Vonnegut, Kurt, Jr.
  Slaughterhouse-Five: V3
Wright, Richard
  Black Boy: V1

Asian American

Tan, Amy
  The Joy Luck Club: V1

Asian Canadian

Kogawa, Joy
   Obasan: V3

British

Austen, Jane
   Pride and Prejudice: V1
Blair, Eric Arthur
   Animal Farm: V3
Brontë, Charlotte
   Jane Eyre: V4
Brontë, Emily
   Wuthering Heights: V2
Conrad, Joseph
   Heart of Darkness: V2
Dickens, Charles
   Great Expectations: V4
Forster, E. M.
   A Passage to India: V3
Golding, William
   Lord of the Flies: V2
Hardy, Thomas
   Tess of the d'Urbervilles: V3
Marmon Silko, Leslie
   Ceremony: V4
Orwell, George
   Animal Farm: V3
Shelley, Mary
   Frankenstein: V1

Canadian

Atwood, Margaret
   The Handmaid's Tale: V4
Kogawa, Joy
   Obasan: V3

Colombian

García Márquez, Gabriel
   Love in the Time of Cholera: V1

German

Remarque, Erich Maria
   All Quiet on the Western Front: V4

Hispanic American

Cisneros, Sandra
   The House on Mango Street: V2

Jewish

Bellow, Saul
   Seize the Day: V4
Malamud, Bernard
   The Natural: V4
Wiesel, Eliezer
   Night: V4

Native American

Dorris, Michael
   A Yellow Raft in Blue Water: V3
Marmon Silko, Leslie
   Ceremony: V4

Nigerian

Achebe, Chinua
   Things Fall Apart: V3

Romanian

Wiesel, Eliezer
   Night: V4

Russian

Dostoyevsky, Fyodor
   Crime and Punishment: V3

South African

Gordimer, Nadine
   July's People: V4
Paton, Alan
   Cry, the Beloved Country: V3

West Indian

Kincaid, Jamaica
   Annie John: V3

Subject/Theme Index

*Boldface denotes discussion in
Themes section.

A

Abandonment
    Ceremony: 21, 26
    Great Expectations: 90–91, 102
    Night: 244
    The Women of Brewster Place:
      359–60
Abortion
    The Handmaid's Tale: 114, 116,
      125–26
Abuse
    Great Expectations: 102
Adulthood
    Jane Eyre: 180–84
Adventure and Exploration
    Winesburg, Ohio: 340–41
Africa
    July's People: 189–91, 196,
      201–02
African-American Heritage
    The Women of Brewster Place: 355
Alienation
    Seize the Day: 276–77, 281–83,
      286
    Winesburg, Ohio: 330
Alienation and Loneliness
    All Quiet on the Western Front: 7
    Great Expectations: 97
    The Red Badge of Courage: 260
    Seize the Day: 281
    The Women of Brewster Place: 354
Allegory
    The Natural: 211, 217–19
    Seize the Day: 295

American Civil War
    The Red Badge of Courage:
      253–55, 261, 263, 265, 267
    The Sound and the Fury: 298,
      307–08
American Dream
    Seize the Day: 281
American Northeast
    Go Tell It on the Mountain: 74
    The Red Badge of Courage: 263
American South
    In Country: 137–38, 144, 148
    The Sound and the Fury: 297–98,
      307
American Southwest
    Ceremony: 20
Anger
    The Red Badge of Courage:
      268–69
    Seize the Day: 287–88
    The Sound and the Fury: 312–13,
      319–20
Apartheid
    July's People: 188–89, 194–97
Apathy
    The Red Badge of Courage:
      267–69
Appearance vs. Reality
    The Red Badge of Courage: 260
Arthurian Legend
    The Natural: 211, 217, 220–25
Asia
    In Country: 137–39, 145–47
      151–56
Atonement
    Go Tell It on the Mountain: 67–68
    Great Expectations: 99–101, 104

    Jane Eyre: 159, 170–71, 177
    Night: 249–51
    The Sound and the Fury: 314–17
Atonement and Forgiveness
    Jane Eyre: 170
Austria
    All Quiet on the Western Front: 9
Authoritarianism
    The Chosen: 49, 51–53
    Night: 229, 235, 237–38

B

Beauty
    In Country: 155, 157
    Winesburg, Ohio: 339, 341–42
Belgium
    All Quiet on the Western Front: 9
Berlin
    All Quiet on the Western Front:
      11, 13
Betrayal
    The Red Badge of Courage:
      271–73
Bildungsroman
    All Quiet on the Western Front:
      8, 12
    Night: 238, 241
Body
    July's People: 193

C

Catharsis
    Seize the Day: 283–84
Childhood
    Go Tell It on the Mountain: 65,
      67, 72–73, 77

Great Expectations: 88–89,
    97–99, 101
Jane Eyre: 161, 169, 171–72,
    174, 180–84
Choices and Consequences
    The Natural: 216
Christianity
    Jane Eyre: 161, 170, 175, 177
    Night: 249–51
    The Sound and the Fury: 313–17
City Life
    The Red Badge of Courage: 262
Cold War
    Night: 238–39
Coming of Age
    The Chosen: 49
    The Red Badge of Courage: 259
Communism
    In Country: 146–47
    Seize the Day: 284–85
Community
    The Women of Brewster Place: 354
Courage
    The Handmaid's Tale: 129
    The Natural: 221–22
    The Red Badge of Courage:
        255–56, 260–61, 265–67,
        269–73
    Seize the Day: 277–78
Creativity
    The Sound and the Fury: 309
    Winesburg, Ohio: 339–42
Crime and Criminals
    Ceremony: 22, 29, 31
    Go Tell It on the Mountain: 68, 76
    Great Expectations: 90–91,
        99–101, 103, 105–06, 109–112
    The Handmaid's Tale: 116–17,
        122, 126, 130–32
    July's People: 188, 191, 195–96
    The Natural: 217–18
    The Sound and the Fury:
        299–300, 306
Cruelty
    Ceremony: 21, 25
    Great Expectations: 99–100
    The Handmaid's Tale: 130–31, 133
    July's People: 188–90, 195–99
    The Sound and the Fury: 318–20
    The Women of Brewster Place:
        354–56, 358–59 366–69
Cuba
    The Red Badge of Courage:
        262–63
Culture Clash
    July's People: 195
Cynicism
    Jane Eyre: 181–83

D

Dance
    Ceremony: 25–26, 28–29

Death
    Night: 231–32, 235–38, 241,
        243–51
Death
    All Quiet on the Western Front:
        3, 4, 6–8 11, 13–15
    Ceremony: 22, 26, 28–29, 36–40
    The Chosen: 45, 53
    Go Tell It on the Mountain:
        67–68, 73–74, 76
    Great Expectations: 91–92, 97,
        99–100, 102
    The Handmaid's Tale: 117, 122,
        124, 131–33
    In Country: 137–39, 143–47, 151,
        153–54
    Jane Eyre: 161–62, 170–72, 174,
        182
    July's People: 190, 195–98
    The Red Badge of Courage:
        255–56, 260–61, 263–70
    Seize the Day: 276, 279, 282–84,
        287–91
    The Sound and the Fury:
        299–300, 314–17
    Winesburg, Ohio: 324–25, 330, 333
    The Women of Brewster Place:
        349–51, 356, 358, 362–63, 366
Depression and Melancholy
    Jane Eyre: 181–82
Description
    The Women of Brewster Place:
        367–68
Dialogue
    Go Tell It on the Mountain: 83
    In Country: 148
Disease
    Ceremony: 31
Divorce
    Seize the Day: 278, 285
Doubt and Ambiguity
    Winesburg, Ohio: 330
Dreams and Visions
    Ceremony: 39–40
    Great Expectations: 88, 101–03
    Night: 245–48
    Winesburg, Ohio: 339–40, 342
    The Women of Brewster Place:
        348, 351, 356, 359–66
Duty and Responsibility
    Go Tell It on the Mountain: 73

E

Emotions
    All Quiet on the Western Front:
        3, 7
    Great Expectations: 104, 107, 110
    The Handmaid's Tale: 131, 135
    In Country: 143, 155–56
    Jane Eyre: 171, 177, 181–82,
        184–86
    July's People: 196, 201

Night: 235, 245
    The Red Badge of Courage: 264,
        266, 269
    Seize the Day: 281–83, 286
    The Sound and the Fury: 307,
        310, 315, 318–19
    Winesburg, Ohio: 340–42
    The Women of Brewster Place:
        358, 365
England
    All Quiet on the Western Front: 9
    Great Expectations: 102
    Jane Eyre: 159–60, 172, 174–76
Essay
    The Sound and the Fury: 310
Eternity
    Night: 246, 248
    The Sound and the Fury: 306
Europe
    All Quiet on the Western Front:
        2, 3, 6, 8, 10, 12
    The Chosen: 44, 51, 53
    Go Tell It on the Mountain: 76
    Great Expectations: 102
    Jane Eyre: 160, 176
    Night: 239
    The Red Badge of Courage: 264
    Winesburg, Ohio: 331–33
Evil
    Ceremony: 25
Evil
    Ceremony: 21–22, 25–26, 36–38
    Go Tell It on the Mountain: 67,
        78–79
    Great Expectations: 99, 101,
        109–10
    The Handmaid's Tale: 122–23
    Jane Eyre: 161–62, 170, 180–81
    The Natural: 211, 217
    Night: 249
    The Sound and the Fury: 315,
        317, 319
Execution
    Night: 249–51
Exile
    The Handmaid's Tale: 130–31,
        133
    Night: 231, 235, 238, 243–44, 247
    The Red Badge of Courage:
        271–72
    The Sound and the Fury: 309
    The Women of Brewster Place:
        360, 362

F

Failure
    The Natural: 216
Fall From Grace
    Go Tell It on the Mountain: 67
Family Life
    Go Tell It on the Mountain: 65, 86
    Seize the Day: 285

Fanaticism
The Chosen: 59–61, 63

Farm and Rural Life
Ceremony: 22, 28–30
Great Expectations: 102
Winesburg, Ohio: 324–25, 332–33

Fate and Chance
Great Expectations: 88, 97, 99–100
Jane Eyre: 181–83
July's People: 203–05
The Red Badge of Courage: 267, 269

Father and Son
Seize the Day: 282

Fear and Terror
All Quiet on the Western Front: 3–4, 7, 12
Go Tell It on the Mountain: 83, 86
Great Expectations: 88, 100–01
The Handmaid's Tale: 116–17, 122–23, 133–35
Jane Eyre: 181–83
Night: 229, 231–32, 235, 237–38, 240–41, 245–48
The Red Badge of Courage: 255–56, 262, 268–69, 271–73
Seize the Day: 282–85
The Sound and the Fury: 317–20

Female Bonding
The Women of Brewster Place: 354

Female Sexuality
The Women of Brewster Place: 356

Feminism
The Handmaid's Tale: 114, 127, 133–36

Folklore
Ceremony: 29
The Natural: 222

Forgiveness
Great Expectations: 91, 99–100
Jane Eyre: 170

France
All Quiet on the Western Front: 9, 13

Free Will
The Handmaid's Tale: 122

Free Will vs. Determinism
The Red Badge of Courage: 253, 259, 261

Friendship
All Quiet on the Western Front: 7
The Chosen: 44–45, 48–49, 57–59

G

Germany
All Quiet on the Western Front: 1, 7, 9–13
The Chosen: 51
Night: 243

Ghost
Ceremony: 25–26, 30, 32
Jane Eyre: 181–182

God
The Chosen: 55, 57, 59
Go Tell It on the Mountain: 67–68, 73, 78–81, 84–86
Jane Eyre: 162, 170
Night: 231, 234–36, 238, 241–45, 247–48
The Sound and the Fury: 314–16
The Women of Brewster Place: 354

God and Religion
Go Tell It on the Mountain: 73
Jane Eyre: 170
Night: 235

Good and Evil
The Natural: 217

Gothicism
Jane Eyre: 159, 172–73, 175, 177

Graphic and Visual Arts
The Sound and the Fury: 308

Great Depression
The Sound and the Fury: 297, 308

Grief and Sorrow
Night: 231–32, 235, 239
The Sound and the Fury: 317, 319–20
The Women of Brewster Place: 350, 354, 358

Grotesque
Winesburg, Ohio: 324, 331, 337

Growth and Development
The Natural: 217

Guilt
Great Expectations: 100, 103, 109–12

Guilt and Innocence
Great Expectations: 100
The Handmaid's Tale: 122

H

Happiness and Gaiety
Great Expectations: 88–90, 99–100, 103, 108–09
The Handmaid's Tale: 115–16, 122, 124
Jane Eyre: 162, 170–71, 181–84

Hatred
Ceremony: 36–38
The Chosen: 52
Go Tell It on the Mountain: 65, 67, 74, 83, 86
Great Expectations: 99–100
July's People: 194–95, 206, 208
Night: 237
The Red Badge of Courage: 255–56, 268
The Sound and the Fury: 319–20
The Women of Brewster Place: 367

Havana
The Red Badge of Courage: 262

Heaven
Go Tell It on the Mountain: 82, 84
The Sound and the Fury: 314

Heroism
Night: 241
Seize the Day: 283
Ceremony: 28, 32
Great Expectations: 107, 109
The Handmaid's Tale: 127, 129–30, 134–36
Jane Eyre: 173, 177–81, 183, 185–86
The Natural: 211, 221–27
The Red Badge of Courage: 255, 260–61, 270, 273

History
All Quiet on the Western Front: 18
The Chosen: 44, 50, 53
Go Tell It on the Mountain: 66, 74–75
In Country: 143, 148–50
July's People: 196, 199
The Sound and the Fury: 306, 310
Winesburg, Ohio: 334

The Holocaust
The Chosen: 44, 49, 51, 53
Night: 229, 236–44

Honor
Great Expectations: 88, 101
The Red Badge of Courage: 272–73
The Sound and the Fury: 312, 316

Hope
All Quiet on the Western Front: 1, 7
Great Expectations: 99, 103
Jane Eyre: 181–83
July's People: 206–09
Seize the Day: 282
The Women of Brewster Place: 348, 355–56, 358–59, 363–65

Human Condition
Seize the Day: 281

Humiliation and Degradation
Great Expectations: 88, 90–91, 98–99

Humor
Ceremony: 35–38
Great Expectations: 101, 103–04, 106
The Natural: 225–26
Seize the Day: 293, 295

I

Identity
The Chosen: 49
In Country: 144

Identity (Search for Self)
  Go Tell It on the Mountain: 72
  Great Expectations: 98
Imagery and Symbolism
  The Chosen: 51, 55, 57, 60, 62
  Great Expectations: 111–12
  The Handmaid's Tale: 124, 126
  In Country: 144–45, 148
  Jane Eyre: 169, 174
  The Natural: 217
  Night: 243–45, 248
  The Red Badge of Courage: 254, 260, 264
  The Sound and the Fury: 315–17
  Winesburg, Ohio: 340–41
Imagination
  Winesburg, Ohio: 340
Incest
  The Sound and the Fury: 299, 306
Independence
  Jane Eyre: 169
The Individual and Society
  Go Tell It on the Mountain: 73
Individual vs. Machine
  All Quiet on the Western Front: 6
Individual vs. Society
  Seize the Day: 282
Industrial Revolution
  The Red Badge of Courage: 262
Insanity
  Night: 231, 235–37
  The Sound and the Fury: 306
Irony
  All Quiet on the Western Front: 13–15
  Ceremony: 37
  Go Tell It on the Mountain: 82–86
  The Handmaid's Tale: 135–36
  The Natural: 226–27
  The Red Badge of Courage: 260–61, 272–73
Israel
  The Chosen: 50–52

J

Japan
  In Country: 146
Judaism
  The Chosen: 42–45, 48–58, 60, 62–64
  Night: 229–30, 231, 235, 241, 243, 249–51
  Seize the Day: 277, 290–91

K

Killers and Killing
  All Quiet on the Western Front: 4, 7–8, 10, 12
  Ceremony: 21–22, 38–40
  Go Tell It on the Mountain: 76

  In Country: 154
  Night: 231–32, 235–36, 239–41, 243–44, 249–50
  Seize the Day: 292
  The Sound and the Fury: 315
  Winesburg, Ohio: 324, 331–32
Kindness
  Ceremony: 38–40
  Great Expectations: 105–06
  Winesburg, Ohio: 340–42
Knowledge
  Great Expectations: 101
  Jane Eyre: 175
  Night: 245–49
  The Red Badge of Courage: 264

L

Landscape
  Ceremony: 21–22, 29–30, 39–40
  Great Expectations: 101
  In Country: 139, 145, 148, 152–57
  Jane Eyre: 179
  The Red Badge of Courage: 256, 259, 265–69, 272
Law and Order
  Ceremony: 19–20, 22, 26, 29, 31, 36, 38
  Go Tell It on the Mountain: 75–77
  Great Expectations: 88, 90–91, 98, 100, 102, 110–11
  The Handmaid's Tale: 114–16, 122, 125–26, 130–31
  Jane Eyre: 162, 169, 174
  July's People: 191, 194, 196–98
Limitations and Opportunities
  Go Tell It on the Mountain: 84–85
  Jane Eyre: 172, 175–76
Literary Criticism
  Winesburg, Ohio: 335
Literature
  Jane Eyre: 186
  Winesburg, Ohio: 341
London
  Great Expectations: 90–92, 98–99, 101–03
  Jane Eyre: 160–61, 176
Loneliness
  All Quiet on the Western Front: 7
  Great Expectations: 88, 97–98
  In Country: 155
  The Red Badge of Courage: 255, 260, 264, 271–73
  Seize the Day: 281, 283–84, 287–88
  The Sound and the Fury: 299
  Winesburg, Ohio: 325, 330
  The Women of Brewster Place: 348, 354, 359
Loneliness and Alienation
  Winesburg, Ohio: 330

Lost Generation
  All Quiet on the Western Front: 1, 7
Love and Passion
  Jane Eyre: 168
  The Sound and the Fury: 306
Love and Passion
  Ceremony: 39–40
  Go Tell It on the Mountain: 67, 74, 82–83, 86
  Great Expectations: 89–90, 98–99, 101, 107–08
  The Handmaid's Tale: 116–17, 122
  In Country: 155–56
  Jane Eyre: 159, 161–62, 169–72, 174, 177, 180, 182–86
  Night: 231, 238, 241
  Seize the Day: 282, 292, 294
  The Sound and the Fury: 299, 305–06, 311–19
  Winesburg, Ohio: 324–25, 338–41
  The Women of Brewster Place: 350, 354–56, 358–61
Lower Class
  Great Expectations: 102
Loyalty
  Go Tell It on the Mountain: 66–67, 74, 78, 80
  The Sound and the Fury: 314, 316–17
  The Women of Brewster Place: 361

M

Magic
  Ceremony: 21–22, 26
Marriage
  Great Expectations: 99
  Jane Eyre: 162, 169–76, 179–80, 183, 185–86
  July's People: 195–96
  Seize the Day: 285
  The Sound and the Fury: 299
  Winesburg, Ohio: 339–40
Memory and Reminiscence
  Go Tell It on the Mountain: 74
  The Sound and the Fury: 299, 305, 307, 310
Mental Instability
  The Sound and the Fury: 317
Middle Class
  Seize the Day: 284, 285
Middle East
  Night: 231, 239
  The Chosen: 45, 48–49, 51–52
Miracle
  July's People: 206, 208
Money and Economics
  Go Tell It on the Mountain: 75–76
  Great Expectations: 90–91, 98–100, 102–03

Jane Eyre: 162, 175–76
The Natural: 213, 216–19
Seize the Day: 278, 282, 285, 287
The Sound and the Fury: 300, 305, 308–09
Winesburg, Ohio: 331, 333

Monologue
The Sound and the Fury: 299, 306–07, 311–12

Mood
Winesburg, Ohio: 335

Morals and Morality
Ceremony: 26, 31, 37
Go Tell It on the Mountain: 72–73, 84–86
Great Expectations: 99–100, 110
The Handmaid's Tale: 122–23, 125–26, 133–35
Jane Eyre: 169–70, 173–74, 177, 184–86
The Natural: 211, 216–19, 222–24
The Red Badge of Courage: 267–70, 272–73
The Sound and the Fury: 308, 310, 314, 317–18

Music
All Quiet on the Western Front: 10, 12
The Sound and the Fury: 309
Night: 232–33, 235

Mystery and Intrigue
Jane Eyre: 159, 162, 172–73

Myths and Legends
Ceremony: 22, 26, 29, 31–32, 34
July's People: 195, 199, 204–05
The Natural: 211, 217, 219–20, 222–27
The Sound and the Fury: 313–15, 317
The Women of Brewster Place: 365–66

N

Narration
All Quiet on the Western Front: 4, 8, 12–14
Ceremony: 20, 28, 31–32, 34, 36–38
The Chosen: 50, 53, 58
Go Tell It on the Mountain: 66–68, 74, 78–80, 83–86
Great Expectations: 100, 104–05
The Handmaid's Tale: 114, 117, 119–24, 126–27, 134–36
In Country: 145, 148–49, 151
Jane Eyre: 161, 171–72, 181–83
July's People: 195–96, 199
The Natural: 211, 218–19
Night: 237, 240, 245–48, 250–51
Seize the Day: 283
The Sound and the Fury: 299, 306–07, 313–15, 317

Winesburg, Ohio: 324, 331, 335–38
The Women of Brewster Place: 362–64, 367–69

Nationalism and Patriotism
All Quiet on the Western Front: 6–9, 11

Naturalism
The Red Badge of Courage: 253, 259, 261, 264

Nature
July's People: 194

Nature
All Quiet on the Western Front: 8
Ceremony: 35, 38–40
Jane Eyre: 174
July's People: 194
The Red Badge of Courage: 254, 256, 259–61, 264, 266, 269, 272
Winesburg, Ohio: 341

Nightmare
The Women of Brewster Place: 359–60, 362

1920s
All Quiet on the Western Front: 10

1950s
The Natural: 217–19
Seize the Day: 284–85

North America
Ceremony: 26, 29–31
The Handmaid's Tale: 124–25
The Red Badge of Courage: 263

Novel
All Quiet on the Western Front: 18
The Chosen: 53, 63–64
Great Expectations: 111
Jane Eyre: 176
The Red Badge of Courage: 264
The Sound and the Fury: 299, 309–10

Nuclear War
Night: 239–40
Seize the Day: 285–86

Nurturance
Ceremony: 39–40

O

Obsession
Winesburg, Ohio: 324–25

Old Age
Great Expectations: 91, 97, 99, 103
Seize the Day: 283, 287

Order and Disorder
In Country: 144

P

Painting
Night: 249, 251

The Red Badge of Courage: 266
Winesburg, Ohio: 325, 334, 339, 343

Perception
Jane Eyre: 170
July's People: 188, 194–95, 197, 199
Winesburg, Ohio: 339, 341–42

Performing Arts
The Sound and the Fury: 309

Permanence
The Sound and the Fury: 306, 309–10

Persecution
The Chosen: 49, 51–52
Great Expectations: 99–100
The Handmaid's Tale: 134–35
Night: 236, 239, 241, 249–51
The Women of Brewster Place: 366–69

Perseverance
All Quiet on the Western Front: 2, 4
Jane Eyre: 181, 183
The Women of Brewster Place: 363–66

Personal Identity
Go Tell It on the Mountain: 72
July's People: 206–08

Personification
Jane Eyre: 177

Philosophical Ideas
Jane Eyre: 181, 183
The Red Badge of Courage: 259, 264

Pleasure
The Women of Brewster Place: 367–69

Plot
Jane Eyre: 177
Winesburg, Ohio: 323–24, 331

Poetry
Ceremony: 19–22, 29
Night: 237, 241
The Red Badge of Courage: 254
The Women of Brewster Place: 363–66

Point of View
All Quiet on the Western Front: 2, 3, 8, 12
Go Tell It on the Mountain: 83–84
The Red Badge of Courage: 255, 260
The Sound and the Fury: 306, 310

Politicians
The Handmaid's Tale: 116, 124, 126
The Natural: 217–19
The Red Badge of Courage: 263

Politics
The Chosen: 49

Subject/Theme Index

Politics
  All Quiet on the Western Front:
     7–11, 18
  Ceremony: 19, 26–32
  The Chosen: 45, 49–50, 52–55
  Go Tell It on the Mountain:
     76–77
  The Handmaid's Tale: 114–16,
     121–27, 130–33
  In Country: 146–48
  July's People: 190, 195–99
  The Natural: 217–19
  The Red Badge of Courage: 263
  Winesburg, Ohio: 325, 332–33
Pornography
  The Handmaid's Tale: 114,
     125–27
Poverty
  Great Expectations: 98, 100, 102
  Jane Eyre: 169–72, 174
  The Red Badge of Courage: 262
Pride
  The Sound and the Fury: 305
Pride
  The Red Badge of Courage: 255,
     261, 264
Prophecy
  July's People: 188, 198–99
Psychology and the Human Mind
  Ceremony: 21–22
  The Chosen: 42, 44–45, 49, 54,
     56–57, 63
  Go Tell It on the Mountain: 65,
     74, 77–78, 83–84, 86
  In Country: 139, 143–44, 147
  Jane Eyre: 181–84
  July's People: 207, 208
  The Sound and the Fury: 307
  Winesburg, Ohio: 334
Punishment
  The Handmaid's Tale: 131
  Jane Eyre: 161, 169–70

R

Race
  Go Tell It on the Mountain: 73
Race
  Ceremony: 19–21, 25–32, 34–38
  The Chosen: 52, 64
  Go Tell It on the Mountain: 67,
     73–78
  July's People: 188, 190–91, 194,
     196–99
  The Sound and the Fury: 306–09
  The Women of Brewster Place:
     348, 350, 355, 357–59
Racism
  Ceremony: 26
Racism and Prejudice
  Go Tell It on the Mountain: 73,
     75–80

  July's People: 196–97
  The Women of Brewster Place:
     354–56, 358
Realism
  The Natural: 211, 217–18
  The Red Badge of Courage: 266
Religion
  Ceremony: 26
Religion and Religious Thought
  Ceremony: 29–30
  The Chosen: 42, 44–45, 48–53,
     55–58, 61, 63–64
  Go Tell It on the Mountain: 65,
     70, 72–74, 77–78, 80–86
  The Handmaid's Tale: 114, 122,
     125, 126–27, 133
  Jane Eyre: 159, 161, 170, 178,
     180, 184
  Night: 229, 235–36, 243, 249,
     251
  The Red Badge of Courage: 254,
     256, 264, 267, 270
  Seize the Day: 291–92, 295
  The Sound and the Fury: 305–06,
     310, 313–17
  Winesburg, Ohio: 324
  The Women of Brewster Place:
     358
Religious Works
  The Chosen: 44–45, 51, 53,
     55–57
  The Handmaid's Tale: 130,
     132–33
Remorse and Regret
  Great Expectations: 90, 100–01
Revenge
  Great Expectations: 92, 99, 101
  The Sound and the Fury: 312–13,
     319–20
Rite of Passage
  Winesburg, Ohio: 329
Rites of Passage
  Ceremony: 27
Romanticism
  The Red Badge of Courage: 266

S

Saints
  Go Tell It on the Mountain: 82–84
Salvation
  Go Tell It on the Mountain:
     78–80, 82, 85–86
  The Sound and the Fury: 314–17
Sanity and Insanity
  Night: 236
  The Sound and the Fury: 306
Science and Technology
  All Quiet on the Western Front:
     7, 10–12, 14
  The Red Badge of Courage: 259,
     262–64

Sea and Sea Adventures
  The Red Badge of Courage:
     262–64
Search for Home and Family
  Jane Eyre: 171
Search for Knowledge
  Great Expectations: 102
  In Country: 155, 157
  Jane Eyre: 174–76
  The Natural: 222–24
  The Sound and the Fury:
     309–10
Setting
  Go Tell It on the Mountain:
     73–74
  The Handmaid's Tale: 117, 123
  Jane Eyre: 159, 172–73, 177
  The Red Badge of Courage: 255,
     261
  The Sound and the Fury: 307
Sex and Sexuality
  The Handmaid's Tale: 117, 122,
     126
  Jane Eyre: 177
  The Sound and the Fury:
     299–300, 311–13, 316–18
  Winesburg, Ohio: 322, 324–25,
     330, 334–35, 339–42
  The Women of Brewster Place:
     356–58, 366–69
Sex Roles
  The Handmaid's Tale: 121
  July's People: 194
Sexism
  The Handmaid's Tale: 133–35
Sexual Abuse
  The Handmaid's Tale: 114,
     116–17, 122, 127
  The Women of Brewster Place:
     350, 354, 356, 358, 366–69
Sickness
  Ceremony: 22, 28
Sin
  Go Tell It on the Mountain:
     67–68, 78–80
  Great Expectations: 100, 109–10
  The Handmaid's Tale: 122
  Jane Eyre: 161, 170–71
  Night: 249
Social Order
  Great Expectations: 99
Solitude
  The Red Badge of Courage: 271,
     273
  Winesburg, Ohio: 325, 332
Soul
  The Chosen: 44–45, 56–57
  Seize the Day: 281, 283, 292–94
South Africa
  July's People: 188–89, 196,
     198–99, 202, 206–09
Soviet Union
  The Chosen: 52, 54

Spain
  The Red Badge of Courage:
    262–63
Spanish-American War
  The Red Badge of Courage: 262
Spiritual Leaders
  The Chosen: 42, 44–45, 49–51,
    53, 55–57, 64
  Go Tell It on the Mountain:
    66–67, 73
  Jane Eyre: 160–61, 162, 170–73
  The Sound and the Fury: 314–17
Spirituality
  The Chosen: 53–57
  Go Tell It on the Mountain:
    78–80, 84–86
  Jane Eyre: 159, 162, 170
  Night: 229, 232, 235–37, 241–44,
    247–51
  Winesburg, Ohio: 324
Sports and the Sporting Life
  The Chosen: 42, 44, 48, 50–51
  The Natural: 211–12, 217–27
Storms and Weather Conditions
  Ceremony: 21, 26, 28, 30–31,
    39–40
  Jane Eyre: 174
  The Women of Brewster Place:
    363–64
Stream of Consciousness
  The Sound and the Fury: 299,
    307, 310
Structure
  All Quiet on the Western Front:
    13–14
  The Handmaid's Tale: 122
  Night: 248
  The Sound and the Fury: 299,
    306, 308–10
Suburban Life
  Seize the Day: 284
Success and Failure
  The Natural: 212, 216–17,
    220–22
  Seize the Day: 278, 281–83, 285

Suicide
  The Sound and the Fury: 299,
    305–07

T

Time
  The Sound and the Fury: 305
Time and Change
  The Sound and the Fury: 298,
    305, 307–09
Tolerance
  The Chosen: 59, 61–63
Tradition
  Ceremony: 26
Transcendentalism
  The Red Badge of Courage: 266
Trust
  Seize the Day: 289, 292, 294

U

Understanding
  Winesburg, Ohio: 339–42
United States
  The Chosen: 51–52
  The Red Badge of Courage:
    262–63
Utopianism
  The Handmaid's Tale: 115,
    126–27

V

Victim and Victimization
  Great Expectations: 99
Vietnam
  In Country: 139, 143–47
Vietnam War
  In Country: 139, 143–45, 147,
    149–51
Violence Against Women
  The Women of Brewster Place: 354

W

War and Peace
  In Country: 143
War, the Military, and Soldier Life
  All Quiet on the Western Front:
    1–4, 6–18
  Ceremony: 21–22, 25–26,
    28–35
  The Chosen: 51–52, 64
  Go Tell It on the Mountain: 65, 74
  The Handmaid's Tale: 116,
    120–22, 124, 129–31
  In Country: 137–41, 143–57
  July's People: 188–89, 196–99
  Night: 229, 231–32, 238–39
  The Red Badge of Courage:
    253–56, 260–73
  Seize the Day: 285
  Winesburg, Ohio: 324, 331–33
Wealth
  Great Expectations: 97–101, 103
Wildlife
  Ceremony: 22, 25–26
  In Country: 145, 155–57
  The Red Badge of Courage: 256,
    264
Wisdom
  Seize the Day: 290–92
Witch
  Ceremony: 25, 28–29
World War I
  All Quiet on the Western Front:
    1–4, 8, 10, 12–15, 18
  The Sound and the Fury: 298, 308
  Winesburg, Ohio: 323, 331–34
World War II
  Ceremony: 21, 28, 30–31
  The Chosen: 44–45, 48–53
  The Sound and the Fury: 308

Z

Zionism
  The Chosen: 45, 48–52, 55–56